# Social Statistics for a Diverse Society

## THE PINE FORGE PRESS SERIES IN RESEARCH METHODS AND STATISTICS

*edited by Kathleen S. Crittenden*

Through its unique modular format, this Series offers an unmatched flexibility and coherence for undergraduate methods and statistics teaching. The two "core" volumes, one in methods and one in statistics, address the primary concerns of undergraduate courses, but in less detail than found in existing texts. The smaller "satellite" volumes in the Series can either supplement these core books, giving instructors the emphasis and coverage best suited for their course and students, or be used in more advanced, specialized courses.

# Social Statistics for a Diverse Society

**Chava Frankfort-Nachmias**
*University of Wisconsin–Milwaukee*

**with contributions by Mark Rodeghier**
*University of Illinois–Chicago*

**Pine Forge Press**
Thousand Oaks, California ■ London ■ New Delhi

For information, address:

 **Pine Forge Press**
A Sage Publications Company
2455 Teller Road
Thousand Oaks, California 91320
(805) 499-4224
e-mail: sales@pfp.sagepub.com

Sage Publications Ltd.
6 Bonhill Street
London EC2A 4PU
United Kingdom

Sage Publications India Pvt. Ltd.
M-32 Marker
Greater Kailash I
New Delhi 110 048 India

*Production,* Mary Douglas, Rogue Valley Publications; *Copy Editor,* Lura Harrison; *Interior Designer,* Lisa Mirski Devenish; *Artist,* Natalie Hill; *Typesetter,* ExecuStaff Composition Services; *Cover Designer,* Paula Shuhert and Graham Metcalfe; *Production Manager,* Anne Draus, Scratchgravel Publishing Services; *Print Buyer,* Anna Chin

*Printed in the United States of America*
99 00 01 10 9 8 7 6 5 4 3 2 1

**Library of Congress Cataloging-in-Publication Data**
Frankfort-Nachmias, Chava.
   Social statistics for a diverse society / Chava Frankfort-Nachmias with contributions by Mark Rodeghier.
       p.    cm. — (Pine Forge Press series on research methods and statistics)
   Includes index.
   ISBN 0-7619-8621-9 (p : alk. paper)
   1. Social sciences—Statistical methods.  2. Statistics.
 I. Rodeghier, Mark.  II. Title.  III. Series.
HA29.N25  1997
519.5—dc21                           96-45371
                                           CIP

*To all my friends*

## About the Author

**Chava Frankfort-Nachmias** is Associate Professor of Sociology at the University of Wisconsin–Milwaukee, where she teaches courses in statistics and research methods. She is the author of *Research Methods in the Social Sciences* (with David Nachmias) and numerous publications on ethnicity and development, urban revitalization, and science and gender. She was the recipient of the University of Wisconsin System Teaching Improvement Grant on integrating race, ethnicity, and gender into the social statistics and research methods curriculum.

## About the Publisher

Pine Forge Press is a new educational publisher, dedicated to publishing innovative books and software throughout the social sciences. On this and any other of our publications, we welcome your comments and suggestions.

Please call or write us at:

**Pine Forge Press**
A Sage Publications Company
2455 Teller Road
Newbury Park, CA 91320
(805) 499-4224
E-mail: sales@pfp.sagepub.com

Visit our new World Wide Web site, your direct link to a multitude of on-line resources: http://www.sagepub.com/pineforge

# Brief Contents

# Detailed Contents

## 2 Organization of Information: Frequency Distributions

## 3 Graphic Presentation

## 4 Measures of Central Tendency

## 8 Bivariate Regression and Correlation

## 13 Testing Hypotheses: The Basics

## 14 Testing Hypotheses About Two Samples

# Series Foreword

The *Pine Forge Series in Research Methods and Statistics*, consisting of core books in methods and statistics in the social sciences and a series of satellite volumes on specialized topics, allows instructors to create a customized curriculum. The authors of the core volumes are both seasoned researchers and distinguished teachers, and the more specialized texts are written by acknowledged experts in their fields. To date, the series offers the core texts in research methods and introductory statistics courses and three satellite volumes focusing on sampling, field methods, and survey research. To be published soon are satellite volumes on regression analysis, experimental design and analysis of variance, and evaluation research.

In *Social Statistics for a Diverse Society,* Chava Frankfort-Nachmias provides a core introduction to statistics that is strongly grounded in important social issues. Although the typical treatment chooses examples to illustrate particular statistical techniques, Frankfort-Nachmias organizes statistical topics around the tasks of describing the variety of social groupings in society and asking questions about issues of social stratification and inequality. Two "integration and review" chapters and an extensive set of computational and SPSS® exercises, all using real world data, continue the focus on statistics as a tool for understanding the major social divisions in contemporary society.

Kathleen S. Crittenden
*Series Editor*

# Preface

If you had been following the 1996 presidential elections, you might have noticed that voting patterns varied considerably by factors such as gender, race, family income, education, and age. For example, Clinton's coalition relied on overwhelming support from women, blacks, and low-income voters. Fifty-four percent of women, 84% of blacks, and 60% of low-income voters supported Bill Clinton for president. Not only were these important differences revealed after the election, but they were estimated with impressive accuracy months before the elections took place!

The increased prominence of women in Clinton's coalition and the continued support of blacks and less affluent voters raise questions about the direction of the Democratic party during the 1998 Congressional elections and the 2000 presidential elections. Should the party protect programs traditionally supported by women and less affluent voters, such as Medicare and education; or should it follow more conservative trends and emphasize budget balancing and welfare and entitlement reforms?

Statistics provides the tools which enable us to analyze and understand differences in voting patterns and how they might influence the direction of a political party. Statistics also allows us to gain insight into other real-life problems that shape our lives. My goal in this book is to show you that statistics is both useful and interesting and a lot easier to understand than you may have been led to believe.

This book is an introduction to statistics for students in the social sciences (sociology and related fields, such as criminal justice, political science, social work, public administration, communication, and nursing) who have not had extensive training in mathematics and are taking an introductory course in statistics.

## Teaching and Learning Goals

This book has three related goals. The first goal is to introduce you to social statistics and demonstrate its value. While most of you will not use statistics in your own research, you will be expected to read and interpret statistical information presented by others in professional and scholarly publications, in the workplace, or in the popular media. This book will help you understand the concepts behind the statistics you encounter so that you will be able to assess the circumstances in which certain statistics should and should not be used.

The second goal of this book is to demonstrate to you that substance and statistical techniques are truly related in social science research. A special quality of this book is its integration of statistical techniques with substantive issues of particular relevance in the social sciences. Because the world you live in is characterized by a growing diversity, where personal and social realities are increasingly shaped by race, class, and gender, as well other categories of experience, this book teaches you basic statistics while incorporating research related to the dynamic interplay of race, class, and gender. You will become proficient in statistics while learning about social differences and inequality through the substantive examples as well as through the organization and emphasis of statistical concepts and procedures. It is my hope that this approach will make the learning of statistics interesting and relevant to you.

Many of you may lack substantial math background, and some of you may suffer from the "math anxiety syndrome." This anxiety often leads to a less-than-optimum learning environment, with students trying to memorize every detail of a statistical procedure rather than attempting to understand the general concept involved.

Hence, the third goal of this book is to address math anxiety by using straightforward prose to explain statistical concepts and by emphasizing intuition, logic, and common sense over rote memorization and derivation of formulas.

## Distinctive Features of This Book

The three goals outlined above are accomplished through a variety of special features:

*A Close Link Between the Practice of Statistics and Important Social Issues*
The examples throughout the book, most taken from news stories, government reports, scholarly research, and the General Social Survey, are formulated to emphasize to students that they live in a world in which statistical arguments are common. Statistical concepts and procedures are illustrated with real data and interesting research studies,

providing students with a clear sense of how questions about important social issues can be studied with various statistical techniques.

*A Focus on Diversity*  A strong emphasis on race, class, and gender as central substantive concepts is mindful of a trend in the social sciences toward integrating issues of diversity in the curriculum. This focus on the richness of social differences within the United States is manifested in the application of statistical tools to examine how race, class, gender, and other categories of experience shape our social world and explain social behavior.

*Intuitive Multivariate Approach to Statistical Understanding*  The book introduces the broad concept of multivariate analysis without actually dealing with its complex technical detail. The concept is introduced early on and throughout the text by the frequent comparison of the experiences of people with diverse and multiple social statuses. Through the use of simple statistical concepts, students are exposed to the complex notion of the interconnected nature of social systems.

*Statistics in Practice*  Most chapters include one or several application sections that show how the statistical concepts covered in the chapter can be applied to examine social issues. The Statistics in Practice sections use real data from the General Social Survey or other sources.

*Reading the Research Literature*  While many students will not use statistics in their own research, they will be expected to read and interpret statistical information presented by others in professional and scholarly publications. The statistical analyses presented in these publications are a good deal more complex than most classroom and textbook presentations. To guide students in reading and interpreting research reports written by social scientists, most chapters include a section in which excerpts of published research reports utilizing the statistical concepts under discussion are presented.

*Integration and Review Chapters*  Two special review chapters are included. The first is a review of descriptive statistical methods, and the second, as the final chapter of the book, reviews inferential statistics. The review and integration chapters provide students with an overview of the interconnectedness of the statistical concepts and help them test their abilities to cumulatively apply the knowledge they have acquired. Students learn to recognize, given the data and research purpose at hand, the best statistical procedure to apply, in order to analyze the data properly. Both chapters include flowcharts that summarize the systematic approach utilized in the selection of statistical techniques as well as exercises that require the use of several different procedures.

*Learning by Doing*  A rich variety of exercises at the end of each chapter and special exercises at the end of both integration and review chapters are of three kinds: (1) traditional exercises to help students understand basic principles and procedures using, at most, simple calculators; (2) computer exercises involving students' use of SPSS; (3) group exercises promoting *cooperative learning*, so that students can learn to work in "teams"—the way most social science projects are conducted.

---

*Special care has been taken to ensure the accuracy of the calculations and notations throughout this book. Each page was carefully proofread, independent of the author, by two experienced statistics instructors. Every example in the book was independently checked by working through it, and every exercise in the book was also worked out, step by step, to ensure the accuracy of the answers at the back of this book and in the instructor's manual.*

---

*Creative Use of Graphics*  The book makes plentiful and sparkling use of graphics, both to teach students statistical understanding and to relate graphics presented in the popular media to academic statistics teaching.

*Computer Applications and Data Set*  SPSS for Windows is used throughout the book, although the use of computers is not required to teach and learn from the text. Special demonstrations at the end of each chapter help students interpret SPSS output. Real data from a wealth of interesting research projects are used to motivate and make concrete the coverage of statistical topics. These data, from the General Social Survey and other sources, are included in a diskette packaged with every copy of the text. The diskette includes "movies" created with Lotus ScreenCam that illustrate and annotate the operation of key statistical techniques in SPSS for Windows from each chapter of the book.

*Additional Supplementary Texts on Important Topics*  The Pine Forge Press Series in Research Methods and Statistics, of which this book is a part, includes additional supplementary volumes covering regression and analysis of variance in more detail than is available in this book. These supplements were written to closely coordinate with our text.

*Tools to Promote Effective Study*  Each chapter closes with a list of main points and key terms discussed in that chapter. Boxed definitions of the key terms also appear in the body of the chapter and in the index/glossary. In addition, boxed learning checks dispersed throughout serve to emphasize to students the important points discussed in a particular section of the chapter. Answers to all the odd-numbered problems in the text are included in back of the book. Complete step-by-step solutions are in the manual for instructors, available upon adoption of the text.

## Acknowledgments

I am grateful to Steve Rutter, the president of Pine Forge Press. His deep understanding of the changing world of college teaching and his remarkable involvement in every phase of this project have made it all possible.

My largest single debt is to our series editor, Kathleen S. Crittenden. In her detailed comments on many drafts of this book, countless contributions at every step of the way, and her support and unflagging patience, she has seen me through the completion of this book.

I am intellectually indebted to Elizabeth Higginbotham and Lynn Weber Cannon for an instructive and inspiring SWS workshop on integrating race, class, and gender in the sociological curriculum. At that workshop the idea to work on this book began to emerge. I was also greatly influenced by the pioneering work of Margaret L. Andersen and Patricia Hill Collins, who developed an interdisciplinary and inclusive framework for transforming the curriculum.

My profound gratitude goes to friends and colleagues who have stood by me, cheered me on, and understood when I was unavailable for long periods due to the demands of this project. Special thanks to Stacey Oliker and Eleanor Miller for supporting my work and offering personal encouragement throughout. I am indebted to Shani Beth Halachmy and Marilyn Kraar, my closest friends, for their support and encouragement. I am also grateful to Joanna Spiro, who encouraged me to begin this project, and to Carole Warshaw, who helped me see my way through a difficult period.

Many manuscript reviewers recruited by Pine Forge provided invaluable feedback. I thank:

Catherine W. Berheide, *Skidmore College*
Terry Besser, *University of Kentucky*
Lisa Callahan, *Russell Sage College*
Ashley "Woody" Doane, *University of Hartford*
James Ennis, *Tufts University*
Kristin Esterberg, *University of Missouri–Kansas City*
Gary Gorham, *North Dakota State University*
Barbara Hart, *University of Texas, Tyler*
Colleen Johnson, *University of Memphis*
Barbara R. Keating, *Mankato State University*
Alice Kemp, *University of New Orleans*
John Light, *Vermont Alcohol Research Center*
Thomas J. Linneman, *University of Washington*
Joan Morris, *University of Central Florida*
Chandra Muller, *University of Texas*
Edward Nelson, *California State University, Fresno*
Jeff Pounders, *Ouachita Baptist University*
Josephine A. Ruggiero, *Providence College*
Valerie Schwebach, *Rice University*
Judith Stull, *Lasalle University*
Ira M. Wasseman, *Eastern Michigan University*
Janet Wilmoth, *Purdue University*
Cathy Zimmer, *North Carolina State University*

Special thanks to Thomas J. Linneman for his generous comments and valuable suggestions for the graphics.

I wish to express my indebtedness to Chris Roerden for editing an earlier draft and to Lura Harrison for careful editing of the final version of the manuscript. Many thanks to Anne Draus at Scratchgravel and Mary Douglas at Rogue Valley Publications for guiding the book through the production process. I also thank the staff of Pine Forge Press for their patience and support throughout the project.

Indispensable assistance in preparing the manuscript was provided at every step by my research assistant, Pat Pawasarat, who is also the co-author of two chapters in this book. I would like to express my gratitude to Pat for her thoroughness and patience. I also thank Mark Rodeghier, who wrote the exercises and helped with many of the examples from the General Social Survey, in addition to creating the SPSS demonstrations and the Lotus ScreenCam "movies." I also thank Helen Miller for her work on the instructor's manual, James Harris for help in preparing the final version of the manuscript, and Lisa Amoroso for help in preparing the instructor's manual.

I am grateful to my students at the University of Wisconsin–Milwaukee, who taught me that even the most complex statistical ideas can be simplified. The ideas presented in this book are the products of many years of classroom testing. I thank my students for their patience and contributions.

Finally, I thank Marlene Stern, whose love and support made it possible for me to finish the book, and my daughters, Anat and Talia, for their extraordinary patience, sense of humor, and faith in me.

Chava Frankfort-Nachmias
*University of Wisconsin–Milwaukee*

# Social Statistics for a Diverse Society

# 1     The What and the Why of Statistics

**Introduction**

**The Research Process**

**Asking Research Questions**

**The Role of Theory**

**Formulating the Hypotheses**

Independent and Dependent Variables: Causality

Independent and Dependent Variables: Guidelines

**Collecting Data**

Levels of Measurement

*Nominal Level of Measurement*

*Ordinal Level of Measurement*

*Interval-Ratio Level of Measurement*

*Cumulative Property of Levels of Measurement*

*Levels of Measurement of Dichotomous Variables*

Discrete and Continuous Variables

**Analyzing Data and Evaluating the Hypotheses**

Descriptive and Inferential Statistics: Principles

Descriptive and Inferential Statistics: Illustration

*Organization of Information: Frequency Distributions*

*Graphic Presentation*

*Measures of Central Tendency*

*Measures of Variability*

*Bivariate Methods*

*Statistical Inference*

Evaluating the Hypotheses

**Looking at Social Differences**

**Box 1.1   A Tale of Simple Arithmetic: How Culture May Influence How We Count**

## Box 1.2  Are You Anxious About Statistics?

■  ■  ■  ■   **Introduction**

Are you taking this course in statistics because it is required in your major—not because you find the subject interesting? If so, you may be feeling somewhat intimidated right now because you know that statistics involves numbers and math. Perhaps you feel intimidated by statistics not only because you're uncomfortable with math, but also because you probably suspect that numbers and math don't leave room for human judgment or have any relevance to your own personal experience. In fact, you may even question the relevance of statistics to understanding people, social behavior, or society.

In this course, we will attempt to show you that statistics can be a lot more interesting and easy to understand than you may have been led to believe. In fact, as we draw upon your previous knowledge and experience and relate materials to interesting and important social issues, you'll begin to see that statistics is not just a course you have to pass but a useful tool as well.

There are two major reasons why learning statistics may be of value to you. First, you are constantly exposed to statistics every day of your life. Marketing surveys, voting polls, and the findings of social research appear daily in newspapers and popular magazines. By learning statistics you will become a sharper consumer of statistical material. Second, as a major in the social sciences, you may be expected to read and interpret statistical information presented to you in the workplace. Even if conducting research is not a part of your job, you may still be expected to understand and learn from other people's research or to be able to write reports based on statistical analyses.

Just what *is* statistics anyway? Your familiar association with the word may be numbers that indicate birth rates, conviction rates, per-capita income, marriage and divorce rates, and so on. But the word **statistics** also refers to a set of procedures used by social scientists. They use these procedures to organize, summarize, and communicate information. Only information represented by numbers can be the subject of statistical analysis. Such information is called **data**; researchers use statistical procedures to analyze data to answer research questions and test theories. It is the latter usage—answering research questions and testing theories—that this textbook explores.

---

*Statistics*   A set of procedures used by social scientists to organize, summarize, and communicate information.

---

## The Research Process

To give you a better idea of the role of statistics in social research, I'd like to start by looking at the **research process**. We can think of the research process as a set of activities in which social scientists engage so they can answer questions, examine ideas, or test theories.

As illustrated in Figure 1.1, the research process consists of five main stages:

1. Asking the research question
2. Formulating the hypotheses
3. Collecting data
4. Analyzing data
5. Evaluating the hypotheses

Figure 1.1   **The Research Process**

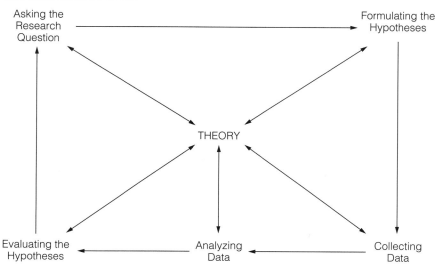

Each stage affects the *theory* and is affected by it as well. Statistics are most closely tied to the data analysis stage of the research process. As we will see in later chapters, statistical analysis of the data helps researchers test the validity and accuracy of their hypotheses. Let's briefly discuss each of the stages illustrated in Figure 1.1.

---

*Research Process* A set of activities in which social scientists engage to answer questions, examine ideas, or test theories.

---

> **Learning Check.** *Make sure you understand the research process described in Figure 1.1. Whenever you are asked to evaluate others' research, your first step will be to determine whether the researchers followed this process. Read on for more explanation of each stage.*

## Asking Research Questions

The starting point for most research is asking a *research question*. Consider the following research questions taken from a number of social science journals:

"Does cost control influence the quality of health care?"

"Has sexual harassment become more widespread during the last decade?"

"Does social class influence voting behavior?"

"What factors influence the economic mobility of women workers?"

These are all questions that can be answered by conducting **empirical research**. Empirical research is based on information that can be verified by using our direct experience. To answer research questions we cannot rely on reasoning, speculation, moral judgment, or subjective preference. For example, the questions "Is racial equality good for society?" or "Is an urban lifestyle better than a rural lifestyle?" cannot be answered empirically because the terms *good* and *better* are concerned with values, beliefs, or subjective preference and, therefore, cannot be independently verified. One way to study these questions is by defining "good" and "better" in terms that can be verified empirically. For example, we can define "good" in terms of economic growth and "better" in terms of psychological well-being. These questions could then be verified by conducting empirical research.

You may wonder how to come up with a research question. The first step is to pick a question that interests you. If you are not sure, look around! Ideas for research problems are all around you, from newspapers, magazines, and television to personal experience or your own intuition. Talk to other people, write down your own observations and ideas, or learn what other social scientists have written about.

Take, for instance, the issue of gender and work. As a college student about to enter the labor force, you may wonder about the similarities and differences between women's and men's work experiences and about the opportunities that will become available to you when you graduate. Here are some facts and observations based on only newspaper and research reports and my own personal experience: In 1993 women who were employed full-time earned $416 per week on average; men who were employed full-time earned $559 per week on average. Women's and men's work is also very different. Men and women are usually segregated into different types of work, and women remain a minority in many of the higher ranking and higher salaried positions in professional and managerial occupations.[1] For example, in 1993 women made up 21.8 percent of physicians, 22.8 percent of lawyers and judges, 18.6 percent of architects, and 31.2 percent of managers in marketing and advertising.[2] In contrast, of all women in the labor force, 44.6 percent were employed in either clerical or service jobs.[3] Some of the research questions these observations may inspire us to ask include: Are women paid, on average, less than men for the same types of work? How much change has there been in women's work over time? Does the fact that women and men work in gender-segregated settings relate to the disparity in earnings between men and women?

> **Learning Check.** *Can you think of one or two social science questions amenable to empirical research? You can almost bet that you will be required to do a research project sometime in your college career. Get a head start and start thinking about a good research question now.*

[1]U.S. Bureau of Labor Statistics. 1993. Full-time wage and salary workers: 1994. *Statistical Abstract of the United States*. Bulletin No. 2307. Washington, DC: GPO.

[2]U.S. Bureau of the Census. 1993. Employed persons, by sex, race, and occupation: 1994. *Statistical Abstract of the United States*. Washington, DC: GPO.

[3]Margaret L. Andersen, *Thinking about Women*. New York: MacMillan, 1993, 115.

## The Role of Theory

You may have noticed that each of the preceding research questions is expressed in terms of a *relationship*. This relationship may be between two or more attributes of individuals or groups, such as gender and income or gender segregation in the workplace and income disparity. The relationship between attributes or characteristics of people and groups lies at the heart of social scientific inquiry. We will have more to say about relationships later in this chapter as well as throughout this book. But for now, let's move on and discuss the role of theory in the research cycle.

Most of us use the term *theory* quite casually to explain events and experiences in our daily life. We may have a "theory" about why our boss has been so nice to us lately or why we didn't do so well on our last history test. In a somewhat similar manner, social scientists attempt to explain the nature of social reality. Whereas our theories about events in our lives are commonsense explanations based on educated guesses and personal experience, to the social scientist a theory is a more precise explanation that is frequently tested by conducting research.

A **theory** is a fairly elaborate explanation of the relationship between two or more observable attributes of individuals or groups. The goal of scientific theory is to establish a link between what we observe (the data) and our conceptual understanding of why certain phenomena are related to each other in a particular way. For instance, suppose we wanted to understand the reasons for the income disparity between men and women; we may wonder whether the types of jobs men and women have and the organizations in which they work have something to do with their wages.

One explanation for gender inequality in wages is *gender segregation in the workplace*. Gender segregation in the workplace refers to the concentration of men and women in different occupations and jobs.[4] Most American men and women are concentrated in different kinds of jobs and occupations. For example, in 1990, one-third of all women who were in the labor force worked in only 10 of the 503 occupations listed by the census, and only 11 percent worked in occupations that were at least 75 percent male.

What is the significance of gender segregation in the workplace? In our society, people's occupations and jobs are closely associated with their level of prestige, authority, and income. The jobs in which women and men are segregated are not only different but unequal. Although the proportion of women in the labor force has markedly increased, women are still concentrated in occupations with low pay, low prestige, and few opportunities for promotions. Thus, gender segregation in the workplace

[4]Barbara Reskin and Irene Padavic, *Women and Men at Work*. Thousand Oaks, CA: Pine Forge Press, 1994, 45.

is associated with unequal earnings, authority, and status. In particular, women's and men's segregation into different jobs and occupations is the most immediate cause of the pay gap. Women receive lower pay than men even when they have the same level of education, skills, and experience as men in comparable occupations.

---

*Theory*  An elaborate explanation of the relationship between two or more observable attributes of individuals or groups.

---

> **Learning Check.**  *Make sure you understand the importance of theory in research. The purpose of empirical research is to provide support for an existing theory, modify a theory to fit new evidence, or refute a theory.*

## Formulating the Hypotheses

So far we have come up with a number of research questions about the income disparity between men and women in the workplace. We have also discussed a possible explanation—a theory—that helps us make sense of many interrelated observations about gender inequality in wages. Is that enough? Where do we go from here?

Our next step is to test some of the ideas suggested by the gender segregation theory. This can be accomplished by doing some research. But this theory, even if it sounds reasonable and logical to us, is much too general and does not contain enough specific information to be directly tested. Instead, theories suggest specific, concrete predictions about the way observable attributes of people or groups are interrelated in real life. These predictions, called **hypotheses**, are tentative answers to research problems. Hypotheses are tentative because they can be verified only after they have been tested empirically.[5] For example, one hypothesis we can derive from the gender segregation theory is that wages in occupations in which the majority of workers are female are lower than the wages in occupations in which the majority of workers are male.

Not all hypotheses are derived directly from theories, as in the preceding example. We can generate hypotheses in many ways—from theories, directly from observations, or from intuition. Probably the greatest source for hypotheses is the professional literature. A critical review of the

[5]Chava Frankfort-Nachmias and David Nachmias, *Research Methods in the Social Sciences.* New York: St. Martin's Press, 1996, 62.

professional literature will familiarize you with the current state of knowledge and with hypotheses that others have studied.

---

*Hypothesis*   A tentative answer to a research problem.

---

But let's go back to our hypothesis and examine it carefully:

Wages in occupations in which the majority of workers are female are lower than the wages in occupations in which the majority of workers are male.

Notice that this hypothesis is a statement of a relationship between two characteristics that vary: *wages* and *gender composition* of occupations. Such characteristics are called variables. A **variable** is a property of people or objects that takes on two or more values. For example, a variable you hear about a lot as a student in the social sciences is "social class." People can be classified into a number of social class categories, such as upper class, middle class, or lower class. Similarly, people have different levels of education; therefore, "education" is a variable. "Family income" is a variable; it can take on values from zero to thousands of dollars or more. "Wages" is a variable; it also can take on values from zero to hundreds of thousands of dollars or more. Similarly, "gender composition" is a variable. The percentage of females (or males) in an occupation can vary from 0 to 100. (See Figure 1.2 for examples of some variables and their values.)

---

*Variable*   A property of people or objects that takes on two or more values.

---

Every variable must include categories that are both *exhaustive* and *mutually exclusive.* Exhaustiveness means that there should be enough categories composing the variables to enable us to classify every observation. For example, the common classification of the variable "marital status" into the categories "married," "single," "divorced," and "widowed" violates the requirement of exhaustiveness because it does not allow us to classify same-sex couples or heterosexual couples who are not legally married. (We can make every variable exhaustive by adding the category "other" to the list of categories. However, this practice is not recommended if it leads to the exclusion of categories that have theoretical significance or a substantial number of observations.)

Mutual exclusiveness refers to the need to classify every observation into one and only one category. Thus, for example, we need to define

Figure 1.2 **Variables and Value Categories**

| Variable | Categories |
|---|---|
| Social class | Upper class<br>Middle class<br>Lower class |
| Religion | Christian<br>Jewish<br>Muslim |
| Income | $ 1,000<br>$ 2,500<br>$10,000<br>$15,000 |
| Gender | Male<br>Female |

"religion" in such a way that no one would be classified into more than one category. For instance, the categories "Protestant" and "Methodist" are not mutually exclusive because Methodists are also considered Protestant and, therefore, could be classified into both categories.

Social scientists can choose which level of social life to focus their research on. They can focus on individuals or groups of people like families, organizations, nations, and so on. These distinctions are referred to as **units of analysis**. A variable will be a property of whatever the unit of analysis is for the study. Variables can be a property of individuals, of groups (such as the family or a social group), of organizations (such as a hospital or university), or of societies (such as a country or a nation). For example, in a study that looks at the relationship between the level of education of individuals and their income, the variable "income" refers to the income level of an individual. On the other hand, a study that compares how differences in corporations' revenues relate to differences in the fringe benefits they provide to their employees uses the variable "revenue" as a characteristic of an organization (the corporation). The variables "wages" and "gender composition" in our example are characteristics of occupations. Figure 1.3 illustrates different units of analysis frequently employed by social scientists.

Figure 1.3   **Examples of Units of Analysis**

*Individual as unit of analysis:*
How old are you?
What are your political views?
What is your occupation?

*Family as unit of analysis:*
How many children are in the family?
Who does the housework?
How many wage earners are there?

*Organization as unit of analysis:*
How many employees are there?
What is the gender composition?
Do you have a diversity office?

*City as unit of analysis:*
What was the crime rate last year?
What is the population density?
What type of government runs things?

---

*Unit of Analysis*   The level of social life on which social scientists focus. Examples of different levels are individuals and groups.

---

*Learning Check.*   *Remember that research question you came up with? Can you formulate a hypothesis you could test? Remember, the variables must take on two or more values and you must determine the unit of analysis.*

## Independent and Dependent Variables: Causality

Our hypotheses are usually stated in terms of a relationship between an *independent* and a *dependent variable*. The distinction between an independent and a dependent variable is an important one in the language of research. Social theories are often intended to provide an explanation for social patterns. The explanations often involve the notion of causal relations between variables. For example, according to the gender-segregation theory, gender segregation in the workplace is the primary explanation (although certainly not the only one) of the male/female earning gap. Why should jobs where the majority of workers are female pay less than jobs that employ mostly men? One explanation is that "societies undervalue the work women do, regardless of what those tasks are, because women do them. . . . Physical strength, for example, in which men tend to excel over women, commands premium pay in metal working industries. But manual dexterity, allegedly more common in women than men, does not raise workers' pay in assembly-line jobs."[6] Similarly, "In the United States, where most dentists are male, dentists are near the top of the income hierarchy; in Europe, where most dentists are female, dentists' incomes are much closer to the average income. In general, the more women in an occupation, the lower its average pay."[7]

In the language of research, the variable the researcher wants to explain (the effect) is called the **dependent variable**. The variable that is expected to "cause" or account for the dependent variable is called the **independent variable**. Therefore, in our example, "gender composition of occupations" is the independent variable, while "wages" is the dependent variable.

---

*Dependent Variable*   The variable to be explained (the "effect") by the researcher.

*Independent Variable*   The variable expected to account for (the "cause" of) the dependent variable.

---

Cause-and-effect relationships between variables are *not* easy to infer in the social sciences. You need to meet three conditions to establish that two variables are causally related: (1) the cause has to precede the effect in time, (2) there has to be an empirical relationship between the cause and the effect, and (3) this relationship cannot be explained by other factors.

Let's consider the decades-old debate about controlling crime through the use of prevention versus punishment as an example of how to evaluate cause-and-effect relationships. Some people argue that special counseling for youths at the first sign of trouble and strict controls on access to firearms would help reduce crime. Others argue that overhauling federal and state sentencing laws to stop early prison releases is the solution. Here's an example from the state of Washington, which in 1994 adopted a new

---

[6]Reskin and Padavic, pp. 118–119.
[7]Ibid.

measure—"three strikes and you're out"—imposing life prison terms on three-time felons. Let's suppose that two years after the measure was introduced the crime rate in Washington declined somewhat. Does the observation that the incidence of crime declined mean that the new measure caused this reduction? Not necessarily! Perhaps the rate of crime had been going down for other reasons, such as improvement in the economy, and the new measure had nothing to do with it. To demonstrate a cause-and-effect relationship, we would need to show three things: (1) the enactment of the "three strikes and you're out" measure was associated with a decrease in crime; (2) the reduction of crime actually occurred *after* the enactment of this measure; and (3) the relationship between the reduction in crime and the "three strikes and you're out" policy is not due to the influence of another variable (for instance, the improvement of overall economic conditions).

The three conditions required to establish cause-and-effect relationships are not always easy to meet in the real world. Even though it can be relatively easy to show that two variables are empirically correlated, for many variables investigated in the social sciences the time order is unclear. For instance, it would be difficult to establish which comes first: political party identification or attitudes toward gay rights, or level of education or self-esteem. Does a person with high self-esteem go to college or does a person who goes to college develop high self-esteem? Similarly, because of the complex nature of social reality, many empirical relationships we observe can be attributed to other factors. For example, suppose you observed a relationship between the number of firefighters at a fire site and the amount of damage.[8] The more firefighters at the site, the greater the amount of damage. This association might lead you to infer that the number of firefighters affects the amount of damage at a fire site. However, a third factor—the size of the fire—explains both the number of firefighters at the site and the amount of damage. When the fire is large, more firefighters are sent to the site and there is a great deal of damage. Similarly, when the fire is small, fewer firefighters are at the site and there is probably very little damage. But, if you limit your observations to only large fires or to only small fires, you will not find an association between the number of firefighters and the amount of damage. The empirical relationship between the number of firefighters in different sites and the amount of damage is *spurious* (fake). A relationship is **spurious** when it can be "explained away" by another variable. (In Chapter 6 we will learn about a statistical procedure, elaboration, that can help us uncover spurious relationships.)

[8]Frankfort-Nachmias and Nachmias, p. 57.

## Independent and Dependent Variables: Guidelines

Because of the limitations in inferring cause-and-effect relationships in the social sciences, be cautious about using the terms *cause* and *effect* when examining relationships between variables. However, using the terms *independent variable* and *dependent variable* is still appropriate even when this relationship is not articulated in terms of direct cause and effect. Here are a few guidelines that may help you to identify the independent and dependent variables:

1. The dependent variable is always the property you are trying to explain; it is always the object of the research.
2. The independent variable usually occurs earlier in time than the dependent variable.
3. The independent variable is often seen as influencing, directly or indirectly, the dependent variable.

To determine which is the independent variable and which is the dependent variable, be guided by the purpose of the research. In the real world, variables are neither dependent nor independent; they can be switched around depending on the research problem. A variable defined as independent in one research investigation may be a dependent variable in another.[9] For instance, "formal education" may be an independent variable in a study attempting to explain how education influences political attitudes. However, in an investigation of whether a person's level of education is influenced by the social status of his or her family of origin, "formal education" will be the dependent variable. Some variables, such as "sex," "race," "age," or "ethnicity," because they are primordial characteristics that cannot be explained by social scientists, are never considered dependent variables in a social science analysis.

---

**Learning Check.** *Try to identify the independent and dependent variables in the following hypotheses:*

- *Children who attended preschool day-care centers earn better grades in first grade than children who received home preschool care.*
- *People who attend church regularly are more likely to oppose abortion than people who do not attend church regularly.*

*What are the independent and dependent variables in* your *hypotheses?*

---

[9]Frankfort-Nachmias and Nachmias, p. 56.

### Collecting Data

Once we have decided on the research question, the hypothesis, and the variables to be included in the study, we proceed to the next stage in the research cycle. This step includes measuring our variables and collecting the data. As researchers, we must decide how to measure the variables of interest to us, how to select the cases for our research, and what kind of data collection techniques we will be using. A wide variety of data collection techniques are available to us, from direct observations to survey research, experiments, or secondary sources. Similarly, we can construct numerous measuring instruments. These instruments can be as simple as a single question included in a questionnaire or as complex as a composite measure constructed through the combination of two or more question-naire items. The choice of a particular data collection method or instrument to measure our variables depends on the study objective. For instance, say we decide to study how social class position is related to attitudes about abortion. Since attitudes about abortion are not directly observable, we need to collect data by asking a group of people questions about their attitudes and opinions. A suitable method of data collection for this project would be a *survey* that uses some kind of questionnaire or interview guide to elicit verbal reports from respondents. The questionnaire could include numerous questions designed to measure attitudes toward abortion, social class, and other variables relevant to the study.

Now let's go back to our earlier example and see how we would go about collecting data to test the hypothesis relating the gender composition of occupations to wages. We want to gather information on the proportion of men and women in different occupations and the average earnings for these occupations. This kind of information is routinely collected by the government and published in sources such as bulletins distributed by the U.S. Department of Labor's Bureau of Labor Statistics and the *Statistical Abstract of the United States*. The data obtained from these sources could then be analyzed and used to test our hypothesis.

### Levels of Measurement

The statistical analysis of data involves many mathematical operations, from simple counting to addition and multiplication. However, not every operation can be freely used with every variable. The type of statistical operations we employ will depend on how our variables are measured. For example, for the variable "gender," we can use the number "1" to represent females and the number "2" to represent males. Similarly, "1" can also be used as a numerical code for the category "one child" in the variable "number of children." Clearly, in the first example the number is an arbitrary symbol that does not correspond to the property "female," whereas in the second example the number "1" has a distinct numerical meaning that does correspond to the property "one child." The correspondence between the properties we measure and the numbers representing these properties determines the type of statistical operations we use in our numerical calculations. The degree of correspondence also leads to a distinction among different ways of measuring—that is, to distinct *levels of measurement*. In this section we will discuss three levels of measurement—*nominal, ordinal,* and *interval-ratio*.

*Nominal Level of Measurement* At the **nominal** level of measurement numbers or other symbols are assigned to a set of categories for the purpose of naming, labeling, or classifying the observations. "Gender" is an example of a nominal level variable. Using the numbers "1" and "2," for instance, we can classify our observations into the categories "females" and "males," with "1" representing females and "2" representing males. We could use any of a variety of symbols to represent the different categories of a nominal variable; however, when numbers are used to represent the different categories, we do not imply anything about the magnitude or quantitative difference between the categories. Because the different categories (males vs. females, for instance) vary in the quality inherent in each but not in quantity, nominal variables are often called *qualitative*. Other examples of nominal level variables are "political party," "religion," and "race."

*Ordinal Level of Measurement* Whenever we assign numbers to rank-ordered categories ranging from low to high, we have an **ordinal** level variable. "Social class" is an example of an ordinal variable. We might classify individuals with respect to their social class status as "upper class," "middle class," or "working class." We can say that a person in the category of "upper class" has a higher class position than a person in a "middle class" category (or that a "middle class" position is higher than a "lower class" position), but we do not know the magnitude of the differences between each of these categories. That is, we don't know how much higher "upper class" is compared with "middle class."

Many attitudes we measure in the social sciences are ordinal level variables. Take, for instance, the following question used to measure attitudes toward same-sex marriages: "Same-sex couples should have the right to marry one another." Respondents are asked to mark the number representing their degree of agreement or disagreement with this statement. One form in which a number might be made to correspond

Table 1.1 **Ordinal Ranking Scale**

| Rank | Value |
| --- | --- |
| 1 | Strongly agree |
| 2 | Agree |
| 3 | Neither agree nor disagree |
| 4 | Disagree |
| 5 | Strongly disagree |

with the answers can be seen in Table 1.1. Although the differences between these numbers represent higher or lower degrees of agreement with same-sex marriages, the distance between any two of those numbers does not have a precise numerical meaning.

*Interval-Ratio Level of Measurement* If the categories (or values) of a variable can be rank-ordered, and if the measurements for all the cases are expressed in the same units, then an **interval-ratio** level of measurement has been achieved. Examples of variables measured at the interval-ratio level are "age," "birth rate," "income," and "SAT scores." With all these variables we can compare values, not only in terms of which is larger or smaller, but also in terms of *how much* larger or smaller one is compared with another. In some discussions of levels of measurement you will see a distinction made between interval-ratio variables that have a natural zero point (where zero means the absence of the property) and those variables that have zero as an arbitrary point. For example, "weight" and "length" have a natural zero point, whereas "temperature" has an arbitrary zero point. Variables with a natural zero point are also called *ratio variables*. In statistical practice, however, ratio variables are subjected to operations that treat them as interval and ignore their ratio properties. Therefore, no distinction between these two types is made in this text.

*Nominal Measurement* Numbers or other symbols are assigned to a set of categories for the purpose of naming, labeling, or classifying the observations.

*Ordinal Measurement* Numbers are assigned to rank-ordered categories ranging from low to high.

*Interval-Ratio Measurement* Measurements for all cases are expressed in the same units.

Table 1.2  **Gender Composition in Four Major Occupational Groups (in percentages)**

| Occupational Group | Women in Occupation |
| --- | --- |
| Executive, administrative, and managerial | 42 |
| Administrative support | 79 |
| Transportation workers | 4 |
| Service workers | 60 |

*Cumulative Property of Levels of Measurement* Variables that can be measured at the interval-ratio level of measurement can also be measured at the ordinal and nominal levels. As a rule, properties that can be measured at a higher level (interval-ratio is the highest) can also be measured at lower levels, but not vice versa. Let's take for example "gender composition" of occupations, the independent variable in our research example. Table 1.2 shows the percentage of women in four major occupational groups as reported in the 1994 *Statistical Abstract of the United States*.[10]

The variable "gender composition" (measured as the percentage of women in the occupational group) is an interval-ratio variable and, therefore, has the properties of nominal, ordinal, and interval-ratio measures. For example, we can say that the transportation group differs from the service workers group (a nominal comparison), that service occupations have more women than transportation occupations (an ordinal comparison), and that service occupations have 56 percentage points more women (60 minus 4) than transportation occupations (an interval-ratio comparison).

The type of comparisons possible at each level of measurement are summarized in Table 1.3 and Figure 1.4. Notice that whereas differences can be established at each of the three levels, only at the interval-ratio level can we establish the magnitude of the difference.

> **Learning Check.** *Make sure you understand these levels of measurement. In the not too distant future, your instructor is likely to ask you what statistical procedure you would use to describe or analyze a set of data. To make the proper choice, you must know the level of measurement of the data.*

[10]*Statistical Abstract of the United States*, 1994.

Table 1.3  **Levels of Measurement and Possible Comparisons**

| Level | Different or Equivalent | Higher or Lower | How Much Higher |
|-------|------------------------|-----------------|-----------------|
| Nominal | Yes | No | No |
| Ordinal | Yes | Yes | No |
| Interval-ratio | Yes | Yes | Yes |

Figure 1.4  **Levels of Measurement and Possible Comparisons: Education Measured on Nominal, Ordinal, and Interval-Ratio Levels**

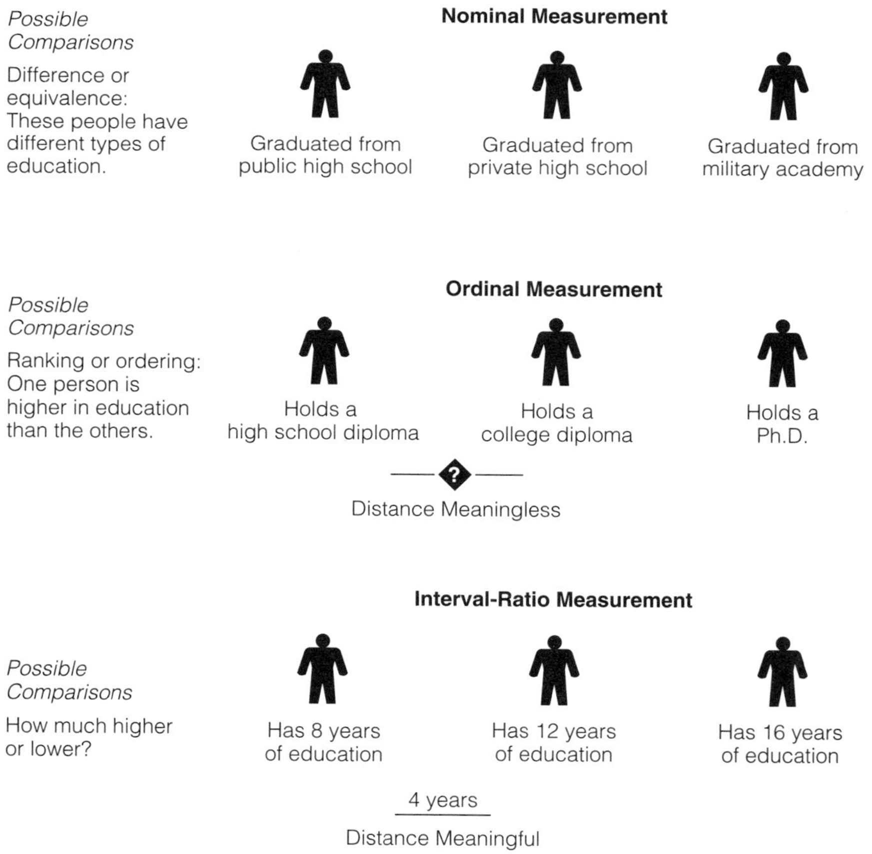

*Possible Comparisons*

**Nominal Measurement**

Difference or equivalence: These people have different types of education.

Graduated from public high school

Graduated from private high school

Graduated from military academy

*Possible Comparisons*

**Ordinal Measurement**

Ranking or ordering: One person is higher in education than the others.

Holds a high school diploma

Holds a college diploma

Holds a Ph.D.

 ? Distance Meaningless

*Possible Comparisons*

**Interval-Ratio Measurement**

How much higher or lower?

Has 8 years of education

Has 12 years of education

Has 16 years of education

 4 years Distance Meaningful

*Levels of Measurement of Dichotomous Variables* A variable that has only two values is called a *dichotomous variable*. Several key social factors like "gender," "employment status," and "marital status" are dichotomies. For example, you are either male or female; employed or unemployed; married or not married. Such variables may seem to be measured at the nominal level: you either fit in the male category or the female category. No category is naturally higher or lower than the other so they can't be ordered.

However, because there are only two possible values for a dichotomy, we can measure it at the ordinal or the interval-ratio level. For example, we can think of "femaleness" as the ordering principle for gender, so that "female" is higher and "male" is lower. Using "maleness" as the ordering principle, "female" is lower and "male" is higher. In either case, with only two classes there is no way to get them out of order, and, therefore, gender could be considered at the ordinal level.

Dichotomous variables can also be considered to be interval-ratio level. Why is this? In measuring interval-ratio data, the size of the interval between the categories is *meaningful*: the distance between 4 and 7, for example, is the same as the distance between 11 and 14. But with a dichotomy, there is only one interval. Therefore, there is really no other distance to which we can compare it:

 ————————    HIV+ ——————— HIV–

Mathematically, this gives the dichotomy more power than other nominal level variables (as you will notice later in the text).

This is why researchers "dichotomize" some of their variables, turning a multicategory nominal variable into a dichotomy. For example, you may see "race" (originally divided into many categories) dichotomized into "white" and "nonwhite." Though this is substantively suspect, it may be the most logical statistical step to take.

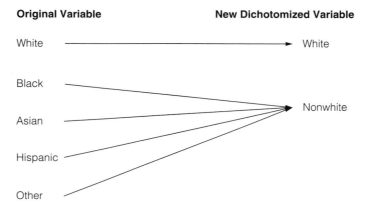

Just be sure that the grouping into two categories (for example, White vs. Nonwhite) captures a distinction that is important to your research question.

### Discrete and Continuous Variables

The statistical operations we can perform are also determined by whether the variables are continuous or discrete. *Discrete* variables have a minimum-sized unit of measurement, which cannot be subdivided. The number of children per family is an example of a discrete variable because the minimum unit is one child. Families may have 2 or 3 children but not 2.5 children. The variable "wages" in our research example is a discrete variable because currency has a minimum unit (1 cent), which cannot be subdivided. One can have $101.21 or $101.22 but not $101.21843. Wages cannot differ by less than 1 cent—the minimum-sized unit.

Unlike discrete variables, *continuous* variables do not have a minimum-sized unit of measurement and, therefore, their range of values can be subdivided into increasingly smaller fractional values. "Length" is an example of a continuous variable because there is no minimum unit of length. A particular object may be 12 inches long, it may be 12.5 inches long, or it may be 12.532011 inches long. Although we cannot always measure all possible length values with absolute accuracy (some values will be too small for any measuring instrument to register), it is possible for objects to exist at an infinite number of lengths.[11] In principle, we can speak of a tenth of an inch, a ten-thousandth of an inch, or a ten-trillionth of an inch. The variable "gender composition of occupation" is a continuous variable because it is measured in proportions or percentages (for example, the percentage of women in medicine), which can be subdivided into smaller and smaller fractions.

This attribute of variables—whether they are continuous or discrete—affects subsequent research operations, particularly measurement procedures, data analysis, and methods of inference and generalizations. However, please keep in mind that, in practice, some discrete variables can be treated as if they were continuous, and vice versa.

> ***Learning Check.*** *Name three continuous and three discrete variables. Determine whether each of the variables in your hypothesis is continuous or discrete.*

---

[11]Frankfort-Nachmias and Nachmias, p. 58.

## Analyzing Data and Evaluating the Hypotheses

Following the data collection stage, researchers analyze their data and evaluate the hypotheses of the study. The data consist of codes and numbers used to represent our observations. In our example, each occupational group would be represented by two scores: (1) the percentage of women and (2) the average wage. If, for instance, we had collected information on 100 occupations, we would end up with 200 scores, 2 per occupational group. However, the typical research project includes more variables; therefore, the amount of data the researcher confronts is considerably larger. We now must find a systematic way to organize these data, analyze them, and use some set of procedures to decide what they mean. These last steps make up the *statistical analysis* stage, which is the main topic of this textbook. It is also at this point in the research cycle where statistical procedures will help us *evaluate* our research hypothesis and assess the theory from which the hypothesis was derived.

## Descriptive and Inferential Statistics: Principles

Statistical procedures can be divided into two major categories: *descriptive statistics* and *inferential statistics*. Before we can discuss the difference between these two types of statistics we need to understand the terms *population* and *sample*. A **population** is the total set of individuals, objects, groups, or events in which the researcher is interested. For example, if we were interested in looking at voting behavior in the last presidential election, we would probably define our population as all citizens who voted in the election. If we wanted to understand the employment patterns of Hispanic women in our state, we would include in our population all Hispanic women in our state who are in the labor force.

Although we are usually interested in a population, quite often, because of limited time and resources, it is impossible to study the entire population. Imagine interviewing all the citizens of the United States who voted in the last election, or even all the individuals who are in the labor force in our state. Not only would that be very expensive and time consuming, but we would probably have a very hard time locating everyone! Fortunately, we can learn a lot about a population if we carefully select a subset from that population. This subset is called a *sample*. A **sample** is a relatively small subset selected from a population. Researchers usually collect their data from a sample and then generalize their observations to the larger population.

*Population*   The total set of individuals, objects, groups, or events in which the researcher is interested.

*Sample*   A relatively small subset selected from a population.

**Descriptive statistics** includes procedures that help us organize and describe data collected from either a sample or a population. (Occasionally data are collected on an entire population.) **Inferential statistics**, on the other hand, is concerned with making predictions or inferences about a population from observations and analyses of the sample. For instance, the General Social Survey (GSS), from which numerous examples presented in this book are drawn, is conducted every year by the National Opinion Research Center (NORC) on a representative sample of about 1500 respondents. The survey, which includes several hundred questions, is designed to provide social science researchers with a readily accessible database of socially relevant attitudes, behaviors, and attributes of a cross-section of the U.S. adult population. NORC has verified that the composition of the GSS samples closely resembles census data. But because the data are based on a sample rather than on the entire population, the average for the sample will not equal the average of the population as a whole. For example, in the 1991 GSS respondents were asked what they think is the ideal number of children for a family. In analyzing the responses (using a descriptive statistical procedure to calculate averages), researchers found the average to be 3.4. This average will probably differ from the average of the population from which the GSS sample was drawn. The tools of statistical inference help determine the accuracy of the sample average obtained by the researchers. We show in later chapters (11 and 12) that the sample average for any given sample (here, 3.4) is likely to be fairly close to the actual "true" average in the population.

*Descriptive Statistics*   Procedures that help us organize and describe data collected from either a sample or a population.

*Inferential Statistics*   The logic and procedures concerned with making predictions or inferences about a population from observations and analyses of the sample.

### Descriptive and Inferential Statistics: Illustration

Let's now go back to our research example on gender segregation in the workplace to illustrate some descriptive statistical procedures and the role of inferential statistics. Numerous statistical procedures can be applied to data collected on the gender composition of occupations and the wages associated with these occupations. We will begin to look at some of the options in the next chapter. For now, let's review briefly some of the statistical procedures we can apply with the data we have collected.

*Organization of Information: Frequency Distributions* At the completion of the data collection phase of our study we will have accumulated a great deal of information typically represented by thousands of numbers. To make sense out of these data we will want to organize and summarize them in some systematic way. For example, we may want to count how many women worked in the top occupations for women in recent years. In Chapter 2, we will learn about a device called a *frequency distribution*, which allows us to perform such analyses. Table 1.4 is an example of a frequency distribution taken from the 1992 Census Bureau (this is an example of population data). It lists the number of women who work in the top five primarily female occupations in the United States. (For more on frequency distributions see Chapter 2.)

*Graphic Presentation* We can also organize and summarize the information using visual aids such as charts and graphs. For example, Figure 1.5 is a graph displaying the percentage of females employed in selected occupations in 1992. We will learn more about some of the graphic techniques available to us in Chapter 3.

Table 1.4    **Top Five Occupations for Women, 1990**

| Occupation | Number of Women |
|---|---|
| Total women in labor force | 56,487,249 |
| Secretary | 3,966,179 |
| Elementary schoolteacher | 2,372,174 |
| Cashier | 2,259,316 |
| Registered nurse | 1,777,885 |
| Bookkeeper, accounting clerk | 1,721,202 |

*Source:* U.S. Bureau of the Census, 1992a: Table 1.

Figure 1.5 **Percentage of Selected Managerial and Professional Specialists Who Are Female**

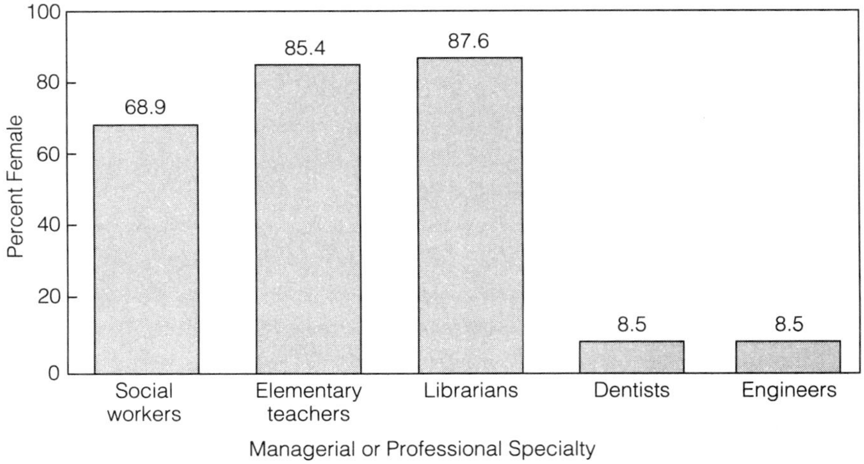

Source: *Statistical Abstract of the United States,* 1993.

*Measures of Central Tendency*  Another way to summarize quantitative information is by calculating measures that inform us about some central trends in our data. For example, we may want to find the average wage in each of the five occupations listed in Figure 1.5. Measures that tell us what is average or typical about a distribution are described in Chapter 4.

*Measures of Variability*  Social researchers are usually interested not only in what is average or typical in a set of observations, but also in the degree of differences displayed in these data. For example, we may be interested in measuring the extent of racial diversity in each of the occupational groups examined in our study. Measures that describe diversity and variation in a set of observations are described in Chapter 5.

*Bivariate Methods*  To examine the relationship between the gender composition of occupations (the independent variable) and wages (the dependent variable) we can calculate a measure of association. Bivariate methods for describing associations between variables are described in Chapters 6, 7, and 8.

*Statistical Inference*  Our research on the gender composition of occupations was based on a *sample* of occupations selected from all occupational groups in the United States. Whenever statistical analyses are based on samples rather than on the entire population findings may not reflect the actual trends in the whole population. *Statistical inference* will help us decide how closely our sample can be expected to resemble the population from which it was drawn. Statistical inference is discussed in Chapters 11 through 16.

### Evaluating the Hypotheses

At the completion of these descriptive and inferential procedures we can move to the next stage of the research process—the assessment and evaluation of our hypotheses and theories in light of the analyzed data. At this next stage new questions might be raised about unexpected trends in the data and about other variables that may have to be considered in addition to our original variables. For example, we may have found that the relationship between gender composition of occupations and earnings can be observed with respect to some groups of occupations but not others. Similarly, the relationship between these variables may apply for some racial/ethnic groups but not for others.

Those findings will provide evidence to help us decide how our data relate to the theoretical framework that guided our research. We may decide to revise our theory and hypothesis to take account of those later findings. Recent studies[12] are actually modifying what we know about gender segregation in the workplace. These studies suggest that race, as well as gender, shapes the occupational structure in the United States and explains disparities in income. This reformulation of the theory calls for a modified hypothesis and new research, which will start the circular process of research all over again.

Statistics provides an important link between theory and research. As our example on gender segregation demonstrates, the application of statistical techniques is an indispensable part of the research process. The results of statistical analyses help us evaluate our hypotheses and theories, discover unanticipated patterns and trends, and provide the impetus for shaping and reformulating our theories. Nevertheless, the importance of statistics should not diminish the significance of the preceding phases of the research process. Nor does the use of statistics lessen the importance of our own judgment in the entire process. Statistical analysis is a relatively small part of the research process, and even the most rigorous statistical procedures cannot speak for themselves. If our research questions are poorly conceived or our data are flawed due to errors in our design and measurement procedures, our results will be useless.

[12]For example, see Wu Xu and Ann Leffler, "Gender and Race Effects on Occupational Prestige, Segregation, and Earnings." *Gender and Society*, Vol. 6, No. 3, September 1992.

## Looking at Social Differences

By the middle of the next century, if current trends continue unchanged, the United States will no longer be a predominantly white society. Due mostly to renewed immigration and higher birth rates, the United States is being transformed into "a global society" in which nearly half of all Americans will be African Americans, Asian Americans, Hispanic Americans, or Native Americans.

Is the increasing diversity of American society relevant to social scientists? What impact will such diversity have on the research methodologies we employ?

In a diverse society stratified by race, ethnicity, class, and gender, less partial and distorted explanations of social relations tend to result when researchers, research participants, and the research process itself reflect that diversity. Such diversity shapes the research questions we ask, how we observe and interpret our findings, and the conclusions we draw.

How does a consciousness of social differences inform social statistics? How can issues of race, class, gender, and other categories of experience shape the way we approach statistics? A statistical approach that focuses on social differences uses statistical tools to examine how variables such as race, class, and gender, as well as other categories of experience such as age, religion, and sexual preference, shape our social world and explain social behavior. Numerous statistical procedures can be applied to describe these processes, and we will begin to look at some of those options in the next chapter. For now, let's preview briefly some of the procedures that can be employed to analyze social differences.

In Chapter 2, we will learn how to organize information using descriptive techniques, such as frequency distributions, percentage distributions, ratios, and rates. These statistical tools can also be employed to learn about the characteristics and experiences of groups in our society

---

### Box 1.1  A Tale of Simple Arithmetic: How Culture May Influence How We Count

A second-grade schoolteacher posed this problem to the class: "There are four blackbirds sitting in a tree. You take a slingshot and shoot one of them. How many are left?"

"Three," answered the seven-year-old European with certainty. "One subtracted from four leaves three."

"Zero," answered the seven-year-old African with equal certainty. "If you shoot one bird, the others will fly away." *

*Working Woman, January 1991, 45.

that have not been as visible as other groups. For example, in a series of special reports published by the Census Bureau over the last few years, these descriptive statistical techniques were used to describe the characteristics and experiences of Native Americans, Hispanics, and the elderly in America.

In Chapter 3, we illustrate how graphic devices can highlight diversity. In particular, graphs help us to (1) explore the differences and similarities between the many social groups coexisting within American society and (2) emphasize the rapidly changing composition of the U.S. population. Using data published by the Census Bureau on the elderly in America, we discuss various graphic devices that can be used to describe differences and similarities among the elderly. For instance, by employing a simple graphic device called a bar chart, we depict variations in the living patterns of the elderly and show that in every age category elderly females are more likely than elderly males to live alone. Another graphic device, called a time series chart, shows changes over time in the percentages of divorced white, African American, and Hispanic women.

Whereas the similarities and commonalities in social experiences can be depicted using measures of central tendency (Chapter 4), the differences and diversity within social groups can be described using statistical measures of variation. For instance, we may want to analyze the changing age composition in the United States, or compare the degree of racial/ethnic or religious diversity in the fifty states. Measures such as the standard deviation and the index of qualitative variation (IQV) are calculated for these purposes. For example, using IQV, we can demonstrate that Vermont is the least diverse state, whereas New Mexico is the most diverse (Chapter 5).

Finally, in Chapter 6, we discuss a method of bivariate analysis (cross-tabulation), which is especially suitable for examining the association between different social behaviors and variables such as race, class, ethnicity, gender, or religion. We use this method of analysis to show not only how each of these variables operates independently in shaping behavior, but also how they interlock in shaping our experience as individuals in society.[13]

Finally, a word of caution about all applications of statistics. Whatever model of social research you use, whether you follow a traditional model of research or integrate your analysis with qualitative data, and whether you focus on social differences or on other aspects of social behavior that

---

[13]Patricia Hill Collins, "Toward a New Vision: Race, Class, and Gender as Categories of Analysis and Connection." Keynote address at Integrating Race and Gender into the College Curriculum: A workshop sponsored by the Center for Research on Women, Memphis State University, Memphis, TN, 1989.

## Box 1.2  Are You Anxious About Statistics?

Some of you are probably taking this introductory course in statistics with a great deal of suspicion and very little enthusiasm. The word *statistics* may make you anxious because you associate statistics with numbers, formulas, and abstract notations that seem inaccessible and complicated. It appears that statistics is not as integrated into the rest of your life as are other parts of the college curriculum.

Statistics is perhaps the most anxiety-provoking course in any social science curriculum. This anxiety often leads to a less than optimum learning environment with students often trying to memorize every detail of a statistical procedure rather than trying to understand the general concept involved.

After many years of teaching statistics, I have learned that what underlies many of the difficulties students have in learning statistics, is the belief that it involves mainly memorization of meaningless formulas.

There is no denying that statistics involves many strange symbols and unfamiliar terms. It is also true that you need to know some math to do statistics. But although the subject involves some mathematical computations, you will not be asked to know more than four basic operations: addition, subtraction, multiplication, and division. The language of statistics may appear difficult because these operations (and how they are combined) are written in a code that is unfamiliar to you. Those abstract notations are simply part of the language of statistics; much like learning any foreign language, you need to learn the alphabet before you can "speak the language." Once you understand the vocabulary and are able to translate the symbols and codes into terms that are familiar to you, you will feel more relaxed and begin to see how statistical techniques are just one more source of information.

For me, the key to enjoying and feeling competent in statistics is to frame anything I do in a familiar language and in a context that is relevant and interesting. Therefore, you will find that this book emphasizes intuition, logic, and common sense over rote memorization and derivation of formulas. I have found that this approach reduces statistics anxiety for most students and improves learning.

Another strategy that will help you develop confidence in your ability to do statistics is working with other people. This book encourages collaboration in learning statistics as a strategy designed to help you overcome statistics anxiety. Over the years I have learned that students who are intimidated by statistics do not like to admit it or talk about it. This avoidance mechanism may be an obstacle to overcoming statistics anxiety. Talking about your feelings with other students will help you realize that you are not the only one who suffers from fears of inadequacy about statistics. This sharing process is at the heart of the treatment of statistics anxiety, not because it will help you realize that you are not the "dumbest" one in the class after all, but because talking to others in a "safe" group setting will help you take risks and trust your own intuition and judgment. Ultimately, your judgment and intuition lie at the heart of your ability to translate statistical symbols and concepts into a language that makes sense and to interpret data using newly acquired statistical tools. *

*This discussion is based on Sheila Tobias' pioneering work on mathematics anxiety. See especially Sheila Tobias, *Overcoming Math Anxiety*. New York: Norton, 1978, Chapters 2 and 8.

may interest you, any application of statistical procedures requires a basic understanding of the statistical concepts and techniques. This text, as an introductory book to social statistics, is intended to familiarize you with the range of descriptive and inferential statistics widely applied in the social sciences. But this emphasis on statistical techniques should not diminish the importance of human judgment and your awareness of the personmade quality of statistics. Only with this awareness can statistics become a useful tool for viewing social life.

## MAIN POINTS

- Statistics are procedures used by social scientists to organize, summarize, and communicate information. Only information represented by numbers can be the subject of statistical analysis.

- The research process is a set of activities in which social scientists engage to answer questions, examine ideas, or test theories. It consists of the following stages: asking the research question, formulating the hypotheses, collecting data, analyzing data, and evaluating the hypotheses.

- A theory is a fairly elaborate explanation of the relationship between two or more observable attributes of individuals or groups.

- Theories offer specific concrete predictions about the way observable attributes of people or groups would be interrelated in real life. These predictions, called hypotheses, are tentative answers to research problems.

- A variable is a property of people or objects that takes on two or more values. The variable the researcher wants to explain (the "effect") is called the dependent variable. The variable that is expected to "cause" or account for the dependent variable is called the independent variable.

- Three conditions are required to establish causal relations: (1) the cause has to precede the effect in time, (2) there has to be an empirical relationship between the cause and the effect, and (3) this relationship cannot be (spurious) explained by other factors.

- At the nominal level of measurement, numbers or other symbols are assigned to a set of categories to name, label, or classify the observations. At the ordinal level of measurement, categories can be rank-ordered from low to high (or vice versa). At the interval-ratio level of measurement, measurements for all cases are expressed in the same unit.

- A population is the total set of individuals, objects, groups, or events in which the researcher is interested. A sample is a relatively small subset selected from a population.

■ Descriptive statistics includes procedures that help us organize and describe data collected from either a sample or a population. Inferential statistics is concerned with making predictions or inferences about a population from observations and analyses of the sample.

### KEY TERMS

| | |
|---|---|
| *data* | *ordinal measurement* |
| *dependent variable* | *population* |
| *descriptive statistics* | *research process* |
| *empirical research* | *sample* |
| *hypothesis* | *statistics* |
| *independent variable* | *theory* |
| *inferential statistics* | *unit of analysis* |
| *interval-ratio measurement* | *variable* |
| *nominal measurement* | |

### SPSS DEMONSTRATIONS

The data that you will use in the computer exercises for this text are designed to be used with the program SPSS for Windows. There are two versions of the program, a standard version with no limitations on the number of variables or cases (respondents), and a student version, with a limitation of 1,500 cases and 50 variables. The data files included with this book have been constructed so that they can be used with either version of SPSS.

The data that you will use are included in two files: GSS94.SAV and GSS87_91.SAV. The "SAV" extension tells you the file is an SPSS data file stored in a format that the program can easily read. The files contain responses from the General Social Survey (GSS). See Appendix F for a full description of the GSS.

The file GSS94.SAV contains a selection of variables from the full 1994 file and a random sample of 1,000 respondents from the file, rather than all the respondents (which number about 3,000). The file GSS87_91.SAV contains responses from the years 1987 to 1991, inclusive. This will allow you to look at changes over time. The file contains 1400 cases, randomly selected from each of these five years, and, again, a small selection of variables from the full files for each year.

Appendix E explains the basic operation of SPSS for Windows and shows how to run the program. You may need to refer to that appendix before proceeding further.

When you begin to use a new data set, one of the first tasks is to review the definitions of the variables. Appendix F includes this information for each variable, but you can also access the information directly in SPSS. There are two ways this can be accomplished.

First, of course, you have to open a data file. As with all Windows programs, files are opened in SPSS by clicking on *File*, then on *Open*, then on *Data*. After switching directories and drives to the location of the files (which may be on a hard disk or a floppy drive), you can select either of the two GSS files and click on *OK*.

One way to review the list of variables in an SPSS file is to click on the *Utilities* choice from the main menu, then on *Variables* in the list of submenu choices. When you do so, a dialog box opens (depicted, showing the 1994 file). The SPSS variable names, which are limited to eight characters or less, are listed in the scroll box. When a variable is highlighted, the descriptive label for the variable is listed, along with any missing values that have been defined, plus value labels for the categories of the variable, if necessary.

A second way to see the same information, and also be able to print it so that you have a hard copy of the data definitions, is to click on *Utilities*, then on *File Info*. This choice tells SPSS to place variable definition information in the Output window. You can scroll up and down in the Output window to see the variables, and you can print the Output window

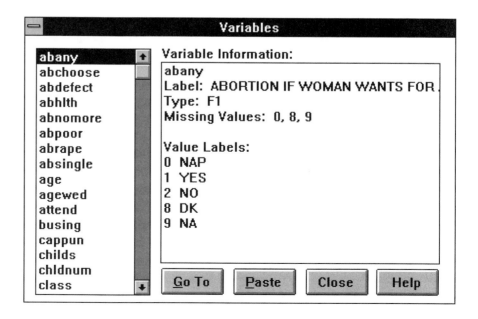

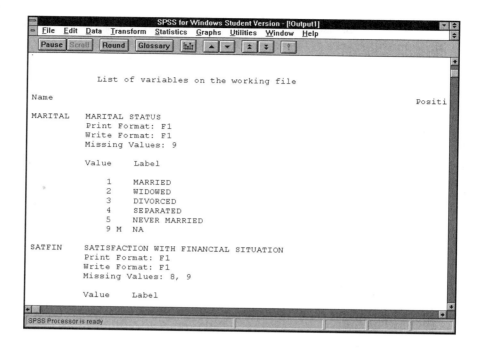

to keep a printed version of this information. The order of variables in this second option matches that in the Data Editor window, whereas the first option lists the variables in alphabetical order.

### EXERCISES

1. Review Figure 1.1 in the chapter (it describes the research process). Why are arrows shown going in both directions between the Evaluating the Hypotheses and Theory stages?

2. Construct potential hypotheses or research questions to relate the variables in each of the following examples. Also, write a brief statement explaining why you believe there is a relationship between the variables as specified in your hypotheses.
   a. Gender and educational level; gender and retirement age
   b. Income and race (define race in whatever categories you wish)
   c. The murder rate and the number of executions in a state; the crime rate and the number of police in a city
   d. The percentage of the gross national product (GNP) for a nation spent on military expenditures and the overall level of security for that nation

3. Determine the level of measurement for each of these variables.
   a. The number of people in your family
   b. Place of residence, classified as urban, suburban, or rural
   c. The percentage of a college's students who attended public high schools
   d. The rating of the overall quality of a textbook, on a scale from "Excellent" to "Poor"
   e. The type of transportation a person takes to work (for example, bus, walk, car)
   f. The highest educational degree earned
   g. The unemployment rate in the United States

4. Develop a theory to explain the amount of education that people attain. Use at least three independent variables in your theory, with "education" as the dependent variable. Construct hypotheses to link each of the independent variables with educational attainment.

5. For each of the variables in exercise 3 that you classified as interval-ratio, indicate whether it is discrete or continuous.

6. For each of the following examples, indicate whether it involves the use of descriptive or inferential statistics. Justify your answer.
   a. Estimating the number of unemployed people in the United States
   b. Asking all the students at a college their opinion about the quality of food at the cafeteria
   c. Calculating the profit of a business
   d. Conducting a study to determine the rating of the quality of a new automobile, gathered from 1000 new buyers
   e. The average salaries of various categories of employees (for example, tellers and loan officers) at a large bank
   f. The change (increase or decrease) in the number of immigrants coming to the United States from Asian countries between 1980 and 1995

7. List three research questions you find interesting that can be investigated with statistics. Find sources for the questions in your daily life, in what you see on television or read about in the newspaper or magazines, or from classes you've taken at school. Which one of these would be the most difficult to study? Why?

8. Construct measures of political participation at the nominal, ordinal, and interval-ratio levels. (*Hint:* You can use such behaviors as voting frequency or political party membership in constructing these measures.) Discuss the advantages and disadvantages of each.

9. Propose a possible spurious relationship between two variables. To do so, suggest a third variable that affects both variables and thus causes them to appear to be related (as with the firefighter example in the text, you don't have to use only social variables in your answer).

## GROUP PROBLEMS

To make the most of the group exercises in each chapter, work should be shared as much as possible between group members. Some exercises only involve a group discussion, but many others require the gathering of information from the library or your classmates. Make sure that each group member has a specific task that he or she must complete to help the group finish the exercise.

1. Locate an article in a social science journal that uses statistics. In sociology, you could first try looking in a journal from the regional societies, such as the *Sociological Quarterly* (and the same is true for other social science disciplines). Have everyone in the group read the article, then discuss the following points or questions.
   a. Which variables are included in the study? For each, indicate its level of measurement and whether it is discrete or continuous. Discuss whether (and how) you might change how some of these variables were measured and still be able to conduct the study.
   b. What hypotheses were tested by the researchers? Which variables were the dependent variables? Were these hypotheses developed from previous research, theory, logic, or a combination of these?
   c. Were descriptive statistics used? If so, which ones? How about inferential statistics (you aren't expected to understand most of these statistics yet)?
   d. Given the results of this research, suggest another study to follow up, extend, or further test the findings in the article.

2. As a group, design a study to investigate the relationship between income level and physical health in your community or your state. Propose a sample you could construct to use in this study. What is your hypothesis about the relationship between health and income? Suggest several ways to measure health, including both ordinal and interval-ratio measures. Suggest several ways to measure income, again including both ordinal and interval-ratio measures. What other independent variables might you want to include besides income? Can the results of your proposed study be generalized beyond your own community or state? Why or why not?

After the group has developed plans for the study, send some group members to the library to find data relating health to income, either for your state or the United States as a whole. Do these data support your hypothesis? Use this information to write a report or present the results of the project to the entire class.

# 2 Organization of Information: Frequency Distributions

**Introduction**

**Frequency Distributions**

**Proportions and Percentages**

**Percentage Distributions**

**Comparisons**

**Statistics in Practice: Labor Force Participation of Native Americans**

**The Construction of Frequency Distributions**

Frequency Distributions for Nominal Variables

Frequency Distributions for Ordinal Variables

Frequency Distributions for Interval-Ratio Variables

**Cumulative Distributions**

**Box 2.1   Real Limits, Stated Limits, and Midpoints of Class Intervals**

**Rates**

**Statistics in Practice: Marriage and Divorce Rates over Time**

**Reading the Research Literature: Statistical Tables**

Basic Principles

Tables with a Different Format

**Conclusion**

MAIN POINTS

KEY TERMS

SPSS DEMONSTRATIONS

EXERCISES

SPSS PROBLEMS

GROUP PROBLEMS

## Introduction

As social researchers we often have to deal with very large amounts of data. For example, by completion of the data collection phase of a typical survey, you will have accumulated thousands of individual responses represented by a jumble of numbers. To begin to make sense out of these data you will have to organize and summarize them in some systematic fashion. The most basic method for organizing data is to classify the observations into a frequency distribution. A **frequency distribution** is a table that reports the number of observations that fall into each category of the variable we are analyzing. Constructing a frequency distribution is usually the first step in the statistical analysis of data.

---

*Frequency Distribution*   A table reporting the number of observations falling into each category of the variable.

---

## Frequency Distributions

Let's begin with an example of a frequency distribution of a variable described in a study on Native Americans. When Columbus first encountered "the original inhabitants of the Americas," people he later described as "Indios," nothing was known about their numbers, where they lived, or the characteristics of their social structure.[1] During the last 200 years we have gathered a wealth of information about other immigrant groups who settled in North America. Yet, in comparison, until a few years ago we knew little more about Native Americans than Columbus did 500 years ago.

---

[1]C. Matthew Snipp, *American Indians: The First of This Land.* New York: Russell Sage Foundation, 1989, 1.

In 1980, the U.S. Bureau of the Census went to great lengths to collect data on the Native American population. Because so little is known about their contemporary experiences, this information presents an opportunity for significantly advancing the current state of knowledge. A summary and analysis of these data appeared in a book published in 1989, *American Indians: The First of This Land.*[2] In its exposition, the book relies heavily on some of the techniques we will discuss in this chapter.

Native Americans are not one group but many, extremely diverse, groups. There are today about 200 different Native American tribes characterized by distinct lifestyles and cultural practices. Therefore, the question of who is a Native American is not a simple matter: Native American identity also depends on personal perception of Indian race and ethnicity. Table 2.1 shows the frequency distribution of the variable "identity categories of Native Americans." These categories are based on several different patterns of self-identified race and ethnic background. The first category includes persons who disclose their race and ethnic background as Native American. This group is referred to as *Native American.* The second category includes persons who report their race as Native American but include non-Indian ancestry in their ethnic background. The designation for these individuals is *Native American of multiple ancestry.* A third category contains persons who cite a non-Indian race yet claim Native American ancestry for their ethnic background.[3] These individuals are known as *Native Americans of Indian descent.*

Notice that the frequency distribution is organized in a table, which has a number (2.1) and a descriptive title. The title indicates the kind of data presented here—"Categories of Native American Identity." The table consists of two columns. The first column identifies the variable (categories

Table 2.1 **Frequency Distribution for Categories of Native American Identity**

| Identity | Frequency (f) |
| --- | --- |
| Native American | 947,500 |
| Native American of multiple ancestry | 269,700 |
| Native American of Indian descent | 5,537,600 |
| Total (N) | 6,754,800 |

*Source:* Adapted from C. Matthew Snipp, *American Indians: The First of This Land.* New York: Russell Sage Foundation, 1989, 51. Based on 1980 census data.

[2]Ibid.
[3]Snipp, pp. 50–51.

of Native American identity) and its categories (Native American, Native American of multiple ancestry, and Native American of Indian descent). The second column, headed "Frequency ($f$)," tells the number of cases in each category as well as the total number of cases ($N = 6{,}754{,}800$). Notice also that the source of the table is clearly identified as a source note in the table. It shows that the table was adapted from a book by C. Matthew Snipp, *American Indians: The First of This Land,* and that the data come from the 1980 census. In general, the source of data for a table should appear as a source note in the table unless it is clear from the general discussion of the data.

What can you learn from the information presented in Table 2.1? The table shows that in 1980, about 6.8 million persons (6,754,800) reported that their race and/or ethnic ancestry was Native American. Out of this group, the majority, about 5.5 million persons (5,537,600) cite a non-Indian race yet claim Native American ancestry for their ethnic background (Native American of Indian descent), 947,500 report their race and ethnic background as Native American, and the remaining 269,700 include persons who identify themselves as Native American but are of multiple ancestry (Native American of multiple ancestry).

---

**Learning Check.**   *You will see frequency distributions throughout this book. Take the time to familiarize yourself with the parts in this basic example; they will get more complicated as we go on.*

---

## Proportions and Percentages

Frequency distributions are helpful in presenting information in a compact form. However, when the number of cases is large the frequencies may be difficult to grasp. Even though there is nothing wrong in concluding that out of 6.8 million Native Americans (6,754,800) 5.5 million (5,537,600) cite a non-Indian race yet claim Native American ancestry for their ethnic background (Native American of Indian descent), most of us find it difficult to think of the relative sizes of such large numbers. *Proportions* and *percentages* provide a way to standardize each raw frequency by translating it into a *relative frequency*—that is, a proportion or a percentage. A **proportion** is a relative frequency obtained by dividing the frequency in each category by the total number of cases. You may have learned to calculate proportions before, but just in case you have forgotten: to find a proportion ($P$) divide the frequency ($f$) in each category by the total number of cases ($N$)

or

$$P = \frac{f}{N}$$

where

$f$ = frequency
$N$ = total number of cases

Therefore, the proportion of Native American respondents who in 1980 identified themselves as simply "Native American" is

$$\frac{947,500}{6,754,800} = .14$$

The proportion who identified themselves as "Native American of multiple ancestry" is

$$\frac{269,700}{6,754,800} = .04$$

and finally, the proportion who identified themselves as "Native American of Indian descent" is

$$\frac{5,537,600}{6,754,800} = .82$$

Proportions should always sum to 1.00 (allowing for some rounding errors). Thus for our example, the sum of the three proportions is

.14 + .04 + .82 = 1.00

We can easily determine a frequency from a proportion by multiplying the proportion by the total $N$:

$$f = P(N)$$

Thus, the frequency of Native American respondents who in 1980 identified themselves as simply "Native American" is

.14(6,754,800) = 945,672

Note that the obtained frequency differs somewhat from the actual frequency of 947,500. This difference is due to rounding of the proportion. If we use the actual proportion instead of the rounded proportion, we obtain the correct frequency:

.140270622(6,754,800) = 947,500

---

**Learning Check.** *Compare group A with group B in Figure 2.1 and answer the following questions: Which group has the greatest number of women? Which group has the largest proportion of women?*

Figure 2.1   **Numbers and Proportions**

Group A                                    Group B

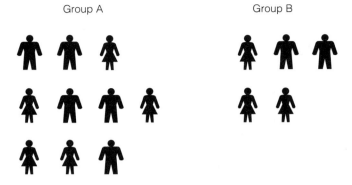

We can also express frequencies as percentages. A **percentage** is a relative frequency obtained by dividing the frequency in each category by the total number of cases and multiplying by 100. In most statistical reports, frequencies are presented as percentages rather than proportions. Percentages express the size of the frequencies as if there were a total of 100 cases.

To calculate a percentage, simply multiply the proportion by 100:

$$\text{Percentage } (\%) = \frac{f}{N}(100)$$

or

$$\text{Percentage } (\%) = P(100)$$

Therefore, the percentage of Indian respondents who identified themselves as "Native American" is

$.14(100) = 14\%$

The percentage who identified themselves as "Native American of multiple ancestry" is

$.04(100) = 4\%$

and finally, the percentage who identified themselves as "Native American of Indian descent" is

$.82(100) = 82\%$

---

*Proportion*   A relative frequency obtained by dividing the frequency in each category by the total number of cases.

*Percentage*   A relative frequency obtained by dividing the frequency in each category by the total number of cases and multiplying by 100.

---

> **Learning Check.** *Calculate the proportion of males and females in your statistics class. What percentage is female?*

## Percentage Distributions

Percentages are usually displayed as *percentage distributions*. A **percentage distribution** is a table showing the percentage of observations falling into each category of the variable. For example, Table 2.2 presents the frequency distribution of categories of Native American identity (Table 2.1) and the corresponding percentage distribution. Percentage distributions (or proportions) should always show the base (*N*) on which they were computed. Thus, in Table 2.2 the base on which the percentages were computed is *N* = 6,754,800.

> *Percentage Distribution* A table showing the percentage of observations falling into each category of the variable.

## Comparisons

In Table 2.2 we illustrated that there are three different categories of Native American identity: Native American, Native American of multiple ancestry, and Native American of Indian descent. These distinctions among the Native American population raise important questions about our understanding of who is considered Native American. For instance,

Table 2.2   **Frequency and Percentage Distributions for Categories of Native American Identity**

| Identity | Frequency (*f*) | Percentage (%) |
|---|---|---|
| Native American | 947,500 | 14 |
| Native American of multiple ancestry | 269,700 | 4 |
| Native American of Indian descent | 5,537,600 | 82 |
| Total (*N*) | 6,754,800 | 100 |

*Source:* Adapted from C. Matthew Snipp, *American Indians: The First of This Land.* New York: Russell Sage Foundation, 1989, 51. Based on 1980 census data.

population estimates vary considerably from fewer than 1 million Native Americans, if we restrict our definition to only persons who consistently identify their race and ethnicity as Native American, to almost 7 million persons if all three identity categories are pooled.

The decision to consider these groups separately or to pool them in considering the Native American population depends to a large extent on our research question. For instance, we know that 274,775 persons who identify their race and ethnicity as Native American were below the poverty line in 1980 and 288,988 were not in the labor force during the same period. Are these figures high or low? What do they tell us about the socioeconomic characteristics of Native Americans?

To answer these questions and determine whether the three categories of Native American identity have markedly different social characteristics we need to *compare* them. How do the numbers describing the poverty levels and unemployment rates of self-identified Native Americans compare with those numbers for Native Americans of multiple ancestry, Native Americans of Indian descent, or the population at large?

As students, as social scientists, and even as consumers, we are frequently faced with problems that call for some way to make a clear and valid comparison. For example, in 1990, 28 percent of the elderly lived alone. Is this figure high or low? Similarly, in 1990, 53 percent of mothers with a child under the age of 1 were in the labor force. Does this reflect a change in the American family? In each of these cases comparative information is required to answer the question and reach a conclusion.

These examples also illustrate several ways in which comparisons can be made. What we compare depends largely on the question we are posing. Without a clearly formulated research question it is difficult to decide which of numerous possible comparisons to make.

Several types of comparison are quite common in the social sciences. One type is the comparison between groups that have different characteristics. These include, for example, comparisons between old and young, between white and Hispanic, or as in our example, between different categories of Native American identity. Sometimes we may be interested in looking at regional differences among groups or in comparing groups from different segments of society. You may have read news stories about contrasts in voting patterns between the North and the South, or the percentage of homeowners in central cities and suburbs. In addition, we are often interested in comparing changes in the same group over time, such as changes in the percentage of foreign-born residents in the United States over the last decade or how the population has shifted from the cities toward the suburbs.

In this chapter, we look at some of the many techniques that can be used to make comparisons. In Chapter 3, we learn to illustrate comparisons by means of graphs. Finally, in Chapter 4 we explore averages and other measures of central tendency as another set of tools that can be used to make comparisons.

## Statistics in Practice: Labor Force Participation of Native Americans

Very often we are interested in comparing two or more groups that differ in size. Percentages are especially useful for making such comparisons. For example, we know that differences in socioeconomic status mark divisions between populations, indicating differential access to economic opportunities. Labor participation is an important indicator of access to economic opportunities and is strongly associated with socioeconomic status. Table 2.3 shows the raw frequency distributions for the variable "labor force participation" for all three categories of Native American identity.

Which group has the highest relative number of persons who are not in the labor force? Due to the differences in the population sizes of the three groups, this is a difficult question to answer based on only the raw frequencies. To make a valid comparison we have to compare the percentage distributions for all three groups. These are presented in Table 2.4. Notice that the percentage distributions make it easier to identify differences between the groups. Compared with Native Americans of multiple ancestry or Native Americans of Indian descent, Native Americans have the highest percentage not in the labor force (30.5% vs. 21.6% and

Table 2.3 **Labor Force Participation among Householders of Native American Background (raw frequencies)**

| Labor Force Participation | Native American | Native American of Multiple Ancestry | Native American of Indian Descent |
|---|---|---|---|
| Employed | 583,660 | 183,666 | 4,064,598 |
| Unemployed | 63,482 | 21,846 | 282,418 |
| Not in labor force | 288,988 | 58,255 | 1,101,982 |
| Military and other | 11,370 | 5,933 | 88,602 |
| Total (N) | 947,500 | 269,700 | 5,537,600 |

*Source:* Adapted from C. Matthew Snipp, *American Indians: The First of This Land.* New York: Russell Sage Foundation, 1989, 55. Based on 1980 census data.

Table 2.4  **Labor Force Participation Among Householders of Native American Background (in percentages)**

| Labor Force Participation | Native American | Native American of Multiple Ancestry | Native American of Indian Descent |
|---|---|---|---|
| Employed | 61.6% | 68.1% | 73.4% |
| Unemployed | 6.7% | 8.1% | 5.1% |
| Not in labor force | 30.5% | 21.6% | 19.9% |
| Military and other | 1.2% | 2.2% | 1.6% |
| Total | 100.0% | 100.0% | 100.0% |
| (N) | 947,500 | 269,700 | 5,537,600 |

*Source:* Adapted from C. Matthew Snipp, *American Indians: The First of This Land.* New York: Russell Sage Foundation, 1989, 55. Based on 1980 census data.

19.9%). Conversely, among the three groups, Native Americans of Indian descent have the highest percentage (73.4% vs. 68.1% and 61.6%) of persons who are employed.

> **Learning Check.** *Examine Table 2.4 and try to answer the following questions: What is the percentage of Native Americans who are employed? What is the base (N) for this percentage? What is the percentage of Native Americans of multiple ancestry who are not in the labor force? What is the base (N) for this percentage?*

Whenever one group is compared with another, the most meaningful conclusions can usually be drawn based on comparison of the relative frequency distributions. In fact, we are seldom interested in a single distribution. Most interesting questions in the social sciences are about differences between two or more groups.[4] The finding that the labor force participation patterns of Native Americans vary depending on their race and ethnic identity raises a serious doubt about whether American Indians can be legitimately regarded as a single, relatively homogeneous ethnic group. Further analyses could examine *why* differences in Native American identity are associated with differences in labor force participation patterns. Other variables that explain these differences could be identified. These kinds of questions can be answered using more complex multivariate statistical techniques, but the comparison of percentage distributions is

[4]David Knoke and George W. Bohrnstedt, *Basic Social Statistics.* New York: Peacock Publishers, 1991, 25.

an important foundation to those more complex techniques. Percentage comparison is used, for example, in Chapter 6 to establish relationships between two variables. At this point, however, it is important to remember the significance of the technique of comparison to most scientific investigations.

Before we continue, keep in mind that although we encourage you to begin thinking analytically about complex data, the basic procedures discussed in the first ten chapters of this book only allow you to draw some tentative conclusions about differences between groups. To make valid comparisons you will need to consider the more complex techniques of sampling and statistical inference, which are discussed in the last six chapters. As you proceed through this book and beyond and master all the statistical concepts necessary for valid inference, you will be able to provide more complex interpretations of the data.

## The Construction of Frequency Distributions

Up to now you have been introduced to the general concept of a frequency distribution. We saw that data can be expressed as raw frequencies, proportions, or percentages. We also saw how to use percentages to compare distributions in different groups.

In this section, you will learn how to construct frequency distributions. While most often this will be done by your computer, it is important to go through this process to understand how frequency distributions are actually put together.

For nominal and ordinal variables, constructing a frequency distribution is quite simple. Count and report the number of cases that fall into each category of the variable along with the total number of cases ($N$). For the purpose of illustration, let's take a small subsample of forty cases from our 1982 to 1990 GSS sample and record their scores on the following variables: "gender," a nominal level variable; "job security," an ordinal level variable; "hours worked" and "number of children," both interval-ratio level variables.

The gender of the respondents was recorded by the interviewer at the beginning of the interview. To measure job security, respondents were asked, "Thinking about the next 12 months, how likely do you think it is that you will lose your job or be laid off—very likely, fairly likely, not too likely, or not at all likely?" Four categories (very likely, fairly likely, not too likely, or not at all likely) were offered for response. The last category represented the highest level of job security. The number of hours worked was obtained by asking respondents, "How many hours did you work last week at all jobs?" The number of children was determined by the question, "How many children have you ever had?" The answers given by a subsample of forty respondents are displayed in Table 2.5. Note that each row in the table represents a respondent, whereas each column represents a variable. (This format is conventional in the social sciences.)

You can see that it is going to be difficult to make sense of these data just by eyeballing Table 2.5. How many of these forty respondents are males? How many said they are very likely to lose their jobs? How many work 40 hours a week? To try and answer these questions we will construct the frequency distributions for all four variables.

Table 2.5 **A Subsample from the General Social Survey**

| Gender | Job Security | Number of Children | Hours Worked |
|--------|-------------|--------------------|--------------|
| Male | Not at all likely | 0 | 4 |
| Male | Fairly likely | 0 | 31 |
| Male | Not at all likely | 1 | 11 |
| Male | Very likely | 0 | 40 |
| Male | Not at all likely | 2 | 34 |
| Male | Not at all likely | 1 | 50 |
| Male | Not at all likely | 3 | 40 |
| Male | Very likely | 0 | 50 |
| Male | Fairly likely | 0 | 1 |
| Female | Fairly likely | 1 | 40 |
| Male | Not too likely | 2 | 40 |
| Male | Fairly likely | 0 | 40 |
| Male | Not too likely | 1 | 42 |
| Female | Not at all likely | 4 | 10 |
| Female | Not at all likely | 0 | 49 |
| Male | Not at all likely | 1 | 40 |
| Male | Not at all likely | 2 | 40 |
| Male | Not at all likely | 5 | 82 |
| Female | Not too likely | 3 | 40 |
| Female | Fairly likely | 4 | 42 |
| Female | Not at all likely | 2 | 16 |
| Female | Not at all likely | 0 | 21 |
| Male | Fairly likely | 2 | 21 |
| Male | Not too likely | 4 | 24 |
| Female | Very likely | 2 | 31 |
| Female | Not too likely | 2 | 34 |
| Male | Not at all likely | 4 | 40 |

Table 2.5    **(continued)**

| | | | |
|------|------------------|---|----|
| Male | Not at all likely | 3 | 40 |
| Male | Not at all likely | 2 | 40 |
| Male | Not at all likely | 1 | 40 |
| Male | Not at all likely | 0 | 40 |
| Male | Very likely | 5 | 42 |
| Male | Not at all likely | 0 | 42 |
| Male | Not too likely | 3 | 49 |
| Male | Not at all likely | 2 | 53 |
| Male | Not at all likely | 2 | 60 |
| Male | Not too likely | 1 | 60 |
| Male | Not too likely | 1 | 70 |
| Female | Not at all likely | 0 | 70 |
| Female | Not at all likely | 0 | 76 |

## Frequency Distributions for Nominal Variables

Let's begin with the nominal variable, "gender." First, we tally the number of males, then the number of females (the column of tallies has been included in Table 2.6 for the purpose of illustration). The tally results are then used to construct the frequency distribution presented in Table 2.6. The table has a title describing its content (Frequency Distribution of the Variable Gender: GSS Subsample). Its categories (male and female) and their associated frequencies are clearly listed; in addition, the total number of cases ($N$) is also reported. The Percentages column is the percentage distribution for this variable. To convert the Frequency column to percentages, simply divide each frequency by the total number of cases and multiply by 100. Percentage distributions are routinely added to almost any frequency table and are especially important if comparisons with other groups are to be considered. We can immediately see that it is easier now

Table 2.6    **Frequency Distribution of the Variable Gender: GSS Subsample**

| Gender | Tallies | Frequency (f) | Percentages (%) |
|--------|---------|---------------|-----------------|
| Male | ///// ///// ///// ///// ///// //// | 29 | 72.5 |
| Female | ///// ///// / | 11 | 27.5 |
| Total (N) | | 40 | 100.0 |

to read the information. There are 11 females and 29 males in this sample. Based on this frequency distribution we can also conclude that the majority of this subsample of 40 respondents are males.[5]

---

**Learning Check.** *Construct a frequency distribution for males and females in your statistics class.*

---

### Frequency Distributions for Ordinal Variables

To construct a frequency distribution for ordinal level variables, follow the same procedures outlined for nominal level variables. Table 2.7 presents the frequency distribution for the variable "job security" for the forty GSS respondents. The table shows that 55 percent, the majority of respondents, feel that they are not at all likely to lose their jobs.

The major difference between frequency distributions for nominal and ordinal variables is the order in which the categories are listed. The categories for nominal level variables do not have to be listed in any particular order. For example, we could list females first and males second without changing the nature of the distribution. However, since the categories or values of ordinal variables are rank-ordered, they must be listed in a way that reflects their rank—from the lowest to the highest or from the highest to the lowest. Thus, the data on job security in Table 2.7 are presented in declining order from "very likely" (least secure) to "not at all likely" (most secure).

Table 2.7 **Frequency Distribution of Job Security: GSS Subsample**

| Job Security | Frequency (f) | Percentages (%) |
|---|---|---|
| Very likely | 4 | 10 |
| Fairly likely | 6 | 15 |
| Not too likely | 8 | 20 |
| Not at all likely | 22 | 55 |
| Total (N) | 40 | 100 |

---

[5]Remember that we are working here with a very small subsample from the GSS. The actual gender breakdown for the 1994 GSS is 43 percent males and 57 percent females.

**Learning Check.** *Figures 2.2a, 2.2b, and 2.2c illustrate the gender and job security data in stages as presented in Tables 2.5, 2.6, and 2.7. To convince yourself that classifying the respondents by gender (Figure 2.2b) and by job security (Figure 2.2c) makes the job of counting much easier, turn to Figure 2.2a and answer these questions: How many men are in the group? How many women? How many said they are very likely to lose their job? Now turn to Figure 2.2b: How many men are in the group? Women? Finally, examine Figure 2.2c: How many said they are very likely to lose their jobs? Not at all likely to lose their jobs?*

Figure 2.2a   **Forty Respondents from the GSS Subsample, Their Gender, and Their Level of Job Security (data from Table 2.5)**

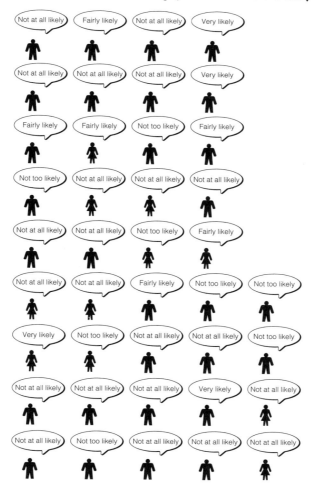

Figure 2.2b **Forty Respondents from the GSS Subsample, Classified by Their Gender (see Table 2.6)**

Figure 2.2c **Forty Respondents from the GSS Subsample, Classified by Their Gender, and Their Level of Job Security (see Table 2.7)**

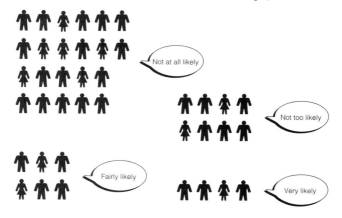

## Frequency Distributions for Interval-Ratio Variables

I hope you agree by now that constructing frequency distributions for nominal and ordinal level variables is rather straightforward. Simply list the categories and count the number of observations that fall into each category. Building a frequency distribution for interval-ratio variables with relatively few values is also easy. For example, when constructing a frequency distribution for the "number of children," simply list the number of children and report the corresponding frequency as shown in Table 2.8.

Very often, interval-ratio variables have a wide range of values, which makes simple frequency distributions very difficult to read. For example, take a look at the frequency distribution for the variable "hours worked" in Table 2.9. The distribution contains values varying from 1 to 82, making

Table 2.8 **Frequency Distribution for the Number of Children: GSS Subsample**

| Number of Children | Frequency (f) | Percentages (%) |
|---|---|---|
| 0 | 12 | 30 |
| 1 | 8 | 20 |
| 2 | 10 | 25 |
| 3 | 4 | 10 |
| 4 | 4 | 10 |
| 5 | 2 | 5 |
| Total (N) | 40 | 100 |

Table 2.9 **Frequency Distribution for Hours Worked: GSS Subsample**

| Hours Worked | Frequency (f) |
|---|---|
| 1 | 1 |
| 4 | 1 |
| 10 | 1 |
| 11 | 1 |
| 16 | 1 |
| 21 | 2 |
| 24 | 1 |
| 31 | 2 |
| 34 | 2 |
| 40 | 13 |
| 42 | 4 |
| 49 | 2 |
| 50 | 2 |
| 53 | 1 |
| 60 | 2 |
| 70 | 2 |
| 76 | 1 |
| 82 | 1 |

it difficult to establish a pattern. For a more concise picture, the separate possible scores must be reduced into a number of smaller groups, each containing a number of scores. Table 2.10 displays the now grouped frequency distribution of the data in Table 2.9. Each group, known as a class interval, now contains ten possible scores instead of one. Thus, the scores 40, 42, and 49 all fall into the class interval of 40–49. The second column of Table 2.10, Frequency, tells us the number of respondents that fall into each of the intervals. Thus, the 19 respondents that fall into the class interval of 40–49 include the 13 respondents represented in Table 2.9 who have a score of 40, the 4 respondents who have a score of 42, and the 2 respondents who have a score of 49. Having grouped the scores we can now clearly see that the biggest single group (19, or 47.5%) works between 40 and 49 hours a week. The percentage distribution we have added to Table 2.10 displays the relative frequency of each interval and emphasizes this trend as well.

The class intervals presented in Table 2.10 are the ones actually used in the GSS survey. The decision as to how many groups to use and, therefore, how wide the intervals should be is usually up to the researcher and depends on what makes sense in terms of the purpose of the research. Ten hours might be a reasonable interval when you are looking at, say, the average workweek for single parents, but it probably would be too wide for a study that looked at how many hours a day people who are on a flextime schedule actually work. The rule of thumb is that an interval width should be large enough to avoid too many categories but not so large that

Table 2.10 **Grouped Frequency Distribution of Hours Worked: GSS Subsample**

| Hours Worked | Frequency (f) | Percentages (%) |
|---|---|---|
| 00–09 | 2 | 5.0 |
| 10–19 | 3 | 7.5 |
| 20–29 | 3 | 7.5 |
| 30–39 | 4 | 10.0 |
| 40–49 | 19 | 47.5 |
| 50–59 | 3 | 7.5 |
| 60–69 | 2 | 5.0 |
| 70–79 | 3 | 7.5 |
| 80 or more | 1 | 2.5 |
| Total (N) | 40 | 100.0 |

significant differences between observations are concealed.[6] Obviously, the number of intervals to use will depend on the width of each. For instance, if you are working with scores ranging from 10 to 60 and you establish an interval width of 10, you will have 5 intervals.

---

**Learning Check.** *Can you verify that Table 2.10 was constructed correctly? Use Table 2.9 to determine the frequency of cases that fall into the categories of Table 2.10.*

---

**Learning Check.** *If you are having trouble distinguishing between nominal, ordinal, and interval-ratio variables, go back to Chapter 1 and review the section on levels of measurement.*

---

## Cumulative Distributions

Sometimes we may be interested in locating the relative position of a given score in a distribution. For example, we may be interested in finding out how many of our sample worked fewer than 20 hours a week. Or, how many worked fewer than 40 hours. Frequency distributions can be presented in a cumulative fashion to answer such questions. A **cumulative frequency distribution** shows the frequencies at or below each category (or class interval or score) of the variable.

Cumulative frequencies are appropriate only for variables that are measured at an ordinal level or higher. They are obtained by adding to the frequency in each category the frequencies of all the categories below it. Alternatively, you can cumulate frequencies by adding to the frequency in each category the frequencies of all the categories above it.

Let's look at Table 2.11. It shows the cumulative frequencies added to Table 2.10. The cumulative frequency column denoted by $Cf_{below}$ describes the number of persons at or below each interval. For example, you can see that 5 of the 40 respondents listed in Table 2.11 worked 19 hours or less and 12 worked 39 hours or less.

To construct a cumulative frequency distribution (at or below each class interval), start with the frequency in the lowest class interval (or with the lowest score, when the data are ungrouped) and add to it the frequencies in the next highest class interval. Continue adding the frequencies until

[6]Knoke and Bohrnstedt, p. 41.

### Box 2.1   Real Limits, Stated Limits, and Midpoints of Class Intervals

The class intervals presented in Table 2.10 constitute the categories of the variable "hours worked" that we used to classify the survey's respondents. In Chapter 1, we noted that our variables need to be both exhaustive and mutually exclusive. These principles apply to the class intervals here as well. This means that each of the forty respondents can be classified into one and only one category. In addition, we should be able to classify all the possible scores.

In our example, these requirements are met: Each observation score fits into only one class interval, and there is an appropriate category to classify each individual score as recorded in Table 2.10. However, if you looked closely at Table 2.10 you may have noticed that there is actually a gap of one hour between adjacent intervals. A gap could create a problem with scores that have fractional values. For example, let's suppose for a moment the number of hours worked had been reported with more precision. Where would you classify a woman who worked 49.3 hours? Notice that her scores would actually fall between the intervals 40–49 and 50–59! To avoid this potential problem use the real limits rather than the stated limits listed in Table 2.10. Real limits extend the upper and lower limits of the intervals by .5. For instance, the real limits for the interval 40–49 are 39.5–49.5; the real limits for the interval 50–59 are 49.5–59.5; and so on. (Scores that fall exactly at the upper real limit or the lower real limit of the interval [for example, 59.5 or 49.5] are usually rounded to the closest even number. The number 59.5 would be rounded to 60 and would thus be included in the interval 59.5–69.5.) In the following table we include both the stated limits and real limits for the grouped frequency distribution of hours worked. So where would you classify a respondent who worked 49.3 hours? (Answer: in the interval 39.5–49.5) How about 19.9? (in the interval 19.5–29.5)

### Frequency Distribution of Hours Worked: Stated Limits, Real Limits, and Midpoints

| Hours Worked Stated Limits | Hours Worked Real Limits | Midpoint | Frequency (f) |
|---|---|---|---|
| 00–09 | −00.5–09.5 | 4.50 | 2 |
| 10–19 | 09.5–19.5 | 14.50 | 3 |
| 20–29 | 19.5–29.5 | 24.50 | 3 |
| 30–39 | 29.5–39.5 | 34.50 | 4 |
| 40–49 | 39.5–49.5 | 44.50 | 19 |
| 50–59 | 49.5–59.5 | 54.50 | 3 |
| 60–69 | 59.5–69.5 | 64.50 | 2 |
| 70–79 | 69.5–79.5 | 74.50 | 3 |
| 80 or more | 79.5 or more | | 1 |
| Total (N) | | | 40 |

Even though grouped frequency distributions are very helpful in summarizing information, remember that they are only a summary and therefore involve a considerable loss of detail. Since most researchers and students have access to computers, grouped frequencies are used only when the raw data are not available. Most of the statistical procedures described in later chapters are based on the raw scores.

### Midpoints

The *midpoint* is a single number that represents the entire interval. A midpoint is calculated by adding the lower and upper real limits of the interval and dividing by 2. The midpoint of the interval 19.5–29.5, for instance, is (19.5 + 29.5) ÷ 2 = 24.5. The midpoint for all the intervals of the preceding table are displayed in the third column. Notice that the last interval is open-ended and therefore is not represented by a midpoint. To calculate a midpoint for an open-ended interval, you must estimate its upper limit.

you reach the last class interval. The frequency in the last class interval will be equal to the total number of cases. In Table 2.11 the frequency associated with the first class interval (00–09) is 2. The cumulative frequency associated with this interval is also 2 since there are no cases below this class interval. The frequency for the second class interval (10–19) is 3. The cumulative frequency for this interval is 2 + 3 = 5. To obtain the cumulative frequency of 8 for the third interval we add its frequency (3) to the cumulative frequency associated with the second class interval (5). Continue this process until you reach the last class interval. Its cumulative frequency is the sum of its frequency plus the frequencies of all the

Table 2.11 **Frequency Distribution and Cumulative Frequency of Hours Worked**

| Hours Worked | Frequency (f) | $Cf_{below}$ | $Cf_{above}$ |
|---|---|---|---|
| 00–09 | 2 | 2 | 40 |
| 10–19 | 3 | 5 | 38 |
| 20–29 | 3 | 8 | 35 |
| 30–39 | 4 | 12 | 32 |
| 40–49 | 19 | 31 | 28 |
| 50–59 | 3 | 34 | 9 |
| 60–69 | 2 | 36 | 6 |
| 70–79 | 3 | 39 | 4 |
| 80 or more | 1 | 40 | 1 |
| Total (N) | 40 | | |

preceding intervals. Therefore, the cumulative frequency for the last interval is equal to the total number of cases ($N$).

The second type of cumulative distribution shows the cumulative frequencies at or above each interval. To construct this type of distribution you begin with the frequency in the highest class interval and add to it the frequency in the next lowest class interval. Continue adding the frequencies until you reach the lowest class interval. This type of cumulative distribution is denoted by the $Cf_{above}$ column in Table 2.11.

We can also construct a cumulative percentage distribution ($C\%$), which has wider applications than the cumulative frequency distribution ($Cf$). A **cumulative percentage distribution** shows the percentage at or below (or at or above) each category (class interval or score) of the variable. A cumulative percentage distribution is constructed using the same procedure as for a cumulative frequency distribution except that the percentages—rather than the raw frequencies—for each category are added to the total percentages for all the categories below it (or above it).

In Table 2.12 we have added the percentage distribution and the cumulative percentage distribution based on the data in Table 2.11 for "hours worked" (only the cumulative percentages at or below an interval are shown here). The table shows that almost one-third of the sample (30%) worked less than full-time—that is, 39 hours or less.

Like the percentage distributions described earlier, cumulative percentage distributions are especially useful when you want to compare differences between groups. For an example of how cumulative

Table 2.12 **Cumulative Frequencies and Cumulative Percentages for Hours Worked**

| Hours Worked | Frequency (f) | Cf_below | Percentages (%) | C% |
|---|---|---|---|---|
| 00–09 | 2 | 2 | 5.0 | 5.0 |
| 10–19 | 3 | 5 | 7.5 | 12.5 |
| 20–29 | 3 | 8 | 7.5 | 20.0 |
| 30–39 | 4 | 12 | 10.0 | 30.0 |
| 40–49 | 19 | 31 | 47.5 | 77.5 |
| 50–59 | 3 | 34 | 7.5 | 85.0 |
| 60–69 | 2 | 36 | 5.0 | 90.0 |
| 70–79 | 3 | 39 | 7.5 | 97.5 |
| 80 or more | 1 | 40 | 2.5 | 100.0 |
| Total (N) | 40 | | | |

percentages are used in a comparison, we have used the 1987 to 1991 GSS data to contrast the opinions of black women and white men about their family income relative to other families. Respondents were asked the following question: "Compared with American families in general, would you say your family income is far below average, below average, average, above average, or far above average?"

*Cumulative Frequency Distribution*  A distribution showing the frequency at or below (or at or above) each category (class interval or score) of the variable.

*Cumulative Percentage Distribution*  A distribution showing the percentage at or below (or at or above) each category (class interval or score) of the variable.

The percentage distribution and the cumulative percentage distribution for black women and white men is shown in Table 2.13. The cumulative percentage distributions suggest that relatively more black women than white men consider their relative family income average or lower. Whereas only 68 percent of the white males consider their family income average or lower (where lower includes the categories below average and far below average), 82 percent of the black women ranked their income average or lower. What might explain these differences? Both gender and racial discrimination might play a role in the income gap between black women and white men. Black women experience a double disadvantage in income: the lower income associated with race and the lower wage of women. These data prompt many other questions about the role that both race and

Table 2.13  **Relative Family Income—White Men and Black Women**

| | White Men | | Black Women | |
|---|---|---|---|---|
| **Relative Family Income** | % | C% | % | C% |
| Far below average | 1 | 1 | 11 | 11 |
| Below average | 16 | 17 | 25 | 36 |
| Average | 51 | 68 | 46 | 82 |
| Above average | 28 | 96 | 17 | 99 |
| Far above average | 4 | 100 | 1 | 100 |
| Total | 100 | | 100 | |
| (N) | (621) | | (342) | |

*Source:* GSS data from 1987–1992.

gender play in income inequality. For instance, are these differences primarily because of gender or because of race? Begin to explore these questions by comparing the responses to this GSS question given by white and black respondents (regardless of gender) and by men and women (regardless of race). Exercise 15 supplies the data that will help you pursue these questions.

Racial and gender inequalities in income follow similar trends in other related areas such as occupation and education. Are there similar differences in the occupational and educational distributions of men and women? blacks and whites? You may be able to answer some of these questions by doing exercise 16 and group problem 2.

> **Learning Check.** *Cumulative frequencies and percentages have applications in some of the statistical procedures we will discuss later in this book. You might want to review this section and make sure you know the difference between* at or below *and* at or above.

## Rates

"More than a decade has passed since the 1970s' dramatic decline in marriage and rise in divorce revolutionized the American family. But echoes of those changes are still reverberating," states a report released by the Census Bureau in 1992. The report, "Marriage, Divorce, and Remarriage in the 1990s"[7] finds that marriage rates, falling since World War II, continue to drop and divorce rates are twice the 1950s' level.

I am sure you have heard of *rates* before. Terms such as *birth rate, unemployment rate,* and *marriage rate* are often used by social scientists and demographers and then quoted in the popular media to describe population trends. But what exactly are rates, and how are they constructed? A **rate** is a number obtained by dividing the number of actual occurrences in a given time period by the number of possible occurrences. For example, to determine the rate of marriage for 1990, the U.S. Census Bureau took the number of marriages performed in 1990 (actual occurrence) and divided it by the total population in 1990 (possible occurrences). The marriage rate for 1990 can be expressed as:

$$\text{Marriage rate, } 1990 = \frac{\text{Number of marriages in 1990}}{\text{Total population in 1990}}$$

[7]U.S. Bureau of the Census. 1992. Marriage, divorce, and remarriage in the 1990s. *Current Population Reports,* P23-180. Washington, DC: GPO.

Since 2,448,000 marriages were performed in 1990 and the number for the total population was 250,000,000, the marriage rate for 1990 can be expressed as:

$$\text{Marriage rate, } 1990 = \frac{2,448,000 \text{ marriages}}{250,000,000 \text{ Americans}} = .0098$$

This means that for every person in the United States, .0098 marriages occurred during 1990.

Rates are often expressed as rates per thousand or hundred thousand to eliminate decimal points and make the number easier to interpret. For example, to express the marriage rate per thousand we multiply it by 1,000:

$$\text{Marriage rate, } 1990 = \frac{2,448,000 \text{ marriages}}{250,000,000 \text{ Americans}} \times 1,000$$

$$= .0098 \times 1,000 = 9.8$$

This means that for every 1,000 people, 9.8 marriages occurred during 1990.

Similarly, the divorce rate for the U.S. population during 1990 was obtained as follows:

$$\text{Divorce rate, } 1990 = \frac{1,175,000 \text{ divorces}}{250,000,000 \text{ Americans}} \times 1,000$$

$$= .0047 \times 1,000 = 4.7$$

Or, for every 1,000 people, 4.7 divorces occurred in 1990.

The preceding marriage and divorce rates are referred to as "crude rates" because they are based on the total population. Rates can be calculated on the general population or on a more narrowly defined select group. For instance, marriage rates are often given for the number of people who are 15 years or older—people who are considered of "marriageable age." Rates can also be calculated separately for men and women. For example, the 1990 marriage rate for men who are 15 and older was obtained as follows:

$$\text{Marriage rate, men 15 and older, } 1990 = \frac{2,448,000}{94,339,000} \times 1,000 = 25.9$$

and for women in the same age group:

$$\text{Marriage rate, women 15 and older, } 1990 = \frac{2,448,000}{101,457,000} \times 1,000 = 24.1$$

---

***Rate*** A number obtained by dividing the number of actual occurrences in a given time period by the number of possible occurrences.

---

*Learning Check.* Law enforcement agencies routinely record crime rates (the number of crimes committed relative to the size of a population), arrest rates (the number of arrests made relative to the number of crimes reported), and conviction rates (the number of convictions relative to the number of cases tried). Can you think of some variables that could be expressed as rates?

## Statistics in Practice: Marriage and Divorce Rates over Time

So have marriage rates really declined? How about divorce rates? How can we examine the shifting marriage and divorce rates? Like percentages, rates are useful in making comparisons between different groups and over time. The crude marriage rate of 9.8 for 1990 might be difficult to interpret by itself and will not answer our question of whether or not marriage rates have really changed. To illustrate how rates have changed over time, let's look at Table 2.14, which reports the marriage rates and divorce rates since 1970 for women 15 years and older. The table shows that over the last two decades marriage has declined rather steadily, whereas the divorce rate in 1990 was roughly the same as it was in 1975 but much higher than it was in 1970.

*Learning Check.* Make sure you understand how to read tables. Can you explain how we reached the preceding conclusions based on the information in Table 2.14?

Table 2.14 **Marriage and Divorce Rates per 1,000 Women 15 Years Old and Over**

| Year | Marriage Rate | Divorce Rate |
|------|---------------|--------------|
| 1970 | 28.4 | 14.9 |
| 1975 | 25.6 | 20.3 |
| 1980 | 26.1 | 22.6 |
| 1985 | 24.8 | 21.7 |
| 1990 | 24.1 | 20.1 |

*Source:* Data from U.S. Bureau of the Census report, "Marriage, Divorce, and Remarriage in the 1990s," 1992.

### Reading the Research Literature[8]: Statistical Tables

Statistical tables that display frequency distributions or other kinds of statistical information are found in virtually every book, article, or newspaper report that makes any use of statistics. However, the inclusion of statistical tables in a report or an article doesn't necessarily mean that the research is more scientific or convincing. You will always have to ask what the tables are saying and judge for yourself whether the information is relevant or accurately presented and analyzed. Most statistical tables presented in the social science literature are a good deal more complex than those we describe in this chapter. The same information can sometimes be organized in many different ways, and that because of space limitations the researcher may present the information with minimum detail.

In this section, we present some guidelines for how to read and interpret statistical tables displaying frequency distributions. The purpose is to help you see that some of the techniques described in this chapter are actually used in a meaningful way. Remember, it takes time and practice to develop the skill of reading tables. Even experienced researchers sometimes make mistakes when interpreting tables. So take the time to study the tables presented here; do the chapter problems; and you will find that reading, interpreting, and understanding tables will in time become easier.

### Basic Principles

The first step in reading any statistical table is to understand what the researcher is trying to tell you. There must be a reason for including the information, and usually the researcher tells you what it is. Begin your inspection of the table by reading its title. It usually describes the central contents of the table. Check for any source notes to the table. These tell the source of the data or the table and any additional information the author considers important. Next, examine the column and row headings and subheadings. These identify the variables, their categories, and the kind of statistics presented, such as raw frequencies or percentages. The main body of the table includes the appropriate statistics (frequencies, percentages, rates, and so on) for each variable and/or group as defined by each heading and subheading.

Table 2.15 was taken from an article written by Professor Marie Withers Osmond et al. about AIDS risks among women. In their study, Professor Osmond and her co-authors examined the ways that high-risk sexual behaviors are related to decisions about using condoms by low-income, culturally diverse women in South Florida. The study focused on two

[8]The idea for "Reading the Research Literature" sections that appear in most chapters was inspired by Joseph F. Healey, *Statistics: A Tool for Social Research* (4th edition). Belmont, California: Wadsworth, 1996.

Table 2.15  **Frequency and Percentage Distribution for Race, Education, Income, Frequency of Condom Use, and the Decision to Use a Condom for Main Partner and Client Subsamples**

| | GROUP | | | |
| | Main Partner | | Client | |
| VARIABLES | f | % | f | % |
|---|---|---|---|---|
| **Frequency of condom use:** | | | | |
| More than half the time | 69 | 26 | 76 | 70 |
| Less than half the time | 199 | 74 | 33 | 30 |
| Total (N) | 268 | 100 | 109 | 100 |
| **Decision to use condom:** | | | | |
| Self | 55 | 20 | 61 | 56 |
| Both | 123 | 46 | 20 | 18 |
| Partner | 17 | 6 | 9 | 8 |
| Never discuss | 73 | 27 | 19 | 17 |
| Total (N) | 268 | 99 | 109 | 99 |
| **Race/Ethnicity:** | | | | |
| White | 92 | 34 | 32 | 29 |
| African American | 127 | 47 | 59 | 54 |
| Hispanic | 35 | 13 | 18 | 17 |
| Haitian | 14 | 5 | 0 | 0 |
| Total (N) | 268 | 99 | 109 | 100 |
| **Education:** | | | | |
| Some college | 47 | 17 | 19 | 17 |
| High school | 106 | 40 | 38 | 35 |
| Less than high school | 115 | 43 | 52 | 48 |
| Total (N) | 268 | 100 | 109 | 100 |
| **Income:** | | | | |
| Job | 99 | 37 | 19 | 17 |
| Welfare, government, or unemployment | 26 | 10 | 7 | 6 |
| Family, friends | 63 | 23 | 16 | 15 |
| Tricks, illegal | 80 | 30 | 67 | 62 |
| Total (N) | 268 | 100 | 109 | 100 |

*Source:* Adapted from Marie Withers Osmond et al., "The Multiple Jeopardy of Race, Class, and Gender for AIDS Risk among Women," *Gender and Society,* Vol. 7, No. 1, March 1993, 105.

subsamples of women who were randomly selected from various agencies including county jails, public and community health services, and drug and alcohol treatment centers. The first subsample ($N = 268$), which became known as the "main partner" group, included women who stated that they had a main sexual partner with whom they were sexually active. The second subsample ($N = 109$), which was known as the "client" group, included women who stated that they had sex in exchange for money or drugs.

In Table 2.15, the researchers display the frequencies and percentages for the major variables included in the study. Even though the table is quite simple, it is important to examine it carefully, including its title and headings, to make sure you understand what the information means.

---

**Learning Check.** *Inspect Table 2.15 and try to answer the following questions:*

1. *What is the source of this table?*
2. *How many variables are presented? What are their names?*
3. *What is represented by the numbers presented in the first column? In the second column?*

---

What does the author tell us about the table? The researcher uses Table 2.15 to describe the social class and the racial/ethnic composition in the main partner and client subsamples. By analyzing the percentage columns, a number of observations can be made about the characteristics of the respondents included in the study and the differences between the two groups. First, note that the largest single group among both the main partner and client subsamples is African Americans (47% and 54%, respectively). Second, more than one-third (40 percent) of the women in the main partner subsample graduated from high school and another 17 percent gained some additional trade or college training. Among the client subsample the corresponding figures are 35 percent and 17 percent. Third, with regard to income, 37 percent of the main partner subsample reported job or business as their primary source, whereas "tricks" or other illegal activities (30%) were more common than welfare, government, or unemployment (10%). Among the client subsample 17 percent report jobs as their primary source of income and 62 percent say that their income came primarily from tricks or other illegal activities. What do these numbers tell us about the differences in the background of the women in the two groups? The main partner group is slightly more educated than the client group. Moreover, for relatively more women in the client group, the primary sources of income are tricks and other illegal activities.

The two central variables in this study are "frequency of condom use" and "decision to use condom." The researchers use the first as a measure of AIDS risk and the second to assess what power these women could assert in their relationships. Women who reported that they (self) made the decision to use a condom during sexual intercourse were seen as having more power than women whose response was either "both," "partner," or "never discuss."

A close examination of the percentages in Table 2.15 reveals some differences between the client and main partner subsamples regarding these two variables. Among the main partner subsample 26 percent use condoms more than half the time, but among women in the client subsample 70 percent report such frequency of use. Regarding the decision to use condoms, 20 percent of the women in the main partner subsample reported that they made this decision themselves, whereas 46 percent said the decision was made by both themselves and their partner. Among the client subsample these percentages are reversed: 56 percent of the women reported "self," whereas 18 percent said that "both" made the decision. The researchers conclude that power relations are different with clients than with the main partners: women find it especially difficult to negotiate condom use with intimate sexual partners (that is, main partners). Thus, the women are more assertive and the men more compliant in the client relationship.

Finally, Table 2.15 provides some preliminary evidence that the two groups investigated here are different in terms of their power relations with their sexual partner and the extent to which they engage in high-risk sexual behavior. For a more detailed analysis of the relationships between these variables you need to consider some of the more complex techniques of bivariate analysis and statistical inference. We consider these more advanced techniques beginning in Chapter 6.

## Tables with a Different Format

Tables can sometimes present data for only a subset of the sample. For example, Table 2.16, based on 1994 census data of white Americans, shows the percentages of a number of variables. However, only partial information on each of the variables is included, and therefore the percentages do not add up to 100 percent. For instance, 18.0 percent of white Americans have had less than twelve years of school. The remaining 82.0 percent who have had twelve or more years of school are omitted from the table. Similarly, 67.8 percent owned homes in 1994; the 32.2 percent who are not homeowners are omitted from the table. In addition, Table 2.16 also presents the homicide rate (per 100,000) for white male Americans in 1992.

Table 2.16    **Selected Economic and Social Indicators for White Americans, 1994**

| Indicators | Percentages (%) |
|---|---|
| Less than twelve years of school | 18.0 |
| Unemployed | 5.3 |
| Female-headed households | 14.0 |
| Own their homes | 67.8 |
| Families below poverty level | 9.4 |
| Homicide rate (1992, for males, per 100,000) | 9.1 |

*Source:* U.S. Bureau of the Census. *Statistical Abstract of the United States,* 1995.

Table 2.17    **Selected Quality-of-Life Indicators for White and Black Americans, 1994**

| Indicators | Percentage of Whites (%) | Percentage of Blacks (%) |
|---|---|---|
| Less than twelve years of school | 18.0 | 27.1 |
| Unemployed | 5.3 | 11.5 |
| Female-headed households | 14.0 | 48.0 |
| Own their homes | 67.8 | 42.5 |
| Families below poverty level | 9.4 | 31.3 |
| Homicide rate (1992, for males, per 100,000) | 9.1 | 67.5 |

*Source:* U.S. Bureau of the Census, *Statistical Abstract of the United States,* 1995.

Although the data displayed in Table 2.16 provide useful information, we are usually interested in answering questions that go beyond a simple description of how the variables are distributed. Most research usually goes on to make comparisons between groups or to compare one group at different time periods. For instance, to put the information on white Americans presented in Table 2.16 into a more meaningful context we may want to compare it with that of other groups in America. Such a comparison allows us to answer questions such as how "high" is a 67 percent home ownership rate, and is the 14 percent female-headed households figure "high" or "low"?

Take a look at Table 2.17. It includes information previously included in Table 2.16, with additional information on black Americans. This table is used by its authors to demonstrate that living conditions for black Americans in the 1990s remained substantially below those of white Americans. This fact is reflected by notable differences in the proportion of black and white families (31.3% compared with 9.4%) who are living below the poverty line. It is also manifested in substantially higher rates of unemployment for blacks (11.5% in 1994 vs. 5.3% for whites) and in notably higher rates of homicide (more than seven times as high).

## Conclusion

In the introduction to this chapter we told you that constructing a frequency distribution is usually the first step in the statistical analysis of data; we hope that by now you agree that constructing a basic frequency or percentage distribution is a fairly straightforward task. As you have seen in the examples in this chapter, distribution tables help researchers to organize, summarize, display, and describe data. Trends within groups and differences or similarities between groups can be identified using a simple distribution table.

In the chapters that follow you will find that frequency distribution tables provide the basic information for graphically displaying data and calculating measures of central tendency and variability. In other words, you will see frequency and percentage distributions again and again, so make sure you have confidence in your ability to construct and read distribution tables before you proceed to the next chapters.

### MAIN POINTS

- The most basic method for organizing data is to classify the observations into a frequency distribution, a table that reports the number of observations that fall into each category of the variable we are analyzing.

- Constructing a frequency distribution is usually the first step in the statistical analysis of data.

- To obtain a frequency distribution for nominal and ordinal variables, the number of cases that fall into each category of the variable is counted and reported along with the total number of cases ($N$).

- To construct a frequency distribution for interval-ratio variables that have a wide range of values, the scores are reduced into a number of smaller groups, each containing a number of scores. Each group is known as a class interval.

- Proportions and percentages are relative frequencies. To construct a proportion you divide the frequency ($f$) in each category by the total number of cases ($N$). To obtain a percentage you divide the frequency ($f$) in each category by the total number of cases ($N$) and multiply by 100.

- Percentage distributions are tables that show the percentage of observations that fall into each category of the variable. Percentage distributions are routinely added to almost any frequency table and are especially important if comparisons between groups are to be considered.

- One other method of expressing raw frequencies in relative terms is known as a rate. Rates are defined as the number of actual occurrences in a given time period divided by the number of possible occurrences. Rates are often multiplied by some power of 10 to eliminate decimal points and make the number easier to interpret.

- Cumulative frequency distributions allow us to locate the relative position of a given score in a distribution. They are obtained by adding to the frequency in each category the frequencies of all the categories below it (or above it).

- Cumulative percentage distributions have wider applications than cumulative frequency distributions. A cumulative percentage distribution is constructed by adding to the percentages in each category the percentages of all the categories below it (or above it).

## KEY TERMS

*cumulative frequency distribution*  
*cumulative percentage distribution*  
*frequency distribution*  
*percentage*

*percentage distribution*  
*proportion*  
*rate*

## SPSS DEMONSTRATIONS

*Demonstration 1: Producing a Listing of Data Values*  
*for Selected Variables and Cases*

The SPSS Data Editor window displays all the information for a file. Each row corresponds to a case in the file (for the 1994 General Social Survey, each row corresponds to a person). Each column in the window corresponds to one of the variables, such as SEX or RACE. Although it is possible to examine the information in the file by scrolling through the Data Editor window, that procedure is awkward when you wish to examine variables whose columns are not located close together. In those instances, it is easier and better to use the SPSS procedure List Cases to produce a formatted list of cases and variables.

We will be studying the items that ask about various attitudes toward abortion, so we include these items in our List Cases request. But we will also include the variable SEX, which is located far from the columns for the abortion items. The List Cases procedure can be found by clicking on *Statistics*, then on *Summarize*, and finally on *List Cases*. When you do so, you will see the following dialog box.

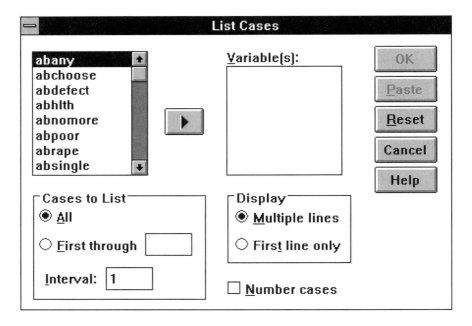

Place the variable SEX in the Variable(s) box, then place the variables ABDEFECT, ABHLTH, ABPOOR, and ABRAPE in the Variable(s) box underneath SEX. Since the file has 1,000 cases and we don't want to see the data for all 1,000 respondents, click under the "First through" choice in the Cases to List box, and type "20" in the text box. This tells SPSS to display the information for only the first twenty cases in the file. When you've done this, click on *OK*. The output from the List Cases command is placed in the output window, as shown.

```
SPSS for Windows Student Version - [!Output1]
 File   Edit   Data   Transform   Statistics   Graphs   Utilities   Window   Help

 Pause  Scroll   Round   Glossary

SEX ABANY ABCHOOSE ABDEFECT ABHLTH ABNOMORE ABPOOR ABRAPE ABSINGLE

  2    1      8        8       8      2        2      8       2
  2    2      4        2       1      2        2      1       2
  1    0      3        0       0      0        0      0       0
  2    1      0        1       1      1        1      1       1
  2    0      0        0       0      0        0      0       0
  2    0      0        0       0      0        0      0       0
  1    1      1        1       1      1        1      1       1
  2    1      0        1       1      1        1      1       1
  1    1      0        1       1      1        1      1       1
  1    1      1        1       1      1        1      1       1
  1    8      0        8       8      8        8      8       8
  1    1      0        1       1      1        1      1       1
  1    0      8        0       0      0        0      0       0
  1    2      5        2       2      2        2      2       2
  2    2      8        1       1      2        8      1       2
  2    1      8        1       1      1        1      1       1
  2    1      0        1       1      1        1      1       1
  2    0      0        0       0      0        0      0       0
  2    0      0        0       0      0        0      0       0
  2    1      0        1       1      1        1      1       1


Number of cases read:  20     Number of cases listed:  20

SPSS Processor is ready
```

When looking at this type of output, you must know what the various codes represent. For SEX, 1 = Male and 2 = Female. The various items about support for abortion are measured in two categories, with 1 = Yes (a woman should be able to obtain a legal abortion in this circumstance) and 2 = No (an abortion should not be available in this circumstance). The exception is for the variable ABCHOOSE (Should a woman be able to get a legal abortion for any reason?), which is measured on a 5-point scale, from 1 = Strongly Agree that abortion is acceptable, to 5 = Strongly Disagree that abortion is acceptable. The other codes, 0, 8, and 9, represent missing data and can be ignored for the moment.

When studying the output, you are searching for possible patterns in the data; for example, do the females seem to have greater support for abortion under these diverse circumstances? If that turned out to be the case, the females would have more values of 1 than do the males (except for ABCHOOSE, of course). There doesn't appear to be much pattern in the data here, but remember that the output only lists the first 20 cases out of 1,000 in the whole file and therefore most likely is not a good representation of the actual data in the total file.

*Demonstration 2: Producing Frequency Tables for the Abortion Items*

The Frequencies procedure in SPSS for Windows is found under the *Statistics* menu in the *Summarize* section. If you click on these menu selections you will see the following dialog box, where we have already placed the abortion items in the Variable(s) box. That's all you have to do before clicking on *OK*.

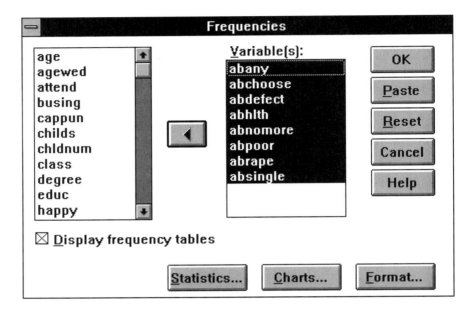

The frequency tables that SPSS has just created are displayed in the Output window; SPSS has scrolled down to the bottom of the Output window. Most people want to start looking at their output from the first variable listed, and the easiest way to do so is to click on the double-headed triangles in the toolbar (between the Utilities and Window choices in the main menu). The button is noted in the screen shown.

```
┌──────────────────────────────────────────────────────────────────────┐
│  ─                    SPSS for Windows Student Version - [!Output1]   ▼ ▲ │
│  ◻  File  Edit  Data  Transform  Statistics  Graphs  Utilities  Window  Help ▲ │
│  ┌────────┬───────┬────────┬─────────┐ ┌────┐ ┌──┬──┐ ┌──┬──┐ ┌───┐     │
│  │ Pause │ Scroll │ Round │ Glossary │ │ ▬▬ │ │ ▲│ ▼│ │ ≛│ ≛│ │ ⚲ │     │
│  └────────┴───────┴────────┴─────────┘ └────┘ └──┴──┘ └──┴──┘ └───┘     │
│  DK                            8         2           2.6    Missing    ▲ │
│                                       ------- -------  -------          │
│                               Total    1000     00.0    100.0          │
│                                                                        │
│  Valid cases    659    Missing cases    341    ┌─────────────┐         │
│                                                │  Click Here  │         │
│  - - - - - - - - - - - - - - - - - - - - - - -└─────────────┘- - - -   │
│                                                                        │
│  ABSINGLE   NOT MARRIED                                                 │
│                                                                        │
│                                               Valid      Cum           │
│  Value Label            Value  Frequency  Percent  Percent   Percent   │
│                                                                        │
│  YES                      1       324      32.4     48.7      48.7      │
│  NO                       2       341      34.1     51.3     100.0      │
│  NAP                      0       315      31.5    Missing             │
│  DK                       8        19       1.9    Missing             │
│  NA                       9         1        .1    Missing             │
│                                 -------  -------  -------              │
│                         Total    1000     100.0    100.0              │
│                                                                        │
│  Valid cases    665    Missing cases    335                           ▼ │
│ ◻▌                                                                    ▼ │
│ ◄ ▐                                                                 ► │
│ SPSS Processor is ready                                                 │
└──────────────────────────────────────────────────────────────────────┘
```

After clicking, SPSS will display the first frequency table we requested, which happens to be for the variable ABANY (should a woman be able to receive an abortion for any reason). You can see this table in the next figure.

```
ABANY       ABORTION IF WOMAN WANTS FOR ANY REASON


                                               Valid      Cum
Value Label              Value  Frequency  Percent  Percent   Percent

YES                        1       315      31.5     47.7      47.7
NO                         2       345      34.5     52.3     100.0
NAP                        0       315      31.5    Missing
DK                         8        24       2.4    Missing
NA                         9         1        .1    Missing
                                 -------  -------  -------
                         Total    1000     100.0    100.0

Valid cases    660    Missing cases    340
```

The variable name, ABANY, is listed in the first line, along with the variable label. The first column lists the Value Label for each category of ABANY. These correspond to the numeric values listed in the next column, so that 1 = YES, 2 = NO, and 8 = DK, which stands for "Don't Know." "NA" means "No Answer" and "NAP" means "Not Applicable."

The next four columns contain the important information in the table. The Frequency column shows the number of respondents who gave a particular response, so we see that 315 people said a woman should be able to have an abortion for any reason, while 345 said no to this question. As you might expect, Americans are about equally divided on this topic. There are a fairly large number of Not Applicable responses because not every respondent was asked this question. Notice also that 24 people said they were unable to say "Yes" or "No" (the DK category).

The next column, "Percent," calculates what percentage of the whole sample (1,000 cases) each of the responses represents. Thus, 31.5 percent of the sample said that a legal abortion should be available for any reason. Normally, though, the Valid Percent column is more useful. This column removes the cases defined as missing (the last three categories) and recalculates percentages based only on the valid responses. You can see in the last line that SPSS reports that there are 660 valid cases and 340 missing cases. Using the Valid Percent column we can see that 47.7 percent of American adults said that abortion was acceptable for any reason, while 52.3 percent said that it was not. As we noted, Americans are about equally divided on this contentious issue. The percentage figures in both columns add to 100 percent.

The last column, "Cum Percent," calculates cumulative percentages beginning with the first response. In this table with only two valid response categories the information in this column is not that useful, but if you look at the frequency table for ABCHOOSE (not pictured), you can see that 46.3 percent of the valid cases either Agree or Strongly Agree that a woman should be able to get a legal abortion for any reason. With ABCHOOSE the cumulative percentages allow us to easily see how many respondents gave a range of responses, beginning with the first category.

## EXERCISES

1. Suppose you have surveyed thirty people and asked them whether they are white (W) or nonwhite (N), and how many traumas (serious accidents, rapes, or crimes) they have experienced in the last year. You also asked them to tell you whether they perceive themselves as being in the upper, middle, working, or lower class. Your survey resulted in the following raw data:

| Race | Class | Traumas | Race | Class | Traumas |
|------|-------|---------|------|-------|---------|
| W | L | 1 | W | W | 0 |
| W | M | 0 | W | M | 2 |
| W | M | 1 | W | W | 1 |
| N | M | 1 | W | W | 1 |
| N | L | 2 | N | W | 0 |
| W | W | 0 | N | M | 2 |
| N | W | 0 | W | M | 1 |
| W | M | 0 | W | M | 0 |
| W | M | 1 | N | W | 1 |
| N | W | 1 | W | W | 0 |
| N | W | 2 | W | W | 0 |
| N | M | 0 | N | M | 0 |
| N | L | 0 | N | W | 0 |
| W | U | 0 | N | W | 1 |
| W | W | 1 | W | W | 0 |

(Data based on General Social Survey files for 1987 to 1991)

    a. What level of measurement is being used for race? for class?
    b. Construct raw frequency tables for race and class.
    c. What proportion of the thirty individuals are nonwhite? What percentage are white?
    d. What proportion are middle class?

2. Using the data and your raw frequency tables from exercise 1, construct a relative frequency table for class. (*Hint:* Use percentages.)
    a. Which is the smallest perceived class?
    b. Which two classes composed the largest percentages of people?

3. Using the data from exercise 1, construct a relative frequency table for trauma.
    a. What level of measurement is used for the trauma variable?
    b. Are people more likely to have experienced no traumas or only one trauma in the last year?
    c. What proportion have experienced one or more traumas in the last year?

4. Many people believe that government programs to help the poor benefit blacks and Hispanics more than whites. You have these four frequency tables that show the ethnic/racial distribution for recipients of welfare, food stamps, Medicaid, and public housing:

| Ethnicity | Welfare | Food Stamps | Medicaid | Public Housing |
|-----------|---------|-------------|----------|----------------|
| White | 84 | 92 | 94 | 76 |
| Black | 64 | 66 | 62 | 86 |
| Hispanic | 30 | 32 | 32 | 28 |

(Data based on a report of the Center on Budget & Policy Priorities, which in turn is based on 1991 census data)

a. Construct relative frequency tables for each of these variables. What is the unit of analysis for these tables?
b. Do whites, blacks, or Hispanics receive more welfare benefits?
c. Blacks receive more of which type of aid than do whites?
d. Most of the recipients of food stamps and Medicaid are of which ethnicity?
e. Do the data support the notion that most government aid goes to blacks and Hispanics? Explain your answer using percentages. What other information would be helpful to answer these questions? (*Hint:* Think about population data.)

5. Suppose you are using General Social Survey (GSS) data from the years 1987 to 1991 for a research project. You are interested in the level of education of the American population, and the GSS includes a question that asks for the number of years of education. The GSS data yield the following frequency distribution for years of education:

| Years of Education | Frequency | $N = 2196$ |
|--------------------|-----------|------------|
| 1 | 4 | |
| 2 | 4 | |
| 3 | 13 | |
| 4 | 18 | |
| 5 | 14 | |
| 6 | 33 | |
| 7 | 30 | |
| 8 | 100 | |
| 9 | 79 | |
| 10 | 123 | |
| 11 | 156 | |
| 12 | 684 | |
| 13 | 194 | |
| 14 | 252 | |
| 15 | 113 | |

| 16  | 214 |
|-----|-----|
| 17  | 53  |
| 18  | 62  |
| 19  | 18  |
| 20+ | 32  |

a. What is the level of measurement of years of education?

b. Construct a frequency table, with relative and cumulative percentages, for years of education.

c. How many respondents have eight or less years of education? What percentage of the sample does this value represent?

d. Assume that you are really more interested in the general level of education rather than in the raw number of years of education, so you would like to group the data into four categories that better reflect your interests. Assume that anyone with twelve years of education is a high school graduate, and that anyone with sixteen years of education is a college graduate. Construct a relative frequency table for education in four categories based on these assumptions.

e. What percentage of the sample has graduated from college?

f. What percentage of the sample has *not* graduated from high school?

6. Suppose that an organization in your state is lobbying to make pornography illegal because they believe that it leads to a breakdown in morals. The leadership of this organization presumes that more women members than men support their stance toward pornography. The following frequency distribution shows how gender is related to belief that pornography leads to a breakdown in morals from a sample of members.

a. Compute relative frequencies for men and women from the table. Use them to describe the relationship between attitude toward pornography and gender.

b. Do these data support the belief of the organization's leadership about their members?

c. What if you were told that there are twice as many female members of the organization? Would that change your answer to (b)?

**Does pornography lead to a breakdown in morals?**

|         | No  | Yes |
|---------|-----|-----|
| Males   | 115 | 120 |
| Females | 120 | 110 |

7. America continues to receive large numbers of immigrants. Often, these immigrants prefer to speak their own language, at least at home. In South River, New Jersey, 3,637 of the 12,788 residents above age 4 speak a language other than English at home, as reported by the U.S. Census Bureau. The following frequency distribution shows the languages:

| | |
|---|---|
| Chinese | 34 |
| French | 55 |
| German | 65 |
| Hungarian | 198 |
| Indic | 34 |
| Italian | 95 |
| Polish | 831 |
| Portuguese | 1,369 |
| Russian | 191 |
| Spanish | 473 |
| Slavic | 279 |
| Other | 13 |

a. Compute the relative frequency distribution for these data. Why would a cumulative frequency distribution be less useful for this table?
b. What percentage of these residents speak Polish at home?
c. What percentage speak Spanish?
d. What are the four most common languages among residents who don't speak English at home?
e. Which two languages are the least common?

8. Suppose you have just finished a survey of 13,986 state prison inmates in the United States (data based on Survey of State Prison Inmates 1991). Your next task is to present a preliminary report to the Bureau of Justice Statistics. This report must include a description of the prison population.
a. Compute relative frequencies for the following raw frequency distributions.

| Gender: | | Ethnicity: | |
|---|---|---|---|
| Male | 665,719 | White | 4,895 |
| Female | 38,462 | Black | 6,433 |
| Age: | | Hispanic | 2,378 |
| 24/younger | 3,077 | Other | 280 |
| 25–34 | 6,434 | Employment status when | |
| 35–44 | 3,217 | committing crime: | |
| 45+ | 1,258 | Full-time job | 7,692 |

Schooling completed:

| | |
|---|---|
| 8th grade/less | 2,657 |
| Some high school | 6,464 |
| High school grad | 3,097 |
| Some college+ | 1,678 |

Income for year before prison:

| | |
|---|---|
| $9,999/less | 7,273 |
| $10,000–$24,000 | 4,615 |
| $25,000+ | 2,098 |

| | |
|---|---|
| Part-time job | 1,678 |
| Looking for job | 2,238 |
| Not looking for job | 2,378 |

Who inmates lived with most as a child:

| | |
|---|---|
| Both parents | 6,014 |
| Mother only | 5,455 |
| Father only | 559 |
| Other relative | 1,538 |
| Foster home | 420 |

b. Write a 300-word paragraph for the Bureau of Justice describing the characteristics of the state prison population, using percentages to support your statements.

9. Have you ever wondered whether television gives an accurate picture of life in America? *USA Today*, July 6, 1993, published the following data about characters appearing on television programs based on a week of watching network television.

Sex:

| | |
|---|---|
| Male | 63% |
| Female | 37% |

Age:

| | |
|---|---|
| Children (0–12) | 4% |
| Teens (13–17) | 6% |
| Young adults (18–35) | 42% |
| Middle age (36–59) | 40% |
| Seniors (60+) | 8% |

Race/Ethnicity:

| | |
|---|---|
| White | 84% |
| Black | 13% |
| Asian | 1% |
| Hispanic | 2% |
| Native American | 0.4% |

Employment:

| | |
|---|---|
| Professional/executive | 60% |
| Labor/service/clerical | 21% |
| Law enforcement | 19% |

Miscellaneous:

| | |
|---|---|
| Are handicapped | 2% |
| Are overweight | 10% |
| Wear glasses | 14% |

Compare these data with the following data describing the actual U.S. population.

Sex:
| | |
|---|---|
| Male | 49% |
| Female | 51% |

Age:
| | |
|---|---|
| Children (0–12) | 19% |
| Teens (13–17) | 7% |
| Young adults (18–35) | 30% |
| Middle age (36–59) | 27% |
| Seniors (60+) | 17% |

Race/Ethnicity:
| | |
|---|---|
| White | 76% |
| Black | 12% |
| Asian | 3% |
| Hispanic | 9% |
| Native American | 1% |

Employment:
| | |
|---|---|
| Professional/executive | 26% |
| Labor/service/clerical | 72% |
| Law enforcement | 2% |

Miscellaneous:
| | |
|---|---|
| Are handicapped | 17% |
| Are overweight | 68% |
| Wear glasses | 38% |

We can see from these data that some groups of people are underrepresented on television, whereas others are overrepresented. Use the percentages from the preceding tables to support your answers to the following questions:

a. Which gender is underrepresented?
b. Which two age groups are greatly overrepresented?
c. Which racial/ethnic group is the most underrepresented?
d. Does television provide an accurate depiction of the distribution of employment status among Americans?
e. Are blacks overrepresented or underrepresented on television?
f. Are handicapped people overrepresented or underrepresented?

10. Advocates of gay rights often argue that homosexuality is not a "preference" or a choice, but rather an "orientation" that cannot be changed. Gay rights advocates also often argue that gays and lesbians should not be barred from military service. Suppose you would like to determine whether most Americans agree with these viewpoints or believe otherwise.

   a. Construct relative frequency tables for the following data (based on a 1992 *New York Times*/CBS News poll of 1154 Americans):

   Believes homosexuality:
   | | |
   |---|---|
   | Is a choice | 508 |
   | Can't be changed | 496 |
   | Don't know | 150 |

   Believes homosexuals should be allowed in the military:
   | | |
   |---|---|
   | Yes | 496 |
   | No | 498 |
   | Don't know | 160 |

   b. Do Americans in general believe that homosexuality is a choice or is something that can't be changed? (Explain your answer using percentages.)

   c. Do Americans in general agree or disagree with the statement that homosexuals should be allowed in the military?

11. In exercise 8, you described some of the demographic characteristics of state prison inmates in the United States. You found that a large proportion of prisoners are male, and now you wonder if there are any other gender differences among prisoners.

   a. Compute relative frequencies for the following raw data:

   | Reasons for incarceration: | Men | Women |
   |---|---|---|
   | Violent crime | 312,888 | 12,308 |
   | Property crime | 166,430 | 11,154 |
   | Drug crime | 139,801 | 12,692 |
   | Other crime | 46,600 | 2,308 |

   b. For what reason are men most likely to be incarcerated?

   c. Most women prisoners are incarcerated for what reason?

   d. Are there any similarities between incarceration reasons for men and women? Explain.

12. Suppose you work at your city's department of health and are interested in mortality rates. You are particularly interested in four different causes of death: heart disease, cancer, stroke, and homicide. You know that the total population of your city is 350,000. Compute mortality rates per 100,000 based on the following numbers of deaths due to the four causes.

Deaths caused by:
| | |
|---|---|
| Heart disease | 697 |
| Cancer | 510 |
| Stroke | 140 |
| Homicide | 49 |

(Statistics based on 1987 data from the National Center for Health Statistics)

13. The birth rate among American women has been quite variable during this century. For example, the so-called baby boom occurred during a period of about fifteen years after World War II in the United States, when the average number of children born to each woman increased dramatically. The following birth rates show the changes in average number of children per female for the last seventy years (Data based on U.S. census reports):

| Year | Birth Rate |
|---|---|
| 1920 | 3.3 |
| 1945 | 2.5 |
| 1958 | 3.8 |
| 1966 | 2.6 |
| 1976 | 1.7 |
| 1991 | 2.1 |

a. How did the birth rate change between 1920 and 1945? 1945 and 1958? 1958 and 1991?
b. Describe the overall trend in birth rates from 1920 to 1991.

14. In exercise 12, you computed mortality rates per 100,000 for the total population of your city. Now you want to compare the mortality rates of whites and blacks for the four different causes of death.

   a. Use the following frequency distributions to compute mortality rates per 100,000 for blacks and whites.

| Population: | 350,000 | |
|---|---|---|
| White | 227,500 | |
| Black | 122,500 | |
| Deaths caused by: | Whites | Blacks |
| Heart disease | 408 | 289 |
| Cancer | 296 | 214 |
| Stroke | 71 | 69 |
| Homicide | 13 | 36 |

   b. Is there a difference in mortality rates between blacks and whites? Explain your answer using the rates and describe the difference if there is one. (Data from the National Center for Health Statistics, 1987)

15. In Table 2.13 in the chapter you saw cumulative frequency tables for how white men and black women believe their family income compares with that for all Americans. The following two tables present relative frequency distributions for this GSS question, first for whites and blacks, then for males and females. Use the tables to answer the questions.

| | Race of Respondent | | | |
|---|---|---|---|---|
| | White | | Black | |
| Opinion of Family Income | Count | % | Count | % |
| Far below average | 31 | 3.8 | 50 | 8.7 |
| Below average | 176 | 21.7 | 193 | 33.4 |
| Average | 424 | 52.2 | 270 | 46.8 |
| Above average | 171 | 21.1 | 55 | 9.5 |
| Far above average | 10 | 1.2 | 9 | 1.6 |

|  | Sex of Respondents | | | |
|  | Male | | Female | |
| Opinion of Family Income | Count | % | Count | % |
| --- | --- | --- | --- | --- |
| Far below average | 21 | 3.8 | 60 | 7.2 |
| Below average | 119 | 21.6 | 250 | 29.8 |
| Average | 285 | 51.8 | 409 | 48.7 |
| Above average | 112 | 20.4 | 114 | 13.6 |
| Far above average | 13 | 2.4 | 6 | .7 |

a. What is the cumulative percentage of females who think their family income is average or below? What is the cumulative percentage of males who believe their family income is below average?

b. Is the cumulative percentage of blacks who believe their family income is average or below greater or less than that for females who hold the same belief?

c. What is the cumulative percentage of whites who believe their family income is average or above?

d. What percentage of males believe their family income is below or far below average? What percentage of males believe their family income is above or far above average? Why might these two values be so close?

16. Building on the previous exercise, the tables below present the frequency distributions for education by gender and race. Use them to answer these questions.

a. Construct frequency tables based on percentages and cumulative percentages of educational attainment for gender and race.

b. What percentage of males have gone beyond a high-school education? What is the comparable percentage for females?

c. What percentage of whites have completed high school or less? What is the comparable percentage for blacks?

d. Are the cumulative percentages more similar for men and women or for blacks and whites? (In other words, where is there more inequality?) Explain.

|  | Gender | |
| Education | Male | Female |
| --- | --- | --- |
| Some high school | 133 | 224 |
| High school graduate | 155 | 271 |
| Some college | 133 | 227 |
| College graduate | 132 | 125 |

|  | Race | |
| Education | White | Black |
| --- | --- | --- |
| Some high school | 174 | 183 |
| High school graduate | 264 | 162 |
| Some college | 195 | 165 |
| College graduate | 186 | 71 |

## SPSS PROBLEMS

1. Imagine that you are conducting a study of marriage and the family. You might want to begin by describing the marital status of contemporary Americans. Use the SPSS Frequencies command with the 1994 GSS data (filename GSS94.SAV) to produce a frequency table for the variable MARITAL. (*Hint:* Using the SPSS Menus, choose *Statistics . . . Summarize . . . Frequencies.*)

   Using the frequency table, answer these questions.
   a. What percentage of the sample is married?
   b. What percentage is divorced?
   c. What percentage is single (has never been married)?
   d. What percentage of the population has ever been married?

2. Suppose you are a political speechwriter for a presidential candidate. You are trying to decide whether to emphasize your candidate's economic platform in the speech you are writing for tomorrow's television broadcast. You would like to know whether most Americans are satisfied with their financial situation or not. A question on the GSS asks respondents how satisfied they are with their financial situations (SATFIN). Using the GSS data and SPSS, generate frequency distributions of the variable SATFIN. Then answer these questions.
   a. What percentage of the population is satisfied with their financial situation?
   b. What percentage is not at all satisfied?

c. What percentage and how many people don't know if they are satisfied with their financial situation?

d. You decide to exclude those who answered "don't know" from the statistics you present in your speech. What percentage is "not at all satisfied" if "don't know" is excluded or considered "missing"?

## GROUP PROBLEMS

1.  This exercise is designed to have you practice reading and interpreting tabular data. Go to the library and search for various published data that are presented in tables, coordinating your work with other group members so you find a variety of tables. You can use U.S. census data available in various publications (such as the *Summary Social, Economic and Housing Characteristics* volume for each state), the tables from the *Statistical Abstract of the United States*, or the *City and County Databook*. Try to find complicated tables rather than simple ones with only a few columns or rows of numbers.

    After you and your group members have selected some tables, pick out one that you want to study and describe. Examine the table closely and make sure you understand the meaning of all the numbers presented in the table as well as definitions of terms, columns, and rows and limitations on the data that are often presented in footnotes.

    After you are satisfied with your knowledge of the table, write a report summarizing your understanding of the table and what it shows about the social world. Then prepare and present a short (5 minutes) informal talk on the table and its key information to your group members to get practice in presenting tabular information. You may also want to discuss the design of the table if you find aspects of it hard to understand. If you believe the design is partially flawed, suggest changes that could be made to improve it.

2.  In exercise 16 you studied the frequency distribution of education for men and women and for blacks and whites. As suggested in the text, you can explore racial and gender inequality further by looking at occupation by gender or by race. Although the GSS file contains a variable measuring occupation, it has too many categories to be useful.

    Instead, find current occupational data by sending some group members to the library to look up census data on occupation for men and women and for blacks and whites. Try to find tables where occupation is coded into no more than ten categories. Make sure that the categories of occupation are listed in order of increasing prestige (such as from blue collar to white collar). Then calculate percentages and cumulative percentages for males and females, then for whites and blacks.

Use these data to have a group discussion on inequality in occupation. Are there greater differences between men and women or between blacks and whites? Compare these results to those for education in exercise 16. Are there similar differences in occupation as there are for education? Why might this be so?

# 3     Graphic Presentation

## Introduction

You have probably heard that "a picture is worth a thousand words." The same can be said about statistical graphs because they summarize hundreds or thousands of numbers. Many people are intimidated by statistical information presented in frequency distributions or in other tabular forms, but they find the same information to be readable and understandable when presented graphically. Graphs tell a story in "pictures" rather than in words or numbers. They are supposed to make us think about the substance rather than the technical detail of the presentation.

In this chapter, you will learn about some of the most commonly used graphical techniques. We concentrate less on the technical details of how to create graphs and more on how to choose the appropriate graphs to make statistical information coherent. We also focus on how to interpret information presented graphically and how to recognize when a graph distorts what the numbers have to say. A graph is a device used to create a visual impression, and that visual impression sometimes may be misleading.

As we introduce the various graphical techniques we also show you how to use graphs to tell a "story." The particular story we tell in this chapter is that of senior citizens in America. The different types of graphs introduced in this chapter demonstrate the many facets of the aging of America over the next four decades. People have tended to talk about seniors as if they composed a homogeneous group, but the different graphical techniques we illustrate here dramatize the wide variations in economic characteristics, living arrangements, and family status among people aged 65 and older. Most of the statistical information presented in this chapter is based on the *1990 Census of Population and Housing* and numerous other reports prepared by statisticians from the Census Bureau and other government agencies that gather information about senior citizens in America.

Table 3.1 **U.S. Population 65 Years and Over by Race and Ethnic Origin, 1990**

| Race/Ethnicity | Frequency (f) | Percentages (%) |
|---|---|---|
| White | 28,020,562 | 90.2 |
| Black | 2,492,221 | 8.0 |
| Native American, Asian, and Other | 566,112 | 1.8 |
| Total (N) | 31,078,895 | 100.0 |

*Source:* U.S. Bureau of the Census. 1992. "Sixty-five plus in America." *Current Population Reports.* Special studies P23-178, Table 2-2.

Numerous graphing techniques are available to you, but here we focus on just a few of the most widely used in the social sciences. The first two, the pie and bar charts, are appropriate for nominal and ordinal variables. The next two, histograms and frequency polygons, are used with interval-ratio variables. We also discuss stem and leaf plots, statistical maps, and time series charts. The stem and leaf plot is used for describing interval-ratio data and the statistical map is most often used with interval-ratio data. Finally, time series charts are used to show how some variables change over time.

## The Pie Chart: The Race and Ethnicity of the Elderly

The elderly population of the United States is racially and ethnically heterogeneous. As the data in Table 3.1 show, of the total elderly population (in this chapter, the elderly are defined as persons 65 years and older) in 1990, about 28.0 million were white[1]; about 2.5 million, black; and 566,112, Native American, Asians, and others.

A **pie chart** shows the differences in frequencies or percentages among categories of a nominal or an ordinal variable. The categories are displayed as segments of a circle whose pieces add up to 100 percent of the total frequencies. The pie chart shown in Figure 3.1 displays the same information that Table 3.1 presents. Although you can inspect these data in Table 3.1, you can interpret the information more easily by seeing it presented in the pie chart in Figure 3.1. It shows that the elderly population is predominantly white (90.2%), followed by black (8%).

[1]The census data group most Hispanic Americans as whites.

Figure 3.1  **U.S. Population 65 Years and Over by Race and Ethnic Origin, 1990**

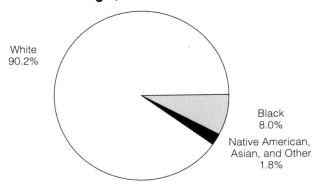

White
90.2%

Black
8.0%

Native American,
Asian, and Other
1.8%

$N = 31{,}078{,}895$
*Source:* U.S. Bureau of the Census. *Current Population Reports,* P23-178.

---

**Learning Check.**  *Notice that the pie chart contains all of the information presented in the frequency distribution. Like the frequency distribution, charts have an identifying number, a title that describes the content of the figure, and a reference to a source. The frequency or percentage is represented both visually and in numbers.*

---

*Pie Chart*  A graph showing the differences in frequencies or percentages among categories of a nominal or an ordinal variable. The categories are displayed as segments of a circle whose pieces add up to 100 percent of the total frequencies.

---

To compare two distributions we can use two pie charts. For example, Figure 3.2 shows two pie charts that display the U.S. population 65 years and older by race and ethnic origin for the years 1990 and 2050. This figure tells us at a glance that between 1990 and 2050 the percentage of blacks is expected to increase from 8 to 14 percent of the total elderly population. Similarly, the percentage of other ethnic groups (such as Asian, Pacific Islander, Native American, Eskimo, and Aleut combined) is expected to increase from 2 to 7 percent of the total elderly population.[2] We can highlight this growing racial diversity of the elderly

[2]U.S. Bureau of the Census. *Current Population Reports,* p23-178, p. 2-11.

Figure 3.2 **U.S. Population 65 Years and Over by Race and Ethnic Origin, 1990 and 2050**

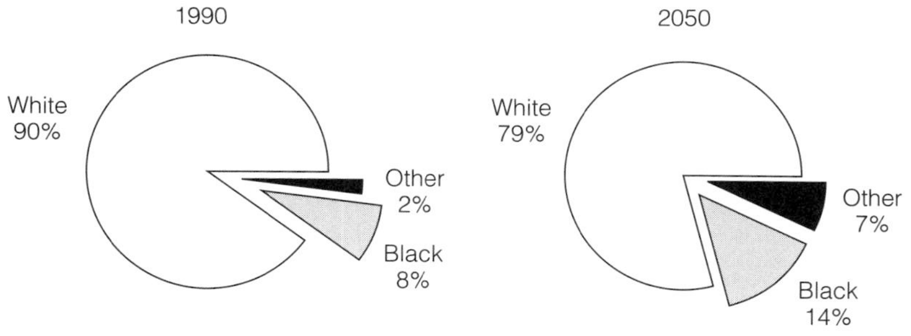

1990

White
90%

Other
2%

Black
8%

2050

White
79%

Other
7%

Black
14%

*Source:* U.S. Bureau of the Census. *Current Population Reports,* P23-178.

population in the coming decades[3] by "exploding" the pie chart, moving the segments representing these groups slightly outward to draw them to the viewer's attention.

> **Learning Check.**  *Note that we could have "exploded" the segment of the pies representing the white population if we had wanted to highlight the shrinking proportion of whites.*

## The Bar Graph: The Living Arrangements and Labor Force Participation of the Elderly

The **bar graph** provides an alternative way to graphically present nominal or ordinal data. It shows the differences in frequencies or percentages among categories of a nominal or an ordinal variable. The categories are displayed as rectangles of equal width with their height proportional to the frequency or percentage of the category.

Let's illustrate the bar graph with an overview of the living arrangements of the elderly. Living arrangements change considerably with advancing age—an increasing number of the elderly live alone or with other relatives. Figure 3.3 is a bar graph displaying the percentage distribution of the living arrangements for the elderly for 1990. This chart is interpreted similarly to a pie chart except that the categories of

---

[3]The 2050 figures are projected by the Census Bureau.

Figure 3.3   **Living Arrangements of the Elderly (65 and Older) in the United States, 1990**

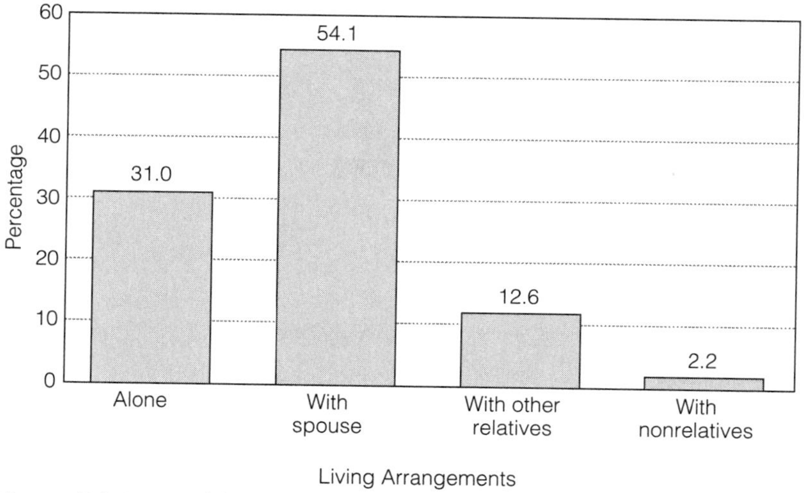

Living Arrangements

*Source:* U.S. Bureau of the Census. *Current Population Reports,* P23-178.

the variable are arrayed along the horizontal axis (sometimes referred to as the *X*-axis) and the percentages along the vertical axis (sometimes referred to as the *Y*-axis). This bar graph is easily interpreted: It shows that in 1990, 54.1 percent of the elderly lived with a spouse; 31.0 percent lived alone; and the remaining 14.8 percent lived with either other relatives or nonrelatives.

Construct a bar graph by first labeling the categories of the variables along the horizontal axis. For these categories, construct rectangles of equal width, with the height of each proportional to the frequency or percentage of the category. Note that a space separates each of the categories to make clear that they are not continuous.

---

*Bar Graph*   A graph showing the differences in frequencies or percentages among categories of a nominal or an ordinal variable. The categories are displayed as rectangles of equal width with their height proportional to the frequency or percentage of the category.

---

Bar graphs are often used to compare one or more categories of a variable among different groups. For instance, as women age, there is an increasing likelihood they will live alone. This fact is related to the shorter

Figure 3.4 **Living Arrangements of U.S. Elderly (65 and Older) by Gender, 1990**

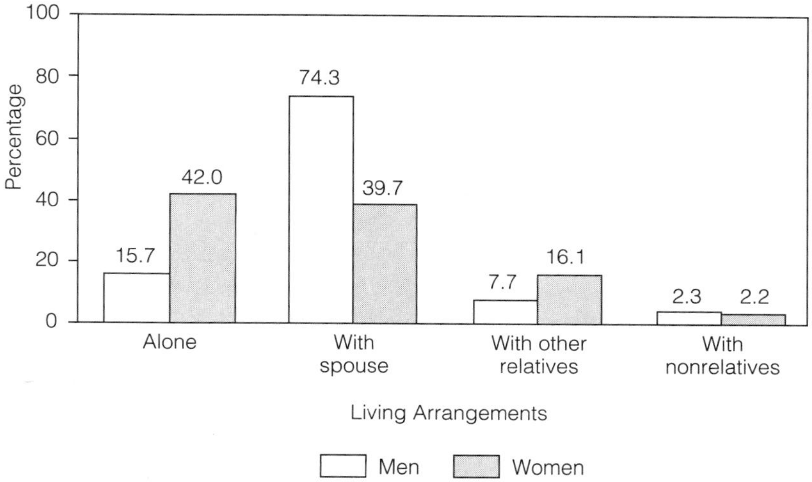

*Source:* U.S. Bureau of the Census. *Current Population Reports,* P23-178.

life expectancies of men and the tendency of men to marry women younger than themselves.[4]

Suppose we want to show how the patterns in living arrangements differ between men and women. Figure 3.4 compares the percentage of women and men 65 years and older who lived with others or alone in 1990. It clearly shows that elderly women are more likely than elderly men to live alone. We can also construct bar graphs horizontally, with the categories of the variable arrayed along the vertical axis and the percentages or frequencies displayed on the horizontal axis. This format is illustrated in Figure 3.5, which compares the 1989 income of elderly men and women by age groups.

From Figure 3.5, we see that the majority of all elderly persons had 1989 income below $20,000. Women living alone were more likely to have low income than men living alone, and people 75 years and over were poorer than people younger than 75 years. In the 65-to-74-year age group, 47.8 percent of the women, compared with 33.8 percent of the men, had income below $10,000; among people 75 years and older, the figures are 58.0 percent for women and 41.9 percent for men.

[4]*Current Population Reports,* pp. 6-3 and 6-4.

Figure 3.5    **Income in 1989 of U.S. Elderly Householders Living Alone by Age and Sex (in percentages)**

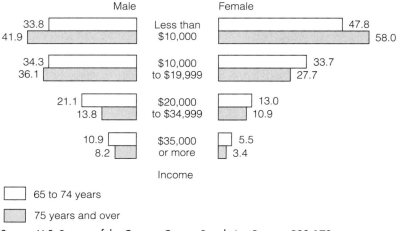

Source: U.S. Bureau of the Census. *Current Population Reports,* P23-178.

---

***Learning Check.***   *When bar charts or histograms (we'll talk about histograms soon) are used to display the frequencies of the categories of a single variable, the categories are shown on the X-axis and the frequencies on the Y-axis. In a horizontal bar chart or histogram this is reversed.*

---

## The Statistical Map: The Geographic Distribution of the Elderly

Since the 1960s, the elderly have been relocating to the South and the West of the United States. It is projected that in the next twenty years these regions will increase their elderly population by about 40 percent. We can display these dramatic geographical changes in American society by using a statistical map. Maps are especially useful for describing geographical variations in variables, such as population distribution, voting patterns, crime rates, or labor force composition.

Let's look at Figure 3.6. It presents a statistical map, by state, of the percent increase from 1980 to 1990 of the population 65 years and older. The variable "percent increase in the elderly population from 1980 to 1990" has three categories: under 14.0 percent, 14.0 to 29.9 percent, and 30.0 percent or more. Each category is represented by a different shading (or color code), and the states are shaded depending on their classification

Figure 3.6 **Percent Increase in U.S. Population 65 Years and Over by State, 1980 to 1990**

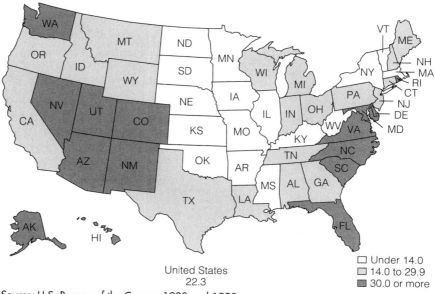

United States
22.3

☐ Under 14.0
☐ 14.0 to 29.9
■ 30.0 or more

*Source:* U.S. Bureau of the Census, 1980 and 1990.

into the different categories. To make it easier to read a map that you construct and to identify its patterns, keep the number of categories relatively small, say, not more than five.

Figure 3.6 emphasizes that over the decade of the 1980s the greatest percentage of increase in the elderly population occurred mainly in the western states and the southern coastal states.

Figures 3.7 and 3.8 are two additional examples of statistical maps. They present a geographical breakdown by state of the distribution of elderly blacks and Hispanics. These maps show that in 1990 the southern and the northeastern states contained the largest concentration of black elderly, whereas the Hispanic elderly were concentrated mainly in the southwestern and the western states.

> **Learning Check.** *Because states vary so much in population, it might be informative to construct maps showing the percentage of the total population in each state that is black elderly (or Hispanic). How might such maps differ from Figures 3.7 and 3.8? Group problem 3 might help you answer this question.*

Figure 3.7 **Percentages of Total U.S. Black Population 65 Years and Over Living in Each State, 1990**

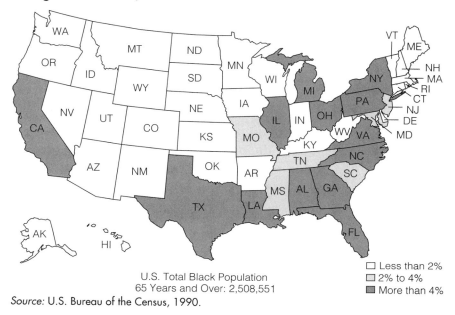

U.S. Total Black Population
65 Years and Over: 2,508,551

☐ Less than 2%
☐ 2% to 4%
■ More than 4%

*Source:* U.S. Bureau of the Census, 1990.

Figure 3.8 **Percentages of Total U.S. Hispanic-Origin Population 65 Years and Over Living in Each State, 1990**

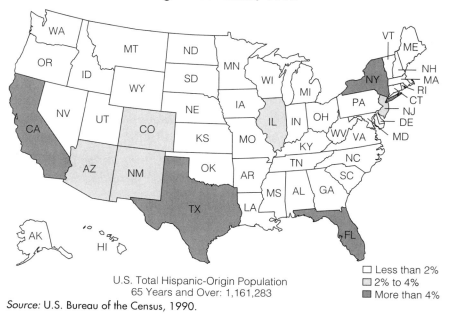

U.S. Total Hispanic-Origin Population
65 Years and Over: 1,161,283

☐ Less than 2%
☐ 2% to 4%
■ More than 4%

*Source:* U.S. Bureau of the Census, 1990.

The examples you have been exploring in this section are all limited to data on the state level. However, maps can also display geographical variations on the level of cities, counties, city blocks, census tracts, and other units. Your choice of whether to display variations on the state level or for smaller units will depend on the research question you wish to explore.

---

**Learning Check.** *Can you think of a few other examples of data that could be described using a statistical map?*

---

## The Histogram

In the previous section you were introduced to the bar chart—a graphical portrayal of nominal and ordinal variables. The **histogram** is used to show the differences in frequencies or percentages among categories of an interval-ratio variable. The categories are displayed as contiguous bars, with width proportional to the width of the category and height proportional to the frequency or percentage of that category. A histogram looks very similar to a bar chart except that the bars are contiguous to each other (touching) and may not be of equal width. In a bar chart, the spaces between the bars visually indicate that the categories are separate. Examples of separate categories are "married" and "single," "male" and "female," and "employed" and "unemployed." In a histogram the touching bars indicate that the categories or intervals are ordered from low to high in a meaningful way. For example, the categories of "hours spent studying," "age," and "years of school completed" are contiguous, ordered intervals.

Figure 3.9 is a histogram displaying the percentage distribution of the population 65 years and over by age. The data on which the histogram is based are presented in Table 3.2. To construct the histogram of Figure 3.9, arrange the age intervals along the horizontal axis and the percentages (or frequencies) along the vertical axis. For each age category, construct a bar with the height corresponding to the percentage of the elderly in the population in that age category. The width of each bar corresponds to the number of years that the age interval represents. The area that each bar occupies tells us the proportion of the population that falls into a given age interval. The histogram is drawn with the bars touching each other to indicate that the intervals are contiguous.

Figure 3.9 **Relative Frequency of U.S. Population 65 Years and Over by Age, 1990**

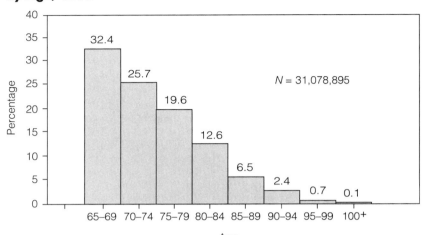

Source: U.S. Bureau of the Census. *Current Population Reports,* P23-178.

Table 3.2 **Percentage Distribution of U.S. Population 65 Years and Over by Age, 1990**

| Age | Percentages (%) |
| --- | --- |
| 65–69 | 32.4 |
| 70–74 | 25.7 |
| 75–79 | 19.6 |
| 80–84 | 12.6 |
| 85–89 | 6.5 |
| 90–94 | 2.4 |
| 95–99 | .7 |
| 100+ | .1 |
| Total | 100.0 |
| (N) | 31,078,895 |

Source: U.S. Bureau of the Census. 1992. "Sixty-five plus in America." *Current Population Reports.* Special studies P23-178.

> *Histogram*  A graph showing the differences in frequencies or percentages among categories of an interval-ratio variable. The categories are displayed as contiguous bars, with width proportional to the width of the category and height proportional to the frequency or percentage of that category.

## Statistics in Practice: The "Graying" of America

We can also use the histogram to depict more complex trends, as, for instance, the "graying" of America. Let's consider for a moment some of these trends: The elderly population today is ten times larger than it was in 1900, and it will more than double by the year 2030. Indeed, as a journalist has pointed out,

> if the automobile had existed in Colonial times, half the residents of the New Land . . . couldn't have taken a spin: One of every two people were under age 16. Most didn't live long enough to reach old age. Today, the population too young to drive has dropped to one in four while adults 65 and over account for one in eight.[5]

The histogram can give us a visual impression of these demographic trends. For an illustration, let's look at Figures 3.10 and 3.11. Both are applications of the histogram and are used to examine, by gender, actual and projected patterns of the age distribution in America in 1955 and 2010. Notice that in both figures, age groups are arranged along the vertical axis, whereas the frequencies (in millions of people) are along the horizontal axis. Each age group is classified by males on the left and females on the right. Because this type of histogram reflects age distribution by gender, it is also called an age-sex pyramid.

Visually compare the different pieces of data presented in these graphs. By observing where age groups are concentrated you can discern major patterns in age distribution over time. Note the different shapes of Figure 3.10 and Figure 3.11. Whereas in 1955 the largest group in the population was 0 to 9 years old, in 2010 the largest group will be 45 to 54 years old. These dramatic changes reflect the "graying" of the baby boom (born 1946 to 1965) generation. Almost 84 million babies were born in the United States from 1946 to 1965—60 percent more than were born during the preceding two decades. By 2010, as the baby boom generation

[5]*USA Today,* 10 November 1992.

Figure 3.10 **U.S. Population by Gender and Age, 1955 (in millions)**

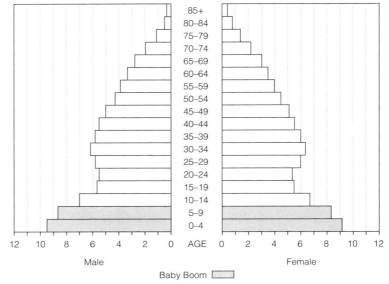

Source: U.S. Bureau of the Census. *Current Population Reports,* P23-178.

Figure 3.11 **U.S. Population by Gender and Age, 2010 (in millions)**

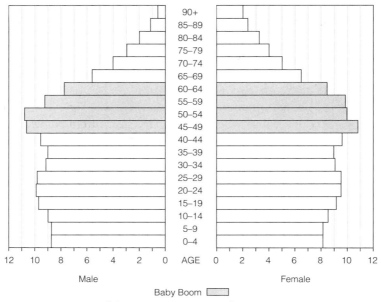

Source: U.S. Bureau of the Census. *Current Population Reports,* P23-178.

reaches 45 to 64, the number of middle-aged and elderly Americans will increase dramatically.

Also observe in Figures 3.10 and 3.11 the differences in the number of men and women as age increases. These differences are especially noticeable in Figure 3.11. For example, between ages 70 and 74, women outnumber men 5 to 4; for those 85 years and over, women outnumber men almost 2 to 1. These differences are due to the fact that at every age, male mortality exceeds female mortality.

> **Learning Check.** *Notice that when we want to use the histogram to compare groups, we must show a histogram for each group (see Figures 3.10 and 3.11). When we compare groups on the bar chart, we are able to compare two or more groups on the same bar chart (see Figure 3.4).*

## The Frequency Polygon

Numerical growth of the elderly population is worldwide, occurring in both developed and developing countries. In 1991, twenty-seven nations had elderly populations of at least 2 million. Demographic projections indicate that there will be forty-nine such nations by 2020. Among the nations experiencing dramatic growth of the elderly population is Japan. Figure 3.12 is a frequency polygon displaying the elderly population of Japan by age.

The **frequency polygon** is another way to display interval-ratio distributions; it shows the differences in frequencies or percentages among categories of an interval-ratio variable. Points representing the frequencies of each category are placed above the midpoint of the category and are joined by a straight line. Notice that in Figure 3.12 the age intervals are arranged on the horizontal axis and the frequencies along the vertical axis. Instead of using bars to represent the frequencies, however, points representing the frequencies of each interval are placed above the midpoint of the intervals. Adjacent points are then joined by straight lines.

Both the histogram and the frequency polygon can be used to depict distributions and trends of interval-ratio variables. How do you choose which one to use? To some extent the choice is a matter of individual preference, but, in general, polygons are better suited for comparing how a variable is distributed across two or more groups or across two or more time periods. For example, Figure 3.13 compares the elderly population in Japan for 1991 with the projected elderly population for the years 2000 and 2020.

Figure 3.12 **Population for Japan, Age 55 and Over, 1991**

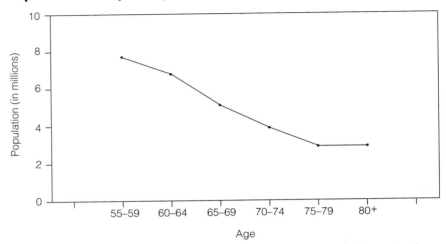

*Source:* Adapted from U.S. Bureau of the Census. Kevin Kinse, Center for International Research, International Data Base.

Figure 3.13 **Population for Japan, Age 55 and Over, 1991, 2000, and 2020**

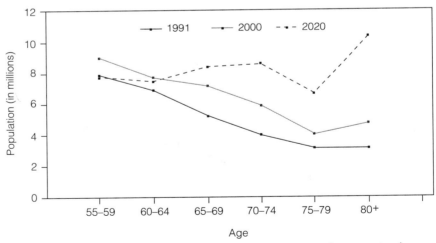

*Source:* Adapted from U.S. Bureau of the Census. Kevin Kinse, Center for International Research, International Data Base.

Let's examine this frequency polygon. It shows that Japan's population age 65 and over is expected to grow dramatically in the coming decades. According to projections, the percentage of Japan's population that is elderly could grow from 15.3 million (8.1 percent of the total population) to 21.4 million (16.7 percent) in 2000 and to 33.4 million (26.2 percent) by 2020.[6] Japan's oldest-old population is also projected to grow rapidly, from about 3.1 million (less than 3 percent of the total population) to 10.3 million (8 percent) by 2020. This projected rise has already led to reduction in retirement benefits and other adjustments to prepare for the economic and social impact of a rapidly aging society.[7]

---

*Frequency Polygon*   A graph showing the differences in frequencies or percentages among categories of an interval-ratio variable. Points representing the frequencies of each category are placed above the midpoint of the category and are joined by a straight line.

---

**Learning Check.**   *Look closely at the frequency polygons shown in Figure 3.13. Verify the frequencies just described for the oldest-old population (80 years and over). Can you recalculate the percentages for these data?*

## The Stem and Leaf Plot

The **stem and leaf plot** is a quick and simple way to organize a set of scores. In a sense it is a visual display of a frequency distribution and can be used as a preliminary step in determining the shape of the distribution. Let's use the data displayed in Table 3.3 to illustrate how to construct a stem and leaf plot. These data represent the population 65 years and older per 10,000 residents in selected cities for 1990. A stem and leaf plot for these data is shown in Figure 3.14.

The first step in constructing a stem and leaf plot from a set of scores is to split each score into two components: a stem and a leaf. The stems are the leading digits and the leaves are the trailing digits. You can see that Table 3.3 includes scores that are either three or four digits long. For three-digit numbers, the stem is the first digit and for the four-digit scores

---

[6]U.S. Bureau of the Census. 1992. "Sixty-five plus in America." *Current Population Reports.* Special studies, p. 2-19.

[7]*Current Population Reports*, p. 2-20.

Table 3.3  **U.S. Population 65 Years and Over per 10,000 Total Residents in Selected Cities of 100,000 or More, 1990**

| WEST | | SOUTH | |
|---|---|---|---|
| Pacific | | West South Central | |
| Honolulu, HI | 1,596 | Oklahoma City, OK | 1,187 |
| Seattle, WA | 1,519 | Little Rock, AK | 1,256 |
| Portland, OR | 1,456 | Houston, TX | 828 |
| Los Angeles, CA | 998 | Dallas, TX | 972 |
| San Francisco, CA | 1,456 | New Orleans, LA | 1,301 |
| San Diego, CA | 1,022 | | |
| | | East South Central | |
| Mountain | | Louisville, KY | 1,659 |
| Boise, ID | 1,191 | Memphis, TN | 1,222 |
| Las Vegas, NV | 1,027 | Jackson, MS | 1,162 |
| Phoenix, AZ | 968 | Birmingham, AL | 1,484 |
| Tucson, AZ | 1,263 | | |
| Salt Lake City, UT | 1,450 | South Atlantic | |
| Denver, CO | 1,386 | Norfolk, VA | 1,051 |
| Albuquerque, NM | 1,112 | Charlotte, NC | 980 |
| | | Atlanta, GA | 1,128 |
| MIDWEST | | Miami, FL | 1,655 |
| West North Central | | Tampa, FL | 1,462 |
| Sioux Falls, ND | 1,168 | Baltimore, MD | 1,371 |
| Omaha, NE | 1,289 | | |
| Kansas City, KS | 1,291 | NORTHEAST | |
| Minneapolis, MN | 1,295 | Middle Atlantic | |
| Des Moines, IA | 1,340 | New York, NY | 1,301 |
| St. Louis, MO | 1,664 | Buffalo, NY | 1,484 |
| | | Philadelphia, PA | 1,518 |
| East North Central | | Pittsburgh, PA | 1,793 |
| Milwaukee, WI | 1,244 | Newark, NJ | 928 |
| Detroit, MI | 1,215 | | |
| Chicago, IL | 1,186 | New England | |
| Indianapolis, IN | 1,144 | Boston, MA | 1,166 |
| Columbus, OH | 915 | Providence, RI | 1,356 |
| Cleveland, OH | 1,399 | Bridgeport, CT | 1,358 |
| | | Springfield, MA | 1,374 |
| | | Hartford, CT | 988 |

*Source:* U.S. Bureau of the Census. *Current Population Reports,* P23-178.

Figure 3.14  **U.S. Population 65 Years and Over per 10,000 Total Residents in Selected Cities of 100,000 or More, 1990**

| | | | | | | | | | |
|----|----|----|----|----|----|----|----|----|----|
| 08 | 28 | | | | | | | | |
| 09 | 15 | 28 | 68 | 72 | 80 | 88 | 98 | | |
| 10 | 22 | 27 | 51 | | | | | | |
| 11 | 12 | 28 | 44 | 62 | 66 | 68 | 86 | 87 | 91 |
| 12 | 15 | 22 | 44 | 56 | 63 | 89 | 91 | 95 | |
| 13 | 01 | 02 | 40 | 56 | 58 | 71 | 74 | 86 | 99 |
| 14 | 50 | 56 | 56 | 62 | 84 | 84 | | | |
| 15 | 18 | 19 | 96 | | | | | | |
| 16 | 55 | 59 | 64 | | | | | | |
| 17 | 93 | | | | | | | | |

Source: *Current Population Reports,* P23-178.

the stem is the first two digits. The leaves (trailing digits) in both cases have two digits. For example, there are 998 older persons per 10,000 residents in Los Angeles. The stem becomes 9 and the leaf, 98. For Detroit, which has 1,215 older persons per 10,000 residents, the stem is 12 and the leaf is 15.

Next, we list the stems from smallest to largest, with each stem beginning a new row. We then draw a vertical line to the right of the stems. Each score is classified into the same row as its stem; its leaf is then written in that row to the right of the vertical line, so the scores are in ascending order.

Let's try and identify the scores for some of the cities listed in Table 3.3 in the resulting stem and leaf plot in Figure 3.14. For example, the third line with a stem of 10 has three leaves: 22, 27, and 51. The scores represented in this row are thus 1,022, 1,027, and 1,051, which are the population numbers for San Diego, CA; Las Vegas, NV; and Norfolk, VA.

Note that the stem and leaf plot looks a lot like a histogram turned on its side (like Figures 3.10 and 3.11 ), except that it displays actual scores. This feature of the stem and leaf plot allows us to quickly identify important properties of the distribution. For instance, from Figure 3.14 we can see that the elderly population figures for the cities represented in the plot range from 828 to 1,793 per 10,000, and that in most cities the number of people 65 years or over is between 1,112 and 1,484 per 10,000.

---

***Stem and Leaf Plot***  A visual display of a frequency distribution.

---

### Time Series Charts

We are often interested in examining how some variables change over time. For example, we may be interested in showing changes in the labor force participation of Hispanic women over the last decade, changes in the public's attitude toward abortion rights, or changes in divorce and marriage rates. A **time series chart** displays changes in a variable at different points in time. It involves two variables: "time," which is labeled across the horizontal axis, and another variable of interest whose values (frequencies, percentages, or rates) are labeled along the vertical axis. To construct a time series chart, use a series of dots to mark the value of the variable at each time interval, and then join the dots by a series of straight lines.

Figure 3.15 shows a time series from 1900 to 2050 of the percentage of the total population that is 65 years or older (the figures for the years 2000 through 2050 are projections made by the Social Security Administration). This time series lets us clearly see the dramatic increase in the elderly population. The number of elderly increased from a little less than 5 percent in 1900 to about 12 percent in 1990. The rate is expected to nearly double by 2050 when almost 25 percent of the total population will be 65 years or older. This dramatic increase in the elderly population, especially beginning in the year 2010, is associated with the "graying" of the baby boom

Figure 3.15 **Percentage of Total U.S. Population 65 Years and Over, 1900 to 2050**

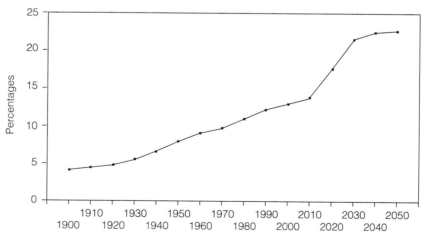

Year

*Source:* U.S. Bureau of the Census. *Current Population Reports,* P23-178.

Figure 3.16 **Percentage of U.S. Population 65 and Over Currently Divorced—by Gender, 1960 to 2040**

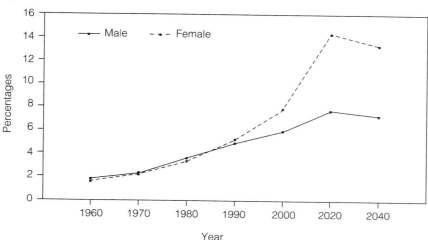

*Source:* U.S. Bureau of the Census. *Current Population Reports,* P23-178.

generation. This group, which was 0 to 9 years old in 1955 (see the age pyramid in Figure 3.10), will be 55 to 64 years old in the year 2010.

The implications of these demographic changes are enormous. To cite just a few, there will be more pressure on the health-care system and on private and public pension systems. Also, because the voting patterns of the elderly differ from those of younger people, the "graying" of America will have major political effects.

Often, we are interested in comparing changes over time for a number of groups. Let's examine Figure 3.16, which charts the trends in the percentage of divorced elderly from 1960 to 2040 for men and women. This time series graph shows that the percentage of divorced elderly men and elderly women was about the same until 1990. For both groups the percentage increased from less than 2 percent in 1960 to about 5 percent in 1990.[8] According to projections, however, there will be significant increases in the percentage of men and women who are divorced: from 5 percent of all the elderly in 1990 to 8 percent of all elderly men and 14 percent of all elderly women by the year 2020. This sharp upturn is clearly emphasized in Figure 3.16.

[8]*Current Population Reports,* p. 6-1.

*Time Series Chart*   A graph displaying changes in a variable at different points in time. It shows time (measured in units such as years and months) on the the horizontal axis and the frequencies (percentages or rates) of another variable on the vertical axis.

---

**Learning Check.**   *How does the time series chart differ from a frequency polygon? The difference is that frequency polygons display frequency distributions of a single variable, whereas time series charts display two variables. Also, time is always one of the variables displayed in a time series chart.*

## Distortions in Graphs

In this chapter, we have seen that statistical graphs can give us a quick sense of the main patterns in the data. But graphs not only quickly inform us; they also can quickly deceive us. Because we are often more interested in general impressions than in detailed analyses of the numbers, we are more vulnerable to being swayed by distorted graphs. But what are graphical distortions? How can we recognize them? In this section, we illustrate some of the most common methods of graphical deception so you will be able to critically evaluate information that is presented graphically. To help you learn more about graphical "integrity," I highly recommend *The Visual Display of Quantitative Information* (1983), by Edward Tufte. This book not only demonstrates the many advantages of working with graphs, but it also contains a detailed discussion of some of the pitfalls in the application and interpretation of graphics.

## Shrinking and Stretching the Axes: Visual Confusion

Probably the most common distortions in graphical representations occur when the distance along the vertical or horizontal axis is altered in relation to the other axis.[10] Axes can be stretched or shrunk to create any desired result. Let's look at the example presented in Figure 3.17a. It is taken from a 1993 issue of *USA Today,* showing changes in cost per child enrolled in Head Start. The impression the graph gives is that from 1966 to 1993, cost per child skyrocketed! However, even though the cost has indeed gone up from $271 to $3,849, these figures are not adjusted for inflation. With such an adjustment the increase may not seem as dramatic. Suppose that we want to make the increase in cost look more moderate without adjusting

[10]R. Lyman Ott et al., *Statistics: A Tool for Social Sciences.* Boston: PWS-Kent Publishing Co., 1992, 92–95.

Figure 3.17  **Cost per Child Enrolled in Head Start, U.S.**

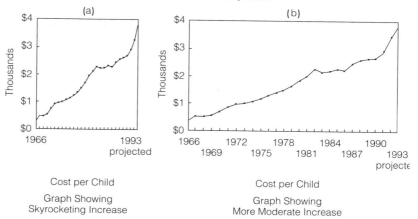

Cost per Child

Graph Showing
Skyrocketing Increase

Cost per Child

Graph Showing
More Moderate Increase

*Source:* Adapted from *USA Today,* March 15, 1993. Copyright 1992 *USA Today.* Used by permission.

for inflation. We can stretch the horizontal axis to enlarge the distance between the years, as shown in Figure 3.17b. As a result of this stretching the trend appears less steep and the increase in cost appears smaller. We have changed the impression considerably without altering the data in any way. Another way to decrease the steepness of the slope is to shrink the vertical axis so that the dollar amounts are represented by smaller heights than they are in Figure 3.17a or 3.17b.

The opposite effect can be obtained by shrinking the horizontal axis and narrowing the distance between the points on the scale. That technique makes the slope look more steep.[11] Consider the graphs in Figures 3.18a and 3.18b, which depict the increase in the number of women elected to state legislatures between 1973 and 1993. In Figure 3.18a the increase of more than 300 percent (from 424 to 1,516), although discernible, does not appear to be very great. This increase can be made to appear more dramatic by shrinking the horizontal axis so the years are moved closer together. This was done in Figure 3.18b, which represents the same data. The steeper slope, created by moving the years closer together, gives the impression of a more substantial increase.

> **Learning Check.** *When you are using a computer software program to draw a graph, the program will automatically adjust the size of the axes to avoid distortion. You will have to be creative to produce a distorted graph on your computer, if you can do it at all.*

[11]Ibid.

Figure 3.18    **Women in U.S. Legislatures, 1973 to 1993**

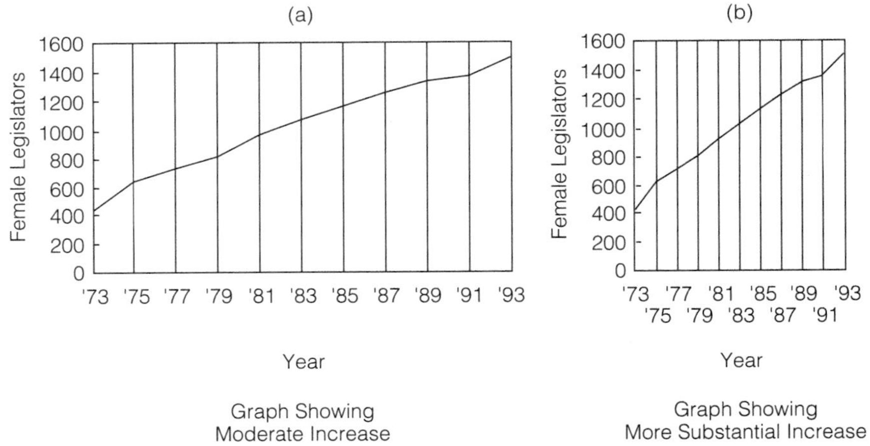

(a)

Graph Showing
Moderate Increase

(b)

Graph Showing
More Substantial Increase

*Source:* Adapted from *USA Today*, February 12, 1993. Copyright 1993 *USA Today*. Used by permission.

## Distortions with Picture Graphs

Another way to distort data with graphs is to use pictures to represent quantitative information. The problem with picture graphs is that the visual impression received is created by the picture's total area rather than by its height (the graphs we have discussed so far rely on height).

Take a look at Figure 3.19. It shows the estimated number of HIV-infected people in 1992 in some of the hardest-hit areas around the world. Note that sub-Saharan Africa, where the virus may have originated, is the hardest hit, with 6.5 million infected men and women. This number is more than six times the number of HIV infections in South and Central America, where the number of infections is about 1 million. Yet the human figures representing the number of infections for Africa are about twenty times larger in total area occupied than the size of the human figures for South and Central America. The reason for this magnified effect is that even though the data are one-dimensional (1 million compared with 6.5 million infected people in sub-Saharan Africa), the human figures representing these numbers are two-dimensional. Therefore, it is not only height that is represented but width as well, creating a false impression of the difference in the number of HIV infections.

These examples illustrate the potential pitfalls in interpreting graphs, emphasizing the point that a graph is a device used to create a visual impression, and that visual impressions sometimes may be misleading. Always interpret a graph in the context of the numerical information the graph represents.

Figure 3.19 **Estimated Number of HIV Infections in 1992**

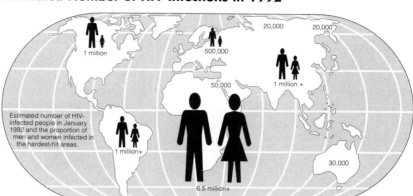

*Source:* Adapted from *New York Times,* June 28, 1992. Copyright © 1992 The New York Times Co. Used by permission.

## Statistics in Practice: Diversity at a Glance

In this chapter, you are learning how to present statistical information using various graphical techniques. Graphs can tell a story in pictures rather than in words or numbers. Because this chapter tells the story of the elderly in America, the different types of graphs you are being introduced to illustrate that the elderly in America are increasing not just in numbers but in diversity as well.

We now illustrate some additional ways in which graphics can be used to visually highlight diversity. In particular, we show how graphs can help us to (1) explore the differences and similarities between the many social groups coexisting within American society and (2) emphasize the rapidly changing composition of the U.S. population. Indeed, because of the heterogeneity of American society, the most basic question to ask when you look at data is "compared to what?" This question not only is at the heart of quantitative thinking[12] but underlies inclusive thinking as well.

Three types of graphs, the bar chart, the frequency polygon, and the time series chart, are particularly suitable for making comparisons among groups. Let's begin with the bar chart displayed in Figure 3.20. It compares elderly males and females who live alone, by age, gender, and race or Hispanic origin. Figure 3.20 shows that the percentage of elderly who live alone varies not only by age but by both race and gender. For instance, we see that in every age category, elderly females are more likely than elderly males to live alone. This trend holds true regardless of race or Hispanic

[12]Edward R. Tufte, *The Visual Display of Quantitative Information.* Cheshire, CT: Graphics Press, 1983, 53.

Figure 3.20 **Percentage of U.S. Population 65 Years and Over Living Alone by Age, Gender, and Race or Hispanic Origin, March 1990**

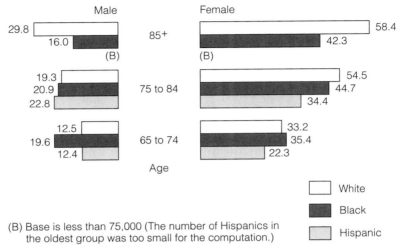

(B) Base is less than 75,000 (The number of Hispanics in the oldest group was too small for the computation.)

*Source:* U.S. Bureau of the Census. *Current Population Reports,* P23-178.

origin. Why the difference? Women who are divorced or widowed late in life have a lower rate of remarriage than men. Therefore, they are more likely to live alone. Figure 3.20 illustrates that by looking at age, race, Hispanic origin, and gender simultaneously we are able to see that elderly people have different experiences depending on these variables.

> **Learning Check.** *Examine Figure 3.20 again. Notice that regardless of their gender elderly Americans of Hispanic origin are less likely to live alone than either black or white elderly. Can you think of possible explanations for these differences?*

The frequency polygon provides another way of looking at differences based on gender and/or race/ethnicity or on other attributes like class, age, or sexual preference. For example, Figure 3.21 compares years of school completed by black Americans ages 25 to 64 and 65 years and older with that of all Americans in the same age groups.

The data illustrate that in the United States the percentage of Americans who have completed only 8 years of education has declined dramatically from about 30 percent among Americans 65 years and older to less than 10 percent for those who are 25 to 64 years old. The decline for black Americans is even more dramatic, from more than half for the black elderly to about

Figure 3.21 **Years of School Completed in the United States by Race and Age, 1989**

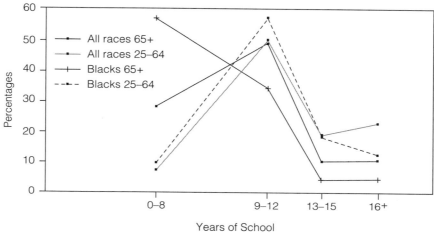

Source: U.S. Bureau of the Census. *Current Population Reports,* P23-178.

10 percent for those who are 25 to 64 years old. The corresponding trend illustrated in Figure 3.21 is the increase in the percentage of Americans (all races as well as black Americans) who have completed between 9 and 12 years of schooling, 13 and 15 years, or 16 years or more. For example, about one-third of black Americans 65 years or older completed 9 to 12 years of schooling, compared with almost 60 percent of those who are 25 to 64 years.

The trends shown in Figure 3.21 reflect the development of mass education in this country during the last fifty years. The percentage of Americans who have completed four years of high school or more has risen from about 40 percent in 1940 to almost 85 percent in 1990. Similarly in 1940 only about 5 percent of Americans completed four or more years of college, compared with about 25 percent in the 1990s.[13]

[13]U.S. Bureau of the Census. 1988. Population estimates and projections. *Current Population Reports,* series P-25, No. 1022; *United States Population Estimates by Age, Sex, and Race, 1980 to 1987.* Washington, DC: GPO, p. 25; U.S. Bureau of the Census. Population characteristics. *Current Population Reports,* series P-20, No. 462; *Educational Attainment in the United States: March 1991 and 1990.* Table 18. Washington, DC: GPO.

---

**Learning Check.** *Figure 3.21 illustrates that overall, younger Americans (25 to 64 years old) are better educated than elderly Americans. However, despite these overall trends there are differences between the number of years of schooling completed by "Blacks" and "All races." Examine Figure 3.21 and find these differences. What do they tell you about schooling in America?*

---

Finally, Figure 3.22 is a time series chart showing changes over time in the percentage of divorced white, black, and Hispanic women. It shows that between 1975 and 1985, the percentage of divorce among white and black women steadily increased. However, between 1985 and 1990 there was a dramatic decline in the percentage of divorce among black women, whereas the percentage of divorce among white women changed very little. In part, the apparent decline in the divorce rate among black women is because they are more likely to separate without divorcing. For whatever reason, however, this has resulted in a convergence in the percentage of divorce among white and black women. In contrast, the percentage of divorce among Hispanic women slightly decreased between 1980 and 1985 and remained almost unchanged between 1985 and 1990.

To conclude, the three examples of graphs in this section as well as some of the examples throughout this chapter have illustrated how

Figure 3.22 **Percentage of Divorced U.S. Women (after first marriage) by Race and Hispanic Origin, 1975, 1980, 1985, and 1990**

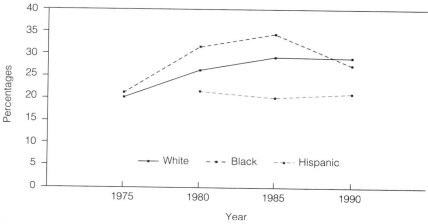

*Note:* Data not available for Hispanic women, 1975.
*Source:* U.S. Bureau of the Census. *Current Population Reports,* P23-178.

graphical techniques can portray the complexities of the social world by emphasizing the distinct characteristics of age, gender, and ethnic groups. By depicting similarities and differences, graphs help us better grasp the richness and complexities of the social world.

## MAIN POINTS

■ A pie chart shows the differences in frequencies or percentages among categories of nominal or ordinal variables. The categories of the variable are segments of a circle whose pieces add up to 100 percent of the total frequencies.

■ A bar graph shows the differences in frequencies or percentages among categories of a nominal or an ordinal variable. The categories are displayed as rectangles of equal width with their height proportional to the frequency or percentage of the category.

■ Histograms display the differences in frequencies or percentages among categories of interval-ratio variables. The categories are displayed as contiguous bars with their height proportional to the frequency or percentage of the category.

■ A frequency polygon shows the differences in frequencies or percentages among categories of an interval-ratio variable. Points representing the frequencies of each category are placed above the midpoint of the category (interval). Adjacent points are then joined by a straight line.

■ A stem and leaf plot is a quick and simple way to organize a set of scores. It can be used as a preliminary step in determining the shape of a distribution.

■ A time series chart displays changes in a variable at different points in time. It displays two variables: time, which is labeled across the horizontal axis, and another variable of interest whose values (for example, frequencies, percentages, or rates) are labeled along the vertical axis.

## KEY TERMS

| | |
|---|---|
| *bar graph* | *pie chart* |
| *frequency polygon* | *stem and leaf plot* |
| *histogram* | *time series chart* |

## SPSS DEMONSTRATIONS

*Demonstration 1: Producing a Bar Chart*

Producing graphics by hand is a tedious job. SPSS for Windows greatly simplifies and improves the production of graphics. The program offers a separate choice from the main menu bar, *Graphs,* that lists fifteen separate types of graphs that SPSS can create. We will use GSS94.SAV for this demonstration.

The first option under the *Graphs* menu is *Bar,* which will produce various types of bar charts. We will use bar charts to display the distribution of the nominal variable ABPOOR. After clicking on *Graphs* and then *Bar,* you will be presented with the following initial dialog box.

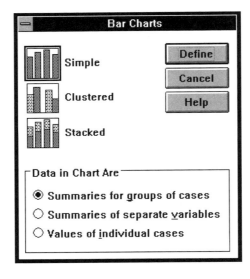

Almost all graphics procedures in SPSS begin with a dialog box that allows you to choose exactly which type of chart you want to construct. Many graph types can display more than one variable (the Clustered or

Stacked choices). We will keep things simple here, so click on the *Simple* choice, then on *Define.* When you do so, the main dialog box for simple bar charts opens.

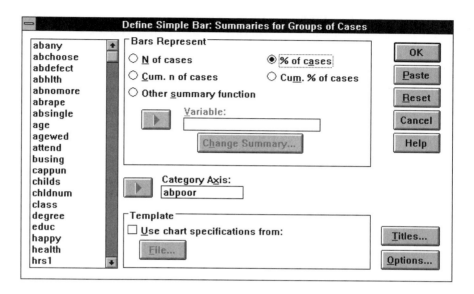

The variable ABPOOR should be placed in the box labeled "Category Axis." In the Bars Represent box, click on the "% of cases" radio button. This choice changes the default statistic from the number of cases to percentages, which are normally more useful for comparison purposes.

There is one more thing to do before telling SPSS to create the bar chart. Unlike the way SPSS works for the statistical procedures, SPSS automatically *includes* missing values in many graphs rather than deleting them. You can, and should, change this by clicking on *Options.* You will see the following dialog box:

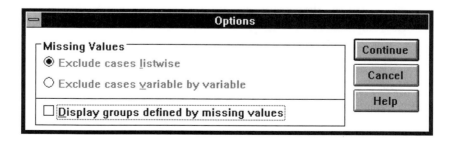

Click in the box labeled "Display groups defined by missing values" to turn off this choice. Then click on *Continue,* then on *OK* to submit your request to SPSS.

The bar chart for ABPOOR has only two bars because the only valid responses to the question of whether it should be possible for a woman to obtain a legal abortion if her family is poor are "yes" and "no."

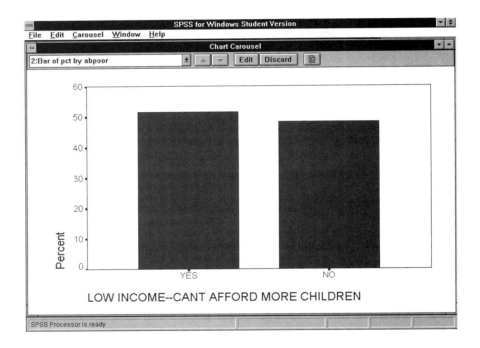

The ambivalence with which abortion is viewed by Americans is well illustrated by this bar chart, as just over 50 percent of the valid responses approve of abortion in this circumstance, while just under 50 percent disapprove of it.

SPSS graphs can be edited by clicking on the button labeled *Edit,* which moves the graph from the Chart Carousel window to its own window and displays various editing tools and choices.

*Demonstration 2: Producing a Histogram*

Histograms are used to display interval or ratio variables. The variable AGE in the 1994 GSS file is coded in years and so is a suitable candidate. Under the *Graphs* menu in SPSS is a *Histogram* option. Click on these choices and you will see this dialog box.

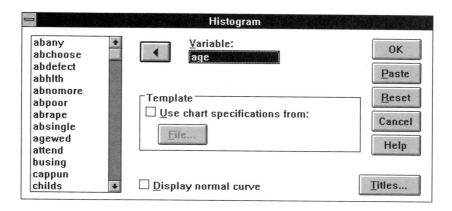

Histograms are created for one variable at a time (that's why there was no opening dialog box as for bar charts). You simply put the variable you want to display in the Variable box. You don't need to worry about missing values in histograms. SPSS automatically deletes them from the display, unlike the bar chart default action. So just click on the *OK* button to process this request.

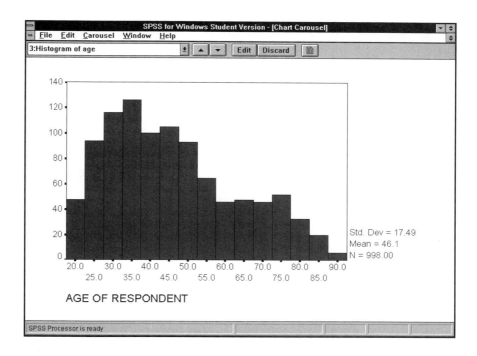

You can immediately see that there are more people at ages below 40 than above. SPSS automatically decided that the appropriate width for each interval was five years, based on the range of the variable AGE and the optimal number of bars to be displayed on a screen. The number displayed under each bar is the midpoint of that interval, so, for example, the bar for 50 years of age includes everyone from 47.5 to 52.5 (which in practice implies that it includes all the respondents who are 48, 49, 50, 51, and 52 years old).

Study this histogram and try to understand why it has the shape it does. Notice also that SPSS calculates three statistics, the standard deviation, mean, and N (the number of cases). We will discuss the first two in the next two chapters. The number of valid cases, 998, means that only two people did not answer this question.

### EXERCISES

1. Consider the following pie charts from the May 20, 1993 issue of *USA Today,* which describe characteristics of state prison inmates.

*Source:* J. L. Albert, *USA Today,* May 20, 1993.

    a.  What proportion of inmates are men?

    b.  What percentage of inmates had a full-time job before being imprisoned?

    c.  What percentage of inmates did not graduate from high school?

    d.  What percentage of inmates are people of color?

2.  In Chapter 2, exercise 1, you surveyed thirty people and asked them whether they were white or nonwhite and how many traumas they had experienced in the last year. You also asked them to tell you whether they perceived themselves as being in the upper, middle, working, or lower class. The survey resulted in the following raw data:

| Race | Class | Trauma | Race | Class | Trauma |
|------|-------|--------|------|-------|--------|
| W | L | 1 | W | W | 0 |
| W | M | 0 | W | M | 2 |
| W | M | 1 | W | W | 1 |
| N | M | 1 | W | W | 1 |
| N | L | 2 | N | W | 0 |
| W | W | 0 | N | M | 2 |
| N | W | 0 | W | M | 1 |
| W | M | 0 | W | M | 0 |
| W | M | 1 | N | W | 1 |
| N | W | 1 | W | W | 0 |
| N | W | 2 | W | W | 0 |
| N | M | 0 | N | M | 0 |
| N | L | 0 | N | W | 0 |
| W | U | 0 | N | W | 1 |
| W | W | 1 | W | W | 0 |

(Data based on General Social Survey files for 1987 to 1991)

    a.  Construct a pie chart depicting the percentage distribution of race. (*Hint:* Remember to include a title, percentages, and appropriate labels.)

    b.  Construct a pie chart showing the percentage distribution of class.

    c.  Construct a graph with two pie charts comparing the percentage distribution of the number of traumas experienced last year by race.

3.  Look at the bar charts from the *USA Today* article in exercise 1.

    a.  What percentage of inmates were using both alcohol and drugs during their criminal act?

    b.  What percentage were using either alcohol or drugs, or both?

    c.  What percentage of women were incarcerated for drug crimes? What percentage of men?

    d.  How many women were incarcerated for drug crimes?

4. Using the data from exercise 2, construct bar graphs showing percentage distributions for race and class. Remember to include appropriate titles, percentages, and labels.

5. Suppose you want to compare the number of traumas experienced last year for blacks and whites.
   a. Using the data from exercise 2, construct a grouped bar graph (similar to Figure 3.4) showing the percentage distribution of the number of traumas experienced last year by race.
   b. Which race is most likely to have experienced two traumas last year?
   c. Why shouldn't you construct a grouped bar chart showing the frequencies rather than the percentages?

6. Imagine that you work for the Food and Drug Administration (FDA) and your current task is to write a report about pesticides found in fruits and vegetables. You've been given the following data to use in the report:

| | Percentage of Produce with Pesticides (%) | Number of Types of Pesticides Detected |
|---|---|---|
| Tomatoes | 47 | 42 |
| Celery | 74 | 16 |
| Strawberries | 73 | 38 |
| Oranges | 71 | 20 |
| Apples | 64 | 34 |
| Cantaloupes | 53 | 33 |
| Pears | 57 | 26 |
| Cherries | 64 | 23 |
| Peaches | 76 | 28 |
| Spinach | 56 | 24 |

(Data from the Environmental Working Group, based on FDA data, 1990 to 1992)

   a. Construct a bar chart showing the distribution of pesticides in various types of produce.
   b. Construct a bar chart showing the number of types of pesticides detected in each food.
   c. Can you think of a way to combine both of these charts into a single graph? Construct such a graph.

7. Assume that you are a newspaper journalist writing an article on government aid programs. You have the data presented in exercise 4 in Chapter 2 for the article, and you wish to graphically represent these data in an easily understood format.
   a. Would you choose to use bar charts or pie charts? Why?
   b. Construct bar or pie charts (depending on your answer) to represent all of the data. Remember to include appropriate titles, percentages, and labels.

8. The *New York Times* constructed the following statistical map to represent the percentage of each state's population that was 65 years or older in 1990, based on U.S. census data.

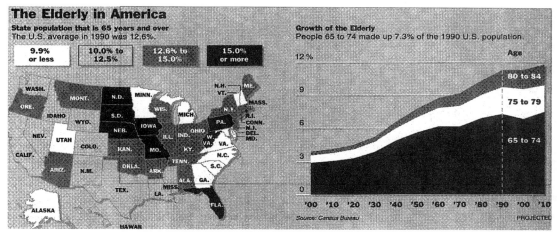

*Source: New York Times,* November 10, 1992.

   a. Write a 200-word report for your local newspaper describing the variation in elderly population across the United States.
   b. Think about what causes some states to have more elderly in their population. Then locate the states with 15.0 percent or more elderly and explain why the reasons for their relatively high proportion of elderly might be the same (or different).

9. You are writing a research paper about teen smoking and have the following data. To make calculations simpler, assume that there were 100 students in each grade level in each year.

| Year | Grade | Percentage Who Smoke Daily |
|------|-------|----------------------------|
| 1992 | 8 | 7 |
| 1992 | 10 | 12 |
| 1992 | 12 | 17 |
| 1993 | 8 | 8 |
| 1993 | 10 | 14 |
| 1993 | 12 | 19 |

(Data from the University of Michigan)

a. Suppose you want to argue that older teens are more likely to smoke daily. Construct a bar chart that supports this argument. (*Hint:* Group by year.)
b. Now suppose you want to argue that more teens are smoking daily in 1993 than in 1992. Construct a bar chart that supports this argument. (*Hint:* Group by grade.)
c. Explain why the graphs in (a) and (b) are appropriate for each situation.

10. Use the data in exercise 5, Chapter 2, on educational level for this problem.
a. What level of measurement is "years of education"? Why can you use a histogram to graph the distribution of education, in addition to a bar chart?
b. Construct a histogram for years of education, using equal-spaced intervals of four years. Don't use percentages in this chart.

11. The 1987 to 1991 GSS data on educational level can be further broken down by race, as follows:

| Years of Education | Whites | Blacks |
|---|---|---|
| 1 | 1 | 3 |
| 2 | 1 | 3 |
| 3 | 3 | 10 |
| 4 | 5 | 13 |
| 5 | 3 | 11 |
| 6 | 19 | 14 |
| 7 | 12 | 18 |
| 8 | 59 | 41 |
| 9 | 37 | 42 |
| 10 | 61 | 62 |
| 11 | 65 | 91 |
| 12 | 417 | 267 |
| 13 | 106 | 88 |
| 14 | 133 | 119 |
| 15 | 58 | 55 |
| 16 | 148 | 66 |
| 17 | 43 | 10 |
| 18 | 45 | 17 |
| 19 | 15 | 3 |
| 20+ | 27 | 5 |
| Total | 1,258 | 938 |

a. Construct two histograms for education, one for blacks and one for whites.

b. Now use the two graphs to describe the differences in educational attainment by race.

12. You are given the following data on the ages for the employees of a small newspaper and are asked to create a stem and leaf plot to graphically depict the age distribution.

Ages:  23, 34, 54, 34, 22, 64, 44, 41, 49, 39, 70, 20, 28, 32, 35, 46, 40, 44, 29, 55, 50, 33, 49, 26, 27, 62, 51, 56, 32, 25, 36, 46, 60, 54, 34

a. Create a stem and leaf plot. How many digits should the stem represent?

b. Describe the distribution of age among the employees, using the chart.

13. Use the data from exercise 13, Chapter 2, on birth rates for this problem.
    a. Construct a time series bar graph showing the change in birth rates over the period from 1920 to 1991.
    b. Next, construct a time series polygon (similar to a frequency polygon) showing the same data. Which of these two graphs would you prefer to include in a report? Why?

14. Examine the time series chart concerning marriage and divorce rates from the December 9, 1992 *USA Today* reproduced here.

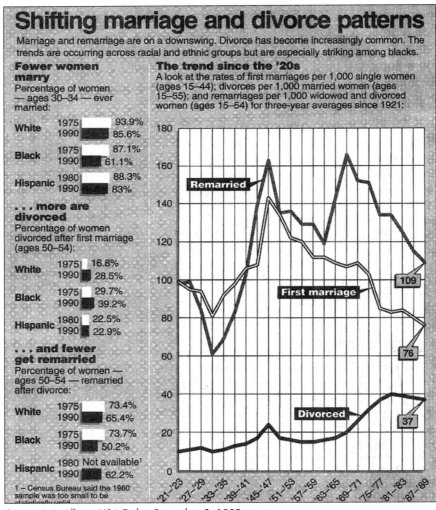

*Source:* J. L. Albert, *USA Today,* December 9, 1992.

a. Describe how the rate of first marriage has changed over the years. In which two periods was the rate of first marriage equal to about 1 per every 10 single women (between the ages of 15 and 44)?

b. Has there been more fluctuation in the divorce rate or the first marriage rate? Which rate has exhibited a greater *percentage* change over time?

c. There are two peaks in the remarriage rate. Can you suggest what might have caused these peaks?

15. As time has gone on, segregation in large American school systems has not decreased, as many expected after the civil rights reforms of the 1950s and 1960s. Evidence for this is provided by the following data, taken from the U.S. Department of Education, for several years. These numbers represent the typical percentage of whites in school districts attended by blacks (so the higher the number, the *more integrated* the district).

| Year | Boston | Chicago | Los Angeles |
|------|--------|---------|-------------|
| 1968 | 27.4% | 5.4% | 7.5% |
| 1974 | 32.8% | 3.2% | 10.2% |
| 1986 | 22.3% | 6.0% | 11.7% |
| 1992 | 18.2% | 4.6% | 9.6% |

a. Construct one time series chart to represent these numbers. Then describe the variation in segregation as measured by these data. Which city has had the most segregated school districts?

b. Let's say you wanted to exaggerate the changes in percentage of whites over time. How would you modify the time series chart to do this?

## SPSS PROBLEMS

1. You have been given the job of making a presentation on attitudes toward the social mingling of whites and blacks, using the 1987 to 1991 General Social Survey data (filename GSS87_91.SAV). In particular, you will use data on whether Americans support racial intermarriage, racial segregation, and busing for racial integration. Variables appropriate for your report include RACMAR, RACSEG, and BUSING (although there are certainly others you could use).

a. Using SPSS, construct pie charts for the variables you have chosen. Be sure to include appropriate labels and to remove any missing responses from the chart. (*Hint:* With the SPSS menus, choose *Graphs . . . Pie* to reach the appropriate dialog box.)

b. Now construct bar charts for the same variables. (*Hint:* From the SPSS menus, choose *Graphs . . . Bar.*)

c. Describe the attitude of Americans toward the social mingling of whites and blacks, using either the pie or bar charts.

2. Use the variable EDUC to construct a histogram for years of education. Compare it with the histogram you constructed for exercise 10. Can you modify the SPSS-generated histogram so that it has the same-sized intervals as the one you created? (*Hint:* Look under the *Chart . . . Axis* menu.)

3. Construct a stem and leaf plot for the age of the respondents in the GSS file (using the variable AGE). Compare its format with the stem and leaf plot you created in exercise 12. What are the differences?

4. The GSS data set actually combines responses from five years, from 1987 to 1991, and thus can be used to construct time series charts.

a. Use the variable YEAR to construct a time series chart showing the percentage of people who have ever been divorced or separated (DIVORCE) for each of these years. (*Hint:* Use the *Line* choice from the Graphs menu, and place YEAR on the Category Axis. You'll also need to make changes in the Bars Represent box.)

b. Are you surprised at the changes by year in the percentage of divorced people? What year had the highest percentage of divorced respondents? the lowest?

c. What might be the cause of these yearly fluctuations?

**GROUP PROBLEMS**

1. Working in small groups to share the workload, search in your local newspapers, national newspapers such as *USA Today* or the *New York Times,* or newsmagazines for articles that use graphics. Choose several articles so the group has a variety of graph types.

Share copies of the graphs with each member of your group. Then discuss how well each of the graphs is constructed, considering such features as appropriate labels, axes, statistics (percentages, rates, and so on), footnotes, color (if applicable), and importantly, the type of graph chosen. Remember that a well-constructed graph should be able to stand on its own, without accompanying text. If some of the graphs seem unsatisfactory, suggest modifications that would improve their functionality.

2. Both pie charts and bar graphs can display the distribution of a nominal or ordinal variable. Nevertheless, perhaps there are situations when one type of graph is better than another (think about variables with

lots of categories). The choice of an appropriate graph or chart is very important when presenting data visually. Have a group discussion about these two types of statistical graphs, concentrating on when each is most appropriate. Summarize your discussion in a brief report that can be given to the other members of the class.

3. Have some group members go to the library and find data from the U.S. census on the percentage of the population in each state that is black and elderly and Hispanic and elderly (elderly is defined as age 65 and over). You might have to get raw numbers and calculate the percentages from census data. Have other group members find blank maps of the United States that can be colored and/or shaded, then have one or two group members construct maps like Figures 3.7 and 3.8 in the chapter. It would be best to use colors, but since each group member will need a copy, it might be better to use different shading or crosshatching. After the maps are constructed, compare them with Figures 3.7 and 3.8 and describe differences in the percentage distribution by state of elderly blacks and Hispanics versus the number of these same groups in each state. Do the states with a greater percentage of these groups for the United States as a whole also have large absolute state populations of elderly blacks and Hispanics? Can you explain or suggest reasons why or why not?

# 4 Measures of Central Tendency

**Introduction**

**The Mode: Foreign Languages Spoken in the United States**

**The Median: Worries About Health Care**
Finding the Median in Sorted Data
*An Odd Number of Cases*
*An Even Number of Cases*
Finding the Median in Frequency Distributions

**Box 4.1   Finding the Median in Grouped Data**
Statistics in Practice: Opinions About National Defense Spending
Statistics in Practice: Changes in Age at First Marriage
Locating Percentiles in a Frequency Distribution

**Box 4.2   Finding Percentiles in Grouped Data**

**The Mean: Murder Rates in Fifteen American Cities**
Using a Formula to Calculate the Mean
Understanding Some Important Properties of the Arithmetic Mean

**Box 4.3   Finding the Mean in a Frequency Distribution**
*Interval-Ratio Level of Measurement*
*Center of Gravity*
*Sensitivity to Extremes*

**The Shape of the Distribution: The Experience of Traumatic Events**
The Symmetrical Distribution
The Positively Skewed Distribution
The Negatively Skewed Distribution
Guidelines for Identifying the Shape of a Distribution

**Considerations for Choosing a Measure of Central Tendency**
Level of Measurement

## Box 4.4  Statistics in Practice: Median Annual Earnings Among Subgroups
Skewed Distribution
Symmetrical Distribution

■  ■  ■  ■   **Introduction**

In Chapters 2 and 3, we learned that frequency distributions and graphical techniques are useful tools for presenting information. The main advantage of using frequency distributions or graphs is to summarize quantitative information in ways that can be easily under-stood even by a lay audience. Often, however, we need to describe a large set of data involving many variables for which graphs and tables may not be the most efficient tools. For instance, let's say we want to present information on the income, education, and political party affiliation of both men and women. Doing so might require up to six frequency distributions or graphs. The more variables we add, the more complex the presentation becomes.

Another way of describing a distribution is by selecting a single number that describes or summarizes the distribution more concisely. Such numbers describe what is typical about the distribution (for example, the average income among Hispanics who are college graduates or the most common party identification among the rural poor), or how much variation there is in the distribution (What is the degree of racial/ethnic diversity on your college campus? or, What is the age range among students in your statistics class?). Numbers that describe what is average or typical of the distribution are called **measures of central tendency**. Numbers that describe diversity or variability are called **measures of variability**. Measures of central tendency are discussed in this chapter, and measures of variability are presented in Chapter 5.

---

*Measures of Central Tendency*   Numbers that describe what is average or typical of the distribution.

---

In this chapter, we will learn about three measures of central tendency—the *mode, median,* and *mean.* You are probably somewhat familiar with these measures—the terms *median* income or *average* income, for example, are used quite a bit even in the popular media. Each describes what is most typical, central, or representative of the distribution. In this chapter, we will also learn about how these measures differ from one another. We will see that the choice of an appropriate measure of central tendency for representing a distribution depends on three factors: (1) the way the variables are measured (their level of measurement), (2) the shape of the distribution, and (3) the purpose of the research.

## The Mode: Foreign Languages Spoken in the United States

The **mode** is the category or score with the largest frequency or percentage in the distribution. Of all the averages discussed in this chapter, the mode is the easiest one to identify. Simply locate the category represented by the highest frequency!

---

*Mode*   The category or score with the largest frequency (or percentage) in the distribution.

---

We can use the mode to determine, for example, the most common foreign language spoken in the United States today. English is clearly the language of choice in public communication in the United States, but you may be surprised by the Census Bureau finding that one out of every seven people living in the United States speaks one of 329 different languages other than English at home. Record immigration from many countries since 1980 has contributed to a sharp increase in the number of people who speak a foreign language.[1]

What is the most common foreign language spoken in the United States today? To answer this question look at Table 4.1, which lists the ten most commonly spoken foreign languages in the United States and the number of people who speak each language. The table shows that Spanish is the most common; more than 17 million people speak Spanish. In this example we refer to "Spanish" as the mode, the category with the largest frequency in the distribution.

[1]*USA Today,* April 28, 1993.

Table 4.1 **Ten Most Common Foreign Languages Spoken in the United States**

| Language | Number of Speakers |
|---|---|
| Spanish | 17,339,000 |
| French | 1,702,000 |
| German | 1,547,000 |
| Italian | 1,309,000 |
| Chinese | 1,249,000 |
| Tagalog | 843,000 |
| Polish | 723,000 |
| Korean | 626,000 |
| Vietnamese | 507,000 |
| Portuguese | 430,000 |

*Source:* U.S. Bureau of the Census. 1994.
*Statistical Abstract of the United States: 1994*
(114th edition). Washington, DC: GPO.

The mode is always a category or score, not a frequency. Do not confuse the two. That is, the mode in the previous example is "Spanish," not the frequency associated with it, 17,339,000.

The mode is not necessarily the category with the majority (that is, more than 50%) of cases, as it is in Table 4.1; it is simply the category in which the largest number (or proportion) of cases fall. For example, Figure 4.1 is a pie chart showing the answers of 1991 GSS respondents to the following question: "Please indicate whether you would like to see more or less government spending on child care for poor children." Note that the highest percentage (45%) of respondents is associated with the answer "spend more." The answer "spend more" is therefore the mode in this instance. Notice that this response category does not include the majority of cases (it includes only 45%).

The mode is used to describe nominal variables. Recall that with nominal variables—such as foreign languages spoken in the United States, race/ethnicity, or religious affiliation—we are only able to classify respondents based on a qualitative and not a quantitative property. By describing the most commonly occurring category of a nominal variable (such as Spanish in our example) the mode thus reflects the most important element of the distribution of a variable measured at the nominal level. The mode is the only measure of central tendency that can be used with nominal level variables. It can, however, be used to describe the most commonly occurring category

Figure 4.1 **Opinion of Government Spending on Child Care for the Poor**

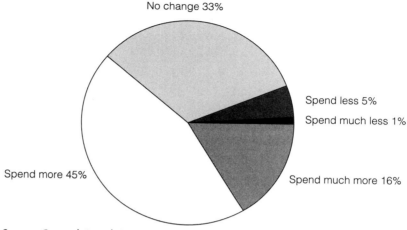

*Source:* General Social Survey, 1991.

Figure 4.2 **Government Should Try to Reduce Income Differences Between the Rich and the Poor**

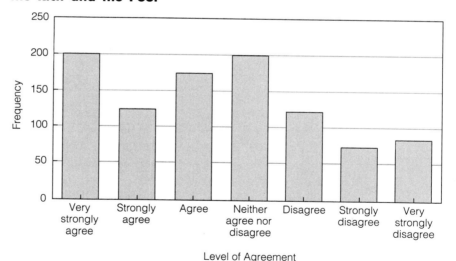

*Source:* General Social Survey, 1991.

in any distribution. For example, the variable "opinion of government spending" presented in Figure 4.1 is an ordinal variable.

In some distributions, there are two scores or categories with the highest frequency. Such distributions have two modes and are said to be *bimodal*. For instance, Figure 4.2 is a bar graph showing the responses of 1991 GSS respondents to the following statement: "Government should try to reduce income differences between the rich and the poor." The same number of respondents (200) "very strongly agreed" and "neither agreed nor disagreed" with this statement. Both response categories have the highest frequency and both are therefore the modes. We can thus describe this distribution as bimodal. When two scores or categories with the highest frequencies are quite close (yet not identical in frequency), the distribution is still "essentially" bimodal. In these situations you should not rely on merely reporting the (true) mode, but instead report the top two highest frequency categories.

---

**Learning Check.** *Listed below is the political party affiliation of fifteen individuals. Find the mode.*

*Democrat, Republican, Democrat, Republican, Republican, Independent, Democrat, Democrat, Democrat, Republican, Independent, Democrat, Independent, Republican, Democrat*

*Why is the mode the only measure of central tendency you can use to describe this distribution?*

---

## The Median: Worries About Health Care

The **median** is a measure of central tendency that can be calculated for variables that are at least at an ordinal level of measurement. The median represents the exact middle of a distribution; it is the score that divides the distribution into two equal parts so that half the cases are above it and half below it. For example, the median household income in 1990 was \$35,350. This means that half the households in the United States earned more than \$35,350 and half earned less than \$35,350. Since many variables used in social research are ordinal, the median is an important measure of central tendency in social science research.

---

*Median*    The score that divides the distribution into two equal parts so that half the cases are above it and half below it.

---

For instance, what are the opinions of Americans about health care in the United States? How can we describe their level of satisfaction with personal health care? with national health-care cost? with health insurance coverage? To answer these questions, a Gallup Poll conducted in 1991[2] asked people whether they were "very satisfied," "somewhat satisfied," "somewhat dissatisfied," or "very dissatisfied" with the quality of health care they receive. Level of satisfaction is an ordered (ordinal) variable. Thus, to estimate the average level of satisfaction of Americans with the quality of health care they receive, we need to use a measure of central tendency appropriate for ordinal variables. The median is a suitable measure for those variables whose categories or scores can be arranged in order of magnitude from lowest to highest. Therefore, the median can be used with ordinal or interval-ratio variables for which scores can be at least rank-ordered but cannot be calculated for variables measured at the nominal level.

## Finding the Median in Sorted Data

It is very easy to find the median. In most cases it can be done by simple inspection of the sorted data. The location of the median score will differ somewhat, depending on whether the number of observations is odd or even. Let's first consider two examples with an odd number of cases.

*An Odd Number of Cases* Suppose we are looking at the responses of five people to the questions "Are you satisfied or dissatisfied with your health insurance coverage? . . . Are you very or somewhat satisfied/dissatisfied?" These questions were part of the Gallup Poll on health care. Following are the responses of five hypothetical persons:

| Response | Person |
|---|---|
| Very dissatisfied | Jim |
| Very satisfied | Sue |
| Very dissatisfied | Bob |
| Somewhat dissatisfied | Jorge |
| Very satisfied | Karen |
| Total (N) | 5 |

[2]*Gallup Poll Monthly,* August 1991.

To locate the median:

1. Arrange the responses in order from lowest to highest (or highest to lowest):

| Response | Person |
|---|---|
| Very dissatisfied | Jim |
| Very dissatisfied | Bob |
| *Somewhat dissatisfied* | *Jorge* |
| Very satisfied | Sue |
| Very satisfied | Karen |
| Total (N) | 5 |

2. The median is the response associated with the middle case. Find the middle case when $N$ is odd by adding 1 to $N$ and dividing by 2, or, $(N + 1) \div 2$. Since $N$ is 5, the middle case is the $(5 + 1) \div 2$, or the third case (Jorge).

3. The response associated with the third case, Jorge, is "somewhat dissatisfied"; therefore, this is the median.

Notice that the median divides the distribution exactly in half so that there are two respondents who are more satisfied and two respondents who are less satisfied.

Now let's look at another example (see Figure 4.3, page 142). The following is a list of the suicide rates per 100,000 population (an interval-ratio variable) in the nine largest cities in the United States for 1989:[3]

| Rate | City |
|---|---|
| 7.44 | New York |
| 13.38 | Los Angeles |
| 10.00 | Chicago |
| 14.11 | Houston |
| 14.78 | Philadelphia |
| 12.61 | San Diego |
| 12.26 | Detroit |
| 14.30 | Dallas |
| 18.37 | Phoenix |
| Total (N) | 9 |

[3]National Center for Health Statistics, 1989. *Vital Statistics of the United States,* Vol. II, Mortality, Part B. DHHS Pub. No. (PHS) 92-1102 Public Health Service. Washington, DC: GPO, 1992.

To locate the median:

1. Arrange the suicide rates in order from lowest to highest:

| Rate | City |
|------|------|
| 7.44 | New York |
| 10.00 | Chicago |
| 12.26 | Detroit |
| 12.61 | San Diego |
| 13.38 | Los Angeles |
| 14.11 | Houston |
| 14.30 | Dallas |
| 14.78 | Philadelphia |
| 18.37 | Phoenix |
| Total (N) | 9 |

2. The middle case is $(9 + 1) \div 2 = 5$, the fifth city, Los Angeles. The median is 13.38, the suicide rate associated with Los Angeles. It divides the distribution exactly in half so that there are four cities with lower suicide rates and four cities with higher suicide rates.

*An Even Number of Cases*  Now let's delete the last score to make the number of cities even. The scores have already been arranged in increasing order:

7.44, 10.00, 12.26, 12.61, 13.38, 14.11, 14.30, 14.78

When $N$ is even we no longer have a single middle case. The median is therefore located halfway between the two middle cases. Find the two middle cases by using the previous formula: $(N + 1) \div 2$, or, $(8 + 1) \div 2 = 4.5$. For our example, this means that you average the scores for the fourth and fifth cities, San Diego and Los Angeles. The suicide rates associated with these cities are 12.61 and 13.38. To get the median, simply average these two middle numbers:

$$\text{Median} = \frac{12.61 + 13.38}{2} = 12.99$$

The median is therefore 12.99.

When our data are ordinal, averaging the two middle scores is no longer appropriate. In that situation the median simply falls between two particular values.

Figure 4.3  **Finding the Median Suicide Rate**

### Finding the Median Suicide Rate for Nine Cities

1. Order the cases from lowest to highest:

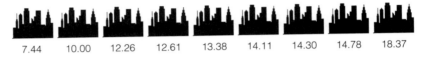

7.44    10.00    12.26    12.61    13.38    14.11    14.30    14.78    18.37

2. In this situation, we need the *5th* case: $(9 + 1) \div 2 = 5$.

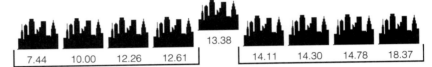

7.44    10.00    12.26    12.61        13.38        14.11    14.30    14.78    18.37

4 cases on this side of the median            4 cases on this side of the median

### Finding the Median Suicide Rate for Eight Cities

1. Order the cases from lowest to highest:

7.44    10.00    12.26    12.61    13.38    14.11    14.30    14.78

2.  In this situation, we need "imaginary" case 4.5: $(8 + 1) \div 2 = 4.5$.

3. To find the value of this case, take the average of the two cases surrounding it:

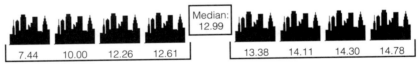

Median:
12.99

7.44    10.00    12.26    12.61        13.38    14.11    14.30    14.78

4 cases on this side of the median            4 cases on this side of the median

---

> **Learning Check.**  *Find the median of the following distribution of an interval-ratio variable:*
> *22, 15, 18, 33, 17, 5, 11, 28, 40, 19, 8, 20*

---

## Finding the Median in Frequency Distributions

Often our data are arranged in frequency distributions. The procedure for locating the median in a frequency distribution is a bit more involved than the procedure we just described. Take, for instance, the frequency distribution displayed in Table 4.2. It shows the political views of GSS respondents in 1991.

To identify the median we have to find the category associated with the observation located at the middle of the distribution. To help locate this observation we construct a cumulative percentage distribution, as shown in column 5 of Table 4.2. In this example, the percentages are cumulated from "extremely liberal" to "extremely conservative." You can also cumulate the other way, from "extremely conservative" to "extremely liberal." The observation located at the middle of the distribution is the one that has a cumulative percentage value equal to 50 percent. The median is the value of the category associated with this observation.[4] This middle observation falls within the category "moderate." The median for this distribution is therefore "moderate." If you are not sure why the middle of the distribution—the 50 percent point—is associated with the category "moderate," look again at the cumulative percentage column (C%) and notice that 27.76 percent of the observations are accumulated below the category "moderate" and that 67.79 percent have been accumulated up to the category "moderate." We know then, that 50 percent is located somewhere within the "moderate" category.

Alternatively, the median can be computed based on the cumulated frequency distribution instead of the cumulated percentage distribution. In that case, you first identify the observation located in the middle of the distribution $((N + 1) \div 2)$ and then find the category associated with this observation. The middle observation is

Table 4.2 **Political Views of GSS Respondents, 1991**

| Political View | Frequency | Cf | Percentages (%) | C% |
|---|---|---|---|---|
| Extremely liberal | 37 | 37 | 2.53 | 2.53 |
| Liberal | 154 | 191 | 10.56 | 13.09 |
| Slightly liberal | 214 | 405 | 14.67 | 27.76 |
| Moderate | 584 | 989 | 40.03 | 67.79 |
| Slightly conservative | 218 | 1207 | 14.94 | 82.73 |
| Conservative | 212 | 1419 | 14.53 | 97.26 |
| Extremely conservative | 40 | 1459 | 2.74 | 100.00 |
| Total (N) | 1,459 | | 100.00 | |

[4]This rule was adapted from David Knoke and George W. Bohrnstedt, *Basic Social Statistics.* New York: Peacock Publishers, 1991, 56–57.

### Box 4.1 Finding the Median in Grouped Data

When interval-ratio variables are arranged in grouped frequency distributions, we use the following formula to locate the median:

$$\text{Median} = L + \left[\frac{N(.5) - Cf_{below}}{f}\right]w$$

where

$L$ = the lower limit of the interval containing the median

$Cf_{below}$ = the cumulative sum of the frequencies below the interval containing the median

$f$ = the frequency of the interval containing the median

$w$ = the width of the interval containing the median

$N$ = the total number of cases

### Grouped Frequency Distribution of Hours Worked: A GSS Subgroup

| Hours Worked Stated Limits | Hours Worked Real Limits | Frequency (f) | Cf_below |
|---|---|---|---|
| 00–09 | –0.5– 9.5 | 2 | 2 |
| 10–19 | 9.5–19.5 | 3 | 5 |
| 20–29 | 19.5–29.5 | 3 | 8 |
| 30–39 | 29.5–39.5 | 4 | 12 |
| 40–49 | 39.5–49.5 | 19 | 31 |
| 50–59 | 49.5–59.5 | 3 | 34 |
| | | Total (N) | 34 |

To illustrate the computation of the median, consider the grouped distribution of the variable "hours worked," which we first presented in Chapter 2 (Box 2.1). Here we have added a cumulated frequencies column ($Cf_{below}$) to the original table.

To locate the median, we first identify the middle case in the distribution by dividing the total number of cases ($N$) by 2. Since $N = 34$, the middle case is $34 \div 2$, or 17. We need to locate the seventeenth case and identify the score corresponding to it. The cumulative frequency column shows that there are twelve observations preceding the interval 39.5–49.5. This interval contains nineteen more observations. Hence, the seventeenth observation is located within that interval and, therefore, we know that the median is located somewhere within that interval. To find the exact value of the median, we apply the formula for medians in grouped data:

$$\text{Median} = 39.5 + \left[\frac{34(.5) - 12}{19}\right]10 = 42.1$$

The median number of hours worked is 42.1.

(1459 + 1) ÷ 2 = 730. The cumulative frequency ($Cf$) of 730 falls in the category "moderate." Therefore, the median is "moderate."

When interval-ratio data are arranged in grouped distributions the procedure for calculating the median is a bit more complicated. In most situations it is unlikely that you will need to calculate the median from grouped distributions by hand. We have presented an example involving a grouped distribution in Box 4.1.

> **Learning Check.** *If you are confused about cumulative distributions, go back to Chapter 2 and review. Remember, we told you they would be useful.*

## Statistics in Practice: Opinions About National Defense Spending

We can use the median to make comparisons between groups or over time. As an example let's examine whether Americans' views on defense spending have shifted over the last five years. Defense spending accounts for the largest single category of expenditure (about 29 percent) in the federal budget. How do Americans feel about the level of military spending? The victory over Iraq in 1991 demonstrated that the world balance of power has shifted toward the United States and its allies. Are Americans less willing to support military spending since the Gulf War? To answer this question we will utilize data from the General Social Survey (GSS). In 1991 and 1994, respondents participating in the GSS were asked to indicate whether they thought "we're spending too much, too little, or about the right amount" on military, armaments, and defense. The percentage and cumulative percentage distributions for 1991 and 1994 are presented in Table 4.3.

Notice that the position of the median has *not* shifted between 1991 and 1994. For both 1991 and 1994 the median is the category "about right" ("we are spending about the right amount on the military, armaments, and defense"). Thus, we can conclude that Americans' opinion regarding defense spending has stayed about the same between 1991 and 1994.

> **Learning Check.** *How did we determine the medians in the preceding example?*

Table 4.3 **Opinions about Defense Spending, 1991 and 1994**

| Response | 1991 Frequency (f) | 1991 Percentages (%) | C% | 1994 Frequency (f) | 1994 Percentages (%) | C% |
|---|---|---|---|---|---|---|
| Too little | 105 | 14.5 | 14.5 | 239 | 16.5 | 16.5 |
| About right | 418 | 57.6 | 72.1 | 715 | 49.3 | 65.8 |
| Too much | 202 | 27.9 | 100.0 | 497 | 34.2 | 100.0 |
| Total (N) | 725 | 100.0 | | 1451 | 100.0 | |
| | Median = About right | | | Median= About right | | |

*Source*: GSS, 1991 and 1994.

## Statistics in Practice: Changes in Age at First Marriage

For another example of how we can use the median to compare groups, consider the significant changes that have taken place during the last two decades in marriage patterns in the United States. They have profoundly influenced our lives both socially and economically. Delayed first marriage is associated with increased education and work experience for both men and women.[5]

Figure 4.4 compares the median age at first marriage for men and women in 1970 and in 1990. Because the median is a single number summarizing central tendency in the distribution, we can use it to note differences between subgroups of the population or changes over time. In this example, the difference in median age at first marriage for both men and women over the last two decades (the median age increased from 1970 to 1990) clearly shows a movement away from first marriage at an early age.

> **Learning Check.** *Examine Figure 4.4 and contrast median ages at first marriage of women and men over the two decades. What can you learn about gender and age at first marriage?*

## Locating Percentiles in a Frequency Distribution

The median is a special case of a more general set of measures of location called *percentiles*. A **percentile** is a score below which a

[5]U.S. Bureau of the Census. 1991. Population profile of the United States, 1991. *Current Population Reports*, ser. P-23, No. 173, July.

Figure 4.4 **Median Age at First Marriage for Men and Women, 1970 and 1990**

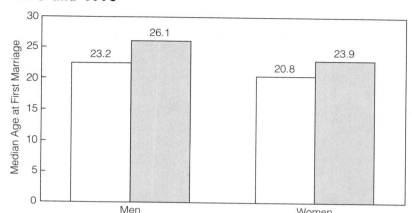

specific percentage of the distribution falls. The *n*th percentile is a score below which *n* percent of the distribution falls. For example, the 75th percentile is a score that divides the distribution so that 75 percent of the cases are below it. The median is the 50th percentile; that is, it is a score that divides the distribution so that 50 percent of the cases fall below it. Like the median, percentiles require that data be ordinal or higher in level of measurement. Percentiles are easy to identify when the data are arranged in frequency distributions.

To help illustrate how to locate percentiles in a frequency distribution, we display in Table 4.4 the frequency distribution, the percentage distribution, and the cumulative percentage distribution for the variable "number of children per family" for the 1991 GSS sample. The 50th percentile (the median) is 2 children, meaning that 50 percent of the respondents have 2 children or less (as you can see from the cumulative percentage column, 50% falls somewhere in the third category, associated with 2 children). Similarly, the 80th percentile is 3 children because 80 percent of the respondents have 3 children or less. The procedure for calculating percentiles from grouped distributions is similar to the one suggested for calculating medians. This procedure is illustrated in Box 4.2.

Table 4.4 **Frequency Distribution for Number of Children: GSS Subsample**

| Number of Children | Frequency (f) | Percentages (%) | C% |
|---|---|---|---|
| 0 | 419 | 28 | 28 |
| 1 | 255 | 17 | 45 |
| 2 | 375 | 25 | 70 |
| 3 | 215 | 14 | 84 |
| 4 | 127 | 8 | 92 |
| 5 | 54 | 4 | 96 |
| 6 | 24 | 2 | 98 |
| 7 | 23 | 1 | 99 |
| 8 or more | 17 | 1 | 100 |
| Total (N) | 1,509 | 100 | |

---

*Percentile*  A score below which a specific percentage of the distribution falls.

---

Percentiles are widely used to evaluate relative performance on standardized achievement tests, such as the SAT or ACT. Let's suppose for a moment that your ACT score was 29. To evaluate your performance for the college admissions officer, the testing service translated your score into a percentile rank. Your percentile rank was determined by comparing your score with the scores of all other seniors who took the test at the same time. Suppose for a moment that 90 percent of all students received a lower ACT score than you (and 10 percent scored above you). Your percentile rank would have been 90. If, however, there were more students who scored better than you, let's say that 15 percent scored above you and 85 percent scored lower than you, your percentile rank would have been only 85.

Another measure of location widely used is the *quartile*. The lower quartile is equal to the 25th percentile and the upper quartile is equal to the 75th percentile. (Can you locate the upper quartile in Table 4.4?). A college admissions office interested in accepting the top 25 percent of its applicants based on their SAT scores could calculate the upper quartile (the 75th percentile) and accept everyone whose score is equivalent to the 75th percentile or higher.

**Box 4.2  Finding Percentiles in Grouped Data**

The formula for medians shown in Box 4.1 can also be used to calculate percentiles from grouped data. The only adjustment required in the formula is to multiply the total number of cases by the desired percentile and determine the interval where the appropriate percentile is located. For instance, the following formula was adapted to find the 25th percentile for the data shown in the table in Box 4.1.

$$\text{25th percentile} \ (Q_1) = L + \left[ \frac{N(.25) - Cf_{below}}{f} \right] w$$

$$= 29.5 + \left[ \frac{34(.25) - 8}{4} \right] 10 = 30.75$$

In other words, 25 percent of the respondents worked less than 30.75 hours.

---

**Learning Check.**  *Can you provide the formula for calculating the 20th percentile? The 20th percentile is sometimes referred to as the lower quintile. Can you determine the percentile that marks the upper quintile?*

## The Mean: Murder Rates in Fifteen American Cities

The arithmetic **mean** is by far the most well known and widely used average. The mean is what most people call the "average." The mean is typically used to describe central tendency in interval-ratio variables such as income, age, and education. You are probably already familiar with how to calculate the mean. Simply add up all the scores and divide by the total number of scores.

---

*Mean*  The arithmetic average obtained by adding up all the scores and dividing by the total number of scores.

---

Crime statistics, for example, are often analyzed using the mean. Each year about 25 percent of U.S households are victims of some form of crime. The rates of both violent and property crimes in the United States have increased since the mid-1980s and reached an all-time high in 1991. While violent crimes in the United States are the least common types of crimes, they are nonetheless the highest of any industrialized nation. For instance, murder rates in the United States are approximately five times as high as those in Europe.

Table 4.5 shows the 1991 murder rates (per 100,000 population) for the fifteen largest cities in the United States. We want to summarize the information presented in this table by calculating some measure of central tendency. Because the variable "murder rate" is an interval-ratio variable, we will select the arithmetic mean as our measure of central tendency.

Table 4.5    **1991 Murder Rate per 100,000 Population for the Fifteen Largest Cities in the United States**

| City | Murder Rate per 100,000 |
|------|-------------------------|
| New York | 29.3 |
| Los Angeles | 28.9 |
| Chicago | 32.9 |
| Houston | 36.5 |
| Philadelphia | 25.0 |
| San Diego | 14.7 |
| Detroit | 58.4 |
| Dallas | 48.6 |
| Phoenix | 12.8 |
| San Antonio | 21.8 |
| Honolulu | 3.4 |
| San Jose | 6.6 |
| Baltimore | 40.6 |
| San Francisco | 12.9 |
| Jacksonville | 19.6 |
| Total | 392.0 |

$$\text{Mean} = \frac{392}{15} = 26.1$$

To find the mean murder rate for the data presented in Table 4.5 add up the murder rates for all the cities and divide the sum by the number of cities:[6]

$$\text{Mean} = \frac{392}{15} = 26.1$$

The mean murder rate for the fifteen largest cities in the United States is 26.1.

> **Learning Check.** *Sociologists hypothesize that violent crime follows certain social and regional patterns. For example, they suggest that large cities have more crime than smaller cities. One way to check these ideas is by calculating and comparing the crime rates for large and small cities. Exercise 14 provides the murder rates for large and small cities in the United States. Calculate the mean for each group of cities separately. What is your conclusion?*

## Using a Formula to Calculate the Mean

Another way to calculate the arithmetic mean is to use a formula. Beginning with this section, we introduce a number of formulas that will help you calculate some of the statistical concepts we are going to present. A *formula* is a shorthand way to explain what operations we need to follow to obtain a certain result. So instead of saying "add all the scores together and then divide by the number of scores," we can define the mean by the following formula:

$$\overline{Y} = \frac{\sum Y}{N} \tag{4.1}$$

Let's take a moment to consider these new symbols because we continue to use them in later chapters. We use $Y$ to represent the raw scores in the distribution of the variable $y$; $\overline{Y}$ is pronounced as "Y-bar" and is the mean of the variable $y$. The symbol represented by the Greek letter $\sum$ is pronounced as "sigma," and it is used often from now on. It is a summation sign (just like the + sign) and directs us to sum

---

[6]The rates presented in Table 4.5 are computed for aggregate units (cities) of different sizes. The mean of 26.1 is therefore called an *unweighted* mean. It is not the same as the murder rate for the population in the combined cities.

whatever comes after it. Therefore, $\Sigma Y$ means "add up all the raw $y$ scores." Finally, the letter $N$, as you know by now, represents the number of cases (or observations) in the distribution.

Let's summarize:

$Y$ = the raw scores of the variable $y$

$\overline{Y}$ = the mean of $y$

$\Sigma Y$ = the sum of all the $y$ scores

$N$ = the number of observations

Now that we know what the symbols mean, let's work through another example.

The following are the ages of the ten students in my graduate research methods class:

21, 32, 23, 41, 20, 30, 36, 22, 25, 27

What is the mean age of my students?

For these data the ages included in this group are represented by $Y$; $N = 10$, the number of students in the class; and $\Sigma Y$ is the sum of all the ages:

$$\Sigma Y = 21 + 32 + 23 + 41 + 20 + 30 + 36 + 22 + 25 + 27 = 277$$

Thus, the mean age is

$$\overline{Y} = \frac{\Sigma Y}{N} = \frac{277}{10} = 27.7$$

The mean can also be calculated when the data are arranged in a grouped distribution. However, in most situations you will not need to calculate the mean from a grouped distribution by hand. We have presented an example involving a grouped distribution in Box 4.3.

---

*Learning Check.* The following distribution is the same as the one you used to calculate the median in an earlier Learning Check.

22, 15, 18, 33, 17, 5, 11, 28, 40, 19, 8, 20

Can you calculate the mean? Is it the same as the median or is it different?

---

## Understanding Some Important Properties of the Arithmetic Mean

The following three mathematical properties make the mean the most important measure of central tendency. It is, in fact, a concept that is basic to numerous and more complex statistical operations.

## Box 4.3  *Finding the Mean in a Frequency Distribution*

When data are arranged in a frequency distribution, we must give each score its proper weight by multiplying it by its frequency. We can use the following modified formula to calculate the mean:

$$\overline{Y} = \frac{\sum fY}{N}$$

where

$\overline{Y}$ = the mean
$fY$ = a score multiplied by its frequency
$\sum fY$ = the sum of all the $fY$'s
$N$ = the total number of cases in the distribution

### Ideal Number of Children: GSS 1988

| Number of Children (Y) | Frequency (f) | Frequency × Y (fY) |
|---|---|---|
| 0 | 12 | 0 |
| 1 | 25 | 25 |
| 2 | 733 | 1466 |
| 3 | 333 | 999 |
| 4 | 183 | 732 |
| 5 | 26 | 130 |
| 6 | 15 | 90 |
| 7 | 12 | 84 |
| Total | N = 1,339 | $\sum fY$ = 3,526 |

We now illustrate how to calculate the mean from a frequency distribution using the preceding formula. In the 1988 General Social Survey respondents were asked what they think is the ideal number of children for a family. Their responses are presented in the table. Notice that to calculate the value of $\sum fY$ (column 3), each score (column 1) is multiplied by its frequency (column 2), and the products are then added together.

Thus, when we apply the formula:

$$\overline{Y} = \frac{\sum fY}{N}$$

$$\overline{Y} = \frac{3,526}{1,339} = 2.6$$

we find that the mean for the ideal number of children is 2.6.

**Learning Check.** If you are having difficulty understanding how to find the mean in a frequency distribution examine this table. It explains the process without using any notation.

**Finding the Mean in a Frequency Distribution**

| Number of people per house | Number of houses like this | Number of people such houses contribute |
|---|---|---|
| 1 | 3 | 3 |
| 2 | 5 | 10 |
| 3 | 1 | 3 |
| 4 | 1 | 4 |

Total number of people: 20  Total number of houses: 10
Mean number of people per house: 20 ÷ 10 = 2

Here is another example that requires finding the average education of working-class and middle-class African American women.* We will calculate the mean from the following frequency distributions. The tables are frequency distributions of years of education of middle-class and working-class African American women. Try to apply the formula for means in a frequency distribution to the two tables to find the mean education for the two groups.

## Years of Education of Working-Class African American Women: GSS 1988 to 1990

| Education ($Y$) | Frequency ($f$) | Frequency × $Y$ ($fY$) |
|---|---|---|
| 4 | 1 | 4 |
| 6 | 3 | 18 |
| 7 | 2 | 14 |
| 8 | 2 | 16 |
| 9 | 5 | 45 |
| 10 | 3 | 30 |
| 11 | 9 | 99 |
| 12 | 16 | 192 |

*Social class rank is based on the respondents' self-identification.

| | | |
|---|---|---|
| 13 | 4 | 52 |
| 14 | 8 | 112 |
| 15 | 1 | 15 |
| 16 | 4 | 64 |
| 17 | 1 | 17 |
| 18 | 2 | 36 |
| 20 | 1 | 20 |
| Total | 62 | 734 |

$$\overline{Y} = 11.8$$

## Years of Education of Middle-Class African American Women: GSS 1988 to 1990

| Education (Y) | Frequency (f) | Frequency × Y (fY) |
|---|---|---|
| 4 | 1 | 4 |
| 6 | 3 | 18 |
| 7 | 1 | 7 |
| 8 | 2 | 16 |
| 9 | 2 | 18 |
| 10 | 3 | 30 |
| 11 | 7 | 77 |
| 12 | 12 | 144 |
| 13 | 6 | 78 |
| 14 | 10 | 140 |
| 15 | 2 | 30 |
| 16 | 6 | 96 |
| 17 | 0 | 0 |
| 18 | 6 | 108 |
| 20 | 2 | 40 |
| Total | 63 | 806 |

$$\overline{Y} = 12.8$$

Examine the tables showing years of education for working-class and middle-class African American women. Note how similar working-class and middle-class African American women are on education. This similarity is striking given that education is a major component of social class. You may want to explore this issue further by comparing the level of education of working-class and middle-class white women or of working-class and middle-class African American and white men. SPSS problem 4 provides specific instructions that will help you explore this question further.

*Interval-Ratio Level of Measurement* Because it requires the mathematical operations of addition and division, the mean can only be calculated for variables measured at the interval-ratio level. This is the only level of measurement that provides numbers that can be added and divided.

*Center of Gravity* Because the mean incorporates *all* the scores in the distribution (unlike the mode and median), we can think of it as the *center of gravity* of the distribution. That is, the mean is the point that perfectly balances all the scores in the distribution. If we subtract the mean from each score and add up all the differences, the sum will always be zero!

---

**Learning Check.** *Why is the mean considered the center of gravity of the distribution? Think of the last time you were in a park on a seesaw (it may have been a long time ago) with a friend who was much heavier than you. You were left hanging in the air until your friend moved closer to the center. In short, to balance the seesaw a light person far away from the center (the mean) can balance a heavier person who is closer to the center. Can you illustrate this principle with a simple income distribution?*

**Illustrating the Seesaw Principle**

**a.** Three men, weights 60, 120, and 180, all stand on a seesaw. The fulcrum is placed at 120. The mean is (60 +120 + 180)/3. The seesaw balances.

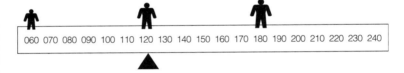

**b.** The 180-pound man is replaced by a 240-pound man, but we do not move the fulcrum. The seesaw slowly falls to the right.

**c.** We move the fulcrum to 140. The new mean is (60 + 120 + 240)/3. The seesaw balances again.

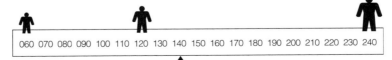

*Sensitivity to Extremes* The mean is based on every score in the distribution (the examples we have used to show how to compute the mean demonstrate that, unlike with the mode or the median, every score enters into the calculation of the mean). This property makes the mean sensitive to extreme scores in the distribution. The mean is pulled in the direction of either very high or very low values. A glance at Figure 4.5 should convince you of that. Figures 4.5a and 4.5b each show the incomes of ten individuals. In Figure 4.5b, the income of one

Figure 4.5 **The Value of the Mean Is Affected by Extreme Scores**

**a.** No extreme scores: the mean is $3,000

| Income ($Y$) | | Frequency ($f$) | $fY$ |
|---|---|---|---|
| 1,000 | | 1 | 1,000 |
| 2,000 | | 2 | 4,000 |
| 3,000 | | 4 | 12,000 |
| 4,000 | | 2 | 8,000 |
| 5,000 | | 1 | 5,000 |
| | | $N = 10$ | $\Sigma fY = 30,000$ |

$$\text{Mean} = \frac{\Sigma fY}{N} = \frac{30,000}{10} = \$3,000$$

Median = $3,000

**b.** One extreme score: the mean is $6,000

| Income ($Y$) | | Frequency ($f$) | $fY$ |
|---|---|---|---|
| 1,000 | | 1 | 1,000 |
| 2,000 | | 2 | 4,000 |
| 3,000 | | 4 | 12,000 |
| 4,000 | | 2 | 8,000 |
| 35,000 | | 1 | 35,000 |
| | | $N = 10$ | $\Sigma fY = 60,000$ |

$$\text{Mean} = \frac{\Sigma fY}{N} = \frac{60,000}{10} = \$6,000$$

Median = $3,000

individual shifted from $5,000 to $35,000. Notice the effect it had on the mean; it shifted from $3,000 to $6,000! The mean is disproportionately affected by the relatively high income of $35,000 and is misleading as a measure of central tendency for this distribution. Notice that the median's value is not affected by this extreme score; it remained at $3,000. Thus, the median gives us better information on the typical income for this group. In the next section, we will see that because of the sensitivity of the mean, it is not suitable as a measure of central tendency in distributions that have a few very extreme values on one side of the distribution (a few extreme values are no problem if they are not mostly on one side of the distribution).

*Learning Check.* *When asked to choose the appropriate measure of central tendency for a distribution, remember that the level of measurement is not the only consideration. When variables are measured at the interval-ratio level, the mean is usually the measure of choice, but remember that extreme scores in one direction make the mean unrepresentative and the median or mode may be the better choice.*

## The Shape of the Distribution: The Experience of Traumatic Events

In this chapter we have looked at the way in which the mode, median, and mean reflect central tendencies in the distribution. Distributions (this discussion is limited to distributions of interval-ratio variables) can also be described by their general shape, which can be easily represented visually. A distribution can be either *symmetrical* or *skewed,* depending on whether there are a few extreme values at one end of the distribution.

A distribution is **symmetrical** (Figure 4.6a) if the frequencies at the right and left tails of the distribution are identical, so that if it is divided into two halves, each will be the mirror image of the other. In a *unimodal* symmetrical distribution the mean, median, and mode are identical.

In **skewed** distributions, there are a few extreme values on one side of the distribution. Distributions that have a few extremely high values are said to be **positively skewed** (Figure 4.6c), and those with a few extremely low values are referred to as **negatively skewed** (Figure 4.6b). In a negatively skewed distribution, the mean will be pulled in the direction of the lower scores; in a positively skewed distribution, it will be pulled toward the high scores.

Figure 4.6 **Types of Frequency Distributions**

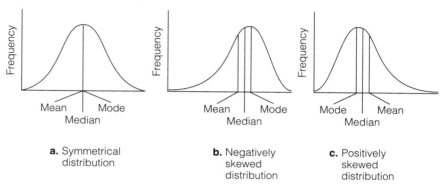

**a.** Symmetrical distribution

**b.** Negatively skewed distribution

**c.** Positively skewed distribution

We can illustrate the differences among symmetrical and positively and negatively skewed distributions by comparing how different groups in our society experience traumatic events. Severe illness, death in the family, divorce, and unemployment are traumatic events that are a part of life. But are some of us more prone to trauma than others? Are some groups likely to suffer more traumatic events than others?

Every year the GSS asks a sample of respondents to report on the number of different traumatic events (deaths, divorces, unemployment, and hospitalizations or disabilities) that happened to them during the previous five years. Here we look at the responses to this question by the following three groups: (1) working-class black males, (2) middle-class black males, and (3) working-class black females. The frequency distributions for the number of traumas for these three groups are presented in Tables 4.6 through 4.8, and the corresponding bar graphs are depicted in Figures 4.7a through 4.7c.

*Symmetrical Distribution*  The frequencies at the right and left tails of the distribution are identical. Each half of the distribution is the mirror image of the other.

*Skewed Distribution*  A distribution with a few extreme values on one side of the distribution.

*Positively Skewed Distribution*  A distribution with a few extremely high values.

*Negatively Skewed Distribution*  A distribution with a few extremely low values.

## The Symmetrical Distribution

First, let's examine Table 4.6 and Figure 4.7a displaying the distribution of trauma reported by working-class black males. Notice that the largest number (31) experienced 1 trauma during the last five years (mode = 1), and about an equal number (23 and 20, respectively) reported either 0 or 2 traumas. As shown in Figure 4.7a, the mode, median, and mean are almost identical, and they coincide at about the middle of the distribution.

The distribution of traumas for working-class black males as depicted in Table 4.6 and Figure 4.7a is a nearly symmetrical distribution. The mean, median, and mode are almost identical and the distribution below the center (where the mean, median, and mode are located) is almost a mirror image of that above the center.

## The Positively Skewed Distribution

Now let's examine Table 4.7 and Figure 4.7b, displaying the distribution of traumas reported by middle-class black males. Note that the largest number of respondents (22) is concentrated at the low end of the scale (0 traumas), with few people reporting that they experienced a high number of traumas (3+ traumas). Notice also that in this distribution, the mean, median, and mode have different values, with the mean having the highest value ($\overline{Y} = 1.12$), the median the second

Table 4.6  **Number of Traumas During the Last Five Years: Working-Class Black Males**

| Number of Traumas (Y) | Frequency (f) | fY | Percentages (%) | C% |
|---|---|---|---|---|
| 0 | 23 | 0 | 29.9 | 29.9 |
| 1 | 31 | 31 | 40.2 | 70.1 |
| 2 | 20 | 40 | 26.0 | 96.1 |
| 3+* | 3 | 9 | 3.9 | 100.0 |
| Total | 77 | 80 | 100.0 | |

$$\overline{Y} = \frac{\sum fY}{N} = \frac{80}{77} = 1.04$$

Median = 1.00
Mode = 1.00

*The category 3+ is assumed to be 3 for the purpose of calculating the mean.

Figure 4.7 **Number of Traumas During the Last Five Years for Three Groups**

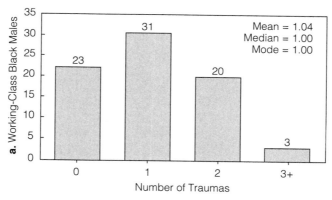

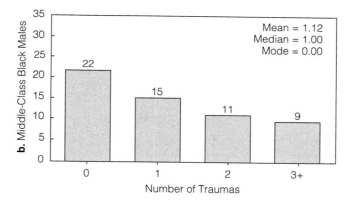

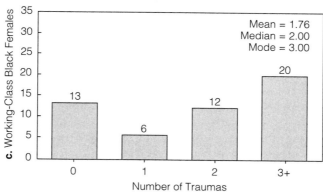

Source: General Social Survey, 1988 to 1990.

Table 4.7  **Number of Traumas During the Last Five Years: Middle-Class Black Males**

| Number of Traumas (Y) | Frequency (f) | fY | Percentages (%) | C% |
|---|---|---|---|---|
| 0 | 22 | 0 | 38.6 | 38.6 |
| 1 | 15 | 15 | 26.3 | 64.9 |
| 2 | 11 | 22 | 19.3 | 84.2 |
| 3+ | 9 | 27 | 15.8 | 100.0 |
| Total | 57 | 64 | 100.0 | |

$$\overline{Y} = \frac{\sum fY}{N} = \frac{64}{57} = 1.12$$

Median = 1.00
Mode = 0.00

highest value (median = 1.00), and the mode the lowest value (mode = 0.00). The distribution of traumas for middle-class black males as depicted in Table 4.7 and Figure 4.7b is positively skewed. As a general rule, for skewed distributions the mean, median, and mode do not coincide. The mean, which is always pulled in the direction of extreme scores, falls closest to the tail of the distribution where a small number of extreme scores are located.

## The Negatively Skewed Distribution

Now turn to Table 4.8 and Figure 4.7c for working-class black females; you can see the opposite pattern. The distribution of the number of traumas reported by working-class black women in the General Social Survey is a negatively skewed distribution. First, note that the largest number of women are concentrated at the high end (3+ traumas) of the scale, and that there are fewer women at the low end. The mean, median, and mode also differ in values as they did in the previous example. However, here the mode has the highest value (mode = 3.00), the median has the second highest (median = 2.00), and the mean has the lowest value ($\overline{Y}$ = 1.76).

## Guidelines for Identifying the Shape of a Distribution

Following are some useful guidelines for identifying the shape of a distribution.

Table 4.8 **Number of Traumas During the Last Five Years:
Working-Class Black Females**

| Number of Traumas (Y) | Frequency (f) | f Y | Percentages (%) | C% |
|---|---|---|---|---|
| 0 | 13 | 0 | 25.5 | 25.5 |
| 1 | 6 | 6 | 11.8 | 37.3 |
| 2 | 12 | 24 | 23.5 | 60.8 |
| 3+ | 20 | 60 | 39.2 | 100.0 |
| Total | 51 | 90 | 100.0 | |

$$\overline{Y} = \frac{\Sigma fY}{N} = \frac{90}{51} = 1.76$$

Median = 2.00
Mode = 3.00

1. In unimodal distributions, when the median, mode, and mean coincide or are almost identical, the distribution is symmetrical.

2. When the mean is higher than the median (or is positioned to the right of the median) the distribution is positively skewed.

3. When the mean is lower than the median (or is positioned to the left of the median) the distribution is negatively skewed.

> **Learning Check.** *A tip. To identify positively and negatively skewed distributions, look at the tail on the chart. If the tail points to the right (the positive end of the X-axis) the distribution is positively skewed. If the tail points to the left (the negative, or potentially negative, end of the X-axis) the distribution is negatively skewed.*

## Considerations for Choosing a Measure of Central Tendency

So far we have considered three basic kinds of averages, the mode, the median, and the mean. Each can represent a central tendency of a distribution. But which one should we use? the mode? the median? the mean? Or, perhaps, all of them? There is no simple answer to this question. However, in general, we tend to use only one of the three measures of central tendency, and the choice of the appropriate one involves a number of considerations. These considerations and how they affect our choice of the appropriate measure are presented in a decision tree shown in Figure 4.8.

## Level of Measurement

One of the most basic considerations in choosing a measure of central tendency is the variable's level of measurement. Valid use of any of the three measures requires that the data be measured at the level appropriate for that measure or higher. Thus, as shown in Figure 4.8, with nominal variables, our choice is restricted to the mode as a measure of central tendency.

However, with ordinal data we have two choices: the mode or the median (or sometimes both). Our choice will depend on what we want to know about the distribution. If we are interested in showing what is the most common or typical value in the distribution, then our choice is the mode. If, however, we want to show which value is located exactly in the middle of the distribution, then the median is our measure of choice.

When the data are measured on an interval-ratio level, the choice between the appropriate measures is a bit more complex and is restricted by the shape of the distribution.

Figure 4.8 **How to Choose a Measure of Central Tendency**

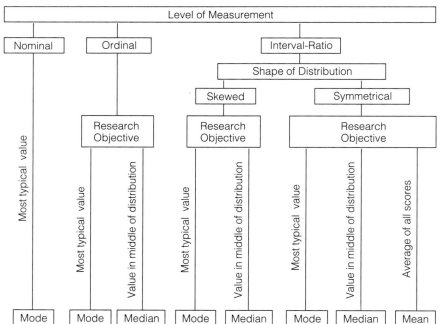

## Box 4.4 *Statistics in Practice: Median Annual Earnings Among Subgroups*

Personal income is frequently positively skewed because there are fewer people with high income; therefore, studies on earnings often report median income. The mean tends to overestimate both the earnings of the most typical earner (the mode) and the earnings represented by the 50th percentile (the median). In the following example the median is used to compare annual earnings of white, black, and Hispanic men and women.

Figure 4.9 **Median Annual Earnings by Race and Gender, 1993**

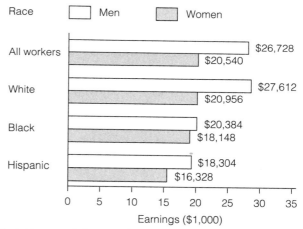

*Source: Statistical Abstract of the United States, 1994.*

In Figure 4.9 we compare the 1993 median annual earnings of full-time men and women workers in the entire population and among white, black, and Hispanic workers. Since the earnings of white males are the highest in comparison with all other groups, it is useful to look at each group's median earnings relative to the earnings of white males. For example, white women today are paid just 76 cents for every $1 paid to white men ($20,956 ÷ $27,612 = 0.76). For women of color, the gap is greater. In 1993, black women were paid approximately 66 cents ($18,148 ÷ $27,612 = 0.66) and Hispanic women 59 cents ($16,328 ÷ $27,612 = 0.59) for every $1 paid to white men.

## Skewed Distribution

When the distribution is skewed the mean may give misleading information on the central tendency, since its value is affected by extreme scores in the distribution. Therefore, the median (see, for example, Box 4.4) or the mode can be chosen as the preferred measure of central tendency because neither is influenced by extreme scores. For instance, for both middle-class black males and working-class black females (Figures 4.7b and 4.7c), the mean does not provide as accurate a representation of the "typical" number of traumas an individual has experienced during the last five years as the median and the mode. Thus, either one could be used as an "average," depending on our research objective.

## Symmetrical Distribution

When the distribution we want to analyze is symmetrical we can use any of the three averages. Again, our choice depends on the research objective and what we want to know about the distribution. In general, however, the mean will be our best choice because it contains the greatest amount of information and is easier to use in more advanced statistical analyses.

### MAIN POINTS

- The mode, the median, and the mean are measures of central tendency—numbers that describe what is average or typical about the distribution.

- The mode is the category or score with the largest frequency (or percentage) in the distribution. It is often used to describe the most commonly occurring category of a nominal level variable.

- The median is a measure of central tendency that represents the exact middle of the distribution. It is calculated for variables measured on at least an ordinal level of measurement.

- The mean is typically used to describe central tendency in interval-ratio variables, such as income, age, or education. We obtain the mean by summing all the scores and dividing by the total ($N$) number of scores.

- In a symmetrical distribution the frequencies at the right and left tails of the distribution are identical. In skewed distributions there are either a few extremely high (positive skew) or a few extremely low (negative skew) values.

## KEY TERMS

*mean*

*measures of central tendency*

*median*

*mode*

*negatively skewed distribution*

*percentile*

*positively skewed distribution*

*skewed distribution*

*symmetrical distribution*

## SPSS DEMONSTRATIONS

*Demonstration 1: Producing Measures of Central Tendency with Frequencies*

We previously used the Frequencies procedure in Chapter 2 to look at the categories of variables measuring attitude toward abortion. Frequencies also has the ability to produce the three measures of central tendency discussed in this chapter. We will use Frequencies to calculate measures of central tendency for AGE and ABCHOOSE. (Should a woman be able to get a legal abortion for any reason?)

Click under *Statistics*, *Summarize*, then *Frequencies*. Place AGE and ABCHOOSE in the Variable(s) box. Then click on the *Statistics* button.

The Central Tendency box lists four choices, and we will click on the first three. Then click on *Continue*, then on *OK* to process this request.

```
┌─────────────────────────────────────────────────────────────────────────┐
│ ▬                 SPSS for Windows Student Version - [!Output1]      ▼ ▲│
│ ▬  File  Edit  Data  Transform  Statistics  Graphs  Utilities  Window  Help      ▲│
│ ┌──────┐ ┌──────┐ ┌──────┐ ┌────────┐ ┌───┐ ┌──┐┌──┐ ┌──┐┌──┐ ┌──┐          │
│ │Pause │ │Scroll│ │Round │ │Glossary│ │▐▌▌│ │▲ ││▼ │ │▲ ││▼ │ │  │          │
│ └──────┘ └──────┘ └──────┘ └────────┘ └───┘ └──┘└──┘ └──┘└──┘ └──┘          │
│                              75        10      1.0      1.0     91.8        │
│                              76        13      1.3      1.3     93.1        │
│                              77        10      1.0      1.0     94.1        │
│                              78         8       .8       .8     94.9        │
│                              79         6       .6       .6     95.5        │
│                              80         9       .9       .9     96.4        │
│                              81         4       .4       .4     96.8        │
│                              82         6       .6       .6     97.4        │
│                              83         3       .3       .3     97.7        │
│                              84         3       .3       .3     98.0        │
│                              85         7       .7       .7     98.7        │
│                              86         4       .4       .4     99.1        │
│                              87         3       .3       .3     99.4        │
│                              88         1       .1       .1     99.5        │
│                              89         5       .5       .5    100.0        │
│  NA                          99         2       .2    Missing               │
│                                      -------  -------   -------              │
│                            Total     1000    100.0    100.0                 │
│                                                                             │
│  Mean        46.086     Median     43.000     Mode        32.000            │
│                                                                             │
│                                                                             │
│  Valid cases     998    Missing cases       2                               │
│                                                                             │
│ SPSS Processor is ready                                                     │
└─────────────────────────────────────────────────────────────────────────┘
```

The frequency table for AGE is quite lengthy, so only the bottom portion is displayed here. Note that the oldest age appears to be 89, but that is because all ages of 90 and above have been recoded to 89 for ease of analysis.

AGE is an interval-ratio variable, which means that the mode, median, and mean are all appropriate measures of central tendency. The mean of AGE is about 46.1, but remember that the GSS file includes only adults, so the mean value (and the other measures of central tendency) should not be taken as representative of the American population as a whole.

The median is 43, which is close to the mean value. Roughly half of the respondents are above the age of 43 and half are below. However, since the median is lower than the mean, it implies that the distribution of age is positively skewed. Look back at the SPSS example in Chapter 3 (p. 121) where the histogram for AGE was displayed and see if you can observe the positive skewness.

The mode is 32, so more people are 32 years old than any other age (35 people, to be exact). This is another indication of the positive skewness in the distribution of age.

The output from Frequencies for ABCHOOSE shows that SPSS has no idea that this variable is measured on an ordinal scale. In other words, SPSS produces exactly the output we asked for, without regard for whether the output is correct for this type of variable. It's up to you, the user, to select the proper measure of central tendency.

ABCHOOSE    SHOULD A WOMAN GET AN ABORTION FOR ANY R

| Value Label | Value | Frequency | Percent | Valid Percent | Cum Percent |
|---|---|---|---|---|---|
| STRONGLY AGREE | 1 | 93 | 9.3 | 20.8 | 20.8 |
| AGREE | 2 | 114 | 11.4 | 25.5 | 46.3 |
| NEITHER AGREE NOR DI | 3 | 47 | 4.7 | 10.5 | 56.8 |
| DISAGREE | 4 | 90 | 9.0 | 20.1 | 77.0 |
| STRONGLY DISAGREE | 5 | 103 | 10.3 | 23.0 | 100.0 |
| NAP | 0 | 508 | 50.8 | Missing | |
| CAN'T CHOOSE | 8 | 10 | 1.0 | Missing | |
| NA | 9 | 35 | 3.5 | Missing | |
| | | ------- | ------- | ------- | |
| | Total | 1000 | 100.0 | 100.0 | |

| Mean | 2.991 | Median | 3.000 | Mode | 2.000 |
|---|---|---|---|---|---|

Valid cases    447    Missing cases    553

Since ABCHOOSE is an ordinal variable we can use the median and mode to summarize its distribution. The median is 3, which corresponds to the response "Neither Agree nor Disagree," so there is roughly an equal split between those agreeing or disagreeing that abortion should be legal for any reason. This illustrates further how Americans are divided on this issue. The mode is 2, which means that the most frequent response is to "Agree" that abortion should be legal for any reason (114 responses).

## Demonstration 2: Producing Measures of Central Tendency with Descriptives

When you want to calculate the mean of interval-ratio variables but you don't need to view the actual frequency table listing the responses in each category, the Descriptives procedure is often the best choice. Descriptives can be found in the *Statistics . . . Summarize* menu.

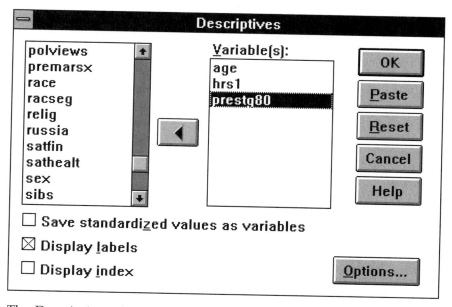

The Descriptives dialog box is uncomplicated and only requires that you place the variables of interest in the Variable(s) box. By default, Descriptives will calculate the mean, standard deviation (to be discussed in the next chapter), minimum, maximum, and the number of cases with a valid response.

We will view these descriptive statistics for AGE, HRS1 (hours worked last week), and PRESTG80 (the respondent's occupational prestige score in 1980, which varies on a scale from 1 to 99).

```
Number of valid observations (listwise) =        633.00

                                                 Valid
Variable      Mean     Std Dev   Minimum  Maximum    N   Label

HRS1         41.44      13.95        4       89     636   NUMBER OF HOURS WOR
PRESTG80     43.92      13.72       17       86     959   RS OCCUPATIONAL PRE
AGE          46.09      17.49       18       89     998   AGE OF RESPONDENT
```

The output from Descriptives automatically lists the variables in the order of the value of their means, from low to high, rather than the order we specified in the dialog box. The mean of AGE is the same as SPSS calculated in Frequencies (except for rounding). For HRS1, hours worked last week, we can see that the mean value of 41.44 is close to the standard or "normal" value of 40 hours per week, with a minimum of 4 (people not working are excluded), and a maximum of 89 (someone was obviously very busy that week). The mean for PRESTG80 is around 44, about halfway between 1 and 99.

The Descriptives procedure has other options that we will explore in later chapters that allow us to modify the output by requesting additional statistics, a different display order, or the creation of new variables that are mathematically related to the existing variables.

## EXERCISES

1. In Chapter 2, exercise 1, you surveyed thirty people about their race (white or nonwhite) and how many traumas they had experienced in the last year. You also asked each about his or her self-perceived social class. Find the mode for all three variables in the survey.

2. You are interested in understanding whether public opinion has any influence on government spending for the poor. Fortunately, the General Social Survey contains a question about whether the respondent agrees or disagrees that government should spend less on the poor. Here is a small random sample of 100 responses to this question for the years 1987 to 1991.

| Attitude | Frequency |
| --- | --- |
| Strongly agree | 15 |
| Agree | 15 |
| Neither | 20 |
| Disagree | 25 |
| Strongly disagree | 25 |

 a. At what level is this variable measured? What is the mode for attitude toward government spending for the poor?
 b. If the level of measurement is appropriate, calculate the median for this variable. (*Hint:* The number of cases is even.) In general, how would you characterize the public's attitude toward spending for the poor?

3. In Chapter 2, exercise 5, we looked at the level of education of the American population, using GSS data from the years 1987 to 1991.
 a. What is the level of measurement for "years of education"? What is the mode for education? What is the median for education?
 b. Construct quartiles for education. What is the 25th percentile? the 50th percentile? the 75th percentile? Why don't you need to calculate the 50th percentile to answer this question?

4. Using the GSS for all the years from 1987 to 1991, you find the following grouped distribution for the respondent's age:

| Age Category | Frequency |
|---|---|
| 18–29 | 476 |
| 30–39 | 567 |
| 40–49 | 384 |
| 50–59 | 251 |
| 60-69 | 257 |
| 70–89 | 272 |

   a. Calculate the median for age, using the formula for a grouped distribution. What is its value?
   b. Now also calculate the 20th and 80th percentile values for age.

5. Religion has been and continues to be important to many Americans. Nevertheless, there are demographic differences in religious behavior, including age. The following table, taken from the GSS from 1987 to 1991, depicts how often people pray within various age groups (not all ages are displayed).

| | Age Group | | |
|---|---|---|---|
| Prayer Frequency | 18–29 | 50–59 | 70–89 |
| Several times a day | 45 | 67 | 86 |
| Once a day | 108 | 44 | 47 |
| Several times a week | 62 | 24 | 12 |
| Once a week | 30 | 8 | 4 |
| Less than once a week | 92 | 23 | 17 |

   a. Calculate the median and mode for each age group.
   b. Use this information to characterize how prayer behavior varies by age. Does the median or mode provide a better description of the data? Do the statistics support the idea that there is a prayer "generation gap," such that some age groups engage in more prayer than others?

6. AIDS is a serious health problem for this country (and many others). Data from the National Centers for Disease Control for 1992 and 1993 show the number of children living with AIDS in various Metropolitan Statistical Areas (the top ten MSAs are listed).

| Metropolitan Statistical Area | June 1992 | June 1993 |
|---|---|---|
| New York | 348 | 423 |
| Miami | 87 | 100 |
| Newark | 73 | 79 |
| Washington, DC | 40 | 75 |
| Baltimore | 43 | 71 |
| Chicago | 53 | 69 |
| Los Angeles | 50 | 55 |
| Boston | 34 | 45 |
| Fort Lauderdale | 30 | 38 |
| Philadelphia | 30 | 38 |

a. Calculate the mean number of children with AIDS in these urban areas in both 1992 and 1993. Did AIDS cases among children increase from one year to the next? Does the mean adequately represent the central tendency of the distribution of AIDS cases in each year? Why or why not?

b. Recalculate the mean for each year after removing the New York MSA. Is the mean now a better representation of central tendency for the remaining nine MSAs?

7. U.S. households have become smaller over the years. The following table from the 1989 GSS lists the number of people of all ages living in a household.

| Number of People | Frequency |
|---|---|
| 1 | 103 |
| 2 | 112 |
| 3 | 78 |
| 4 | 70 |
| 5 | 18 |
| 6 | 13 |
| 7 | 7 |
| 8 | 4 |
| 9 | 2 |

Calculate the mean number of people living in a U.S. household in 1989. (*Hint:* Use the formula for calculating the mean from a frequency distribution.)

8. In exercise 6 you calculated the mean for the number of children with AIDS. We now want to test whether the distribution of AIDS cases is symmetrical or skewed.
   a. To do so, calculate the median and mode for each year, using all MSAs. Based on these results and the means, how would you characterize the distribution of AIDS cases for each year?
   b. What value best represents the central tendency of each distribution?
   c. If you found the distributions to be skewed, what is the (statistical) cause?

9. In exercise 7 you examined U.S. household size in 1989. Use these data again and construct a bar chart to represent the distribution of household size.
   a. From the appearance of the bar chart, would you say the distribution is positively or negatively skewed? Why?
   b. Now calculate the median and mode for the distribution. Do these numbers provide further evidence to support your decision about how the distribution is skewed? Why do you think the distribution of household size is asymmetrical?

10. Exercise 3 used GSS data on the educational level of U.S. adults.
    a. Calculate the mean for years of education.
    b. Compare the value of the mean with that for the median and mode you have already calculated. Without constructing a bar chart, describe whether and how the distribution of years of education is skewed.

11. You listen to a debate between two politicians discussing the economic health of the United States. One politician says that the average income of U.S. adults is $25,000; the other says that the average American makes only $20,000, so Americans are not as well off as the first politician claims. Is it possible for both these politicians to be correct? If so, explain how.

12. Picking an appropriate statistic to describe the central tendency of a distribution is a critical skill. For the following situations, choose the statistic you believe most suitable to answer the problem posed. Justify your answer. If it is difficult to answer some items because of a lack of information, describe what other information you believe is needed.
    a. Using GSS sample data, determine the most common religious denomination in the United States.

b. With responses given on a scale from 1 to 5 (where 1 = Not Effective and 5 = Very Effective), find the overall opinion about the effectiveness of the U.S. Congress in doing its job.

c. Find the typical number of cars owned by an average American household.

d. Find the average number of hours Americans watch television every day.

e. Determine the best measure of central tendency to compare the wages of males with those of females.

f. From a GSS sample, determine the overall political position of Americans, with responses on a scale from 1 = Very Conservative to 7 = Very Liberal.

g. Find the most common length of sentence for a group of individuals incarcerated for the crime of burglary.

13. You have examined the educational level of Americans in several previous exercises. Discuss the advantages and disadvantages of all three measures of central tendency when they are used to summarize with one number the years of education of American adults. Are you confident that one of these three is the best measure of central tendency for education? If so, why?

14. Do murder rates in cities vary with city size? Investigate this question using the data in the table for large and small cities. Calculate the mean and median for each group of cities. Where is the murder rate highest? Do the mean and median have the same pattern for the two groups?

### Murder Rate per 100,000 in 1992

| Large Cities | | Small Cities | |
|---|---|---|---|
| New York | 27.1 | Colorado Springs | 5.7 |
| Los Angeles | 30.3 | Arlington, TX | 5.9 |
| Chicago | 33.1 | Louisville | 14.2 |
| Houston | 27.4 | St. Paul | 11.8 |
| Philadelphia | 26.5 | Corpus Christi | 11.2 |
| San Diego | 12.7 | Mesa, AZ | 3.0 |
| Dallas | 37.0 | Wichita | 9.4 |
| Phoenix | 13.6 | Fresno, CA | 22.0 |
| Detroit | 57.0 | Tulsa | 8.8 |
| San Antonio | 22.5 | Santa Ana, CA | 19.0 |

## SPSS PROBLEMS

1. In exercise 2 we used a sample of data on whether Americans agree or disagree that government should spend less on the poor. If we ran a Frequencies command on this same GSS data in SPSS, we would obtain the following output:

GOVLESS  Government  should  spend  less  on  the  poor

| Value Label | Value | Frequency | Percent | Valid Percent | Cum Percent |
|---|---|---|---|---|---|
| Strongly Agree | 1.00 | 15 | 15.0 | 15.0 | 15.0 |
| Agree | 2.00 | 15 | 15.0 | 15.0 | 30.0 |
| Neither | 3.00 | 20 | 20.0 | 20.0 | 50.0 |
| Disagree | 4.00 | 25 | 25.0 | 25.0 | 75.0 |
| Strongly Disagree | 5.00 | 25 | 25.0 | 25.0 | 100.0 |
| | Total | 100 | 100.0 | 100.0 | |

Mean      3.300    Median    3.500          Mode          4.000

*Multiple  modes  exist.  The  smallest  value  is  shown.

Valid  cases      100        Missing  cases      0

    a. Did SPSS calculate the same values for the mode and median as you did by hand? If not, why?

    b. Which measure of central tendency, mean or median, is most appropriate to summarize the distribution of GOVLESS? Explain why.

2. We are interested in investigating whether males or females have a higher level of education. Use the GSS data from 1994 and the variable EDUC with the Frequencies procedure to produce frequency tables and the mean, median, and mode separately for males and females.

The most straightforward way to produce this output is to first split the file into groups and have SPSS analyze each separately. To do this choose *Data . . . Split File* from the menu, then choose "Repeat Analysis for each group" in the dialog box and place SEX in the Groups Based on box (and click on *OK*). All procedures run after this will be done separately for males and females.

    a. Do you think that, on the average, males have more education than females? Use all the available information to answer this question.

b. When we use statistics to describe the social world, we should always go beyond merely using statistics to describe the condition of various social groups. Just as important is our interpretation of the statistics and some judgment as to whether any differences we find between groups seem of practical importance; that is, do they make a practical difference in the world. Do you think any differences you discovered between male and female educational levels are important enough to have an effect on such things as the ability to get a job or the salary that someone makes? Defend your answer.

3. Some people believe that minorities have more children than whites. Use SPSS to investigate this question with either GSS data file. (The variable CHILDS records the respondent's number of children.) To get the necessary information, have SPSS split the file by race, then run Frequencies for CHILDS.

   a. What is the best measure of central tendency to represent the number of children in a household? Why?

   b. Which race has more children per respondent?

4. (Extra credit) The educational attainment of working-class and middle-class African American women was compared in this chapter. You can use SPSS to do the same for white women and African American and white men. There is more than one method to get the frequency distribution of education for these groups, but the easiest might be to use the *Split File* menu choice. Use the 1987–1991 GSS file for this exercise.

   a. In the Split File dialog box (found under the *Data* menu), place the variables RACESEX and CLASS (in that order) in the Groups Based on box, after clicking on the "Repeat Analysis for each group" button. RACESEX has four categories, for white males, black males, white females, and black females, respectively. CLASS has five valid values, with working-class = 2 and middle-class = 3. After you run the Split File procedure, SPSS will create a separate set of output for each group defined by the combination of the values of RACESEX and CLASS.

   b. Now run Frequencies on the variable EDUC. SPSS will create a great deal of output; all you need to do is find the appropriate frequency tables and calculate the mean from the table. For example, to find the frequency table for middle-class black males, look for the section with values of RACESEX = 2 and CLASS = 3.

   c. Is the gap in education between African American working-class and middle-class men greater than that between white working-class and middle-class men? How about for females?

## GROUP PROBLEMS

1. Working in a small group, decide on three items of information that you would like to collect from each member of your class. These could be attitude toward some timely and interesting issue, political party preference, type of neighborhood or town in which someone lives, number of books currently checked out of the library, favorite type of food, and so forth. After choosing three variables, define appropriate response categories (for example, for education, years of education; for place of residence, city, suburban, or rural), then collect the information from all of your classmates, including your group members, in whatever manner you and your instructor deem most suitable. After collecting the data, describe the distribution and central tendency of all three variables. Decide which measure of central tendency is most appropriate for each variable for the goal of best describing your classmates. Present your work in the form of a short report.

2. Collect articles from national newsmagazines such as *Time, Newsweek,* or *U.S. News and World Report* that use measures of central tendency to discuss the distribution and level of income of Americans by race (or gender) and how it has changed over the years. The question of whether differences in income have decreased or not between these groups has been hotly debated among economists, politicians, and others for several years. You and your other group members should find several articles discussing this topic, from both the 1980s and 1990s (share the workload to make the task easier). Make copies for everyone.

   Each group member should then take one article and prepare a written report that explains how the measures of central tendency have been used to consider the matter of income distribution by race (or gender). Does each article correctly use and explain the statistics it presents? Consider whether a reader who isn't taking this class would have some trouble fully understanding parts of the article based on the statistics.

   Finally, meet as a group to discuss how the choice of a measure of central tendency can affect the estimate of race (or gender) differences in income. Prepare a brief report, as a group, summarizing this discussion and any conclusions you reach.

# 5     Measures of Variability

## Introduction

In the last chapter, we looked at measures of central tendency: the mean, the median, and the mode. With these measures we can describe with a single number what is average for or typical of a distribution. Even though measures of central tendency can be very helpful, they tell us only part of the story. In fact, when used alone they often mislead rather than inform us. An alternative way of summarizing a distribution is by selecting a single number that describes how much variation and diversity there is in the distribution. Numbers that describe diversity or variability are called **measures of variability**.

---

*Measures of Variability*   Numbers that describe diversity or variability in the distribution.

---

In this chapter, we discuss five measures of variability: the index of qualitative variation, the range, the interquartile range, the standard deviation, and the variance. But before we discuss these measures, let's explore why they are important.

## The Importance of Measuring Variability

The importance of looking at variation and diversity can be illustrated by thinking about the vast differences in the experiences of women in the United States. Are U.S. women united by their similarities or divided by their differences? The answer is *both*. To address the similarities without dealing with differences is "to misunderstand and distort that which separates as well as that which binds women together."[1] Even when we focus on one particular group of women it is important to look at the differences as well as the commonalities. Take, for example, Asian American women. As a group they share a number of characteristics.

> Their participation in the workforce is higher than that of women in any other ethnic group. Many . . . live life supporting others, often allowing their lives to be subsumed by the needs of the extended family. . . . However, there are many circumstances when these shared experiences are not sufficient to accurately describe the condition of a particular Asian American woman. Among Asian American women there are those who were born in the United States . . . and . . . those who recently arrived in the United States. Asian American women are diverse in their heritage or country of origin: China, Japan, the Philippines, Korea . . . and . . . India. . . . Although the majority of Asian American women are working class—contrary to the stereotype of the "ever successful" Asians—there are poor, "middle-class," and even affluent Asian American women.[2]

As this example illustrates, one basis of stereotyping is treating a group as if it is totally represented by its central value, ignoring the diversity within the group. Sociologists often contribute to this type of stereotyping when their empirical generalizations, based on a statistical difference between averages, are interpreted in this overly simplistic way. All this argues for the importance of using measures of variability as well as central tendency whenever we want to characterize or compare groups.

Thus, whereas the similarities and commonalities in the experiences of Asian American women are depicted by a measure of central tendency like the median, the mode, or the mean, the differences and diversity of their experiences can be described only by using measures of variation.

The concept of variability has implications not only for describing differences and diversity of social groups like Asian American women, but also for issues that are important in your everyday life. One of the most important issues facing the academic community today is how to reconstruct the curriculum to make it more responsive to the needs of students. Let's take the issue of statistics instruction on the college level.

[1] Johnneta B. Cole, "Commonalities and Differences." In *Race, Class, and Gender,* edited by Margaret L. Andersen and Patricia Hill Collins. Belmont, CA: Wadsworth, 1992, 128–129.
[2] Ibid., pp. 129–130.

In the social sciences, statistics courses are often the last "road-block" preventing students from successfully completing their requirement in the major. One factor identified in numerous studies as a handicap for many students is the "math anxiety syndrome." Statistics is perhaps the most anxiety-provoking course in any social science curriculum. This anxiety often leads to a less than optimum learning environment with students often trying to memorize every detail of a statistical procedure rather than understand the general concept involved. Let's suppose that a university committee is examining the issue of how to better respond to the needs of students. In its attempt to evaluate statistics courses offered in different departments, the committee compares the grading policy in two courses. The first, offered in the sociology department, is taught by Professor Brown; the second, offered through the school of social work, is taught by Professor Yamato. The committee finds that over the years the average grade for Professor Brown's class has been C+. The average grade in Professor Yamato's class is also C+. We could easily be misled by these statistics into thinking that the grading policy of both instructors is about the same. However, we need to look more closely into how the grades are distributed in each of the classes to obtain more complete information about them. The differences in the distribution of grades are illustrated in Figure 5.1, which displays the frequency polygon for the two classes.

Figure 5.1 **Distribution of Grades for Professors Brown and Yamato's Statistics Classes**

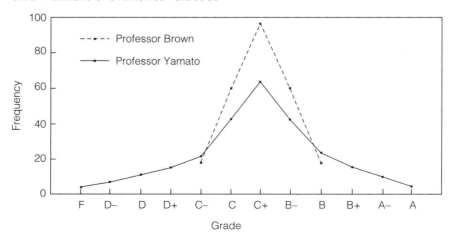

Compare the shapes of these two distributions. Notice that while both distributions have the same mean they are shaped very differently. The grades in Professor Yamato's class are more spread out and range from A to F, while the grades for Professor Brown's class are clustered around the mean and range only from B to C−. Even though the means for both distributions are identical, the distribution of grades in Professor Yamato's class varies considerably more than the grades given by Professor Brown. We see the comparison between the two classes is more complex than we first thought it would be.

As this example demonstrates, information on how scores are spread from the center of a distribution is as important as information about the central tendency in a distribution. This type of information is obtained by measures of variability.

> **Learning Check.**   Look closely at Figure 5.1. Whose class would you choose to take? If you fear you are likely to fail statistics, your best bet would be Professor Brown's class where no one fails. But, if you want to keep up your GPA and are willing to work, Professor Yamato's class is the better choice. If you had to choose one of these classes based solely on the average grades, your choice would not be well informed. We think everyone should be able to get an A in statistics.

## The Index of Qualitative Variation (IQV)

The United States is undergoing a demographic shift from a predominantly white/European population to one characterized by increased racial, ethnic, and cultural diversity. These changes challenge us to rethink every conceptualization of society based solely on the experiences of white/European populations and force us to ask questions that focus on the experiences of different racial/ethnic groups. For instance, we may want to compare the racial/ethnic diversity in different cities, regions, or states or to find out if a group has become more racially and ethnically diverse over time.

The **index of qualitative variation (IQV)** is a measure of variability for nominal variables like race and ethnicity. The index can vary from 0.00 to 1.00. When all the cases in the distribution are in one category, there is no variation (or diversity) and IQV is 0.00. In contrast, when the cases in the distribution are distributed evenly across the categories, there is maximum variation (or diversity) and IQV is 1.00.

*Index of Qualitative Variation (IQV)*   A measure of variability for nominal variables. It is based on the ratio of the total number of differences in the distribution to the maximum number of possible differences within the same distribution.

Suppose that you attend "Northeastern College," a small college where the majority of students are white and a small minority are either black or Hispanic. In contrast, your best friend is going to "Southwestern College," a small liberal arts college, where the number of white, black, and Hispanic students is about equal. The frequency and percentage distributions for the two colleges are presented in Table 5.1. Which college is more diverse? Clearly, Southwestern College, where whites, blacks, and Hispanics are more or less equally represented, is more diverse than Northeastern College, where blacks and Hispanics are but a small minority. You can also get a visual feel for the relative diversity in the two colleges by examining the two bar charts presented in Figure 5.2.

## Steps for Calculating the IQV

To substantiate these observations let's compute and compare the IQV for the two colleges. The IQV is based on the ratio of the total number of differences in the distribution to the maximum number of possible differences within the same distribution.

Table 5.1   **Racial/Ethnic Groups in Two Colleges**

| Race/Ethnicity | Northeastern College | | Southwestern College | |
| --- | --- | --- | --- | --- |
| | Frequency (f) | Percentages* (%) | Frequency (f) | Percentages* (%) |
| White | 480 | 90 | 224 | 34 |
| Black | 31 | 6 | 200 | 30 |
| Hispanic | 23 | 4 | 236 | 36 |
| Total (N) | 534 | 100 | 660 | 100 |

*Rounded

Figure 5.2 **Racial/Ethnic Groups in Northeastern and Southwestern Colleges**

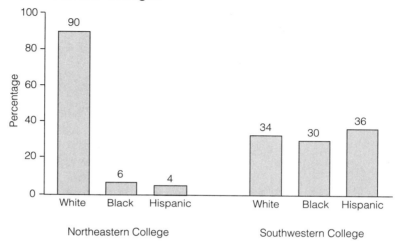

Table 5.2 **The Student Council at Northeastern College**

| Race | Student | Frequency |
|------|---------|-----------|
| White | Ruth, Justin | 2 |
| Black | Gabriel | 1 |
| Hispanic | Rachel | 1 |
| Total (N) | | 4 |

*Calculating the Total Number of Differences*[3] Suppose the student council at Northeastern College included four students divided into three racial groups. For the purpose of illustration we have assigned names to each of the students. Our hypothetical data are presented in Table 5.2.

Whereas Ruth and Justin are both white, Ruth differs racially from Gabriel, who is black, and from Rachel, who is Hispanic. Similarly, Justin differs racially from both Gabriel and Rachel. Finally, Gabriel differs racially from Rachel. Computing the index of qualitative variation (IQV) involves counting these differences. To help us count the total number of racial differences, let's list all the pairs that differ racially:

[3]The following discussion is based on John H. Mueller et al., *Statistical Reasoning in Sociology.* New York: Houghton Mifflin Company, 1970, 174–178.

1. Ruth, Gabriel
2. Ruth, Rachel
3. Justin, Gabriel
4. Justin, Rachel
5. Gabriel, Rachel

Counting each pair as one difference, we come up with a total of five differences.

> **Learning Check.** *Figure 5.3 illustrates how to count the total number of racial differences in the student council of Northeastern College. Examine this figure and determine the total number of gender differences for the same individuals.*

A simpler method of finding the total number of differences in the distribution is to multiply the frequency in each category by the frequency in every other category in the distribution and sum the products. Thus, if we use the frequencies listed in Table 5.2 to count the total number of differences we have: $(2 \times 1) + (2 \times 1) + (1 \times 1) = 2 + 2 + 1 = 5$.

We can express the procedure for finding the total number of differences in a distribution with this formula:

$$\text{Total observed differences} = \sum f_i f_j$$

where

$f_i$ = the frequency of category $i$
$f_j$ = the frequency of category $j$

Applying this formula, let's count the total number of racial differences at Northeastern College:

$$\text{Total observed differences} = (480 \times 31) + (480 \times 23) + (31 \times 23) = 26{,}633$$

And now let's count the differences at Southwestern College:

$$\text{Total observed differences} = (224 \times 200) + (224 \times 236) + (200 \times 236)$$
$$= 144{,}864$$

*Calculating the Maximum Possible Differences* The total number of differences at the colleges is not only a function of the degree of racial/ethnic diversity, but also of the total number of students in each college. (It is also a function of the number of racial/ethnic groups in each college; in this example the number of racial and ethnic categories

Figure 5.3 **Counting the Total Number of Racial Differences: The Student Council at Northeastern College**

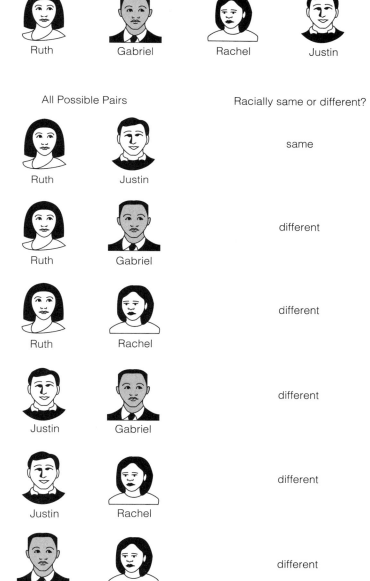

Total number of racial differences: 5

is identical in both colleges.) Therefore, the number of differences in each college can only be interpreted relative to the maximum diversity possible in each college. Maximum diversity would be attained if there were an equal number of students in each racial/ethnic group. For example, Southwestern would reach maximum diversity if its 660 students were equally divided among the three racial groups (220 in each racial group).

To calculate the maximum possible differences follow this formula:

$$\text{Maximum possible differences} = \frac{K(K-1)}{2}\left(\frac{N}{K}\right)^2$$

where

$K$ = the number of categories in the distribution
$N$ = the total number of cases in the distribution

For Northeastern the maximum possible differences are

$$\frac{3(3-1)}{2}\left(\frac{534}{3}\right)^2 = 95,052$$

and for Southwestern

$$\frac{3(3-1)}{2}\left(\frac{660}{3}\right)^2 = 145,200$$

*Computing the Ratio* The IQV is the ratio between the total observed differences and the maximum possible differences:

$$\text{IQV} = \frac{\text{Total observed differences}}{\text{Maximum possible differences}}$$

$$= \frac{\sum f_i f_j}{\frac{K(K-1)}{2}\left(\frac{N}{K}\right)^2} \tag{5.1}$$

The IQV for Northeastern is

$$\text{IQV} = \frac{(480 \times 31) + (480 \times 23) + (31 \times 23)}{\frac{3(3-1)}{2}\left(\frac{534}{3}\right)^2} = 0.28$$

and for Southwestern it is

$$\text{IQV} = \frac{(224 \times 200) + (224 \times 236) + (200 \times 236)}{\frac{3(3-1)}{2}\left(\frac{660}{3}\right)^2} = 0.998$$

Notice that the values of the IQV for the two colleges support our earlier observation: At Southwestern College with an IQV = 0.998 there is considerably more racial/ethnic variation than at Northeastern College, where the IQV = 0.28.

To summarize, these are the steps we follow to calculate the IQV:

1. Find the total number of observed differences: Multiply the frequency in each category by the frequency in every other category in the distribution and sum the products:

$$\text{Total observed differences} = \sum f_i f_j$$

2. Find the maximum possible differences:

$$\text{Maximum possible differences} = \frac{K(K-1)}{2}\left(\frac{N}{K}\right)^2$$

3. Find the IQV:

$$\text{IQV} = \frac{\text{Total observed differences}}{\text{Maximum possible differences}}$$

*Expressing the IQV as a Percentage* The IQV can also be expressed as a percentage, rather than a proportion: simply multiply the IQV by 100. Expressed as a percentage, the IQV would reflect the percentage of racial/ethnic differences relative to the maximum possible differences in each distribution. Thus, an IQV of 0.28 indicates that the number of racial/ethnic differences in Northeastern College is 28 percent (0.28 × 100) of the maximum possible differences. Similarly, for Southwestern College, an IQV of 0.998 means that the number of racial/ethnic differences is 99.8 percent (0.998 × 100) of the maximum possible differences.

*Calculating the IQV from Percentage or Proportion Distributions* The IQV can also be calculated from percentage or proportion distributions by substituting these percentages or proportions for $f$'s into the formula and 100 or 1.00 for $N$. For instance, we can calculate the IQV for Northeastern College using the percentage distribution (from Table 5.1) instead:

$$\text{IQV} = \frac{(90 \times 6) + (90 \times 4) + (6 \times 4)}{\dfrac{3(3-1)}{2}\left(\dfrac{100}{3}\right)^2} = 0.28$$

As you can see, the IQV is the same whether we use the frequency or the percentage distribution.

### Box 5.1   The IQV Formula: What's Going On Here?

At first, the denominator of the IQV formula looks mean and nasty. However, it is actually quite easy to understand what it's doing. Let's say we have a frequency distribution that looks like this:

| | |
|---|---|
| Whites | 8 |
| Blacks | 4 |
| Asians | 2 |
| Hispanics | 2 |
| Total | 16 |

Observed Differences = 84

It's pretty easy to tell that the situation with the maximum possible differences would be this:

| | |
|---|---|
| Whites | 4 |
| Blacks | 4 |
| Asians | 4 |
| Hispanics | 4 |

Maximum Differences = 96

Now let's look at the formula's denominator:

$$\frac{K(K-1)}{2}\left(\frac{N}{K}\right)^2$$

Let's look at what's in parentheses first. $N \div K$ in this case is $16 \div 4$, or 4, so $N \div K$ is simply the frequency in each cell when we have maximum differences.

Now let's tackle that exponent. Why square 4? Well, in the frequency distribution with maximum differences, instead of multiplying $8 \times 4$, $8 \times 2$, and so on, we will be multiplying $4 \times 4$, or 4 squared to count differences.

But how many times do we multiply 4 by 4? If we look at the figure, we can easily see that it's six. That's exactly what the left side of the formula is telling us: $K(K-1) \div 2$ in this case is $4(4-1) \div 2$, or 6. This tells us the number of $4 \times 4$'s we need:

So don't let formulas scare you. They're only systematic ways of doing things you are already doing intuitively.

> **Learning Check.** *Calculate the maximum possible differences for the data shown in Table 5.2 (racial makeup of the student council at Northeastern College). Calculate the IQV for the student council (we have already calculated total differences).*

> **Learning Check.** *Examine Box 5.2 and consider the impact that the number of categories of a variable has on the IQV. What would happen to the Berkeley case in 1994 if Asians were broken down into two categories with 20 percent in one and 19 percent in the other? (To answer this question you will need to recalculate the IQV for 1994 with these new data.)*

## Statistics in Practice: Diversity in U.S. Society

According to demographers' projections, by the middle of the next century the United States will no longer be a predominantly white society. The combined population of the four largest minority groups—African Americans, Asian Americans, Hispanic Americans, and Native Americans—reached an estimated 64.3 million in 1993.[4] If the current trends of new immigration and higher birth rates continue, the United States will be transformed into 'a global society' in which nearly half of all Americans will be from today's racial and ethnic minorities.[5] The arrival of millions of immigrants during the 1980s increased the diversity of many states and cities. Moreover, some cities and states attracted more new immigrants than others. Demographers call it chain migration: "Migrants don't go randomly to various spots in the USA. They use friends, neighbors and relatives to locate their new residences."[6] The immigrant meccas also changed: as many immigrants entered California during the 1980s as entered New York State from 1901 to 1910.[7]

How do you compare the amount of diversity in different cities or states? Diversity is a characteristic of a population many of us can sense intuitively. For example, the ethnic diversity of a large city is seen in the many members of various groups encountered when walking down its streets or traveling through its neighborhoods.[8]

[4]*Milwaukee Journal,* June 12, 1993.

[5]*New York Times,* November 16, 1993.

[6]*USA Today,* June 9, 1993.

[7]*New York Times,* November 16, 1993.

[8]Michael White, "Segregation and Diversity Measures in Population Distribution," *Population Index,* Vol. 52, No. 2, 198–221.

### Box 5.2  Statistics in Practice: Diversity at Berkeley Through the Years*

"BERKELEY, Calf.—The photograph in Sproul Hall of the 10 Cal 'yell leaders' from the early 1960's, in their Bermuda shorts and letter sweaters, leaps out like an artifact from an ancient civilization. They are all fresh-faced, and in a way that is unimaginable now, they are all white."[†]

On the flagship campus of the University of California system, the center of the affirmative action debate in higher education today, the ducktails and bouffant hairdos of those 1960s cheerleaders seems indeed out of date. The University of California's Berkeley campus was among the first of the nation's leading universities to embrace elements of affirmative action in its admission policies and now boasts that it has one of the most diverse campuses in the United States.

The following pie charts show the racial and ethnic breakdown of undergraduates at U.C. Berkeley for 1984 and 1994. The IQVs were calculated using the percentage distribution (as shown in the pie charts) for race and ethnicity for each year. The IQVs illustrate the changes in Berkeley's student body from mostly white in 1984 to one of the most diverse campuses in the United States.

Figure 5.4  **Racial/Ethnic Composition of Student Body at U.C. Berkeley, 1984 and 1994**

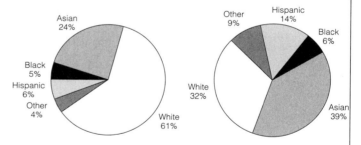

1984: Mostly White          1994: A Diverse Student Body

*Source: New York Times,* June 4, 1995. Copyright © 1995 by The New York Times Co. Reprinted by permission.

$$
IQV_{1984} = \frac{\begin{array}{c}(61 \times 24) + (61 \times 5) + (61 \times 6) + (61 \times 4) + (24 \times 5)\\ + (24 \times 6) + (24 \times 4) + (5 \times 6) + (5 \times 4) + (6 \times 4)\end{array}}{\frac{5(5-1)}{2}\left(\frac{100}{5}\right)^2}
$$

$$
= \frac{2,813}{4,000} = 0.70
$$

$$IQV_{1994} = \frac{\begin{array}{c}(32 \times 39) + (32 \times 6) + (32 \times 14) + (32 \times 9) + (39 \times 6) \\ + (39 \times 14) + (39 \times 9) + (6 \times 14) + (6 \times 9) + (14 \times 9)\end{array}}{\frac{5(5-1)}{2}\left(\frac{100}{5}\right)^2}$$

$$= \frac{3,571}{4,000} = 0.89$$

*Adapted from the *New York Times*, June 4, 1995.
†Ibid.

We can use the IQV to measure the amount of diversity in different states. Table 5.3 displays population by race and ethnicity for all fifty states. Based on the data in Table 5.3 and using formula 5.1 as in our earlier example, we have calculated the IQV for each state in Table 5.4.

Table 5.3  **Population by Race and Ethnicity for the Fifty States**

| State | White | Black | Native American, Eskimo, or Aleut | Asian or Pacific Islander | Other | Hispanic |
|---|---|---|---|---|---|---|
| Alabama | 2,960,167 | 1,017,713 | 16,221 | 21,217 | 640 | 24,629 |
| Alaska | 406,722 | 21,799 | 84,594 | 18,730 | 395 | 17,803 |
| Arizona | 2,626,185 | 104,809 | 190,091 | 51,530 | 4,275 | 688,338 |
| Arkansas | 1,933,082 | 372,762 | 12,393 | 12,144 | 468 | 19,876 |
| California | 17,029,126 | 2,092,446 | 184,065 | 2,710,353 | 56,093 | 7,687,938 |
| Colorado | 2,658,945 | 128,057 | 22,068 | 56,773 | 4,249 | 424,302 |
| Connecticut | 2,754,184 | 260,840 | 5,950 | 49,114 | 3,912 | 213,116 |
| Delaware | 528,092 | 111,011 | 1,938 | 8,854 | 453 | 15,820 |
| Florida | 9,475,326 | 1,701,103 | 32,910 | 146,159 | 8,285 | 1,574,143 |
| Georgia | 4,543,425 | 1,737,165 | 12,621 | 73,725 | 2,358 | 108,922 |
| Hawaii | 347,644 | 25,916 | 4,001 | 646,404 | 2,874 | 81,390 |
| Idaho | 928,661 | 3,211 | 12,418 | 9,053 | 479 | 52,927 |
| Illinois | 8,550,208 | 1,673,703 | 18,213 | 275,568 | 8,464 | 904,446 |
| Indiana | 4,965,242 | 428,612 | 11,999 | 36,618 | 2,900 | 98,788 |
| Iowa | 2,663,840 | 47,493 | 6,765 | 24,926 | 1,084 | 32,647 |
| Kansas | 2,190,524 | 140,761 | 20,363 | 30,814 | 1,442 | 93,670 |

(table continued on next page)

Table 5.3 **Continued**

| State | White | Black | Native American, Eskimo, or Aleut | Asian or Pacific Islander | Other | Hispanic |
|-------|-------|-------|-----------------------------------|---------------------------|-------|----------|
| Kentucky | 3,378,022 | 261,360 | 5,518 | 17,201 | 1,211 | 21,984 |
| Louisiana | 2,776,022 | 1,291,470 | 17,539 | 39,302 | 2,596 | 93,044 |
| Maine | 1,203,357 | 4,937 | 5,898 | 6,505 | 402 | 6,829 |
| Maryland | 3,326,109 | 1,177,823 | 12,143 | 136,619 | 3,672 | 125,102 |
| Massachusetts | 5,280,292 | 274,464 | 10,545 | 140,338 | 23,237 | 287,549 |
| Michigan | 7,649,951 | 1,282,744 | 52,571 | 102,506 | 5,929 | 201,596 |
| Minnesota | 4,101,266 | 93,040 | 48,251 | 76,229 | 2,429 | 53,884 |
| Mississippi | 1,624,198 | 911,891 | 8,316 | 12,543 | 337 | 15,931 |
| Missouri | 4,448,465 | 545,527 | 18,873 | 40,087 | 2,419 | 61,702 |
| Montana | 733,878 | 2,242 | 46,475 | 4,123 | 173 | 12,174 |
| Nebraska | 1,460,095 | 56,711 | 11,719 | 12,026 | 865 | 36,969 |
| Nevada | 946,357 | 76,503 | 17,480 | 35,897 | 1,177 | 124,419 |
| New Hampshire | 1,079,484 | 6,749 | 2,042 | 9,197 | 447 | 11,333 |
| New Jersey | 5,718,966 | 984,845 | 12,490 | 264,341 | 9,685 | 739,861 |
| New Mexico | 764,164 | 27,642 | 128,068 | 12,587 | 3,384 | 579,224 |
| New York | 12,460,189 | 2,569,126 | 50,540 | 666,843 | 29,731 | 2,214,026 |
| North Carolina | 4,971,127 | 1,449,142 | 78,930 | 50,593 | 2,119 | 76,726 |
| North Dakota | 601,592 | 3,451 | 25,590 | 3,345 | 157 | 4,665 |
| Ohio | 9,444,622 | 1,147,440 | 19,137 | 89,195 | 7,025 | 139,696 |
| Oklahoma | 2,547,588 | 231,462 | 246,631 | 32,366 | 1,378 | 86,160 |
| Oregon | 2,579,732 | 44,982 | 35,749 | 67,422 | 1,729 | 112,707 |
| Pennsylvania | 10,422,058 | 1,072,459 | 13,505 | 134,056 | 7,303 | 232,262 |
| Rhode Island | 896,109 | 34,283 | 3,629 | 17,584 | 6,107 | 45,752 |
| South Carolina | 2,390,056 | 1,035,947 | 8,004 | 21,304 | 841 | 30,551 |
| South Dakota | 634,788 | 3,176 | 49,648 | 3,013 | 127 | 5,242 |
| Tennessee | 4,027,631 | 774,925 | 9,685 | 30,938 | 1,265 | 32,741 |
| Texas | 10,291,680 | 1,976,360 | 52,803 | 303,825 | 21,937 | 4,339,905 |
| Utah | 1,571,254 | 10,868 | 22,748 | 32,490 | 893 | 84,597 |
| Vermont | 552,184 | 1,868 | 1,651 | 3,159 | 235 | 3,661 |
| Virginia | 4,701,650 | 1,153,133 | 14,347 | 154,183 | 3,757 | 160,288 |
| Washington | 4,221,622 | 146,000 | 76,397 | 203,668 | 4,435 | 214,570 |
| West Virginia | 1,718,896 | 55,986 | 2,363 | 7,252 | 491 | 8,489 |
| Wisconsin | 4,464,677 | 241,697 | 37,769 | 52,284 | 2,148 | 93,194 |
| Wyoming | 412,711 | 3,426 | 622 | 2,622 | 221 | 33,986 |

*Source:* U.S. Bureau of the Census. 1990. General population characteristics. *Current Population Reports,* ser. P-25. Washington, DC: GPO.

Table 5.4 **Racial and Ethnic Diversity as Measured by the IQVs for Fifty States**

| State | IQV | State | IQV | State | IQV |
|---|---|---|---|---|---|
| New Mexico | 0.70 | Virginia | 0.46 | Oregon | 0.21 |
| California | 0.69 | Delaware | 0.43 | South Dakota | 0.20 |
| Hawaii | 0.66 | Nevada | 0.43 | Kentucky | 0.19 |
| Texas | 0.66 | Oklahoma | 0.40 | Wisconsin | 0.19 |
| New York | 0.58 | Colorado | 0.39 | Nebraska | 0.18 |
| Louisiana | 0.57 | Michigan | 0.36 | Utah | 0.18 |
| Mississippi | 0.57 | Tennessee | 0.35 | Idaho | 0.17 |
| Maryland | 0.54 | Arkansas | 0.35 | Montana | 0.17 |
| Arizona | 0.53 | Connecticut | 0.34 | Minnesota | 0.14 |
| South Carolina | 0.53 | Washington | 0.29 | Wyoming | 0.13 |
| Florida | 0.52 | Missouri | 0.28 | North Dakota | 0.12 |
| Georgia | 0.52 | Ohio | 0.28 | West Virginia | 0.10 |
| New Jersey | 0.51 | Massachusetts | 0.27 | Iowa | 0.09 |
| Illinois | 0.49 | Pennsylvania | 0.26 | Maine | 0.06 |
| Alabama | 0.48 | Kansas | 0.25 | New Hampshire | 0.06 |
| Alaska | 0.48 | Indiana | 0.23 | Vermont | 0.04 |
| North Carolina | 0.47 | Rhode Island | 0.23 | | |

The advantage of using a single number to express diversity is demonstrated in Figure 5.5, which depicts the regional variations in diversity as expressed by the IQVs from Table 5.4. Figure 5.5 shows the wide variation in racial/ethnic diversity that exists in the United States. Notice that New Mexico, with an IQV of 0.70, is the most diverse state. At the other extreme, Vermont, where the majority of the population is white, has an IQV of 0.04 and is the most homogeneous of the states.

> **Learning Check.** *What regional variations in racial/ethnic diversity are depicted in Figure 5.5? Can you think of at least two explanations for these patterns?*

Figure 5.5 **Racial/Ethnic Diversity in the United States, 1990 IQV**

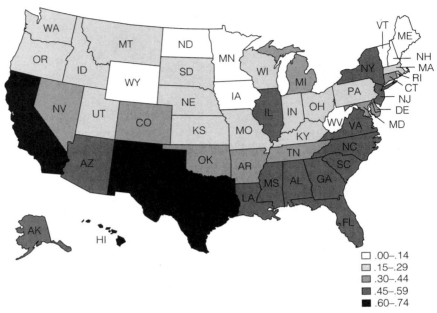

.00–.14
.15–.29
.30–.44
.45–.59
.60–.74

*Source:* U.S. Bureau of the Census, 1990.

## The Range

The simplest and most straightforward measure of variation is the **range**, which measures variation in interval-ratio variables. It is the difference between the highest (maximum) and lowest (minimum) scores in the distribution:

Range = highest score – lowest score

In the 1994 GSS, the oldest person included in the study was 84 years old and the youngest was 20. Thus, the range was 84 – 20, or 64 years.

---

*Range* A measure of variation in interval-ratio variables. It is the difference between the highest (maximum) and lowest (minimum) scores in the distribution.

---

The range can also be calculated on percentages. For example, since the 1980s, relatively large communities of the elderly have become noticeable, not just in the traditional retirement meccas of the Sun Belt,

### Box 5.3 Using the IQV: American Attitudes About Spending

As part of the 1994 General Social Survey, respondents were asked a set of ten questions about government spending. For each question, the respondent was given a particular issue and asked whether the country was spending too much, too little, or about the right amount on that issue. The ten issues were the environment, space exploration, health care, the problems of big cities, welfare, crime, drugs, education, defense, and improving the conditions of blacks.

Using the frequency distribution for each variable, we can calculate the IQV for each issue.

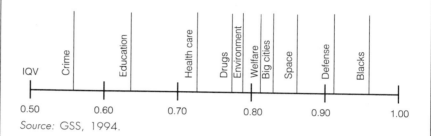

Source: GSS, 1994.

As you can tell from this graphic, Americans have differing opinions about spending. However, the amount of variation differs from issue to issue, and the IQV helps us to see this. For example, the IQVs for crime and education are a relatively low 0.56 and 0.64, respectively. A strong majority of Americans (72% for education and 77% for crime) feel that we are spending too little on these issues. On the other end of the IQV spectrum, we have such issues as defense and improving the conditions of blacks. The IQV for defense is 0.92. The IQV for spending on blacks is 0.96. This implies that Americans are divided in their thinking: some Americans think that we're spending too little, some think we're spending too much, and some think we're spending the right amount.

Does controversy exist where you expect it would exist?

but also in the Ozarks of Arkansas and the mountains of Colorado and Montana. The number of elderly persons *increased* in every state during the 1980s. Table 5.5 displays the percent increase in the elderly population from the 1980s to the 1990s by region and by state.[9] What

[9]The percent increase in the population 65 years and over for each state and region was obtained by the following formula:

$$\text{Percent increase} = \left( \frac{1990 \text{ population} - 1980 \text{ population}}{1980 \text{ population}} \right) 100$$

Table 5.5  **Percent Increase in the Population 65 Years and Over by Region, Division, and State, 1980 to 1990**

| Region, Division, and State | Percentages (%) | Region, Division, and State | Percentages (%) |
|---|---|---|---|
| UNITED STATES | 22.3 | SOUTH (cont.) | |
| | | South Atlantic (cont.) | |
| NORTHEAST | 15.2 | Virginia | 31.5 |
| New England | 16.4 | West Virginia | 13.0 |
| Maine | 15.9 | North Carolina | 33.3 |
| Vermont | 13.7 | South Carolina | 38.1 |
| New Hampshire | 21.4 | Georgia | 26.6 |
| Massachusetts | 12.8 | Florida | 40.4 |
| Rhode Island | 18.6 | | |
| Connecticut | 22.2 | East South Central | 16.5 |
| | | Kentucky | 13.9 |
| Middle Atlantic | 14.8 | Tennessee | 19.6 |
| New York | 9.4 | Alabama | 18.9 |
| New Jersey | 20.0 | Mississippi | 11.0 |
| Pennsylvania | 19.5 | | |
| | | West South Central | 20.1 |
| MIDWEST | 15.8 | Arkansas | 12.0 |
| East North Central | 17.9 | Louisiana | 16.0 |
| Ohio | 20.3 | Oklahoma | 12.8 |
| Indiana | 18.9 | Texas | 25.2 |
| Illinois | 13.8 | | |
| Michigan | 21.5 | WEST | 34.3 |
| Wisconsin | 15.4 | Mountain | 43.6 |
| | | Montana | 25.9 |
| West North Central | 11.4 | Idaho | 29.4 |
| Minnesota | 14.0 | Wyoming | 27.0 |
| Iowa | 9.9 | Colorado | 33.2 |
| Missouri | 10.7 | New Mexico | 40.7 |
| North Dakota | 13.2 | Arizona | 55.8 |
| South Dakota | 12.4 | Utah | 37.3 |
| Nebraska | 8.5 | Nevada | 94.1 |
| Kansas | 11.9 | | |
| | | Pacific | 31.3 |
| SOUTH | 26.3 | Washington | 33.3 |
| South Atlantic | 33.6 | Oregon | 29.0 |
| Delaware | 36.4 | California | 29.9 |
| Maryland | 30.8 | Alaska | 93.7 |
| Washington, DC | 4.8 | Hawaii | 64.2 |

*Source:* U.S. Bureau of the Census. 1992. "Sixty-five plus in America." *Current Population Reports.* Special studies P23-178. Table 5-1.

is the range in the percent increase in state elderly population for the United States? To find the range in a distribution simply pick out the highest and lowest scores in the distribution and subtract. Nevada has the highest percent increase, with 94.1 percent, and the District of Columbia has the lowest increase, with 4.8 percent. The range is therefore 94.1 percent − 4.8 percent, or 89.3 percent.

Although the range is simple and quick to calculate it is a rather crude measure because it is based on only the lowest and highest scores. These two scores might be extreme and rather atypical, which might make the range a misleading indicator of the variation in the distribution. For instance, notice that among the fifty states and the District of Columbia listed in Table 5.5, no other has a percent increase nearly as low as the District of Columbia's and only Alaska has a percent increase nearly as high as Nevada's. The range of 89.3 percent does not give us information about the variation in states between the District of Columbia and Alaska.

> **Learning Check.** *Why can't we use the range to describe diversity in nominal variables? The range can be used to describe diversity in ordinal variables (for example, we can say that responses to a question ranged from "somewhat satisfied" to "very dissatisfied"), but it has no quantitative meaning. Why not?*

## The Interquartile Range: Increases in Elderly Populations

To remedy this limitation we can employ an alternative to the range—the *interquartile range (IQR)*. The **interquartile range**, a measure of variation for interval-ratio variables, is the width of the middle 50 percent of the distribution. It is defined as the difference between the lower and upper quartiles ($Q1$ and $Q3$).

$$IQR = Q3 - Q1$$

Recall that the first quartile ($Q1$) is the 25th percentile (p. 148), the point at which 25 percent of the cases fall below it and 75 percent above it. The third quartile ($Q3$) is the 75th percentile, the point at which 75 percent of the cases fall below it and 25 percent above it. The interquartile range, therefore, defines variation for the middle 50 percent of the cases. Like the range, the interquartile range is based on only two scores. However, because it is based on intermediate rather than on the most extreme scores in the distribution, it avoids some of the instability associated with the range.

These are the steps for calculating the IQR:

1. To find Q1 and Q3 order the scores in the distribution either from the highest to the lowest score or vice versa. Table 5.6 presents the data of Table 5.5 arranged in order from Nevada, with the highest percent increase (94.1%), listed first, to the District of Columbia, with the lowest percent increase (4.8%), listed last.

2. Next, identify the first and third quartiles. That means we have to identify the percent increase in the elderly population associated with the state that divides the distribution so that 25 percent of the states are below it and 75 percent of the states are above it (Q1, or the 25th percentile). Next, we have to identify the state that divides the distribution in such a way that 75 percent of the states are below it and 25 percent of the states are above it (Q3, or the 75th percentile). To find Q1 we then multiply N by .25:

$$(N) (.25) = (51) (.25) = 12.75$$

Table 5.6 **Percent Increase of the Population 65 Years and Over, 1980 to 1990, by State, Ordered from Lowest to Highest**

| State | Percentages (%) | State | Percentages (%) | State | Percentages (%) |
|---|---|---|---|---|---|
| Nevada | 94.1 | Wyoming | 27.0 | Minnesota | 14.0 |
| Alaska | 93.7 | Georgia | 26.6 | Kentucky | 13.9 |
| Hawaii | 64.2 | Montana | 25.9 | Illinois | 13.8 |
| Arizona | 55.8 | Texas | 25.2 | Vermont | 13.7 |
| New Mexico | 40.7 | Connecticut | 22.2 | North Dakota | 13.2 |
| Florida | 40.4 | Michigan | 21.5 | West Virginia | 13.0 |
| South Carolina | 38.1 | New Hampshire | 21.4 | Massachusetts | 12.8 |
| Utah | 37.3 | Ohio | 20.3 | Oklahoma | 12.8 |
| Delaware | 36.4 | New Jersey | 20.0 | South Dakota | 12.4 |
| North Carolina | 33.3 | Tennessee | 19.6 | Arkansas | 12.0 |
| Washington | 33.3 | Pennsylvania | 19.5 | Kansas | 11.9 |
| Colorado | 33.2 | Indiana | 18.9 | Mississippi | 11.0 |
| Virginia | 31.5 | Alabama | 18.9 | Missouri | 10.7 |
| Maryland | 30.8 | Rhode Island | 18.6 | Iowa | 9.9 |
| California | 29.9 | Louisiana | 16.0 | New York | 9.4 |
| Idaho | 29.4 | Maine | 15.9 | Nebraska | 8.5 |
| Oregon | 29.0 | Wisconsin | 15.4 | Washington, DC | 4.8 |

*Interquartile Range (IQR)*   The width of the middle 50 percent of the distribution. It is defined as the difference between the lower and upper quartiles ($Q1$ and $Q3$).

The first quartile falls between the 12th and 13th states. Counting up from the bottom, the 12th state is West Virginia and the percent increase associated with it is 13.0. The 13th state is North Dakota with a percent increase of 13.2. To find the first quartile we take the average of 13.0 and 13.2. Therefore, $(13.0 + 13.2) \div 2 = 13.1$ is the first quartile: $Q1 = 13.1$.

To find $Q3$ we multiply $N$ by .75:

$(N)(.75) = (51)(.75) = 38.25$

The third quartile falls between the 38th and 39th states. Counting up from the bottom, the 38th state is Maryland and the percent increase associated with it is 30.8. The 39th state is Virginia, with a percent increase of 31.5. To find the third quartile we take the average of 30.8 and 31.5. Therefore, $(30.8 + 31.5) \div 2 = 31.1$ is the third quartile: $Q3 = 31.1$.

3. We are now ready to find the interquartile range:

   IQR = $Q3 - Q1 = 31.1 - 13.1 = 18.0$

The interquartile range of percent increase in the elderly population is 18 percent.

Notice that the IQR gives us better information than the range. The range gave us an 89.3 percent spread from 94.1 percent to 4.8 percent, but the IQR tells us that half the states are clustered between 31.1 and 13.1—a much narrower spread. The extreme scores represented by Nevada (94.1%) and the District of Columbia (4.8%) have no effect on the IQR because they fall at the extreme ends of the distribution.

> **Learning Check.**   *Why is the IQR better than the range as a measure of variability, especially when there are extreme scores in the distribution? To answer this question you may want to examine Figure 5.6.*

Figure 5.6  **The Range vs. the Interquartile Range: Childbearing among Two Groups of Women**

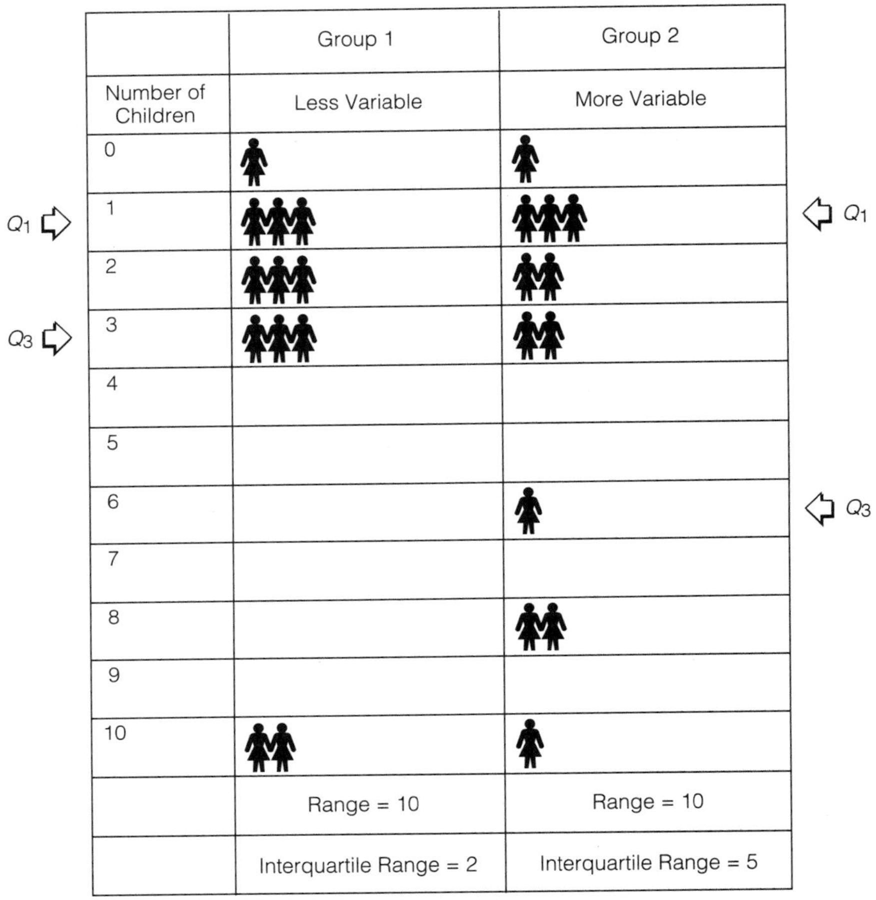

| Number of Children | Group 1 Less Variable | Group 2 More Variable |
|---|---|---|
| 0 | 👤 | 👤 |
| 1 | 👤👤👤 | 👤👤👤 |
| 2 | 👤👤👤 | 👤👤 |
| 3 | 👤👤👤 | 👤👤 |
| 4 | | |
| 5 | | |
| 6 | | 👤 |
| 7 | | |
| 8 | | 👤👤 |
| 9 | | |
| 10 | 👤👤 | 👤 |
| | Range = 10 | Range = 10 |
| | Interquartile Range = 2 | Interquartile Range = 5 |

$Q_1$ ⇨ (at row 1, Group 1)

$Q_3$ ⇨ (at row 3, Group 1)

⇦ $Q_1$ (at row 1, Group 2)

⇦ $Q_3$ (at row 6, Group 2)

## The Box Plot

A graphic device called the *box plot* can visually present the range, the interquartile range, the median, the lowest (minimum) score, and the highest (maximum) score. The box plot provides us with a way to visually examine the center, the variation, and the shape of distributions of interval-ratio variables.

Figure 5.7 is a box plot of the distribution of the percent increase in the elderly population in the 1980s displayed in Table 5.6. To construct the box plot in Figure 5.7 we used the lowest and highest values

Figure 5.7    **Box Plot of the Distribution of the Percent Increase in Elderly Population, 1980s**

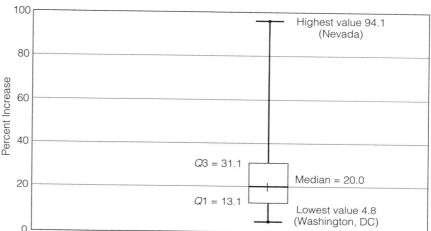

in the distribution, the upper and lower quartiles, and the median. We can easily draw a box plot by hand following these instructions:

1. Draw a box between the lower and upper quartiles.

2. Draw a solid line within the box to mark the median.

3. Draw vertical lines (called whiskers) outside the box, extending to the lowest and highest values.

What can we learn from creating a box plot? We can obtain a visual impression of the following properties: First, the center of the distribution is easily identified by the solid line inside the box. Second, since the box is drawn between the lower and upper quartiles, the interquartile range is reflected in the height of the box. Similarly, the length of the vertical lines drawn outside the box (on both ends) represents the range of the distribution. Both the interquartile range and the range give us a visual impression of the spread in the distribution. Finally, the relative position of the box and/or the position of the median within the box tells us whether the distribution is symmetrical or skewed. A perfectly symmetrical distribution would have the box at the center of the range as well as the median in the center of the box. When the distribution departs from symmetry, the box and/or the median will not be centered; it will be closer to the lower quartile when there are more cases with lower scores or to the upper quartile when there are more cases with higher scores.

Box plots are particularly useful for comparing distributions. To demonstrate box plots that are shaped quite differently, in Figure 5.8 we have used the data on the percent increase in the elderly population (Table 5.5) to compare the pattern of change occurring between 1980 and 1990 in the northeastern and western regions of the United States. As you can see, the box plots differ from each other considerably. What can you learn from comparing the box plots for the two regions? First, the positions of the medians highlight the dramatic increase in the elderly population in the western United States. While the Northeast (median = 18.6%) has experienced a steady rise in its elderly population, the West is showing a much higher percent increase (median = 33.3%). Second, both the range (illustrated by the position of the whiskers in each box plot) and the interquartile range (illustrated by the height of the box) are much wider in the West (range = 68.2%; IQR = 19.05%) than in the Northeast (range = 12.8%; IQR = 6.5%), indicating that there is more variability among states in the West than among those in the Northeast. Finally, the relative positions of the boxes tell us something about the different shapes of these distributions. Because its box is at about the center of its range, the Northeast distribution is almost symmetrical. In contrast, with its box off center and closer to the lower end of the distribution, the distribution of percent change in the elderly population for the western states is positively skewed. (In comparing these two distributions notice that although it is positively skewed, the lowest values in the western distribution are higher than the highest value in the northeastern distribution.)

## The Variance and the Standard Deviation: Changes in the Nursing Home Population

The elderly population in the United States today is ten times as large as in 1900 and is projected to more than double from 1990 to 2030. The pace and direction of these demographic changes will create compelling social, economic, and ethical choices for individuals, families, and governments, especially regarding the living arrangements of the elderly.[10]

Most of the elderly live in households rather than in nursing homes, but the likelihood of living in a nursing home increases with

[10]U.S. Bureau of the Census, 1992. "Sixty-five plus in America." *Current Population Reports.* Special studies, p. 2–19.

Figure 5.8    **Box Plots of the Percent Increase in the Elderly Population (1980s) for Northeast and West Regions**

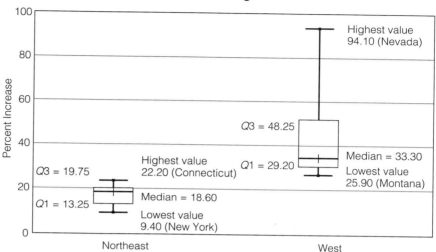

age. Table 5.7 presents the percent change in the nursing home population for all regions of the United States. These percent changes were calculated by the Census Bureau using the following formula:

$$\text{Percent change} = \frac{1990 \text{ population} - 1980 \text{ population}}{1980 \text{ population}} (100)$$

For example, the nursing home population in the Pacific region was 182,791 in 1980. In 1990 the nursing home population increased to 203,829. Therefore, the percent change from 1980 to 1990 is

$$\text{Percent change} = \frac{203,829 - 182,791}{182,791} (100) = 11.51$$

Table 5.7 shows that between 1980 and 1990 the size of the nursing home population in the United States increased by an average of 26.35 percent.[11] But this average increase does not inform us about the regional variation in the nursing home population. For example, do the New England states show a smaller-than-average increase because of the outmigration of the elderly population to the warmer climate of the Sun Belt states? Is the increase higher in the South because of the immigration of the elderly?

---

[11]Because the percent changes in the nursing home population were computed for aggregate units (region), the mean increase of 26.35 percent in the nursing home population is the *unweighted* average of the regional increases.

Table 5.7   **Percent Change in the Nursing Home Population from 1980 to 1990 by Region**

| Region | Percentages (%) |
|---|---|
| Pacific | 11.51 |
| West North Central | 12.41 |
| New England | 12.48 |
| East North Central | 16.87 |
| West South Central | 18.00 |
| Middle Atlantic | 26.59 |
| East South Central | 33.54 |
| Mountain | 39.66 |
| South Atlantic | 66.09 |
| Mean ($\bar{Y}$) | 26.35 |

Even though it is important to know the average percent increase for the nation as a whole, you may also want to know whether regional increases differ from the national average. If the regional increases are close to the national average, the figures will cluster around the mean, but if the regional increases deviate much from the national average, they will be widely dispersed around the mean.

Let's look at the percent change in the nursing home population for all regions in the United States. The data are presented in Table 5.7. Note that there is considerable regional variation. The percent change ranges from 66.09 percent in the South Atlantic states to 11.51 percent in the Pacific states, so the range is 54.58 percent (66.09% − 11.51% = 54.58%). Moreover, except for the Middle Atlantic states, most of the regions deviate considerably from the national average of 26.35 percent. But how large are these deviations on the average? We want a measure that will give us information about the overall variations among all regions in the United States and, unlike the range or the interquartile range, will not be based on only two scores.

Such a measure will reflect how much, on the average, each score in the distribution deviates from some central point, like the mean. We use the mean as this reference point rather than other kinds of averages, like the mode or median, because the mean is based on all the scores in the distribution. Therefore, it is more useful as a basis from which to calculate average deviation. The sensitivity of the mean to extreme values carries over to the calculation of the average deviation, which is based on the mean. Another reason for using the mean as a reference point is that more advanced measures of variation require the use of algebraic properties that can be assumed only by using the arithmetic mean.

The *variance* and the *standard deviation* are two closely related measures of variation that increase or decrease based on how closely the scores cluster around the mean. The **variance** provides a measure of the average of the squared deviations from the center (mean) of the distribution, and the **standard deviation** is equal to the square root of the variance. Both measure variability in interval-ratio variables.

---

*Variance*   A measure of variation for interval-ratio variables; it is the average of the squared deviations from the mean.

*Standard Deviation*   A measure of variation for interval-ratio variables; it is equal to the square root of the variance.

---

## Calculating the Deviation from the Mean

Consider again the distribution of the percent change in the nursing home population for the nine regions of the United States. Because we want to calculate the average difference of all the regions from the national average (the mean), it makes sense to first look at the difference between each region and the mean. This difference is called a *deviation from the mean* and it is symbolized as $(Y - \overline{Y})$. The sum of these deviations can be symbolized as $\Sigma(Y - \overline{Y})$. The calculations of these deviations for each region are displayed in Table 5.8 and Figure 5.9. We also summed these deviations. Note that each region has either a positive or a negative deviation score. The deviation is positive when the percent increase in the nursing home population is above the mean. It is negative when the percent increase is below the mean. Thus, for example, New England's deviation score of −13.87 means that its percent change in the nursing home population was 13.87 below the mean.

You may wonder if we could calculate the average of these deviations by simply adding up the deviations and dividing them? Unfortunately we *cannot* because the sum of the deviations of scores from the mean is always zero, or algebraically $\Sigma(Y - \overline{Y}) = 0$. In other words, if we were to subtract the mean from each score and then add up all the deviations as we did in Table 5.8, the sum would be zero, which in turn would cause the average deviation (that is, average difference)

Table 5.8 **Percent Change in the Nursing Home Population from 1980 to 1990 by Region and Deviations from the Mean**

| Region | Percentages (%) | $Y - \bar{Y}$ |
|---|---|---|
| Pacific | 11.51 | $11.51 - 26.35 = -14.84$ |
| West North Central | 12.41 | $12.41 - 26.35 = -13.94$ |
| New England | 12.48 | $12.48 - 26.35 = -13.87$ |
| East North Central | 16.87 | $16.87 - 26.35 = -9.48$ |
| West South Central | 18.00 | $18.00 - 26.35 = -8.35$ |
| Middle Atlantic | 26.59 | $26.59 - 26.35 = 0.24$ |
| East South Central | 33.54 | $33.54 - 26.35 = 7.19$ |
| Mountain | 39.66 | $39.66 - 26.35 = 13.31$ |
| South Atlantic | 66.09 | $66.09 - 26.35 = 39.74$ |
| | $\sum Y = 237.15$ | $\sum(Y - \bar{Y}) = 0.00$ |

$$\text{Mean} = \bar{Y} = \frac{\sum Y}{N} = \frac{237.15}{9} = 26.35$$

Figure 5.9 **Illustrating Deviations from the Mean**

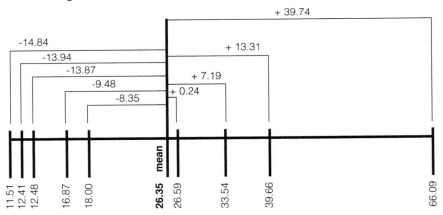

$$-14.84 + -13.94 + -13.87 + -9.48 + -8.35 + 0.24 + 7.19 + 13.31 + 39.74 = 0$$

to compute to zero. This is always true because the mean is the center of gravity of the distribution.

Mathematically, we can overcome this problem by either (1) ignoring the plus and minus signs, using instead the absolute values of the deviations, or (2) squaring the deviations—that is, multiplying each deviation by itself—to get rid of the negative sign. Since absolute values are difficult to work with mathematically, the latter method is used to compensate for the problem.

Table 5.9 presents the same information included in Table 5.8, but here we squared the actual deviations from the mean and added together the squares. The sum of the squared deviations is symbolized as $\Sigma(Y - \bar{Y})^2$. Note that by squaring the deviations we end up with a sum representing the deviation from the mean, which is positive. (Note that this sum will equal zero if all the cases have the same value as the mean case.) In our example, this sum is $\Sigma(Y - \bar{Y})^2 = 2,574.71$.

---

**Learning Check.** *Examine Table 5.9 again and note the disproportional contribution of the South Atlantic region to the sum of the squared deviations from the mean (it actually accounts for about 60% of the sum of squares). Can you explain why? Hint: It has something to do with the sensitivity of the mean to extreme values.*

---

## Calculating the Variance and the Standard Deviation

Remember that we are interested in the *average* of the squared deviations from the mean. Therefore, we need to divide the sum of the

Table 5.9 **Percent Change in the Nursing Home Population from 1980 to 1990 by Region and Deviations and Squared Deviations from the Mean**

| Region | Percentages (%) | $Y - \bar{Y}$ | $(Y - \bar{Y})^2$ |
|---|---|---|---|
| Pacific | 11.51 | $11.51 - 26.35 = -14.84$ | 220.23 |
| West North Central | 12.41 | $12.41 - 26.35 = -13.94$ | 194.32 |
| New England | 12.48 | $12.48 - 26.35 = -13.87$ | 192.38 |
| East North Central | 16.87 | $16.87 - 26.35 = -9.48$ | 89.87 |
| West South Central | 18.00 | $18.00 - 26.35 = -8.35$ | 69.72 |
| Middle Atlantic | 26.59 | $26.59 - 26.35 = 0.24$ | .06 |
| East South Central | 33.54 | $33.54 - 26.35 = 7.19$ | 51.70 |
| Mountain | 39.66 | $39.66 - 26.35 = 13.31$ | 177.16 |
| South Atlantic | 66.09 | $66.09 - 26.35 = 39.74$ | 1,579.27 |
| $\Sigma Y = 237.15$ | | $\Sigma(Y - \bar{Y}) = 0.00$ | $\Sigma(Y - \bar{Y})^2 = 2,574.71$ |

$$\text{Mean} = \bar{Y} = \frac{\Sigma Y}{N} = \frac{237.15}{9} = 26.35$$

squared deviations by the number of scores ($N$) in the distribution. However, unlike with the calculation of the mean, we will use $N - 1$ rather than $N$ in the denominator. Continuing with our illustration in Table 5.9, we divide the sum of the squared deviations by the number of regions minus 1:

$$\frac{\sum (Y - \overline{Y})^2}{N - 1} = \frac{2,574.71}{8} = 321.84$$

The average of the squared deviations from the mean we just calculated is known as the *variance*. The variance is symbolized as $S_Y^2$. In our example, the variance for the percent change in the nursing home population is $S_Y^2 = 321.84$.

The formula for the variance is

$$S_Y^2 = \frac{\sum (Y - \overline{Y})^2}{N - 1} \tag{5.2}$$

where

$S_Y^2$ = the variance

$Y - \overline{Y}$ = the deviations from the mean

$\Sigma(Y - \overline{Y})^2$ = the sum of the squared deviations from the mean

$N$ = the number of scores

Notice that the formula incorporates all the symbols we defined earlier. This formula means: The variance is equal to the average of the squared deviations from the mean.

Follow these steps to calculate the variance:

1. Calculate the mean, $\overline{Y} = \Sigma Y \div N$.

2. Subtract the mean from each score to find the deviation, $(Y - \overline{Y})$.

3. Square each deviation, $(Y - \overline{Y})^2$.

4. Sum the squared deviations, $\Sigma(Y - \overline{Y})^2$.

5. Divide the sum by $N - 1$, $\Sigma(Y - \overline{Y})^2 \div (N - 1)$.

6. The answer is the variance, $S_Y^2$.

To assure yourself that you understand how to calculate the variance, go back to Table 5.7 and follow this step-by-step procedure for calculating the variance. Now plug the required quantities into formula 5.2.

$$S_Y^2 = \frac{\sum (Y - \overline{Y})^2}{N - 1} = \frac{2,574.71}{8} = 321.84$$

This answer is identical to the one we obtained before.

One problem with the variance is that it is based on squared deviations and therefore is no longer expressed in the original units of measurement. For instance, it is difficult to interpret the variance of 321.84, which represents the distribution of the percent change in the nursing home population, because this figure is expressed in squared percentages. Thus, we often will take the square root of the variance and interpret it instead. This gives us the *standard deviation.*

The standard deviation, symbolized as $S_Y$, is the square root of the variance, or

$$S_Y = \sqrt{S_Y^2}$$

The standard deviation for our example is

$$S_Y = \sqrt{S_Y^2} = \sqrt{321.84} = 17.94$$

The formula for the standard deviation uses the same symbols used in the formula for the variance:

$$S_Y = \sqrt{\frac{\sum (Y - \overline{Y})^2}{N - 1}} \tag{5.3}$$

The formula means: The standard deviation is equal to the square root of the average of the squared deviations from the mean.

The advantage of the standard deviation is that it is measured in the same units as in the original data, unlike the variance. For instance, the standard deviation for our example is 17.94. Because the original data were expressed in percentages, this number is expressed as a percentage as well. In other words, you could say "the standard deviation is 17.94 percent." But what does this mean? The actual number tells us very little by itself, but it allows us to evaluate the relative dispersion of the scores around the mean. In a distribution in which all the scores are identical, the standard deviation is zero. The more the standard deviation departs from zero the more variation there is in the distribution. Therefore, a standard deviation of 17.94 percent means that on average the percent change in the nursing home population for the nine regions of the United States is widely dispersed around the mean of 26.35 percent.

Another way to interpret the standard deviation is to compare it with another distribution. For instance, Table 5.10 and Figure 5.10 display the means and standard deviations for years of education for a sample of middle-class white women and middle-class black males from the GSS. Note that the mean scores are about the same—around twelve years of education. However, the information provided by the standard deviation suggests that the *distribution* of education in the

Table 5.10 **Means and Standard Deviations for Years of Education: Middle-Class White Women and Middle-Class Black Men**

|  | Mean | Standard Deviation |
|---|---|---|
| Middle-class white women (N = 321) | 12.8 | 2.2 |
| Middle-class black men (N = 178) | 12.4 | 3.9 |

*Source:* General Social Survey, 1988 to 1991.

Figure 5.10 **Illustrating the Means and Standard Deviations for Years of Education**

Middle-class white women: mean = 12.8, standard deviation = 2.2

Middle-class black men: mean = 12.4, standard deviation = 3.9

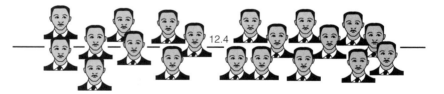

> ***Learning Check.*** *Take time to understand the section on standard deviation and variance. You will see these statistics again and again in more advanced statistical procedures. Although your instructor may require you to memorize the formulas, it is more important for you to understand how to interpret standard deviation and variance and when they can be appropriately used. Many hand calculators and all statistical computer software programs will calculate these measures of diversity for you, but they won't tell you what they mean. Once you understand the meaning behind these measures, the formulas will be easier to remember.*

## Box 5.4 Computational Formula for the Variance and Standard Deviation

We have learned how to use the definitional formulas for the standard deviation and the variance. These formulas are easy to follow conceptually, but they are tedious to compute, especially when working with a large number of scores. The following computational formulas are easier and faster to use and give exactly the same result:

$$S_Y^2 = \left(\frac{\sum Y^2}{N-1}\right) - \left(\frac{N}{N-1}\right)\left(\frac{\sum Y}{N}\right)^2$$

$$S_Y = \sqrt{\left(\frac{\sum Y^2}{N-1}\right) - \left(\frac{N}{N-1}\right)\left(\frac{\sum Y}{N}\right)^2}$$

where

$\sum Y^2$ = the sum of the squared scores (find this by first squaring each score and adding up the squared scores)

$N$ = the number of scores in the distribution

$\left(\frac{\sum Y}{N}\right)^2$ = the sum of the scores divided by $N$ and then squared (find this quantity by first dividing the sum of the scores by $N$ and then squaring the answer, which is equivalent to squaring the mean)

To illustrate how to calculate the variance and standard deviation using the computational formula, we will use data on the suicide rates per 100,000 population in the nine largest cities in the United States. These data were presented earlier in Chapter 4 (p. 140). In the following table we add an additional column to the original data to help us generate the following quantities required by the formula: $\sum Y^2$ and $\sum Y$.

### Suicide Rates per 100,000 Population in the Nine Largest U.S. Cities for 1989

| City | Suicide Rate ($Y$) | $Y^2$ |
|---|---|---|
| New York | 7.44 | 55.35 |
| Los Angeles | 13.38 | 179.02 |
| Chicago | 10.00 | 100.00 |
| Houston | 14.11 | 199.09 |
| Philadelphia | 14.78 | 218.45 |
| San Diego | 12.61 | 159.01 |
| Detroit | 12.26 | 150.31 |
| Dallas | 14.30 | 204.49 |
| Phoenix | 18.37 | 337.46 |
| | $\sum Y = 117.25$ | $\sum Y^2 = 1,603.18$ |

$$\text{Mean} = \overline{Y} = \frac{\sum Y}{N} = \frac{117.25}{9} = 13.03$$

Now plug the results into the formula for the variance:

$$S_Y^2 = \left(\frac{\sum Y^2}{N-1}\right) - \left(\frac{N}{N-1}\right)\left(\frac{\sum Y}{N}\right)^2 = \frac{1,603.18}{8} - \left(\frac{9}{8}\right)\left(\frac{117.25}{9}\right)^2$$

$$= 200.40 - 190.94 = 9.46$$

The standard deviation can be found by taking the square root of the variance. For our example, the standard deviation is

$$S_Y = \sqrt{9.46} = 3.08$$

Hence, for the nine largest cities in the United States, the suicide rate has a mean* of 13.03 suicides per 100,000 population and a standard deviation of 3.08 suicides per 100,000 population.

*Unweighted mean

two groups is not that similar. The relatively low standard of deviation among middle-class white women indicates that this group is relatively homogeneous in its educational level. Conversely, the standard deviation for middle-class black males is larger, suggesting wider dispersion around the mean. A sizable number of middle-class black males have an educational level quite a bit lower than twelve years, but an also notable number have an educational level higher than twelve years.

## Considerations for Choosing a Measure of Variation

So far we have considered five measures of variation: the IQV, the range, the interquartile range, the variance, and the standard deviation. Each measure can represent the degree of variability in a distribution. But which one should we use? There is no simple answer to this question. However, in general, we tend to use only one measure of variation, and the choice of the appropriate one involves a number of considerations. These considerations and how they affect our choice of the appropriate measure are presented in a decision tree shown in Figure 5.11.

Figure 5.11 **How to Choose a Measure of Variation**

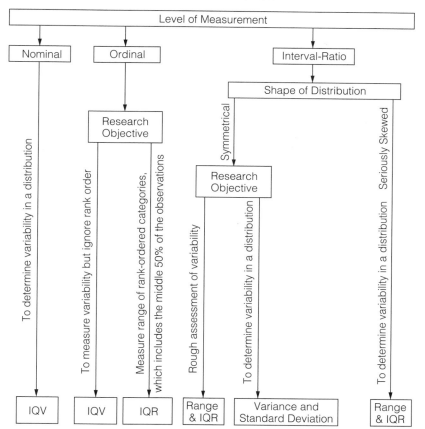

As in choosing a measure of central tendency, one of the most basic considerations in choosing a measure of variability is the variable's level of measurement. Valid use of any of the measures requires that the data are measured at the level appropriate for that measure or higher, as shown in Figure 5.11.

- *Nominal level* With nominal variables, your choice is restricted to the IQV as a measure of variability.

- *Interval-ratio level* For these variables, the variance (or standard deviation), range, or interquartile range can be chosen. Because the range, and to a lesser extent the interquartile range, is based on only two scores in the distribution (and therefore tends to be sensitive if either of the two points is extreme), the variance and/or standard deviation is usually preferred. However, if a distribution is extremely skewed so that the mean is no longer representative of the central tendency in the distribution, the range and the interquartile range can be used. The range and the interquartile range will also be useful when you are reading tables or quickly scanning data to get a rough idea of the extent of dispersion in the distribution.

■ *Ordinal level* The choice of measure of variation for ordinal variables is more problematic. The IQV can be used to reflect variability in distributions of ordinal variables, but because it is not sensitive to the rank-ordering of values implied in ordinal variables, it loses some information. Another possibility is to use the interquartile range. However, the interquartile range relies on distance between two scores to express variation, information that cannot be obtained from ordinally measured scores. The compromise is to use the interquartile range alongside the median, interpreting the interquartile range as the range of rank-ordered values that include the middle 50 percent of the observations.[12]

## Reading the Research Literature: Gender Differences in Caregiving

In Chapter 2 we discussed how frequency distributions are presented in the professional literature. We noted that most statistical tables presented in the social science literature are considerably more complex than those we describe in this book. The same can be said about measures of central tendency and variation. Most research articles use measures of central tendency and variation in ways that go beyond describing the central tendency and variation of a single variable. In this section, we refer to both the mean and standard deviation because in most research reports the standard deviation is reported along with the mean.

Table 5.11, taken from an article by Professors Naomi Gerstel and Sally Gallagher,[13] illustrates a common research application of the

---

[12]Herman J. Loether and Donald G. McTavish, *Descriptive and Inferential Statistics: An Introduction.* Boston: Allyn and Bacon, Inc., 1980, 160–161.

[13]Naomi Gerstel and Sally Gallagher, "Caring for Kith and Kin: Gender, Employment, and Privatization of Care." *Social Problems,* Vol. 41, No. 4, November 1994, 519–537.

Table 5.11 **Gender and Caregiving: Number and Hours Helped per Month[a]**

| | Wives | | Husbands | |
|---|---|---|---|---|
| | Mean | Standard Deviation | Mean | Standard Deviation |
| I. INFORMAL CAREGIVING | | | | |
| Number Helped: | | | | |
| Kin[b] | 5.25 | 2.86 | 4.02 | 2.59 |
| Friends | 3.44 | 2.54 | 2.26 | 2.17 |
| Total people | 8.71 | 5.34 | 6.29 | 3.58 |
| Hours Helped: | | | | |
| All Kin[b] | 42.77 | 30.82 | 15.06 | 14.02 |
| Parents | 11.52 | 19.10 | 3.76 | 3.74 |
| Parents-in-law | 6.20 | 12.23 | 3.95 | 7.47 |
| Adult children | 20.79 | 37.27 | 4.60 | 10.45 |
| Friends | 10.93 | 14.48 | 6.35 | 10.30 |
| II. FORMAL CAREGIVING | | | | |
| Number of groups | 2.08 | 2.26 | 3.14 | 3.54 |
| Volunteer hours | 8.09 | 13.68 | 9.41 | 13.67 |
| III. TOTAL CAREGIVING | | | | |
| Total hours[c] | 61.79 | 60.49 | 30.82 | 27.76 |

a. Measures computed for all respondents ($N = 273$), except Hours Helped Parents (includes only those with at least one living parent, $N = 165$). Parents-in-law (includes only those with at least one living parent-in-law, $N = 162$), and Adult Children (includes only those with at least one adult child, $N = 126$).

b. Kin includes parents, parents-in-law, adult children, siblings, grandparents, aunts, uncles, and any other kin mentioned.

c. Total Hours = Informal (Hours for All Kin and Friends) + Formal (Volunteer Hours).
*Source:* Adapted from Naomi Gerstel and Sally Gallagher, "Caring for Kith and Kin: Gender, Employment, and the Privatization of Care." *Social Problems,* Vol. 41, No. 4, November 1994, 525.

mean and standard deviation. Professors Gerstel and Gallagher examined gender differences in caregiving to relatives and friends, as well as in volunteering to groups. Despite growing acceptance among Americans for governmental aid for the disabled, the majority of Americans continue to believe it is the responsibility of women to provide personal and household assistance to elderly parents and in-laws, as well as to aging siblings and adult children.

Gerstel and Gallagher's major hypothesis is "that wives will give care in far greater breadth . . . and depth than husbands. That is, wives are far more likely to give help to a larger number of people than husbands, including to more relatives, more friends, as well as more volunteer groups."[14] The researchers (1) assess the amount and types of care provided by wives compared with husbands and (2) look at the relevance of employment status on the amount and type of care provided by wives and husbands.

Data for this study come from household interviews conducted in 1990 with 273 married respondents—179 married women and 94 of their husbands. The sample was limited to whites (86 percent) and blacks (14 percent) over the age of 21 in Springfield, Massachusetts. Table 5.11 lists the most important variables used in the study. It presents the means and standard deviations for the breadth and depth of informal and formal caregiving.

To measure the breadth of informal caregiving, interviewers named a number of different categories of people—including mother and father, adult children, other relatives, and friends. After naming a category (for example, mother), the interviewer gave the respondent a list of tasks and asked if she or he had done each task for the person named within the last month. The total number of people given care and the number of people in each category provide a measure of the "breadth of informal caretaking." In addition, respondents were asked how many hours in the last month they provided care to each category of person. The total number of hours of care given to all kin and hours given to people in each category (parents, parents-in-law, adult children) is a measure of the "depth of informal caregiving." To measure the "breadth and depth of formal caregiving," respondents were asked to list the number of voluntary organizations they belonged to and in which they did charity and volunteer work, and how many hours they spent on that work. Finally, because gender is a central focus of this study, the means and standard deviations are reported separately for men (husbands) and women (wives).

In describing the data displayed in Table 5.11, the researchers focused on the differences between men and women for each of the variables:

> The table shows striking differences between wives and
> husbands in the breadth, depth, and distribution of caregiving.
> Compared to husbands, wives help . . . a larger number of
> people, both kin and friends. Moreover, wives give . . . more

[14]Ibid., p. 522.

hours of care to friends. The differences in the amount of time wives, compared to husbands, spend providing for their own parents are even larger . . . Mothers spend more than four times more hours than fathers helping their adult children. Overall, wives give help to more relatives and spend almost three times as much time doing so. Clearly, wives are the major caregivers.[15]

What can you conclude from examining the standard deviations for these variables? The first thing to look for are variables with a great deal of variation. This is the case with the variable "hours helped" in all categories, as well as with both aspects of formal caregiving. Notice that for both men and women (except for parents-in-law for men), the standard deviations are larger than the mean. This indicates that there is a great deal of variation in the breadth and depth of caregiving among both men and women.

## MAIN POINTS

- Measures of variability are numbers that describe how much variation and diversity there is in a distribution.

- The index of qualitative variation (IQV) is used to measure variation in nominal variables. It is based on the ratio of the total number of differences in the distribution to the maximum number of possible differences within the same distribution. IQV can vary from 0.00 to 1.00.

- The range measures variation in interval-ratio variables and is the difference between the highest (maximum) and lowest (minimum) scores in the distribution. To find the range simply subtract the lowest from the highest score in a distribution.

- The interquartile range (IQR) measures the width of the middle 50 percent of the distribution. It is defined as the difference between the lower and upper quartiles ($Q1$ and $Q3$).

- The box plot is a graphical device that visually presents the range, the interquartile range, the median, the lowest (minimum) score, and the highest (maximum) score. The box plot provides us with a way to visually examine the center, the variation, and the shape of a distribution.

- The variance and the standard deviation are two closely related measures of variation for interval-ratio variables that increase or decrease based on how closely the scores cluster around the mean.

[15]Ibid., p. 525.

The variance provides a measure of the average of the squared deviations from the center (mean) of the distribution; the standard deviation is equal to the square root of the variance.

## KEY TERMS

*index of qualitative variation (IQV)*  *range*

*interquartile range (IQR)*  *standard deviation*

*measures of variability*  *variance*

## SPSS DEMONSTRATIONS

*Demonstration 1: Producing Measures of Variability with Frequencies*

SPSS can produce all the measures of variability discussed in this chapter except the index of qualitative variation. SPSS can be programmed to calculate the IQV, but that would take us into SPSS operations that are beyond the scope of this textbook.

The Frequencies procedure that we have used before calculates several measures of variability. We'll begin with Frequencies and calculate various statistics for AGE. If we click on *Frequencies,* then on the *Statistics* button, we can select the appropriate statistics.

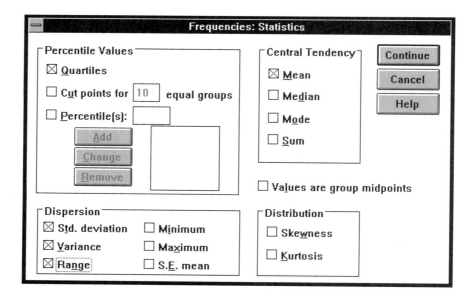

The measures of variability available are listed in the Dispersion box. We've selected the standard deviation, variance, and range, plus the mean (in the Central Tendency box) for reference. In the Percentile Values box, we've selected Quartiles to tell SPSS to calculate the values for the 25th, 50th, and 75th percentiles. SPSS also allows us to specify exact percentiles in this section (such as the 34th percentile) by typing a number in the box after "Percentile(s)" and then clicking on the *Add* button. Notice also that there is a separate checkbox ("Values are group midpoints") to tell SPSS that we are using grouped data.

We have already seen the frequency table for the variable AGE, so after clicking on *Continue,* we click on *Format* to turn off the display of the table. This is done by clicking on the radio button for "Suppress tables with more than 10 categories." There are other formatting options here that you may wish to explore when using SPSS.

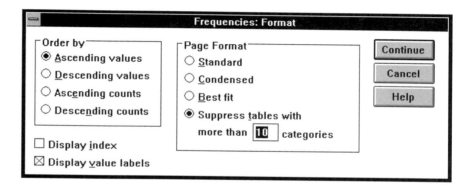

Click on *Continue,* then *OK* to run the procedure. SPSS once again produces the mean and also includes the other statistics we requested. The range of age is 71 years (from 18 to 89). The standard deviation is 17.485, which indicates that there is a moderate amount of dispersion in the ages (this is also visible if the histogram of AGE is reviewed from Chapter 3). The variance, 305.726, is the square of the standard deviation.

```
AGE          AGE OF RESPONDENT


Mean          46.086     Std dev     17.485      Variance      305.726
Range         71.000


Percentile     Value      Percentile    Value      Percentile      Value

  25.00       32.000        50.00      43.000        75.00        58.000

Valid cases     998      Missing cases      2
```

The value of the 25th percentile is 32; the value of the 50th percentile (which is also the median) is 43; and the value of the 75th percentile is 58. Although Frequencies does not calculate the interquartile range, it can easily be calculated by subtracting the value of the 25th percentile from the 75th percentile, which yields a value of 26 years. Compare this value with the standard deviation.

*Demonstration 2: Producing Variability Measures and Box Plots with Explore*

Another procedure in SPSS that can produce the usual measures of variability is Explore, which also produces stem and leaf plots and box plots. The Explore procedure is located in the *Summarize* section of the Statistics menu. In its main dialog box, the variables for which you want to produce statistics are placed in the Dependent List box. You have the option of putting one or more categorical variables in the Factor List box. If you do so, Explore will display separate statistics for each category of the Factor variables.

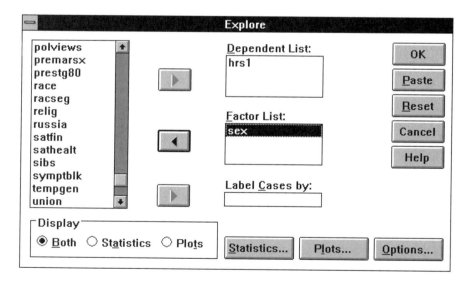

Place the variable "hours worked last week" (HRS1) in the Dependent box and SEX in the Factor box, to provide separate output for males and females. By default, Explore will produce statistics and plots, so we don't need to make any other choices. Although our request will not produce percentiles or create a histogram, Explore has options to do both these tasks plus several others.

The output for males follows. There were 307 males who were working last week and who answered this question. The mean number of hours worked was slightly larger than 44. The standard deviation is about 14.31, the range is 85, and the IQR is 10 hours, which is quite narrow compared with the range or standard deviation. The stem and leaf plot is also displayed. We will not discuss it here, but you may wish to refer to the discussion in Chapter 3 about this type of graph.

```
┌──────────────────────────────────────────────────────────────────────────────┐
│                    SPSS for Windows Student Version - [!Output1]          ▼ ▲  │
│  File  Edit  Data  Transform  Statistics  Graphs  Utilities  Window  Help      │
│                                                                                │
│       HRS1        NUMBER OF HOURS WORKED LA                                     │
│  By   SEX      1          MALE                                                  │
│                                                                                │
│  Valid cases:        307.0   Missing cases:      128.0   Percent missing:   29 │
│                                                                                │
│                                                                                │
│  Mean        44.0619  Std Err     .8165  Min        4.0000  Skewness    .09    │
│  Median      40.0000  Variance 204.6661  Max       89.0000  S E Skew    .13    │
│  5% Trim     43.9987  Std Dev   14.3062  Range     85.0000  Kurtosis   1.03    │
│  95% CI for Mean (42.4552, 45.6685)      IQR       10.0000  S E Kurt    .27    │
│                                                                                │
│                                                                                │
│  Frequency     Stem &  Leaf                                                    │
│                                                                                │
│     14.00  Extremes    (4), (5), (8), (9), (10), (12), (13), (14), (15), (16)  │
│     19.00  Extremes    (18), (19), (20), (22), (24), (25)                      │
│      2.00        2 .   &                                                        │
│     11.00        3 *   000&                                                     │
│     18.00        3 .   55788&                                                   │
│    108.00        4 *   000000000000000000000000000000000024&                   │
│     34.00        4 .   55555678888&                                            │
│     36.00        5 *   000000000024&                                           │
│     15.00        5 .   5568&                                                    │
│     26.00        6 *   000000000                                               │
│     24.00  Extremes    (65), (70), (72), (75), (76), (78), (80), (84), (89)    │
│                                                                                │
│  Stem width:   10                                                              │
│  Each leaf:       3 case(s)                                                     │
│                                                                                │
│  SPSS Processor is ready                                                        │
└──────────────────────────────────────────────────────────────────────────────┘
```

Although not displayed, the mean of HRS1 for females was about 39; the median was identical to that for males (40). The standard deviation was 13.17, the IQR was 9, and the range 81—values close to those for males but slightly smaller. The variation in hours worked last week for females is somewhat lower than for males.

Explore displays separate box plots for males and females in the same window for easy comparison. The SPSS box plot has some differences from those discussed in this chapter. Some things are the same, though. The solid dark line is the value of the median. The width of the shaded box (in color on the screen) is the IQR (10 hours for males and 9 hours for females). Notice that the median is centered in the box for females but not for males. This is partially because so many males report working 40 hours last week.

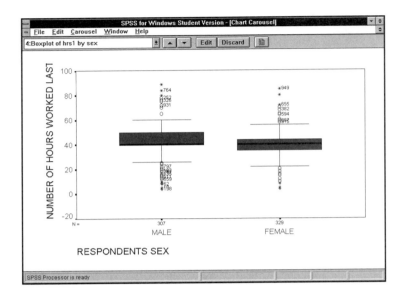

Unlike the box plots in this chapter, SPSS extends "Whiskers" from the box edges to 1½ times the box width (the IQR). In the text, the whiskers extend out to the minimum and maximum values. Instead, if there are additional values beyond 1½ times the IQR, SPSS displays the individual cases. Those that are somewhat extreme are marked with an open circle, and those considered very extreme are marked with an asterisk. The former falls from 1½ to 3 box widths from the edge of the box; the latter group falls more than 3 box widths from the box edge. The number of valid cases in each group is listed at the bottom of each box plot. There is no way to force SPSS to produce a box plot similar to that produced in the text.

The box plot shows us that variability in hours worked last week for males and females is similar, although the IQR for males runs from 40 hours to 50 hours, while the IQR for females runs from 35 to 44 hours. Both genders have outlying cases beyond the edge of the whiskers for people who worked many hours, or few hours, last week. The number next to the outlying case refers to the SPSS case ID, or row number, in the Data Editor window.

**EXERCISES**

1. Americans often think of themselves as quite diverse in their political opinions, falling all along a continuum of the political spectrum from liberal to conservative. Let's use the data from the

GSS for 1994 to quantitatively investigate the diversity of political views. The frequency table displays respondents' self-rating of their political position (the cases with no response were removed for this example).

POLVIEWS  THINK  OF  SELF  AS  LIBERAL  OR  CONSERVATIVE

| Value Label Percent | Value | Frequency | Percent | Valid Percent | Cum Percent |
|---|---|---|---|---|---|
| Extremely liberal | 1 | 23 | 2.3 | 2.4 | 2.4 |
| Liberal | 2 | 110 | 11.0 | 11.4 | 13.8 |
| Slightly liberal | 3 | 120 | 12.0 | 12.4 | 26.2 |
| Moderate | 4 | 361 | 36.1 | 37.2 | 63.4 |
| Slightly conservative | 5 | 156 | 15.6 | 16.1 | 79.5 |
| Conservative | 6 | 161 | 16.1 | 16.6 | 96.1 |
| Extremely conservative | 7 | 38 | 3.8 | 3.9 | 100.0 |
| | Total | 969 | 100.0 | 100.0 | |

Valid  cases    969 Missing  cases  31

a. What is the maximum possible number of differences, given this table?
b. What is the observed number of differences?
c. What is the IQV for this variable? Do you find it to be higher (closer to 1) or lower (closer to 0) than you might have expected for political views? Put another way, do you expect that Americans are diverse in their political views, or more narrowly concentrated in certain categories? And does this value of IQV support your expectation and what you observe from the table?

2. Traditionally, minorities and females have had few jobs in the construction trades. Even in 1990, most construction workers were still male and white. Perhaps, as females have recently been hired into construction jobs, there has been more racial diversity. That is, perhaps there are higher percentages of blacks and Hispanics among female construction workers than among male workers. U.S. census data from 1990 provide the following frequency distributions for male and female carpenters in a large midwestern city.

### Number of Carpenters

| | Male | Female |
|---|---|---|
| White | 6,448 | 101 |
| Black | 1,458 | 35 |
| Hispanic | 2,156 | 26 |
| Total | 10,062 | 162 |

a. Calculate the total number of observed differences for males and females separately.
b. Calculate the maximum number of possible differences for each gender.
c. Use the values you calculated in (a) and (b) to calculate the IQV for males and females. Is there more diversity by race for male or female carpenters? Notice that there are more Hispanic than black male carpenters, but more black than Hispanic female carpenters.

3. The Census Bureau annually estimates the percentage of Americans below the poverty level for various geographic areas. Use the information provided by state to characterize poverty in the southern versus the western portion of the United States. The table displays the percentage of Americans below the poverty level in these two regions in 1991.

| South | Percentage | West | Percentage |
|---|---|---|---|
| Alabama | 18.8 | Alaska | 18.8 |
| Florida | 15.4 | Arizona | 14.8 |
| Georgia | 17.2 | California | 15.7 |
| Kentucky | 18.8 | Idaho | 14.9 |
| Louisiana | 19.0 | Montana | 15.4 |
| Mississippi | 23.7 | Nevada | 11.4 |
| North Carolina | 14.5 | New Mexico | 22.4 |
| South Carolina | 16.4 | Oregon | 13.5 |
| Tennessee | 15.5 | Utah | 12.9 |
| | | Washington | 8.9 |

a. What is the range of poverty rates in the South? the West? Which is greater?
b. What is the interquartile range (IQR) for the South? for the West? Which is larger?

c. Using these calculations, compare the variability of the poverty rate of the states in the West with those in the South.

4. Use the data from exercise 3 again. This time your task is to create box plots to display the variation in poverty level by region.
    a. First, combine both regions and create a box plot for all the states. What is the 75th percentile for poverty rate? Are there any outlying cases (that is, outside the whiskers)?
    b. Now create a separate box plot for the West and one for the South. Do these box plots add to your discussion from exercise 3? If so, how?

5. Use Table 5.5 for this exercise to continue comparisons by region. Use only the information for states in the West (Mountain) and Midwest (West North Central).
    a. Compare the Mountain states with those in the West North Central on the percent increase in the elderly population by calculating the range. Which region had a greater range?
    b. Calculate the IQR for each region. Which is greater?
    c. Use the statistics to characterize the variability in population increase of the elderly in the two regions. Why do you think one region is more variable than another?

6. "Occupational prestige" is a statistic developed by sociologists to measure the status of one's occupation. It is measured on a scale from 1 to 100 (though no occupation has a score at either extreme). Occupational prestige is also a component of what sociologists call "socioeconomic status," a composite measure of one's status in society. Blacks, on average, have lower occupational prestige, but given that, is it still possible that the variation among prestige scores for blacks is no greater than for whites? We investigate this question, using 1994 GSS data to generate the following SPSS output from the Explore procedure.

```
        PRESTG80  RS  OCCUPATIONAL  PRESTIGE
By      RACE      1            WHITE


Valid cases: 810.0        Missing cases: 33.0    Percent missing: 3.9



Mean      44.6346   Std Err     .4791   Min    17.0000   Skewness     .3510
Median    44.0000   Variance 185.9058   Max    86.0000   S E Skew   .0859
5% Trim  44.3361   Std Dev   13.6347   Range 69.0000   Kurtosis   -.4680
95% CI  for  Mean  (43.6942, 45.5749) IQR   17.2500   S E  Kurt   .1716
```

```
              PRESTG80    RS  OCCUPATIONAL  PRESTIGE
By            RACE    2            BLACK


Valid  cases: 114.0Missing  cases: 4.0  Percent  missing: 3.4



Mean      39.7982  Std  Err    1.3531  Min    17.0000  Skewness    .6214
Median    38.5000  Variance 208.7111  Max    74.0000  S E  Skew   .2265
5%  Trim  39.1852  Std  Dev   14.4468  Range 57.0000  Kurtosis   -.4490
95%  CI  for  Mean  (37.1176, 42.4789)  IQR    18.0000  S E  Kurt   .4493
```

(*Note:* The Explore procedure produces a variety of statistics, including some we have not discussed, including skewness, kurtosis, and the standard error ("Std Err"). Don't worry about these in this exercise.)

    a. Notice that SPSS supplies the interquartile range (IQR), the median, and the minimum and maximum values for each race. Use this information to construct box plots for whites and blacks, placing them side by side on the same graph.

    b. Looking at the values of the mean and median, do you think the distribution of prestige is skewed for blacks? for whites? Why or why not? Is this evident from the box plots?

    c. Explain why you think there is more variability of prestige for whites or for blacks, or why the variability of prestige is similar for the two groups.

7. In exercise 3 you studied the variation in poverty rates among states in the South and West, using the range and the IQR.

    a. Use the same data, but now calculate the standard deviation for each region.

    b. Which region appears to have more variability as measured by the standard deviation? Are these results consistent with what you found using the range and the IQR?

8. A child psychologist is studying the behavior of children during play by unobtrusively observing them during recess periods at an elementary school. Her work is part of a long–term study on how cooperation develops among humans and how a person's characteristics are related to cooperative behavior. In this phase of the study, she has recorded the number of incidents of cooperative behavior among two groups of children over a 15-day period:

    GROUP 1:  4 9 11 3 10 12 6 9 11 9 4 12 20 8 9

    GROUP 2:  9 4 13 2 5 10 6 4 7 7 12 8 5 10 8

The psychologist's first task is to study the average level of cooperation and its dispersion in each group before she takes into account group differences.

a. Calculate the mean and standard deviation for the number of incidents of cooperative behavior in each group.

b. Use these values to discuss differences in cooperative behavior between the two groups of children, from a statistical standpoint.

c. What if you learn that there are twice as many children in group 1 as in group 2? Would that new information modify your answer to (b)? Why or why not?

9. A group of investigators have just finished a study that measured the amount of time each member of a marriage spends doing housework. The investigators classified each couple as traditional or nontraditional, depending on the attitudes of both partners. (Traditional couples commonly grant more authority to the male; nontraditional couples share more in decision making.) The investigators provide you with the following data for males only.

**Hours of Housework per Week**

| Traditional Family | Nontraditional Family |
|---|---|
| $\overline{Y} = 6.3$ | $\overline{Y} = 12.4$ |
| $\Sigma Y^2 = 1,104$ | $\Sigma Y^2 = 2,889$ |
| $\Sigma Y = 63$ | $\Sigma Y = 186$ |
| $N = 10$ | $N = 15$ |

a. Calculate the variance and standard deviation from these statistics for each family type.

b. What can you say about the variability in the amount of time men spend doing housework in traditional versus nontraditional marriages? Why might there be a difference? Why might there be more variability for one type of family than another?

c. Was it necessary in this problem to provide you with the value of $\overline{Y}$ to calculate the variance and standard deviation?

10. Use the data in exercise 7 in Chapter 4 on the number of people living in U.S. households in 1989.

a. Calculate the standard deviation for this variable, using the formula for grouped frequency distributions. Is the standard deviation larger or smaller than the value of the mean?

b. Why do you think the mode and median for household size are lower than the mean? Does this fact have any implication for housing policy in the United States?

11. You are interested in studying the variability of violent crime and the rate of incarceration in the eastern and midwestern United States. The U.S. Census Bureau collected the following statistics on these two variables for twenty-one states in the East and Midwest in 1992.

|  | Violent Crime Rate per 100,00 People | Federal and State Prisoners per 1,000 People |
|---|---|---|
| Maine | 131 | 1.2 |
| New Hampshire | 126 | 1.6 |
| Vermont | 109 | 2.2 |
| Massachusetts | 779 | 1.7 |
| Rhode Island | 395 | 2.8 |
| Connecticut | 495 | 3.5 |
| New York | 1,122 | 3.4 |
| New Jersey | 626 | 2.9 |
| Pennsylvania | 427 | 2.1 |
| Ohio | 526 | 3.5 |
| Indiana | 508 | 2.5 |
| Illinois | 977 | 2.7 |
| Michigan | 770 | 4.1 |
| Wisconsin | 276 | 1.8 |
| Minnesota | 338 | 0.9 |
| Iowa | 278 | 1.6 |
| Missouri | 740 | 3.1 |
| North Dakota | 83 | 0.8 |
| South Dakota | 195 | 2.1 |
| Nebraska | 349 | 1.6 |
| Kansas | 511 | 2.4 |

a. Calculate the mean for each variable.
b. Calculate the standard deviation for each variable.
c. Calculate the interquartile range for each variable.
d. Compare the mean with the standard deviation and IQR for each variable. Does there appear to be more variability of the rate of violent crime or of the incarceration rate in these states? What states contribute more to the greater variability for each variable?

e. Suggest why one variable has more variability than the other. In other words, what social forces would cause one variable to have a relatively larger standard deviation than its mean?

12. Construct a box plot for both variables in exercise 11. Discuss how the box plot reinforces the conclusions you drew about the variability of the rates of violent crime and incarceration.

13. Use the data in Table 5.6 for this exercise.
   a. Calculate the standard deviation for the percent increase in the elderly population from 1980 to 1990 by state.
   b. Compare this statistic with the IQR and the box plot shown in Figure 5.7. Which is larger, the IQR or the standard deviation?
   c. Would the standard deviation lead you to the same conclusion about the variability of the increase in the elderly population as the IQR and the box plot?

14. You decide to use GSS data from 1994 to investigate how Americans feel about spending federal government money on welfare and to improve the condition of blacks. By using the Frequencies procedure, you obtain the following output on these two variables, where "Too little" means that the federal government is spending too little, "About right" means that the level of government spending on this issue is about right, and "Too much" means the government is spending too much.

NATFARE   WELFARE

| Value Label | Value | Frequency | Percent | Valid Percent | Cum Percent |
|---|---|---|---|---|---|
| Too little | 1 | 64 | 6.4 | 12.3 | 12.3 |
| About right | 2 | 138 | 13.8 | 26.5 | 38.8 |
| Too much | 3 | 319 | 31.9 | 61.2 | 100.0 |
| NAP | 0 | 461 | 46.1 | Missing | |
| DK | 8 | 17 | 1.7 | Missing | |
| NA | 9 | 1 | .1 | Missing | |
| | Total | 1,000 | 100.0 | 100.0 | |

Valid cases  521      Missing cases  479

NATRACE   IMPROVING  THE  CONDITIONS  OF  BLACKS

| Value Label | Value | Frequency | Percent | Valid Percent | Cum Percent |
|---|---|---|---|---|---|
| Too little | 1 | 155 | 15.5 | 31.0 | 31.0 |
| About right | 2 | 221 | 22.1 | 44.2 | 75.2 |
| Too much | 3 | 124 | 12.4 | 24.8 | 100.0 |
| NAP | 0 | 461 | 46.1 | Missing | |
| DK | 8 | 39 | 3.9 | Missing | |
| Total | | 1,000 | 100.0 | 100.0 | |

Valid  cases  500      Missing  cases  500

(*Note:* The label of "NAP" stands for "Not Applicable," "DK" stands for "Don't Know," and "NA" for "No Answer.")

a.  What would an appropriate measure of variability be for these variables?

b.  Calculate the appropriate measure of variability for each variable.

c.  In 1994, was there more variability for attitudes toward spending on welfare or improving the conditions of blacks?

**SPSS PROBLEMS**

1.  Use the 1994 GSS file to investigate the variability of the age of the respondent (AGE) and the age at which the respondent was first married (AGEWED). You can use either the Frequencies or the Explore procedure.

a.  Which variable has more variability? Use more than one statistic to answer this question.

b.  Why should one variable have more variability than the other, from a societal perspective?

2.  Use the 1994 GSS file to study the number of hours that males and females work each week. The variable HRS1 measures the number of hours a respondent worked the week before the interview.

a.  Use the Explore procedure to study the variability of hours worked, comparing males with females. Be sure to request a box plot by leaving the "Both" choice selected in the Display box.

b.  Is there much difference in the variability of men's and women's hours worked? Do you find this result surprising?

c. Write a short paragraph describing the box plot that SPSS created as if you were writing a report and had included the box plot as a chart to support your conclusions about the variability (and central tendency) of hours worked between males and females.

3. Has the size of families decreased over time? Or to put it another way, is the ideal family size smaller than the family in which someone grew up? To investigate this question, use the variables SIBS (the number of brothers and sisters) and CHLDNUM (how many children a person expects to have).
   a. Which variable has the greater mean? Which has greater variability?
   b. What do these statistics tell you about the preferred size of American families from one generation to another? What factors might complicate your interpretation?

## GROUP PROBLEMS

1. Use the data from group problem 1 in Chapter 4 that you collected from your classmates.
   a. Calculate an appropriate measure of variability for each of the three variables. Add this information to the report that you prepared in Chapter 4, which described the central tendency and distribution of each variable.

2. Working with other group members, find articles or published government data that report on the change in some statistics over time, such as the rate of violent crime, the percentage of Americans living in poverty, or unemployment rates. Pick three or four statistics to study. The *Statistical Abstract of the United States* is one source for this information. Have some group members go to the library to get the information. Then have other group members use the data to calculate the standard deviation for each data series (thus, if you have crime rates for each year from 1980 to 1995, you would have sixteen data points or sixteen cases). Have a group discussion concerning these questions:
   a. Are the yearly changes generally greater or lower than the standard deviation for each data series? What might this be telling you about the yearly fluctuations in the series? Why might one data series have less variability than others?
   b. What might this be telling you about the yearly fluctuations in the series?

3. Can you guess (or do you know) the percentage distribution of racial or ethnic groups in the United States, in the nearest major city, and in the state where your school is located? Have each group member guess what the distribution of race or ethnicity is in these three geographical and political divisions. Record the guesses. To keep the problem manageable, choose only the major categories of ethnicity or race when making your guesses (you can jointly decide with other group members which categories to include). Then have one or two group members go to the library and obtain the actual values for the population from U.S. census or other appropriate publications. After you've got this information, meet again and compare the guesses with the actual values. Were most people close or far off in their predictions? Also, compare the predicted *variability* in racial or ethnic composition of the population by you and other group members with the actual variability. (*Hint:* Calculate the IQV.) Did most people predict more or less heterogeneity than exists in the population?

# 6 Relationships Between Two Variables: Cross-Tabulation

■ ■ ■ ■ **Introduction**

In the second part of this book we turn our attention to bivariate methods of analysis. **Bivariate analysis** is a method designed to detect and describe the relationship between two variables. Thus far, you may have had an intuitive sense of the terms "relationship" and "association." We have seen in earlier chapters that by comparing the properties of different groups one can often think in terms of "relationships." But in this and the following two chapters we look at the concept of relationships between variables in more depth.

---

*Bivariate Analysis*    A statistical method designed to detect and describe the relationship between two variables.

---

Certainly you are familiar with the idea of "relationship" simply because you are aware that in the world around you things (and people) "go together." For example, as children grow their weight increases; larger cities have more crime than smaller cities. In fact, many of the reports in our daily newspapers are statements about relationships. For example, a news story based on a census report on immigration to the United States documents the struggles many new immigrants have with the English language.[1] The article compares the English proficiency of native-born Americans with that of foreign-born Americans by using a set of simple bar charts (Figure 6.1). Notice that there is a pattern in Figure 6.1. More native born than foreign born

---

[1]*USA Today*, November 5, 1993.

Figure 6.1 **English Proficiency and Nativity**

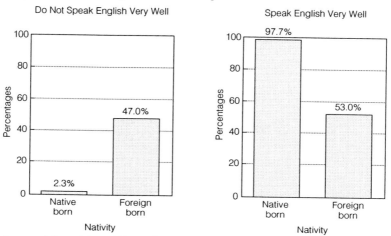

Source: Adapted from USA Today, November 5, 1993. Copyright 1993, USA TODAY. Used by permission.

speak English well; more foreign born than native born don't speak English well. This simple example illustrates a relationship or association between the variables "nativity" (native born vs. foreign born) and "English proficiency" (speak English well, do not speak English well).

One of the main objectives of social science is to make sense out of human and social experience by uncovering regular patterns among events. Therefore, the language of relationships is at the heart of social science inquiry. See the following examples from articles and research reports:

*Example 1* Students who had a history of earning good grades were less likely to miss class than students who did not.[2] (This example indicates a relationship between grade point average and absenteeism among college students.)

*Example 2* Contrary to the stereotype, whites use government safety net programs more than blacks or Hispanics, and they are more likely than minorities to be lifted out of poverty by the taxpayer money they get.[3] (This example indicates a relationship between race and receipt of government aid.)

[2]Gary Wyatt, "Skipping Class: An Analysis of Absenteeism among First-Class College Students." *Teaching Sociology,* Vol. 20, July 1992, 201–207.
[3]*USA Today,* 9 October 1992.

*Example 3* "Puerto Rican men were less likely than whites (but more likely than blacks) to be in the labor force."[4] (This example indicates a relationship between race/ethnicity and labor force participation.)

In each of these examples a relationship means that certain values of one variable tend to "go together" with certain values of the other variable. In Example 1, lower grades "go together" with irregular class attendance; higher grades go with regular class attendance. In Example 2, being white "goes together" with more frequent use of government aid; being black or Hispanic goes with less frequent use of government aid. Finally, in Example 3, white "goes together" with greater likelihood of employment; being black or Puerto Rican "goes together" with less likelihood of employment.

In this chapter, we introduce one of the most common techniques for the analysis of relationships between two variables—*cross-tabulation.* **Cross-tabulation** is a technique for analyzing the relationship between two variables that have been organized in a bivariate table. (Bivariate tables are defined later.) We demonstrate not only how to detect whether two variables are associated, but also how to determine the strength of the association and, when appropriate, its direction. We will also see how these methods are applied in "real" research situations.[5]

---

*Cross-Tabulation*   A technique for analyzing the relationship between two variables that have been organized in a bivariate table.

---

In Chapters 7 and 8, we discuss special measures of association for nominal, ordinal, and interval-ratio variables. Finally, in a special review chapter (Chapter 9), we discuss how to choose the most appropriate measure of association.

## Independent and Dependent Variables

In the social sciences, an important aspect of the language of relationship between two variables is the distinction between the *independent*

---

[4]Cordella W. Reimers, "Hispanic Earnings and Employment in the 1980s." In *Hispanics in the Workplace,* edited by Stephen B. Knouse et al. Newbury Park, CA: Sage, 1992.

[5]Full consideration of the question of detecting the presence of a bivariate relationship requires the use of inferential statistics. Inferential statistics is discussed in chapters 11 through 16.

*variable* and the *dependent variable*. These terms, first introduced in Chapter 1, are used throughout this chapter as well as in the following chapters, and therefore it is important that you understand the distinction between them. Let's take our example about nativity and English proficiency, in which nativity—whether native born or foreign born—has some influence on the level of English proficiency. Even though immigration status is not necessarily a direct cause of language ability (see the discussion of causality in Chapter 1), immigration status is assumed to be connected to English proficiency through a complex set of experiences—such as education, employment, and other socialization experiences—all of which do have an influence on the acquisition of language. If we then hypothesize that English proficiency (which is the variable to be explained by the researcher) varies by whether a person is native born or foreign born (which is the variable assumed to influence English proficiency), then "English proficiency" is the dependent variable and "nativity" is the independent variable.

In each of the illustrations given, there are two variables, an independent and a dependent variable. In Example 1, the purpose of the research is to explain absenteeism. One of the variables hypothesized as being connected to absenteeism is grades. Therefore, "absenteeism" is the dependent variable and "grades" the independent variable. In Example 2, the object of the investigation is to examine the common stereotype that people of color use government aid more than white Americans. The investigator is trying to explain differences in utilization of government aid using race as an explanatory variable. Therefore, the "utilization of government aid" is the dependent variable and "race" is the independent variable. Similarly, in Example 3, "labor force participation" is the dependent variable because it is the variable to be explained, whereas "race," the explanatory variable, is the independent variable.

The statistical techniques discussed in this and the following two chapters help the researcher decide the strength of the relationship between the independent and dependent variables.

> **Learning Check.**   *If you are still having trouble distinguishing between an independent and a dependent variable, go back to Chapter 1 (pp. 10–13) for a detailed discussion.*

## The Bivariate Table: Safety in Cities

Many of you are aware of the problem of safety in our cities. The level of perceived safety in large cities is rather low because of the high rates of crime and violence. But are some of us more vulnerable than others? Do men and women have a different sense of safety? To answer this, let's examine the replies of men and women to the survey question, "Is there any area right around here—that is, within a mile—where you would be afraid to walk alone at night?" A simple way to determine if there are gender differences in perceived safety is to compare the answers given by women with those given by men.

Tables 6.1 and 6.2 provide the information we need. They show the frequency distributions (in both absolute frequencies and percentages) for men and women in the 1987 to 1992 General Social Survey (GSS). Comparing the "yes" responses given by the two groups, we can see that women feel less safe than men. Sixty-two percent of the women compared with only 25 percent of the men are afraid to walk alone in their neighborhoods at night. A comparison of the "no" responses reinforces this observation: more men than women feel safe. It seems reasonable to say then, based on these comparisons, that level of fear

Table 6.1 **Afraid to Walk Alone in Neighborhood at Night (men)**

| Afraid | Frequency (f) | Percentages (%) |
| --- | --- | --- |
| No | 186 | 75 |
| Yes | 62 | 25 |
| Total (N) | 248 | 100 |

*Source:* General Social Survey, 1987 to 1992.

Table 6.2 **Afraid to Walk Alone in Neighborhood at Night (women)**

| Afraid | Frequency (f) | Percentages (%) |
| --- | --- | --- |
| No | 94 | 38 |
| Yes | 153 | 62 |
| Total (N) | 247 | 100 |

*Source:* General Social Survey, 1987 to 1992.

is associated with gender. This conclusion is based on comparing the percentages rather than the absolute frequencies because the number of men and the number of women surveyed differ.

A more efficient way to examine the hypothesis that there are gender differences in perceived safety is to combine the two separate distributions into one table or one graph, as shown in Table 6.3 and Figure 6.2. Both make it easier to observe the connection between gender and fear. Here again, you can see that women are more likely to feel unsafe (62% afraid) than men (25% afraid). Note that Figure 6.2 shows only the percentage of men and women who are *afraid*. Since the percentages of *afraid* and *not afraid* sum to 100 percent in each group (men and women), there is no need to show both.

Table 6.3 is known as a *bivariate table*. A **bivariate table** displays the distribution of one variable across the categories of another variable.

Table 6.3  **Percentage of Men and Women Afraid to Walk Alone in Neighborhood at Night**

| Afraid | Men | Women |
|--------|-----|-------|
| No | 75% | 38% |
| Yes | 25% | 62% |
| Total | 100% | 100% |
| (N) | (248) | (247) |

Figure 6.2  **Percentage of Men and Women Afraid to Walk Alone at Night**

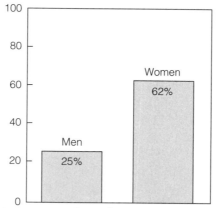

*Source:* General Social Survey, 1987 to 1992.

It can be thought of as a series of frequency distributions joined together to make one table. Table 6.3 shows the frequency distribution of "fear" among males, compared with a frequency distribution of "fear" for females. These frequency distributions are presented in percentage form.

---

*Bivariate Table*   A table that displays the distribution of one variable across the categories of another variable.

---

### How to Construct a Bivariate Table: Race and Home Ownership

Although we can construct bivariate tables simply by attaching together a series of frequency distributions like the one presented in Table 6.3, bivariate tables are obtained by classifying cases based on their joint scores for two variables. The data in Table 6.4 represent a sample of respondents by race and whether they own or rent their homes (home ownership).

Table 6.4   **Race and Home Ownership for Fifteen GSS Respondents**

| Respondent | Race | Home Ownership |
|---|---|---|
| 1 | Black | Own |
| 2 | Black | Own |
| 3 | White | Rent |
| 4 | White | Rent |
| 5 | White | Own |
| 6 | White | Own |
| 7 | White | Own |
| 8 | Black | Rent |
| 9 | Black | Rent |
| 10 | Black | Rent |
| 11 | White | Own |
| 12 | White | Own |
| 13 | White | Rent |
| 14 | White | Rent |
| 15 | Black | Rent |

To make sense out of these data we must first construct the table in which these individual scores will be classified. In Table 6.5, the fifteen respondents were classified according to joint scores on race and home ownership. The table has the following features typical of most bivariate tables:

1. It has a title describing its content in terms of the two variables.

2. It has two dimensions, one for race and one for home ownership.

   The variable "home ownership" is represented in the rows of the table, with one row for owners and another for renters. The variable "race" makes up the columns of the table, with one column for each racial group included. A table may have more columns and more rows, depending on how many categories the variables represent. For example, had we included a group of Hispanics, there would have been three columns (not including the Row Total column). Usually, the independent variable is the **column variable** and the dependent variable is the **row variable**.

---

*Column Variable*   A variable whose categories are the columns of a bivariate table.

*Row Variable*   A variable whose categories are the rows of a bivariate table.

---

Table 6.5   **Home Ownership by Race (absolute frequencies)**

| HOME OWNERSHIP | RACE Black | White | |
|---|---|---|---|
| Own | 2 | 5 | 7 Row Marginals (Row total) |
| Rent | 4 | 4 | 8 |
| | 6 | 9 | 15 Total Cases (N) |

Column Marginals (Column total)

3. The intersection of a row and a column is called a **cell**. For example, the two individuals represented in the upper left cell are blacks who are also homeowners.

---

*Cell*   The intersection of a row and a column in a bivariate table.

---

4. The *column and row totals* are the frequency distribution for each variable, respectively. The column total is the frequency distribution for "race," the row total for "home ownership." Row and column totals are sometimes called **marginals**. The total number of cases (*N*) is the number reported at the intersection of the row and column total (these elements are labeled in the table).

---

*Marginals*   The row and column totals in a bivariate table.

---

5. The table is a 2 × 2 table because it has two rows and two columns (not counting the marginals). We usually refer to this as an *r* × *c* table, in which *r* represents the number of rows and *c* the number of columns. Thus, a table in which the row variable has three categories and the column variable two categories would be designated as a 3 × 2 table.

---

**Learning Check.**   *Examine Table 6.5 carefully. Make sure you can identify all of the parts just described and that you understand how the numbers were obtained. Can you identify the independent and dependent variables in the table? You will need to know this to convert the frequencies to percentages.*

---

## How to Compute Percentages in a Bivariate Table

To compare home ownership status for blacks and whites, we need to convert the raw frequencies to percentages because the column totals are not equal. Recall from Chapter 2 that percentages are especially useful for comparing two or more groups that differ in size. There are two basic rules for computing and analyzing percentages in a bivariate table:

1. Calculate percentages within each category of the independent variable.

2. Interpret the table by comparing the percentages for different categories of the independent variable.

*Calculating Percentages Within Each Category of the Independent Variable*
This rule means that we have to calculate percentages within each category of the variable that the investigator defines as the independent variable. When the independent variable is arrayed in the *columns* we compute percentages within each column separately. The frequencies within each cell and the row marginals are divided by the total of the column in which they are located, and the column totals should sum to 100 percent. When the independent variable is arrayed in the *rows* we compute percentages within each row separately. The frequencies within each cell and the column marginals are divided by the total of the row in which they are located, and the row totals should sum to 100 percent.

In our example, we are interested in "race" as the independent variable and in its relationship with "home ownership." Therefore, we are going to calculate percentages by using the column total of each racial group as the base of the percentage. For example, the percentage of black respondents who own their homes is obtained by dividing the number of black homeowners by the total number of blacks in the sample:

$$(100)\frac{2}{6} = 33\%$$

Table 6.6 presents percentages based on the data in Table 6.5. Notice that the percentages in each column add up to 100 percent.

Table 6.6 **Home Ownership by Race (in percentages)**

| HOME OWNERSHIP | RACE Black | White | Total |
|---|---|---|---|
| Own | 33% | 56% | 47% |
| Rent | 67% | 44% | 53% |
| Total | 100% | 100% | 100% |
| | (6) | (9) | (15) |

*Comparing the Percentages Across Different Categories of the Independent Variable* The second rule tells us to compare how home ownership varies between blacks and whites. Comparisons are made by examining differences between percentages across different categories of the independent variable. In this case, we simply compare the percentage of blacks and whites who are homeowners. We can see that the percentage is larger (56%) among whites than among blacks (33%). In other words, in this group[6] whites are more likely to be homeowners than blacks. Therefore, we can conclude that one's race appears to be associated with the likelihood of being a homeowner.

Notice that the same conclusion, that race may be associated with the likelihood of being a homeowner, would be drawn had we compared the percentage of black and white renters. But, since the percentages of homeowners and renters within each racial group sum to 100 percent, we need to make only one comparison. In fact, for any 2 x 2 table only one comparison needs to be made to interpret the table. For larger tables there is more than one comparison that can be made and used in interpretation.

---

**Learning Check.**   *Practice constructing a bivariate table. Use Table 6.4 to create a percentage bivariate table. Compare your table with Table 6.6. Did you remember all of the parts? Are your calculations correct? If not, go back and review this section. It might be helpful to examine Box 6.1. It illustrates the process of constructing and percentaging bivariate tables. Remember, you must correctly identify the independent variable so you know whether to percentage across the rows or down the columns.*

---

## How to Deal with Ambiguous Relationships Between Variables

Sometimes it is not apparent which variable is independent or dependent; sometimes the data can be viewed either way. In this case, you might compute both row and column percentages. For example, Table 6.7 presents three sets of figures: the absolute frequencies (6.7a), the column percentages (6.7b), and the row percentages (6.7c) for the variables "attitude toward abortion" and "job security" for a sample

---

[6]Note that this group is but a small sample taken from the GSS national sample. The relationship between home ownership and race noted here may not necessarily hold true in other (larger) samples.

## Box 6.1  *Percentaging a Bivariate Table*

**1.** Black and white homeowners and renters:

Owners

Renters

**2.** Divide respondents into two groups by race (the independent variable); count the number in each group to get the column totals.

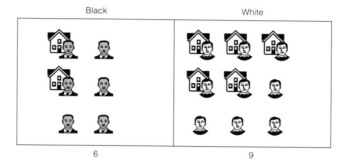

| Black | White |
|:---:|:---:|
| 6 | 9 |

**3.** Divide each group into homeowners and renters (the dependent variable); count the number in each group to get the row totals.

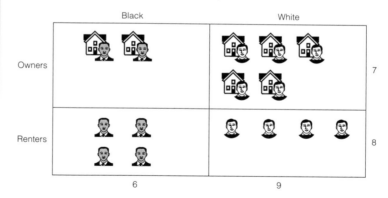

| | Black | White | |
|---|:---:|:---:|---|
| Owners | | | 7 |
| Renters | | | 8 |
| | 6 | 9 | |

**4.** Count each cell:

| | Black | White | |
|---|:---:|:---:|---|
| Owners | 2 | 5 | 7 |
| Renters | 4 | 4 | 8 |
| | 6 | 9 | |

**5.** % of blacks who are owners: (100)2/6 = 33%
% of whites who are owners: (100)5/9 = 56%
% of blacks who are renters: (100)4/6 = 67%
% of whites who are renters: (100)4/9 = 44%

**6.** Compare percentages: 33% vs. 56%
67% vs. 44%

Table 6.7 **The Different Ways Percentages Can Be Computed: Attitudes Toward Abortion by Job Security ("Job Find")**

a. **Absolute Frequencies**

| | JOB FIND | | Row |
|---|---|---|---|
| ABORTION | Easy | Not Easy | Total |
| Yes | 28 | 35 | 63 |
| No | 33 | 46 | 79 |
| Column Total | 61 | 81 | 142 |

b. **Column Percentages (column totals as the base)**

| | JOB FIND | | |
|---|---|---|---|
| ABORTION | Easy | Not Easy | Total |
| Yes | 46% | 43% | 44% |
| No | 54% | 57% | 56% |
| Total | 100% (61) | 100% (81) | 100% (142) |

c. **Row Percentages (row totals as the base)**

| | JOB FIND | | |
|---|---|---|---|
| ABORTION | Easy | Not Easy | Total |
| Yes | 44% | 56% | 100% (63) |
| No | 42% | 58% | 100% (79) |
| Total | 43% | 57% | 100% (142) |

*Source:* General Social Survey, 1987 to 1992.

of GSS female respondents. "Job security" (labeled as "Job Find") is measured with the survey question "About how easy would it be for you to find a job with another employer with approximately the same income and fringe benefits you now have?" The variable "attitude toward abortion" is measured in terms of the respondent's approval or disapproval of three reasons for obtaining an abortion: (1) the woman does not want the baby because the family has a very low income and cannot afford more children; (2) the woman is not married and does not want to marry the father; and (3) the woman does not want to have more children. Table 6.7b shows that women who feel more secure economically are slightly more likely to support the right to abortion than women who feel less secure economically (46% compared with 43%). Table 6.7c shows that women who support abortion are slightly more likely to feel economically secure than women who are against abortion (44% compared with 42%).

Thus, percentaging within each *column* (Table 6.7b) allows us to examine the hypothesis that job security (the independent variable) is associated with support for abortion (the dependent variable). When we percentage within each *row* (Table 6.7c) the hypothesis is that attitudes toward abortion (the independent variable) may be related to one's sense of job security (the dependent variable).[7] Figures 6.3a and 6.3b are simple bar charts illustrating the two methods of calculating and comparing percentages as depicted in Tables 6.7b and 6.7c.

Finally, it is important to understand that ultimately what guides the construction and interpretation of bivariate tables is the theoretical question posed by the researcher. Although the particular example in Table 6.7 makes sense if interpreted using either row or column percentages, not all data can be interpreted this way. For example, a table comparing women's and men's attitudes toward the Equal Rights Amendment could provide a sensible explanation in only one direction. Gender might influence a person's attitude toward the amendment, but a person's attitude toward the amendment certainly couldn't influence her or his gender. Therefore, either row or column percentages are appropriate, depending on the way the variables are arrayed, but not both.

---

[7]One other way in which percentages are sometimes expressed is with the total number of cases (N) as the base for the percentages. These overall percentages express the proportion of the sample who share two properties. For example, 28 of 142 women (19.7%) are for abortion and have job security. Overall percentages do not have as much research utility as row and column percentages and are used less frequently.

Figure 6.3 **Charts Comparing Column and Row Percentages Shown in Tables 6.7b and 6.7c**

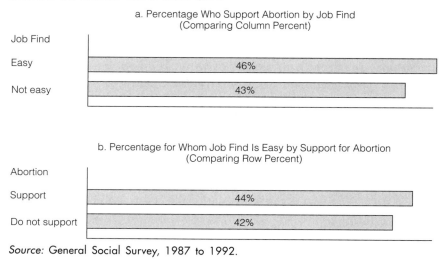

a. Percentage Who Support Abortion by Job Find
(Comparing Column Percent)

Job Find

Easy        46%

Not easy    43%

b. Percentage for Whom Job Find Is Easy by Support for Abortion
(Comparing Row Percent)

Abortion

Support         44%

Do not support  42%

*Source:* General Social Survey, 1987 to 1992.

---

***Learning Check.*** *Figures 6.3a and 6.3b both show only one set of bars. Figure 6.3a shows only the percentage who support abortion in each group. What are the percentages of those who do not support abortion? Figure 6.3b shows only the percentages with job security (easy). What are the percentages of those who do not have job security (not easy)?* Hint: *The percentages add to 100 percent within each category of the variable treated as independent.*

---

## Reading the Research Literature: Medicaid Use Among the Elderly

The guidelines for constructing and interpreting bivariate tables discussed in this chapter are not always strictly followed. Moreover, most bivariate tables presented in the professional literature are a good deal more complex than those we have just been describing. Let's conclude this section with a fairly typical example of how bivariate tables are presented in social science literature. The following example is drawn from a study by Madonna Harrington Meyer on Medicaid use among the elderly.[8]

Access to health care for all Americans is at the top of the U.S. domestic agenda today. The rise of long-term care as a politically salient topic is fueled by the increase in the elderly population, which is ten times larger than it was in 1900 and will more than double by the year 2030. Financing of long-term care is a problem for most older persons because Medicare, the universal health care program for the aged, excludes most long-term care. Only Medicaid, the poverty-based health care program, includes long-term care coverage. Therefore, only the poor elderly receive assistance from the state for long-term care.[9]

In this study, Professor Meyer explores the distribution of Medicaid benefits to the frail elderly. She examines the hypothesis that gender and race are important determinants of Medicaid use "because the U.S. long term care system stratifies by gender and race by perpetuating, rather than alleviating, inequality created by social and market forces."[10]

The study examines differences in Medicaid use in 1984, by age, education, marital status, gender, and race. Meyer analyzed data from the National Long Term Care survey conducted by the Department of Health and Human Services in 1982 and 1984. The data set is based on a national random sample of 6,000 functionally impaired older persons who resided in the community in 1982. By 1984, respondents had either continued to live in the community, entered a nursing home, or died.

Table 6.8 shows the results of the survey. Follow these steps in examining it:

1. Identify the dependent variable and the type of unit of analysis it describes (such as individual, city, or child). Here, the dependent variable is "Received Medicaid in 1984." The categories for this variable are "yes" and "no." The type of unit used in this table is individuals.

2. Identify the independent variables included in the table and the categories of each. There are five independent variables: age, education, marital status, gender, and race. Age consists of three categories: 65–74, 75–84, and 85+. Education consists of the categories "8th grade or less," "9–12 grade," and "some college." "Married,"

[8]Madonna Harrington Meyer, "Gender, Race, and the Distribution of Social Assistance: Medicaid Use among the Frail Elderly." *Gender & Society,* Vol. 8, No. 1, 1994, 8–28.

[9]Ibid., p. 9.

[10]Ibid., p. 12.

Table 6.8  **Percentage Medicaid Use in 1984, by Age, Education, Marital Status, Gender, and Race of Functionally Impaired Older Persons**

| | RECEIVED MEDICAID IN 1984 | | |
| --- | --- | --- | --- |
| | Yes | No | N |
| **Age** | | | |
| 65–74 | 19.5 | 80.5 | 1,561 |
| 75–84 | 23.8 | 76.2 | 1,943 |
| 85+ | 25.4 | 74.6 | 1,007 |
| **Education** | | | |
| 8th grade or less | 29.5 | 70.5 | 2,326 |
| 9–12 grade | 16.5 | 83.5 | 1,523 |
| Some college | 8.1 | 91.5 | 530 |
| **Marital Status** | | | |
| Married | 13.7 | 86.3 | 1,947 |
| Widowed | 28.6 | 71.4 | 2,079 |
| Divorced, separated, never married | 34.6 | 65.4 | 437 |
| **Gender** | | | |
| Men | 17.1 | 82.9 | 1,488 |
| Women | 25.4 | 74.6 | 3,024 |
| **Race** | | | |
| White | 19.1 | 80.9 | 3,942 |
| Black and Hispanic | 47.7 | 52.3 | 570 |

*Source:* Adapted from Madonna Harrington Meyer, "Gender, Race, and the Distribution of Social Assistance: Medicaid Use among the Frail Elderly." *Gender & Society*, Vol. 8, No. 1, 1994, 8–28. Used by permission of Sage Publications, Inc.

"widowed," and "divorced, separated, never married" are the categories for marital status. Gender consists of "men" and "women"; and finally, "white" and "black and Hispanic" are the categories for race.

3. Clarify the structure of the table. Note that the independent variables are arrayed in the rows of the table, while the dependent variable, "received Medicaid in 1984," is arrayed in the columns. The table is divided into five panels, one for each independent variable. There are actually five bivariate tables here, one for each independent variable.

Since the independent variables are arrayed in the rows, percentages are calculated within each row separately, with the row totals serving as the base for the percentages. For example, there were 1561 respondents who were 65 to 74 years old. Of these, 19.5 percent received Medicaid in 1984 and 80.5 percent did not. Similarly, of the 1,943 respondents who were 75 to 84, 23.8 percent received Medicaid in 1984 and 76.2 percent did not. Even though not shown in the table, the percentages within each row add to 100 percent.

4. Following the rules we learned earlier in this chapter, after calculating percentages within each category of the independent variable, we compare them for different categories of the independent variable. Using Table 6.8, we can make a number of comparisons, depending on which independent variable we are examining. For example, to determine the relationship between age and the propensity to use Medicaid, compare the percentages of respondents of the different age groups who received Medicaid in 1984 (19.5% with 23.8% and 25.4%). Alternatively, you can compare the percentages of respondents in the three age groups who did not receive Medicaid (80.5% vs. 76.2% and 74.6%).

Based on these percentage comparisons here is what you can conclude about the relation between age and the propensity to use Medicaid: Among the frail elderly age is associated with Medicaid use; the oldest-old are more likely than the youngest-old to receive Medicaid.

Next, look at the relationship between education and the propensity to use Medicaid. You can compare percentages of respondents with 8th-grade education or less who received Medicaid (29.5%) with those of respondents with 9th- to 12th-grade education (16.5%) and some college (8.1%) who received Medicaid. You can make similar comparisons to determine the association between marital status, gender, or race and the receipt of Medicaid.

The bivariate relations between age, education, marital status, gender, and receipt of Medicaid presented in Table 6.8 are also illustrated in Figure 6.4. Notice that only the percentages of elderly who have received Medicaid in 1984 ("yes") are shown. Since the percentage of elderly who responded "yes" and the percentage who responded "no" sum to 100, there is no need to show both sets of figures.

5. Finally, what conclusion can you draw about variations in the propensity to use Medicaid? The author offers this interpretation of the findings presented in the table:

Figure 6.4 **Percentage Who Received Medicaid in 1984 by Age, Education, Marital Status, Gender, and Race**

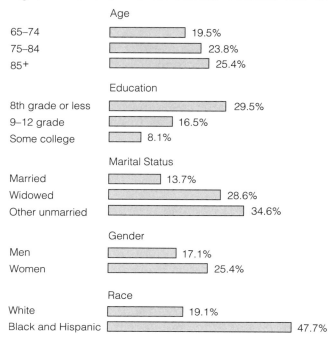

Age
- 65–74    19.5%
- 75–84    23.8%
- 85+    25.4%

Education
- 8th grade or less    29.5%
- 9–12 grade    16.5%
- Some college    8.1%

Marital Status
- Married    13.7%
- Widowed    28.6%
- Other unmarried    34.6%

Gender
- Men    17.1%
- Women    25.4%

Race
- White    19.1%
- Black and Hispanic    47.7%

Advancing age is a . . . determinant of Medicaid use, because with age, the need for chronic care increases while available resources decrease. The magnitude of the relationship is small, however; Medicaid use is only slightly higher for the oldest old than for the youngest old. Level of education is also . . . related to Medicaid use, in part because of the link between education and income. Those with an 8th grade level of education or less are nearly 4 times as likely as those with some college education to receive Medicaid. Marital status is . . . (also) related to Medicaid use. Widowed persons, for example, are more than twice as likely as married persons to rely on Medicaid. Older persons who are divorced, separated, or never married are most likely to receive Medicaid. . . . Finally, gender and race are also . . . predictors of Medicaid use. Women are somewhat more likely than men to rely on Medicaid, and other races are considerably more likely than whites to rely on Medicaid.[11]

[11]Ibid., pp. 14–15.

> **Learning Check.** *Use Table 6.8 to verify each of the following conclusions drawn by the researcher about Medicaid use among the elderly: (1) advancing age is a determinant of Medicaid use; (2) level of education is related to Medicaid use; (3) marital status is related to Medicaid use; and (4) gender and race are also related to Medicaid use. Can you explain these patterns? What other questions do these patterns raise about Medicaid use among the elderly?*

## The Properties of a Bivariate Relationship

So far we have looked at the general principles of a bivariate relationship as well as the more specific "mechanics" involved in examining bivariate tables. In this next section, we present some detailed observations we may want to make about the "properties" of a bivariate association. These properties can be expressed as three questions to ask when examining a bivariate relationship:[12]

1. Does there appear to be a relationship?
2. How strong is it?
3. What are the pattern and the direction of the relationship?

## The Existence of the Relationship

We have seen earlier in this chapter that calculating percentages and comparing them are the two operations necessary to analyze a bivariate table. Let's discuss that now in a bit more detail. Look at Table 6.9. Here we want to examine whether the frequency of traumatic events experienced by women during the preceding five-year period had an effect on their support for abortion. Support for abortion was measured with the following question: "Please tell me whether or not you think it should be possible for a pregnant woman to obtain a legal abortion if the woman wants it for any reason." The frequency of traumatic events was determined by asking respondents to indicate the number of traumas they had experienced during the preceding five years. Among the traumatic events considered were death in the family, unemployment, and hospitalizations.

---

[12]The same three properties are also discussed by Joseph F. Healey in *Statistics: A Tool for Social Research,* 4th ed. New York: Wadsworth, 1996, 308–314.

Table 6.9 **Support for Abortion by Trauma (women)**

| ABORTION | NUMBER OF TRAUMAS | | | Total |
|---|---|---|---|---|
| | 0 | 1 | 2+ | |
| Yes | 19% | 41% | 76% | 46% |
| No | 81% | 59% | 24% | 54% |
| Total | 100% | 100% | 100% | 100% |
| (N) | (27) | (44) | (33) | (104) |

*Source:* General Social Survey, 1982 to 1990.

Let's hypothesize that women who have suffered more traumatic events in their lives are more likely to be pro-choice. We are not suggesting that suffering trauma necessarily "causes" pro-choice attitudes, but that perhaps there is an indirect connection between the two. For example, perhaps women who suffered more traumas feel a loss of control over their lives and are thus more likely to want to control their own bodies through the right to choose an abortion. (Indirect associations often can be elaborated further by looking at other variables. We discuss elaboration in more detail later in this chapter.)

In this formulation trauma is said to "influence" attitudes toward abortion, so it is the independent variable; therefore, percentages are calculated within each category of trauma (trauma is the column variable). We now want to establish whether a relationship exists between the two variables.

A relationship is said to exist between two variables in a bivariate table if the percentage distributions vary across the different categories of the independent variable. In our example we would expect the percentages of those who support abortion and those who oppose it to differ across the three categories of trauma. We can easily see that the percentage who support abortion changes across the different levels of trauma. For women experiencing 0 traumas, 19 percent are pro-choice; for women experiencing 1 trauma, 41 percent are pro-choice; and for those experiencing 2 or more traumas, 76 percent are pro-choice.

Table 6.9 indicates that trauma and support for abortion are associated, as hypothesized.

If the number of traumas were unrelated to attitudes toward abortion among women, then we would expect to find the percentages of women who are pro-choice (or anti-choice) to be equal, regardless of the number of traumas experienced. Table 6.10 is a fictional representation of a strictly hypothetical pattern of no association between abortion attitudes and traumas. The percentage of women who are pro-choice in each category of trauma is equal to the overall percentage of women in the sample who are pro-choice (46%). But looking at the actual data in the original table, Table 6.9, it's clear that the observed percentages of women who are pro-choice differ widely across the three categories of trauma, thereby indicating that the two variables are, in fact, related.

## The Strength of the Relationship

In the preceding section, we saw how to establish whether an association exists in a bivariate table. We now need to establish how to determine the strength of an association between the two variables. A quick method is to examine the percentage difference across the different categories of the independent variable. The larger the percentage difference across the categories, the stronger the association.

In the hypothetical example of no relationship between trauma and attitude toward abortion (Table 6.10) there is a 0 percent difference between the columns. At the other extreme, if all women who suffered 1 or more traumas were pro-choice, and none of the women with 0 traumas was pro-choice, a perfect relationship would be manifested in a 100 percent difference. Most relationships, however, will be somewhere

Table 6.10 **Support for Abortion by Trauma (a hypothetical illustration of no relationship)**

|  | NUMBER OF TRAUMAS | | | |
| --- | --- | --- | --- | --- |
| ABORTION | 0 | 1 | 2+ | Total |
| Yes | 46% | 46% | 46% | 46% |
| No | 54% | 54% | 54% | 54% |
| Total | 100% | 100% | 100% | 100% |
| (N) | (27) | (44) | (33) | (104) |

in between these two extremes. In fact, we rarely see a situation with either a 0 percent or a 100 percent difference. Going back to the observed percentages in Table 6.9, we find the largest percentage difference between 0 and 2+ traumas (76% − 19% = 57%). The differences between 0 and 1 trauma (41% − 19% = 22%) and between 1 and 2+ traumas (76% − 41% = 35%), though not as large, are nonetheless substantial, indicating a strong relationship between number of traumas experienced by women and their attitudes toward abortion.

Percentage differences are but a *rough* indicator of the strength of a relationship between two variables. In later chapters, we discuss measures of association that provide a more standardized indicator of the strength of an association.

## The Direction of the Relationship

When both the independent and dependent variables in a bivariate table are measured at the ordinal level or higher, we can talk about the relationship between the variables as being either positive or negative. A **positive** bivariate relationship exists when the variables vary in the same direction. Higher values of one variable "go together" with higher values of the other variable. In a **negative** bivariate relationship the variables vary in opposite directions: higher values of one variable "go together" with low values of the other variable (and the lower values of one go together with the high values of the other).

---

*Positive Relationship*   A bivariate relationship between two variables measured at the ordinal level or higher in which the variables vary in the same direction.

*Negative Relationship*   A bivariate relationship between two variables measured at the ordinal level or higher in which the variables vary in opposite directions.

---

Table 6.11 from the GSS survey displays a positive relationship between health condition and social class. Examine each class category separately. For individuals in the lower social class (lowest score), a poor health condition is most typical (39%); for the middle-class group, fair health is most common (45%); and finally, the high social class (the highest score) exhibits the highest percentage (63%) of instances of good health. This is a positive relationship, with higher class

Table 6.11　**Health Condition by Social Class: A Positive Relationship**

| HEALTH | CLASS | | |
|---|---|---|---|
| | Low | Middle | High |
| Poor | 39% | 12% | 9% |
| Fair | 36% | 45% | 28% |
| Good | 25% | 43% | 63% |
| Total | 100% | 100% | 100% |
| (N) | (39) | (254) | (202) |

*Source:* General Social Survey, 1987 to 1992.

positions associated with better health condition and lower class positions associated with poorer health.

Table 6.12 from the GSS shows a negative association between the frequency of trauma and social class. For individuals in the lower social class, a frequency of 2+ is the most typical (47%); for the middle-class group the most common (42%) trauma level is 1, and finally 0 trauma is most frequently associated (48%) with the upper social class. The relationship is a negative one because as class position increases the frequency of trauma decreases.[13]

In the next chapter, we will see that measures of relationship for ordinal or interval-ratio variables take on a positive or a negative value, depending on the direction of the relationship.

> **Learning Check.** Look back at Table 6.8. Does a relationship exist between education and Medicaid use among the elderly? How strong is the relationship?

---

[13]Note that the statement "as class position increases the frequency of trauma decreases" applies to the category 2+ only in a limited sense: the frequency (percentage) of trauma *decreases* as class position increases from low to middle class (from 47% to 17%) or from low to high class (from 47% to 32%), but not from middle to high class, where the percentages actually increase (from 17% to 32%).

Table 6.12  **Frequency of Trauma by Social Class: A Negative Relationship**

| TRAUMA | CLASS | | |
| --- | --- | --- | --- |
| | Low | Middle | High |
| 0 | 31% | 41% | 48% |
| 1 | 22% | 42% | 20% |
| 2+ | 47% | 17% | 32% |
| Total | 100% | 100% | 100% |
| (N) | (48) | (220) | (180) |

*Source:* General Social Survey, 1987 to 1992.

## Elaboration

In the preceding sections we have looked at relationships between two variables—an independent and a dependent variable. The examination of a possible relationship between two variables is, however, only a first step in data analysis. Having established through bivariate analysis that the independent and dependent variables are associated, we seek to further interpret and understand the nature of this relationship. In this section, we discuss a procedure called *elaboration*. **Elaboration** is a process designed to further explore a bivariate relationship; it involves the introduction of additional variables, called control variables. Each potential control variable represents an alternative explanation for the bivariate relationship under consideration.

---

*Elaboration*  A process designed to further explore a bivariate relationship; it involves the introduction of additional variables, called control variables. Each potential control variable represents an alternative explanation for the bivariate relationship under consideration.

---

The introduction of additional, control variables into a bivariate relationship serves three primary goals in data analysis.

■ Elaboration allows us to *test for nonspuriousness.* As we saw in Chapter 1, to establish cause-and-effect relations we need to show

not only that an independent and a dependent variable are associated, but also to establish the time order between them and
provide theoretical and empirical evidence that the association is
nonspurious; that is, that it cannot be "explained away" by other
variables.

■ Elaboration *clarifies the causal sequence* of bivariate relationships by
introducing variables hypothesized to intervene between the independent and dependent variable.

■ Elaboration *specifies the different conditions* under which the original
bivariate relationship might hold.

In the preceding sections we learned how to establish that two
variables are associated; in this section we explore the theoretical and
statistical considerations involved in elaborating bivariate relationships. We illustrate the process of elaboration using three examples.
The first is an example of testing for nonspuriousness; the second is
a research example illustrating a causal sequence in which a third
variable intervenes between the independent and dependent variables;
finally, the third research example illustrates how elaboration can
uncover conditional relationships.

## Testing for Nonspuriousness: Firefighters and Property Damage

Let's begin with a favorite example of a spurious relationship. Researchers
have confirmed a strong bivariate relationship between the "number
of firefighters" (the independent variable) at a fire site and the "amount
of property damage" (the dependent variable). The more firefighters
at the site, the greater the amount of damage. This association might
lead you to the embarrassing conclusion (depicted in Figure 6.5) that
firefighters cause property damage at fire sites.

Figure 6.5 depicts what might be a *direct causal relationship* between
firefighters and the amount of damage. The relationship between two
variables is said to be a **direct causal relationship** when it cannot be

Figure 6.5  **The Bivariate Relation Between Number of
Firefighters and Property Damage**

Number of Firefighters ⟶ Property Damage

independent variable                    dependent variable

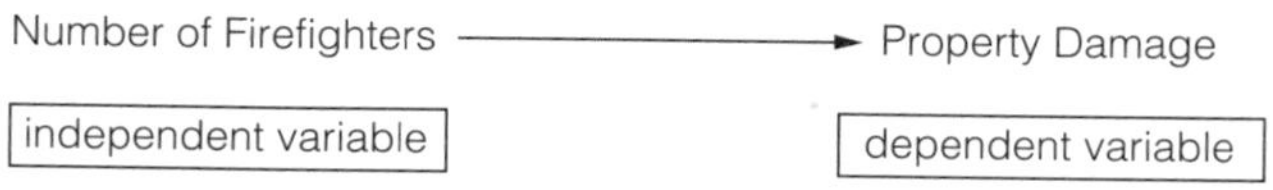

accounted for by other theoretically relevant variables. Clearly, in this case, the relationship between the number of firefighters and damage can be accounted for by a third, causally prior variable—the size of the fire. When the fire is large, more firefighters are sent to the site and there is a great deal of property damage. Similarly, when the fire is small, fewer firefighters are at the site and there is probably very little damage.

This alternative explanation is shown in Figure 6.6. Note that according to the hypothesized causal order suggested in Figure 6.6, both the number of firefighters and the extent of property damage are related to the variable the "size of the fire," but not to each other. The size of the fire is called a *control variable,* and the relation between the number of firefighters and property damage as depicted in Figure 6.6 is *spurious.* A **spurious relationship** is a relationship between two variables in which both the independent and dependent variables are influenced by a causally prior control variable and there is no causal link between them. The bivariate relationship between the independent and dependent variables can thus be "explained away" through the introduction of the control variable.

---

*Direct Causal Relationship*   A bivariate relationship that cannot be accounted for by other theoretically relevant variables.

*Spurious Relationship*   A relationship in which both the independent and dependent variables are influenced by a causally prior control variable and there is no causal link between them. The relationship between the independent and dependent variables is said to be "explained away" by the control variable.

---

Figure 6.6   **Spurious Relationship**

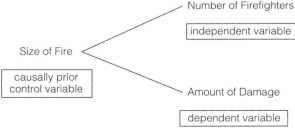

How do you go about testing for the spuriousness of the relationship between the number of firefighters and the extent of property damage as suggested in Figure 6.6? Researchers have adopted the following rule of thumb for determining whether a relationship between two variables is either direct (causal) or spurious: If the bivariate relationship between the two variables remains about the same after controlling for the effect of one or more causally prior and theoretically relevant variables, then the original bivariate relationship is said to be a direct (causal relationship) association. However, if the original bivariate relationship decreases considerably (or vanishes), then the bivariate relationship is said to be spurious.

Let's see how we can apply this rule of thumb to the firefighter example. One way to control for the effect of the size of the fire on the relationship between the number of firefighters and the extent of damage is to divide the fire sites into large and small fires and then reexamine the bivariate association between the other two variables within each group of fire sites. If the original bivariate relationship vanishes (or diminishes considerably), then the explanation suggested by Figure 6.6 would seem more likely. If, however, the original relationship is maintained, then we may need to hold on to the original explanation suggested by Figure 6.5 or go back to the drawing board and think of other alternative explanations for the puzzling relationship between the number of firefighters and the extent of property damage.

Figure 6.7 illustrates the bivariate association between the number of firefighters and the extent of property damage (6.7a), and the process of controlling for the variable "size of fire" (6.7b). Note that the control for size of fire resulted in a substantial decrease (from 40% to 12% difference) in the size of the relationship between the number of firefighters and property damage. This result supports the notion, as depicted in Figure 6.6, that the size of the fire explains both the number of firefighters and the extent of property damage, and that the relationship between the number of firefighters and property damage is therefore spurious.

The introduction of the control variable "size of the fire" into the original bivariate relationship between "number of firefighters" and "property damage" illustrates the process of elaboration. These are the steps:

1. Divide the observations into subgroups on the basis of the control variable. We have as many subgroups as there are categories in the control variable. (In our case there were two subgroups: small and large fires.)

Figure 6.7 **Elaborating a Bivariate Relationship**

**1.** A bivariate relationship between the number of firefighters and the extent of the property damage at 20 fire sites.

(a)

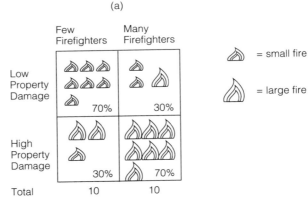

Total     10     10

% difference = 70% − 30% = 40% (column percentages)

**2.** Control for size of fire: divide fire sites into small and large fires. In each group, recalculate the bivariate relationship between the number of firefighters and the extent of the property damage.

(b)

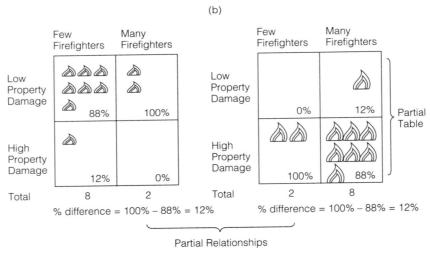

**3.** Compare the partial relationships with the original relationship: 40% compared with 12%.

2. Reexamine the relationship between the original two variables separately for each of the subgroups. The bivariate relationship in each of the separate tables is called a **partial relationship**. The tables are called **partial tables**.

3. Compare the partial relationships with the original bivariate relationship for the total group. In a direct causal pattern, the partial relationships will be very close to the original bivariate relationship. In a spurious pattern, the partial relationship will be much weaker than in the original bivariate relationship.

---

*Partial Relationship*   The relationship between the independent and dependent variables shown in a partial table.

*Partial Tables*   Bivariate tables produced when controlling for a third variable.

---

We employed the elaboration procedure to test for the spurious relationship between the number of firefighters and property damage. Now let's see how elaboration is employed to interpret the causal sequence of bivariate relationships by introducing a control variable hypothesized to *intervene* between the independent and dependent variables.

## An Intervening Relationship: Religion and Attitude Toward Abortion

The research on the relationship between religious affiliation and attitudes toward abortion has shown a consistent pattern: religious affiliation is related to the level of support for abortion.[14] In particular, it has been shown that Catholics oppose abortion more than Protestants or Jews.[15]

To test the hypothesis that religion and abortion attitudes are related, we used data from the 1988 to 1991 GSS sample. We limited the analysis to Catholics and Protestants because of the small numbers of respondents with other religious affiliations. Attitudes toward abortion are measured in terms of the respondent's approval or disapproval of the following three situations:[16] (1) the woman does not want the baby because the family has a very low income and cannot afford more children; (2) the woman is not married and does not

---

[14]For example, see Harris Mills, "Religion, Values and Attitudes Toward Abortion." *Journal for the Scientific Study of Religion,* Vol. 24, No. 2, 1985, 119–236.

[15]Mario Renzi, "Ideal Family Size as an Intervening Variable Between Religion and Attitudes Towards Abortion." *Journal for the Scientific Study of Religion,* Vol. 14, 1975, 23–27.

[16]We have included in the analysis only respondents who either approved ("yes") or disapproved ("no") of all three conditions.

want to marry the father; and (3) the woman does not want to have more children.

The findings are presented in Table 6.13 and illustrated in Figure 6.8. Since, according to the hypothesis, religious affiliation is the independent variable, we use column percentages for our analysis. The

Table 6.13 **Religious Affiliation and Support for Abortion**

|  | RELIGIOUS AFFILIATION | | |
|---|---|---|---|
| SUPPORT | Catholic | Protestant | Total |
| Yes | 34% (56) | 45% (109) | 41% |
| No | 66% (107) | 55% (131) | 59% |
| Total (N) | 100% (163) | 100% (240) | 100% (403) |

*Source:* General Social Survey, 1988 to 1991.

Figure 6.8 **Percentage Who Support Abortion by Religious Affiliation**

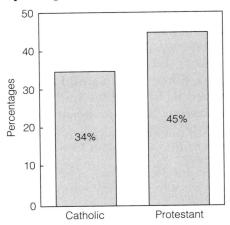

*Source:* General Social Survey, 1988 to 1991.

Figure 6.9 **The Bivariate Relationship Between Religion and Support for Abortion**

results support the hypothesis that religion is related to attitudes toward abortion. Forty-five percent of Protestants, compared with only 34 percent of Catholics, support a woman's right to a legal abortion for the three cited reasons.

These results may suggest the existence of a direct causal relationship between religion and attitudes toward abortion. According to this interpretation of the relationship, being either Protestant or Catholic leads to a different abortion orientation regardless of other factors. Graphically, this hypothesized relationship is shown in Figure 6.9.

Another body of research findings dealing with religion challenges the conclusion that there is a direct causal link (as suggested by Figure 6.9) between religious affiliation and support for abortion. According to this research literature, some of the differences between Catholics and Protestants can be explained by the variable "preferred family size."[17] It is argued that religion is systematically related to desired family size; Catholics prefer larger numbers of children than non-Catholics. Similarly, if one conceptualizes abortion as an alternative device to control family size, then support for abortion may also be associated with preferred family size. Therefore, preferred family size operates as an intervening mechanism through which the relationship between religion and abortion attitudes occurs.

To check these ideas, we analyzed the bivariate associations between preferred family size and religion (Table 6.14) and between preferred family size and support for abortion (Table 6.15).[18] Notice that because the theory suggests that preferred family size operates as an intervening mechanism between religious affiliation and support for abortion, it is analyzed as the dependent variable in Table 6.14 and as the independent variable in Table 6.15.

---

[17]Mario Renzi, pp. 23–27.

[18]Preferred family size was measured by responses to a question about the ideal number of children for a family. Those respondents who said 2 or fewer children as ideal were classified as preferring small families; those who answered 3 or more were classified as preferring large families.

Table 6.14  **Religious Affiliation and Preferred Family Size**

| | RELIGIOUS AFFILIATION | | |
|---|---|---|---|
| SIZE | Catholic | Protestant | Total |
| Large | 52% (85) | 27% (65) | 37% (150) |
| Small | 48% (78) | 73% (175) | 63% (253) |
| Total (N) | 100% (163) | 100% (240) | 100% (403) |

*Source:* General Social Survey, 1988 to 1991.

Table 6.15  **Preferred Family Size and Support for Abortion**

| | PREFERRED FAMILY SIZE | | |
|---|---|---|---|
| SUPPORT | Large | Small | Total |
| Yes | 25% (38) | 50% (127) | 41% (165) |
| No | 75% (112) | 50% (126) | 59% (238) |
| Total (N) | 100% (150) | 100% (253) | 100% (403) |

*Source:* General Social Survey, 1988 to 1991.

The data in Tables 6.14 and 6.15 confirm the linkages between preferred family size and religion and preferred family size and support for abortion. First, more Catholics (52%) than Protestants (27%) tend to prefer larger families (Table 6.14). Second, more respondents who prefer smaller families support a woman's right to abortion (50%) compared with those who prefer larger families (25%) (Table 6.15).

According to this interpretation of the relationship between religion and abortion attitudes, not only is preferred family size associated with both religious affiliation and support for abortion, but it also intervenes between religious affiliation and support for abortion. Thus, it is hypothesized that the relation between religion and attitudes toward abortion is *indirect,* and *linked* via the control variable—preferred family size.

The hypothetical causal sequence suggested by this interpretation is shown in Figure 6.10. In this formulation the control variable (preferred family size) is called an *intervening variable.* An **intervening variable** is a control variable that follows an independent variable but precedes the dependent variable in a causal sequence. Because preferred family size follows the independent variable, religion, but precedes the dependent variable, abortion attitudes, it is considered an intervening variable. The relationship between religion and support for abortion shown in Figure 6.10 is called an *intervening relationship.* An **intervening relationship** is one between two variables in which a control variable intervenes between the independent and dependent variables.

---

*Intervening Variable*  A control variable that follows an independent variable but precedes the dependent variable in a causal sequence.

*Intervening Relationship*  A relationship in which the control variable intervenes between the independent and dependent variables.

---

We can test the implication suggested by the model shown in Figure 6.10 by controlling for preferred family size and repeating the original bivariate analysis between religious affiliation and support for abortion. We control for family size by separating the respondents who indicated that they preferred larger families from those who prefer smaller families. If the causal sequence hypothesized by Figure 6.10

Figure 6.10  **Intervening Relationship**

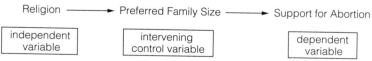

is correct, then the association between religion and abortion attitudes should disappear or diminish considerably once preferred family size has been controlled.

The results presented in Table 6.16 and Figure 6.11 support the notion, as depicted in Figure 6.10, that preferred family size intervenes

Table 6.16 **Religious Affiliation and Support for Abortion After Controlling for Desired Family Size**

| SUPPORT ABORTION | SMALL FAMILY | | | LARGE FAMILY | | |
| | RELIGIOUS AFFILIATION | | | RELIGIOUS AFFILIATION | | |
| | Catholic | Protestant | Total | Catholic | Protestant | Total |
| Yes | 46%<br>(36) | 52%<br>(91) | 50%<br>(127) | 24%<br>(20) | 28%<br>(18) | 25%<br>(38) |
| No | 54%<br>(42) | 48%<br>(84) | 50%<br>(126) | 76%<br>(65) | 72%<br>(47) | 75%<br>(112) |
| Total<br>(N) | 100%<br>(78) | 100%<br>(175) | 100%<br>(253) | 100%<br>(85) | 100%<br>(65) | 100%<br>(150) |

*Source:* General Social Survey, 1988 to 1991.

Figure 6.11 **Percentage Supporting Abortion by Religious Affiliation After Controlling for Preferred Family Size**

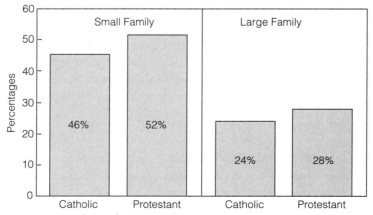

*Source:* General Social Survey, 1988 to 1991.

between religion and abortion attitudes. The associations between religion and abortion attitudes in the two partial tables are smaller than the association in the original bivariate table (Table 6.13). Among respondents who prefer larger families there are smaller differences between Catholics and Protestants regarding a woman's right to an abortion. Twenty-eight percent of Protestants and 24 percent of Catholics support legal abortion. Among those who prefer smaller families, there are also rather small differences between the two religious groups regarding support for legal abortion. Fifty-two percent of Protestants and 46 percent of Catholics are in support of abortion. Thus, we would conclude that Catholics are less favorable to abortion (than Protestants) because they prefer larger families. These findings increase our understanding of the original bivariate relationship between religious affiliation and attitudes toward abortion.

---

**Learning Check.**  *You may have noticed that the tests for spuriousness and for an intervening relationship are identical: they both require that the partial associations disappear or diminish considerably! So how can you differentiate between the two? The differentiation is made on a theoretical rather than on an empirical ground. When a relationship is spurious, there is no causal link between the independent and dependent variables, and both are influenced by a causally prior control variable. In contrast, in an intervening relationship there is an indirect causal link between the independent and dependent variables, and the control variable follows the independent variable but precedes the dependent variable in the causal sequence.*

---

## Conditional Relationships: More on Abortion

What other variables may explain the relationship between religion and attitudes toward abortion? One possible variable is "religious participation." In their research on abortion attitudes, Arney and Trescher[19] found that when religious participation is controlled for, there is little difference in abortion attitudes between Catholics and Protestants who attend church less than once a month. In contrast, among Catholics and Protestants who attend church more than once a month, Catholics were more likely than Protestants to oppose abortion.[20] Other researchers

[19]William R. Arney and William H. Trescher. "Trends in Attitudes Toward Abortion, 1972–1975." *Family Planning Perspective*, Vol. 8, 1976, 117–124.

[20]William V. D'Antonio and Steven Stack, "Religion, Ideal Family Size, and Abortion: Extending Renzi's Hypothesis." *Journal for the Scientific Study of Religion*, Vol. 19, 1980, 397–408.

note that age and gender may also influence the relationship between religion and abortion attitudes. The differences in abortion attitudes between Catholics and Protestants may differ depending on their age and/or gender.

What do these examples have in common? They all specify different conditions under which the relationship between religion and abortion attitudes are expected to hold. For example, Arney and Trescher indicate that the differences in abortion attitudes between Protestants and Catholics might only hold under one condition (attend church more than once a month) of the control variable "religious participation" but not under another (attend church less than once a month). Similarly, the relationship may differ for men and women, or for older and younger individuals. When a bivariate relationship differs for different conditions of the control variable we say that it is a **conditional relationship**. Another way to describe a conditional relationship is to say that there is a *statistical interaction* between the control variable and the independent variable.

Because conditional relationships are very common there are many research examples in sociology illustrating this pattern of elaboration. One such example comes from a study on the relationship between stance on legal abortion and opinions about the morality of abortion. The study shows that although nearly all opponents of abortion view abortion as morally wrong, not all pro-choice supporters view abortion as morally right. Instead, many pro-choice supporters favor legal abortion despite personal moral reservations.[21] This bivariate relationship between abortion morality and stance on legal abortion is displayed in Table 6.17.

---

*Conditional Relationship*  A relationship between the independent and dependent variables that differs for different conditions of the control variable.

---

Because stance on legal abortion is the independent variable, percentages are calculated in the columns. The results of this analysis support Scott's hypothesis: there is almost unanimous agreement among those who oppose abortion (98%) that abortion is morally wrong. Among those who favor legal abortion, however, the level of

[21]Jacqueline Scott, "Conflicting Belief about Abortion: Legal Approval and Moral Doubts." *Social Psychology Quarterly,* Vol. 52, No. 4, 1989, 319–326.

Table 6.17 **Abortion Morality and Stance on Legal Abortion**

| | STANCE ON LEGAL ABORTION | | |
| ABORTION MORALITY | Pro-Choice | Pro-Life | Total |
|---|---|---|---|
| Always wrong or depends | 37% | 98% | 57% |
| Not wrong | 63% | 2% | 43% |
| Total | 100% | 100% | 100% |
| (N) | (337) | (162) | (499) |

*Source:* Adapted from Jacqueline Scott, "Conflicting Belief about Abortion: Legal Approval and Moral Doubts." *Social Psychology Quarterly,* Vol. 52, No. 4, 1989, 319–326. Copyright 1989 by the American Sociological Association. Reprinted by permission.

incongruence is relatively high: 37 percent support legal abortion despite viewing it as morally wrong.[22]

Although there is little difference between men's and women's attitudes toward the legality of abortion, some argue that women are far more likely to feel that abortion is morally wrong. For example, Gilligan[23] argues that whereas men tend to be more concerned with rights and rules, women are more concerned with caring and relationships. Abortion, therefore, may pose a greater moral dilemma for women than for men. To examine the hypothesis that women are more likely than men to favor legal abortion despite moral reservations, the researcher controlled for gender and compared the original relationship between stance on legal abortion and abortion morality among men and women. The cross-tabulation of abortion morality by stance on legal abortion, controlling for gender, is given in Table 6.18. The table shows a marked gender difference in the relationship between abortion morality and stance on legal abortion. Although we can still conclude from Table 6.18 that stance on legal abortion and abortion morality are associated, we need to qualify this conclusion by saying that this association is stronger for men (percentage difference is 96% − 29% = 67%) than for women (percentage difference is 100% − 46% = 54%).

Because the relationship between the independent and dependent variables is different in each of the partial tables, the relationship is

[22]Ibid., p. 322.

[23]Carol Gilligan, *In Different Voice.* Cambridge: Harvard University Press, 1982.

Table 6.18 **Abortion Morality and Stance on Legal Abortion after Controlling for Gender**

| | MEN | | | WOMEN | | |
| | STANCE ON ABORTION | | | STANCE ON ABORTION | | |
| ABORTION MORALITY | Pro-Choice | Pro-Life | Total | Pro-Choice | Pro-Life | Total |
|---|---|---|---|---|---|---|
| Always wrong or depends | 29% | 96% | 50% | 46% | 100% | 64% |
| Not wrong | 71% | 4% | 50% | 54% | 0% | 36% |
| Total | 100% | 100% | 100% | 100% | 100% | 100% |
| (N) | (172) | (78) | (250) | (165) | (84) | (249) |

*Source:* Adapted from Jacqueline Scott, "Conflicting Belief about Abortion: Legal Approval and Moral Doubts." *Social Psychology Quarterly,* Vol. 52, No. 4, 1989, 319–326. Copyright 1989 by the American Sociological Association. Reprinted by permission.

said to be a conditional relationship; that is, the original bivariate relationship depends upon the control variable. In our example, the strength of the relationship between abortion morality and stance on legal abortion is conditioned on gender. The conditional relationship between stance on abortion and abortion morality is depicted in Figure 6.12.

## The Limitations of Elaboration

The elaboration examples discussed in this section point to the complexity of the social world. We started this chapter by stating that most things around us "go together." It is more accurate to say that most things around us are "tangled," and one of the goals of social science is to "untangle" them. Elaboration is a procedure that helps us "untangle" bivariate relations.

In the illustrations presented in this section we looked at bivariate relationships that were clarified and reinterpreted when a control variable was introduced. But how do we know which variables to control for? In reality, theory provides significant guidance both to relationships we look for and the sorts of variables that should be introduced as controls. Without theory as a guide, elaboration can become a series of exercises that more closely resemble random shots in the dark than scientific analysis. But even with theory as our guide,

Figure 6.12 **A Conditional Relationship**

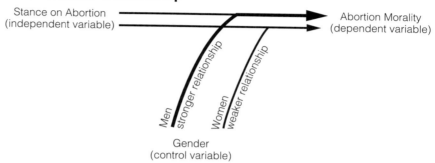

the statistical analysis is often more complex than the presentation in this section may suggest. In our examples, when the control variable was introduced, the "real" nature of the relationship "jumped right out at us." But it's not always that easy. In fact, most often there is a perilous gap between theory and analysis. This does not mean that you have to abandon your effort to "untangle" bivariate relationships, only that you should be aware of both the importance of theory as a guide to your analysis and the limitations of the statistical analysis.

> **Learning Check.**   *In this section, you have been introduced to a number of important new terms. See if you can write out definitions for the following terms: elaboration, control variable, intervening variable, causally prior variable, spurious relationship, partial relationship, partial table, and conditional relationship. If you cannot provide a definition for each of these terms, you are not clear on the process of elaboration. Go back and review.*

## Statistics in Practice: Family Support for the Transition from High School

In earlier chapters we saw that statistics helps us analyze how race, class, age, or gender shapes our experiences. However, we focused primarily on how these categories of experience operate separately (we compared men and women; the young and the old; the working class and the middle class; and so on). Now we need to think about how these systems interlock in shaping our experience as individuals in society.[24] Everyone has his or her own particular combination of a race, a social class, an age, and a gender. These factors act as lenses through which we experience the world. Through analysis of the intersecting effects of these factors we can understand the ways that others experience the world from their different or similar perspectives.

When we start to see race, class, and gender as intersecting systems of experience, we see, for example, that while white women and women of color may share some common experience based on their gender, their racial experiences are distinct. Similarly, depending on their race and class, men experience gender differently. For example, we know that the removal of manufacturing jobs has increased black and Hispanic male job loss. At the same time, many women of color have found their work opportunities expanded in service and high-tech jobs.[25]

The methods of bivariate analysis and, in particular, the statistical technique of elaboration are especially suitable for the examination of how race, class, and gender are linked with social behavior. In Table 6.19 we present the findings of a study that examined the kind of family support women who are now in professional and managerial positions received when they made their transition from high school to college. This example illustrates how to analyze the simultaneous operation of race and class using the method of elaboration. The example also demonstrates the drastic differences in conclusions that would have been drawn had either or both of these factors been ignored.[26]

Table 6.19 includes five types of family support, representing five dependent variables: (1) information on entrance examinations and colleges; (2) information on admission requirements; (3) financial support in paying tuition and fees; (4) emotional support; and (5) encouragement for career. Only one category is given for each dependent variable. This category represents the percentage of women having received family support in each of the specified areas. For example, 42 percent (of the 50) of black women who were raised in middle-class families reported that family members had helped them in procuring information on

---

[24]Patricia Hill Collins, "Toward a New Vision: Race, Class, and Gender as Categories of Analysis and Connection." Keynote address at Integrating Race and Gender into the College Curriculum: A workshop sponsored by the Center for Research on Women, Memphis State University, Memphis, TN, 1989.

[25]D. Stanley Eitzen and Maxine Baca Zinn, "Structural Transformation and Systems of Inequality" in Margaret L. Andersen and Patricia Hill Collins, *Race, Class, and Gender*, 178–183.

[26]Lynn Weber Cannon, Elizabeth Higginbotham, and Marianne L. A. Leung, "Race and Class Bias in Research on Women: A Methodological Note." Research paper 5, presented at the Center for Research on Women, Memphis, 1987.

Table 6.19 **Race and Class Origin Differences in Percentage Reporting Family Support for the Transition from High School to College**

| | BLACK | | WHITE | |
|---|---|---|---|---|
| | Working Class | Middle Class | Working Class | Middle Class |
| TYPE OF FAMILY SUPPORT | (N = 50) | (N = 50) | (N = 50) | (N = 50) |
| **Information** | | | | |
| Entrance exams and colleges | 22% | 42% | 24% | 40% |
| Admission requirements | 20% | 34% | 20% | 30% |
| **Financial** | | | | |
| Paid tuition and fees | 56% | 90% | 62% | 88% |
| **Emotional** | | | | |
| Emotional support | 64% | 86% | 56% | 70% |
| Encouragement for career | 56% | 60% | 40% | 52% |

*Source:* Adapted from Lynn Weber, Elizabeth Higginbotham, and Marianne L. A. Leung, "Race and Class Bias in Research on Women: A Methodological Note." Research Paper 5 presented at the Center for Research on Women, University of Memphis, 1987.

entrance examinations and colleges. The remaining 58 percent of this group (not shown) did not receive family help in this area.

Race and class origin are the two independent variables in this analysis. To estimate the effect of class on family support we compare middle class–raised women with working class–raised women among black and white women. The data show that there are large class differences in all types of family support provided to these women by their families. For example, whereas 90 percent of black middle-class families paid tuition for their daughters, only 56 percent of black working-class families did so. A similar pattern is observed among the white women. Similarly, more middle-class families, both black (86%) and white (70%), provided emotional support to their daughters during the transition from high school to college.

The second step involved in looking at a table like this one is to examine whether there are racial differences in family support. To estimate the effect of race we compare black and white women who were raised in working-class and in middle-class families. This comparison reveals virtually no relationship between race and either procurement of information or financial support. For instance, 20 percent of working-class blacks and 20 percent of working-class whites were provided help with information on college admissions requirements; similarly, 34 percent of middle-class blacks and 30 percent of middle-class whites were provided support in this category. However, examination of the emotional support category reveals fairly substantial race differences: 86 percent of respondents report that their middle-class black families provided emotional support compared with only 70 percent of the middle-class white families. Similarly, more working-class blacks (64% vs. 56%) provided emotional support to their daughters in the transition from high school to college.

The group that differs most from the others on both emotional support and encouragement for career are black middle-class women, who received the highest degree of family support in each of these categories.

In conclusion, the data reveal a strong relationship between class origin and both information and financial support provided by the family. Also, the data show relationships between both race and class and emotional encouragement and support. Had the study failed to address both the race and class background of the professional and managerial women, we would have drawn very different conclusions about the role of families in supporting women as they moved from high school to college.[27]

This is another example of the pattern of elaboration examined earlier. In this case, class origin is used as a control variable to elaborate on the relationship between race and family support. In this society, race is associated with class (blacks are more likely to be raised in a working-class family), and class is associated with family support (working-class families are less likely to provide family support). Had we not analyzed the effect of the class background of the women as well as their race, we would have concluded that black women receive far less support in all areas than white women. Such a conclusion could have reinforced a stereotype—that black families are less supportive of their children's education. Such a conclusion would represent a distortion of the real process since it is working-class women, both black and white, who receive less family support.[28]

[27]Ibid.
[28]Ibid.

Finally, this example demonstrates the importance of looking at the simultaneous effects of race and class on the lives of women. This is only one among many ways in which race, class, and gender comparisons can be incorporated in a statistical analysis. Moreover, examining the linkages between race, class, and gender cannot be limited to women. While integrating these variables into our analysis introduces complexity to our research, it also suggests new possibilities for thinking that will enrich us all.

## MAIN POINTS

- Bivariate analysis is a statistical technique designed to detect and describe the relationship between two variables. A relationship is said to exist when certain values of one variable tend to "go together" with certain values of the other variable.

- A bivariate table displays the distribution of one variable across the categories of another variable. It is obtained by classifying cases based on their joint scores for two variables.

- Percentaging bivariate tables is a method used to examine the relationship between two variables that have been organized in a bivariate table. The percentages are always calculated within each category of the independent variable.

- Bivariate tables are interpreted by comparing percentages across different categories of the independent variable. A relationship is said to exist if the percentage distributions vary across the categories of the independent variable.

- Variables measured at the ordinal or interval-ratio levels may be positively or negatively associated. With a positive association, higher values of one variable correspond to higher values of the other variable. When there is a negative association between variables, higher values of one variable correspond to lower values of the other variable.

- Elaboration is a technique designed to clarify bivariate associations. It involves the introduction of control variables to interpret the links between the independent and dependent variables.

- In a spurious relationship both the independent and dependent variables are influenced by a causally prior control variable, and there is no causal link between them.

- In an intervening relationship the control variable follows the independent variable but precedes the dependent variable in the causal sequence.
- In a conditional relationship the bivariate relationship between the independent and dependent variables is different in each of the partial tables.

## KEY TERMS

| | |
|---|---|
| *bivariate analysis* | *intervening variable* |
| *bivariate table* | *marginals* |
| *cell* | *negative relationship* |
| *column variable* | *partial relationship* |
| *conditional relationship* | *partial table* |
| *cross-tabulation* | *positive relationship* |
| *direct causal relationship* | *row variable* |
| *elaboration* | *spurious relationship* |
| *intervening relationship* | |

## SPSS DEMONSTRATIONS

*Demonstration 1: Producing Bivariate Tables*

SPSS has a separate procedure designed specifically to produce cross-tabulation tables. Perhaps not surprisingly, it is called the Crosstabs procedure and can be found under *Summarize* in the *Statistics* menu. The dialog box for Crosstabs requires us to specify both a variable that will define the rows and one that defines the columns of a table. We will investigate the relationship between support for a legal abortion for a woman who is not married and religious affiliation.

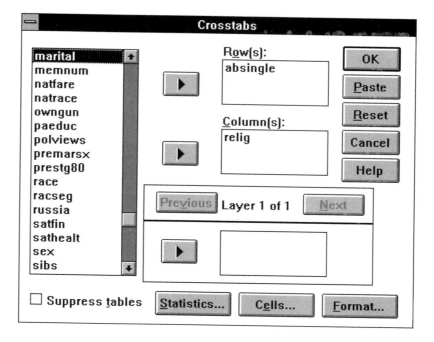

By default, SPSS displays the count in each cell of the table. Normally, then, you should click on the *Cells* button to request percentages. As usual, we percentage the table based on the independent or predictor variable, which is religious affiliation in this example. Since that variable defines the columns, we click on the checkbox for "Column" (note that "Observed" is already checked by default in the Counts section).

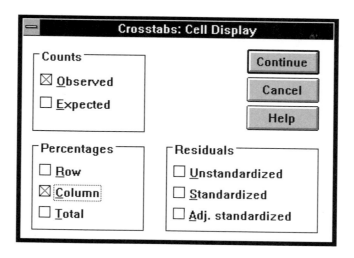

Click on *Continue*, then *OK*, to see the following table displayed. SPSS displays both the count and column percentage in each cell. In the upper left corner of the table, the labels "Count" and "Col Pct" are displayed as a reminder of what SPSS has placed in each cell. Row totals and column totals are supplied automatically, as is the overall total (665 respondents gave valid responses to both questions). The number of missing responses on one or both variables is also displayed.

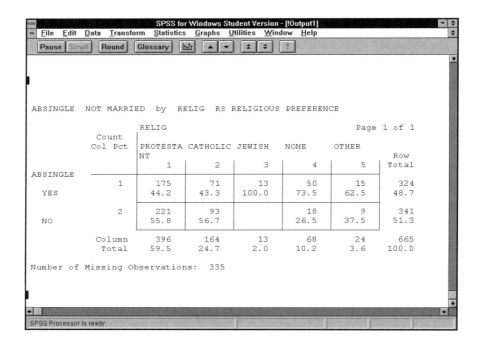

The table shows great differences in support across religious categories for a legal abortion for a single woman. A majority of Protestants and Catholics oppose abortion in this instance, but a majority of Jews, the nonreligious, and others (Hindus, Buddhists, Muslims, and others) support abortion. Do you find these differences surprising, or are they consistent with your understanding of the social world?

*Demonstration 2: Producing Tables with a Control Variable*

As we've seen in this chapter, the analysis of data is enhanced when a third variable—a control variable—is added to a bivariate table. In the Crosstabs procedure, the third variable is added in the Layer section of the main dialog box (this box is labeled "Layer 1 of 1" because it is possible to have additional levels of control, which are accessed by clicking on the *Next* button). We will keep the same dependent variable, ABSINGLE, but make RACE the column variable and SEX the control variable.

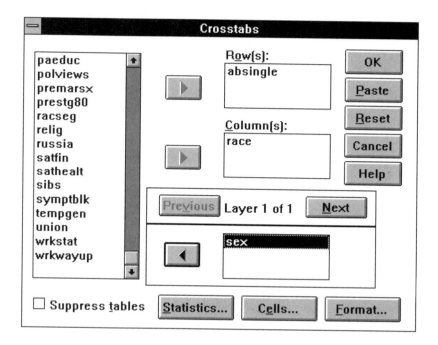

There is no need to change the numbers displayed in the cells: the count and column percentage are still correct choices. The next two figures show the bivariate tables of support for legal abortions for single women by race, separately for males and females.

```
ABSINGLE  NOT MARRIED  by  RACE  RACE OF RESPONDENT
Controlling for..
SEX  RESPONDENTS SEX  Value = 1  MALE
```

|  | | RACE | | | |
|---|---|---|---|---|---|
|  | Count | WHITE | BLACK | OTHER | |
|  | Col Pct | | | | |
|  | | 1 | 2 | 3 | Row Total |
| ABSINGLE | | | | | |
| YES | 1 | 140 | 7 | 2 | 149 |
|  | | 54.1 | 28.0 | 28.6 | 51.2 |
| NO | 2 | 119 | 18 | 5 | 142 |
|  | | 45.9 | 72.0 | 71.4 | 48.8 |
| | Column | 259 | 25 | 7 | 291 |
| | Total | 89.0 | 8.6 | 2.4 | 100.0 |

Page 1 of 1

```
ABSINGLE   NOT MARRIED   by   RACE   RACE OF RESPONDENT
Controlling for..
SEX   RESPONDENTS SEX   Value = 2   FEMALE

                         RACE                    Page 1 of 1
             Count
             Col Pct  WHITE      BLACK      OTHER
                                                      Row
                        1          2          3      Total
 ABSINGLE         ─────────────────────────────────
                  1      145        18        12       175
      YES                47.9       34.0      66.7     46.8

                  2      158        35        6         199
      NO                 52.1       66.0      33.3      53.2

             Column      303        53        18        374
             Total       81.0       14.2      4.8      100.0

Number of Missing Observations:   335
```

SPSS labels each table with the value of the control variable for easy reference.

In the first table (for males), we see that a majority of whites support abortion for single women, but a larger majority of blacks do not, nor do those of other races (although there are only 7 respondents). In the second table (for females), a majority of whites oppose abortion, and blacks continue to oppose it, but now those of other races are more likely to support abortion. Finding differences like these are one reason why researchers use control variables in analyses. These tables display a conditional relationship between race and support for abortion for single women when sex is introduced as a control variable.

In later chapters, we will use the *Statistics* button in the Crosstabs dialog box to request additional output to further interpret and evaluate bivariate tables.

## EXERCISES

1. An example in the chapter showed that more women than men were afraid to walk alone in their neighborhoods at night. Use the data below on fear, race, and home ownership for this exercise.
   a. Construct a bivariate table of frequencies for race and fear of walking alone at night. Which is the independent variable?
   b. Calculate percentages for the table based on the independent variable. Describe the relationship between race and fear of walking alone using the table. What social factors might account for the relationship?

Race: B = black, W = white; Fear: Y = yes, N = no; R = rent, O = own

| Respondent | Race | Fear of Walking Alone | Rent/Own |
|---|---|---|---|
| 1 | B | N | O |
| 2 | B | Y | O |
| 3 | W | N | R |
| 4 | W | N | O |
| 5 | W | Y | R |
| 6 | B | N | R |
| 7 | W | N | O |
| 8 | B | N | R |
| 9 | W | Y | O |
| 10 | B | Y | R |
| 11 | W | N | O |
| 12 | B | Y | O |
| 13 | B | Y | R |
| 14 | W | Y | O |
| 15 | W | N | R |
| 16 | B | N | R |
| 17 | W | N | O |
| 18 | B | Y | R |
| 19 | W | N | O |
| 20 | B | Y | R |
| 21 | W | Y | O |

(Data based on the 1987 to 1991 GSS)

2. The following bivariate table shows the relationship between support for school busing for racial purposes (reducing segregation at school) and the race of the respondent.
   a. Which is the independent variable?
   b. Is there a difference in attitude between whites and blacks? What is the percentage difference?
   c. What might account for the differences you see in the table? Suggest at least two reasons.

| BUSING | RACE WHITE | BLACK | Total |
|---|---|---|---|
| Favor | 28.6% | 59.3% | 45.2% |
| Oppose | 71.4% | 40.7% | 54.8% |
| Total | 57.9% | 42.1% | 100.0% |

(Data based on the 1994 GSS)

3. More people are attending college in the United States now than in the first half of the twentieth century. Many students consider a college education a means of preparing for an occupation. Let's suppose that you are involved in an orientation program for freshmen on your campus. One of these new students asks for your advice in choosing a major, saying that she wants to study something that is likely to lead to a job related to her major. Based on the following data from a survey of students who graduated between July 1989 and June 1990, which majors would you suggest for her? Why? Which major might you discourage her from pursuing?

| Job Related to Major? | Major | | | |
|---|---|---|---|---|
| | Engineering | Business | Social Service | Humanities |
| Yes | 89% | 81% | 71% | 57% |
| No | 11% | 19% | 29% | 43% |

(Data from the *1991 Recent College Graduates Survey*, U.S. Dept of Education)

4. Use the data from exercise 1 to construct a bivariate table to compare fear of walking alone at night between people who own their homes and those who rent. Use percentages to show whether there is a difference between homeowners and renters in fear of walking alone.

5. Advocates of gay rights often argue that homosexuality is not a "preference" or a choice, but rather an "orientation" that cannot be changed. However, in exercise 10 in Chapter 2, we found that Americans are equally split on this issue. Suppose one of your classmates has a close friend or family member who is gay or lesbian, and he thinks people who don't have similar relationships have different beliefs about the origins of homosexuality than people who do have a gay or lesbian friend or family member. Use the following table to answer the questions.
   a. What is the dependent variable? the independent variable?
   b. What proportion of those polled have a close friend or family member who is gay or lesbian?
   c. Are people who have a close relationship with a gay or a lesbian more likely to believe that homosexuality is a choice or that it is something that cannot be changed? (*Hint:* Calculate percentages.)

| Homosexuality Is | Has Gay or Lesbian Close Friend or Family Member? | | |
| --- | --- | --- | --- |
| | Yes | No | Total |
| Choice | 81 | 427 | 508 |
| Can't change | 144 | 352 | 496 |
| Don't know | 29 | 121 | 150 |
| Total | 254 | 900 | 1,154 |

(Data based on 1992 *New York Times*/CBS News poll)

6. Refer to exercise 5. Suppose another of your classmates says that it can't be very significant to know whether a person believes homosexuality is a choice or not, since people are equally split (44% and 43%, respectively) between the two positions. Your professor presents the following table based on the same survey.

| Should Gays and Lesbians Be Allowed in the Military? | Is Homosexuality a Choice or Is It an Orientation That Cannot Change? | | | |
| --- | --- | --- | --- | --- |
| | Choice | Can't change | Don't know | Total |
| Yes | 162 | 268 | 66 | 496 |
| No | 276 | 160 | 62 | 498 |
| Don't know | 70 | 68 | 22 | 160 |
| Total | 508 | 496 | 150 | 1,154 |

(Data based on 1992 *New York Times*/CBS News poll)

a. Which is the dependent variable in this table? Which is the independent variable? Discuss why assigning the variables to these categories is problematic.

b. Is there a relationship between people who believe that homosexuality is a choice and attitude toward allowing gays and lesbians in the military? (Use percentages to support your answer.)

7. Americans are very concerned about their health-care system. Everyone would like to feel that their health is good, but some groups may have more difficulty in dealing with their health-care problems. A neighborhood clinic wants to develop a health promotion program aimed at people in the community who don't feel their health is good. The clinic conducted a survey to measure the perceived health of people in their community by gender.

a. What proportion of the community feels that they are in good health? What proportion are in excellent health? What proportion feel that their health is only fair or poor?

b. Is there a difference in perceived health of women versus men? What is the difference?

c. Should the clinic focus their health promotion program on men or women? Why? (Use percentages to support your answer.)

HEALTH  CONDITION  OF  HEALTH  by  SEX  RESPONDENTS  SEX

|  | Count | SEX MALE 1 | SEX FEMALE 2 | Row Total |
|---|---|---|---|---|
| HEALTH | | | | |
| EXCELLENT | 1 | 98 | 118 | 216 31.5 |
| GOOD | 2 | 136 | 181 | 317 46.3 |
| FAIR | 3 | 60 | 67 | 127 18.5 |
| POOR | 4 | 8 | 17 | 25 3.6 |
| Column Total | | 302 44.1 | 383 55.9 | 685 100.0 |

(Data  from  the  1994  General  Social  Survey)

8. Throughout the twentieth century, the educational level of Americans has been increasing. The following U.S. census data show the relationship between time and the level of education attained by American adults over the age of 25 for two periods.

| | **Education Level** | | |
|---|---|---|---|
| **Year** | Less than 9th grade | High school graduate or more | Bachelor's degree or more |
| 1980 | 18.3% | 66.5% | 16.2% |
| 1990 | 10.4% | 75.2% | 20.3% |

    a. What is the direction of this relationship?

    b. Use percentage differences to describe the relationship. Why don't the percentages add to 100 percent by year? Is this a problem in analyzing the table?

    c. Do these data support the idea that Americans were getting more education in 1990 than ten years before?

9. One aspect of a "generation gap" is that parents and their children often have different values. Use the following data from the 1987 to 1991 GSS to investigate this topic.

    a. Is there a relationship between age and attitude about premarital sex? Compute appropriate percentages and marginal totals to investigate this question.

    b. If there is a relationship, is it strong or weak? What is the direction of the relationship?

| | Age | | | | | |
|---|---|---|---|---|---|---|
| **Is Premarital Sex** | 20–29 | 30–39 | 40–49 | 50–59 | 60–69 | 70+ |
| Always wrong | 37 | 45 | 45 | 32 | 40 | 72 |
| Almost always wrong | 12 | 19 | 20 | 21 | 18 | 21 |
| Sometimes wrong | 57 | 59 | 39 | 16 | 32 | 16 |
| Not wrong at all | 104 | 134 | 86 | 52 | 39 | 26 |

10. Refer to exercise 9. What happens to the strength of the relationship between age and attitude toward premarital sex if age is grouped by twenty-year intervals rather than ten-year intervals? (*Hint:* Combine cells so that the age groups are "20–39," "40–59," and "60+.")

11. A census of Los Angeles County shows the following data for the proportion of people living in neighborhoods where they are of the same race/ethnicity as most of their neighbors. Thus, for example, 35 percent of blacks in 1980 lived in neighborhoods that were predominantly black.

    a. Have residential segregation patterns changed over the last decade for blacks? What is the direction of the change? How about for Hispanics? How has their residential segregation pattern changed?

    b. Is there a relationship between ethnicity and the direction of the changes in segregation?

**Percentage of Each Race Living in Neighborhoods Where Most People Are of the Same Ethnicity**

| | Race | |
|---|---|---|
| **Year** | Black | Hispanic |
| 1980 | 35% | 17% |
| 1990 | 13% | 27% |

(Based on U.S. census data as reported in the *Los Angeles Times*, May 6, 1991)

12. In exercise 1 you found that blacks are more likely than whites to fear walking alone in their neighborhoods. You now wonder if this difference exists because whites are more likely to own their own homes and so live in safer neighborhoods. In other words, you want to try some elaboration.
    a. Use the data from exercise 1 to construct tables showing the relationship between fear of walking alone and race, controlling for whether the individual rents or owns his or her dwelling.
    b. Does renting versus owning one's dwelling "explain" the difference in fear between whites and blacks (use percentage differences to support your answer)?
    c. Has introducing home ownership shown that the relationship between race and fear is spurious, or is home ownership an intervening variable? Explain.

13. Black students in the United States typically attend public schools in which they are a majority (and therefore white students a minority). In the last three decades, in many large cities, such as New York, black students have been attending schools with a decreasing proportion of white students.
    a. Based on the following data for Los Angeles, New York, Dallas, and Chicago, is the direction of the trend the same or different in these four cities?
    b. Is the trend stronger in New York or Dallas?
    c. If the trends are different, use the column percentages to describe the differences in each city.

| A Typical Black Student's Classmates Are | Los Angeles | | | | New York | | | |
|---|---|---|---|---|---|---|---|---|
| | 1968 | 1974 | 1986 | 1992 | 1968 | 1974 | 1986 | 1992 |
| White Students | 7.5% | 10.2% | 11.7% | 9.6% | 23.2% | 16.5% | 10.4% | 8.4% |
| Students of Color | 92.5% | 89.8% | 88.3% | 90.4% | 76.8% | 83.5% | 89.6% | 91.6% |

| A Typical Black Student's Classmates Are | Dallas | | | | Chicago | | | |
|---|---|---|---|---|---|---|---|---|
| | 1968 | 1974 | 1986 | 1992 | 1968 | 1974 | 1986 | 1992 |
| White Students | 5.6% | 14.4% | 11.8% | 9.3% | 5.4% | 3.2% | 6.0% | 4.6% |
| Students of Color | 94.4% | 86.6% | 88.2% | 90.7% | 94.6% | 98.8% | 94.0% | 95.4% |

(Data from a *USA Today* article from 12 May 1994, based on 1991/92 U.S. Department of Education and National School Boards Association data)

14. An organization in your state is lobbying to make pornography illegal because its members believe that pornography leads to a breakdown in morals. You believe that people with conservative views about women are more likely to hold such beliefs about pornography and that people with liberal views about women are more likely to disagree with this view. The GSS has a question about whether people believe that pornographic materials lead to a breakdown in morals, and a question about whether people approve or disapprove of women working (the liberal position is to approve).

a. Do the GSS data support your beliefs or not? Why?

**Should Women Work Outside the Home?**

| Does Pornography Lead to a Breakdown in Morals? | | Approve | Disapprove | Total |
|---|---|---|---|---|
| | Yes | 251 | 71 | 322 |
| | No | 175 | 28 | 203 |
| | Total | 426 | 99 | 525 |

(Data from the 1987 to 1991 GSS)

b. Your friend argues that there are gender differences in the effect that attitude about women working outside the home has on views about pornography. Do the GSS survey data in the following table support her belief? Why or why not?

c. What can you conclude about the relationship between views about women working and attitudes about pornography? Is this an example of a conditional relationship?

**Should women work outside the home?**

| Does pornography lead to a breakdown in morals? | | Males | | Females | |
|---|---|---|---|---|---|
| | | Approve | Disapprove | Approve | Disapprove |
| | Yes | 86 | 29 | 165 | 42 |
| | No | 90 | 15 | 85 | 13 |

15. In the previous exercise you examined the relationship between liberal attitudes about women and the belief that pornographic materials lead to a breakdown in morals. The relationship was not different for men and women. Do liberal attitudes about women working have a conditional effect for whites and blacks?
   a. Use the following table to answer this question and describe the relationship between race, attitude toward women working, and attitude toward the effect of pornography.
   b. Does race show that the relationship between attitude toward women working and attitude toward the effect of pornography is spurious? Why or why not?

**Should women work outside the home?**

| Does pornography lead to a breakdown in morals? | | White | | Black | |
|---|---|---|---|---|---|
| | | Approve | Disapprove | Approve | Disapprove |
| | Yes | 157 | 36 | 94 | 35 |
| | No | 102 | 14 | 73 | 14 |

(Data from the 1987 to 1991 GSS)

## SPSS PROBLEMS

1. The sample 1994 GSS data contain responses to questions about the respondent's general happiness (HAPPY) and his or her subjective class identification (CLASS). Analyze the relationship between responses to these two questions with the SPSS Crosstabs procedure, requesting counts and appropriate cell percentages.
   a. What percentage of working-class people responded that they were "very happy"?

b. What percentage of the upper class were "very happy"?

c. What percentage of those who were "pretty happy" were also middle class?

d. Most of the people who said they were "very happy" were from which two classes?

e. Is there a relationship between perceived class and perceived happiness? If there is a relationship, describe it. Is it strong or weak?

2. Suppose an editorial in your local newspaper reports that people with more education oppose busing as a means of reducing racial segregation in schools. You decide to use the 1987 to 1991 GSS data to verify the relationship between attitude toward busing (BUSING) and the level of education reported in the newspaper (use the variable EDLEV4, which groups educational attainment in four categories).

a. Create the appropriate table using SPSS and the Crosstabs procedure.

b. Create a bar chart grouped by EDLEV4 to graphically display this same table. (*Hint:* In SPSS, use a clustered bar chart.)

c. Is there a relationship between the variables? What is its direction?

d. Do the data support the newspaper's assertion?

Next you recall from exercise 2 (p. 285) that there was a strong relationship between attitude toward busing and race. You wonder if the relationship between attitude toward busing and education holds true if one controls for race.

e. Use the Crosstabs procedure with RACE as a control variable to create separate tables of EDLEV4 by BUSING for blacks and whites.

f. Is there a difference in support for busing between blacks with different levels of education?

g. Is there a difference in attitude between whites with different levels of education?

h. Is the relationship between attitude toward busing and level of education a spurious one?

3. In other exercises, you examined the relationship between liberal views about the role of women and attitudes about pornography among men and women. You and your friend decide to see if the same kind of relationship holds for other independent variables. Use the 1987 to 1991 GSS data for this exercise.

a. Use SPSS to construct a table showing the relationship between attitudes about women working (FEWORK) and attitudes about women having access to abortion for any reason (ABANY). (*Hint:* Use ABANY as the dependent variable.)

Next, use SPSS to construct tables showing the same relationship controlling for sex. Then answer these questions.

  b. Overall, are women or men more likely to agree that a woman should be able to have an abortion if she wants to for any reason?

  c. Do men who approve of women working have different opinions about women having abortions for any reason than men who disapprove of women working?

  d. Is there a difference in support for abortion between women who approve of women working and those who disapprove? If so, describe the relationship.

  e. Finally, use SPSS to construct tables showing the relationship between attitude toward abortion and women working, controlling for race. Does attitude toward women working have a different effect on beliefs about abortion for whites and blacks?

## GROUP PROBLEMS

1. Use the data from group problem 1 in Chapter 4 that you collected from your classmates. Also, arrange to receive data from other groups in the class so that you have a wide range of variables to choose from.

  a. Select several variables whose relationships you would like to investigate. Construct bivariate tables relating these variables to each other, selecting a dependent variable when appropriate.

  b. Characterize the relationships in the tables using appropriate percentages.

  c. Each group member can then select one of the bivariate tables and add a control variable to the table, perhaps gender. Are there any differences in the bivariate relationship after adding the control variable? If so, describe them with appropriate percentages.

  d. Write a report or provide a verbal report to the class summarizing your group's findings.

2. Work with other group members to gather information from the library on the relationship between employment (and unemployment), age, and race. One possible source is from the government publication *Employment and Earnings*, but there are others as well. Use the information to write a report characterizing the relationship between age, race, and employment. What type of person is most likely to be employed? What type is most likely to be unemployed? Be sure to mention which groups are more likely to be unemployed in your report.

3. How well do newspapers and magazines use and report on data displayed in bivariate tables? Assign some group members the job of looking in back issues of newspapers or national newsmagazines to find stories that used bivariate tables, or better yet, tables with control variables, to support or illustrate the subject of the article. Then have other group members calculate the percentage differences in the tables if that wasn't done in the article. Have a group discussion, covering at least the following points, and then write a summary of your findings or present them to the whole class.

   a. Do the articles identify independent and dependent variables? An article doesn't have to (and probably won't) use this terminology, but it can suggest which variable affects another. If the variables in the table are not linked in this fashion, how does the article connect them?

   b. Is the discussion of the table accurate and complete? Are the differences between categories large enough (or small enough) to support the article's conclusions?

   c. Could the presentation of the table have been improved? How?

   d. Suggest a few variables that could have been included as control variables in the table.

**7** ## Measures of Association for Nominal and Ordinal Variables

**Using Ordinal Measures with Dichotomous Variables**

**Box 7.2  What Is Strong? What Is Weak? A Guide to Interpretation**

**Reading the Research Literature: Worldview and Abortion Beliefs**
Examining the Data
Interpreting the Data

MAIN POINTS
KEY TERMS
SPSS DEMONSTRATION
EXERCISES
SPSS PROBLEMS
GROUP PROBLEMS

## Introduction

In Chapter 6, we focused on one bivariate technique—the method of cross-tabulation—in which the pattern of relationship between two variables was analyzed by making a number of percentage comparisons. In Chapters 7 and 8, we discuss special **measures of association** for nominal, ordinal, and interval-ratio variables. These measures enable us to use a single summarizing measure for analyzing the pattern of relationship between two variables. Such measures of association reflect the strength of the relationship and, at times, its direction (whether it is positive or negative). They also indicate the usefulness of predicting the dependent variable from the independent variable.

In this chapter, we discuss three measures of association: lambda, a measure of association for nominal variables; gamma; and Somers' *d*, suitable for measuring associations between ordinal variables. In Chapter 8, we introduce Pearson's correlation coefficient, measuring bivariate association between interval-ratio variables.

---

*Measure of Association*   A single summarizing number that reflects the strength of the relationship, indicates the usefulness of predicting the dependent variable from the independent variable, and often shows the direction of the relationship.

---

To introduce the logic of the measures of association discussed here, let's use an example. Imagine for a moment that we are asked to identify or predict the abortion stance of each of 20 entering freshmen. Let's suppose that we know nothing about these students individually, but we find out that about 60 percent of all students on our campus tend to be pro-choice. One simple way would be to identify all 20 (prediction 1 in Figure 7.1) freshmen as pro-choice. Chances are that we will make about 12 correct guesses or predictions (60% of 20 = 12), but we will make about 8 errors. Suppose instead that we

Figure 7.1 **Reducing Prediction Error**

**Prediction 1: All students are pro-choice.**

choice choice choice anti choice anti choice anti anti choice

anti anti choice choice choice anti choice choice choice anti

Using this prediction, we would make 8 errors.

**Prediction 2: All Republicans are anti-abortion; all Democrats are pro-choice.**

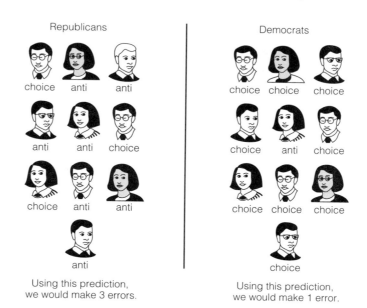

Republicans

choice anti anti

anti anti choice

choice anti anti

anti

Democrats

choice choice choice

choice anti choice

choice choice choice

choice

Using this prediction, we would make 3 errors.

Using this prediction, we would make 1 error.

Total number of errors using Prediction 2: 4 errors

are told that half the students (10) identify themselves as Republicans and half (10) as Democrats. We could try to improve our predictions by identifying all Democrats as pro-choice and all Republicans as anti-abortion. Although not all Democrats are pro-choice and some Republicans identify themselves as pro-choice, chances are that we will reduce the number of errors by using political party affiliation to identify who is pro-choice. Let's assume that 3 students who identify themselves as Republicans are indeed pro-choice, while 1 of those who self-identifies as a Democrat is anti-abortion. Although we will still end up with 4 errors (prediction 2 in Figure 7.1), this second method is nevertheless an improvement over our earlier method of guessing. We will have reduced the number of errors by 4 (or 8 − 4), a 50 percent improvement [(4 ÷ 8)100]! This 50 percent improvement represents the *proportional reduction of error* when political party affiliation is used to identify students who are pro-choice.

## Proportional Reduction of Error

All the measures of association discussed in this and the next chapter are based on the concept of the **proportional reduction of error**, which is often abbreviated as **PRE**. According to the concept of PRE, two variables are associated when information about one can help us improve our prediction of the other. The variables "political party affiliation" and "position on abortion" are associated because political party affiliation helped improve our prediction of the students' positions on abortion by 50 percent.

Table 7.1 may help us grasp intuitively the general concept of PRE. This table presents the bivariate relationship between trauma history and position on abortion among a subsample of women from the GSS survey. The relationship between these two variables was discussed earlier in Chapter 6 (see Table 6.9).[1] Table 7.1 shows a strong relationship between the independent variable "number of traumas" ("traumas" refers to traumatic events such as death in the family, serious illness, and hospitalization experienced by respondents during the previous five years), and the dependent variable, "position on abortion." Thirty-two percent of the women who experienced 1 or fewer traumas are pro-choice compared with 76 percent of the women who had suffered 2 or more traumas.

---

[1]Table 7.1 is actually a simplified version of Table 6.9. For illustration purposes we have combined women who experienced 0 or 1 trauma into one category, *1 or fewer.*

Table 7.1  **Support for Abortion by Trauma (women)**

|  | NUMBER OF TRAUMAS | | |
| ABORTION | 1 or fewer | 2 or more | Total |
|---|---|---|---|
| Yes (pro-choice) | 32% (23) | 76% (25) | 46% (48) |
| No (anti-abortion) | 68% (48) | 24% (8) | 54% (56) |
| Total (N) | 100% (71) | 100% (33) | 100% (104) |

*Source:* General Social Survey, 1982 to 1990.

Let's say that we want to predict a woman's position on abortion but we do not know anything about her trauma history. Based on the row totals in Table 7.1 we could predict that every woman in the sample is anti-abortion because this is the modal category of the variable "abortion" position. With this prediction we would be making 48 errors, because, in fact, 48 out of the 104 women included in this group are pro-choice and only 56 are anti-abortion. (These numbers are shown in the column marginals of Table 7.1.) Now let's see if we could improve this prediction by utilizing the information we have on each woman's trauma history. For this prediction we are going to employ the following rule: If a woman experienced 2 or more traumatic events in the last five years we predict that she will be pro-choice. If a woman experienced 1 or fewer traumatic events we predict that she is anti-abortion. It makes sense to use this rule because we know, based on Table 7.1, that women who suffered 2 or more traumas are more likely to be pro-choice, whereas women who suffered 1 or fewer traumas are more likely to be anti-abortion. Using this prediction rule, we will make 31 errors instead of 48 because 23 of the women who experienced 1 or fewer traumas are actually pro-choice, whereas 8 of the women who experienced 2 or more traumas are anti-abortion (23 + 8 = 31). In other words, we are better off predicting women's positions on abortion by looking at their trauma history than by ignoring this information; we reduce our errors from 48 to 31. This difference represents a proportional reduction of error of .35:

$$\frac{48 - 31}{48} = .35$$

*Proportional Reduction of Error (PRE)*   The concept that underlies the definition and interpretation of several measures of association. PRE measures are derived by comparing the errors made in predicting the dependent variable while ignoring the independent variable with errors made when making predictions that use information about the independent variable.

## PRE and Degree of Association

All PRE measures are based on comparing predictive error levels that result from each of two methods of prediction. With the first method, predictions are made while ignoring the independent variable (we predicted position on abortion while ignoring trauma history; this method resulted in 48 errors of prediction). With the second method, predictions are made based on using information we have about the independent variable (we predicted position on abortion based on trauma history; this method resulted in 31 errors of prediction). If the variables are *associated,* the second method will result in fewer errors of prediction than the first method. The stronger the relationship between the variables, the larger the reduction in the number of errors of prediction. The reduction in errors can vary from 0.0—which represents *no association* between the variables, and therefore no reduction in prediction error—to 1.0 in the case of a *perfect association*—which represents a 100 percent reduction in the number of errors of prediction. Intermediate values of PRE will reflect the strength of the association between the two variables and therefore the utility of using one to predict the other.

## A General Formula for PRE Measures

The conceptual formula for all[2] PRE measures of association is

$$\text{PRE} = \frac{E1 - E2}{E1} \tag{7.1}$$

[2]Even though this general formula provides a framework for all PRE measures of association, only lambda is illustrated with this formula. Gamma and Somers' *d,* which are discussed in the next section, are calculated with a different formula. Yet they are still interpreted as PRE measures.

where

$E1$ = errors of prediction made when the independent variable is ignored

$E2$ = errors of prediction made when the prediction is based on the independent variable

Let's recalculate the proportional reduction of error for Table 7.1 using formula 7.1.

1. We ignored trauma history and predicted that every woman in our sample is anti-abortion. This prediction resulted in 48 errors. Therefore,

   $E1 = 48$

2. We predicted that women who suffered 1 or fewer traumas were anti-abortion, whereas women who had suffered 2 or more traumas were pro-choice. This prediction resulted in 31 errors. Therefore,

   $E2 = 31$

The proportional reduction of error resulting from using trauma history to predict position on abortion is

$$\text{PRE} = \frac{48 - 31}{48} = .35$$

PRE measures of association may range from 0.0 to ±1.0. A PRE of zero indicates that the two variables are not associated; information about the independent variable will not improve predictions about the dependent variable. A PRE of ±1.0 indicates a perfect positive or negative association between the variables; we can predict the dependent variable without error using information about the independent variable. The more the measure of association departs from 0.00 in either direction, the stronger the association. A PRE of .35 indicates that there is a moderate relationship between women's position on abortion and their trauma history.

PRE measures of association can be multiplied by 100 to indicate the percentage improvement in prediction. Thus, a PRE of .35 also means that we have improved our prediction of women's position on abortion by 35 pecent (.35 × 100 = 35%) by using information on their trauma history.

## Lambda: A Measure of Association for Nominal Variables

Few phenomena exemplify the American dream as well as home ownership. For most Americans, owning a home is a source of security both psychologically and financially. Psychologically, ownership provides stability and privacy. Financially, ownership not only is a symbol of wealth, but also represents the primary means of accumulating wealth in this society.

If home ownership is a primary source of psychological and financial security would it be associated with a sense of financial satisfaction? To examine this question, let's look at Table 7.2, which shows ninety-four GSS respondents classified by home ownership status (whether they own or rent) and their satisfaction with their financial situation. In this example, we will consider home ownership status to be the independent variable, and level of financial satisfaction, which may be explained or predicted by the independent variable, to be the dependent variable.

Because "home ownership" is a nominal variable, we need to apply a measure of association suitable for calculating relationships between nominal variables. Such a measure will help us determine how strongly associated home ownership is with financial satisfaction. **Lambda** is such a measure; it is also a PRE measure that follows the basic formula

$$\frac{E1 - E2}{E1}$$

## A Method for Calculating Lambda

Take a look at Table 7.2, but try to ignore the information in the body of the table. Instead, examine the row totals, which show the distribution of the variable "financial satisfaction." Note that the mode of this distribution is the category "satisfied." If we had to predict the level of financial satisfaction of the ninety-four persons presented here, our best bet would be to guess the mode, which is that everyone is "satisfied." Because this category has the highest number of people in it, this prediction will result in the smallest possible error. The number of wrong predictions we make using this method is actually 53, since out of 94 people only 41 were in fact satisfied (94 − 41 = 53).

Now take another look at Table 7.2, but this time let's consider home ownership status when we predict financial satisfaction. Once again, we can use the mode of financial satisfaction, but this time we

Table 7.2 **Financial Satisfaction by Home Ownership\***

| FINANCIAL SATISFACTION | HOME OWNERSHIP | | |
| --- | --- | --- | --- |
| | Own | Rent | Row Total |
| Satisfied | 33 | 8 | 41 |
| More or less | 17 | 17 | 34 |
| Not satisfied | 5 | 14 | 19 |
| Column total | 55 | 39 | 94 |

\*The shaded frequencies are the modes of the three distributions: Own, Rent, and Row Total.
*Source:* General Social Survey, 1982 to 1990.

apply it separately to renters and homeowners. The mode for homeowners is "satisfied" (33 homeowners are satisfied); therefore, we can predict that all homeowners are "satisfied." With this method of prediction we make 22 errors, since only 33 out of 55 homeowners were in fact satisfied (55 − 33 = 22). Next, do the same for renters. The mode for this group is "more or less satisfied"; this will be our prediction for the entire group of renters. This method of prediction results in 22 errors (39 − 17 = 22).

Let's now put it all together and state the procedure for calculating lambda in more general terms.

1. Find $E1$, the errors of prediction made when the independent variable is ignored. To find $E1$, subtract the mode of the dependent variable from $N$. For Table 7.2, $E1$ is

   $$E1 = N - Mo$$
   $$E1 = 94 - 41 = 53$$

2. Find $E2$, the errors made when the prediction is based on the independent variable. To find $E2$, subtract the mode for each category of the independent variable from the total for that category and add the subtotals. For Table 7.2, $E2$ is

   Own   55 − 33 = 22

   Rent   39 − 17 = 22

   $E2$        = 44

3. Calculating lambda using formula 7.1:

   $$\text{Lambda} = \frac{E1 - E2}{E1}$$

$$\text{Lambda} = \frac{53 - 44}{53} = .17$$

By comparing $E1$ with $E2$, we can determine whether using the independent variable to predict the dependent variable results in fewer errors. In our example, there is clearly an advantage in using home ownership status to predict financial satisfaction because we have reduced the number of errors of prediction by 9, from 53 to 44.

The proportional reduction of error indicated by lambda, when multiplied by 100, can be interpreted as follows: by using information on respondents' home ownership status to predict their level of financial satisfaction, we have improved our prediction of financial satisfaction by 17 percent (.17 × 100 = 17%).

Lambda may range from 0.0 to 1.0. Zero indicates that there is nothing to be gained by employing the independent variable to predict the dependent variable; 1.0 indicates that by using the independent variable as a predictor we are able to predict the dependent variable without any error. A lambda of .17 is less than one-quarter of the distance between 0.0 and 1.0, and it indicates that for this subsample of GSS respondents, home ownership status and financial satisfaction are only slightly associated.

---

**Learning Check.** *Explain why lambda would not assume negative values.*

---

## Statistics in Practice: Home Ownership, Financial Satisfaction, and Race

Historically, home ownership has been as important in the black community as in society as a whole. The home has served as the center of black family life in a society in which racial segregation was practiced in public places. Researchers have found that home ownership has a positive effect on the social participation of black residents.[3]

Despite the value that blacks place on home ownership, evidence exists that they do not receive the economic returns from home ownership that are experienced by whites. Therefore, the association between

---

[3]Hayward Derrick Horton, "Race and Wealth: A Demographic Analysis of Black Homeownership." *Sociological Inquiry*, Vol. 62, No. 4, November 1992, 480–489.

home ownership and financial satisfaction may differ for black and white respondents. To check this out we selected another sample from our GSS data file and divided it into two groups by race. Let's examine the association between home ownership and financial satisfaction, as measured with lambda, in the two groups. Tables 7.3 and 7.4 present the bivariate tables for black and white respondents. Let's see how well home ownership predicts financial satisfaction in each of the groups.

Using formula 7.1 and the information in Table 7.3, we find that $E1 = 32$ and $E2 = 32$. Plugging these figures into the formula for lambda, we find:

$$\text{Lambda} = \frac{E1 - E2}{E1} = \frac{32 - 32}{32} = 0$$

Table 7.3 **Financial Satisfaction by Home Ownership among Blacks**

| FINANCIAL SATISFACTION | HOME OWNERSHIP | | Row Total |
|---|---|---|---|
| | Own | Rent | |
| Satisfied | 5 | 7 | 12 |
| More or less | 11 | 12 | 23 |
| Not satisfied | 10 | 10 | 20 |
| Column total | 26 | 29 | 55 |

*Source:* General Social Survey, 1982 to 1990.

Table 7.4 **Financial Satisfaction by Home Ownership among Whites**

| FINANCIAL SATISFACTION | HOME OWNERSHIP | | Row Total |
|---|---|---|---|
| | Own | Rent | |
| Satisfied | 23 | 2 | 25 |
| More or less | 10 | 3 | 13 |
| Not satisfied | 3 | 8 | 11 |
| Column total | 36 | 13 | 49 |

*Source:* General Social Survey, 1982 to 1990.

Now let's do the same for Table 7.4. Since $E1 = 24$ and $E2 = 18$:

$$\text{Lambda} = \frac{24 - 18}{24} = .25$$

---

***Learning Check.*** *Use formula 7.1 to calculate E1 and E2 for each table. Are our answers correct?*

---

A lambda of 0.0 for blacks means that home ownership status has no association with financial satisfaction. Knowledge of black respondents' home ownership status does not improve the prediction of their level of financial satisfaction. In contrast, home ownership and financial satisfaction are moderately associated among whites. A lambda of .25 reflects a proportional reduction of error of 25 percent.

---

***Learning Check.*** *Understanding PRE measures is important because the concept of PRE is used quite often in statistics (it will come up again in Chapter 8). To get a better grasp of what PRE means, investigate the following crosstabs and accompanying pie charts.*

Hypothetical Strong Relationship: Stress Level by Dog Ownership
Lambda = .80

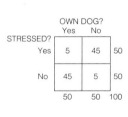

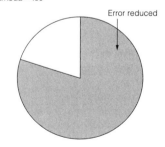

Hypothetical Moderate Relationship: Stress Level by Dog Ownership
Lambda = .40

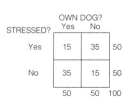

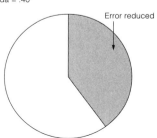

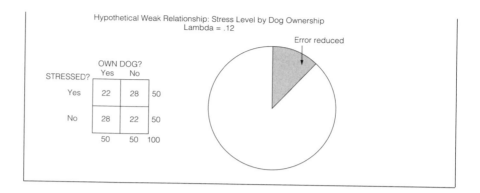

Hypothetical Weak Relationship: Stress Level by Dog Ownership
Lambda = .12

## Some Guidelines for Calculating Lambda

Lambda is an **asymmetrical measure of association**. This means that lambda will vary depending on which variable is considered the independent variable and which the dependent variable. In our example, we predicted financial satisfaction based on home ownership, and not vice versa. Had we instead considered financial satisfaction the independent variable and home ownership the dependent variable, the value of lambda for blacks would have been .38.

---

*Asymmetrical Measure of Association*  A measure whose value may vary depending on which variable is considered the independent variable and which the dependent variable.

---

The method of calculation follows the same guidelines even when the variables are switched. However, exercise caution in calculating lambda, especially when the independent variable is arrayed in the rows rather than in the columns. To avoid confusion we can switch the variables and follow the convention of arraying the independent variable in the columns; then follow the exact guidelines suggested for calculating lambda. Remember, however, that although lambda can be calculated either way, ultimately what guides the decision of which variables to consider as independent or dependent is the theoretical question posed by the researcher.

Lambda is always zero in situations in which the modes for each category of the independent variable fall into the same category of the dependent variable. This condition is illustrated in Table 7.3, where the modes for both Own and Rent fall into the category More or less. A problem with interpreting lambda arises in situations in which lambda is zero, while other measures of association indicate that the variables are associated (see exercise 7). To avoid this potential problem examine the percentage differences in the table whenever lambda is exactly equal to zero. If the percentage differences are very small (usually 5% or less) lambda is an appropriate measure of association for the table. However, if the percentage differences are larger, indicating that the two variables may be associated, lambda will be a poor choice as a measure of association. In such a case, we may want to discuss the association in terms of the percentage differences or select an alternative measure of association. Alternatively, when nominal variables have only two categories (dichotomous variables), we may use ordinal measures—such as gamma (discussed next)—to measure the association.

> **Learning Check.** *Calculate lambda using "financial satisfaction" as the independent variable and "home ownership" as the dependent variable. Is your answer .38?*
>
> *Now calculate the percentage difference for Table 7.3. (Don't forget to percentage the table first.) Is it safe to use lambda as a measure of association?*

---

*Lambda* An asymmetrical measure of association, lambda is suitable for use with nominal variables and may range from 0.0 to 1.0. It provides us with an indication of the strength of an association between the independent and dependent variables.

---

## Gamma and Somers' *d*: Ordinal Measures of Association

In the last section, we looked at a method for measuring the strength of association between *nominal* variables. The method was based on calculating the proportionate reduction in error that occurs when the independent variable is used to predict the dependent variable. In this section, we discuss how to measure and interpret an association between two *ordinal* variables. The two measures we discuss—*gamma* and *Somers' d*—are both PRE measures. This means that if there is an association between the two variables, knowledge of one variable will enable us to make better predictions of the other variable.

Before we illustrate how measures of association between ordinal variables are calculated and interpreted, let's review for a moment the definition of ordinal level variables (first defined in Chapter 1). Whenever we assign numbers to rank-ordered categories ranging from low to high, we have an ordinal level variable. "Social class" is an example of an ordinal variable. We might classify individuals with respect to their social class status as "upper class," "middle class," or "working class." We can say that a person in the category of "upper class" has a higher class position than a person in a "middle class" category (or that a "middle class" position is higher than a "lower class" position).

Ordinal variables are very common in social science research. For example, the General Social Survey contains many questions that ask people to indicate their response on an ordinal scale. An example is

"very often," "fairly often," "occasionally," "almost never"

## Analyzing the Association Between Ordinal Variables: Job Security and Job Satisfaction

Let's look at a research example in which the association between two ordinal variables is considered. Over the past five years, a major transformation has occurred in the American workplace. Driven by the need to cut business costs, be more competitive, and raise profits, corporate America is restructuring, downsizing, and laying off millions of workers. Even though there are some good economic reasons for the current restructuring, the human costs are enormous. An extensive body of literature has documented that employees who survive downsizing have to work longer and harder. The resulting decrease in job security and the increase in stress lead to discontent, lower creativity, and generally reduced job satisfaction.

We want to examine the hypothesis that the higher a person's job security, the higher his or her job satisfaction. To examine this hypothesis we selected two questions from the General Social Survey. The following question is a measure of "job satisfaction":

On the whole, how satisfied are you with the work you do— would you say you are very satisfied, moderately satisfied, a little dissatisfied, or very dissatisfied?[4]

---

[4]We have recoded the original response categories for this question into the following new categories: very satisfied = high, moderately satisfied = moderate, a little dissatisfied or very dissatisfied = low.

To measure "job security" they asked:

> Thinking about the next 12 months, how likely do you think it is that you will lose your job or be laid off—very likely, fairly likely, not too likely, or not at all likely?[5]

Table 7.5 displays the cross-tabulation of these two variables, with "job security" as the independent variable and "job satisfaction" as the dependent variable. Thirty-six percent of those who indicate high job security, but only 11 percent of those who indicate low job security, are "satisfied" with their job. The percentage differences (36% − 11% = 25%) indicate that the variables are related. There are several other percentage differences that can be computed on these data (for example, 36% − 22% = 14%; 22% − 11% = 11%) that yield smaller percentage differences but that lead to the same conclusion that job satisfaction and job security are associated.

Table 7.5   **Job Satisfaction by Job Security***

| JOB SATISFACTION (Y) | JOB SECURITY (X) | | | |
| | High | Medium | Low | Total |
|---|---|---|---|---|
| High | a<br>36%<br>(16) | b<br>22%<br>(8) | c<br>11%<br>(14) | 18%<br>(38) |
| Moderate | d<br>43%<br>(19) | e<br>47%<br>(17) | f<br>46%<br>(60) | 46%<br>(96) |
| Low | g<br>20%<br>(9) | h<br>31%<br>(11) | i<br>43%<br>(56) | 36%<br>(76) |
| Total (N) | 100%<br>(44) | 100%<br>(36) | 100%<br>(130) | 100%<br>(210) |

*The cells in this table have been labeled from a through i.

[5]We have recoded responses to this question into three levels of job security: not at all likely = high job security, not too likely = medium job security, and very likely and fairly likely = low job security.

*Comparison of Pairs*  Let's explore this relationship a bit further. To understand the logic of the ordinal measures of association discussed in this section, we have to restate the relationship not in terms of individual observations but in terms of **paired observations** and their relative position (or rank order) on the two variables. To make the discussion a bit more concrete, let's suppose that we narrow each variable into only two categories, high and low job security and high and low job satisfaction, and that there are only four people involved, one in each cell. For the purpose of this illustration we have assigned names to each individual. Our hypothetical data are presented in Figure 7.2. We now pair these four people (six combinations can be created) and describe their rank order on the question of job security and job satisfaction. These results are presented in Figure 7.3.

---

**Paired Observations**  Observations compared in terms of their relative rankings on the independent and dependent variables.

---

Let's consider the first pair, John and Arturo. Notice that John, who is high on job security, is also high on job satisfaction, and that Arturo, who has low job security, is also low on job satisfaction. When we consider this pair we can say that the person who has higher job security (John) is also the more satisfied of the two. This pair would lead us to conclude that the higher one's job security the higher one's job satisfaction, or that job satisfaction increases with job security.

Next consider Ruth and May. Ruth, who has low job security, is satisfied with her job. On the other hand, May, who has high job security, is not satisfied with her job. Regarding this pair we could

Figure 7.2  **Job Satisfaction by Job Security of Four People (hypothetical)**

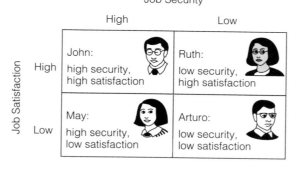

Figure 7.3 **Rank Order of Four People on Job Security and Job Satisfaction**

Pair                                                         Type of Pair

| John: high security, high satisfaction | Arturo: low security, low satisfaction | Same Order (*Ns*) |

| John: high security, high satisfaction | Ruth: low security, high satisfaction | Tied on the dependent variable, job satisfaction (*Nty*) |

| John: high security, high satisfaction | May: high security, low satisfaction | Tied on the independent variable, job security (*Ntx*) |

| Ruth: low security, high satisfaction | Arturo: low security, low satisfaction | Tied on the independent variable, job security (*Ntx*) |

| Ruth: low security, high satisfaction | May: high security, low satisfaction | Inverse Order (*Nd*) |

| Arturo: low security, low satisfaction | May: high security, low satisfaction | Tied on the dependent variable, job satisfaction (*Nty*) |

say that the person who has the lower job security is the more satisfied. This pair would lead us to conclude that the lower one's job security the higher one's job satisfaction, or that job satisfaction decreases with job security.

*Types of Pairs* Because ordinal variables have direction—that is, their categories can range from low to high, the relationship between ordinal variables also has direction. The direction of the relationship can be *positive* or *negative*. With a positive relationship, if one person is ranked above another on one variable, he or she would rank above the other person on the second variable. Such a relative ranking of two observations is called a **same order pair**. We label the count of these types of pairs as **Ns**. Same order pairs show a positive association. John and Arturo are a same order pair, displaying a positive association because John, who is higher than Arturo on job security, is also more satisfied than Arturo. For John and Arturo, job satisfaction increases with job security.

---

*Same Order Pair (Ns)*   Paired observations that show a positive association; the member of the pair ranked higher on the independent variable is also ranked higher on the dependent variable.

---

With a negative relationship, if one person is ranked above another on one variable, he or she ranks below the other person on the second variable. Such relative ranking of a pair of observations is called an **inverse order pair** (their count is labeled as **Nd**). Inverse order pairs show a negative association. Ruth and May are an inverse order pair who display a negative association because Ruth, who is lower than May on job security, is higher (more satisfied) than May on job satisfaction. For Ruth and May, job satisfaction decreases with job security.

---

*Inverse Order Pair (Nd)*   Paired observations that show a negative association; the member of the pair ranked higher on the independent variable is ranked lower on the dependent variable.

---

Note that there are four other pairs in Figure 7.3. These pairs all have the same value on either job satisfaction or job security. For example, whereas Ruth and Arturo have different levels of job satisfaction (Ruth's level of job satisfaction is high while Arturo's is low), they each have low job security. Pairs that have the same value on a variable are called **tied pairs**. If the pairs share the same value on the independent variable (X), they are called pairs *tied on the independent variable* (their count is designated as **Ntx**); if the pairs are tied on the dependent variable (Y), they are called pairs *tied on the dependent variable* (**Nty**). Pairs can also share the same value on both the independent and the dependent variables; such pairs are designated as **Ntxy**.

---

*Tied Pairs (Ntx, Nty, or Ntxy)*   Paired observations that share the same value on the independent variable (*Ntx*), the dependent variable (*Nty*), or both variables (*Ntxy*).

---

*Uses for Information About Pairs*  We now discuss two ordinal measures of association that use the information about these types of pairs—gamma and Somers' *d*. **Gamma**, the most frequently used measure of association for ordinal variables, considers only untied pairs—that is, *same order* and *inverse order* pairs. **Somers' *d*** includes pairs that are tied on the dependent variable. Therefore, our discussion will be limited to same order pairs, inverse order pairs, and pairs tied on the dependent variable.

To calculate gamma you must first count the number of same order (*Ns*) pairs and inverse order (*Nd*) pairs that can be obtained from a bivariate table. To calculate Somers' *d* you must also count the number of pairs that are tied on the dependent variable (*Nty*). Once we find *Ns, Nd,* and *Nty,* the calculation of gamma and Somers' *d* is pretty straightforward.

Because our illustration is based on only four cases (Figure 7.2), the number of pairs involved is very small and can easily be identified (as in Figure 7.3) and counted. However, because the number of cases in most bivariate tables is considerably larger (as it is in our original table, Table 7.5), the number of pairs that can be generated becomes very large, and the process of identifying the types of pairs becomes a bit more complicated.

## Counting Pairs

To illustrate the process of identifying and counting all the same order pairs (*Ns*), inverse order pairs (*Nd*), and pairs tied on the dependent variable (*Nty*) that can be generated from a bivariate table,[6] let's go back to Table 7.5, which presents the original bivariate distribution of job satisfaction by job security. Note that the table is constructed so that the cell in the upper left corner represents the highest category on both *X* and *Y* (*high* job security and *high* job satisfaction), with levels of *X* decreasing from left to right, and the levels of *Y* decreasing from top to bottom. Always make sure tables you analyze are arranged in this

---

[6]This process of counting pairs also appears in Chava Frankfort-Nachmias and David Nachmias, *Research Methods in the Social Sciences.* New York: St. Martin's Press, 1996, 408–412.

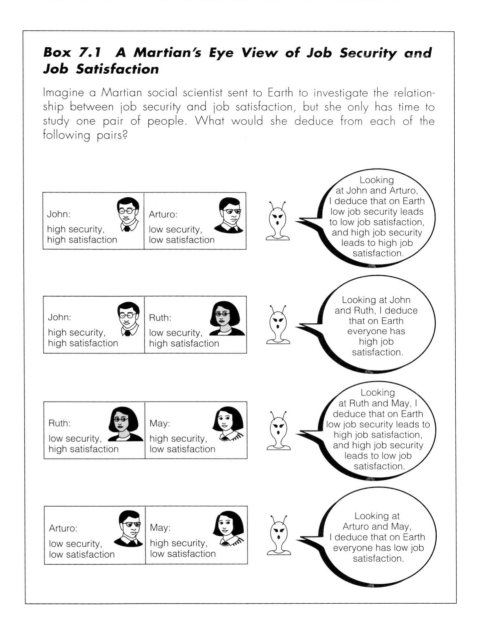

**Box 7.1  A Martian's Eye View of Job Security and Job Satisfaction**

Imagine a Martian social scientist sent to Earth to investigate the relationship between job security and job satisfaction, but she only has time to study one pair of people. What would she deduce from each of the following pairs?

way before following the procedure outlined here to find *Ns* and *Nd*. If your table is not arranged in this way, you can always rearrange it to follow this format.

*Same Order Pairs (Ns)*  To find the number of same order (*Ns*) pairs, multiply the frequency in each cell in the table by the sum of the frequencies of all the cells that are lower on both variables, that is, both below and to the right of that cell. Repeat this process for each cell that has cells below it and to its right, and then sum the products. The total of these products is $Ns$.

Let's begin with the upper left cell, $a$, in Table 7.5. The frequency (16) is multiplied by the sum of the frequencies in cells $e$, $f$, $h$, and $i$ (17 + 60 + 11 + 56). These are the cells that lie below and to the right of cell $a$. The product equals 2,304 pairs.

This computation is illustrated in Figure 7.4, in which cell $a$ and the cells that lie below it and to its right ($e$, $f$, $h$, $i$) are shaded. Move to the next cell, cell $d$. Its frequency, 19, is multiplied by (11 + 56), the sum of the frequencies in cells $h$ and $i$, and the result equals 1,273 pairs. (The direction of the multiplication is illustrated in Figure 7.4.) This procedure is repeated for cells $b$ and $e$. Because cells $g$ and $h$ have no cells below them and cells $c$, $f$, and $i$ have no cells to the right of them, they are not included in the computations of $Ns$. Now let's sum the total number of same order ($Ns$) pairs:

Figure 7.4 **Counting All Same Order Pairs ($Ns$) from Table 7.5**

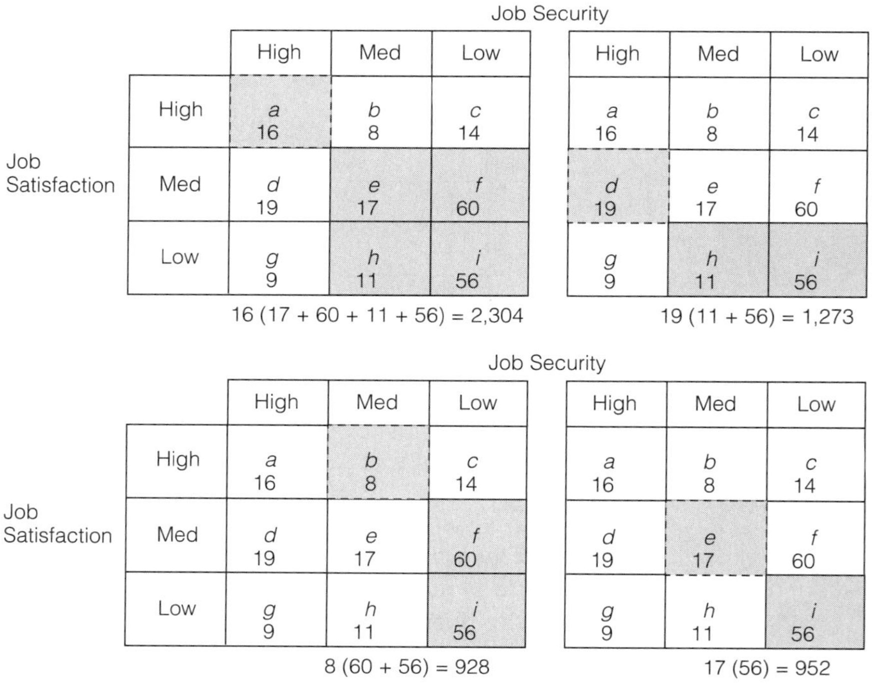

$$Ns = 2{,}304 + 1{,}273 + 928 + 952 = 5{,}457$$

$Ns = 2{,}304 + 1{,}273 + 928 + 952 = 5{,}457$

Each one of these 5,457 pairs follows the definition of $Ns$ pairs presented earlier. For instance, take a pair formed from cell $a$ and cell $h$. The member of the pair from cell $a$ is high on job security and high on job satisfaction, whereas the member of the pair from cell $h$ is medium on job security and low on job satisfaction. Therefore, we can say that the member of the pair that is higher on job security (high versus medium) is also higher on job satisfaction (high versus low).

---

**Learning Check.** *To convince yourself that each of the 5,457 Ns pairs we counted is indeed a same order pair, try for yourself any of the combinations as depicted in Figure 7.4.*

---

*Inverse Order Pairs (Nd)* To calculate the number of inverse order pairs ($Nd$) we proceed in exactly the same way, except for one difference. Because we are interested in pairs in which the relative ranking of the variables is reversed, we reverse our process and begin with the upper right cell (cell $c$). We then multiply its frequency by the cells below it and to its left. Repeat this process for each cell that has cells below it and to its left and then sum the products. The total of these products is $Nd$. (The computations are illustrated in Figure 7.5.) Now let's sum the total number of $Nd$ pairs:

$Nd = 784 + 1{,}200 + 224 + 153 = 2{,}361$

All these pairs follow the definition of $Nd$ pairs. Take a pair formed from cells $c$ and $g$. The member of the pair from cell $c$ is low on job security and high on job satisfaction. Conversely, the member of the pair from cell $g$ is high on job security and low on job satisfaction. Therefore, we can say that the member of the pair that is lower on job security is higher on job satisfaction.

*Pairs Tied on the Dependent Variable (Nty)* In Table 7.5 the dependent variable is the row variable, so all pairs from the same row will be tied on the dependent variable. For example, if we select two cases from Table 7.5, one from cell $a$ and one from cell $b$, each has a high level of job satisfaction. Therefore, we will define these as tied on $Y$. Similarly, if we pair someone from cell $g$ with someone from cell $i$, each has a low level of job satisfaction; therefore, we will define these as tied on $Y$.

Figure 7.5   **Counting All Inverse Order Pairs (*Nd*) from Table 7.5**

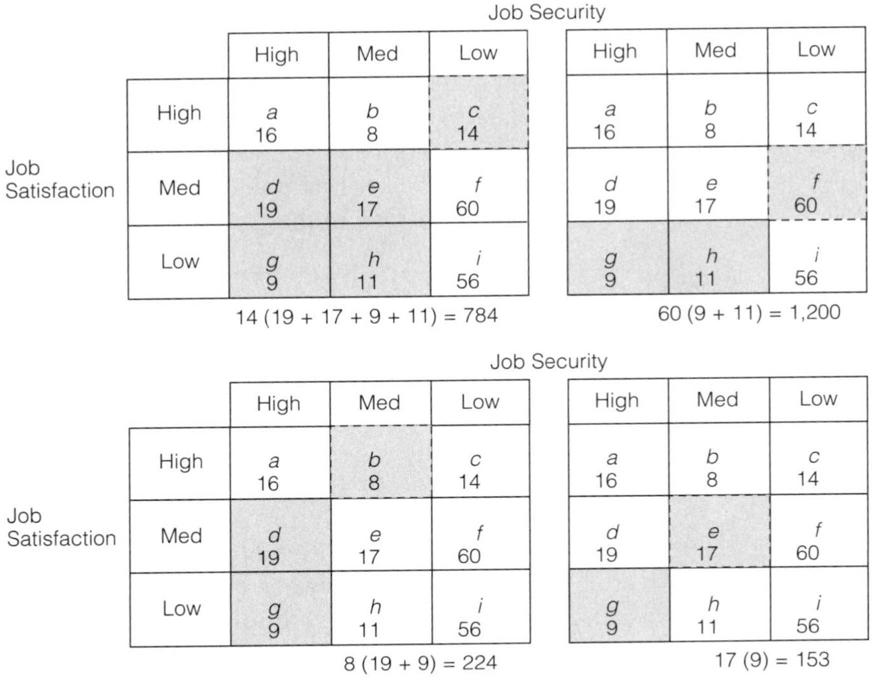

Job Security

|  | High | Med | Low |
|---|---|---|---|
| High | *a* 16 | *b* 8 | *c* 14 |
| Med | *d* 19 | *e* 17 | *f* 60 |
| Low | *g* 9 | *h* 11 | *i* 56 |

14 (19 + 17 + 9 + 11) = 784

60 (9 + 11) = 1,200

8 (19 + 9) = 224

17 (9) = 153

*Nd* = 784 + 1,200 + 224 + 153 = 2,361

To count all the pairs that are tied on the dependent variable (*Nty*), the frequency in each cell is multiplied by the sum of the frequencies in the cells both in that row and to its right, and the products are added. (The computations are illustrated in Figure 7.6.) Let's sum the total number of pairs tied on the dependent variable (*Nty*):

*Nty* = 352 + 112 + 1,463 + 1,020 + 603 + 616 = 4,166

Before we discuss gamma, let's look again at the meaning of same order and inverse order pairs. (Pairs that are tied on the dependent variable *Nty* are not included in the calculation of gamma; they will be discussed later when we introduce Somers' *d*.) *Same order* pairs are all the pairs of observations formed from Table 7.5 that show a positive relationship between the variables—the higher your job security the higher your job satisfaction, or job satisfaction increases with job security. Inverse order pairs are all the pairs of observations that show a negative relationship between the variables—the higher your job security the lower your job satisfaction, or job satisfaction decreases

Figure 7.6 **Counting All Pairs Tied on the Dependent Variable (*Nty*) from Table 7.5**

Job Security

| | | High | Med | Low | | High | Med | Low |
|---|---|---|---|---|---|---|---|---|
| | High | *a* 16 | *b* 8 | *c* 14 | | *a* 16 | *b* 8 | *c* 14 |
| Job Satisfaction | Med | *d* 19 | *e* 17 | *f* 60 | | *d* 19 | *e* 17 | *f* 60 |
| | Low | *g* 9 | *h* 11 | *i* 56 | | *g* 9 | *h* 11 | *i* 56 |

16 (8 + 14) = 352          8 (14 ) = 112

Job Security

| | | High | Med | Low | | High | Med | Low |
|---|---|---|---|---|---|---|---|---|
| | High | *a* 16 | *b* 8 | *c* 14 | | *a* 16 | *b* 8 | *c* 14 |
| Job Satisfaction | Med | *d* 19 | *e* 17 | *f* 60 | | *d* 19 | *e* 17 | *f* 60 |
| | Low | *g* 9 | *h* 11 | *i* 56 | | *g* 9 | *h* 11 | *i* 56 |

19 (17 + 60) = 1,463          17 (60) = 1,020

Job Security

| | | High | Med | Low | | High | Med | Low |
|---|---|---|---|---|---|---|---|---|
| | High | *a* 16 | *b* 8 | *c* 14 | | *a* 16 | *b* 8 | *c* 14 |
| Job Satisfaction | Med | *d* 19 | *e* 17 | *f* 60 | | *d* 19 | *e* 17 | *f* 60 |
| | Low | *g* 9 | *h* 11 | *i* 56 | | *g* 9 | *h* 11 | *i* 56 |

9 (11 + 56) = 603          11 (56) = 616

*Nty* = 352 + 112 + 1,463 + 1,020 + 603 + 616 = 4,166

with job security. Our purpose in this analysis is to determine whether there is an association between job security and job satisfaction. If there is such an association, we want to be able to determine which of these statements best describes the association—that is, whether the association is *positive* or *negative*. Gamma can help us answer these questions.

## Calculating Gamma

**Gamma** is a symmetrical measure of association suitable for use with ordinal variables or with dichotomous nominal variables. It can vary from 0.0 to ±1.0 and provides us with an indication of the strength and direction of the association between the variables. When there are more $Ns$ pairs gamma will be positive; when there are more $Nd$ pairs gamma will be negative.

Gamma[7] is calculated using the following formula:

$$\text{Gamma} = \frac{Ns - Nd}{Ns + Nd} \tag{7.2}$$

Using this formula and the pairs calculations we made earlier, let's now find the association between job security and job satisfaction:

$$\text{Gamma} = \frac{5,457 - 2,361}{5,457 + 2,361} = .396$$

A gamma of .396 indicates that there is a moderate and a positive association between job security and job satisfaction. We can conclude that using information on respondents' job security helps us improve the prediction of their job satisfaction by almost 40 percent.

Gamma is a **symmetrical measure of association**. This means that the value of gamma will be the same regardless of which variable is the independent variable or the dependent variable. Thus, if we had wanted to predict job security from job satisfaction rather than the opposite, we would have obtained the same gamma.

---

*Symmetrical Measure of Association*   A measure whose value will be the same when either variable is considered the independent variable or the dependent variable.

---

## Positive and Negative Gamma

Gamma can vary from 0.0 to ±1.0. It reflects the proportional reduction in prediction error when incorporating information on the independent variable to predict the dependent variable. Note from formula 7.2 that the size and the direction of gamma (whether positive or

---

[7]For 2 × 2 tables, a measure identical to gamma—Yule's *Q*—was first introduced by the statistician Udny Yule. However, whereas gamma is suitable for any size of table, Yule's *Q* is appropriate only for 2 × 2 tables. When gamma is calculated for 2 × 2 tables it is sometimes referred to as Yule's *Q*.

negative) are functions of the relative number of same order (*Ns*) versus the number of inverse order (*Nd*) pairs. More *Ns* pairs makes gamma positive; more *Nd* pairs makes gamma negative. The larger the difference between the number of *Ns* and *Nd* pairs, the larger the size of the coefficient (irrespective of sign). For example, when all the pairs are *Ns* (*Nd* = 0), gamma equals 1.00:

$$\text{Gamma} = \frac{Ns - 0}{Ns + 0} = 1.0$$

A gamma of 1.0 indicates that the relationship between the variables is positive, and the dependent variable can be predicted without any error on the basis of the independent variable. When *Ns* is zero, gamma will be −1.0, indicating a perfect and a negative association between the variables:

$$\text{Gamma} = \frac{0 - Nd}{0 + Nd} = -1.0$$

When *Ns* = *Nd*, gamma will equal zero:

$$\text{Gamma} = \frac{Ns - Nd}{Ns + Nd} = \frac{0}{Ns + Nd} = 0.0$$

A gamma of zero reflects no association between the two variables; hence, there is nothing to be gained by using order on the independent variable to predict order on the dependent variable.

---

*Gamma*  A symmetrical measure of association suitable for use with ordinal variables or with dichotomous nominal variables. It can vary from 0.0 to ±1.0 and provides us with an indication of the strength and direction of the association between the variables. When there are more *Ns* pairs gamma will be positive; when there are more *Nd* pairs gamma will be negative.

---

## Gamma as a PRE Measure

Like all PRE measures, gamma is based on two methods of prediction. The first method ignores the relative order of pairs on the independent variable (only untied pairs are included in the computation of gamma), whereas the second method takes this information into account. Suppose that we had tried to predict the rank order of each of the 7,818 pairs (the sum of *Ns* and *Nd* pairs: *Ns* + *Nd* = 5,457 + 2,361 = 7,818) while ignoring information on their relative rank order on job security. If we had used a random method to make these predictions for each of the pairs, chances are that only about 50 percent of our guesses would have been right. Therefore, we would have made errors about half the time or $(Ns + Nd) \div 2 = (5,457 + 2,361) \div 2 = 3,909$.

Now let's see if we can improve this prediction by taking the rank order on job security into consideration when predicting the rank order on job satisfaction. The likelihood of improving the prediction depends on the number of $Ns$ versus $Nd$ pairs. When $Ns$ is greater than $Nd$, as it is in our example, it makes sense to predict that if respondents are higher on job security, they will also be higher on job satisfaction. That is, job satisfaction increases with job security (this is the order displayed by all the $Ns$ pairs). With this prediction we will be making 2,361 errors—the number of $Nd$ pairs for which this prediction is not correct—or 1,548 fewer errors than before $(3,909 - 2,361 = 1,548)$. When we divide this number by 3,909 (the original number of errors)

$$\frac{1,548}{3,909} = .396$$

we obtain a proportionate reduction of error of .396, which is equal to the gamma coefficient we obtained with formula 7.2.

### Statistics in Practice: Trauma by Social Class

When the number of $Nd$ pairs is larger than the number of $Ns$ pairs, gamma is negative and the prediction is that if a person has a higher rank on the independent variable, she or he will have a lower rank on the dependent variable. This order is illustrated in Table 7.6, which displays the cross-tabulation of social class and the frequency of traumas of 448 GSS respondents, with social class treated as the independent variable. This table, which was examined earlier in Chapter 6 (see Table 6.12) shows a negative association between the frequency of trauma and social class. Remember that with a negative relationship, higher values of one variable tend to go together with lower values of the other, and vice versa. In this table, for instance, most (48%) upper-class respondents have experienced 0 traumas, whereas most (47%) lower-class respondents have experienced 2+ traumas. To calculate gamma we must first count the number of $Ns$ and $Nd$ pairs.

The number of same order ($Ns$) pairs that can be formed from Table 7.6 is

$$Ns = 58(92 + 11 + 90 + 15) + 38(11 + 15) + 36(90 + 15) + 92(15)$$
$$= 18,212$$

Table 7.6 **Frequency of Trauma by Social Class**

| | SOCIAL CLASS | | | |
|---|---|---|---|---|
| TRAUMA | Upper | Middle | Lower | Total |
| 2+ | 32% (58) | 17% (38) | 47% (22) | 43% (118) |
| 1 | 20% (36) | 42% (92) | 22% (11) | 31% (139) |
| 0 | 48% (86) | 41% (90) | 31% (15) | 26% (191) |
| Total (N) | 100% (180) | 100% (220) | 100% (48) | 100% (448) |

*Source:* General Social Survey, 1987 to 1992.

The number of inverse order ($Nd$) pairs that can be formed from Table 7.6 is

$$Nd = 22(36 + 92 + 86 + 90) + 38(36 + 86) + 11(86 + 90) + 92(86)$$
$$= 21,172$$

Gamma is

$$\text{Gamma} = \frac{Ns - Nd}{Ns + Nd}$$

$$= \frac{18,212 - 21,172}{18,212 + 21,172} = -.075$$

In this example, the number of inverse order pairs ($Nd$ = 21,172) is larger than the number of same order pairs ($Ns$ = 18,212) and therefore we can predict: if your social class rank is higher than that of the other member of your pair, then your frequency of trauma will be lower— or frequency of trauma decreases with social class. This is the order displayed by all the inverse order pairs. With this prediction we would make 18,212 errors, the number of same order ($Ns$) pairs for which this prediction is not correct.

A gamma of −.075 means that as expected, the relationship between social class and frequency of trauma is negative; that is, as social class increases, frequency of trauma decreases. However, the relationship between these variables is rather weak: Using social class to predict frequency of trauma results in a proportionate reduction of error of only 7.5 percent (.075 × 100 = 7.5%).

## Calculating Somers' *d*

**Somers'** *d* is an asymmetrical measure of association suitable for ordinal variables or for dichotomous nominal variables. This means that its value may be different, depending on which variable is the dependent variable. Because Somers' *d* is asymmetric—it predicts order of pairs on the dependent variable from their order on the independent variable—it counts as predictive errors all pairs that are tied on the dependent variable ($Nty$). Like gamma, Somers' *d* varies from 0.0 to ±1.0 and reflects both the strength and the direction of the association between the variables. The formula for Somers' *d* is

$$\text{Somers'}\ d = \frac{Ns - Nd}{Ns + Nd + Nty}$$

---

*Somers' **d*** An asymmetrical measure of association suitable for ordinal variables or for dichotomous nominal variables. It varies from 0.0 to ±1.0 and reflects both the strength and the direction of the association between the variables. The greater the number of tied pairs, the smaller the value of Somers' *d* compared with the value of gamma.

---

### Tied Pairs and Somers' *d*

To illustrate how tied pairs may affect the strength of the association as reflected in the value of Somers' *d*, let's go back to Figure 7.3, in which we designated the relative rankings of pairs of observations on the two variables of job satisfaction and job security. Notice that four pairs were tied: John and Ruth and Arturo and May had the same rank on job satisfaction, the dependent variable ($Nty$), whereas John and May and Ruth and Arturo had the same rank on job security, the independent variable ($Ntx$). Because Somers' *d* includes only pairs that are tied on the dependent variable ($Nty$), we will consider only the first two pairs.

Comparing the ranking of these two pairs on job satisfaction and job security would lead us to conclude, contradictorily, that higher (or lower) rank on job security is associated with the same level of job satisfaction. This conclusion indicates that there is no relationship between job security and job satisfaction for these pairs. Including such tied pairs in the calculation of Somers' *d* (in the denominator) will decrease the magnitude of the coefficient. The larger the number of ties on the dependent variable ($Nty$), the smaller Somers' $d$ will be relative to gamma. Based on Table 7.5 we took the following counts of the different types of pairs: $Nty$ = 4,166, $Ns$ = 5,457, and $Nd$ = 2,361. Using this information, we can now calculate Somers' $d$:

$$\text{Somers' } d = \frac{5,457 - 2,361}{5,457 + 2,361 + 4,166} = .258$$

## Somers' $d$ Compared with Gamma

Note that for the same data, Somers' $d$ is smaller than gamma (gamma was .396). The inclusion of pairs that are tied on $Y$ in the denominator of the formula for Somers' $d$ means that the value of Somers' $d$ will always be less than the value of gamma. The larger the number of pairs tied on the dependent variable ($Nty$), the smaller will be the size of Somers' $d$ relative to Gamma.

Like gamma, Somers' $d$ is a PRE measure of association. Therefore, the more it departs from 0.0 in either direction, the greater the proportional reduction of error when information about the independent variable is used to predict values of the dependent variable. A Somers' $d$ of .258 indicates that using relative rankings on job security to predict relative ranking on job satisfaction (and by considering tied pairs) results in a proportional reduction of error of .258, or, alternatively, in 25.8% (.258 × 100 = 25.8%) fewer errors.

Because Somers' $d$ considers pairs that are tied on the dependent variable, a change in the definition of the dependent variable will change the computation of ties. For example, a Somers' $d$ in which job security is the dependent variable would include ties on job security rather than on job satisfaction, as we had calculated.

Finally, since both gamma and Somers' $d$ are appropriate to use with ordinal variables or with dichotomous nominal variables, how should we choose between them? Gamma is most often used by social scientists, but Somers' $d$ is preferable to gamma in situations when we can clearly distinguish between the independent and dependent variables. For example, let's say that we wanted to look at the relationship between people's family income while growing up and their political views as adults. Clearly, only family income while growing up can influence political views, and *not* vice versa. In this situation, Somers' $d$ would be preferable to gamma as a measure of association. In contrast, take the variables "attitudes toward gun control" and "attitudes toward abortion." Both could be considered as either the independent or the dependent variable and therefore gamma should be chosen as a measure of association.

---

**Learning Check.**    *Note that we illustrated how to count tied pairs within rows. If the dependent variable is arranged in the columns, you should calculate ties within columns. We have illustrated only how to calculate ties within rows and not within columns. If your dependent variable is the column variable, simply switch the table and make it the row variable. You can then follow the procedure suggested here.*

---

## Using Ordinal Measures with Dichotomous Variables

Measures of association for ordinal data are not influenced by the modal category as is lambda. Consequently, an ordinal measure of association might be preferable for tables when an association cannot be detected by lambda. We can use an ordinal measure for some tables where one or both variables would appear to be measured on a nominal scale. Dichotomous variables (those with only two categories) can be treated as ordinal variables for most purposes. In this chapter, we calculated lambda to examine the association between financial satisfaction and home ownership (Tables 7.2, 7.3, and 7.4). Although home ownership might be considered a nominal variable—because it is dichotomized (own/rent)—it might also be treated as an ordinal variable. Thus, the association between home ownership and financial satisfaction (an ordinal variable) might also be examined using an ordinal measure of association.

Let's calculate gamma for Table 7.3. The number of $Ns$ pairs that can be formed from Table 7.3 is

$$Ns = 5(12 + 10) + 11(10) = 220$$

The number of $Nd$ pairs that can be formed from Table 7.3 is

$$Nd = 7(11 + 10) + 12(10) = 267$$

Gamma is

$$\text{Gamma} = \frac{Ns - Nd}{Ns + Nd}$$

$$= \frac{220 - 267}{220 + 267} = -.096$$

A gamma of −.096 confirms our earlier conclusion that for blacks, home ownership is a very poor predictor of financial satisfaction. To interpret this negative coefficient, think of ownership as the ordering

### Box 7.2  What Is Strong? What Is Weak?
### A Guide to Interpretation

The more you work with various measures of association, the better feel you will have for what particular values mean. Until you develop this instinct, though, here are some guidelines regarding what is generally considered a strong relationship and what is considered a weak relationship.

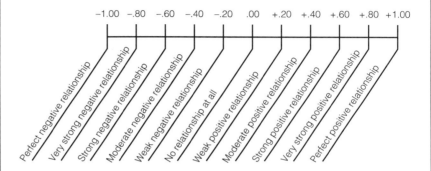

Keep in mind that these are only rough guidelines. Often, the interpretation for a measure of association will depend on the research context. A +.30 in one research field will mean something a little different from a +.30 in another research field. Zero, however, always means the same thing: no relationship.

principle, with "own" as higher and "rent" as lower. Thus, a negative association between home ownership and financial satisfaction among blacks means that greater satisfaction would be expressed by those who do not own their homes.

### Reading the Research Literature:
### Worldview and Abortion Beliefs

Let's conclude this chapter with a fairly typical example of how gamma is presented and interpreted in the social science research literature. The following example is drawn from a study that examines the idea that beliefs about abortion are influenced by a coherent view of the world. It is argued in this study that "each side of the abortion debate has an internally coherent and mutually shared view of the world that is tacit, never fully articulated, and most importantly completely at odds with the world view held by their opponents."[8] In general, if a person is religious, views the primary role of women as one of taking care of the home and raising the children, thinks that sex should be practiced for procreation only, and has a conservative political viewpoint, then this person also tends to disapprove of abortion under almost any circumstances. Conversely, a person who is not religious, has an egalitarian view of gender roles, has liberal attitudes toward sexuality, and identifies himself or herself as left of center on the political spectrum probably believes in a woman's right to choose whether or not to have an abortion.[9] The major hypothesis of this study is "the more conservative a person's world view, the greater his or her disapproval of abortion."[10]

To test this hypothesis, the researcher used data from the 1990 General Social Survey, which is based on a representative sample of all the noninstitutionalized adult residents of the continental United States. To measure worldview the researcher selected six variables: attitudes toward premarital sex, conception of sex roles, religious intensity, political views, fundamentalism, and biblical interpretation. For the purpose of this discussion we have considered only the first three variables.

Measurement of these variables was based on responses to the following questions:

■ *Conception of sex roles* "Do you agree or disagree with this statement? Women should take care of the home and leave running the country up to men."

■ *Premarital sex views* "There's been a lot of discussion about the way morals and attitudes about sex are changing in this country. If a man and a woman have sex relations before marriage, do you think it is always wrong, usually wrong, somewhat wrong, or acceptable?"

■ *Religious intensity* "Would you call yourself a strong, moderate, or weak (stated religion)?"

The dependent variable "abortion belief" was constructed from responses to four questions dealing with the following circumstances under which the person believed it is acceptable or unacceptable for a woman to have an abortion:

[8]Kristin Luker, *Abortion and the Politics of Motherhood.* Berkeley: University of California Press, 1984, 159.

[9]Daniel N. Spicer, "World View and Abortion Beliefs: A Replication of Luker's Implicit Hypothesis." *Sociological Inquiry,* Vol. 64, No. 1, February 1994, 115.

[10]Ibid., pp. 115–116.

If she is married and does not want any more children

If the family has a very low income and cannot afford any more children

If she is not married and does not want to marry the man

The woman wants it for any reason

Based on their response to all four questions, respondents were classified into one of two categories: "approve" or "disapprove" of abortion. The bivariate percentage distributions and the gamma for each of the independent variables and abortion belief are presented in Table 7.7.

### Examining the Data

Begin by examining the structure of the table. Note that it is divided into three parts, one for each independent variable. Each part can be read as a separate table displaying the bivariate percentage and the

Table 7.7 **Percentage Approval of Abortion by Selected Independent Variables (GSS, 1990)**

| Variable | Category | N | Abortion Approval | Gamma |
|---|---|---|---|---|
| **Premarital sex views** | Always wrong | 92 | 15% | −.644 |
| | Usually wrong | 42 | 36% | |
| | Somewhat wrong | 75 | 51% | |
| | Acceptable | 141 | 71% | |
| **Sex role views** | Traditional | 58 | 21% | −.625 |
| | Liberal | 292 | 53% | |
| **Religious intensity** | Strong | 261 | 28% | −.433 |
| | Moderate | 97 | 55% | |
| | Weak | 312 | 59% | |

*Source:* Adapted from Daniel N. Spicer, "World View and Abortion Beliefs: A Replication of Luker's Implicit Hypothesis." *Sociological Inquiry,* Vol. 64, No. 1, February 1994, 120. Used by permission.

gamma for each of the independent variables and abortion beliefs. The independent variables and their categories are arrayed in rows of the table; the dependent variable, "abortion approval," is arrayed in the columns. For each category of the independent variables, the number of people who responded ($N$) and the percentage who approved of abortion are listed. For example, the variable "sex role views" has two categories, Traditional and Liberal. Twenty-one percent of the 58 traditionals approved of abortion. Similarly, among the 292 liberals, 53 percent approved of abortion.

> **Learning Check.** *The percentages who disapproved of abortion are not listed in the table. However, it is very easy to obtain the numbers: simply subtract the percentage who approved from 100 percent for each category. For example, of the 58 traditionals, 79 percent (100% − 21%) disapproved of abortion. Try to complete the table by calculating the percentages who disapproved of abortion for all the variables.*

### Interpreting the Data

Next, interpret the data presented in Table 7.7. In reading the table and interpreting the relationship between each of the independent variables and beliefs about abortion, look at both the percentage differences and the value of gamma. Let's begin by comparing the percentages. Following the rules we learned in Chapter 6, when percentages are calculated within rows (as they are in this table), comparisons are made down the column. For instance, to interpret the relationship between religious intensity and abortion beliefs, compare 28 percent with 55 percent and 59 percent. Similarly, to examine the relationship between sex role views and abortion belief, compare 21 percent with 53 percent. Based on the percentage comparisons for each independent variable, the researcher offers the following interpretation of these findings:

> As shown in [Table 7.7], . . . as the idea of premarital sex becomes more acceptable, the approval of the practice of abortion increases . . . people with traditional sex role conceptions tended to disapprove of abortion and those with a modern, liberal conception of the sexes were in favor of abortion rights. Respondents with a high religious intensity disapproved of

abortion, while those with weak religious ties were much more liberal on the question of abortion.[11]

The detailed summary of the relationships between the variables is confirmed by the values of gamma displayed in the table. The gamma values range from −.433 for religious intensity to −.644 for attitudes toward premarital sex. These values indicate a moderate to strong relationship between various aspects of one's worldview and abortion beliefs.

Notice that all the gamma values are negative. A negative gamma indicates that low values of one variable "go together" with high values of the other variable, and vice versa.

Often it is tricky to interpret the direction of a relationship between ordinal variables because what is considered "low" or "high" is often a function of arbitrary coding by the researcher. However, a researcher will often specify his or her coding in the text. Spicer makes this statement about the direction of these relationships:

> As high scores on . . . the (independent) variables (*higher* values indicating "*conservative*" social views) were associated with *low* scores (*disapproval*) on the abortion view variable . . . the Gamma values are negative.[12]

In other words, the negative gamma between premarital sex views, sex role views, and religious intensity means that respondents who have more conservative social views tend to disapprove of abortion. Conversely, a large percentage of those who have more liberal views approve of abortion.

## MAIN POINTS

■ Measures of association are single summarizing numbers that reflect the strength of the relationship between variables, indicate the usefulness of predicting the dependent variable from the independent variable, and often show the direction of the relationship.

■ Proportionatal reduction of error (PRE) underlies the definition and interpretation of several measures of association. PRE measures are derived by comparing the errors made in predicting the dependent variable while ignoring the independent variable with errors made when making predictions that use information about the independent variable.

[11]Ibid., pp. 120–121.
[12]Ibid., p. 121.

- PRE measures may range from 0.0 to ±1.0. A PRE of 0.0 indicates that the two variables are not associated and that information about the independent variable will not improve predictions about the dependent variable. A PRE of ±1.0 means that there is a perfect (positive or negative) association between the variables and that information about the independent variable results in a perfect (without any error) prediction of the dependent variable.

- Measures of association may be symmetrical or asymmetrical. When the measure is symmetrical, its value will be the same regardless of which of the two variables is considered the independent or dependent variable. In contrast, the value of asymmetrical measures of association may vary, depending on which variable is considered the independent variable and which the dependent variable.

- Lambda is an asymmetrical measure of association suitable for use with nominal variables. It may range from 0.0 to 1.0 and provides us with an indication of the strength of an association between the independent and the dependent variables.

- Gamma is a symmetrical measure of association suitable for ordinal variables or for dichotomous nominal variables. It can vary from 0.0 to ±1.0 and reflects both the strength and direction of the association between the variables.

- Somers' *d* is an asymmetrical measure of association suitable for ordinal variables or for dichotomous nominal variables. Somers' *d* varies from 0.0 to ±1.0 and reflects both the strength and direction of the association between the variables. The greater the number of tied pairs, the smaller the value of Somers' *d* compared with the value of gamma.

## KEY TERMS

*asymmetrical measure of association*

*gamma*

*inverse order pair (Nd)*

*lambda*

*measures of association*

*paired observations*

*proportional reduction of error (PRE)*

*same order pair (Ns)*

*Somers' d*

*symmetrical measure of association*

*tied pairs (Ntx, Nty, Ntxy)*

## SPSS DEMONSTRATION

*Demonstration: Producing Nominal Measures of Association for Bivariate Tables*

In Chapter 6 we used the Crosstabs procedure in SPSS to create bivariate tables. That same procedure is used to request measures of association. We'll begin by investigating the same relationship we did in Chapter 6, support for legal abortions for single women among various categories of religious affiliation.

Click on *Statistics, Summarize,* then *Crosstabs* to get to the Crosstabs dialog box. Put ABSINGLE in the Row(s) box and RELIG in the Column(s) box. Then click on the *Statistics* button.

---

**Crosstabs: Statistics**

☐ Chi-square          ☐ Correlations          [ Continue ]

**Nominal Data**                **Ordinal Data**          [ Cancel ]

☐ Contingency coefficient       ☐ Gamma            [ Help ]

☐ Phi and Cramér's V            ☐ Somers' d

☐ Lambda                        ☐ Kendall's tau-b

☐ Uncertainty coefficient       ☐ Kendall's tau-c

**Nominal by Interval**         ☐ Kappa

☐ Eta                           ☐ Risk

---

The Statistics dialog box has about a dozen statistics from which to choose. Notice that four of each are listed in separate categories for "Nominal Data" and "Ordinal Data." Lambda is listed in the former, and gamma and Somers' *d* in the latter. The other measures of association, such as phi and Cramer's *V*, or Kendall's tau-*b*, are other acceptable measures but will not be discussed in this textbook. The chi-square statistic will be discussed in depth in Chapter 14.

Click on the checkbox for lambda since religious affiliation is a nominal variable. It is critical that we, as users of statistical programs, understand which statistics to select in any procedure. SPSS, like most programs, can't help us select the appropriate statistic for an analysis. Now click on *Continue,* then *OK* to create the table.

```
┌─────────────────────────────────────────────────────────────────────────────────────┐
│                        SPSS for Windows Student Version - [!Output1]          ▼ ▲│
│─ File  Edit  Data  Transform  Statistics  Graphs  Utilities  Window  Help          ▲│
│ ABSINGLE  NOT MARRIED  by  RELIG  RS RELIGIOUS PREFERENCE                           ▲│
│                                                                                      │
│                     RELIG                                    Page 1 of 1             │
│              Count                                                                   │
│                    PROTESTA CATHOLIC JEWISH   NONE    OTHER                          │
│                    NT                                            Row                  │
│                       1       2        3       4       5       Total                 │
│           ABSINGLE ─────────────────────────────────────────                        │
│                       1     175      71       13      50      15      324            │
│                YES                                                   48.7            │
│                                                                                      │
│                       2     221      93               18       9      341            │
│                NO                                                    51.3            │
│                                                                                      │
│                 Column      396     164       13      68      24      665            │
│                 Total      59.5    24.7      2.0    10.2     3.6     100.0            │
│                                                                                      │
│                                                                                      │
│                                                             Approximate              │
│              Statistic              Value     ASE1    Val/ASE0  Significance         │
│           -------------------       -------   -------   -------  ------------         │
│                                                                                      │
│                                                                                      │
│           Lambda :                                                                   │
│              symmetric               .08600   .01594   5.07246                       │
│              with ABSINGLE dependent .15741   .02903   5.07246                       │
│              with RELIG    dependent .00000   .00000                                 │
│           Goodman & Kruskal Tau :                                                    │
│              with ABSINGLE dependent .05631   .01343             .00000 *2           │
│              with RELIG    dependent .01172   .00439             .00000 *2           │
│                                                                                      │
│ SPSS Processor is ready                                                              │
└─────────────────────────────────────────────────────────────────────────────────────┘
```

The table is identical to the one in Chapter 6. Below the table is a large amount of new output. In this chapter, we will only concern ourselves with the first two columns (the other information will become more understandable later in the course). Lambda is listed with three values. We've learned that the value of lambda depends on which variable is considered the dependent variable. In our example, "attitude toward abortion for single women" is dependent, so lambda is about .157. This is of modest magnitude, at best. We conclude that knowing the religious affiliation of the respondent increases the ability to predict his or her abortion attitude by 15.7 percent.

SPSS also calculates a symmetrical lambda for those tables where there is no independent or dependent variable. This calculation goes beyond the scope of this book. (Notice that it is not simply an average of the two other values of lambda.) In addition, as a kind of bonus, SPSS provides the Goodman & Kruskal tau statistic, another nominal measure of association, even though it was not requested. It will always be produced when lambda is requested.

**EXERCISES**

1. In exercise 5 in Chapter 6, we investigated the relationship between whether someone has a close friend or family member who is lesbian or gay and whether she or he believes homosexuality is a choice. The data from that exercise are displayed again here for convenience.

| | Has Gay or Lesbian Close Friend or Family Member? | | |
| Homosexuality Is | Yes | No | Total |
| --- | --- | --- | --- |
| Choice | 81 | 427 | 508 |
| Can't Change | 144 | 352 | 496 |
| Don't know | 29 | 121 | 150 |
| Total | 254 | 900 | 1,154 |

a. As before, we will treat whether or not someone has a friend or family member who is lesbian or gay as the independent variable. If we first ignore that variable and try to predict attitude toward homosexuality, how many errors will we make?

b. If we now take into account the independent variable, how many errors of prediction will we make for those who have a gay or a lesbian friend or family member? for those who don't?

c. Combine the answers in (a) and (b) to calculate the proportional reduction in error for this table based on the independent variable. How does this statistic improve our understanding of the relationship between the two variables?

2. In exercise 6 in Chapter 6, we continued the investigation of attitudes toward homosexuality, studying how belief about whether homosexuality is a choice influenced support for gays or lesbians being allowed in the military. That table (minus the "Don't know" responses) is reproduced here.

| Should Gays and Lesbians Be Allowed in the Military? | Is Homosexuality a Choice or an Orientation That Cannot Change? | | |
| | Choice | Can't Change | Total |
| --- | --- | --- | --- |
| Yes | 162 | 268 | 430 |
| No | 276 | 160 | 436 |
| Total | 438 | 428 | 866 |

    a. Treating belief about whether homosexuality is a choice as the independent variable, calculate lambda for the table. How many errors of prediction will be made if the independent variable is ignored? How many fewer errors will be made if the independent variable is taken into account? Use lambda to discuss the relationship between these two beliefs. Why is lambda an appropriate measure of association?

    b. Both variables in this table are attitudes, so we could consider belief about whether gays and lesbians should be allowed in the military as the predictor, or independent, variable. If we do, then lambda must be recalculated because it is not a symmetrical measure of association. What is the value for lambda when belief about allowing gays and lesbians in the military is the independent variable? How does it compare with the lambda calculated in (a)?

3. In exercises 9 and 10 in Chapter 6, we studied the relationship between age and attitude toward premarital sex. There we used only percentages to characterize the relationship, but our investigation can be extended by using a proportional reduction of error measure on the data in the table. Use the following table where age has been grouped into intervals of twenty years.

    a. To calculate a measure of association for ordinal data we need to calculate the number of $N_s$ and $N_d$ pairs. Calculate these quantities for this table. (*Hint:* Consider the highest category of attitude toward premarital sex to be "Always wrong," and reconstruct the table accordingly.)

    b. Using $N_s$ and $N_d$, calculate gamma for this table. Is gamma positive or negative? Using the value of gamma, interpret the relationship between age and attitude toward premarital sex. How does this add to our discussion of this same table in Chapter 6?

| Is Premarital Sex | Age | | |
|---|---|---|---|
| | 20–39 | 40–59 | 60+ |
| Always wrong | 82 | 77 | 112 |
| Almost always wrong | 31 | 41 | 39 |
| Sometimes wrong | 116 | 55 | 48 |
| Not wrong at all | 238 | 138 | 65 |

4. Use the table in exercise 3.
   a. Calculate the number of cases tied on the dependent variable ($Nt_y$). What is the value of $Nt_y$?
   b. Use this number to calculate Somers' $d$ for the table. How does it compare with gamma?
   c. Would your interpretation of the strength of the relationship between age and attitude toward premarital sex be different if you used Somers' $d$ instead of gamma?

5. Women have increasingly been elected to higher political offices in recent years. Given this fact, is it true that the increasing number of women legislators has, in part, led to a higher percentage of bills being passed on women's or family issues? The following table displays data about the number of bills on women's and family issues that were introduced and then passed by the U.S. Congress for 2 two-year periods in the early 1990s.
   a. Calculate lambda to assess the strength of the relationship between time and bill passage. Be sure to use the appropriate independent variable when calculating lambda.
   b. Does the calculated value of lambda seem surprising, given the relationship observed in the table? Can you explain why lambda has the value that it does?

| | Bills Introduced on Women's and Family Issues | |
| --- | --- | --- |
| Time Period | Didn't Pass | Did Pass |
| 1990 and 1991 | 231 | 19 |
| 1992 and 1993 | 437 | 64 |

(Data from the Congressional Caucus for Women's Issues)

6. There has been much debate in the United States about whether or not the federal government should provide a minimum income for every citizen to improve the lot of the poor. Although politicians can attempt to foster public support for particular policies, often they propose programs and bills that already have broad public support. Using SPSS and the 1991 General Social Survey, you decide to investigate support for the provision of a minimum income by race and subjective social class to provide advice to government leaders. You obtain the following results, with separate tables for whites and blacks. (For ease of illustration and because of low numbers, respondents of lower and upper self-rated social classes are not shown.)

```
        GOVMINC GOVMNT SHOULD PROVIDE MINIMUM INCOME BY CLASS
        Subjective Class Identification
        Controlling for . .
        Race Race of Respondent Value = 1 White

                          Class          Page 1 of 1
                  Count  |
                  Col Pct | Working  Middle
                         | Class    Class    Row
                         |   2    |    3   |  Total
        Govminc  -------- +--------+ ------- +
                       1 |    6   |    5   |   11
        Strongly Agree   |  6.0   |  3.5   |   4.5
                         +--------+ ------- +
                       2 |   13   |   16   |   29
        Agree            | 13.0   | 11.3   |  12.0
                         +--------+ ------- +
                       3 |   25   |   25   |   50
        Neither          | 25.0   | 17.6   |  20.7
                         +--------+ ------- +
                       4 |   42   |   63   |  105
        Disagree         | 42.0   | 44.4   |  43.4
                         +--------+ ------- +
                       5 |   14   |   33   |   47
        Strongly Disagre | 14.0   | 23.2   |  19.4
                         +--------+ ------- +
                  Column    100      142      242
                  Total     41.3     58.7    100.0
```

GOVMINC GOVMNT SHOULD PROVIDE MINIMUM INCOME BY CLASS
Subjective Class Identification
Controlling for . .
Race Race of Respondent Value = 2 Black

|  | | Class | | |
|---|---|---|---|---|
| | Count | | | |
| | Col Pct | Working Class | Middle Class | Row |
| | | 2 | 3 | Total |
| Govminc | | | | |
| Strongly Agree | 1 | 14 14.1 | 6 10.7 | 20 12.9 |
| Agree | 2 | 31 31.3 | 20 35.7 | 51 32.9 |
| Neither | 3 | 25 25.3 | 14 25.0 | 39 25.2 |
| Disagree | 4 | 21 21.2 | 13 23.2 | 34 21.9 |
| Strongly Disagre | 5 | 8 8.1 | 3 5.4 | 11 7.1 |
| Column Total | | 99 63.9 | 56 36.1 | 155 100.0 |

Page 1 of 1

a. Use an appropriate PRE measure, plus percentage differences, to summarize the relationship between support for a minimum income and social class, for whites and blacks separately. Can you suggest a reason for any differences you find?

b. Collapse the two tables to create one table that allows you to investigate the relationship between social class and support for a minimum income. Calculate an appropriate PRE measure and interpret the relationship.

c. Collapse the two tables to create one table so that you can investigate the relationship between race and support for a minimum income. Compute an appropriate PRE measure to aid your analysis.

d. Are the results of these three analyses consistent or contradictory? Explain why.

7. In exercise 5 we learned about what might seem an oddity in the calculation of lambda that caused it to exactly equal zero. Measures of association for ordinal data are not influenced by the modal category as is lambda. Consequently, an ordinal measure of association might be preferable for tables like the one in exercise 5.
   a. Calculate an ordinal measure of association for the table in exercise 5.
   b. Use this statistic to discuss the strength and direction of relationship between time period and the passage of bills on women's and family issues.

8. Tolerance of premarital sexual activity is associated with several demographic variables. In this exercise, we will explore how well education predicts this attitude. The following table uses data from the 1994 GSS, with education recoded into the four categories displayed in the columns.
   a. With education as the predictor variable, calculate gamma for this table.
   b. Now calculate Somers' *d*.
   c. Use these two statistics to discuss the relationship between education and attitude toward premarital sex.
   d. Why is Somers' *d* smaller than gamma?

|  | Count | EDUCGRP | | | | Page 1 of 1 |
|---|---|---|---|---|---|---|
|  |  | < high school 1.00 | High school 2.00 | Under Grad 3.00 | Post- Grad 4.00 | Row Total |
| PREMARSX | | | | | | |
| Always Wrong | 1 | 42 | 49 | 50 | 10 | 151 23.8 |
| Almst Always Wrg | 2 | 8 | 21 | 31 | 8 | 68 10.7 |
| Sometimes Wrong | 3 | 18 | 31 | 52 | 23 | 124 19.6 |
| Not Wrong At All | 4 | 39 | 86 | 123 | 43 | 291 45.9 |
| Column Total |  | 107 16.9 | 187 29.5 | 256 40.4 | 84 13.2 | 634 100.0 |

9. Continue your exploration of how education relates to various attitudes by investigating how it influences support for the death penalty for murderers. The following data were also taken from the 1994 GSS file.

   a. Calculate Somers' *d* for this table.

   b. Use it to describe the relationship between education and support for the death penalty for murder. Is this a strong or weak relationship? What is its direction?

CAPPUN FAVOR OR OPPOSE DEATH PENALTY FOR MURDER BY EDUCGRP

| | | EDUCGRP | | | | Page 1 of 1 |
|---|---|---|---|---|---|---|
| Count | | < high school 1.00 | High school 2.00 | Under Grad 3.00 | Post- Grad 4.00 | Row Total |
| CAPPUN | | | | | | |
| Favor | 1 | 129 | 252 | 287 | 78 | 746 80.1 |
| Oppose | 2 | 39 | 44 | 71 | 31 | 185 19.9 |
| Column Total | | 168 18.0 | 296 31.8 | 358 38.5 | 109 11.7 | 931 100.0 |

10. Gun ownership is quite common in the United States, but those who own a gun are not necessarily a cross-section of Americans. One possibility is that there might be a difference in gun ownership by marital status (perhaps married individuals are more likely to own a gun to protect their families). Using the GSS 1994 data you construct this table.

```
OWNGUN  HAVE  GUN  IN  HOME  BY  MARITAL  MARITAL  STATUS

                Marital                                          Page  1  of  1
        Count |
              |                                          Never
              | Married   Widowed   Divorced  Separated  Married       Row
              |    1    |    2    |    3    |    4     |    5     |    Total
OWNGUN  ---- +--------- + -------- + -------- + ---------+ --------- +
          1 |   176    |   23    |   28    |    3     |   41     |     271
 Yes        |          |         |         |          |          |    40.0
            +--------- + -------- + -------- + ---------+ --------- +
          2 |   176    |   48    |   60    |   13     |  109     |     406
 No         |          |         |         |          |          |    60.0
            +--------- + -------- + -------- + ---------+ --------- +
     Column    352        71        88        16        150          677
     Total     52.0      10.5      13.0       2.4      22.2        100.0
```

a. What measure of association is appropriate for this table?

b. Without doing any calculations, you should be able to study this table and provide one possible value for the proper measure of association. What is that value, and why?

c. The number of married respondents who own a gun and the number who do not are equal (176 for each). Does this make any difference in the calculation of the measure of association? If you're not sure, try calculating the statistic using "Yes" as the modal category for married persons.

11. Exercise 14 in Chapter 6 explored the relationship between attitude toward the effect of pornography on morals and support for women working outside the home. Use the data in the first table (without gender) for this exercise.

a. Calculate gamma for the table.

b. Calculate Somers' *d* for the table.

c. Use the two measures of association to further characterize the relationship between the two attitudes. Do your conclusions agree with what you said for exercise 14c in Chapter 6?

12. It wouldn't be too surprising to find that beliefs about whether the government is spending too much, too little, or about the right amount of money on improving the conditions of blacks vary by race. Explore this question with data from the 1994 GSS, as shown in this table.

NATRACE IMPROVING THE CONDITIONS OF BLACKS BY RACE
Race of Respondent

|  | | RACE | | | Page 1 of 1 |
|---|---|---|---|---|---|
| Count | | White | Black | Other | |
| | | 1 | 2 | 3 | Row Total |
| Natrace | | | | | |
| Too Little | 1 | 96 | 51 | 8 | 155 31.0 |
| About Right | 2 | 202 | 10 | 9 | 221 44.2 |
| Too Much | 3 | 117 | 2 | 5 | 124 24.8 |
| Column Total | | 415 83.0 | 63 12.6 | 22 4.4 | 500 100.0 |

a. Calculate an appropriate measure of association for the table and use it to interpret the strength of the relationship between race and attitude toward federal government spending to help blacks.

## SPSS PROBLEMS

1. In SPSS problem 3 in Chapter 6, you examined the relationship between attitudes about women working (FEWORK) and support for women having an abortion for any reason (ABANY).
   a. Study the same relationship, but this time request appropriate measures of association to more fully describe the relationship. Because these are dichotomous variables, you can use ordinal measures of association.
   b. Add SEX as a control variable and calculate the association measures for each subtable. Is the relationship stronger for women or men? Can you think of reasons why this might be so?

2. Investigate the relationship between the abortion items and various demographic variables (you might begin with gender, age, or race). Study the relationship between these variables with the aid of appropriate measures of association. For example, you might examine whether attitude toward each of the abortion items has a similar relationship to gender. That is, if females are more supportive of abortion for rape victims, are they also more supportive of abortion in other circumstances? Try exploring these relationships further by adding control variables. (You might create tables of abortion attitude by race by gender.) When you have finished the analysis, write a short report summarizing the findings. Suggest possible causes for the relationships you found.

## GROUP PROBLEMS

1. Use the data from Chapter 6 that you collected from the class. You can use either the same variables from the Chapter 6 group problems or other categorical variables.
   a. Construct bivariate tables and calculate suitable measures of association for each table.
   b. Characterize the relationships in each table using these statistics.
   c. Add a control variable to one of the tables, perhaps gender, so that you create two tables. Calculate measures of association and discuss the results with the group.
   d. Write a report or provide a verbal report to the class summarizing the group's findings.

2. Gamma and Somers' *d* are both proper measures of association for ordinal data. We have seen in the exercises that gamma is larger than Somers' *d* for the same table. That is generally true for most tables. Thus, using gamma seems to make a relationship stronger than if you use Somers' *d*. Given this fact, discuss with other group members whether gamma or Somers' *d* should be used with ordinal data. Do you think it makes any sense to use both statistics for the same table?

3. Use the articles and tables the group collected in group problem 3 in Chapter 6. Calculate appropriate measures of association for the tables. Do these statistics add support to the assertions in the articles about the relationship between the variables? Have a group discussion about whether newspapers and magazines should routinely include measures of association in their articles when they present bivariate tables. List both advantages and disadvantages.

4. Does the type of television program influence the gender of characters included on the program? One way to study this research question is with a bivariate table. Have each group member watch five to ten television programs over several days. Make sure that everyone watches a wide variety of programs, but that no two people watch the same programs. Include comedies, soap operas, and dramatic series among program types. For each program, count the number of male and female characters. Then get together as a group and discuss your findings, constructing a bivariate table with "type of program" as one variable (what is its level of measurement?) and "gender distribution" on each program as the other variable. A simple way to code gender is *more males than females, equal numbers of males and females,* and *more females than males.* Percentage the table appropriately, calculate a measure of association, then discuss your findings as a group. Suggest hypotheses to explain any relationship you discover.

## 8 Bivariate Regression and Correlation

■ ■ ■ ■  **Introduction**

Many research questions require the analysis of relationships between interval-ratio level variables. Environmental studies, for instance, frequently measure opinions and behavior in terms of quantity, percentages, units of production, consumption, pollution, and dollar amounts. Let's say that we're interested in the relationship between populations' levels of environmental concern, and their wealth. *Bivariate regression analysis* provides us with the tools to express a relationship between two interval-ratio variables in a concise way.

Since 1900, world population has more than tripled and the global economy has expanded twenty times. This growth has resulted in a tremendous increase both in the consumption of oil and natural gas and in the level of environmental pollution worldwide. The decline in environmental resources combined with ecological threat to human security has led to a global environmental movement and considerable support for environmental protection.

In 1992 the Gallup Institute conducted an international survey of environmental concern in twenty-two countries. We have selected eleven of the twenty-two countries included in the original survey for further examination. The survey included a number of questions designed to measure the degree of environmental concern among the general public in each country. One of the questions asked respondents whether they would be "willing to pay higher prices to protect the environment." The percentage of respondents who indicated that they would be willing to pay higher prices is presented in Table 8.1. Also presented are the mean, variance, and range for these data.

Examining Table 8.1 and the descriptive statistics, it is apparent that although the level of environmental concern as measured by the percentage of citizens who are willing to pay higher prices is relatively high in all eleven countries ($\overline{Y} = 56.45\%$), there is a great deal of variability between countries. The percentage of respondents willing to

Table 8.1 **Percentage of Respondents Willing to Pay Higher Prices to Protect the Environment**

| Country | Percentages (%) |
|---|---|
| Denmark | 78 |
| Norway | 73 |
| Korea | 71 |
| Switzerland | 70 |
| Chile | 64 |
| Canada | 61 |
| Ireland | 60 |
| Turkey | 44 |
| Russia | 39 |
| Japan | 31 |
| Philippines | 30 |

$$\text{Mean} = \bar{Y} = \frac{\sum Y}{N} = \frac{621}{11} = 56.45$$

$$\text{Variance } Y = S_Y^2 = \frac{\sum (Y - \bar{Y})^2}{N - 1} = \frac{3,032.7}{10} = 303.27$$

$$\text{Range } Y = 78\% - 30\% = 48\%$$

*Source:* Adapted from Steven R. Brechin and Willett Kempton, "Global Environmentalism: A Challenge to the Postmaterialism Thesis?" *Social Science Quarterly,* Vol. 75, No. 2, June 1994, 245–266.

pay higher prices if it would result in protecting the environment ranges from a low of 30 percent in the Philippines to a high of 78 percent in Denmark.

One possible explanation for the differences is the economic conditions in these countries. It has been argued by scholars of the environmental movement that, because of limited economic resources, citizens of developing and poorer countries cannot afford to pay for environmental protection and, therefore, there is less support for environmental protection in these countries. One important indicator of economic conditions is the GNP per capita in each country. Table 8.2 displays the GNP per capita, recorded in thousands of dollars, for each of the eleven countries surveyed. Note that GNP per capita ranges widely from $700 (0.7 × 1,000) in the Philippines to $30,300 (30.3 × 1,000) in Switzerland.

Table 8.2    **GNP per Capita Recorded for Eleven Countries in 1992 (in $1,000)**

| Country | GNP per Capita |
|---------|---------------:|
| Denmark | 20.0 |
| Norway | 22.0 |
| Korea | 4.4 |
| Switzerland | 30.3 |
| Chile | 2.0 |
| Canada | 19.0 |
| Ireland | 8.0 |
| Turkey | 1.4 |
| Russia | 3.6 |
| Japan | 24.0 |
| Philippines | 0.7 |

$$\overline{X} = \frac{\sum X}{N} = \frac{135.4}{11} = 12.31$$

$$\text{Variance } X = S_x^2 = \frac{\sum (X - \overline{X})^2}{N-1} = \frac{1,175.3}{10} = 117.52$$

$$\text{Range } X = \$30.3 - \$0.7 = \$29.6$$

*Source:* Adapted from Steven R. Brechin and Willett Kempton.

## The Scatter Diagram

Let's examine the possible relationship between the interval-ratio variables "GNP per capita" and the "percentage willing to pay higher prices to protect the environment." One quick visual method used to display such a relationship between two interval-ratio variables[1] is the **scatter diagram**. Scatter diagrams (also called scatterplots), which are often used as a first exploratory step in regression analysis, can suggest to us whether two variables are associated.

The scatter diagram showing the relationship between willingness to pay higher prices for environmental protection and per-capita income for the eleven countries is shown in Figure 8.1. In a scatter diagram the scales for the two variables form the vertical and horizontal axes of a graph. Usually, the independent variable, $X$, is arrayed

---

[1]We are interested in examining the *aggregate* relationship between GNP per capita and attitudes toward the environment.

Figure 8.1  **Scatter Diagram of GNP per Capita (in $1,000) and Percentage Willing to Pay More to Protect the Environment**

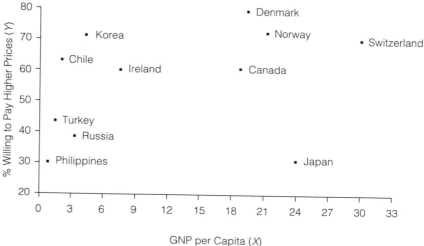

*Source:* Adapted from Steven R. Brechin and Willett Kempton.

along the horizontal axis and the dependent variable, $Y$, along the vertical axis. Because differences in GNP per capita are hypothesized to account for differences in the percentage of those willing to pay higher prices, GNP is assumed to be the independent variable and is arrayed along the horizontal axis. Willingness to pay higher prices, the dependent variable, is arrayed along the vertical axis. In Figure 8.1, each dot represents a country; its location lies at the exact intersection of that country's GNP per capita and the percentage willing to pay higher prices.

---

*Scatter Diagram (Scatterplot)*   A visual method used to display a relationship between two interval-ratio variables.

---

Notice an apparent tendency for countries with lower GNP per capita (for example, the Philippines and Russia) to also have a lower percentage of people willing to pay higher prices for environmental protection, whereas in countries with a higher GNP per capita (for example, Norway and Denmark), a higher percentage of people are willing to pay higher prices. In other words, we can say that GNP per capita and willingness to pay higher prices are *positively associated.* However, there are clearly exceptions to this pattern. For example, with one of the highest GNPs per capita ($24,000), Japan has one of the lowest percentages (31%) of citizens willing to pay higher prices for environmental protection. On the other hand, despite having one of the lowest GNPs per capita ($2,000), a relatively high percentage of Chilean citizens (60%) are willing to pay higher prices for environmental protection.

Scatter diagrams can also illustrate a negative association between two variables. For example, Figure 8.2 displays the association between GNP per capita and the percentage of respondents in fourteen countries who indicated a willingness to volunteer time to help protect the environment. Figure 8.2 suggests that low GNP per capita is associated with a higher percentage of citizens willing to volunteer time for the environment. Conversely, high GNP per capita seems to be associated with a lower percentage of citizens willing to volunteer time for the environment. Figure 8.2 illustrates a *negative association* between GNP per capita and willingness to volunteer time to protect the environment.

Figure 8.2 **GNP per Capita (in $1,000) and Percentage Willing to Volunteer Time for Environmental Protection**

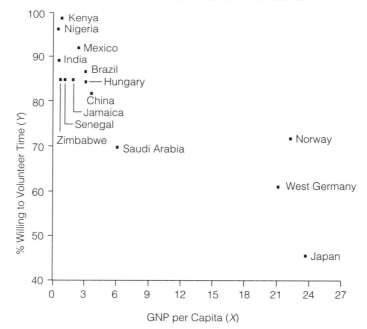

## Linear Relations and Prediction Rules

Scatter diagrams provide a useful but only a preliminary step in exploring a relationship between two interval-ratio variables. We need a more systematic way to express this relationship. Let's examine Figure 8.1 and 8.2 again. Both allow us to see how two sets of measures of environmental concern are related to GNP per capita. The relationships displayed are by no means perfect, but the trends are apparent. In the first case (Figure 8.1), as GNP increases so does the percentage of respondents in each country who are willing to pay higher prices to protect the environment. In the second case (Figure 8.2), as GNP increases the percentage of respondents who are willing to volunteer time decreases.

One way to evaluate these relationships is by expressing them as *linear relationships*. A **linear relationship** allows us to approximate the observations displayed in a scatter diagram with a straight line. In a perfectly linear relationship all the observations (the dots) fall along a straight line (a perfect relationship is sometimes called a **deterministic relationship**), and the line itself provides a predicted value of $Y$ (the vertical axis) for any value of $X$ (the horizontal axis). For example, in Figure 8.3 we superimposed a straight line on the scatterplot

Figure 8.3 **A Straight Line Graph for GNP per Capita (in $1,000) and Percentage Willing to Pay More to Protect the Environment**

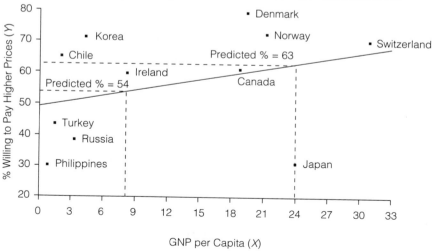

originally displayed in Figure 8.1. Using this line, we can obtain a predicted value of the percentage willing to pay higher prices for any value of GNP, by reading up to the line from the GNP axis and then over to the percentage axis (indicated by the dotted lines). For example, the predicted value of the percentage willing to pay higher prices for a GNP of $8,000 is 54. Similarly, for a GNP of $24,000 we would get a predicted value of 63 percent willing to pay higher prices.

---

*Linear Relationship*   A relationship between two interval-ratio variables in which the observations displayed in a scatter diagram can be approximated with a straight line.

*Deterministic (Perfect) Linear Relationship*   A relationship between two interval-ratio variables in which all the observations (the dots) fall along a straight line. The line provides a predicted value of $Y$ (the vertical axis) for any value of $X$ (the horizontal axis).

---

It is apparent from Figure 8.3 that for the eleven countries surveyed, the actual relationship between GNP per capita and the percentage willing to pay higher prices is not perfectly linear; although some of the countries lie very close to the line, none falls exactly on the line and some deviate from it considerably. Are there other lines that provide a better description of the relationship between GNP per capita and the percentage willing to pay higher prices?

In Figure 8.4 we drew two additional lines that approximate the pattern of relationship shown by the scatter diagram. In each case, notice that even though some of the countries lie close to the line, all fall considerably short of perfect linearity. Is there one line that provides the best linear description of the relationship between GNP per capita and the percentage willing to pay higher prices? How do we choose such a line? What are its characteristics? In the next section, we describe a technique for finding the straight line that most accurately describes the relationship between two variables. But before we do that we need to first review some basic concepts about how straight line graphs are constructed.

**Learning Check.**   *Use Figure 8.3 to predict the percentage willing to pay higher prices in a country with a GNP of $12,000 and one with a GNP of $27,000.*

Figure 8.4 **Alternative Straight Line Graphs for GNP per Capita (in $1,000) and Percentage Willing to Pay More to Protect the Environment**

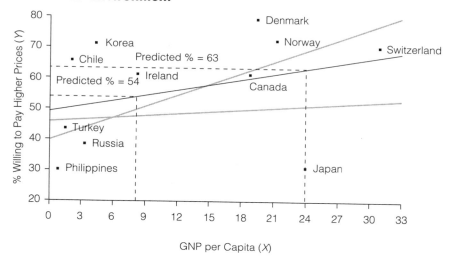

## Constructing Straight Line Graphs

To illustrate the fundamentals of straight line graphs, let's take a simple example. Suppose that in a local school system teachers' salaries are completely determined by seniority. New teachers begin with an annual salary of $12,000, and for each year of seniority their salary increases by $2,000. The seniority and annual salary of six hypothetical teachers are presented in Table 8.3.

Now let's plot the values of these two variables on a graph (Figure 8.5). Because seniority is assumed to determine salary, let it be our independent variable $X$, and let's array it along the horizontal axis. Salary, the dependent variable $Y$, is arrayed along the vertical axis. Connecting the six observations in Figure 8.5 gives us a straight line graph. This graph allows us to obtain a predicted salary value for any value of seniority level simply by reading from the specific seniority level up to the line and then over to the salary axis. For instance, we have marked the lines going up from a seniority of seven years and then over to the salary axis. We can see that a teacher with seven years of seniority is making $26,000.

The relationship between salary and seniority, as depicted in Table 8.3 and Figure 8.5, can also be described with the following algebraic equation:

$$Y = 12,000 + 2,000X$$

where

$X$ = seniority (in years)
$Y$ = salary (in dollars)

Table 8.3 **Seniority and Salary of Six Teachers (hypothetical data)**

| Seniority (in years) X | Salary (in dollars) Y |
|---|---|
| 0 | 12,000 |
| 1 | 14,000 |
| 2 | 16,000 |
| 3 | 18,000 |
| 4 | 20,000 |
| 5 | 22,000 |

Figure 8.5 **A Perfect Linear Relationship Between Seniority (in years) and Annual Salary (in $1,000) of Six Teachers (hypothetical)**

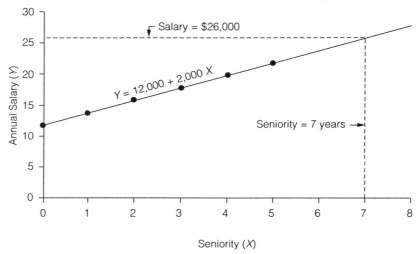

This equation allows us to correctly predict salary ($Y$) for any value for seniority ($X$) that we plug into the equation. For example, the salary of a teacher with five years of seniority is

$Y = 12,000 + 2,000(5) = 12,000 + 10,000 = 22,000$

Note that we can also plug in values of $X$ that are not shown in Table 8.3. For example, the salary of a teacher with ten years of seniority is

$Y = 12,000 + 2,000(10) = 12,000 + 20,000 = 32,000$

The equation describing the relation between seniority and salary is an equation for a straight line. The equations for all straight line graphs have the same general form:

$Y = a + bX$ **(8.1)**

where

$Y$ = the predicted score on the dependent variable
$X$ = the score on the independent variable
$a$ = the **Y-intercept**, or the point where the line crosses the Y-axis; therefore $a$ is the value of $Y$ when $X$ is 0.
$b$ = the **slope** of the line, or the change in $Y$ with a unit change in $X$. For our example, $a$ = 12,000 and $b$ = 2,000. That is, a teacher will make $12,000 with 0 years of seniority, but then her or his salary will go up by $2,000 with each year of seniority.

***Learning Check.*** *For each of these four lines, as X goes up by one unit, what does Y do? Be sure you can answer this question using both the equation and the line.*

Figure 8.6 **Four Lines: Illustrating the Slope and the Y-Intercept**

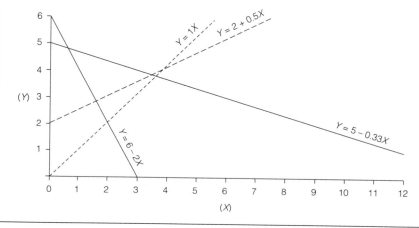

---

*Slope (b)*   The change in variable $Y$ (the dependent variable) with a unit change in variable $X$ (the independent variable).

*Y-intercept (a)*   The point where the line crosses the $Y$-axis, or the value of $Y$ when $X$ is 0.

---

**Learning Check.**   *Use the linear equation describing the relationship between seniority and salary of teachers to obtain the predicted salary of a teacher with twelve years of seniority.*

### Finding the Best-Fitting Line

The straight line displayed in Figure 8.5 and the linear equation representing it ($Y = 12,000 + 2,000X$) provide a very simple depiction of the relationship between seniority and salary because salary (the $Y$ variable) is completely determined by seniority (the $X$ variable). When each value of $Y$ is completely determined by $X$, all the points (observations) lie on the line, and the relationship between the two variables is called a *deterministic relationship,* or a perfectly linear relationship.

Unfortunately, most relationships we study in the social sciences are not deterministic, and we are not able to come up with a linear equation that allows us to predict $Y$ from $X$ with perfect accuracy. We are much more likely to find relationships approximating linearity, but in which numerous cases don't follow this trend perfectly. For instance, in reality teachers' salaries are not completely determined by seniority, and therefore knowing years of seniority will not provide us with a perfect prediction of their salary level.

When the dependent variable ($Y$) is not completely determined by the independent variable ($X$), not all (sometimes none) of the observations will lie exactly on the line. Look back at Figure 8.4, our example of the percentage willing to pay higher prices to protect the environment in relation to GNP per capita. Even though each line represents a linear equation showing us how the percentage of citizens willing to pay higher prices rises with a country's GNP per capita, in none of the cases do we have a perfect prediction. Thus, even though all three lines approximate the linear trend suggested by the scatter diagram, very few of the observations lie exactly on the line and some deviate from it considerably.

Given that none of the lines is perfect, our task is to choose one line—the *best-fitting line*. But which is the best-fitting line?

*Defining Error*  The best-fitting line is the one that generates the least amount of error. Let's think about how this error is defined. Look again at Figure 8.3. For each GNP level, the line (or the equation that this line represents) predicts a value of Y. Ireland, for example, with a GNP of $8,000 gives us a predicted value for Y of 54 percent. But the actual value for Ireland is 60 percent (see also Table 8.1). Thus, we have two values for Y: (1) a predicted Y, which we symbolize as $\hat{Y}$ and which is generated by the prediction equation, also called the *linear regression equation*

$$\hat{Y} = a + bX$$

and (2) the observed Y symbolized simply as Y. Thus, for Ireland, $\hat{Y}$ is 54 percent, whereas Y is 60 percent. We can think of the error as the difference between the observed Y and the predicted Y, or $\hat{Y}$.

If we symbolize error as *e*, then

$$e = Y - \hat{Y}$$

The error for Ireland is 60 percent – 54 percent, or 6 percent.

*The Sum of Squared Error ($\Sigma e^2$)*  We want a line or a prediction equation that minimizes *e* for each individual observation. However, any line we choose will minimize the error for some observations but may maximize it for others. Therefore, we want to find a prediction equation that minimizes the sum of errors over all observations. There are many mathematical ways of defining errors. For example, we may take the algebraic sum of errors $\Sigma(Y - \hat{Y})$, the sum of the absolute errors, $\Sigma(|Y - \hat{Y}|)$, or the sum of the squared errors $\Sigma(Y - \hat{Y})^2$. For mathematical reasons, statisticians prefer to work with the third method— squaring and summing the errors over all observations, obtaining the *sum of the squared errors*, or $\Sigma e^2$. Symbolically, $\Sigma e^2$ is expressed as

$$\Sigma e^2 = \Sigma(Y - \hat{Y})^2$$

*The Least-Squares Line*  The-best fitting regression line is that line where the sum of the squared errors, or $\Sigma e^2$, is at a minimum. Such a line is called the **least-squares line**, and the technique that produces this line is called the **least-squares method**. The technique involves choosing a and b for the equation $\hat{Y} = a + bX$, so that $\Sigma e^2$ will have the smallest possible value. In the next section, we use the data from the eleven countries to find the least-squares equation. But before we continue let's review where we are so far.

---

*Least-Squares Line* (also called the *best-fitting line*)  A line where the sum of the squared error, or $\Sigma e^2$, is at a minimum.

*Least-Squares Method*  The technique that produces the least-squares line.

---

*Review*

1. We examined the relationship between GNP per capita and the percentage willing to pay higher prices to protect the environment, using data collected in eleven countries. We used the *scatter diagram* (*scatterplot*) to display the relationship between these variables.

2. The scatter diagram indicated that the relationship between these variables might be *linear;* as GNP increases so does the percentage of citizens willing to pay higher prices to protect the environment.

3. A more systematic way to analyze the relationship is to develop a *straight line equation* to predict the percentage willing to pay higher prices based on GNP. We saw that there are a number of straight lines that can approximate the data.

4. The *best-fitting line* is one that minimizes $\Sigma e^2$. Such a line is called the *least-squares line,* and the technique that produces this line involves choosing the *a* and *b* for the equation $\hat{Y} = a + bX$ that minimize $\Sigma e^2$.

---

**Learning Check.**  *What is the difference between these two equations: $Y = a + bX$ and $\hat{Y} = a + bX$? Note that both equations are general formulas and that* a *and* b *may not be the same constants in both equations.*

---

## Computing *a* and *b* for the Prediction Equation

Through the use of calculus it can be shown that to figure out the values of *a* and *b* in a way that minimizes $\Sigma e^2$, we need to apply the following formulas:

$$b_{YX} = \frac{S_{YX}}{S_X^2} \tag{8.2}$$

$$a = \overline{Y} - b_{YX}(\overline{X}) \tag{8.3}$$

where

$S_{YX}$ = the covariance of $X$ and $Y$
$S_X^2$ = the variance of $X$
$\overline{Y}$ = the mean of $Y$
$\overline{X}$ = the mean of $X$
$a$ = the $Y$-intercept
$b_{YX}$ = the slope of the line

These formulas assume that $X$ is the independent variable and $Y$ is the dependent variable.

Before we compute $a$ and $b$, let's examine these formulas. The denominator for $b_{YX}$ is the variance of the variable $X$. It is defined as follows:

$$\text{Variance } (X) = S_X^2 = \frac{\sum (X - \overline{X})^2}{N - 1}$$

This formula should be familiar to you from Chapter 5. The numerator $(S_{YX})$, however, is a new term. It is the covariance of $X$ and $Y$ and is defined as

$$\text{Covriance } (X, Y) = S_{YX} = \frac{\sum (X - \overline{X})(Y - \overline{Y})}{N - 1} \tag{8.4}$$

The covariance is a measure of how $X$ and $Y$ vary together. Basically, the covariance tells us to what extent higher values of one variable "go together" with higher values on the second variable (in which case we have a positive covariation) or with lower values on the second variable (which is a negative covariation). Take a look at this formula. It tells us to subtract the mean of $X$ from each $X$ score and the mean of $Y$ from each $Y$ score, and then take the product of the two deviations. The results are then summed for all the cases and divided by $N - 1$.

In Table 8.4 we show the computations necessary to calculate the values of $a$ and $b_{YX}$ for our eleven countries. The means for GNP and percentage willing to pay higher prices are obtained by summing column 1 and column 2, respectively, and dividing each sum by $N$. To calculate the covariance we first subtract $\overline{X}$ from each $X$ score (column 3) and $\overline{Y}$ from each $Y$ score (column 5) to obtain the mean deviations. We then multiply these deviations for every observation. The products of the mean deviations are shown in column 7. For example, for the first observation, Denmark, the mean deviation for GNP is 7.69 ($20 - 12.31 = 7.69$); for the percentage willing to pay higher prices it is 21.55 ($78 - 56.45 = 21.55$). The product of these

Table 8.4 **Worksheet for Calculating a and b for the Regression Equation**

| Country | (1)<br>GNP per<br>Capita<br>(X) | (2)<br>% Willing<br>to Pay<br>(Y) | (3)<br>(X − X̄) | (4)<br>(X − X̄)² | (5)<br>(Y − Ȳ) | (6)<br>(Y − Ȳ)² | (7)<br>(X − X̄)(Y − Ȳ) |
|---|---|---|---|---|---|---|---|
| Denmark | 20.0 | 78 | 7.69 | 59.1 | 21.55 | 464.4 | 165.7 |
| Norway | 22.0 | 73 | 9.69 | 93.9 | 16.55 | 273.9 | 160.4 |
| Korea | 4.4 | 71 | −7.91 | 62.6 | 14.55 | 211.7 | −115.1 |
| Switzerland | 30.3 | 70 | 17.99 | 323.6 | 13.55 | 183.6 | 243.8 |
| Chile | 2.0 | 64 | −10.31 | 106.3 | 7.55 | 57.0 | −77.8 |
| Canada | 19.0 | 61 | 6.69 | 44.8 | 4.55 | 20.7 | 30.4 |
| Ireland | 8.0 | 60 | −4.31 | 18.6 | 3.55 | 12.6 | −15.3 |
| Turkey | 1.4 | 44 | −10.90 | 119.0 | −12.46 | 155.2 | 135.8 |
| Russia | 3.6 | 39 | −8.71 | 75.9 | −17.46 | 304.8 | 152.1 |
| Japan | 24.0 | 31 | 11.69 | 136.7 | −25.47 | 648.7 | −297.7 |
| Philippines | .7 | 30 | −11.61 | 134.8 | −26.46 | 700.1 | 307.2 |
| | ΣX=135.4 | ΣY=621 | 0.00 | 1,175.3 | 0.00 | 3,032.7 | 689.5 |

$$\text{Mean } X = \overline{X} = \frac{\sum X}{N} = \frac{135.4}{11} = 12.31$$

$$\text{Mean } Y = \overline{Y} = \frac{\sum Y}{N} = \frac{621}{11} = 56.45$$

$$\text{Variance } (Y) = S_Y^2 = \frac{\sum (Y - \overline{Y})^2}{N - 1} = \frac{3,032.7}{10} = 303.27$$

$$\text{Standard deviation } (Y) = S_Y = \sqrt{303.27} = 17.41$$

$$\text{Variance } (X) = S_X^2 = \frac{\sum (X - \overline{X})^2}{N - 1} = \frac{1,175.3}{10} = 117.53$$

$$\text{Standard deviation } (X) = S_X = \sqrt{117.53} = 10.84$$

$$\text{Covariance } (X, Y) = S_{YX} = \frac{\sum (X - \overline{X})(Y - \overline{Y})}{N - 1} = \frac{689.5}{10} = 68.95$$

deviations, 165.7 (7.69 × 21.55 = 165.7), is shown in column 7. The sum of these products, shown at the bottom of column 7, is 689.5. Dividing it by 10 ($N - 1$), we get the covariance of 68.95.

The covariance is a measure of the linear relationship between two variables, and its value reflects both the strength and the direction of the relationship. The covariance will be close to zero when $X$ and $Y$ are unrelated; it will be larger than zero when the relationship is positive, and smaller than zero when the relationship is negative.

Now let's substitute the values for the covariance and the variance from Table 8.4 to calculate $b_{YX}$:

$$b_{YX} = \frac{S_{YX}}{S_X^2} = \frac{68.95}{117.53} = 0.59$$

Once $b_{YX}$ has been calculated, finding $a$, the intercept, is simple:

$$a = \overline{Y} - b_{YX}(\overline{X}) = 56.45 - 0.59(12.31) = 56.45 - 7.26 = 49.19$$

The prediction equation is therefore

$$\hat{Y} = 49.19 + 0.59(X)$$

This equation can be used to obtain a predicted value for the percentage of citizens willing to pay higher prices for environmental protection given a country's GNP per-capita level. For example, for a country with a GNP per capita of 2 (in $1,000), the predicted percentage is

$$\hat{Y} = 49.19 + 0.59(2) = 50.37\%$$

Similarly, for a country with a GNP per capita of 12 (in $1,000), the predicted value is

$$\hat{Y} = 49.19 + 0.59(12) = 56.27\%$$

Now, we can plot the straight line graph corresponding to the regression equation. To plot a straight line we need only two points where each point corresponds to an $X, Y$ value predicted by the equation. We can use the two points we just obtained: (1) $X = 2$, $Y = 50.37$ and (2) $X = 12$, $Y = 56.27$. In Figure 8.7, the regression line is plotted over the scatter diagram we first displayed in Figure 8.1.

> **Learning Check.** Use the prediction equation to calculate the predicted values of $Y$ for Chile, Canada, and Japan. Verify that the regression line in Figure 8.7 passes through these points.

## Interpreting $a$ and $b_{YX}$

Now let's interpret the coefficients $a$ and $b_{YX}$ for our equation. The $b_{YX}$ coefficient is equal to 0.59 (in %). This tells us that the percentage of citizens willing to pay higher prices for environmental protection will

Figure 8.7 **The Best-Fitting Line for GNP per Capita and Percentage Willing to Pay More to Protect the Environment**

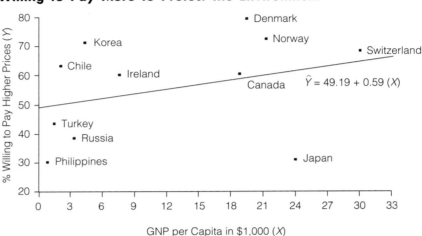

increase by 0.59 percent for every increment of $1,000 in their country's GNP per capita. Similarly, an increase of $10,000 in a country's GNP corresponds to a 5.9 percent (0.59 × 10) increase in the percentage of citizens willing to pay higher prices for environmental protection.

Note that because the relationships between variables in the social sciences are inexact, we don't expect our regression equation to make perfect predictions; neither do we expect it to work for every individual case. Thus, we don't expect an increase of $1,000 in a country's GNP to be associated with an increase of exactly 0.59 percent in the number of its citizens willing to pay higher prices for environmental protection. However, even though the pattern suggested by the regression equation may not hold for every individual country, it gives us a tool by which to make the best possible guess about how a country's GNP per capita is associated, *on average,* with the willingness of its citizens to pay higher prices for environmental protection. Thus, we can say that the slope of 0.59 percent is the estimate of this underlying relationship.

The intercept $a$ is the predicted value of $Y$ when $X = 0$. Thus, it is the point at which the regression line and the $Y$-axis intersect. With $a = 49.19$, a country with a GNP level equal to zero is predicted to have 49.19 percent of its citizens supporting higher prices for environmental protection. Note, however, that no country has a GNP as low as zero, although the Philippines, with a GNP of $700, comes pretty close to it. As a general rule, be cautious when making predictions for $Y$ based on values of $X$ that are outside the range of the data. Thus, when the

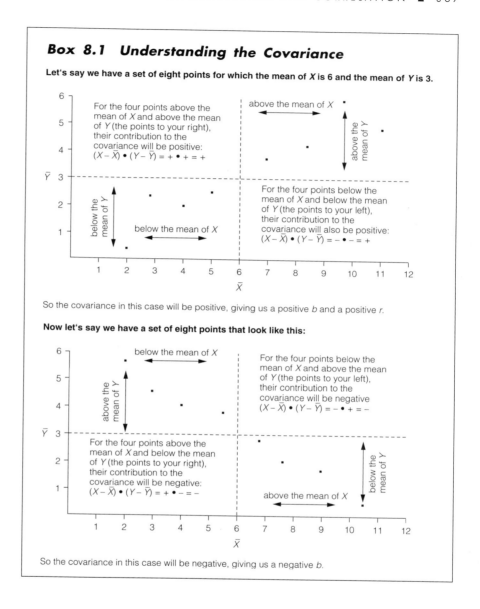

**Box 8.1  Understanding the Covariance**

Let's say we have a set of eight points for which the mean of X is 6 and the mean of Y is 3.

For the four points above the mean of X and above the mean of Y (the points to your right), their contribution to the covariance will be positive: $(X - \bar{X}) \bullet (Y - \bar{Y}) = + \bullet + = +$

above the mean of X

above the mean of Y

$\bar{Y}$  3

below the mean of Y

below the mean of X

For the four points below the mean of X and below the mean of Y (the points to your left), their contribution to the covariance will also be positive: $(X - \bar{X}) \bullet (Y - \bar{Y}) = - \bullet - = +$

$\bar{X}$

So the covariance in this case will be positive, giving us a positive b and a positive r.

**Now let's say we have a set of eight points that look like this:**

below the mean of X

above the mean of Y

For the four points below the mean of X and above the mean of Y (the points to your left), their contribution to the covariance will be negative $(X - \bar{X}) \bullet (Y - \bar{Y}) = - \bullet + = -$

$\bar{Y}$  3

For the four points above the mean of X and below the mean of Y (the points to your right), their contribution to the covariance will be negative: $(X - \bar{X}) \bullet (Y - \bar{Y}) = + \bullet - = -$

above the mean of X

below the mean of Y

$\bar{X}$

So the covariance in this case will be negative, giving us a negative b.

lowest value for X is far above zero, the intercept may not have a clear substantive interpretation.

## Calculating $b_{YX}$ Using a Computational Formula

The formula used to calculate $b_{YX}$—the slope of the regression equation—can become cumbersome to use as N becomes larger. In

### Box 8.2  A Note on Nonlinear Relationships

In analyzing the relationship between GNP and percent willing to pay higher prices for environmental protection, we assumed that the two variables are linearly related. For the most part, social science relationships can be approximated using a linear equation. It is important to note, however, that sometimes a relationship cannot be approximated by a straight line and is better described by some other nonlinear function. For example, Figure 8.8 shows a nonlinear relationship between age and hours of reading (hypothetical data). Hours of reading increase with age until the twenties, remain stable until the forties, and then tend to decrease with age.

One quick way to find out whether your variables form a linear or a nonlinear pattern of relations (or alternatively, the variables may not be related at all!) is to make a scatter diagram of your data. If there is a significant departure from linearity it would make no sense to fit a straight line to the data. There are statistical techniques available for analyzing nonlinear relationships between two variables. They are, however, beyond the scope of this book. Nonetheless, at the very least, you should check for possible departures from linearity when checking your scatter diagram.

Figure 8.8  **A Nonlinear Relationship Between Age and Hours of Reading per Week**

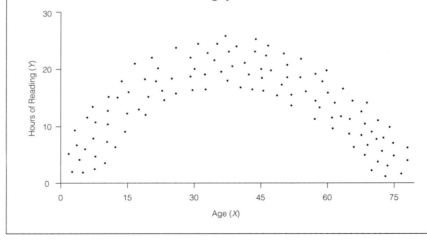

most cases you will use a computer program to find $a$ and $b_{YX}$, but in situations when you have to use a hand calculator to find $b_{YX}$ you can use the following computational formula:

$$b_{YX} = \frac{N\left(\sum XY\right) - \left(\sum X\right)\left(\sum Y\right)}{N\left(\sum X^2\right) - \left(\sum X\right)^2} \tag{8.5}$$

where

$\Sigma X$ = the sum of X
$\Sigma Y$ = the sum of Y
$\Sigma XY$ = the sum of the cross products of the X and Y scores
$\Sigma X^2$ = the sum of the squared X scores

Table 8.5 is a worksheet showing the calculations needed to determine $b_{YX}$, using our data on GNP per capita and the percentage willing to pay higher prices for environmental protection and the computational formula.

**Table 8.5  Worksheet for Calculating $a$ and $b$ Using a Computational Formula**

| Country | (1)<br>GNP<br>(in $1,000)<br>X | (2)<br><br><br>X² | (3)<br>Percentage<br>Willing to Pay<br>Y | (4)<br><br><br>XY | (5)<br><br><br>Y² |
|---|---|---|---|---|---|
| Denmark | 20.0 | 400.00 | 78 | 1,560.0 | 6,084 |
| Norway | 22.0 | 484.00 | 73 | 1,606.0 | 5,329 |
| Korea | 4.4 | 19.36 | 71 | 312.4 | 5,041 |
| Switzerland | 30.3 | 918.09 | 70 | 2,121.0 | 4,900 |
| Chile | 2.0 | 4.00 | 64 | 128.0 | 4,096 |
| Canada | 19.0 | 361.00 | 61 | 1,159.0 | 3,721 |
| Ireland | 8.0 | 64.00 | 60 | 480.0 | 3,600 |
| Turkey | 1.4 | 1.96 | 44 | 61.6 | 1,936 |
| Russia | 3.6 | 12.96 | 39 | 140.4 | 1,521 |
| Japan | 24.0 | 576.00 | 31 | 744.0 | 961 |
| Philippines | 0.7 | 0.49 | 30 | 21.0 | 900 |
| | $\Sigma X = 135.4$ | $\Sigma X^2 = 2,841.86$ | $\Sigma Y = 621$ | $\Sigma XY = 8,333.4$ | $\Sigma Y^2 = 38,089$ |

Mean $X = \bar{X} = \dfrac{\Sigma X}{N} = \dfrac{135.4}{11} = 12.31$

Mean $Y = \bar{Y} = \dfrac{\Sigma Y}{N} = \dfrac{621}{11} = 56.45$

$b_{YX} = \dfrac{N\left(\Sigma XY\right) - \left(\Sigma X\right)\left(\Sigma Y\right)}{N\left(\Sigma X^2\right) - \left(\Sigma X\right)^2} = \dfrac{11(8,333.4) - (135.4)(621)}{11(2,841.86) - (135.4)^2}$

$= \dfrac{91,667.4 - 84,083.4}{31,260.46 - 18,333.16} = \dfrac{7,584}{12,927.3} = 0.59$

$a = \bar{Y} - b_{YX}(\bar{X}) = 56.45 - 0.59(12.31) = 56.45 - 7.26 = 49.19$

## Statistics in Practice: GNP and Willingness to Volunteer Time for Environmental Protection

In our earlier example, we looked at the association between GNP per capita and concern for the environment as measured by the percentage of people willing to pay higher prices to protect the environment. The regression equation we estimated from data collected by the Gallup organization in eleven countries shows that as a country's GNP rises, more citizens in that country are willing to pay higher prices to protect the environment.

What do these findings suggest? The conventional wisdom has been that citizens of poorer countries do not or cannot care about the environment. Indeed, our findings seem to suggest that people in wealthy countries hold stronger environmental values than those in poorer countries. But, one may ask, "Is the only reliable measure of concern for the environment the amount of money one is willing to pay to protect it?"

In an attempt to challenge the conventional wisdom that people in poor countries lack environmental values, Brechin and Kempton[2] argue that even though few people within the poorest countries would offer monetary payment for anything, even for values they hold highly, they are equally or more likely to agree to commit their labor time. The researchers use the results of a survey collected by the Harris organization to examine this argument.[3] The Harris survey asked respondents if they would be willing to volunteer at least 2 hours each week for environmental protection. The percentage of citizens in fourteen countries who indicated that they would agree to such weekly labor requirements is presented in Table 8.6 together with the GNP per capita for each country. The scatter diagram for the data was displayed earlier in Figure 8.2.

Let's examine Figure 8.2 once again. The scatter diagram seems to indicate that the two variables—the percentage agreeing to volunteer time and GNP per capita—are linearly related; it also illustrates that these variables are negatively associated; that is, as GNP per capita rises the percentage of citizens willing to volunteer time to protect the environment declines.

---

[2]Steven R. Brechin and Willett Kempton, "Global Environmentalism: A Challenge to the Postmaterialism Thesis?" *Social Science Quarterly,* Vol. 75, No. 2, June 1994, 245–266.

[3]Both the Harris and the Gallup surveys (discussed in the earlier part of this chapter) examine the relationship between GNP and environmental concerns. However, because the two studies used different samples of countries, we need to be cautious about making generalizations based on looking at them jointly.

Table 8.6    **Percentage of Citizens Willing to Volunteer Time and GNP per Capita for Fourteen Countries**

| Country | GNP (in $1,000) X | Percentage Willing to Volunteer Time Y |
|---|---|---|
| Kenya | .38 | 98 |
| Nigeria | .25 | 95 |
| Mexico | 1.99 | 91 |
| India | .35 | 89 |
| Brazil | 2.55 | 87 |
| Zimbabwe | .64 | 85 |
| Senegal | .65 | 85 |
| Jamaica | 1.26 | 85 |
| Hungary | 2.56 | 84 |
| China | .36 | 83 |
| Norway | 21.85 | 76 |
| Saudi Arabia | 6.23 | 70 |
| West Germany | 20.75 | 62 |
| Japan | 23.73 | 44 |

For a more systematic analysis of the association we need to estimate the least-squares regression equation for this data. Since we want to predict the percentage willing to volunteer time, we treat this variable as our dependent variable $Y$. We use the short cut, the computational formula, to calculate the $b_{YX}$ coefficient.

Table 8.7 shows the calculations necessary to find $b_{YX}$ for our data on GNP per capita in relation to the percentage willing to volunteer time for environmental protection. Using the computational formula (8.5), let's substitute the values for $\Sigma XY$, $\Sigma X$, $\Sigma Y$, and $\Sigma X^2$ from Table 8.7 to calculate $b_{YX}$:

$$b_{YX} = \frac{N\left(\sum XY\right) - \left(\sum X\right)\left(\sum Y\right)}{N\left(\sum X^2\right) - \left(\sum X\right)^2} = \frac{14(5,384.07) - (83.55)(1,134.00)}{14(1,529.78) - (83.55)^2}$$

$$= \frac{75,376.98 - 94,745.70}{21,416.92 - 6,980.60} = \frac{-19,368.72}{14,436.32} = -1.34$$

Table 8.7  **GNP per Capita and Percentage Willing to Volunteer Time for Fourteen Countries**

| Country | GNP (in $1,000) X | X² | Percentage Willing to Volunteer Time Y | XY | Y² |
|---|---|---|---|---|---|
| Kenya | .38 | 0.14 | 98 | 37.24 | 9,604 |
| Nigeria | .25 | 0.06 | 95 | 23.75 | 9,025 |
| Mexico | 1.99 | 3.96 | 91 | 181.09 | 8,281 |
| India | .35 | 0.12 | 89 | 31.15 | 7,921 |
| Brazil | 2.55 | 6.50 | 87 | 221.85 | 7,569 |
| Zimbabwe | .64 | 0.41 | 85 | 54.40 | 7,225 |
| Senegal | .65 | 0.42 | 85 | 55.25 | 7,225 |
| Jamaica | 1.26 | 1.59 | 85 | 107.10 | 7,225 |
| Hungary | 2.56 | 6.55 | 84 | 215.04 | 7,056 |
| China | .36 | 0.13 | 83 | 29.88 | 6,889 |
| Norway | 21.85 | 477.42 | 76 | 1,660.60 | 5,776 |
| Saudi Arabia | 6.23 | 38.81 | 70 | 436.10 | 4,900 |
| West Germany | 20.75 | 430.56 | 62 | 1,286.50 | 3,844 |
| Japan | 23.73 | 563.11 | 44 | 1,044.12 | 1,936 |
| | $\Sigma X =$ 83.55 | $\Sigma X^2 =$ 1,529.78 | $\Sigma Y =$ 1,134 | $\Sigma XY =$ 5,384.07 | $\Sigma Y^2 =$ 94,476 |

Mean $X = \overline{X} = \dfrac{\Sigma X}{N} = \dfrac{83.55}{14} = 5.97$

Mean $Y = \overline{Y} = \dfrac{\Sigma Y}{N} = \dfrac{1,134}{14} = 81.0$

The negative slope of –1.34 confirms our earlier impression; the relationship between wealth and willingness to volunteer time is negative. In other words, the higher the GNP per-capita level, the smaller the percentage of citizens in that country willing to volunteer time to protect its environment. The slope of –1.34 means that an increase of $1,000 in a country's GNP is associated with a decrease of 1.34 percent in the number of people willing to volunteer time for environmental protection.

Now let's find the intercept:

$$a = \overline{Y} - b_{YX}(\overline{X}) = 81.0 - (-1.34)(5.97) = 81.0 + 8.0 = 89.0$$

The prediction equation is therefore

$$\hat{Y} = 89.0 - 1.34(X)$$

In Figure 8.9 this regression line is plotted over the scatter diagram we first displayed in Figure 8.2.

## Methods for Assessing the Accuracy of Predictions

So far we have developed two regression equations that are helping us to make predictions about people's willingness to contribute money or volunteer their time for environmental protection. But, in both cases our predictions are far from perfect. If we examine Figures 8.7 and 8.9, we note that we fail to make accurate predictions in every case! Even though some of the countries lie pretty close to the regression line, none lies directly on the line—an indication that some error of prediction was made. You must be wondering by now, "OK, I understand that the model helps us make predictions, but how can I assess the accuracy of these predictions?"

Figure 8.9 **Regression Line for GNP per Capita (in $1,000) and Percentage Willing to Volunteer Time for Environmental Protection**

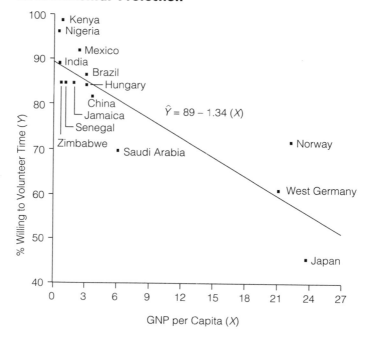

We saw earlier that one way to judge the accuracy of the predictions is to "eyeball" the scatterplot. The closer the observations are to the regression line, the better the "fit" between the predictions and the actual observations. But we want a more systematic method for making such a judgment. We need a measure that tells us how accurate a prediction the regression model provides. The *coefficient of determination*, or $r^2$, is such a measure. It tells us how well the bivariate regression model fits the data. As we will see, the coefficient of determination is related to another measure, *Pearson's correlation coefficient*, or *r*. Both $r^2$ and *r* measure the strength of the association between two interval-ratio variables. Before we discuss these measures, let's first examine the notion of prediction errors.

### Prediction Errors

Examine Figure 8.10. It displays the regression line for the variables "GNP per capita (*X*)" and the "percentage willing to pay higher prices to protect the environment (*Y*)." This regression line and the scatter diagram for the eleven countries surveyed by Gallup were originally presented in Figure 8.7.

In Figure 8.10 we consider the prediction of *Y* for one country, Norway, out of the eleven countries included in the survey. (The *X* and *Y* scores for all eleven countries including Norway are presented in Table 8.4.)

Figure 8.10 **Error Terms for One Observation**

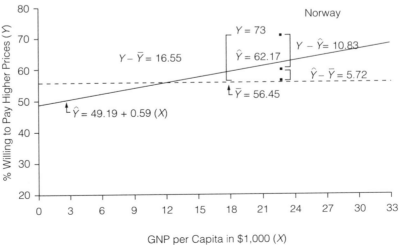

Suppose we didn't know the *actual* Y, the percentage of citizens in Norway who agreed to pay higher prices for environmental protection. Suppose further that we did not have knowledge of X, Norway's GNP per-capita level. Because the mean minimizes the sum of the squared errors for a set of scores, our best guess for Y would be the mean of Y, or $\overline{Y} = 56.45$. The horizontal line in Figure 8.10 represents this mean. Now let's compare the actual Y, 73, with this prediction:

$$Y - \overline{Y} = 73 - 56.45 = 16.55$$

Obviously, with an error of 16.55, our prediction of the average score for Norway is not very accurate (this deviation of $Y - \overline{Y}$ is also illustrated in Figure 8.10). Now let's see if our predictive power can be improved by utilizing our knowledge of X—the GNP per-capita level for Norway—and its linear relation with Y. If we plug Norway's GNP per-capita level of $22,000 into our prediction equation, as follows:

$$\hat{Y} = 49.19 + 0.59(X)$$

$$\hat{Y} = 49.19 + 0.59(22) = 62.17$$

we obtain a predicted Y of 62.17

We can recalculate our new error of prediction by comparing the predicted Y with the actual Y:

$$Y - \hat{Y} = 73 - 62.17 = 10.83$$

Although this prediction is by no means perfect, it is an improvement of 5.72 (16.55 − 10.83 = 5.72) over our earlier prediction.

This improvement is illustrated in Figure 8.10. Note that this improvement of 5.72 is equal to the quantity $\hat{Y} - \overline{Y}$ (62.17 − 56.45 = 5.72). This quantity represents the improvement in the prediction error resulting from utilizing the linear prediction equation.

Let's review what we have done. We have two prediction rules and two measures of error. The first prediction rule is in the absence of information on X, predict $\overline{Y}$. The error of prediction is defined as $Y - \overline{Y}$. The second rule of prediction utilizes X and the regression equation to predict Y. The error of prediction is defined as $Y - \hat{Y}$.

To calculate these two measures of error for all the cases in our sample, we square the deviations and sum them. Thus, for the deviation from the mean of Y we have

$$\sum (Y - \overline{Y})^2$$

and to measure deviation from the regression line, or $\hat{Y}$, we have

$$\sum (Y - \hat{Y})^2$$

(We discussed this error term, the sum of squared errors, earlier in the chapter.)

*The Coefficient of Determination ($r^2$) as a PRE Measure*  The coefficient of determination, $r^2$, is a PRE measure of association. We saw in Chapter 7 that all PRE measures adhere to the following formula:

$$PRE = \frac{E1 - E2}{E1}$$

where

$E1$ = prediction errors made when $X$ is unknown
$E2$ = prediction errors made when $X$ is used to predict $Y$

We have all the elements we need to construct a PRE measure. Because $\Sigma(Y - \overline{Y})^2$ measures the prediction errors when $X$ is unknown we can define

$$E1 = \sum(Y - \overline{Y})^2$$

Similarly, because $\Sigma(Y - \hat{Y})^2$ measures the prediction errors when $X$ is used to predict $Y$, we can define

$$E2 = \sum(Y - \hat{Y})^2$$

We can now calculate the proportional reduction of error associated with using the linear regression equation as a rule for predicting $Y$:

$$PRE = r^2 = \frac{E1 - E2}{E1} = \frac{\sum(Y - \overline{Y})^2 - \sum(Y - \hat{Y})^2}{\sum(Y - \overline{Y})^2} \tag{8.6}$$

The **coefficient of determination**, $r^2$, measures the proportional reduction of error resulting from utilizing the linear regression model. It reflects the proportion of the total variation in the dependent variable, $Y$, explained by the independent variable, $X$.

The coefficient of determination ranges from 0.0 to 1.0; an $r^2$ of 1.0 means that by utilizing the linear regression model we have reduced uncertainty by 100 percent. It also means that the independent variable accounts for 100 percent of the variation in the dependent variable. With an $r^2$ of 1.0, all the observations fall along the regression line, and the prediction error $[\Sigma(Y - \hat{Y})^2]$ is equal to 0.0. An $r^2$ of 0.0 means that using the regression equation to predict $Y$ does not improve the prediction of $Y$. Figure 8.11 shows $r^2$ values near 0.0 and near 1.0, respectively. In Figure 8.11a, where $r^2$ is approximately 1.0, the regression model provides a good fit. In contrast, a very poor fit is shown in Figure 8.11b, where $r^2$ is near zero. An $r^2$ near zero indicates either poor fit or a well-fitting line with a $b_{YX}$ of zero.

Figure 8.11  **Examples Showing $r^2$ Near 1.0 and Near 0**

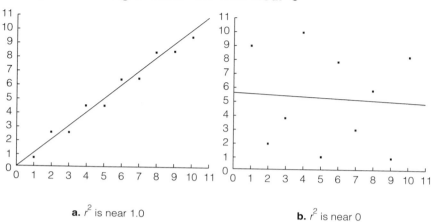

**a.** $r^2$ is near 1.0                    **b.** $r^2$ is near 0

---

***Coefficient of Determination ($r^2$)***  A PRE measure reflecting the proportional reduction of error resulting from utilizing the linear regression model. It reflects the proportion of the total variation in the dependent variable, Y, explained by the independent variable, X.

---

*Calculating $r^2$*  An easier method for calculating $r^2$ uses the following equation:

$$r^2 = \frac{(\text{Covariance}(X,Y))^2}{(\text{Variance}(X))(\text{Variance}(Y))} = \frac{S_{YX}^2}{S_X^2 S_Y^2} \qquad (8.7)$$

This formula tells us to divide the square of the covariance of $X$ and $Y$ by the product of the variance of $X$ and the variance of $Y$.

To calculate $r^2$ for our example we can go back to Table 8.4, where the covariance and the variances for the two variables were already calculated:

Covariance $(X,Y)$ = 68.95
Variance $(X)$     = 117.53
Variance $(Y)$     = 303.27

Therefore,

$$r^2 = \frac{(68.95)^2}{(117.53)(303.27)} = \frac{4,754.10}{35,643.32} = 0.133$$

Figure 8.12 **A Pie Graph Approach to R-Squared ($r^2$)**

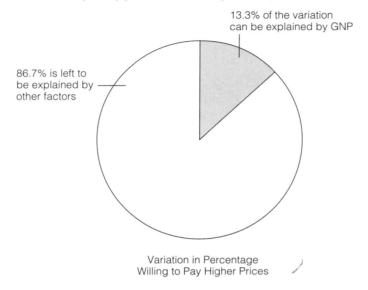

An $r^2$ of 0.133 means that by using GNP per capita and the linear prediction rule to predict $Y$—the percentage willing to pay higher prices—we have reduced uncertainty of prediction by 13.3 percent (0.133 × 100). We can also say that the independent variable—GNP per capita—explains 13.3 percent of the variation in the dependent variable—the percentage willing to pay higher prices (Figure 8.12).

### Pearson's Correlation Coefficient ($r$)

In the social sciences, it is the square root of $r^2$—$r$, also called **Pearson's r** (Pearson's product moment correlation coefficient)—that is most often used as a measure of association between two interval-ratio variables:

$$r = \sqrt{r^2}$$

Pearson's $r$ is usually computed directly[4] by using the following definitional formula:

$$r = \frac{\text{Covariance}(X,Y)}{(\text{Standard deviation}(X))(\text{Standard deviation}(Y))} = \frac{S_{YX}}{S_X S_Y} \quad \textbf{(8.8)}$$

[4]If you obtain $r$ simply by taking the square root of $r^2$ make sure not to lose the sign of $r$ ($r^2$ is always positive but $r$ can also be negative), which can be ascertained by looking at the sign of $S_{YX}$.

Thus, $r$ is defined as the ratio of the covariance of $X$ and $Y$ to the product of the standard deviations of $X$ and $Y$.

*Characteristics of Pearson's r*   Pearson's $r$ is a measure of relationship or association for interval-ratio variables. It is called the correlation coefficient. Like gamma and Somers' $d$ (discussed in Chapter 7; appropriate for nominal and ordinal variables), it ranges from 0.0 to ±1.0, with 0.0 indicating no association between the two variables. An $r$ of +1.0 means that the two variables have a perfect positive association; −1.0 indicates that it is a perfect negative association. The absolute value of $r$ indicates the strength of the linear association between two variables. Thus, a correlation of −0.75 demonstrates a stronger association than a correlation of 0.50. Figure 8.13 illustrates a strong positive relationship, a strong negative relationship, a moderate positive relationship, and a weak negative relationship.

Unlike the $b$ coefficient, $r$ is a symmetrical measure. That is, the correlation between $X$ and $Y$ is identical to the correlation between $Y$ and $X$. In contrast, $b$ may be different when the variables are switched;

Figure 8.13   **Scatter Diagrams Illustrating Weak, Moderate, and Strong Relationships as Indicated by the Absolute Value of *r***

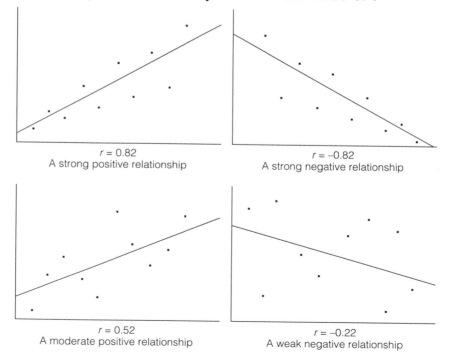

| | |
|---|---|
| $r = 0.82$<br>A strong positive relationship | $r = -0.82$<br>A strong negative relationship |
| $r = 0.52$<br>A moderate positive relationship | $r = -0.22$<br>A weak negative relationship |

that is, when we use $Y$ as the independent variable rather than as the dependent variable.

To calculate $r$ for our example of the relationship between GNP per capita and the percentage of people who support higher prices for environmental protection, let's return to Table 8.4, where the covariance and the standard deviations for $X$ and $Y$ were already calculated:

$$r = \frac{S_{YX}}{S_X S_Y} = \frac{68.95}{(10.84)(17.41)} = \frac{68.95}{188.72} = 0.365$$

A correlation coefficient of 0.365 indicates that there is a weak-to-moderate linear relation between GNP per capita and the percentage of citizens who support higher prices for environmental protection.

Note that we could have just taken the square root of $r^2$ to calculate $r$, because $r = \sqrt{r^2}$. Or, $\sqrt{0.133} = 0.365$. Similarly, if we first calculate $r$ we can obtain $r^2$ simply by squaring $r$ (be careful not to lose the sign of $r$!).

---

***Pearson's Correlation Coefficient (r)***   The square root of $r^2$; it is a measure of association for interval-ratio variables, reflecting the strength of the linear association between two interval-ratio variables.

---

*Calculating r Using a Computational Formula*   The definitional formula for $r$ can become cumbersome to use as $N$ becomes larger. In most cases you will use a computer program to find $r$, but in situations when you have to use a hand calculator, the following computational formula is useful:

$$r = \frac{N\left(\sum XY\right) - \left(\sum X\right)\left(\sum Y\right)}{\sqrt{\left[N\left(\sum X^2\right) - \left(\sum X\right)^2\right]\left[N\left(\sum Y^2\right) - \left(\sum Y\right)^2\right]}} \tag{8.9}$$

where

$\sum X$ = the sum of $X$
$\sum Y$ = the sum of $Y$
$\sum XY$ = the sum of the cross products of the $X$ and $Y$ scores
$\sum X^2$ = the sum of the squared $X$ scores
$\sum Y^2$ = the sum of the squared $Y$ scores

We calculate $r$ for the variables "GNP per capita" and the "percentage willing to volunteer time for environmental protection." The data and the calculations needed to calculate $r$ are shown in Table 8.7. The quantities displayed in the table can be substituted directly into formula 8.9.

$$r = \frac{14(5,384.07) - (83.55)(1,134)}{\sqrt{[14(1,529.78) - (83.55)^2][14(94,476) - (1,134)^2}}$$

$$= \frac{75,376.98 - 94,745.7}{\sqrt{(21,416.92 - 6,980.60)(1,322,664 - 1,285,956)}}$$

$$= \frac{-19,368.72}{\sqrt{(14,436.32)(36,708)}} = \frac{-19,368.72}{\sqrt{529,928,434.6}} = \frac{-19,368.72}{23,020.17}$$

$$= -0.84$$

An $r$ of –0.84 means that there is a strong negative relationship between GNP per capita and the percentage of citizens who are willing to volunteer time for environmental protection.

## Statistics in Practice: Comparable Worth Discrimination

In Chapter 1, we discussed the dual labor market theory as an explanation for the gender gap in earnings. According to the dual labor market theory, men and women are usually segregated into different types of work, with occupations in which the majority of workers are female usually paying less than occupations in which the majority of workers are male. A related explanation of the gender gap in earnings is the idea of comparable worth discrimination. The concept of comparable worth describes a process in which "employers underpay workers who are doing jobs that are different from predominantly male jobs but are of equal value. . . . As a result of comparable worth discrimination, the more female an occupation, the lower its average pay for both female and male workers, after taking into account such factors as education and experience."[5] The comparable worth hypothesis can be stated more succinctly as follows: In occupations that are of comparable worth, the higher the percentage of female workers, the lower the average pay for that occupation.

[5]Barbara Reskin and Irene Padavic, *Women and Men at Work*. Thousand Oaks, CA: Pine Forge Press, 1994, 119.

One way to examine the comparable worth discrimination hypothesis is to compare the pay of predominantly male and female jobs that experts judge to be of comparable worth. Table 8.8 shows the gender composition and average salary of jobs in a New York county in 1988. By eyeballing the data presented in the table we can see clearly that salaries tend to go down as the percentage of women in the job increases.

Given that both "percent female" and "average salary" are interval-ratio variables, we can use bivariate regression analysis to examine the comparable worth hypothesis. Figure 8.14 shows the scatter diagram for percent female and average salary. Because we are assuming that the percentage of female workers in an occupation can predict the average salary for that occupation, we are going to treat it as our independent variable, X. Average salary, then, is our dependent variable, Y. The scatter diagram seems to suggest that the two variables

Table 8.8    **Sex Composition and Salary of Jobs in a New York County, 1988**

| Job Title | Percent Female | Average Salary |
|---|---|---|
| Psychologist II (less than full-time) | 0 | $34,914 |
| Patrol lieutenant | 0 | 32,445 |
| Head groundskeeper II | 0 | 25,140 |
| Respiratory therapy technician | 0 | 21,778 |
| Automotive mechanic | 0 | 21,778 |
| Security aide (part-time) | 0 | 17,205 |
| Public health technician II | 14 | 25,121 |
| Management analyst | 33 | 24,405 |
| Assistant office machine operator | 50 | 14,378 |
| Municipal aide | 59 | 12,716 |
| Mental health worker I | 67 | 14,365 |
| Community service aide | 75 | 14,716 |
| Practical nurse | 93 | 18,082 |
| Community service worker II | 100 | 15,054 |
| Medical technologist | 100 | 24,054 |
| Principal records clerk | 100 | 19,001 |
| Senior accounting clerk/typist | 100 | 15,054 |
| Telephone operator/typist | 100 | 13,100 |
| Accounting clerk/typist | 100 | 13,739 |

*Source:* Adapted from Linda J. Ames, "Erase the Bias: A Pay Equity Guide for Eliminating Race and Sex Bias for Wage-Setting Systems," 1993, Washington DC, National Committee on Pay Equity.

Figure 8.14 **Scatter Diagram for Percent Female and Average Salary**

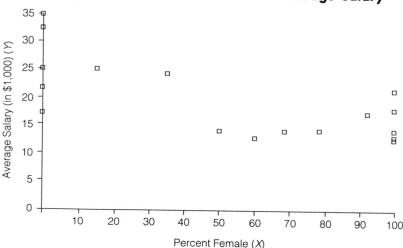

are linearly related. It also illustrates that these variables are negatively associated; that is, as the percentage of women in an occupation rises the average salary declines.

## Computing *a* and *b* for the Prediction Equation

For a more systematic analysis of the association we estimate the following linear regression equation:

$Y = a + bX$

where

$Y$ = the average salary for a respective occupation
$X$ = the percentage of women in a respective occupation

Table 8.9 shows the calculations necessary to find $b$ for the New York county data. Using the computational formula for $b_{YX}$ (formula 8.5), let's substitute the values for $\Sigma XY$, $\Sigma X$, $\Sigma Y$, and $\Sigma X^2$ from Table 8.9 to calculate $b_{YX}$

$$b_{YX} = \frac{N\left(\Sigma XY\right) - \left(\Sigma X\right)\left(\Sigma Y\right)}{N\left(\Sigma X^2\right) - \left(\Sigma X\right)^2} = \frac{19(16,374.184) - (991)(377.045)}{19(86,029) - (991)^2}$$

$$= \frac{311,109.496 - 373,651.595}{1,634,551 - 982,081} = \frac{-62,542.099}{652,470} = -0.096$$

Table 8.9 **Worksheet for Calculating the Regression Equation for Percent Female and Average Salary**

| Occupation | Percent Female X | X² | Average Salary (in $1,000) Y | Y² | XY |
|---|---|---|---|---|---|
| Psychologist II (less than full-time) | 0 | 0 | 34.914 | 1,218.987 | 0.0 |
| Patrol lieutenant | 0 | 0 | 32.445 | 1,052.678 | 0.0 |
| Head groundskeeper II | 0 | 0 | 25.140 | 632.019 | 0.0 |
| Respiratory therapy technician | 0 | 0 | 21.778 | 474.281 | 0.0 |
| Automotive mechanic | 0 | 0 | 21.778 | 474.281 | 0.0 |
| Security aide (part-time) | 0 | 0 | 17.205 | 296.012 | 0.0 |
| Public health technician II | 14 | 196 | 25.121 | 631.064 | 351.694 |
| Management analyst | 33 | 1,089 | 24.405 | 595.604 | 805.365 |
| Assistant office machine operator | 50 | 2,500 | 14.378 | 206.726 | 718.900 |
| Municipal aide | 59 | 3,481 | 12.716 | 161.696 | 750.244 |
| Mental health worker I | 67 | 4,489 | 14.365 | 206.353 | 962.455 |
| Community service aide | 75 | 5,625 | 14.716 | 216.560 | 1,103.700 |
| Practical nurse | 93 | 8,649 | 18.082 | 326.958 | 1,681.626 |
| Community service worker II | 100 | 10,000 | 15.054 | 226.622 | 1,505.400 |
| Medical technologist | 100 | 10,000 | 24.054 | 578.594 | 2,405.400 |
| Principal records clerk | 100 | 10,000 | 19.001 | 361.038 | 1,900.100 |
| Senior accounting clerk/typist | 100 | 10,000 | 15.054 | 226.622 | 1,505.400 |
| Telephone operator/typist | 100 | 10,000 | 13.100 | 171.610 | 1,310.000 |
| Accounting clerk/typist | 100 | 10,000 | 13.739 | 188.760 | 1,373.900 |
| | $\sum X =$ 991 | $\sum X^2 =$ 86,029 | $\sum Y =$ 377.045 | $\sum Y^2 =$ 8,246.465 | $\sum XY =$ 16,374.184 |

Mean $X = \bar{X} = \dfrac{\sum X}{N} = \dfrac{991}{19} = 52.157$

Mean $Y = \bar{Y} = \dfrac{\sum Y}{N} = \dfrac{377.045}{19} = 19.844$

*Source:* Adapted from Ames, 1993.

The negative slope of −0.096 confirms our earlier impression, based on the scatter diagram and Table 8.8, that the relationship between the percentage of women in an occupation and the average salary in that occupation is negative. In other words, the higher the percentage of women in an occupation, the lower the average salary in that occupation. A $b_{YX}$ equal to −.096 means that every 1 percent increase in the representation of women in an occupation is associated with a decrease of about $96 (−0.096 × $1,000 = −$96) in the average salary for that occupation.

Now let's find the intercept:

$$a = \overline{Y} - b_{YX}(\overline{X}) = 19.844 - (-.096)(52.157) = 19.844 + 5.007 = 24.851$$

The prediction equation is therefore

$$\hat{Y} = 24.851 - 0.096(X)$$

The regression line corresponding to this linear regression equation is shown in Figure 8.15.

Based on this linear regression equation, we could predict the average salary in an occupation that is, say, 25 percent female, to be

$$\hat{Y} = 24.851 - .096(25) = 24.851 - 2.4 = 22.451 \text{ or } \$22,451$$

In contrast, the average salary for occupations that are 75 percent female would be

$$\hat{Y} = 24.851 - 0.096(75) = 24.851 - 7.2 = 17.651 \text{ or } \$17,651$$

Figure 8.15 **Scatter Diagram Showing Regression Line for Percent Female and Average Salary**

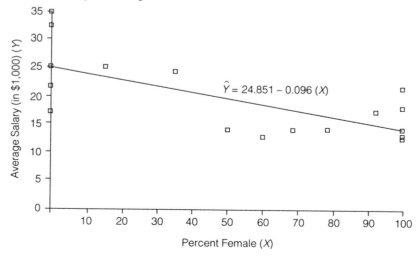

### Computing $r$ and $r^2$

We now find $r$ and $r^2$ for these data. The quantities needed to calculate $r$ are shown in Table 8.9. These quantities can be substituted directly into the computational formula for $r$ (formula 8.9):

$$r = \frac{N\left(\sum XY\right) - \left(\sum X\right)\left(\sum Y\right)}{\sqrt{\left[N\left(\sum X^2\right) - \left(\sum X\right)^2\right]\left[N\left(\sum Y^2\right) - \left(\sum Y\right)^2\right]}}$$

$$= \frac{19(16,374.184) - (991)(377.045)}{\sqrt{[19(86,029) - (991)^2][19(8,246.465) - (377.045)^2]}}$$

$$= \frac{311,109.496 - 373,651.595}{\sqrt{(1,634,551 - 982,081)(156,682.835 - 142,162.932)}}$$

$$= \frac{-62,542.099}{\sqrt{(652,470)(14,519.902)}} = \frac{-62,542.009}{97,333.449} = -0.642$$

Next, $r^2$ can be easily calculated by squaring $r$:

$$r^2 = (-0.642)^2 = 0.412$$

An $r$ of –0.642 means that the two variables—the percentage of women and average salary—are strongly associated. An $r^2$ of 0.412 means that by utilizing the percentage of women to predict the average salary of occupations in one New York county, we have reduced the error of prediction by 41.2 percent. We can also say that the percentage of women in an occupation explains 41.2 percent of the variation in the average salary associated with that occupation.

### Statistics in Practice: The Marriage Penalty in Earnings

Among factors commonly associated with earnings are human capital variables (for example, age, education, work experience, and health) and labor market variables (like the unemployment rate or the structure of occupations). Individual characteristics, such as gender, race, and ethnicity, also explain disparities in earnings. In addition, marital status has been linked to differences in earnings. However, even though marriage is associated with higher earnings for men, for women it carries a penalty; married women tend to earn less at every educational level than single women.

The lower earnings of married women have been related to differences in labor force experience. Marriage and the presence of young children tend to limit women's choice of jobs to those that may offer flexible working hours but are generally low paying and offer fewer opportunities for promotion. Moreover, married women tend to be out of the labor market longer and have fewer years on the job than single women. When they reenter the job market or begin their career after their children are grown, they compete with co-workers with considerably more work experience and on-the-job training. (Women who need to become financially independent after divorce or widowhood may share some of the same liabilities as married women.)

This all suggests that the returns for formal education will be generally lower for married women. Thus, we would expect single women to earn more for each year of formal education than married women. We explore this issue by analyzing the bivariate relationship between level of education and personal income among single and married females (working full-time) who were included in the 1991 GSS sample. We are assuming that level of education (measured in years) can predict personal income, and therefore we treat it as our independent variable, $X$. Personal income (measured in dollars), then, is the dependent variable, $Y$. Since both are interval-ratio variables, we can use bivariate regression analysis to examine the difference in returns for education.

Thus, our bivariate regression equation for single females working full-time is

$$\hat{Y} \text{(single)} = -\$2,559.10 + \$2,948.47X$$

The regression equation tells us that for every unit increase in education—the unit is one year—we can predict an increase of $2,948.47 in the annual income of single women in our sample who work full-time.

The bivariate regression equation for married females working full-time is

$$\hat{Y} \text{(married)} = -\$1,892.02 + \$1,420.54X$$

The regression equation tells us that for every unit increase in education, we can predict an increase of $1,420.54 in the annual income of married women in our sample who work full-time.

This analysis indicates that, as we suggested, the returns for education are considerably lower for married women. For every year of education single women earn more than twice as much as married women!

Let's use these regression equations to predict the difference in annual income between a single woman and a married woman, both with a high school (12 years) education and working full-time:

$$\hat{Y} \text{(married)} = -\$1,892.02 + \$1,420.54(12) = \$15,154.46$$

$$\hat{Y} \text{(single)} = -\$2,559.12 + \$2,948.47(12) = \$32,822.52$$

The predicted difference in annual income between a single and a married woman with a high school education, both working full-time, is $17,668.06 ($32,822.52 − $15,154.46).

We also calculated the $r$ and $r^2$ for these data. For married women $r = 0.336$; for single women, $r = 0.449$. These coefficients indicate that for both groups there is a moderate (the relationship is slightly higher for single women) and positive relationship between education and earnings.

To determine how much of the variation in income can be explained by education we need to calculate $r^2$. For married women:

$$r^2(\text{married}) = (r)^2 = (0.336)^2 = 0.113$$

and for single women:

$$r^2(\text{single}) = (r)^2 = (0.449)^2 = 0.202$$

Using the regression equation, our prediction of income for married women is improved by 11.3 percent ($0.113 \times 100$) over the prediction we would make using the mean alone. For single women there is a slightly better improvement in prediction, 20.2 percent ($0.202 \times 100$).

Finally, the present analysis deals only with one factor affecting earnings—the level of education. Other important factors associated with earnings (occupation, seniority, race and ethnicity, age, and so on) need to be considered for a complete analysis of the differences in earnings between single and married women.

## MAIN POINTS

- A scatter diagram (also called scatterplot) is a quick visual method used to display relationships between two interval-ratio variables. It is used as a first exploratory step in regression analysis and can suggest to us whether two variables are associated.

- Equations for all straight lines have the same general form

    $$Y = a + bX$$

    where

    $Y$ = the predicted score on the dependent variable
    $X$ = the score on the independent variable
    $a$ = the $Y$-intercept, or the point where the line crosses the $Y$-axis; therefore $a$ is the value of $Y$ when $X$ is 0
    $b$ = the slope of the line, or the change in $Y$ with a unit change in $X$

- The best-fitting regression line is that line where the sum of the squared error, or $\Sigma e^2$, is the minimum. Such a line is called the least-squares line, and the technique that produces this line is called the least-squares method.

- The coefficient of determination ($r^2$) and Pearson's correlation coefficient ($r$) measure how well the regression model fits the data. Pearson's $r$ also measures the strength of the association between the two variables. The coefficient of determination, $r^2$, can be interpreted as a PRE measure. It reflects the proportional reduction of error resulting from utilizing the linear regression model.

## KEY TERMS

coefficient of determination ($r^2$)

deterministic (perfect) linear relationship

least-squares line (best-fitting line)

least-squares method

linear relationship

Pearson's correlation coefficient ($r$)

scatter diagram (scatterplot)

slope (b)

Y-intercept (a)

## SPSS DEMONSTRATIONS

*Demonstration 1: Producing Scatterplots (Scatter Diagrams)*

Do people with more education work longer hours at their jobs? This question can be explored with SPSS using the techniques discussed in this chapter for interval-ratio data because "hours worked" and "education" are both coded at an interval-ratio level in the 1994 GSS file.

We begin by looking at a scatterplot of these two variables. The Scatter procedure can be found under the *Graphs* menu choice. In the opening dialog box, click on *Simple* (which means we want to produce a standard scatterplot with two variables), then click on *Define*.

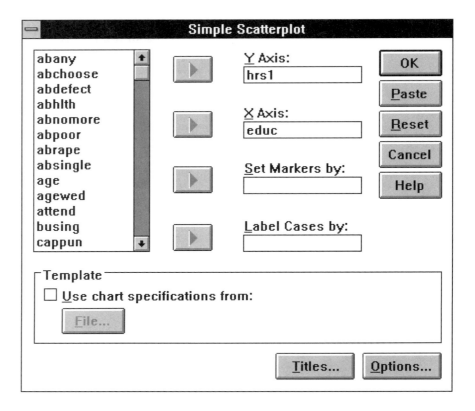

The Scatterplot dialog box requires that we specify a variable for both the *X*- and *Y*-axes. We place EDUC in the *X*-axis because we consider it the independent variable and HRS1 in the *Y*-axis because it is the dependent variable. Then click on *OK*.

SPSS creates the requested graph and places it in a window called the Chart Carousel. This is a temporary holding area for graphs. From here charts can be saved, discarded, or edited. It is difficult to tell, by eye, whether or not there is a relationship between the two variables, so we will ask SPSS to place the regression line on the plot.

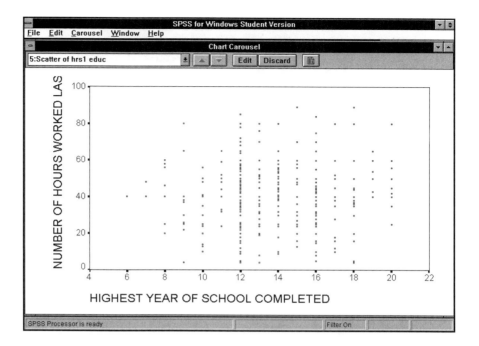

Clicking on the *Edit* button places a graphic in its own window and changes the menu and toolbar so that choices appropriate for the editing of graphics are available. To add a regression line to the plot, we click on *Chart* from the main menu, then *Options*. After a dialog box opens, we click on *Total* in the Fit Lines section. The result of these actions, plus a minor adjustment of the X-axis and the size of the symbols, is shown next.

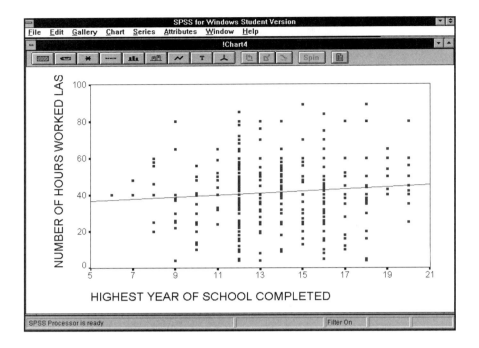

It is now easy to observe that there is a positive relationship between education and number of hours worked each week. However, the relationship doesn't appear that strong; in other words, the predicted value for those with twenty years of education is only a few more hours than those with eight years of education.

*Demonstration 2: Producing Correlation Coefficients*

To further quantify the effect of education on hours worked, we request a correlation coefficient. This statistic is available in the Bivariate procedure, which is located by clicking on *Statistics, Correlate,* then *Bivariate.* Place the variables you are interested in correlating in the Variable(s) box, then click on *OK.*

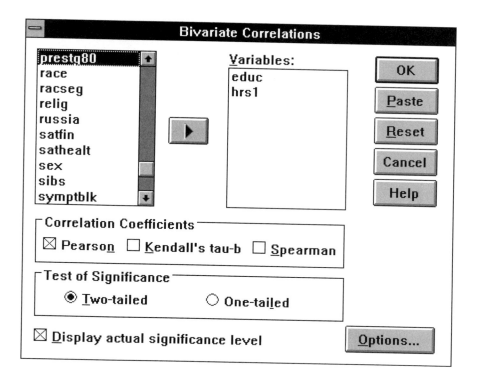

SPSS produces a matrix of correlations, including the uninteresting correlations between education and itself and hours worked and itself (both equal to 1.00). We are interested in the correlation in the bottom left-hand cell, .1058. Since correlations vary from –1 to 1, we see that this is closer to 0 than to 1, so education is not a very good predictor of hours worked, even if it is true that those with more education work longer hours at their job. The number in parentheses under the correlation coefficient is the number of valid cases—those respondents who gave a valid response to both questions. The number is reduced from 1,000 because not everyone in the sample is working. The other bit of output ($p$ = .008) is the probability, which will be discussed in a later chapter.

```
                                - -   Correlation Coefficients   - -
|
                    EDUC          HRS1

EDUC              1.0000          .1058
                 (   996)        (   632)
                 P= .            P= .008

HRS1               .1058         1.0000
                 (   632)        (   632)
                 P= .008         P= .

(Coefficient / (Cases) / 2-tailed Significance)

" . " is printed if a coefficient cannot be computed
```

## Demonstration 3: Producing a Regression Equation

As a final step, we will use SPSS to calculate the best-fitting regression line and the coefficient of determination. This procedure is located by clicking on *Statistics, Regression,* then *Linear.* There is a box in which to place the dependent variable and a box for the independent variables (regression allows more than one). There are many other choices in the Linear Regression dialog box, but the default output from the procedure contains all that we need.

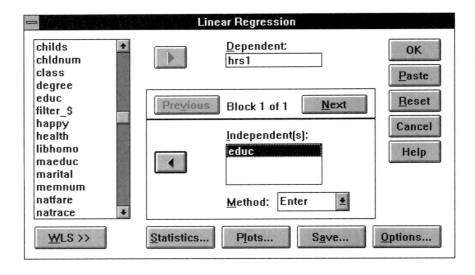

SPSS produces a great deal of output, which is typical for many of the more advanced statistical procedures in the program. The coefficient of determination is labeled "R Square" and its value is .01119, which is very small. Educational attainment explains little of the variation in hours worked. This is probably not too surprising; for example, people who own a small business may have no more than a high school degree but work very long hours in their business.

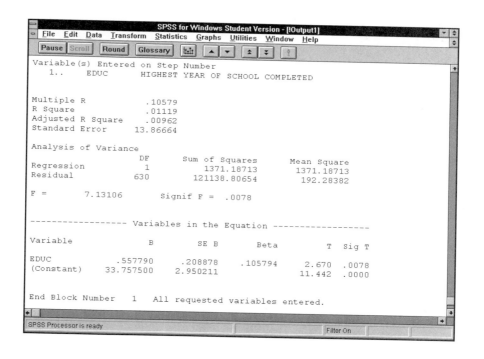

The regression equation results are in the section labeled "Variables in the Equation." The regression equation coefficients are listed in the column headed "B." The coefficient for EDUC, or $b$, is about .558; the intercept term, or $a$, is approximately 33.758. Thus, we would predict that every additional year of education increases the number of hours worked each week by about half an hour. Or we could predict that those with a high school education work, on the average, 33.758 + 12(.558) hours, or about 40.4 hours.

The remaining output from the Regression procedure is generally beyond the scope of this book.

## EXERCISES

1. In exercise 6 in Chapter 3, we examined the distribution of pesticides in produce. Now we can use these same data to study the relationship between the percentage of produce with pesticides and the number of pesticides detected in each food type to see whether food types with more pesticides also have more different types of pesticides.

   a. Construct a scatter diagram (scatterplot) of the two variables, placing the "number of types of pesticides detected" on the horizontal or X-axis, and the "percentage of produce with pesticides" on the vertical, or Y-axis.

   b. Does the relationship between the two variables seem linear? Describe the relationship.

   c. Find the value of the Pearson correlation coefficient that measures the association between the two variables and offer an interpretation.

2. In exercise 6 in Chapter 4, we examined the mean number of children in large metropolitan statistical areas who had AIDS in 1992 and 1993. It seems reasonable to suspect that there should be a relationship between the data for 1992 and 1993, so that areas with a high number of AIDS cases in 1992 would also tend to have a high number of cases in 1993. Test this by using a correlation coefficient.

   a. Calculate the correlation coefficient between the numbers of AIDS cases in 1992 and 1993. Does its value provide statistical evidence that the number of cases in 1993 is closely related to the number of cases in the previous year?

   b. Calculate the coefficient of determination and provide an interpretation of its value.

3. What do you think would happen to the correlation coefficient between two variables if a constant value was added to one of the variables? For example, if a value of 10 was added to each case for a variable, then the mean value of that variable would increase by 10 units. How would its correlation coefficient with another variable also be changed? To investigate this question, use the data from exercise 2.

   a. Add a value of 20 to each MSA's number of AIDS cases in 1992 (leave the values for 1993 unchanged). Now calculate the correlation coefficient between 1992 and 1993. What happened to its value?

   b. Can you think of an explanation? Draw a scatter diagram to illustrate your answer.

4. There is often thought to be a relationship between a person's educational attainment and the number of children he or she has. The hypothesis is that as one's educational level increases, he or she has fewer children. Investigate this conjecture with twenty-five cases drawn randomly from the 1994 GSS file. The following table displays educational attainment, in years, and the number of children for each respondent.

| EDUC | CHILDS |
| --- | --- |
| 12 | 0 |
| 12 | 4 |
| 12 | 3 |
| 18 | 2 |
| 12 | 3 |
| 12 | 3 |
| 18 | 0 |
| 12 | 4 |
| 12 | 3 |
| 17 | 0 |
| 16 | 0 |
| 10 | 2 |
| 16 | 0 |
| 16 | 0 |
| 16 | 2 |
| 18 | 2 |
| 10 | 3 |
| 19 | 1 |
| 17 | 2 |
| 18 | 2 |
| 16 | 3 |
| 12 | 0 |
| 11 | 3 |
| 18 | 2 |
| 12 | 3 |

a. Calculate the Pearson correlation coefficient for these two variables. Does its value support the hypothesized relationship?
b. Calculate the least-squares regression equation using education as a predictor variable. What is the value of the slope $b$? What is the value of the intercept $a$?

c. What is the predicted number of children for a person with a college degree (16 years of education)?

d. Does any respondent actually have this number of children? If so, what is his or her level of education? If not, is this a problem or an indication that the regression equation you calculated is incorrect? Why or why not?

5. Births out of wedlock have been on the rise in the United States for many years. Discussions of this social phenomenon often focus on the greater number of births to unwed minority mothers. However, births to unwed white mothers have also increased. The following data show the percentage of births to mothers who were not married, separately for whites and nonwhites, over a forty-year period.

a. Calculate the correlation coefficient between the percent of unwed births for whites and minorities. What is its value?

b. Provide an interpretation for the coefficient. Substantively, what does the value of the correlation coefficient imply about the similarity in the rate of increase of births out of wedlock for whites and nonwhites?

**Percent of Unwed Births by Year and Race**

| | Race | |
|---|---|---|
| **Year** | White | Nonwhite |
| 1950 | 1.8 | 18.0 |
| 1955 | 1.9 | 20.2 |
| 1960 | 2.3 | 21.6 |
| 1965 | 3.9 | 26.3 |
| 1970 | 5.7 | 37.6 |
| 1975 | 7.3 | 48.8 |
| 1980 | 11.0 | 55.3 |
| 1985 | 14.5 | 60.1 |
| 1989 | 19.2 | 65.7 |

(Data from the National Center for Health Statistics)

6. In exercise 11 in Chapter 5, we studied the variability of the rates of violent crime and incarceration in twenty-one states in the East and the Midwest. We've now been asked to investigate the hypothesis that the number of prisoners is related to the crime rate

because states with higher crime rates are likely to have higher rates of incarceration.

a. Construct a scatter diagram of violent crime rate and incarceration rate, with "crime rate" considered the predictor variable. What can you say about the relationship between these two variables based on the scatterplot?

b. Find the least-squares regression equation that predicts incarceration rate from the crime rate. What is the slope? What is the intercept?

c. Calculate the coefficient of determination ($r^2$) and provide an interpretation.

d. If the crime rate increased by 100 for a state (that is, 100 more crimes per 100,000 people), by how much would you predict the incarceration rate to increase?

e. Does it make sense to predict the incarceration rate when the rate of violent crime is equal to zero? Why or why not?

7. Before calculating a correlation coefficient or a regression equation, it is always important to examine a scatter diagram between two variables to see how well a straight line fits the data. If a straight line does not appear to fit, other curves can be used to describe the relationship (although this subject is not discussed in the textbook).

The following SPSS graph displays the relationship between gross national product (GNP) in dollars for most countries in the world and the infant mortality rate (IMR) for these same countries. The IMR is simply the number of infants who die, standardized by the number of people in a country, so it can be compared across countries (it is defined as the number of deaths per 1,000 births). As the wealth of a country increases—as GNP increases—it seems reasonable to suppose that infant mortality will decrease, due to better medical care and nutrition.

a. The SPSS graph displays the scatterplot for these two variables, with the regression line superimposed on the graph. Also, $r^2$ is displayed in the legend on the right. Is the relationship between these two variables as hypothesized? Is it a negative or positive relationship?

b. Describe the relationship between these two variables, using representative values of GNP and IMR.

c. Does a straight line adequately represent the relationship between GNP and IMR? Why or why not?

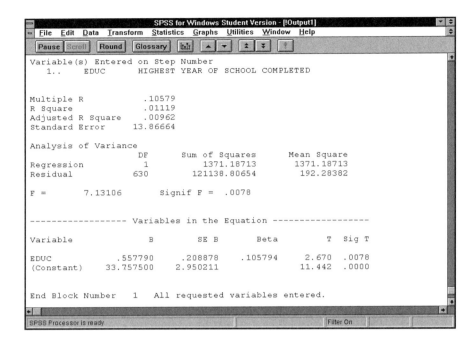

8. In exercise 7, all the countries in the world that reported GNP and infant mortality data were used to construct the scatterplot. Now let's restrict our analysis to countries in South America (ignoring a few small political entities, such as Surinam in northeast South America). For this small group of ten countries, will we find the same relationship between GNP and IMR?

   a. Construct a scatterplot from the following data, predicting IMR from GNP. What is the relationship between GNP and IMR for countries in South America?

   b. Does it appear that a straight line fits these data better than for all countries in the world? Why or why not?

   c. Calculate the correlation coefficient and coefficient of determination. How does the latter value compare with the $r^2$ value in exercise 7? Do these values offer further support for your answer to (b)? How?

   d. (Extra Credit) If you think a linear relationship is a reasonable description of the scatterplot of GNP and IMR for South American countries, why do you think that is not true for the whole world?

| Country | GNP per Capita in 1982 | Infant Mortality in 1983 |
|---|---|---|
| Argentina | 2,520.00 | 35.30 |
| Bolivia | 570.00 | 124.00 |
| Brazil | 2,240.00 | 71.00 |
| Chile | 2,210.00 | 23.60 |
| Colombia | 1,460.00 | 53.00 |
| Ecuador | 1,350.00 | 70.00 |
| Paraguay | 1,610.00 | 45.00 |
| Peru | 1,310.00 | 99.00 |
| Uruguay | 2,650.00 | 33.20 |
| Venezuela | 4,140.00 | 39.00 |

(Data from the Population Reference Bureau and the World Bank)

9. Social scientists have long been interested in various civic, labor, and fraternal organizations in the United States and the role they play in the political, civic, and social life of the country. Alexis de Tocqueville, for example, commented in the nineteenth century about the propensity of Americans to join organizations and work together for the common good. The GSS 1994 data set has information on the total number of formal memberships held by each respondent in various organizations. Use this information for the following selected subsample of respondents to see whether those with more education are more likely to have more organizational memberships.

   a. Construct a scatterplot, predicting the number of memberships with education.

   b. Calculate the regression equation with "education" as the predictor variable and draw the regression line on the scatterplot. What is the slope? What is the intercept? Does a straight line seem to fit the data? Does it fit better for those with more or less education?

   c. What is the error of prediction for the second case (the person with sixteen years of education and five memberships)? What is the error for the person with ten years of education and one membership?

   d. What is the predicted number of memberships for someone with fourteen years of education? with four years of education? Any problems with these predictions?

e. (Extra Credit) Calculate the mean number of years of education and the mean number of memberships. Plot this point on the scatterplot. Where does it fall? Can you think of a reason why this should be true?

| Highest Year of School Completed | Number of Memberships |
|---|---|
| 12 | 0 |
| 16 | 5 |
| 16 | 1 |
| 16 | 1 |
| 11 | 1 |
| 18 | 0 |
| 13 | 5 |
| 10 | 1 |
| 7 | 1 |
| 12 | 3 |
| 14 | 3 |
| 11 | 2 |

10. In exercise 8, we investigated the relationship between infant mortality rate and GNP in South America. The birth rates (number of live births per 1,000 inhabitants) in these same countries follow:

| Country | Birth Rate in 1982 |
|---|---|
| Argentina | 24 |
| Bolivia | 42 |
| Brazil | 31 |
| Chile | 24 |
| Colombia | 28 |
| Ecuador | 41 |
| Paraguay | 35 |
| Peru | 37 |
| Uruguay | 18 |
| Venezuela | 33 |

(Data from the Population Reference Bureau)

a. Construct a scatterplot for birth rate and GNP and one for birth rate and infant mortality rate. Do you think each can be characterized by a linear relationship?

b. Calculate the coefficient of determination and correlation coefficient for each relationship.

c. Use this information to describe the relationship between the variables.

11. Minorities are typically arrested at greater rates than whites, given their proportion in the population. Is it possible that the arrest ratio of minorities to whites is related to the percentage of a city's population that is minority? To answer this question, study the following data for eighteen cities with a population over 100,000. Listed in the table is the percent of the city's population that is black and the arrest ratio for drug crimes (for example, an arrest ratio of 5 means that blacks are five times as likely to be arrested as whites).

a. Construct a scatterplot, predicting the arrest ratio with the percent black population in a city. Does it appear that a straight line relationship will fit the data?

b. Calculate the regression equation with "percent black" as the predictor variable and draw the regression line on the scatter-plot. What is its slope? What is the intercept? Has your opinion changed about whether a straight line seems to fit the data? Are there any cities that fall far from the regression line? Which one(s)?

c. What percent of the black population is required to obtain a predicted value of 1 for the arrest ratio?

d. Predicting a value that falls beyond the observed range of the two variables in a regression is problematic at best, so your answer in (c) isn't necessarily statistically believable. What is a nonstatistical, or substantive, reason why the prediction for an arrest ratio of 1 may be nonsensical?

|  | Percent Black Population | Arrest Ratio |
|---|---|---|
| Livonia, Michigan | 0.0 | 43 |
| Warren, Michigan | 1.0 | 32 |
| Pasadena, Texas | 1.0 | 27 |
| St. Paul, Minnesota | 7.0 | 26 |
| Minneapolis, Minnesota | 13.0 | 22 |
| Madison, Wisconsin | 4.0 | 21 |
| Alexandria, Virginia | 22.0 | 18 |
| Columbus, Ohio | 23.0 | 18 |
| Evansville, Indiana | 10.0 | 17 |
| Hialeah, Florida | 2.0 | 17 |
| Sterling Heights, Michigan | 0.0 | 16 |
| Grand Rapids, Michigan | 19.0 | 15 |
| Pittsburgh, Pennsylvania | 26.0 | 14 |
| Little Rock, Arkansas | 34.0 | 13 |
| Peoria, Illinois | 21.0 | 13 |
| Seattle, Washington | 10.0 | 13 |
| Rockford, Illinois | 15.0 | 12 |
| Lansing, Michigan | 19.0 | 12 |

(Data from *USA Today*, July 26, 1993; calculated from the FBI's Uniform Crime Report)

## SPSS PROBLEMS

1. Use the 1987 to 1991 GSS data file to study the relationship between years of education (EDUC) and the prestige of the respondent's job (PRESTIGE).
   a. Construct a scatterplot of these two variables in SPSS and place the best-fit linear regression line on the scatterplot. Describe the relationship between education and prestige.
   b. Have SPSS calculate the regression equation predicting prestige with education. What are the intercept and the slope? What are the coefficient of determination and the correlation coefficient?
   c. What is the predicted job prestige for someone with a college degree (sixteen years of education)?
   d. (Extra Credit) Can you find a way for SPSS to calculate the error of prediction and predicted value for each respondent and save them as new variables?

2. Use the same variables but do the analysis separately for blacks and whites.
    a. Have SPSS calculate the regression equation for blacks and whites. How similar are they?
    b. What is the predicted job prestige for a black with fourteen years of education? For a white respondent with the same amount of education? Which is greater?

3. Use the 1994 GSS file to investigate the relationship between the respondent's education and the education received by his father and mother (PAEDUC and MAEDUC, respectively).
    a. Construct scatterplots for these variables, using "mother's education" and "father's education" as predictor variables.
    b. Use SPSS to find the correlation coefficient, the coefficient of determination, and the regression equation predicting the respondent's education with father's, then mother's, education. Which variable is the better predictor?
    c. Do these same analyses separately for males and females. What differences, if any, do you find? Can male or female education better be predicted by parent's education?

## GROUP EXERCISES

1. Use the data that your group and the other groups have collected from your classmates. Choose variables that are measured on an interval-ratio scale. If you don't have some of these variables in the data, collect additional information from the class on either an interval or a ratio scale. Share the workload by having two or so people do (a) and another two do (c), and another two (d), then combine everyone's work.
    a. Construct scatterplots to relate one variable to another. You don't have to select a dependent variable, but you must find two variables that might reasonably be related (for example, you would probably not study the relationship between the number of times someone in the class ate pizza last year and that person's number of brothers and sisters).
    b. Do the relationships seem linear in the scatterplots? Describe the relationships.
    c. Calculate the correlation coefficient for each scatterplot and coefficient of determination and use these to further describe the relationships.

    d. Calculate the regression equation for each scatterplot. Then find, for each scatterplot, which cases fit well (have little error of prediction) and which do not fit very well (have a large error of prediction).

    e. Use all these results in a group discussion of why the variables you studied are related (or not related) and why some points fall far from the regression line (or fall close to the line). You may want to write a report describing your findings.

2. In exercise 6, we studied the relationship between rates of violent crime and incarceration in several states in the Midwest and the East.

    a. Locate two or three other measures of the crime rates in these same twenty-one states to supplement the existing data.

    b. Construct scatter diagrams and calculate correlation coefficients and regression equations to relate the new variables to the two rate variables you have already used. Decide whether you think a straight line is a good description for these relationships.

    c. Calculate the errors of prediction for each state for each regression equation. Do some states, in general, have smaller errors of prediction than other states? Which ones? Or do some states have greater errors of prediction? Can you think of any reason why this might be so?

    d. Prepare a group report describing how different types of crime are related to each other.

# 9

# Organization of Information and Measurement of Relationships: A Review of Descriptive Data Analysis

**Introduction**

**Descriptive Data Analysis for Nominal Variables**

Statistics in Practice: Gender and Local Political Party Activism
  *Organize the Data into a Frequency Distribution*
  *Display the Data in a Graph*
  *Describe What Is Average or Typical of a Distribution*
  *Describe Variability Within a Distribution*
  *Describe the Relationship Between Two Variables*

**Descriptive Data Analysis for Ordinal Variables**

Gender and Local Political Party Activism: Continuing Our
  Research Example
  *Organize the Data into a Frequency Distribution*
  *Display the Data in a Graph*
  *Describe What Is Average or Typical of a Distribution*
  *Describe Variability Within a Distribution*
  *Describe the Relationship Between Two Variables*

**Descriptive Data Analysis for Interval-Ratio Variables**

Statistics in Practice: Education and Income
  *Organize the Data into a Frequency Distribution*
  *Display the Data in a Graph*
  *Describe What Is Average or Typical of a Distribution*
  *Describe Variability Within a Distribution*
  *Describe the Relationship Between Two Variables*

**A Final Note**

EXERCISES

SPSS PROBLEMS

## Introduction[1]

In the preceding eight chapters we introduced you to numerous methods researchers use to organize data and describe relationships between variables. We presented the chapters sequentially to reflect the five cumulative stages of data analysis:

1. organizing the data using frequency distributions (Chapter 2),
2. displaying the data using graphic techniques (Chapter 3),
3. determining what is average or typical about a distribution (Chapter 4),
4. determining variation within a distribution (Chapter 5), and
5. measuring the association between two variables (Chapters 6, 7, and 8).

Within the chapters we described alternative methods used in each stage, depending on:

1. the level of data measurement (nominal, ordinal, or interval-ratio), and
2. the purpose of the analysis.

At each of the stages, researchers must decide which technique is appropriate for the data and the research goal. Figure 9.1 presents a flowchart that you can use in this decision-making process. It shows the techniques available at each stage for each of the levels of data—nominal, ordinal, and interval-ratio—and the circumstances that determine the appropriate technique.

The flowchart provides the map for this review chapter. In the sections that follow we examine real research reports that illustrate the use of one or more of the methods appropriate for the level of data

[1]This chapter was co-authored with Pat Pawasarat.

Figure 9.1 **Flowchart of the Systematic Approach to Descriptive Data Analysis**

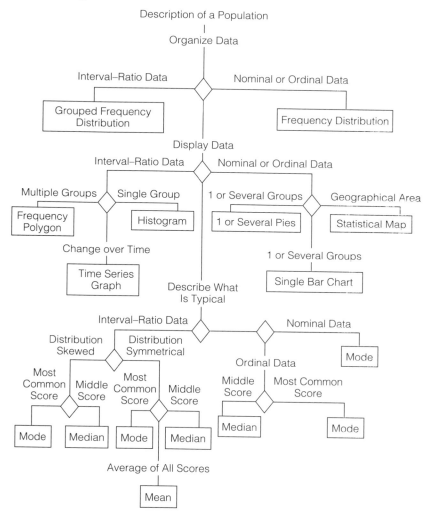

*(figure continued on next page)*

Figure 9.1    **(Continued)**

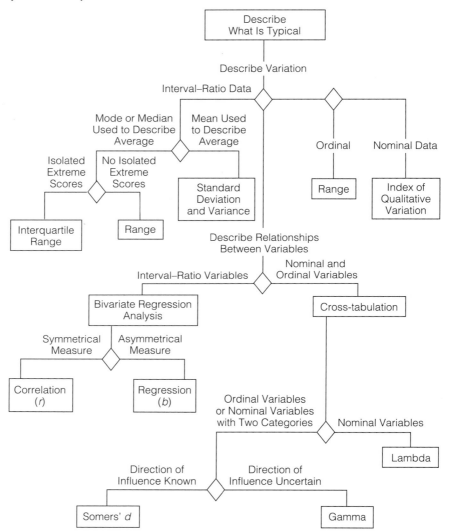

under discussion. The presentation of each application follows the five cumulative steps of descriptive statistical analysis.

## Descriptive Data Analysis for Nominal Variables

We begin our review with the lowest level of measurement—the nominal level. Remember, variables measured at the nominal level are categorized by qualitative differences. "Gender," "race," "religious preference," and "political party" are examples of nominal variables. The categories of nominal variables are discrete, and although we can say that each category is different, we cannot measure the difference between the categories quantitatively.

## Statistics in Practice: Gender and Local Political Party Activism

The 1992 presidential election campaign brought the role of women in politics to the attention of the public and created renewed interest in the subject among social scientists. In Chapter 1, we suggested that research questions are frequently derived through familiarity with professional literature. Laura van Assendelft and Karen O'Connor[2] examined existing literature on women in politics and discovered the following: most studies found that women lack the political ambition to run for public office; the majority of women who do run for office have been active in local political party organizations; and male and female party activists differ in many ways, including in political ambition, education, and employment experience. They also found that most of the research in this area was nearly twenty years old and did not take into account the effects of the women's rights movement in recent years.

Van Assendelft and O'Connor reasoned that since local party activity is an apparent stepping-stone to political office for women, it was important to reanalyze women's activity in local party organizations. The purpose of their research was to describe who party activists are and their reasons for participation and to examine the similarities and differences between male and female party activists. Based on the existing literature, they hypothesized that female activists differ from male activists in level of education and income, employment experience, and political ambition as well as their reasons for participation in political activity. They obtained their data using a mail survey sent to all members of the local Democratic and Republican parties in the metropolitan Atlanta, Georgia, area.

Van Assendelft and O'Connor used eight dependent variables in their study. Two—occupation and marital status—were measured at the nominal level. We will discuss these variables in this section. The other six—level of education, strength of party identification, motivation,

---

[2]Laura van Assendelft and Karen O'Connor, "Backgrounds, Motivations and Interests: A Comparison of Male and Female Local Party Activists." *Women & Politics*, Vol. 14, No. 3, 1994, 77–91.

years of activism, hours spent on party work, and political ambition—
were measured at the ordinal level and will be discussed later. Here
we will follow the five steps of descriptive data analysis as we discuss
their findings.

---

**Learning Check.** *What is the independent variable in van Assendelft and O'Connor's study?*

---

*Organize the Data into a Frequency Distribution* Tables 9.1 and 9.2 show
the distributions for occupation and marital status for men and women.
Notice that in the tables the frequencies are expressed as percentages
rather than as raw frequencies. Remember, we use percentages to
compare groups with unequal *N*'s. (Notice, also, that the total percentage for females in Table 9.1 does not add up to 100 percent. The
difference of 0.1 percent is due to rounding. Small differences such as
this frequently occur in real research applications.)

An examination of Table 9.1 shows us that, in general, the occupational differences between men and women activists are not great. Two
exceptions are noted by van Assendelft and O'Connor: a much higher
percentage of women are employed in the educational sector, and
women are underrepresented in the self-employed professional sector.

Table 9.1  **Occupational Differences among Male and Female Local Party Activists (in percentages)**

| Occupation | Males | Females |
|---|---|---|
| Small business | 21.7 | 18.6 |
| Large business | 31.8 | 29.4 |
| Educational | 3.8 | 13.7 |
| Government | 5.7 | 5.9 |
| Self-employed (business) | 13.4 | 12.7 |
| Self-employed (professional) | 21.7 | 4.9 |
| Homemaker | 0.0 | 12.7 |
| Student | 1.9 | 2.0 |
| Total | 100.0 | 99.9 |
| (N) | (157) | (102) |

*Source:* Laura van Assendelft and Karen O'Connor, "Backgrounds,
Motivations and Interests: A Comparison of Male and Female Local Party
Activists." *Women & Politics,* Vol. 14, No. 3, 1994, 77–91.

Table 9.2   **Marital Status of Male and Female Local Party Activists (in percentages)**

| Marital Status | Males | Females |
|---|---|---|
| Married | 84.5 | 68.6 |
| Single | 15.5 | 31.4 |
| Total | 100.0 | 100.0 |

*Source:* Laura van Assendelft and Karen O'Connor, "Backgrounds, Motivations and Interests: A Comparison of Male and Female Local Party Activists." *Women & Politics,* Vol. 14, No. 3, 1994, 77–91.

The authors point out that the self-employed professional sector includes lawyers—a profession from which many political candidates are drawn—and imply that more women will emerge as candidates as their representation in this sector increases.[3] A third category that shows differences, homemaker, is not discussed by the researchers in this study. Notice that 12.7 percent of the women and 0.0 percent of the men fall into this category.

The distributions in Table 9.2 show that the majority of both males and females are married, but a higher percentage of women (31.4% of women vs. 15.5% of men) are single.

*Display the Data in a Graph*   Figures 9.2 and 9.3 graphically represent the data shown in Tables 9.1 and 9.2. We have chosen to represent occupational differences in a bar graph (Figure 9.2) because the number of categories would make a pie chart somewhat difficult to read. The bar graph allows direct comparison of the percentages of males and females in each occupational category, making it easy to identify the categories where the percentage difference is relatively large— education and homemaker (both higher percentages of women) and self-employed professional (a higher percentage of men).

Both the pie chart and the bar graph are suitable for comparing the two categories of the variable "marital status." In Figure 9.3 we use two pie charts to compare males and females. We can easily see that the percentage of men who are married is greater than the percentage of women who are married.

[3]Ibid., pp. 80–81.

Figure 9.2 **Occupational Differences Among Male and Female Local Party Activists**

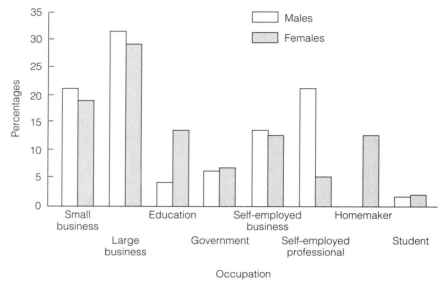

Figure 9.3 **Marital Status of Male and Female Local Party Activists**

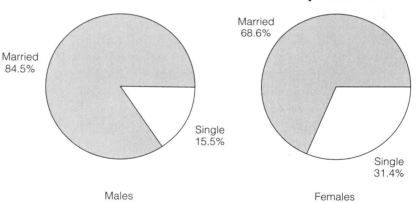

*Describe What Is Average or Typical of a Distribution* These are nominal variables so we can only use the mode to describe the average. Looking at Table 9.1, we can see that the modal occupational sector for both men and women is "large business." Table 9.2 shows that the mode of marital status is "married" for both men and women.

*Describe Variability Within a Distribution* For nominal variables, we can use the index of qualitative variation (IQV) to describe variation within a distribution and to compare distributions. Let's calculate the IQVs for marital status of male and female party activists:

$$IQV = \frac{\sum f_i f_j}{\frac{K(K-1)}{2}\left(\frac{N}{K}\right)^2}$$

$$IQV\ (men) = \frac{84.5 \times 15.5}{\frac{2(2-1)}{2}\left(\frac{100}{2}\right)^2} = \frac{1,309.75}{2,500} = 0.52$$

$$IQV\ (women) = \frac{68.6 \times 31.4}{\frac{2(2-1)}{2}\left(\frac{100}{2}\right)^2} = \frac{2,154.04}{2,500} = 0.86$$

The comparison of the IQVs for men (0.52) and for women (0.86) shows that there is considerably more variability in marital status among female party activists than among the males.

---

**Learning Check.**  *Where did the numbers used to calculate the IQVs for marital status come from? The numbers come from the percentage distributions displayed in Table 9.2. Remember that the IQV can be computed using either frequency or percentage distributions. Practice calculating IQVs using Table 9.1, which shows occupational differences between male and female activists. The IQV for occupational differences among males is 0.87; for females it is 0.94. What do these IQVs tell us about variability within and between the distributions?*

---

*Describe the Relationship Between Two Variables* Table 9.3 shows the bivariate table for marital status of male and female party activists. Bivariate tables are typically constructed with the independent variables as the column variables and the dependent variables as the row variables. To perform a cross-tabulation, we then compare the rows. Table 9.3 shows us that female party activists are much more likely to be single than male party activists (31.4% of females vs. 15.5% of males). This finding may result from married women—who often perform most of the tasks within the home and work outside of the home as well—having more difficulty finding time to participate in political activities. However, the percentage differences we see here

Table 9.3  **Marital Status of Male and Female Local Party Activists**

| MARITAL STATUS | GENDER | | Total |
| | Males | Females | |
| --- | --- | --- | --- |
| Married | 84.5% (136) | 68.6% (70) | 78.3% (206) |
| Single | 15.5% (25) | 31.4% (32) | 21.7% (57) |
| Total (N) | 100.0% (161) | 100.0% (102) | 100.0% (263) |

*Source:* Adapted from Laura van Assendelft and Karen O'Connor, "Backgrounds, Motivations and Interests: A Comparison of Male and Female Local Party Activists." *Women & Politics,* Vol. 14, No. 3, 1994, 77–91.

may simply reflect the relationship between gender and marital status in the total population of the United States.

Notice that the mode in both distributions is "married"; thus, we cannot use lambda to summarize the relationship between the variables. We will rely on cross-tabulation to describe the relationship between gender and marital status.

## Descriptive Data Analysis for Ordinal Variables

The next highest level of measurement is the ordinal level. As with nominal variables, the categories of ordinal variables are discrete; unlike with nominal variables, the categories of ordinal variables can be ranked or ordered from high to low or vice versa. Even though there is a quantitative difference between the categories of an ordinal variable (upper class indicates higher status than lower class), the magnitude of difference is not knowable.

## Gender and Local Political Party Activism: Continuing Our Research Example

Let's return to van Assendelft and O'Connor's study of gender and political party activism and examine some of the variables measured at the ordinal level.

*Organize the Data into a Frequency Distribution* Tables 9.4 through 9.6 show the frequency distributions for education, strength of party identification, and years active in the political organization. Table 9.4 shows that the percentage of male and female party activists who have completed college is nearly equal (35.8% of males and 35.0% of females). However, a much higher percentage of males than females have completed graduate school (43.2% vs. 29.1%). The cumulative percentages show that few male political party activists (3.7%) have a high school education or less compared with female activists (12.6%).

Table 9.5 shows that men and women are very similar in their identification with their chosen political party, and nearly three-quarters of both men and women feel their ties are strong. Notice that the total percentage for both men and women is 98.1 percent rather than 100.0 percent. This difference is too large to be due to rounding. The authors have apparently left out some responses, but the nature of those responses is not apparent from the table or their text.

Look carefully at Table 9.6. Why are we considering the number of years to be an ordinal variable? Measures of time are usually considered to be interval-ratio level variables. The reason time is considered as an ordinal variable here is because the intervals of the categories are unequal. The categories "0–5" and "5–10" contain fewer units than the category "10–20," and the category "20+" may contain

Table 9.4 **Educational Differences Among Male and Female Local Party Activists**

|  | Males | | Females | |
|---|---|---|---|---|
| **Level of Education** | % | C% | % | C% |
| Less than high school | 1.8 | 1.8 | 0.0 | 0.0 |
| High school | 1.9 | 3.7 | 12.6 | 12.6 |
| Some college | 17.3 | 21.0 | 23.3 | 35.9 |
| College | 35.8 | 56.8 | 35.0 | 70.9 |
| Graduate school | 43.2 | 100.0 | 29.1 | 100.0 |
| Total | 100.0 | | 100.0 | |
| (N) | (162) | | (103) | |

*Source:* Laura van Assendelft and Karen O'Connor, "Backgrounds, Motivations and Interests: A Comparison of Male and Female Local Party Activists." *Women & Politics,* Vol. 14, No. 3, 1994, 77–91.

Table 9.5  **Strength of Party Identification of Male and Female Local Party Activists (in percentages)**

| Strength of Party Identification | Males | Females |
|---|---|---|
| Strong | 74.4 | 74.3 |
| Not so strong | 15.6 | 11.9 |
| Weak | 8.1 | 11.9 |
| Total | 98.1 | 98.1 |
| (N) | (160) | (101) |

*Source:* Laura van Assendelft and Karen O'Connor, "Backgrounds, Motivations and Interests: A Comparison of Male and Female Local Party Activists." *Women & Politics,* Vol. 14, No. 3, 1994, 77–91.

Table 9.6  **Years Active in Local Party Organization (in percentages)**

| Years | Males | Females |
|---|---|---|
| 0–5 | 31.6 | 33.3 |
| 5–10 | 20.3 | 19.6 |
| 10–20 | 18.4 | 24.5 |
| 20+ | 29.7 | 22.5 |
| Total | 100.0 | 99.9 |
| (N) | (158) | (102) |

*Source:* Laura van Assendelft and Karen O'Connor, "Backgrounds, Motivations and Interests: A Comparison of Male and Female Local Party Activists." *Women & Politics,* Vol. 14, No. 3, 1994, 77–91.

either fewer or more units than the other categories. Thus, for example, we cannot say how much difference there is between "0–5" and "20+."

Table 9.6 shows that men and women have been involved in party activity for a similar number of years. It is important to note that van Assendelft and O'Connor report that the average age for both male and female activists was 50 years, and a majority of both men and women were older than 50 years.[4] Thus, age differences did not have an effect on the number of years of activity.

[4]Ibid., p. 80.

*Display the Data in a Graph*  Recall from Chapter 3 that one of the primary reasons researchers use graphs in presentations is to make it easier for readers to understand data. We can also use graphs when we want to emphasize some aspect of the data. Table 9.4 shows educational differences between male and female party activists. One of van Assendelft and O'Connor's arguments is that fewer women than men run for political office because fewer women are employed in occupations from which many political candidates are drawn. Such occupations—practicing law, for example—generally require a graduate school education. Thus, we may want to emphasize the finding that a higher percentage of men than women activists have completed graduate school. We can see from Figure 9.4 that few men or women have less than a high school education. The differences between men and women become apparent at the high school level, with a higher percentage of women than men having only a high school education. At the college levels the percentages become more similar, and the largest percentage difference occurs at the graduate school level.

Table 9.7 shows the hours men and women spent per week on party work during elections; this is also displayed in Figure 9.5. At the low end of the hours, the percentage of men exceeds the percentage of women. At the high end the percentage of women exceeds the

Figure 9.4  **Educational Differences Among Male and Female Local Party Activists**

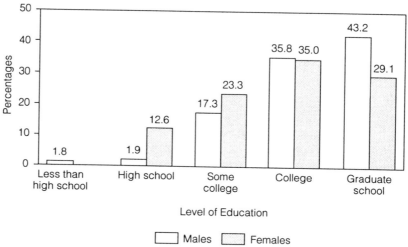

Table 9.7 **Hours Spent per Week on Party Work During Elections (in percentages)**

| Hours | Males | Females |
|-------|-------|---------|
| 0–5 | 60.0 | 42.6 |
| 5–10 | 23.9 | 23.8 |
| 10–20 | 7.7 | 15.8 |
| 20+ | 8.4 | 17.8 |
| Total | 100.0 | 100.0 |
| (N) | (155) | (101) |

*Source:* Laura van Assendelft and Karen O'Connor, "Backgrounds, Motivations and Interests: A Comparison of Male and Female Local Party Activists." *Women & Politics,* Vol. 14, No. 3, 1994, 77–91.

Figure 9.5 **Hours Spent per Week on Party Work During Elections**

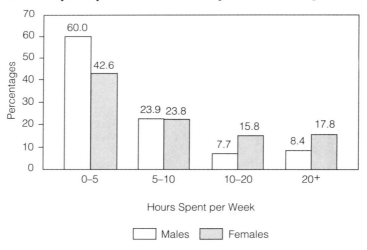

percentage of men. This distribution has few categories, so we could choose to use a pie chart rather than a bar graph to display it.

> **Learning Check.** *Draw a pie chart and compare it with the bar graph shown in Figure 9.5. Which do you think better emphasizes the data? Remember, you can "explode" slices on a pie chart.*

*Describe What Is Average or Typical of a Distribution* With ordinal data we can choose to report either the median or the mode. The deciding criterion is the purpose of the research. Let's look at the variable "level of education" shown in Table 9.4 and decide if we will report the median or the mode. The cumulative percentage columns in Table 9.4 show that the 50th percentile for both males and females falls in the College category. Thus, the median level of education for both males and females is "college." The modes, however, differ—"graduate school" for men and "college" for women. The purpose of this research is to describe both similarities and differences between male and female party activists, so which do we choose? Our inclination would be to report the mode for two reasons. First, when we examine the tables for the other variables we find many areas in which men and women are similar. This makes it all the more important to determine how they differ. Second, reporting the mode supports the argument that women run for political office less frequently than men because—due to lack of educational credentials—they are underrepresented in the professions from which many candidates are chosen. Another option is to report both the mode and the median.

*Describe Variability Within a Distribution* For most of the variables used in this study, the range of categories for men and women is the same. Thus, there is little utility in reporting a range. However, for "level of education" the range differs for men and women. As Table 9.4 shows, the range of education for men is less than high school through graduate school; for women it is high school through graduate school. The range shows us that there is more variability among men than among women.

*Describe the Relationship Between Two Variables* Throughout this discussion we have been performing cross-tabulations of a number of variables. For a more detailed discussion of cross-tabulation as a technique for determining the relationship between variables, let's examine Table 9.8, which shows motivation for party activism for male and female party activists. Before we discuss what this table shows, we need to look at the way the table is constructed.

First, notice that both "gender" and "degree of importance"—the dependent variable—are arrayed in the columns of Table 9.8 instead of in rows as is typical. This suggests that we should compare down the columns. However, if we total the columns, we find that they do not add up to 100 percent. They are not even close. Why? Because in Table 9.8 each row actually represents a separate table, with

Table 9.8 **Motivations for Party Activism Among Males and Females (in percentages)**

| | DEGREE OF IMPORTANCE | | | | | |
| | Very | | Fairly/Not Very | | Not at All | |
| MOTIVATION | (M) | (F) | (M) | (F) | (M) | (F) |
|---|---|---|---|---|---|---|
| Supporting a particular candidate | 53.3 | 68.8 | 42.1 | 29.2 | 4.6 | 2.1 |
| My political philosophy | 77.3 | 82.1 | 22.0 | 17.9 | 0.6 | 0.0 |
| Party loyalty | 36.4 | 33.7 | 57.1 | 61.0 | 6.5 | 5.3 |
| Interest in a government job or political appointment | 5.4 | 8.7 | 32.6 | 25.0 | 61.9 | 66.3 |
| Interest in elected office | 16.4 | 18.1 | 43.6 | 33.0 | 40.0 | 48.9 |
| Friendship or opportunities for meeting people | 14.0 | 14.1 | 72.7 | 67.4 | 13.3 | 18.5 |
| A specific issue that I care about | 35.3 | 49.5 | 56.8 | 45.3 | 7.8 | 5.3 |

*Source:* Laura van Assendelft and Karen O'Connor, "Backgrounds, Motivations and Interests: A Comparison of Male and Female Local Party Activists." *Women & Politics,* Vol. 14, No. 3, 1994, 77–91.

the independent variable in each case being gender. Table 9.9 shows how a table representing one row (interest in elected office) of Table 9.8 can be constructed. When we compare Table 9.9 with the appropriate row in Table 9.8, we can see that in Table 9.9 we make comparisons across the rows in groups of two.

Table 9.8 shows that generally males and females are similarly motivated to participate in party activity. For both males and females political philosophy appears to be the strongest motivator (very important for 77.3% of men and 82.1% of women). Supporting a particular candidate (very important—53.3% for men; 68.8% for women) and specific issues they care about (very important—35.3% for men; 49.5% for women) are stronger motivators for women than for men.

Gamma and Somers' *d* are appropriate for use with ordinal level variables or with dichotomous nominal variables. However, because the independent variable in this example is always "gender"—a dichotomous

Table 9.9 **Importance of Interest in Elected Office in Motivating Party Activism Among Males and Females (in percentages)**

| Degree of Importance | Males | Females |
|---|---|---|
| Very | 16.4 | 18.1 |
| Fairly/Not very | 43.6 | 33.0 |
| Not at all | 40.0 | 48.9 |
| Total | 100.0 | 100.0 |

*Source:* Adapted from Laura van Assendelft and Karen O'Connor, "Backgrounds, Motivations and Interests: A Comparison of Male and Female Local Party Activists." *Women & Politics,* Vol. 14, No. 3, 1994, 77–91.

nominal level variable—we can use both lambda (in cases where the modes of the distributions differ) and gamma or Somers' *d* to measure the association between gender and any of the dependent variables examined earlier.

For example, let's look at the association between gender and the level of education of local party activists shown in Table 9.4. First, we must convert the percentages into frequencies and construct a bivariate table as shown in Table 9.10.

Now let's first calculate lambda:

$$\text{Lambda} = \frac{E1 - E2}{E1}$$

$$E1 = N - Mo = 265 - 100 = 165$$

$$E2 = (162 - 70) + (103 - 36) = 159$$

$$\text{Lambda} = \frac{165 - 159}{165} = .04$$

A lambda of .04 shows us that there is a very weak positive relationship between education and gender. Knowing the gender of an activist will do little to improve our prediction of the level of his or her education.

Next, let's calculate Somers' *d*. Because we are sure about the direction of influence in this relationship (clearly only gender, and not education, can be the independent variable) we choose Somers' *d* rather than gamma:

$$\text{Somers' } d = \frac{Ns - Nd}{Ns + Nd + Nty}$$

Table 9.10 **Educational Differences Among Male and Female Local Party Activists**

|  | GENDER | | |
| --- | --- | --- | --- |
| **LEVEL OF EDUCATION** | Males | Females | Total |
| Less than high school | 3 | 0 | 3 |
| High school | 3 | 13 | 16 |
| Some college | 28 | 24 | 52 |
| College | 58 | 36 | 94 |
| Graduate school | 70 | 30 | 100 |
| Total | 162 | 103 | 265 |

*Source:* Laura van Assendelft and Karen O'Connor, "Backgrounds, Motivations and Interests: A Comparison of Male and Female Local Party Activists." *Women & Politics,* Vol. 14, No. 3, 1994, 77–91.

The number of same order ($Ns$) pairs that can be formed from Table 9.10 is

$$Ns = 3(13 + 24 + 36 + 30) + 3(24 + 36 + 30) + 28(36 + 30) + 58(30) = 4,167$$

The number of inverse order ($Nd$) pairs that can be formed from Table 9.10 is

$$Nd = 0(3 + 28 + 58 + 70) + 13(28 + 58 + 70) + 24(58 + 70) + 36(70) = 7,620$$

The number of pairs tied on the dependent variable ($Nty$) that can be formed from Table 9.10 is

$$Nty = 3(0) + 3(13) + 28(24) + 58(36) + 70(30) = 4,899$$

Thus, Somers' $d$ is

$$\text{Somers' } d = \frac{4,167 - 7,620}{4,167 + 7,620 + 4,899} = -.21$$

A Somers' $d$ of −.21 indicates that there is a weak association between gender and education of local party activists. Using gender to predict level of education results in a proportional reduction of error of 21 percent (−.21 × 100 = 21%). We may designate "femaleness" as the ordering principle for gender, so that "female" is higher and "male" is lower (using "maleness" as the ordering principle, "female" would be lower and "male" higher). The negative sign of Somers' *d* can thus be interpreted to mean that male activists tend to have higher levels of education than female activists.

## Descriptive Data Analysis for Interval-Ratio Variables

The highest level of measurement is the interval-ratio level. The categories of interval-ratio variables are continuous and can be ranked from highest to lowest. The measurements for all the cases are expressed in the same units, and the magnitude of difference between categories can be calculated.

## Statistics in Practice: Education and Income

The purpose of teaching you how to calculate the statistics presented in this book is to help increase your understanding of the procedures and techniques used in statistical analysis. However, you have also learned that computer software, such as SPSS, can quickly and accurately provide researchers with frequency distributions, graphs, and statistical output. In this section, we use output generated by SPSS to analyze the relationship between education and income for a data from the 1987 to 1991 General Social Survey. This research example will review both SPSS output and the procedures for analyzing interval-ratio data.

Although we will not manually calculate our statistics, we still follow the five basic steps of descriptive data analysis to examine the relationship between education and income for respondents to the General Social Survey.

*Organize the Data into a Frequency Distribution*  Table 9.11 shows the output generated by SPSS when frequency distributions of the variables income and education are requested. Let's review the parts of this table.

At the top of each section of the table the code name, or variable name, for the variable and a variable label are listed. This substitutes for the more formal title used in the frequency distributions we constructed manually.

Next, look at the column headings. In the section for income, the column headed "Value Label" indicates the class intervals for the variable RINCOME. The column headed "Value" indicates the code

Table 9.11    **Frequency Distributions for Income and Education**

RINCOME    RESPONDENTS    INCOME

| Value Label | Value | Frequency | Percent | Valid Percent | Cum Percent |
|---|---|---|---|---|---|
| LT $1000 | 1 | 29 | 2.1 | 3.3 | 3.3 |
| $1000  TO  2999 | 2 | 35 | 2.5 | 4.0 | 7.4 |
| $3000  TO  3999 | 3 | 29 | 2.1 | 3.3 | 10.7 |
| $4000  TO  4999 | 4 | 38 | 2.7 | 4.4 | 15.1 |
| $5000  TO  5999 | 5 | 35 | 2.5 | 4.0 | 19.1 |
| $6000  TO  6999 | 6 | 22 | 1.6 | 2.5 | 21.7 |
| $7000  TO  7999 | 7 | 27 | 1.9 | 3.1 | 24.8 |
| $8000  TO  9999 | 8 | 46 | 3.3 | 5.3 | 30.1 |
| $10000  -  14999 | 9 | 138 | 9.9 | 15.9 | 46.0 |
| $15000  -  19999 | 10 | 132 | 9.4 | 15.2 | 61.2 |
| $20000  -  24999 | 11 | 103 | 7.4 | 11.9 | 73.1 |
| $25000  OR  MORE | 12 | 233 | 16.6 | 26.9 | 100.0 |
| NAP | 0 | 487 | 34.8 | Missing | |
| REFUSED | 13 | 46 | 3.3 | Missing | |
| | Total | 1,400 | 100.0 | 100.0 | |

Valid  cases    867      Missing  cases    533

EDUC    HIGHEST  YEAR  OF  SCHOOL  COMPLETED

| Value Label | Value | Frequency | Percent | Valid Percent | Cum Percent |
|---|---|---|---|---|---|
| | 0 | 3 | .2 | .2 | .2 |
| | 1 | 1 | .1 | .1 | .3 |
| | 2 | 4 | .3 | .3 | .6 |
| | 3 | 8 | .6 | .6 | 1.1 |
| | 4 | 10 | .7 | .7 | 1.9 |
| | 5 | 10 | .7 | .7 | 2.6 |
| | 6 | 22 | 1.6 | 1.6 | 4.2 |
| | 7 | 19 | 1.4 | 1.4 | 5.5 |
| | 8 | 65 | 4.6 | 4.7 | 10.2 |
| | 9 | 47 | 3.4 | 3.4 | 13.6 |
| | 10 | 69 | 4.9 | 4.9 | 18.5 |
| | 11 | 99 | 7.1 | 7.1 | 25.6 |
| | 12 | 426 | 30.4 | 30.6 | 56.2 |
| | 13 | 129 | 9.2 | 9.3 | 65.4 |
| | 14 | 160 | 11.4 | 11.5 | 76.9 |
| | 15 | 71 | 5.1 | 5.1 | 82.0 |
| | 16 | 138 | 9.9 | 9.9 | 91.9 |
| | 17 | 34 | 2.4 | 2.4 | 94.3 |
| | 18 | 47 | 3.4 | 3.4 | 97.7 |
| | 19 | 12 | .9 | .9 | 98.6 |
| | 20 | 20 | 1.4 | 1.4 | 100.0 |
| NAP | 97 | 6 | .4 | Missing | |
| | Total | 1,400 | 100.0 | 100.0 | |

Valid  cases  1394  Missing  cases  6

used by interviewers to represent the class interval when marking the original surveys. In the case of RINCOME, the Value Label column is necessary because the code value does not indicate the respondents' actual income. In the case of education (EDUC), however, there is no entry in the Value Label column because the code values directly represent the number of years of school completed by the respondents (with the exception of code 97, which we will discuss in a moment).

The "Frequency," "Percent," and "Cum (Cumulative) Percent" columns are similar to those we have seen in other frequency distributions. The "Valid Percent" column, however, is different. Notice that for income the categories REFUSED and NAP are included in the value labels and for education NAP is shown as a value label for the code value 97. Responses coded as NAP and REFUSED are defined as missing cases, which means that the respondent either was not asked the question or refused to answer, respectively. These cases are not included in any statistical calculations. (Generally, SPSS will not omit these cases unless the value is designated as missing.) When a statistical procedure involves more than one variable, cases missing data for any of the variables—either refused or NAP—are deleted before the statistic is calculated.

*Display the Data in a Graph* To display the data for both education and income we use histograms. SPSS generates histograms as well as a variety of other graphs. However, software graphic packages often allow researchers to produce more professional-looking charts for presentation purposes, and some graphics programs allow the user to directly import data from other sources, such as statistics programs, eliminating the need for manually entering data. Figure 9.6 shows a histogram for the income of GSS respondents. Notice that we have collapsed the categories into equal-width intervals to make the graph easier to read and to maintain the interval-ratio level of measurement. Note that the income category "$25,000+" is not equal in width to the other categories. The fact that it contains so many cases also indicates that it probably should have been divided into several response categories in the original interview. Figure 9.6 shows that the highest percentage of respondents (26.9%) earns more than $25,000 per year. However, a substantial percentage (15.1%) earns less than $5,000 per year.

*Describe What Is Average or Typical of a Distribution* With interval-ratio data we can choose between the mode, the median, and the mean as a measure of central tendency. Whenever possible, the mean is the

Figure 9.6 **Histogram of Income for Respondents to the General Social Survey**

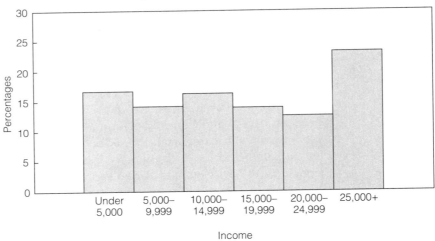

measure of choice because it allows more advanced statistical analysis than either the mode or the median. Looking at the data for education and income using the frequency distribution for education and the histogram for income, we can see that neither distribution is strongly skewed. For both of these variables the mean can be used to describe central tendency. However, as we indicated earlier, it is generally a good idea to also compute and interpret the median for interval-ratio data.

*Describe Variability Within a Distribution* Because we have chosen to use the mean to describe central tendency for each of our two variables, we can use the standard deviation to describe variability. SPSS provides both the mean and the standard deviation for our variables[5] and displays them in the format shown in Table 9.12.

Let's look at this information more closely. The first line tells us that in 886 cases the respondents provided usable answers to both survey questions. These are the cases SPSS will use in any future statistical calculations involving both of the variables. The column headed "Valid N" indicates the number of usable responses for the individual variables. Verify this by looking at Table 9.11. The valid N should be equal to the total frequency minus REFUSED and NAP frequencies.

[5]To calculate these statistics, RINCOME was recoded to the midpoint for each category. Thus, category 1 was coded to 500, and so on.

Table 9.12  **SPSS Output of Means and Standard Deviations**

```
Number  of  valid  observations  (listwise)  =     66.00
                                 Valid
Variable Mean        Std Dev   N      Label
EDUC          12.53     3.11  1,394  HIGHEST  YEAR  OF  SCHOOL
COMPLETED
RINCOME  16,227.22  9,025.35   867   RESPONDENTS  INCOME
```

SPSS has calculated both the mean and the standard deviation for education and income. The mean for education is 12.53 years, with a standard deviation of 3.11 years. The mean indicates that the average respondent has just over a high school education (12 years is equal to completing high school). The standard deviation of 3.11 years, when compared with a mean of 12.53 years, shows that a fairly large number of respondents have either less than or more than a high school education. We conclude that this distribution is moderately diverse.

The mean income for this sample is $16,227.22, with a standard deviation of $9,025.35. The standard deviation is very high in comparison with the mean income and indicates that there is a great deal of diversity in the sample distribution.

> ***Learning Check.***   *The median is not reported in the SPSS output. However, we can easily determine the median for the variables EDUC and RINCOME from Table 9.11. (Hint: Examine the Cum Percent columns.) Compare the median with the mean for each variable. What can you conclude about the shape of the two distributions from this comparison? What can you learn from the medians about the income and education of GSS respondents?*

*Describe the Relationship Between Two Variables*  We have chosen to explore the relationship between education and income because we know that, in general, better-paying jobs require more education than poorer-paying jobs. Because the relationship between these variables is linear, we can use bivariate regression to make determinations about the relationship between education and income.

SPSS produces the regression calculation shown in Table 9.13. At the top of the body of the table SPSS identifies the calculation as a multiple regression. The difference between multiple regression and bivariate regression is that in multiple regression more than one independent variable is used to predict the value of the dependent

Table 9.13 **SPSS Output for the Bivariate Regression of Income and Education**

```
* * * * M U L T I P L E   R E G R E S S I O N * * *
                      *
Listwise  Deletion  of  Missing  Data
Equation  Number  1 Dependent  Variable..  RINCOME
Block  Number  1.    Method:  Enter    EDUC
Variable(s)  Entered  on  Step  Number
1..    EDUC      HIGHEST  YEAR  OF  SCHOOL  COMPLETED
Multiple  R            .36803
R  Square              .13545
Adjusted  R  Square    .13445
Standard  Error    8401.49448

Analysis  of  Variance
                    DF          Sum  of  Squares           Mean  Square
Regression           1          9554581120.62682       9554581120.62682
Residual           864        60985534641.49790         70585109.53877
F  =      135.36256          Signif  F  =  .0000

— — — — — — Variables  in  the  Equation — — — — — — —

Variable              B            SE  B        Beta          T    Sig  T

EDUC          1227.136679      105.473573    .368034   11.635    .0000
(Constant)     −52.940144     1427.998988               −.037    .9704
End  Block  Number    1    All  requested  variables  entered.
```

variable. SPSS uses the multiple regression program to calculate both bivariate and multivariate regression and does not distinguish between the two when it titles the output.

Reading down the table, the first lines tells us that cases missing values for one or both of the variables have been deleted from the calculation. The next line tells us that the dependent variable ($Y$) in the calculation is income, RINCOME. Under "Variable(s) Entered on Step Number," we see that the independent variable is education, EDUC.

The SPSS program for multiple regression produces information on a variety of tests not required for a simple bivariate regression. So where in all those numbers do we find what we need to produce a bivariate regression equation? Look under the section "Variables in the Equation." Producing the regression equation is actually very simple. The value of $b$ is listed in column B and row EDUC. Thus, the value of $b$ is about \$1,227.14. The value of $a$ is found in column B and row (Constant). Thus, our bivariate regression equation is

$$\hat{Y} = -\$52.94 + \$1,227.14$$

(The rest of the material in the table can be ignored.)

The regression equation tells us that for every unit increase in education—the unit is one year—we can predict an increase of $1,227.14 in annual income for the respondents in our sample. Let's use the regression equation to predict the difference in annual income between respondents with a high school (12 years) and a college (16 years) education:

$$\hat{Y} \text{(high school)} = -\$52.94 + \$1,227.14(12) = \$14,672.74$$

$$\hat{Y} \text{(college)} = -\$52.94 + \$1,227.14(16) = \$19,581.30$$

The predicted difference in annual income between high school and college graduates is $4,908.56 ($19,581.30 − $14,672.74 = $4,908.56). Over the course of a normal lifetime of work we would expect college graduates to earn almost a quarter of a million dollars more than high school graduates.

SPSS can also calculate Pearson's correlation coefficient, $r$. The output produced by SPSS is shown in Table 9.14. The output is arranged in a matrix that resembles a bivariate table. Each variable is listed in a row and a column. To find the value of $r$, we need to locate the intersection of the two variables. Since $r$ is a symmetrical measure, it does not matter which variable we consider the independent variable, so we can read either down the columns or across the rows. The correlation coefficient for each pair of variables is the first number in the cell. For EDUC and RINCOME, $r$ is equal to 0.3680. Remember, $r$ can range from 0.0 to ±1.0, with 0.0 indicating no relationship between

Table 9.14 **SPSS Output of Correlation Coefficients**

|  | - - Correlation Coefficients - - | |
|  | EDUC | RINCOME |
| --- | --- | --- |
| EDUC | 1.0000 | .3680 |
|  | (1394) | (866) |
|  | p= . | p= .000 |
| RINCOME | .3680 | 1.0000 |
|  | (866) | (867) |
|  | p= .000 | p= . |

(Coefficient / (Cases) / 2-tailed Significance

the variables and ±1.0 indicating a perfect positive or negative relationship between the variables. An $r$ of 0.3680 indicates a moderate positive relationship between education and income. To determine how much of the variation in income can be explained by education we need to calculate $r^2$:

$$r^2 = (r)^2 = (0.3680)^2 = 0.135$$

Using the regression equation, our prediction of income is improved by 13.5 percent ($0.135 \times 100$) over the prediction we would make using the mean alone. We can also say that education explains 13.5 percent of the variation in income in our sample.

## A Final Note

Many people find that the most difficult part of statistics is determining the proper procedures and techniques to use with the data. This review chapter has been designed as a reference tool for you to use in making those decisions when performing descriptive data analysis.

In Chapters 11, 12, 13, 14, and 15, we will introduce you to inferential statistics—procedures researchers use to make predictions about a population using data collected from a sample of the population. We close this book with a final review chapter (Chapter 16), which will provide you with a reference tool to use when performing inferential statistics.

### EXERCISES

1. Indicate whether the following types of data are nominal, ordinal, or interval-ratio and explain your answer.
   a. The eye color of a person
   b. The number of general elections in which a person has voted in his or her lifetime
   c. Ranking of school quality as below average, average, or above average
   d. Political party membership
   e. The time people have dinner each night
   f. The classification of burns as first, second, or third degree

2. A question from the 1993 GSS asks about one's willingness to accept a cut in living standards to help the environment. Following is a portion of the output from the SPSS Frequencies procedure.

GRNSOL ACCEPT CUT IN LIVING STNDS TO HELP ENVIR

| Value Label | Value | Frequency | Percent | Valid Percent | Cum Percent |
|---|---|---|---|---|---|
| VERY WILLING | 1 | 91 | | | |
| FAIRLY WILLING | 2 | 410 | | | |
| NEITHER WILLING NOR UNWILLING | 3 | 353 | | | |
| NOT VERY WILLING | 4 | 385 | | | |
| NOT AT ALL WILLING | 5 | 229 | | | |
| NAP | 0 | 49 | | | |
| DK | 8 | 36 | | | |
| NA | 9 | 53 | | | |
| | Total | 1606 | | | |

Valid cases  1468      Missing cases  138

a. On what scale of measurement is GRNSOL measured?
b. The values of 0, 8, and 9 should be coded as missing because they correspond to responses of "Not Applicable," "Don't Know," and "No Answer." Taking this into account, calculate values for the columns labeled Percent, Valid Percent, and Cum(ulative) Percent.
c. Is cumulative percentage proper to calculate for GRNSOL? Why or why not?

3. Construct an appropriate graph to display the categories of GRNSOL.

4. For the variable GRNSOL:
   a. Calculate the mode and median. (*Hint:* Don't use the missing data.)
   b. Calculate the IQV. Calculate the range.
   c. Use this information to describe the distribution of responses to this question.

5. The following table shows the relationship between GRNSOL and race of the respondent. Use it to answer these questions.
   a. Describe the relationship you observe in the table using percentage.
   b. What is the strength of the relationship between race and willingness to accept a cut in living standard for the environment? Is the value you calculated consistent with your description in (a)?

```
GRNSOL ACCEPT CUT IN LIVING STNDS TO HELP ENVIR
by RACE RACE OF RESPONDENT
                         RACE           Page 1 of 1
              Count   |
              Col Pct | WHITE   BLACK   OTHER
                      |                            Row
GRNSOL                |   1   |   2   |   3   | Total
             ------ + ----- + ----- + ------+
                  1  |  75   |  13   |   3   |    91
VERY  WILLING        |  6.0  |  8.3  |  4.3  |   6.2
                     + ----- + ----- + ------+
                  2  |  357  |  33   |  20   |   410
FAIRLY  WILLING      | 28.7  | 21.0  | 29.0  |  27.9
                     + ----- + ----- + ------+
                  3  |  311  |  29   |  13   |   353
NEITHER  WILLING     | 25.0  | 18.5  | 18.8  |  24.0
                     + ----- + ----- + ------+
                  4  |  324  |  41   |  20   |   385
NOT  VERY  WILLING   | 26.1  | 26.1  | 29.0  |  26.2
                     + ----- + ----- + ------+
                  5  |  175  |  41   |  13   |   229
NOT  AT  ALL  WILLI  | 14.1  | 26.1  | 18.8  |  15.6
                     + ----- + ----- + ------+
              Column   1,242    157     69    1,468
              Total     84.6   10.7    4.7    100.0
```

6. A poll of white and black Americans in 1993 asked, "Is racial discrimination against blacks where you live serious?" Here are the results:

| Race | Serious | Not Serious |
|------|---------|-------------|
| Whites | 33% | 67% |
| Blacks | 68% | 32% |

(Data from a *USA Today*/CNN/Gallup Poll of 840 adults on February 8–9, 1993. Missing data have been removed.)

a. Use these data to construct a clustered bar chart of the seriousness of racial discrimination against blacks.
b. Describe the relationship between race and belief about discrimination against blacks. Why might the two variables be related?
c. Calculate an appropriate measure of association for this table to measure the strength of the relationship. If you don't think this can be done, explain why.

7. The following table displays the amount 284 people in a large city paid in sales tax in 1995. Calculate the median amount of sales tax paid.

| Amount Paid | Frequency |
|-------------|-----------|
| 0 to $99.99 | 34 |
| $100 to $199.99 | 52 |
| $200 to $499.99 | 121 |
| $500 to $1,000 | 77 |

8. Calculate the mean sales tax paid using the table in exercise 7.

9. Calculate the IQR for the sales tax data.

10. You and a friend are discussing measures of central tendency (you are both very diligent students). Your friend says, "No distribution of an interval-ratio variable is ever truly symmetrical. All of them are skewed to a certain extent." You admit this is probably true. Your friend goes on to make this claim, "Therefore, given Figure 9.1 in the textbook, I think we should never use the mean as a measure of central tendency for interval-ratio data. Instead, it's safer to use the median." Do you agree or disagree with your friend? Provide reasons for your answer.

11. This bar chart displays mean self-rated physical health by gender. (Health is measured on a scale of 1 to 7, where lower numbers mean better health.) Explain what error has been made in creating this chart and what its effect might be on an unsuspecting reader.

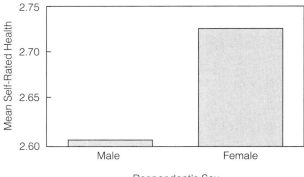

12. In 1990 the United States had 248,709,873 residents according to the Census Bureau. And also in 1990, the U.S. Department of Justice reported that there were 292 federal and state prisoners per 100,000 persons in the United States.
    a. How many total federal and state prisoners were there in 1990?
    b. What was the proportion of the U.S. population in federal and state prison?

13. In the National Election Study of 1994, respondents were asked their feelings toward eventual 1996 presidential contenders Bill Clinton and Bob Dole on a scale of 0 to 100, where a higher score means warmer, more positive feelings. A score of –99 means a non-response. A subsample of the responses follows:

| Clinton | Dole |
|---------|------|
| 30 | 70 |
| 15 | 70 |
| 0 | 85 |
| 40 | 50 |
| 30 | 60 |
| 30 | −99 |
| 85 | −99 |
| 0 | 85 |
| 75 | 20 |
| 70 | 70 |
| 50 | 50 |
| 70 | 50 |
| 70 | 70 |
| 100 | 70 |
| 100 | −99 |
| 80 | 0 |
| 60 | 60 |
| 70 | 70 |
| 90 | 0 |
| 70 | 50 |
| 85 | 0 |
| 85 | 15 |
| 85 | 70 |
| 60 | 70 |

   a. Calculate the mean feelings toward Clinton and toward Dole.
   b. Calculate the variance and standard deviation for the feelings toward Clinton.
   c. Calculate the IQR for feelings toward Dole.

14. What is the relationship between feelings toward Bill Clinton and those toward Bob Dole?
   a. Investigate this question by calculating the correlation coefficient between feelings toward each politician.
   b. Use this statistic to describe how the two variables are related. Does the result make sense?

15. The 1994 National Election Study included a question about approval of President Bill Clinton on a four-point scale. The following contingency table shows the relationship between approval of Clinton and whether a respondent classified himself or herself as middle or working class.

| Approval of Clinton | Lower Class | Middle Class | Total |
|---|---|---|---|
| Strongly disapprove | 175 | 303 | 478 |
| Not strongly disapprove | 150 | 166 | 317 |
| Not strongly approve | 280 | 250 | 530 |
| Strongly approve | 174 | 136 | 310 |

a. Assume that class can be used to predict approval rating. Calculate appropriate percentages and describe the relationship in the table.

b. Calculate a measure of association to further characterize this relationship.

16. A child psychologist measured the amount of time parents spent talking to their young children each day and then, several years later, gave the students a standardized achievement test (the test is measured on a scale from 0 to 50). She obtained these results.

| Time Spent Talking to Child (in minutes) | Test Score |
|---|---|
| 15 | 34 |
| 45 | 47 |
| 9 | 27 |
| 60 | 49 |
| 22 | 29 |
| 30 | 39 |
| 5 | 18 |
| 20 | 26 |
| 25 | 33 |
| 40 | 42 |
| 30 | 36 |

a. Construct a scatterplot of time spent talking and test score. Use it to describe the relationship between these two variables.

b. Calculate the coefficient of determination between these two variables.

c. Calculate the regression equation.

d. What is the predicted test score for a child whose parents talked with her for 50 minutes per day?

## SPSS PROBLEMS

1. The 1987 to 1991 GSS file contains three questions asking how satisfied a respondent was with his or her friends, family, and health (called SATFRND, SATFAM, and SATHEALT, respectively). Each is measured on a scale of 1 to 7, where low scores mean more satisfaction. Use SPSS to answer these questions.

   a. Characterize the distribution of these variables, using measures of central tendency and variability.

   b. What percentage of the sample said they had "A Great Deal" or more satisfaction with their friends? How about with their family?

   c. Create a chart to display SATFAM by SEX. Describe the resulting graph.

2. Continue your exploration of the satisfaction variables by examining their relationship to each other and to other items.

   a. Create a cross-tabulation of SATFAM by SEX and SATFRND by SEX. Have SPSS calculate appropriate percentages, statistics, and measures of association. Use these results to describe the relationships between SEX and the two variables.

   b. Calculate the correlation coefficient between all three satisfaction variables (you will have three coefficients for the three possible pairs). Is there a positive or a negative relationship between these variables? Can you suggest why? Although these variables are measured on a seven-point ordinal scale, it is quite common in the social sciences to use interval-ratio techniques with such data.

   c. Perhaps age is related to satisfaction with one's health. To investigate this, first create a scatterplot of the two variables. Do you find this useful? Why or why not? Have SPSS place a regression line on the plot.

   d. Now have SPSS calculate the regression equation to predict health satisfaction with age. What is the regression equation? What is the coefficient of determination? Describe the relationship between the two variables. Is age a strong predictor of satisfaction with one's health?

   e. What is the predicted health satisfaction rating for a person who is 30 years old? 70 years old?

3. a. Although the satisfaction variables are measured on an ordinal scale, it is much easier to study their relationship to age with interval-ratio techniques. Why is that? What problem would you encounter if you tried to use a cross-tabulation instead?

   b. As an alternative, use the variable AGE3 to study the relationship between age and health satisfaction with a cross-tabulation. Calculate appropriate statistics to describe the relationship. Are your results consistent with what you learned in exercise 2(d) using regression?

# 10     The Normal Distribution

■ ■ ■ ■   **Introduction**

In the preceding chapters we have learned some important things about distributions: how to organize them into frequency distributions; how to display them using graphs; and how to describe their central tendencies and variation using measures such as the mean and the standard deviation. We have also learned that distributions can have different shapes. Some distributions are symmetrical; others are negatively or positively skewed. The distributions we have described so far are all *empirical distributions;* that is, they are all based on real data.

The distribution we describe in this chapter—commonly known as the *normal curve* or the **normal distribution**—is a theoretical rather than an empirical distribution. A *theoretical distribution* is similar to an empirical distribution in that it can be organized into frequency distributions, displayed using graphs, and described by its central tendency and variation using measures such as the mean and the standard deviation. However, unlike an empirical distribution, a theoretical distribution is based on theory rather than on real data. The value of the theoretical normal distribution lies in the fact that many empirical distributions we study seem to approximate it. Therefore, we can often learn a lot about the characteristics of these empirical distributions based on our knowledge of the theoretical normal distribution.

In this chapter, we learn that the normal distribution is central to the theory of inferential statistics, and that it is used as a model to help researchers generalize their research results from samples to populations. In the following chapters, we will discuss some of the principles involved in generalizing results from samples to the population (see page 481 for a definition of *population*). In our discussion, we will use different notation when referring to population parameters. In Table 10.1 we present the sample notation and the corresponding population notation. Note that sample statistics are denoted with italicized letters and the population parameters that correspond to them are denoted with Greek letters. The subscript $Y$ refers to the variable described by these statistics and parameters.

Table 10.1  **Sample and Population Notations**

| Measure | Notations for Sample Statistics | Notations for Population Parameters |
|---|---|---|
| Mean | $\bar{Y}$ | $\mu_Y$ |
| Standard deviation | $S_Y$ | $\sigma_Y$ |
| Variance | $S_Y^2$ | $\sigma_Y^2$ |

Figure 10.1  **The Normal Curve**

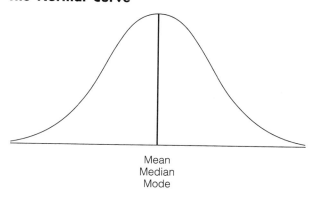

Mean
Median
Mode

## Properties of the Normal Distribution

Let's see what a typical normal distribution looks like. The normal curve (Figure 10.1) looks like a bell-shaped frequency polygon. Because of this property it is sometimes called the *bell-shaped curve.* One of the most striking characteristics of the normal distribution is its perfect symmetry. Notice that if you fold Figure 10.1 exactly in the middle, you have two equal halves, each the mirror image of the other. This means that precisely half the observations fall on each side of the middle. In addition, the midpoint of the normal curve is the point having the maximum frequency. This is also the point at which three measures coincide: the mode (the point of the highest frequency), the median (the point that divides the distribution into two equal halves), and the mean (the average of all the scores). Notice also that most of the observations are clustered around the middle, with the frequencies gradually decreasing at both ends of the distribution.

---

*Normal Distribution*   A bell-shaped and symmetrical theoretical distribution, with the mean, the median, and the mode all coinciding at its peak and with the frequencies gradually decreasing at both ends of the curve.

---

## Empirical Distributions Approximating the Normal Distribution

The normal curve is a theoretical ideal, and real-life distributions never perfectly match this model. However, researchers study many variables (for example, standardized tests like the SAT, ACT, or GRE; height; athletic ability; and numerous social and political attitudes) that closely resemble this theoretical model. When variables are normally distributed, a graphic display will reveal an approximately bell-shaped and symmetrical distribution closely resembling the idealized model shown in Figure 10.1. This property makes it possible for us to describe many empirical distributions based on our knowledge of the normal curve.

### An Example: Final Grades in Statistics

It is easier to understand the properties of a normal curve if we think in terms of a real distribution that is near normal. Let's examine the frequencies and the bar chart presented in Table 10.2. These data are the final scores of 1,200 students who took my class in social statistics at the University of Wisconsin-Milwaukee between 1983 and 1993. To convince you that the variable "final score in statistics" is normally distributed, we overlaid a normal curve on the distribution shown in Table 10.2. Notice how closely our empirical distribution of statistics scores approximates the normal curve!

Notice that 70 is the most frequent score obtained by the students, and therefore it is the mode of the distribution. Because about half the students are either above (49.99%) or below (50.01%) this score, both the mean (70.07) and the median (70) are approximately 70. Also shown in Table 10.2 is the gradual decrease in the number of students who scored either above or below 70. Very few students scored higher than 90 or lower than 50.

When we use the term *normal curve,* we are not referring to identical distributions. The shape of a normal distribution varies, depending on the mean and standard deviation of the particular distribution. For example, in Figure 10.2 we present two normal distributions with

Table 10.2    **Final Grades in Social Statistics of 1,200 Students (1983–1993): A Near Normal Distribution**

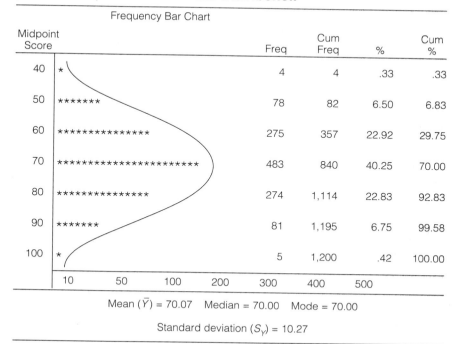

| Midpoint Score | Frequency Bar Chart | Freq | Cum Freq | % | Cum % |
|---|---|---|---|---|---|
| 40 | * | 4 | 4 | .33 | .33 |
| 50 | ******* | 78 | 82 | 6.50 | 6.83 |
| 60 | *************** | 275 | 357 | 22.92 | 29.75 |
| 70 | ************************ | 483 | 840 | 40.25 | 70.00 |
| 80 | *************** | 274 | 1,114 | 22.83 | 92.83 |
| 90 | ******* | 81 | 1,195 | 6.75 | 99.58 |
| 100 | * | 5 | 1,200 | .42 | 100.00 |
| | 10    50    100    200    300    400    500 | | | | |

Mean ($\bar{Y}$) = 70.07    Median = 70.00    Mode = 70.00

Standard deviation ($S_Y$) = 10.27

Figure 10.2    **Two Normal Distributions with Equal Means But Different Standard Deviations**

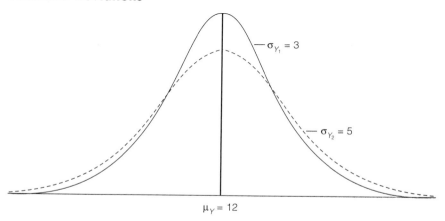

$\sigma_{Y_1} = 3$

$\sigma_{Y_2} = 5$

$\mu_Y = 12$

identical means ($\mu_Y = 12$) but with different standard deviations ($\sigma_{Y_1} = 3$; $\sigma_{Y_2} = 5$). Notice that the distribution with the largest standard deviation appears wider and flatter.

## Areas Under the Normal Curve

Regardless of the precise shape of the distribution, in all normal or nearly normal curves we find a constant proportion of the area under the curve lying between the mean and any given distance from the mean when measured in standard deviation units. The area under the normal curve may be conceptualized as a proportion or a percentage of the number of observations in the sample. Thus, the entire area under the curve is equal to 1.00, or 100 percent ($1.00 \times 100$) of the observations. Because the normal curve is perfectly symmetrical, exactly 0.5000 or 50 percent of the observations lie above or to the right of the center, which is the mean of the distribution, and 50 percent lie below or to the left of the mean.

In Figure 10.3, note the percentage of cases that will be included between the mean and 1, 2, and 3 standard deviations above and below the mean. The mean of the distribution divides it exactly in half: 34.13 percent is included between the mean and 1 standard deviation to the right of the mean; the same percentage is included between the mean and 1 standard deviation to the left of the mean. The plus signs indicate standard deviations above the mean; the minus signs denote standard deviations below the mean. Thus, between the mean and ±1 standard deviations, 68.26 percent of all the observations in the distribution occur; between the mean and ±2 standard deviations, 95.46 percent of all observations in the distribution occur; and between

Figure 10.3 **Percentages Under the Normal Curve**

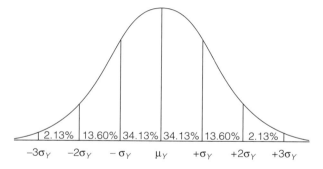

the mean and ±3 standard deviations, 99.72 percent of the observations occur. Verify this by summing the percentages in Figure 10.3.

## Interpreting the Standard Deviation

The fixed relationship between the distance from the mean, measured in standard deviation units, and the areas under the curve represents a property of the normal curve that has highly practical applications. As long as a distribution is normal and we know the mean and the standard deviation, we can determine the relative frequency (proportion or percentage) of cases that fall between any score and the mean.

This property provides an important interpretation for the standard deviation of empirical distributions that are approximately normal. For such distributions, when we know the mean and the standard deviation, we can determine the percent of scores that are within any distance, measured in standard deviation units, from that distribution's mean. For example, we know that college entrance tests like the SAT and ACT are normally distributed. The SAT, for instance, has a mean of 500 and a standard deviation of 100. This means that approximately 68 percent of the students who take the test obtain a score between 400 (1 standard deviation below the mean) and 600 (1 standard deviation above the mean). We can also anticipate that approximately 95 percent of the students who take the test will score between 300 (2 standard deviations below the mean) and 700 (2 standard deviations above the mean).

Not all empirical distributions are normal. We learned that the distributions of some common variables like "income" are skewed and therefore not normal. The fixed relationship between the distance from the mean, measured in standard deviation units, and the areas under the curve applies *only* to distributions that are normal or approximately normal.

## Standard (Z) Scores

We can express the difference between any score in a distribution and the mean in terms of *standard scores,* also known as *Z scores.* A **standard (Z) score** is the number of standard deviations that a given raw score is above or below the mean. A raw score can be transformed into a Z score to find how many standard deviations it is above or below the mean.

---

*Standard (Z) Score*   The number of standard deviations that a given raw score is above or below the mean.

---

### Transforming a Raw Score into a Z Score

To transform a raw score into a Z score, we divide the difference between the score and the mean by the standard deviation. For instance, to transform a final score in my statistics class into a Z score, we subtract the mean of 70.7 from that score and divide the difference by the standard deviation of 10.27. Thus, the Z score of 80 is

$$\frac{80 - 70.07}{10.27} = 0.97$$

or 0.97 standard deviations above the mean. Similarly, the Z score of 60 is

$$\frac{60 - 70.07}{10.27} = -0.98$$

or 0.98 standard deviations below the mean; the negative sign indicates that this score is below the mean. This procedure, in which the difference between a raw score and the mean is divided by the standard deviation, gives us a method of standardization known as *transforming a raw score into a Z score* (also known as a standard score). The Z score formula is

$$Z = \frac{Y - \overline{Y}}{S_Y} \qquad (10.1)$$

A Z score allows us to represent a raw score in terms of its relationship to the mean and to the standard deviation of the distribution. It represents the number of standard deviations that a given raw score is above or below the mean. A positive Z indicates that a score is larger than the mean, and a negative Z indicates that it is smaller than the mean. The larger the Z score the larger the difference between the score and the mean. To go back to our example of the final scores in statistics, we can convert the students' final scores into Z scores using formula 10.1 as shown in Table 10.3.

Table 10.3 **Final Social Science Statistics Scores Converted to Z Scores**

| Final Score | Z Score |
|---|---|
| 40 | $Z = \dfrac{40 - 70.07}{10.27} = \dfrac{-30.07}{10.27} = -2.93$ |
| 50 | $Z = \dfrac{50 - 70.07}{10.27} = \dfrac{-20.07}{10.27} = -1.95$ |
| 60 | $Z = \dfrac{60 - 70.07}{10.27} = \dfrac{-10.07}{10.27} = -0.98$ |
| 70 | $Z = \dfrac{70 - 70.07}{10.27} = \dfrac{-.07}{10.27} = -0.01$ |
| 80 | $Z = \dfrac{80 - 70.07}{10.27} = \dfrac{9.93}{10.27} = 0.97$ |
| 90 | $Z = \dfrac{90 - 70.07}{10.27} = \dfrac{19.93}{10.27} = 1.94$ |
| 100 | $Z = \dfrac{100 - 70.07}{10.27} = \dfrac{29.93}{10.27} = 2.91$ |
| $\overline{Y} = 70.07$ | $S_Y = 10.27$ |

**Learning Check.** *Refer to the data in Table 10.3. How many standard deviations above the mean is a score of 90? Below is a visual interpretation of what this question is asking.*

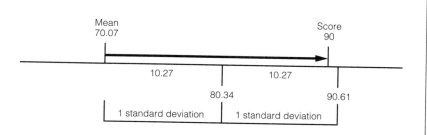

*It is obvious from the figure that a score of 90 is almost 2 standard deviations above the mean. When we use the simple formula, we find that, indeed, the Z score for a score of 90 is 1.94.*

## Transforming a Z Score into a Raw Score

For some applications of the normal curve we need to reverse the process, transforming a Z score into a raw score instead of transforming a raw score into a Z score. A Z score can be converted to a raw score to find the score associated with a particular distance from the mean when this distance is expressed in standard deviation units. For example, suppose we are interested in finding out the final score in the statistics class that lies 1 standard deviation above the mean. To solve this problem we begin with the Z-score formula:

$$Z = \frac{Y - \overline{Y}}{S_Y}$$

Note that for this problem we have the values for $Z$ ($Z = 1$), the mean ($\overline{Y} = 70.07$), and the standard deviation ($S_Y = 10.27$), but we need to determine the value of $Y$:

$$1.00 = \frac{Y - 70.07}{10.27}$$

Through simple algebra we solve for $Y$:

$$Y = 70.07 + 1.0(10.27) = 70.07 + 10.27 = 80.34$$

The score of 80.34 lies 1 standard deviation (or 1 Z score) above the mean of 70.07.

The general formula for transforming a Z score into a raw score is

$$Y = \overline{Y} + Z(S_Y) \qquad\qquad \textbf{(10.2)}$$

Thus, to transform a Z score into a raw score, multiply the Z score by the standard deviation and add the product to the mean.

Now, what statistics score lies 1.5 standard deviations below the mean? Because the score lies below the mean the Z score is negative. Thus,

$$Y = 70.07 + (-1.5)(10.27) = 70.07 - 15.41 = 54.66$$

The score of 54.66 lies 1.5 standard deviations below the mean of 70.07.

---

***Learning Check.*** *Transform the Z scores we obtained in Table 10.3 back into raw scores. Your answers should agree with the raw scores listed in the table.*

## The Standard Normal Distribution

When a normal distribution is represented in standard scores (Z scores), we call it the **standard normal distribution**. Standard scores, or Z scores, are numbers that tell us the distance between an actual score and the mean in terms of standard deviation units. The standard normal distribution has a mean of 0.0 and a standard deviation of 1.0.

---

*Standard Normal Distribution*   A normal distribution represented in standard (Z) scores.

---

Figure 10.4 shows a standard normal distribution with areas under the curve associated with 1, 2, and 3 standard scores above and below the mean. To help you understand the relationship between raw scores of a distribution and standard Z scores, we also show the raw scores in the statistics class that correspond to these standard scores. For example, notice that the mean for the statistics score distribution is 70.07; the corresponding Z score—the mean of the standard normal distribution—is 0. The score of 80.34 is 1 standard deviation above the mean (70.07 + 10.27 = 80.34) and therefore its corresponding Z score is +1. Similarly, the score of 59.80 is 1 standard deviation below the mean (70.07 − 10.27 = 59.80), and its Z-score equivalent is −1.

Figure 10.4   **The Standard Normal Distribution**

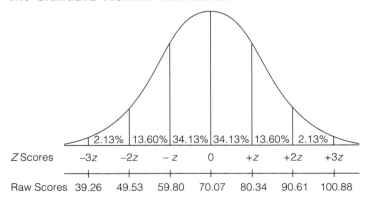

> **Learning Check.** *Go back to Figure 10.3. Compare it with Figure 10.4. Are there differences between these two figures?*

> **Learning Check.** *Can you explain why the mean of the standard normal curve is 0 and the standard deviation is equal to 1?*

## The Standard Normal Table

We can determine the proportion of cases that are included between the mean and any Z score in a normal distribution. The areas or proportions under the standard normal curve, corresponding to any Z score or its fraction, are organized into a special table called the **standard normal table**. The table is presented in Appendix B. In this section, we will discuss how to use this table.

### The Structure of the Standard Normal Table

Table 10.4 reproduces a small part of the standard normal table. Note that the table consists of three columns.

Column A lists positive Z scores. Because the normal curve is symmetrical, the proportions that correspond to positive Z scores are identical to the proportions corresponding to negative Z scores.

Column B shows the area included between the mean and the Z score listed in column A. Note that when Z is positive the area is located on the right side of the mean (Figure a in Table 10.4), whereas for a negative Z score the same area is located left of the mean (Figure b in Table 10.4).

Column C lists the proportion of the area included beyond the Z score that is represented in column A. Areas corresponding to positive Zs are on the right side of the curve (Figure a in Table 10.4). Areas corresponding to negative Z scores are identical except that they are on the left side of the curve (Figure b in Table 10.4).

---

*Standard Normal Table*   A table showing the area (the area shown as a proportion can be translated into a percentage) under the standard normal curve, corresponding to any Z score or its fraction.

---

Table 10.4 **The Standard Normal Table**

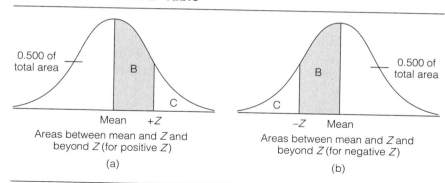

Areas between mean and Z and beyond Z (for positive Z)
(a)

Areas between mean and Z and beyond Z (for negative Z)
(b)

| (A) Z | (B) Area Between Mean and Z | (C) Area Beyond Z | (A) Z | (B) Area Between Mean and Z | (C) Area Beyond Z |
|---|---|---|---|---|---|
| 0.00 | 0.0000 | 0.5000 | 0.21 | 0.0832 | 0.4168 |
| 0.01 | 0.0040 | 0.4960 | 0.22 | 0.0871 | 0.4129 |
| 0.02 | 0.0080 | 0.4920 | 0.23 | 0.0910 | 0.4090 |
| 0.03 | 0.0120 | 0.4880 | 0.24 | 0.0948 | 0.4052 |
| 0.04 | 0.0160 | 0.4840 | 0.25 | 0.0987 | 0.4013 |
| 0.05 | 0.0199 | 0.4801 | 0.26 | 0.1026 | 0.3974 |
| 0.06 | 0.0239 | 0.4761 | 0.27 | 0.1064 | 0.3936 |
| 0.07 | 0.0279 | 0.4721 | 0.28 | 0.1103 | 0.3897 |
| 0.08 | 0.0319 | 0.4681 | 0.29 | 0.1141 | 0.3859 |
| 0.09 | 0.0359 | 0.4641 | 0.30 | 0.1179 | 0.3821 |
| 0.10 | 0.0398 | 0.4602 | | | |
| 0.11 | 0.0438 | 0.4562 | 0.31 | 0.1217 | 0.3783 |
| 0.12 | 0.0478 | 0.4522 | 0.32 | 0.1255 | 0.3745 |
| 0.13 | 0.0517 | 0.4483 | 0.33 | 0.1293 | 0.3707 |
| 0.14 | 0.0557 | 0.4443 | 0.34 | 0.1331 | 0.3669 |
| 0.15 | 0.0596 | 0.4404 | 0.35 | 0.1368 | 0.3632 |
| 0.16 | 0.0636 | 0.4364 | 0.36 | 0.1406 | 0.3594 |
| 0.17 | 0.0675 | 0.4325 | 0.37 | 0.1443 | 0.3557 |
| 0.18 | 0.0714 | 0.4286 | 0.38 | 0.1480 | 0.3520 |
| 0.19 | 0.0753 | 0.4247 | 0.39 | 0.1517 | 0.3483 |
| 0.20 | 0.0793 | 0.4207 | 0.40 | 0.1554 | 0.3446 |

### Transforming Z Scores into Proportions (or Percentages)

We illustrate how to use Appendix B with some simple examples, using our data on students' final statistics scores (see Table 10.2). The examples in this section are applications that require the transformation of Z scores into proportions (or percentages).

*Finding the Area Between the Mean and a Specified Positive Z Score*  Use the standard normal table to find the area between the mean and a specified positive Z score. To find the percentage of students whose scores range between the mean (70.07) and 85, follow these steps.

1. Convert 85 to a Z score:

$$Z = \frac{85 - 70.07}{10.27} = 1.45$$

2. Look up 1.45 in column A (in Appendix B) and find the corresponding area in column B, 0.4265. We can translate this proportion into a percentage ($0.4265 \times 100 = 42.65\%$) of the area under the curve included between the mean and a Z of 1.45 (see Figure 10.5).

3. Thus, 42.65 percent of the students scored between 70.07 and 85.

To find the exact number of students who scored between 70.07 and 85, multiply the proportion 0.4265 by the total number of students. Thus, approximately 512 students ($0.4265 \times 1,200 = 512$) obtained a score between 70.07 and 85.

*Finding the Area Between the Mean and a Specified Negative Z Score*  What is the percentage of students whose scores ranged between 65 and 70.07? We can use the standard normal table and the following steps to find out.

1. Convert 65 to a Z score:

$$Z = \frac{65 - 70.07}{10.27} = -0.49$$

2. Because the proportions that correspond to positive Z scores are identical to the proportions corresponding to negative Z scores, we ignore the negative sign of Z and look up 0.49 in column A. The area corresponding to a Z score of 0.49 is 0.1879. This indicates that 0.1879 of the area under the curve is included between the mean and a Z of −0.49 (see Figure 10.6). We convert this proportion to 18.79 percent ($0.1879 \times 100 = 18.79\%$).

3. Thus, approximately 225 ($0.1879 \times 1,200 = 225$) students obtained a score between 65 and 70.07.

Figure 10.5 **Finding the Area Between the Mean and a Specified Positive Z Score**

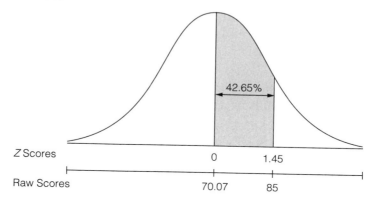

Figure 10.6 **Finding the Area Between the Mean and a Specified Negative Z Score**

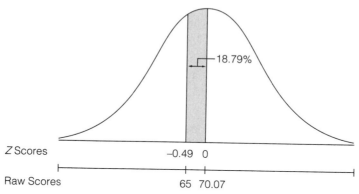

*Finding the Area Between Two Z Scores on the Same Side of the Mean* Suppose the grade of B was assigned to students who scored between 74 and 84. What is the percentage of students who obtained a B during the ten-year period for which the data were collected?

1. First, find the Z scores corresponding to 74 and 84:

$$Z = \frac{74 - 70.07}{10.27} = 0.38 \qquad Z = \frac{84 - 70.07}{10.27} = 1.36$$

2. Look up the areas corresponding to the $Z$ scores and find that 0.38 corresponds to an area of 0.1480 (14.80%) and that the area corresponding to a $Z$ of 1.36 is 0.4131 (41.31%). The area in which we are interested is shown in Figure 10.7.

3. To find the area highlighted in Figure 10.7, subtract the smaller area (the area corresponding to a $Z$ of 0.38 or 14.80%) from the larger area (the area corresponding to a $Z$ of 1.36 or 41.31%). Therefore, the area included between the scores of 74 and 84 is 41.31% − 14.80% = 26.51%.

4. Thus, 26.51 percent of all students scored between 74 and 84.

*Finding the Area Between Two Z Scores on Opposite Sides of the Mean* When the scores we are interested in lie on opposite sides of the mean, we add the areas together rather than subtract one from the other. For example, suppose we want to find the number of students who scored between 62 and 72.

1. First, find the $Z$ scores corresponding to 62 and 72:

$$Z = \frac{72 - 70.07}{10.27} = 0.19 \qquad Z = \frac{62 - 70.07}{10.27} = -0.79$$

2. Look up the areas corresponding to these $Z$ scores; 0.19 corresponds to an area of 0.0753 (or 7.53%) and the area corresponding to a $Z$ of −0.79 is 0.2852 (28.52%) (see Figure 10.8).

3. Because the scores are on opposite sides of the mean, add together the areas obtained in step 2. The total area between these scores is 7.53% + 28.52% = 36.05%.

4. The number of students who scored between 62 and 72 is 433 (1,200 × 0.3605).

*Finding the Area Above a Positive Z Score or Below a Negative Z Score* Over the last few years I have been involved in a project designed to improve the instruction of statistics on my campus. As part of this project I have compared students who have done very well or very poorly to get a better idea of how they compare with other students in the class.

To identify students who did very well, I selected all students who scored above 85. To find how many students scored above 85, I first converted 85 to a $Z$ score:

$$Z = \frac{85 - 70.07}{10.27} = 1.45$$

Thus, the $Z$ score corresponding to a final score of 85 in statistics is equal to 1.45.

Figure 10.7 **Finding the Area Between Two Z Scores on the Same Side of the Mean**

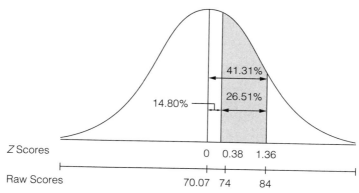

Figure 10.8 **Finding the Area Between Two Z Scores on Opposite Sides of the Mean**

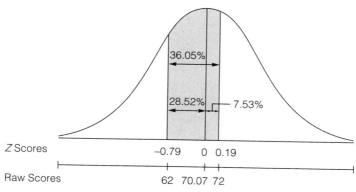

The area beyond a Z of 1.45 includes all students who scored above 85. This area is shown in Figure 10.9. To find the proportion of students whose scores fall into this area refer to the entry in column C that corresponds to a Z of 1.45, 0.0735. This means that 7.35 percent (0.0735 × 100 = 7.35%) of the students scored above 85. To find the exact number of students in this group, multiply the proportion 0.0735 by the total number of students. Thus, there were 1,200 × 0.0735, or about 88 students, who scored above 85 over the ten-year period.

Figure 10.9   **Finding the Area Above a Positive Z Score or Below a Negative Z Score**

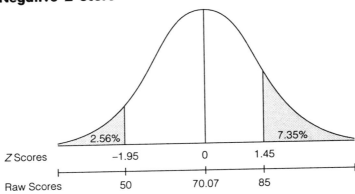

A similar procedure can be applied to identify the number of students who did not do well in the class. My cutoff point for poor performance in this class was the score of 50. To determine how many students did poorly I first converted 50 to a Z score:

$$Z = \frac{50 - 70.07}{10.27} = -1.95$$

The Z score corresponding to a final score of 50 is equal to –1.95. The area beyond a Z of –1.95 includes all students who scored below 50. This area is also shown in Figure 10.9. Locate the proportion of students in this area in column C, in the entry corresponding to a Z of 1.95. (Remember, the proportions corresponding to positive or negative Zs are identical.) This proportion is equal to 0.0256. Thus, 2.56 percent (0.0256 × 100 = 2.56%) of the group, or about 31 (0.0256 × 1,200) students, performed poorly in statistics.

## Transforming Proportions (or Percentages) into Z Scores

The examples in this section are applications that require transforming proportions (or percentages) into Z scores.

*Finding a Z Score Bounding an Area Above It*  Assuming that I assigned an A to the top 10 percent of the students, what would it take to get an A in the class? To answer this question we need to identify the cutoff point for the top 10 percent of the class. This problem involves two steps:

1. Find the $Z$ score that bounds the top 10 percent, or 0.1000 (0.1000 × 100 = 10%), of all the students who took statistics (see Figure 10.10).

    Refer to the areas under the normal curve, shown in Appendix B. First, look for an entry of 0.1000 (or the value closest to it) in column C. The entry closest to 0.1000 is 0.1003. Then locate the $Z$ in column A that corresponds to this proportion. The $Z$ score associated with the proportion 0.1003 is 1.28.

2. Find the final score associated with a $Z$ of 1.28.

    This involves transforming the $Z$ score into a raw score. In formula 10.2 (p. 450), we learned to transform a $Z$ score into a raw score by multiplying it by the standard deviation and adding the product to the mean. Thus,

$$Y = 70.07 + 1.28(10.27) = 70.07 + 13.15 = 83.22$$

The cutoff point for the top 10 percent of the class is the score of 83.22.

*Finding a Z Score Bounding an Area Below It*  Now let's assume that I assigned an F to the bottom 5 percent of the class. What would be the cutoff point for a failing score in statistics? Again, this problem involves two steps:

1. Find the $Z$ score that bounds the lowest 5 percent, or 0.0500, of all the students who took the class (see Figure 10.11).

    Refer to the areas under the normal curve, shown in Appendix B, and look for an entry of 0.0500 (or the value closest to it) in column C. The entry closest to 0.0500 is 0.0495 (0.0505 is equally distant; we choose one). Then locate the $Z$ in column A that corresponds to this proportion, 1.65. Because the area we are looking

Figure 10.10  **Finding a Z Score Bounding an Area Above It**

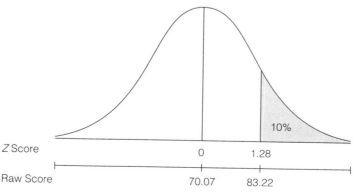

Figure 10.11  **Finding a Z Score Bounding an Area Below It**

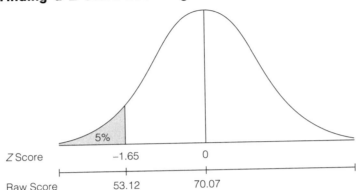

Z Score       −1.65       0

Raw Score     53.12      70.07

for is on the left side of the curve—that is, below the mean—the Z score is negative. Thus, the Z associated with the lowest 0.0500 (or 0.0495) is −1.65.

2. Find the final score associated with a Z of −1.65.
Convert the Z score to a raw score:

$$Y = 70.07 + (-1.65)(10.27) = 70.07 - 16.95 = 53.12$$

The cutoff for a failing score in statistics is 53.12.

---

**Learning Check.** *Can you find the number of students who got an A in the course? How many students failed?*

---

## Working with Percentiles

In Chapter 4 we defined percentiles as scores below which a specific percentage of the distribution falls. For example, the 95th percentile is a score that divides the distribution so that 95 percent of the cases are below it and 5 percent are above it. How are percentile ranks determined? How do you convert a percentile rank to a raw score? To determine the percentile rank of a raw score requires transforming Z scores into proportions or percentages. Converting percentile ranks to raw scores is based on transforming proportions or percentages into Z scores. In the following examples, we illustrate both procedures employing the statistics scores example.

*Finding the Percentile Rank of a Score Higher Than the Mean* Suppose you are one of the 1,200 students who took my statistics course. Your final score in the course was 85. How well did you do relative to the other students who took the class? To evaluate your performance your raw score must be translated into a percentile rank. Figure 10.12 illustrates this problem. To find the percentile rank of a score higher than the mean, follow these steps.

1. Convert the raw score to a Z score:

$$Z = \frac{85 - 70.07}{10.27} = 1.45$$

The Z score corresponding to a raw score of 85 is 1.45.

2. Find the area beyond Z in Appendix B, column C: the area beyond a Z score of 1.45 is 0.0735.

3. Subtract the area from 1.00 and multiply by 100 to obtain the percentile rank:

Percentile rank = (1.0000 − 0.0735 = 0.9265)100 = 92.65%

Being in the 92.65th percentile means that 92.65 percent of all the students enrolled in social statistics scored lower than 85 and 7.35 percent scored higher than 85.

*Finding the Percentile Rank of a Score Lower Than the Mean* Now let's say that you were unfortunate enough to obtain the score of 65 in the class. What is your percentile rank? To evaluate your performance your raw score must be translated into a percentile rank. Figure 10.13

Figure 10.12 **Finding the Percentile Rank of a Score Higher Than the Mean**

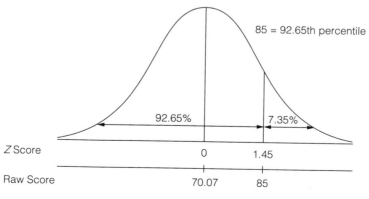

Figure 10.13   **Finding the Percentile Rank of a Score Lower Than the Mean**

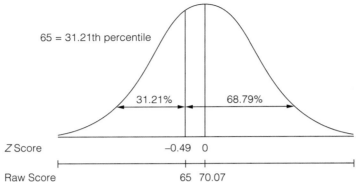

illustrates this problem. To find the percentile rank of a score lower than the mean follow these steps.

1.  Convert the raw score to a Z score:

$$Z = \frac{65 - 70.07}{10.27} = -0.49$$

    The Z score corresponding to a raw score of 65 is –0.49.

2.  Find the area beyond Z in Appendix B, column C: the area beyond a Z score of –0.49 is 0.3121.

3.  Multiply the area by 100 to obtain the percentile rank:

    Percentile rank = 0.3121(100) = 31.21%

    The 31.21th percentile rank means that 31.21 percent of all the students enrolled in social statistics did worse than you (that is, 31.21% scored lower than 65 but 68.79 percent scored higher than 65).

> **Learning Check.**   *In Chapter 4, we learned to identify percentiles using cumulative percentages in a distribution. Examine Table 10.2 and find the 92nd percentile. Does your answer differ from the results we obtained earlier (finding the percentile rank of a score higher than the mean)? If it does, explain why.*

*Finding the Raw Score Associated with a Percentile Higher Than 50*  Now let's assume that our graduate program in sociology will accept only students who scored at the 95th percentile. What is the cutoff point required for admission? Figure 10.14 illustrates this problem. To find the score associated with a percentile higher than 50 follow these steps.

1. Divide the percentile by 100 to find the area below the percentile rank:

$$\frac{95}{100} = 0.9500$$

2. Subtract the area below the percentile rank from 1.00 to find the area above the percentile rank:

$$1.0000 - 0.9500 = 0.0500$$

3. Find the Z score associated with the area above the percentile rank. Refer to the area under the normal curve, shown in Appendix B. First, look for an entry of 0.0500 (or the value closest to it) in column C. The entry closest to 0.0500 is 0.0495. Now locate the Z in column A that corresponds to this proportion, 1.65.

4. Convert the Z score to a raw score:

$$Y = 70.07 + 1.65(10.27) = 70.07 + 16.95 = 87.02$$

The final statistics score associated with the 95th percentile is 87.02. This means that you will need a score of 87.02 or higher to be admitted to the graduate program in sociology.

> **Learning Check.** *In a normal distribution, how many standard deviations from the mean is the 95th percentile? If you can't answer this question review the material in this section.*

Figure 10.14 **Finding the Raw Score Associated with a Percentile Higher Than 50**

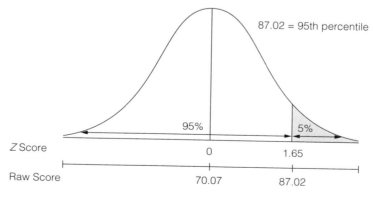

*Finding the Raw Score Associated with a Percentile Lower Than 50* Finally, what is the score associated with the 40th percentile? To find the percentile rank of a score lower than 50 follow these steps (see Figure 10.15).

1. Divide the percentile by 100 to find the area below the percentile rank:

$$\frac{40}{100} = 0.4000$$

2. Find the Z score associated with this area.

    Refer to the area under the normal curve, shown in Appendix B. First, look for an entry of 0.4000 (or the value closest to it) in column C. The entry closest to 0.4000 is 0.4013. Now locate the Z in column A that corresponds to this proportion. The Z score associated with the proportion 0.4013 is –0.25.

3. Convert the Z score to a raw score:

    $Y = 70.07 + (-0.25)(10.27) = 70.07 - 2.568 = 67.50$

The final statistics score associated with the 40th percentile is 67.50. This means that 40 percent of the students scored below 67.50 and 60 percent scored above it.

---

**Learning Check.** *What is the raw score in statistics associated with the 50th percentile?*

---

Figure 10.15 **Finding the Raw Score Associated with a Percentile Lower Than 50**

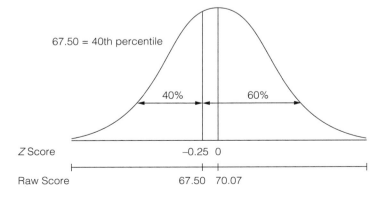

## A Final Note

In this chapter, we learned how the properties of the theoretical normal curve can be applied to describe important characteristics of empirical distributions that are approximately normal. The normal curve has practical applications as well. But the applications of the normal curve extend beyond the description of "real life" distributions. In subsequent chapters, we will see that the normal distribution also enables us to describe the characteristics of a theoretical distribution—the sampling distribution—of great significance in inferential statistics. The techniques learned in this chapter—transforming scores and finding areas under the normal curve—will be used in many of the procedures described in subsequent chapters. Make sure you understand these techniques before you proceed to the next chapter.

## MAIN POINTS

- The normal distribution is central to the theory of inferential statistics. It also provides a model for many empirical distributions that approximate normality.

- In all normal or nearly normal curves, we find a constant proportion of the area under the curve lying between the mean and any given distance from the mean when measured in standard deviation units.

- The standard normal distribution is a normal distribution represented in standard scores, or Z scores. Z scores express the number of standard deviations that a given score is above or below the mean. The proportions corresponding to any Z score or its fraction are organized into a special table called the standard normal table.

## KEY TERMS

*normal distribution*

*standard normal distribution*

*standard normal table*

*standard (Z) score*

## SPSS DEMONSTRATIONS

*Demonstration 1: Producing Z Scores with SPSS*

In this chapter, we discussed the theoretical normal curve, Z scores, and the relationship between raw scores and Z scores. The SPSS Descriptives procedure can calculate Z scores for any distribution. We'll use it to study the distribution of occupational prestige in the

1994 GSS file. Locate the Descriptives procedure within the *Statistics* menu, under *Summarize,* then *Descriptives.* The opening dialog box allows us to place one or more variables in the Variable(s): box, so we place PRESTG80 in this box. A checkbox in the bottom left corner tells SPSS to create standardized values, or *Z* scores, as new variables. Any new variable is placed in a new column in the Data Editor window and will then be available for additional analyses. Click on *OK* to run the procedure.

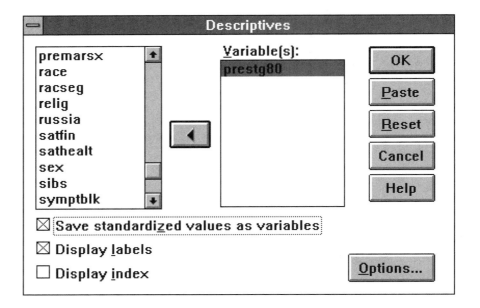

The output from Descriptives is fairly brief, listing the mean and standard deviation for PRESTG80, plus the minimum and maximum values and the number of valid cases. On the bottom half of the output SPSS tells the user that it has created a new *Z* score variable for PRESTG80. By default, SPSS appends a *Z* to the variable name, so the new variable is called ZPRESTG8. Notice how the last character of the old name, a "0," had to be dropped because SPSS has a limit of eight characters for any variable name.

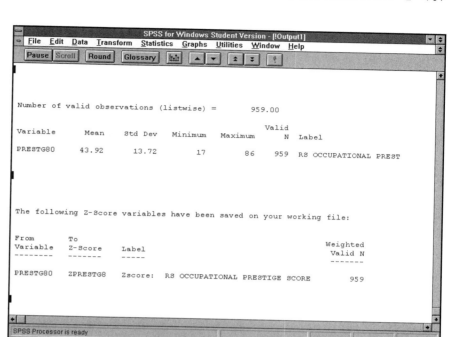

To see this new variable, switch to the Data Editor window by clicking on *Window* from the main menu, then on the file GSS94.SAV. Then go to the last column by pressing the End key.

The first case in the file has a $Z$ score of $-1.08706$, so the prestige score for this person must be below the mean of 43.92. If we scroll to the left, we see that the score for this person was 29 (not pictured), below the mean as we expected. Anywhere SPSS has placed a system missing value in the column for ZPRESTG8 it means that the original prestige score is missing.

If the data file is saved at this point, the new $Z$ score variable will be saved along with the original data and then can be used in analyses. And if we have SPSS calculate the mean and standard deviation of ZPRESTG8, we find that they are equal to 0 and 1.00, respectively.

*Demonstration 2: Producing Z Scores with the Compute Procedure*

SPSS calculated $Z$ scores for PRESTG80 using the same formula that we learned in this chapter. Let's do a bit more work and calculate the $Z$ scores with the standard formula. But in this case, we will tell SPSS the correct formula to use. The Compute procedure lets us define an equation and place the results of the equation in a new variable. To open the dialog box, click on *Transform* from the main menu, then *Compute.* There is a place to specify the name of the new variable (called Target Variable:) and a box, labeled Numeric Expression:, where the user defines the equation.

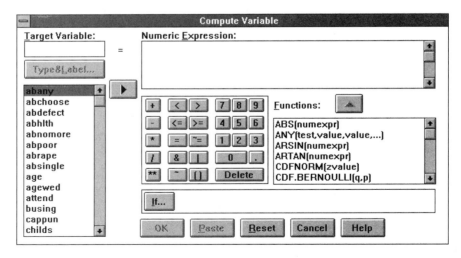

Type ZPREST in the Target Variable: box to name the new variable. Then type the expression *(PRESTG80-43.92/13.72)* in the Numeric Expression: box. If desired, use the list of variables and calculator pad to create the expression to avoid any typing mistakes. The dialog box should now look like the following figure.

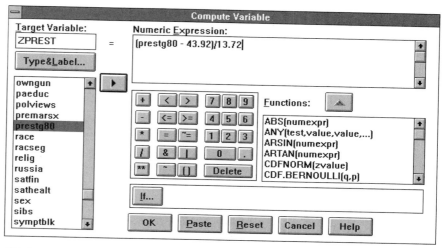

Click on *OK*. SPSS processes the equation and creates another new variable. To prove that this is the same equation used by SPSS in the Descriptives procedure, switch to the Data Editor window if it is not already open, then press the End key to go to the last column. We see that, within rounding error, the variables ZPRESTG8 and ZPREST are identical. Of course, it's usually much easier to have SPSS create the Z scores, but you will find the Compute procedure very helpful as you use SPSS to analyze data.

| | absingle | degree | libhomo | racseg | russia | sathealt | tempgen | union | zprestg8 | zprest | var |
|---|---|---|---|---|---|---|---|---|---|---|---|
| 1 | NO | LT HIG | REMOV | AGREE | DK,NA, | NAP | NAP | NAP | -1.08706 | -1.09 | |
| 2 | NO | HIGH S | NOT RE | DISAG | -1 | NAP | NAP | NAP | -.06680 | -.07 | |
| 3 | NAP | HIGH S | NAP | NAP | DK,NA, | NAP | NAP | NEIT | .00608 | .01 | |
| 4 | YES | HIGH S | REMOV | DISAG | DK,NA, | NAP | SOMEW | NEIT | .15183 | .15 | |
| 5 | NAP | LT HIG | NAP | NAP | DK,NA, | NAP | VERY D | R BE | -1.01418 | -1.01 | |
| 6 | NAP | GRAD | NAP | NAP | DK,NA, | NAP | DK | NEIT | 2.26524 | 2.27 | |
| 7 | YES | BACHE | NOT RE | DISAG | DK,NA, | NAP | NAP | NEIT | .44334 | .44 | |
| 8 | YES | BACHE | NOT RE | DISAG | DK,NA, | NAP | EXTRE | NAP | -.21255 | -.21 | |
| 9 | YES | BACHE | NOT RE | DISAG | DK,NA, | NAP | VERY D | NAP | .15183 | .15 | |
| 10 | YES | BACHE | NOT RE | DISAG | DK,NA, | NAP | NAP | NAP | .22471 | .22 | |
| 11 | DK | GRAD | NOT RE | DISAG | DK,NA, | NAP | VERY D | NEIT | 2.19236 | 2.19 | |
| 12 | YES | BACHE | NOT RE | DISAG | DK,NA, | SOME | NAP | NEIT | .58909 | .59 | |
| 13 | NAP | GRAD | NAP | NAP | -3 | QUITE A | NAP | NEIT | 2.19236 | 2.19 | |
| 14 | NO | LT HIG | REMOV | DISAG | -2 | NAP | NAP | NAP | .00608 | .01 | |
| 15 | NO | HIGH S | NOT RE | DK | +1 | NAP | NAP | NAP | . | . | |
| 16 | YES | BACHE | NOT RE | DISAG | DK,NA, | NAP | NAP | NAP | 1.46360 | 1.46 | |
| 17 | YES | BACHE | NOT RE | DISAG | DK,NA, | NAP | SOMEW | NAP | 1.17210 | 1.17 | |

SPSS for Windows Student Version - [c:\stattext\gss94.sav]

File   Edit   Data   Transform   Statistics   Graphs   Utilities   Window   Help

1:zprest   -1.08746355685131

SPSS Processor is ready

## EXERCISES

1. It is increasingly true that government agencies, on all levels, use examinations to screen applicants and remove bias from the hiring process. Consider a police department in a large midwestern city that uses such an examination to hire new officers. The mean score for all applicants this year on the exam is 98, with a standard deviation of 13. The distribution of scores for the applicants is approximately normal.
   a. Assume that only 12 percent of all applicants can be accepted this year. Will an applicant be accepted if his or her score on the exam is 115?
   b. What is the cutoff score of this year's test? In other words, what score is above 88 percent of all scores in the distribution?
   c. What is the $Z$ value for this score?

2. If a particular distribution you are studying is not normal, it may be difficult to determine the area under the curve of the distribution or translate a raw score into a $Z$ value. Is this statement true? Why or why not?

3. In 1990 the average population of all the countries in the world (192 countries altogether) was 27.3 million, with a standard deviation of 105.7.
   a. China's population in 1990 was 1,101 million (that is, 1 billion, 101 million). Assuming that the population distribution is basically normal, convert the value of China's population to a $Z$ score.
   b. For a normal distribution, what percentage of cases should fall less than 1 standard deviation below the mean, or equivalently, below a $Z$ score of −1? How many countries would fall below this value in 1990? (*Hint:* You don't need a listing of each country's population to answer this question.)
   c. What does your answer in (b) imply about the shape of the distribution of population for the 192 countries? When a distribution isn't normal, what statistic is a better measure of central tendency than the mean?

4. A social psychologist has developed a test to measure gregariousness. The test is normed so that it has a mean of 70 and a standard deviation of 20, and the gregariousness scores are normally distributed in the population of college students used to develop the test.
   a. What is the percentile rank of a score of 40?
   b. What percentage of scores falls between 35 and 90?
   c. What is the standard score for a test score of 65?
   d. What proportion of students should score above 115?

e. What is the cutoff score below which 87 percent of all scores fall?

5. The 1991 General Social Survey provides these statistics for the average income for males and females, plus their associated standard deviations:

| | Mean | Standard Deviation | N |
|---|---|---|---|
| Males | $22,052.51 | $17,734.92 | 434 |
| Females | $14,331.21 | $12,165.89 | 448 |

a. Assuming that income is normally distributed in the population, what proportion of males have incomes between $30,000 and $40,000? What proportion of females have incomes in the same range?

b. What is the probability that a male, drawn at random from the population, will have an income over $50,000? What is the equivalent probability for a female drawn at random?

c. Find the upper and lower income limits, centered around the mean, that will include 50 percent of all females.

d. If income is actually positively skewed in the population, how would that change your other answers?

6. The data in the following table display information for each state on two variables. Use the first variable concerning the living conditions of children in this problem. (Including District of Columbia, there are 51 scores.)

Severely distressed neighborhoods have been defined as having at least four of these five characteristics: a poverty rate above 27.5 percent; at least 39.6 percent of families headed by females; a high school dropout rate above 23.3 percent; more than 17 percent of families on welfare; and more than 46.5 percent of males out of the labor force (not working or seeking work). The percentage of children living in such neighborhoods, by state, is shown in the table.

| | % of Children in Distressed Neighborhoods | % of Eligible Voters Who Voted in the 1992 Election |
|---|---|---|
| Alabama | 9.6 | 54 |
| Alaska | 0.5 | 51 |

(continued)

| Arizona | 5.2 | 51 |
|---|---|---|
| Arkansas | 7.6 | 53 |
| California | 5.1 | 45 |
| Colorado | 2.5 | 62 |
| Connecticut | 5.7 | 63 |
| Delaware | 1.7 | 41 |
| D.C. | 25.2 | 47 |
| Florida | 4.6 | 49 |
| Georgia | 6.2 | 46 |
| Hawaii | 0.5 | 41 |
| Idaho | 0.0 | 53 |
| Illinois | 9.5 | 58 |
| Indiana | 3.0 | 54 |
| Iowa | 1.0 | 64 |
| Kansas | 2.0 | 62 |
| Kentucky | 7.1 | 53 |
| Louisiana | 17.2 | 59 |
| Maryland | 6.2 | 51 |
| Maine | 0.6 | 71 |
| Massachusetts | 5.1 | 60 |
| Michigan | 11.5 | 62 |
| Minnesota | 2.0 | 70 |
| Mississippi | 17.4 | 52 |
| Missouri | 5.2 | 62 |
| Montana | 2.3 | 69 |
| Nebraska | 1.3 | 62 |
| Nevada | 3.3 | 48 |
| New Hampshire | 0.1 | 62 |
| New Jersey | 4.9 | 54 |
| New Mexico | 4.5 | 51 |
| New York | 12.8 | 48 |
| North Carolina | 2.6 | 49 |
| North Dakota | 2.1 | 67 |
| Ohio | 8.1 | 60 |
| Oklahoma | 3.1 | 60 |
| Oregon | 1.1 | 55 |
| Pennsylvania | 6.9 | 54 |
| Rhode Island | 5.1 | 54 |
| South Carolina | 4.4 | 44 |
| South Dakota | 3.6 | 67 |
| Texas | 4.8 | 49 |

| Tennessee | 7.3 | 52 |
| Utah | 0.3 | 62 |
| Vermont | 0.6 | 64 |
| Virginia | 2.8 | 52 |
| Washington | 2.4 | 51 |
| West Virginia | 2.9 | 50 |
| Wisconsin | 5.4 | 68 |
| Wyoming | 0.2 | 62 |

(Data on children in distressed neighborhoods come from the *1994 Kids Count Data Book.*)

a. What are the mean and the standard deviation for the percentage of children in distressed neighborhoods for all states?

b. Using the information from (a), how many states fall more than $1\frac{1}{2}$ standard deviations above the mean? How does this number compare with the number expected from the theoretical normal curve distribution? Can you suggest anything these states have in common that might cause them to have more children in distressed neighborhoods?

c. How many states fall more than 1 standard deviation below the mean? Is this number greater or lower than the expected value from the theoretical normal curve? Again, can you suggest any characteristics these states have in common that might cause them to have fewer children in distressed neighborhoods?

d. (Extra Credit) Create a histogram of the percentages of children in distress. Does the distribution appear to be normal? Use this information to further explain why the number of states falling more than 1 standard deviation below the mean differs from the expected value.

7. Refer to the data in exercise 6 in Chapter 5 on the occupational prestige of whites and blacks. Assume that occupational prestige is normally distributed in each population.

a. What percentage of whites should have occupational prestige scores above 60?

b. What percentage of blacks should have occupational prestige scores above 60?

c. What proportion of whites have prestige scores between 30 and 70?

d. Given that the black sample size is 114, how many blacks in the sample have an occupational prestige score between 50 and 60?

8. SAT scores are normed so that, in any year, the mean of either the verbal or math test should be 500 and the standard deviation 100. Assuming this is true (it is only approximately true, both because of variation from year to year and because scores have decreased since the SAT tests were first developed), answer these questions.
   a. What percentage of students score above 625 on the math SAT in any given year?
   b. What percentage of students score between 400 and 600 on the verbal SAT?
   c. A college decides to liberalize its admission policy. As a first step, the admissions committee decides to exclude only those applicants scoring below the 20th percentile on the verbal SAT. Translate this percentile into a Z score. Then calculate the equivalent SAT verbal test score.

9. The Chicago police department was asked by the mayor's office to estimate the cost of crime to citizens of Chicago. The police began their study with the crime of burglary, taking a random sample of 500 files (there is too much crime to calculate statistics for all the crimes committed). They found the average dollar loss in a burglary was $678, with a standard deviation of $560, and that the dollar loss was normally distributed.
   a. What proportion of burglaries had dollar losses above $1,000?
   b. What percentage of burglaries had dollar losses between $200 and $300?
   c. What is the probability that any one burglary had a dollar loss above $400?

10. There is wide variation in the number of hours people work each week for many reasons. Using the 1994 General Social Survey, you find that the mean number of hours worked last week was 41.44 with a standard deviation of 13.95 hours, based on a sample size of 636.
   a. Assume that "hours worked" is approximately normally distributed in the sample. What is the probability that someone in the sample will work 80 or more hours in a week? How many people in the sample of 636 should have worked 80 or more hours?
   b. What is the probability that someone will work 30 or fewer hours in a week (that is, work part-time)? How many people does this represent in the sample?
   c. What number of hours worked per week corresponds to the 60th percentile?

11. A marketing company did a study of subscribers to magazines. It found that in their sample of 500 the mean number of magazines read each month was 12, with a variance of 16. Answer the questions assuming the distribution of the number of magazines read is normal.
   a. What is the Z score for a person who reads 20 magazines a month?
   b. What proportion of people read less than 10 magazines a month? How many does this correspond to in the sample?
   c. What number of magazines read per month corresponds to a Z score of −1.3?
   d. What is the percentage of people who read between 8 and 16 magazines a month?

12. A company tests applicants for a job by giving writing and software proficiency tests. The means and standard deviations for each exam follow, along with the scores for two applicants, Bill and Ted. Assume test scores are normally distributed.

| Exam | Mean | Standard Deviation | Bill | Ted |
|---|---|---|---|---|
| Writing | 56.4 | 9.3 | 65 | 67 |
| Software use | 68.7 | 5.6 | 70 | 75 |

   a. On which test did Bill do better, relative to the other applicants? Calculate appropriate statistics to answer this question.
   b. On which test did Ted do better, relative to the other applicants? Calculate statistics to answer this question.
   c. What proportion of applicants scored below Bill's Software Use test score?
   d. What is the percentile rank of Ted's Writing score of 67?

13. What is the value of the mean for any standard normal distribution? What is the value of the standard deviation for any standard normal distribution? Explain why this is true for any standard normal distribution.

14. You are asked to do a study of shelters for abused and battered women to determine the necessary capacity in your city to provide housing for most of these women. After recording data for a whole year, you find that the mean number of women in shelters each night is 250, with a standard deviation of 75. Fortunately, the distribution of the number of women in the shelters each night is normal, so you can answer these questions posed by the city council.

a. If the city's shelters have a capacity of 350, will that be enough places for abused women on 95 percent of all nights? If not, what number of shelter openings will be needed?

b. The current capacity is only 220 openings because some shelters have closed. What is the percentage of nights that the number of abused women seeking shelter will exceed current capacity?

## SPSS PROBLEMS

1. The majority of variables that social scientists study are not normally distributed. This doesn't typically cause problems in analysis when the goal of a study is to calculate means and standard deviations— as long as sample sizes are greater than about 50. (This will be discussed in later chapters.) But when characterizing the distribution of scores in *one* sample, or in a complete population (if this information is available), a non-normal distribution can cause complications. We can illustrate this point by examining the distribution of age in the GSS87_91 file.

   a. Access this file, then create a histogram for AGE with a superimposed normal curve. How does the distribution of AGE deviate from the theoretical normal curve?

   b. Calculate the mean and standard deviation for AGE in this sample, using either the Frequencies or Descriptives procedure.

   c. Assuming the distribution of AGE is normal, calculate the number of people who should be 25 years of age or less. SPSS can do this for you with a Compute statement, but it's probably just as easy to use a calculator.

   d. Now use Frequencies to get a table of the percentage of cases at each value of AGE to compare the theoretical calculation in (c) with the actual distribution of age in the sample. What percentage of people in the sample are 25 years old or less? Is this value close to what you calculated? Why might there be a discrepancy?

2. SPSS will calculate standard scores for any distribution. Examine the distribution of HRS1 (number of hours worked last week).

   a. Access the 1994 GSS file. Have SPSS calculate Z scores for HRS1.

   b. What is the equivalent Z score for someone who worked 60 hours last week?

   c. Use the Frequencies procedure to find the percentile rank, in this sample, for a score of 60.

d. Does the percentile rank you found from Frequencies correspond to the Z score for a value of 60? In other words, is the distribution of hours worked last week normal? If so, then the Z score SPSS calculates should be very close, after transforming it into an appropriate area, to the percentile rank for that same score.

e. Create histograms for HRS1 and the new variable ZHRS1. Explain why they have the same shape.

## GROUP PROBLEMS

1. Use the data you have collected from your classmates to examine the distribution of several interval-ratio variables.

    a. Choose several of these variables and calculate the mean and standard deviation.

    b. Assuming the distribution of these variables is normal, calculate Z scores for all the scores in each distribution. Share the workload by assigning one variable to each group member.

    c. Now compare the actual distribution of scores to the theoretical normal curve. Compare the number of scores for each variable 1 standard deviation above the mean and 1 standard deviation below the mean to the expected number from a normal curve. What do you find? Which variables better approximate a normal distribution? Which do not?

    d. Create histograms for each of the variables and examine their shapes in light of your results in (c). Explain how the histograms lead you to the same conclusion as your calculations.

    e. Discuss with group members why some variables more closely approximate a normal distribution than others. What factors might be affecting the shape of each distribution?

2. As you have probably observed in group problem 1, many social variables are not normally distributed. On the other hand, most standardized tests you have taken have distributions that are approximately normal (for example, IQ, ACT, and SAT tests). For that matter, even grades in a statistics class are often close to a normal distribution. Why would test scores be normally distributed but things like income, hours worked per week, and the number of children per family not be normally distributed? Discuss this question with group members and suggest some possible reasons.

## 11 Building Blocks of Inference: Sampling and Sampling Distributions

## ▦ ▦ ▦ ▦  Introduction

In previous chapters we learned about various methods to analyze observations. The examples we used to illustrate these methods were based on observations representing only a tiny fraction of all the observations that we might have chosen. But until now we have ignored the question of who or what should be observed or whether the conclusions based on the observations we chose can be generalized to a larger group of observations. The truth is that we are rarely able to study or observe everyone or everything we are interested in. Consider the following examples.

*Example 1*  The student union on your campus is trying to find out how it can better address the needs of commuter students and has commissioned you to conduct a needs assessment survey. You have been given enough money to survey about 500 students. Given that there are nearly 15,000 commuters on your campus, is this an impossible task?

*Example 2*  Your chancellor appointed a task force to investigate issues of concern to the lesbian, gay, and bisexual community at the university. The task force was charged with assessing the campus climate for members of these university communities and studying the coverage of lesbian, gay, and bisexual subjects in the curriculum. There are about 30,000 students, faculty, and staff on your campus and about 2,000 courses offered every year. How should the task force proceed?

What do these problems have in common? In both situations the major problem is that there is too much information and not enough time and money to collect and analyze all of it.

## Aims of Sampling[1]

Researchers in the social sciences almost never have enough time or money to collect information about the entire group that interests them. Known as the **population**, this group includes all the cases (individuals, objects, or groups) in which the researcher is interested. For example, in our first illustration the population is all 15,000 commuter students; the population in the second illustration consists of all 30,000 faculty, staff, and students on campus. Similarly, the National Opinion Research Center, which conducts the General Social Survey from which many of the examples in this book are selected, is interested in learning about the social and political beliefs of the population of all adult Americans.

Fortunately, we can learn a lot about a population if we carefully select a subset of it. This subset is called a **sample**. Through the process of *sampling*—selecting a subset of observations from the population of interest—we attempt to generalize to the characteristics of the larger group (population) based on what we learn from the smaller group (the sample). The term **parameter**, associated with the population, refers to measures used to describe the distribution of the population we are interested in. For instance, the average commuting time for *all* 15,000 students on your campus is a *population parameter* because it refers to a population characteristic in which you are interested. In previous chapters we learned many ways of describing a distribution, such as a proportion, a mean, or a standard deviation. When they describe the population distribution these measures are referred to as parameters. Thus, a population mean, a population proportion, and a population standard deviation are all population parameters.

---

*Population*   A group that includes all the cases (individuals, objects, or groups) in which the researcher is interested.

*Sample*   A relatively small subset selected from a population.

---

We use the term sample **statistic** when referring to a corresponding characteristic calculated for the sample. For example, the average commuting time for a *sample* of commuter students is a sample

---

[1]This discussion benefited from a more extensive presentation on the aims of sampling, in Richard Maisel and Caroline Hodges Persell, *How Sampling Works.* Thousand Oaks, CA: Pine Forge Press, 1996.

statistic. Similarly, a sample mean, a sample proportion, and a sample standard deviation are all sample statistics. In this and the following chapter we will discuss some of the principles involved in generalizing results from samples to the population. In our discussion we will use different notations when referring to population parameters. The following list presents the sample notation and the corresponding population notation.

| Measure | Sample Notation | Population Notation |
|---|---|---|
| Mean | $\overline{Y}$ | $\mu_Y$ |
| Proportion | $p$ | $\pi$ |
| Standard deviation | $S_Y$ | $\sigma_Y$ |
| Variance | $S_Y^2$ | $\sigma_Y^2$ |

The distinctions between a sample and a population and between a parameter and a statistic are also illustrated in Figure 11.1. For illustration, Figure 11.1 presents both the population and the population

Figure 11.1 **The Proportion of White Respondents in a Population and in a Sample**

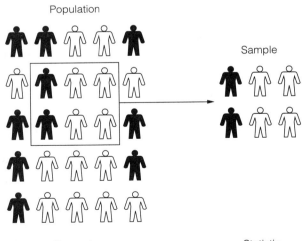

Population

Sample

Parameter

Proportion of white respondents in the population

$$\pi = \frac{15}{25} = .60$$

Statistic

Proportion of white respondents in the sample

$$p = \frac{4}{6} = .67$$

parameter. However, we almost never have enough time or money to collect information about the population. Therefore, we rarely know the value of the parameter. The goal of most research is to find the population parameter. Researchers usually select a sample from the population of interest and obtain an estimate of the population parameter from that sample. The major objective of sampling theory and statistical inference is to provide estimates of unknown parameters from sample statistics that can be easily calculated.

---

*Parameter*   A measure (for example, mean or standard deviation) used to describe the population distribution.

*Statistic*   A measure (for example, mean or standard deviation) used to describe the sample distribution.

---

*Learning Check.*   *It is important that you understand what the terms* population, sample, parameter, *and* statistic *mean. Pretend you are trying to explain these terms to someone else. Use your own words so the meaning makes sense to you. If you cannot clearly define these terms, review the preceding material. You will see these sample and population notations over and over again. If you memorize them, you will find it much easier to understand the formulas used in inferential statistics.*

## Some Basic Principles of Probability

In the following sections, we will discuss a variety of techniques adopted by social scientists to select samples from populations. These techniques all follow a general approach called *probability sampling.* Before we discuss these techniques we will review some basic principles of probability.

We all use the concept of probability in everyday conversation. We might ask, "What is the probability that it will rain tomorrow?" or "What is the likelihood that we will do well on a test?" In everyday conversations our answers to these questions are rarely systematic, but in the study of statistics *probability* has a far more precise meaning.

Probability theory applies to situations in which we can specify the possible outcomes resulting from a certain situation or task. For example, the task of rolling a die has six possible outcomes: 1, 2, 3, 4, 5, 6. The task of flipping a coin results in either of two outcomes: heads or tails. For any such situation or task, the probability of an outcome occurring is defined as the ratio (over the long run) of the number of times the desired outcome can occur relative to the total number of times all the outcomes can occur. Probability estimates outcomes as the number of trials becomes infinite. For instance, over the long run, the probability of getting heads when flipping an evenly balanced coin is 1 to 2, or $\frac{1}{2}$, because heads can occur only once within a total of two possible outcomes (heads and tails). Similarly, over the long run, the probability of rolling a 3 on a die is $\frac{1}{6}$ because the outcome "3" can occur only once within a total of 6 possible equally likely outcomes.

Probabilities are usually measured in terms of proportions. A ratio can be converted to a proportion by dividing its numerator by the denominator. Thus, the probability of $\frac{1}{2}$ is equivalent to .500 ($\frac{1}{2}$ = .500); similarly, .167 corresponds to the ratio $\frac{1}{6}$ ($\frac{1}{6}$ = .167). Probabilities can range from 0 to 1. The closer the probability is to 1, the more likely it is that the event will occur. A probability that is close to 0 means that an event is highly unlikely.

> **Learning Check.**  *What is the probability of drawing an ace out of a normal deck of 52 playing cards? No, it's not $\frac{1}{52}$. There are four aces so the probability of drawing one of them is $\frac{4}{52}$ or $\frac{1}{13}$. The proportion is .077. The probability of drawing the ace of spades is $\frac{1}{52}$.*

## Probability Sampling

Social researchers are usually much more systematic in their effort to obtain samples that are representative of the population than we are when we gather information in our everyday life. Such researchers have adopted a number of approaches for selecting samples from populations. Only one general approach, *probability sampling,* allows the researcher to use the principles of statistical inference to generalize from the sample to the population. **Probability sampling** is a method that enables the researcher to specify for each case in the population the probability of its inclusion in the sample. The purpose of probability sampling is to select a sample that is as representative as possible of the population. The sample is selected in such a way as to allow use of the principles of probability to evaluate the generalizations made from the sample to the population. A probability sample design enables the researcher to estimate the extent to which the findings based on one sample are likely to differ from what would be found by studying the entire population.

---

*Probability Sampling*   A method of sampling that enables the researcher to specify for each case in the population the probability of its inclusion in the sample.

---

Although accurate estimates of sampling error can be made only from probability samples, social scientists often use nonprobability samples because they are more convenient and cheaper to collect. Nonprobability samples are useful under many circumstances for a variety of research purposes. Their main limitation is that they do not allow the use of the method of inferential statistics to generalize from the sample to the population. Because in this and the next chapter we deal only with inferential statistics, we do not discuss nonprobability sampling. In the next two sections,[2] we will learn about three sampling designs that follow the principles of probability sampling: the simple random sample, the stratified random sample, and the systematic random sample.

## The Simple Random Sample

The *simple random sample* is the most basic probability sampling design, and it is incorporated into all the more elaborate probability sampling designs. A **simple random sample** is a sample design chosen in such a way as to ensure that (1) every member of the population has an equal chance of being chosen, and (2) every combination of $N$ members has an equal chance of being chosen.

Let's take a very simple example to illustrate. Suppose we are conducting a cost-containment study of the ten hospitals in our region, and we want to draw a sample of two hospitals to study intensively. We can put into a hat ten slips of paper, each representing one of the ten hospitals and mix the slips carefully. We select one slip out of the hat, identify the hospital it represents and replace it in the hat. We

---

[2]The discussion in these sections is based on Chava Frankfort-Nachmias and David Nachmias, *Research Methods in the Social Sciences.* New York: St. Martin's Press, 1996, 183–194.

then make the second draw and select another slip out of the hat and identify it. The two hospitals we identified on the two draws become the two members of our sample. The sample is a simple random sample because—assuming we made sure the slips were really well mixed—(1) pure chance determined which hospital was selected; (2) every hospital had the same chance of being selected as a member of our sample of two; and (3) every combination of ($N = 2$) hospitals was equally likely to be chosen.

---

**Simple Random Sample**   A sample designed in such a way as to ensure that (1) every member of the population has an equal chance of being chosen, and (2) every combination of $N$ members has an equal chance of being chosen.

---

Researchers usually use computer programs or tables of random numbers in selecting random samples. An abridged table of random numbers is reproduced in Appendix A. To use a random number table, list each member of the population and assign the member a number. Begin anywhere on the table and read each digit that appears in the table in order—up, down, or sideways; the direction does not matter, as long as it follows a consistent path. Whenever we come across a digit in the table of random digits that corresponds to the number of a member in the population of interest, this member is selected for the sample. Continue this process until the desired sample size is reached.

*Example 3*  Selecting a Simple Random Sample.

In your job as a hospital administrator you conduct a cost-containment study by examining patients' records. There are a total of 300 patients' records from which a simple random sample of 5 is to be drawn. You follow these steps:

1. Number the patient accounts, beginning with 001 for the first account and ending with 300, which represents the three-hundredth account.

2. Use some random process to enter Appendix A (you might close your eyes and point a pencil). For our illustration let's start with the first column of numbers. Notice that each column lists five-digit numbers. Because your population contains only three-digit numbers (001–300), drop the last two digits of each number and read only three-digit numbers from the table. Let's read the first three digits in each group of numbers (you could choose any other group of three-digit numbers in this block—for example, the last three digits in the block).

3. Dropping the last two digits of each five-digit block and proceeding down the column, you obtain the following three-digit numbers:

104*
223*
241*
421
375
779
995
963
895
854
289*
635
094*

Among these numbers, five correspond to numbers within the range of numbers assigned to the patient records. They are starred. The last number listed is 094 from line 13. You do not need to list more numbers because you already have five different numbers that qualify for inclusion in the sample. The starred numbers represent the records you will choose for your sample because these are the only ones that fall between 001 and 300, the range you specified.

4. We now have five records in our simple random sample. Let's list them: 104, 223, 241, 289, and 094.

## The Systematic Random Sample

Now let's look at a sampling method that is easier to implement than a simple random sample. The *systematic random sample,* although it is not a true probability sample, provides results very similar to those obtained with a simple random sample. It uses a ratio, K, obtained by dividing the population size by the desired sample size:

$$K = \frac{\text{Population size}}{\text{Sample size}}$$

**Systematic random sampling** is a method of sampling in which every *k*th member in the total population is chosen for inclusion in the sample after the first member of the sample is selected at random from the first *k* members in the population.

For instance, in Example 1 (p. 480), we had 15,000 commuting students in our population and our sample was limited to 500. Therefore:

$$K = \frac{15,000}{500} = 30$$

---

*Systematic Random Sampling*  A method of sampling in which every *k*th member (*K* is a ratio obtained by dividing the population size by the desired sample size) in the total population is chosen for inclusion in the sample after the first member of the sample is selected at random from the first *k* members in the population.

---

Using a systematic random sampling method, we first choose any one student at random from the first 30 students on the list of commuting students. Then we select every 30th student after that until we reach 500, our desired sample size. Suppose that our first student selected at random happens to be the 8th student on the list. The second student in our sample is then 38th on the list (8 + 30 = 38). The third would be 38 + 30 = 68, the fourth, 68 + 30 = 98, and so on. The systematic random sample is illustrated in Figure 11.2.

**Learning Check.**  *How does a systematic random sample differ from a simple random sample?*

## The Stratified Random Sampling

A third type of probability sampling is the *stratified random sample*. We obtain a **stratified random sample** by (1) dividing the population into subgroups based on one or more variables central to our analysis and (2) then drawing a simple random sample from each of the subgroups. We could stratify by race/ethnicity, for example, by dividing the population into different racial/ethnic groups and then drawing a simple random sample from each group. For instance, suppose we want to compare the attitudes of Hispanics toward abortion with the attitudes of white and black respondents. Our population of interest consists of 1,000 individuals, with 700 (or 70%) whites, 200 (20%) blacks, and 100 (10%) Hispanics. Because we know the proportion of

Figure 11.2 **Systematic Random Sampling**

From a population of 40 students, let's select a systematic random sample of 8 students. Our skip interval will be 5 (40 ÷ 8 = 5). Using a random number table, we choose a number between 1 and 5. Let's say we choose 4. We then start with student 4 and pick every 5th student:

Our trip to the random number table could have just as easily given us a 1 or a 5, so all the students do have a chance to end up in our sample.

each subgroup in the population, we may want to draw a stratified sample that would reflect these exact proportions. For instance ,we can draw a stratified sample size of $N = 180$ that includes 126 (70%) whites, 36 (20%) blacks, and 18 (10%) Hispanics. In such a **proportionate stratified sample**, the size of the sample selected from each subgroup is proportional to the size of that subgroup in the entire population.

In a **disproportionate stratified sample**, the size of the sample selected from each subgroup is deliberately made disproportional to the size of that subgroup in the population. For instance, for our example, we could select a sample ($N = 180$) consisting of 90 whites (50%), 45 blacks (25%), and 45 Hispanics (25%). In such a sampling design, even though the sampling probabilities for each population member are not equal (they vary between groups) they are *known* and therefore we can make accurate estimates of error in the inference process.[3] Disproportionate stratified sampling is especially useful when we want to compare subgroups with each other, and when the size

[3]We discuss more on sampling error in the next section.

of some of the subgroups in the population is relatively small. Proportionate sampling can result in the sample having too few members from small subgroup to yield reliable information about them.

---

*Stratified Random Sample*   A method of sampling obtained by (1) dividing the population into subgroups based on one or more variables central to our analysis and (2) then drawing a simple random sample from each of the subgroups.

*Proportionate Stratified Sample*   The size of the sample selected from each subgroup is proportional to the size of that subgroup in the entire population.

*Disproportionate Stratified Sample*   The size of the sample selected from each subgroup is disproportional to the size of that subgroup in the population.

---

**Learning Check.**   *Can you think of some research questions that could best be studied using a disproportionate stratified random sample? When might it be important to use a proportionate stratified random sample?*

---

### Box 11.1  Disproportionate Stratified Samples and Diversity

Disproportionate stratified sampling is especially useful given the increasing diversity of American society. In a diverse society, factors such as race, ethnicity, class, and gender, as well as other categories of experience like age, religion, and sexual preference, become central in shaping our experiences and defining the differences among us. These factors are an important dimension of the social structure, and they not only operate independently but also are experienced simultaneously by all of us.* For example, if you are a white woman you may share some common experiences with a woman of color based on your gender, but your racial experiences are going to be different. Moreover, your experiences within the race/gender system are further conditioned by your social class. Similarly, if you are a man, your experiences are shaped as much by your class, race, and sexual preference as they are by your gender. If you are a black gay man, for instance, you might not benefit equally from patriarchy compared with a classmate who is a white heterosexual male.

What are the research implications of an inclusive approach that emphasizes social differences? Such an approach will include women and men in a study of race; Hispanics and people of color when considering class; and women and men of color when studying gender. Furthermore, such an approach make the experience of previously excluded groups more visible and central because it puts those who have been excluded at the center of the analysis so that we can better understand the experience of all groups, including those with privilege and power.

What are the sampling implications of such an approach? Let's think of an example. Suppose you are looking at the labor force experiences of black and Hispanic women who are over 50 years of age, and you want to compare these experiences with those of white women in the same age group. Both Hispanic and black women compose a small proportion of the population. A proportional sample probably would not include enough Hispanic or black women to provide an adequate basis for comparison with white women. To make such comparisons, it would be desirable to draw a disproportionate stratified sample that deliberately overrepresents both Hispanic and black women so that they are sampled with sufficient size (see Figure 11.3).

**Figure 11.3** **A Random Sample Stratified by Race/Ethnicity**

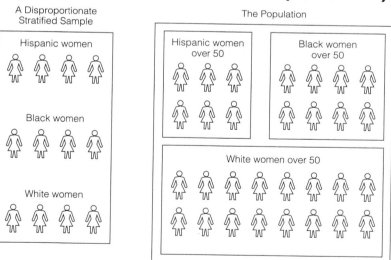

*Margaret L. Andersen and Patricia Hill Collins, *Race, Class, and Gender.* Belmont, CA: Wadsworth, 1992, 1–6.

## The Concept of Sampling Distribution

We began this chapter with a few examples illustrating why researchers in the social sciences almost never collect information on the entire population that interests them. Instead, they usually select a sample from that population and use the principles of statistical inference to estimate the characteristics, or parameters, of that population based on the characteristics, or statistics, of the sample. In this section, we describe one of the most important concepts in statistical inference—*sampling distribution*. The sampling distribution helps estimate the likelihood of our sample statistics and, therefore, enables us to generalize from the sample to the population.

### The Population

To illustrate the concept of the sampling distribution, let's consider as our population the twenty individuals listed in Table 11.1.[4] Our variable, $Y$, is the income (in dollars) for these twenty individuals, and the parameter we are trying to estimate is the mean income.

We use the symbol $\mu_Y$ to represent the population mean; the Greek letter mu ($\mu$) stands for the mean, and the subscript $Y$ identifies the specific variable, income. Using formula 4.1, calculate the population mean:

$$\mu_Y = \frac{\sum Y}{N} = \frac{Y_1 + Y_2 + Y_3 + Y_4 + Y_5 + \cdots + Y_{20}}{20}$$

$$= \frac{11,350 + 7,859 + 41,654 + 13,445 + 17,458 + \cdots + 25,671}{20}$$

$$= 22,766$$

Using formula 5.3, we can also calculate the standard deviation for this population distribution. We use the Greek symbol sigma ($\sigma$) to represent the population's standard deviation and the subscript $Y$ to stand for our variable, income:

$$\sigma_Y = 14,687$$

---

[4]The population of the twenty individuals presented in Table 11.1 is considered a finite population. A finite population consists of a finite (countable) number of elements (observations). Other examples of finite populations include all women in the labor force in 1996 and all public hospitals in New York City. A population is considered infinite when there is no limit to the number of elements it can include. Examples of infinite populations include all women in the labor force, in the past or the future. Most samples studied by social scientists come from finite populations. However, it is also possible to sample from an infinite population.

Table 11.1 **The Population: Personal Income for Twenty Individuals (hypothetical data)**

| Individual | Income ($Y$) |
|---|---|
| Case 1 | 11,350 ($Y_1$) |
| Case 2 | 7,859 ($Y_2$) |
| Case 3 | 41,654 ($Y_3$) |
| Case 4 | 13,445 ($Y_4$) |
| Case 5 | 17,458 ($Y_5$) |
| Case 6 | 8,451 ($Y_6$) |
| Case 7 | 15,436 ($Y_7$) |
| Case 8 | 18,342 ($Y_8$) |
| Case 9 | 19,354 ($Y_9$) |
| Case 10 | 22,545 ($Y_{10}$) |
| Case 11 | 25,345 ($Y_{11}$) |
| Case 12 | 68,100 ($Y_{12}$) |
| Case 13 | 9,368 ($Y_{13}$) |
| Case 14 | 47,567 ($Y_{14}$) |
| Case 15 | 18,923 ($Y_{15}$) |
| Case 16 | 16,456 ($Y_{16}$) |
| Case 17 | 27,654 ($Y_{17}$) |
| Case 18 | 16,452 ($Y_{18}$) |
| Case 19 | 23,890 ($Y_{19}$) |
| Case 20 | 25,671 ($Y_{20}$) |
| Mean ($\mu_Y$) = 22,766 | Standard deviation ($\sigma_Y$) = 14,687 |

Of course, most of the time we do not have access to the population. So instead, we draw one sample, compute the mean—the statistic —for that sample, and use it to estimate the population mean— the parameter.

### The Sample

Let's pretend that $\mu_Y$ is unknown and that we estimate its value by drawing a random sample of three individuals ($N = 3$) from the population of twenty individuals and calculate the mean income for that sample. The incomes included in that sample are as follows:

|  |  |
|---|---|
| Case 8 | 18,342 |
| Case 16 | 16,456 |
| Case 17 | 27,654 |

Now let's calculate the mean for that sample:

$$\overline{Y} = \frac{18,342 + 16,456 + 27,654}{3} = 20,817$$

Notice that our sample mean ($\overline{Y}$), $20,817, differs from the actual population parameter, $22,766. This discrepancy is due to sampling error. **Sampling error** is the discrepancy between a sample estimate of a population parameter and the real population parameter. By comparing the sample statistic with the population parameter we can determine the sampling error. The sampling error for our example is 1,949 (22,766 − 20,817 = 1,949).

Now let's select another random sample of three individuals. This time the incomes included are

| Case 15 | 18,923 |
| Case 5 | 17,458 |
| Case 17 | 27,654 |

The mean for this sample is

$$\overline{Y} = \frac{18,923 + 17,458 + 27,654}{3} = 21,345$$

The sampling error for this sample is 1,421 (22,766 − 21,345 = 1,421), somewhat less than the error for the first sample we selected.

## The Dilemma

Although comparing the sample estimates of the average income with the actual population average is a perfect way to evaluate the accuracy of our estimate, in practice we rarely have information about the actual population parameter. If we did, we would not need to conduct a study! Moreover, few, if any, sample estimates correspond exactly to the actual population parameter. So this then is our dilemma: If sample estimates vary and if most estimates result in some sort of sampling error, how much confidence can we place in the estimate? On what basis can we infer from the sample to the population?

---

*Sampling Error*    The discrepancy between a sample estimate of a population parameter and the real population parameter.

---

## The Sampling Distribution

The answer to this dilemma is to use a device known as the *sampling distribution*. The **sampling distribution** is a theoretical probability distribution of all possible sample values for the statistic in which we are interested. If we were to draw all possible random samples of the same size from our population of interest, compute the statistic for each sample, and plot the frequency distribution for that statistic, we would obtain an approximation of the sampling distribution. Every statistic—for example, a proportion, a mean, or a variance—has a sampling distribution. Because it includes all possible sample values, the sampling distribution enables us to compare our sample result with other sample values and determine the likelihood associated with that result.[5]

---

*Sampling Distribution*    A theoretical probability distribution of all possible sample values for the statistic in which we are interested.

---

## The Sampling Distribution of the Mean

Sampling distributions are theoretical distributions, which means that they are never really observed. Constructing an actual sampling distribution would involve taking all possible random samples of a fixed size from the population. This process would be very tedious because it would involve a very large number of samples. However, to help grasp the concept of the sampling distribution, let's illustrate how one could be generated from a limited number of samples.

## An Illustration

For our illustration we use one of the most common sampling distributions—the sampling distribution of the mean. The **sampling distribution of the mean** is a theoretical distribution of sample means

---

[5]Here we are using an idealized example in which the sampling distribution is actually computed. However, please bear in mind that in practice one never computes a sampling distribution because it is also infinite.

that would be obtained by drawing from the population all possible samples of the same size.

Let's go back to our example in which our population is made up of twenty individuals and their incomes. From that population (Table 11.1), we now randomly draw fifty possible samples of size 3, computing the mean income for each sample and replacing it before drawing another. (In drawing these random samples we follow the procedure for drawing a simple random sample as described on page 486. In our first sample of size 3 we draw the following three incomes: $8,451, $41,654, and $18,923. The mean income for this sample is

$$\overline{Y} = \frac{8,451 + 41,654 + 18,923}{3} = 23,009$$

Now let's restore these individuals to the original list and select a second sample of three other individuals. The mean income for this sample is

$$\overline{Y} = \frac{15,436 + 25,345 + 16,456}{3} = 19,079$$

We repeat this process forty-eight more times, each time computing the sample mean and restoring the sample to the original list. In Table 11.2 we list the means of the first five and the fiftieth samples of $N = 3$ that were drawn from the population of twenty individuals. (Please note that $\Sigma \overline{Y}$ refers to the sum of all the means computed for each of the samples.)

The grouped frequency distribution for all fifty sample means is displayed in Table 11.3, and Figure 11.4 is a histogram of this distribution.

Table 11.2 **Mean Income of Fifty Samples of Size 3**

| Sample | Mean ($\overline{Y}$) |
|---|---|
| First | 23,009 |
| Second | 19,079 |
| Third | 18,873 |
| Fourth | 26,885 |
| Fifth | 21,847 |
| . | . |
| . | . |
| . | . |
| Fiftieth | 26,645 |
| Total ($N$) = 50 | $\Sigma \overline{Y}$ = 1,237,482 |

Table 11.3 **Sampling Distribution of Sample Means for Sample Size N = 3 Drawn for the Population of Twenty Individuals' Incomes**

| Sample Mean Intervals | Frequency | Percentages (%) |
|---|---|---|
| 11,500–15,500 | 6 | 12 |
| 15,500–19,500 | 7 | 14 |
| 19,500–23,500 | 14 | 28 |
| 23,500–27,500 | 4 | 8 |
| 27,500–31,500 | 9 | 18 |
| 31,500–35,500 | 7 | 14 |
| 35,500–39,500 | 1 | 2 |
| 39,500–43,500 | 2 | 4 |
| Total (N) | 50 | 100 |

Figure 11.4 **Sampling Distribution of Sample Means for Sample Size N = 3 Drawn from the Population of Twenty Individuals' Incomes**

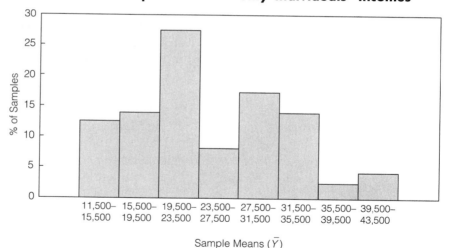

Sample Means ($\bar{Y}$)

This distribution is an example of a sampling distribution of the mean. Notice that in its structure the sampling distribution resembles a frequency distribution of raw scores, except that here each score is a sample mean and the corresponding frequencies are the number of samples with that particular mean value. For example, the third interval in Table 11.3 ranges from $19,500 to $23,500, with a corresponding frequency of 14, or 28 percent. This means that we drew 14 samples (28%) with means ranging between $19,500 and $23,500.

Remember, the distribution depicted in Table 11.3 and Figure 11.4 is an empirical distribution, whereas the sampling distribution is a theoretical distribution. In reality, we never really construct the sampling distribution. However, even this simple empirical example serves to illustrate some of the most important characteristics of the sampling distribution.

---

*Sampling Distribution of the Mean*   A theoretical probability distribution of sample means that would be obtained by drawing from the population all possible samples of the same size.

---

## Review

Before we continue let's take a moment to review the three distinct types of distribution involved in our discussion.

*The Population*   We began with the *population distribution* of twenty individuals. This is a distribution that actually exists; it is an empirical distribution, which usually is unknown to us. We are interested in estimating the mean income for this population.

*The Sample*   We drew a sample from that population. The *sample distribution* is an empirical distribution that is known to us and is used to help us estimate the mean of the population. We selected fifty samples of $N = 3$ and calculated their mean income. We usually use the sample mean ($\overline{Y}$) as an estimate of the population mean ($\mu_Y$).

*The Sampling Distribution of the Mean*   For illustration, we generated an approximation of the sampling distribution of the mean, consisting of fifty samples of $N = 3$. The *sampling distribution of the mean* does not really exist (it is nonempirical).

To help you understand the relationship between the population, the sample, and the sampling distributions, we have illustrated in Figure 11.5 the process of generating an empirical sampling distribution of the mean. From a population of raw scores ($Y$'s), we draw $n$ samples of size $N$ and calculate the mean of each sample. The resulting

Figure 11.5 **Generating the Sampling Distribution of the Mean**

From a population (with a population mean of $\mu_Y$) we start drawing samples and calculating the means for those samples:

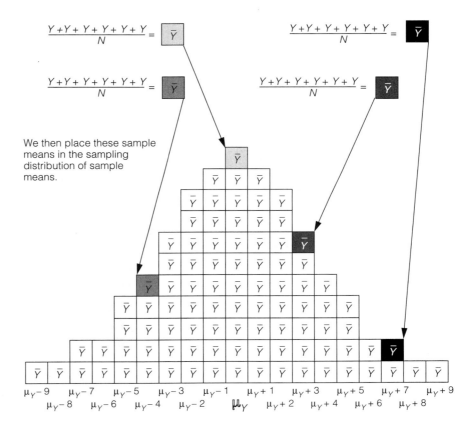

We then place these sample means in the sampling distribution of sample means.

Once we lay all of the sample means out onto the sampling distribution, we notice a few things:

1. The mean of this distribution is $\mu_Y$, the mean for the population of scores.
2. Most of the sample means fall fairly near $\mu_Y$: the probability of pulling such sample means is high.
3. As we move farther and farther away from $\mu_Y$ on either side, we have fewer and fewer sample means: the probability of pulling such sample means is low.

sampling distribution of the mean based on $n$ samples of size $N$, shows the values that the mean could take and the frequency (number of samples) associated with each value. Make sure you understand these relationships. The concept of the sampling distribution is crucial to understanding statistical inference. In this and the next chapter, we learn how to employ the sampling distribution to draw inferences from the sample to the population.

## The Mean of the Sampling Distribution

Like the sample and population distributions, the sampling distribution can be described in terms of its mean and standard deviation. We use the symbol $\mu_{\bar{Y}}$ to represent the mean of the sampling distribution. The subscript $\bar{Y}$ indicates that the variable of this distribution is the mean. To obtain the mean of the sampling distribution, add all the individual sample means ($\sum \bar{Y} = 1{,}237{,}482$) and divide by the number of samples ($N = 50$). Thus, the mean of the sampling distribution of the mean is actually the mean of means:

$$\mu_{\bar{Y}} = \frac{\sum \bar{Y}}{N} = \frac{1{,}237{,}482}{50} = 24{,}750$$

---

*Population, Sample, and Sampling Distribution Symbols*  In the discussions that follow we make frequent references to the mean and standard deviation of the three distributions. To distinguish among the different distributions, the symbols that refer to the means and standard deviations for the sample, population, and sampling distributions follow. Notice that we use Greek letters to refer to both the sampling and the population distributions.

|  | Mean | Standard Deviation |
|---|---|---|
| Sample distribution | $\bar{Y}$ | $S_Y$ |
| Population distribution | $\mu_Y$ | $\sigma_Y$ |
| Sampling distribution of $\bar{Y}$ | $\mu_{\bar{Y}}$ | $\sigma_{\bar{Y}}$ |

---

## The Standard Error of the Mean

The standard deviation of the sampling distribution is called the **standard error of the mean**. The standard error of the mean is a measure we use to describe how much dispersion there is in the sampling distribution of the mean:

$$\sigma_{\bar{Y}} = \frac{\sigma_Y}{\sqrt{N}}$$

This formula tells us that the standard error of the mean is equal to the standard deviation of the population ($\sigma_Y$) divided by the square root of the sample size. For our example, because the population standard deviation is 14,687 and our sample size is 3, the standard error of the mean is

$$\sigma_{\bar{Y}} = \frac{14,687}{\sqrt{3}} = 8,480$$

---

*Standard Error of the Mean*  The standard deviation of the sampling distribution of the mean. It describes how much dispersion there is in the sampling distribution of the mean.

---

## The Central Limit Theorem

In Figures 11.6a and 11.6b we compare the histograms for the population and sampling distributions of Tables 11.1 and 11.3. Figure 11.6a shows the population distribution of twenty incomes, with a mean $\mu_Y = 22,766$ and a standard deviation $\sigma_Y = 14,687$. Figure 11.6b shows the sampling distribution of the means from fifty samples of $N = 3$. It has a mean $\mu_{\bar{Y}} = 24,749$ and a standard deviation (the standard error of the mean) $\sigma_{\bar{Y}} = 8,479$. These two figures illustrate some of the basic properties of sampling distributions in general and the sampling distribution of the mean in particular.

First, as can be seen from Figures 11.6a and 11.6b, the shapes of the two distributions differ considerably. Whereas the population distribution is skewed to the right, the sampling distribution of the mean is less skewed, that is, closer to symmetry and a normal distribution.

Figure 11.6 **Three Income Distributions**

**a.** Population distribution of personal income for twenty individuals (hypothetical data)

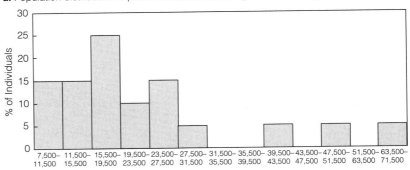

Personal Income ($Y$)

$\mu_Y = \$22,766$ $\qquad$ $\sigma_Y = \$14,687$

**b.** Sampling distribution of sample means for sample size $N = 3$ drawn from the population of twenty individuals' incomes

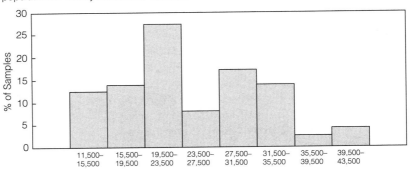

Sample Means ($\bar{Y}$)

$\mu_{\bar{Y}} = \$24,749$ $\qquad$ $\sigma_{\bar{Y}} = \$8,479$

**c.** Sampling distribution of sample means for sample size $N = 6$ drawn from the population of twenty individuals' incomes

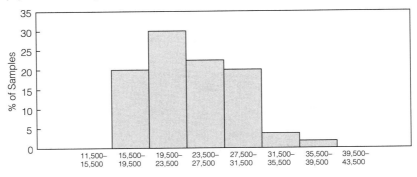

Sample Means ($\bar{Y}$)

$\mu_{\bar{Y}} = \$24,064$ $\qquad$ $\sigma_{\bar{Y}} = \$5,995$

Second, whereas only a few of the sample means coincide exactly with the population mean, $22,766, the sampling distribution centers around this value. The mean of the sampling distribution is a pretty good approximation of the population mean.

Third, the variability of the sampling distribution is considerably smaller than the variability of the population distribution. Notice that the standard deviation for the sampling distribution ($\sigma_{\bar{Y}}$ = 8,479) is almost half that for the population ($\sigma_Y$ = 14,687).

These properties of the sampling distribution are even more striking as the sample size increases. To illustrate the effect of a larger sample on the shape and properties of the sampling distribution, we went back to our population of twenty individual incomes and drew fifty additional samples of $N = 6$. We calculated the mean for each sample and constructed another sampling distribution. This sampling distribution is shown in Figure 11.6c. It has a mean $\mu_{\bar{Y}} = 24,064$ and a standard deviation $\sigma_{\bar{Y}} = 5,995$. Notice that as the sample size increased the sampling distribution became more compact. This decrease in the variability of the sampling distribution is reflected in a smaller standard deviation: with an increase in sample size from $N = 3$ to $N = 6$ the standard deviation of the sampling distribution decreased from 8,479 to 5,995. Furthermore, with an increase in sample size the sampling distribution of the mean is an even better approximation of the normal curve.

These properties of the sampling distribution of the mean are summarized more systematically in one of the most important statistical principles underlying statistical inference. It is called the **Central Limit Theorem**, and it states: If all possible random samples of size $N$ are drawn from a population with a mean $\mu_Y$ and a standard deviation $\sigma_Y$, then as $N$ becomes larger, the sampling distribution of sample means becomes approximately normal, with mean $\mu_{\bar{Y}}$ and standard deviation $\sigma_Y/\sqrt{N}$.

The significance of the Central Limit Theorem is that it tells us that with *sufficient sample size* the sampling distribution of the mean will be normal regardless of the shape of the population distribution. Therefore, even when the population distribution is skewed we can still assume that the sampling distribution of the mean is normal, given random samples of large enough size. Furthermore, the Central Limit Theorem also assures us that (1) as the sample size gets larger the mean of the sampling distribution becomes equal to the population mean; and (2) as the sample size gets larger the standard error of the mean (the standard deviation of the sampling distribution of the mean) decreases in size. The standard error of the mean tells how much variability in the sample estimates there is from sample to sample. The smaller the standard error of the mean the closer (on average) the sample means will be to the population mean. Thus, the larger the sample the more closely the sample statistic clusters around the population parameter.

---

*Central Limit Theorem* An important principle in statistical inference that relates the normal distribution and the sampling distribution of the means with a sufficient sample size.

---

**Learning Check.** *Make sure you understand the difference between the number of samples that can be drawn from a population and the sample size. Whereas the* number of samples *is infinite in theory, the* sample size *is under the control of the investigator.*

## The Size of the Sample

One issue we have not addressed is what is meant by a "sufficient" sample size. Although there is no hard and fast rule, a general rule of thumb is that when $N$ is 50 or more, the sampling distribution of the mean will be approximately normal regardless of the shape of the distribution. However, we can assume that the sampling distribution will be normal even with samples as small as 30 if we know that the population distribution approximates normality.

**Learning Check.** *What is a normal population distribution? If you can't answer this question, go back to Chapter 10. You must understand the concept of a normal distribution before you can understand the techniques involved in inferential statistics.*

## The Significance of the Sampling Distribution and the Central Limit Theorem

In the preceding sections we covered a lot of very abstract material. You probably wonder by now what it all means. In particular you may ask, Why is the concept of the sampling distribution so important? and, What is the significance of the Central Limit Theorem?

To answer these questions, let's go back and review our twenty-income example. To estimate the mean income of a population of twenty individuals we drew a sample of 3 cases and calculated the mean income for that sample. Our sample mean, $\overline{Y} = 24,749$, differs from the actual population parameter, $\mu_Y = 22,766$. Moreover, when we selected different samples we found that each time the sample mean differed from the population mean. These discrepancies are due to sampling errors. Had we taken a number of additional samples we probably would have found that the mean differed each time because every sample differs slightly from every other sample. Few, if any, sample means would correspond exactly to the actual population mean. Although for illustration we define the population's characteristics and therefore can compare the sample statistic with the population parameter, usually we have only one sample statistic as our best estimate of the population parameter. So now let's restate our dilemma: If sample estimates vary and if most result in some sort of sampling error, how much confidence can we place in the estimate? On what basis can we infer from the sample to the population?

The solution to this dilemma lies in the sampling distribution and its properties. Because the sampling distribution is a theoretical distribution that includes all possible sample outcomes, we can compare our sample outcome with it and estimate its likelihood of occurrence.

But, you may ask, since the sampling distribution is theoretical, how can we know its shape and properties so that we can make these comparisons? Our knowledge is based on what the Central Limit Theorem tells us about the properties of the sampling distribution of the mean. We know that if our sample size is large enough, most sample means will be quite close to the true population mean. Therefore, it is highly unlikely that our sample mean would deviate much from the actual population mean.

In Chapter 10, we saw that in all normal or nearly normal curves a constant proportion of the area under the curve lies between the mean and any given distance from the mean when measured in standard deviation units or $Z$ scores. We can find this proportion in a special table, the standard normal table (Appendix B).

Knowing that the sampling distribution of the means is approximately normal, with a mean $\mu_{\overline{Y}}$ and a standard deviation $\sigma_Y / \sqrt{N}$ (the standard error of the mean), we can use Appendix B to determine the probability that a sample mean will fall within a certain distance—measured in standard deviation units or $Z$ scores—of $\mu_{\overline{Y}}$ or $\mu_Y$. For example, we can expect approximately 68 percent (or we can say the probability is approximately .68) of all sample means to fall within ±1 standard error ($\sigma_Y/\sqrt{N}$ or the standard deviation of the sampling distribution of the mean) of $\mu_{\bar{Y}}$ or $\mu_Y$. Similarly, the probability is about .95 that the sample mean will fall within ±2 standard errors of $\mu_{\bar{Y}}$ or $\mu_Y$. In the next chapter, we will see how this information helps us evaluate the accuracy of our sample estimates.

---

***Learning Check.*** *Suppose a population distribution has a mean $\mu_Y = 150$ and a standard deviation $\sigma_Y = 30$ and you draw a simple random sample of $N = 100$ cases. What is the probability that the mean is between 147 and 153? What is the probability that the sample mean exceeds 153? Would you be surprised to find a mean score of 159? Why?* (Hint: *To answer these questions you need to apply what you learned in Chapter 10 about Z scores and areas under the normal curve (Appendix B). Remember, to translate a raw score into a Z score we used this formula:*

$$Z = \frac{Y - \overline{Y}}{S}$$

*However, because here we are dealing with a sampling distribution, substitute Y with the sample mean $\overline{Y}$, $\overline{Y}$ with the population mean $\mu_Y$, and S with the standard error of the mean.*)

$$Z = \frac{\overline{Y} - \mu_{\bar{Y}}}{\sigma_Y/\sqrt{N}}$$

---

## MAIN POINTS

■ Through the process of sampling, researchers attempt to generalize to the characteristics of a larger group (the population) from a subset (sample) selected from that group. The term *parameter,* associated with the population, refers to the information we are interested in finding out. *Statistic* refers to a corresponding calculated sample statistic.

■ A probability sample design allows us to estimate the extent to which the findings based on one sample are likely to differ from what we would find by studying the entire population.

■ A simple random sample is chosen in such a way as to ensure that every member of the population and every combination of *N* members have an equal chance of being chosen.

- In systematic sampling, every $k$th member in the total population is chosen for inclusion in the sample after the first member of the sample is selected at random from the first $k$ members in the population.

- A stratified random sample is obtained by (1) dividing the population into subgroups based on one or more variables central to our analysis and (2) then drawing a simple random sample from each of the subgroups.

- The sampling distribution is a theoretical probability distribution of all possible sample values for the statistic in which we are interested. The sampling distribution of the mean is a frequency distribution of all possible sample means of the same size that can be drawn from the population of interest.

- According to the Central Limit Theorem, if all possible random samples of size $N$ are drawn from a population with a mean $\mu_Y$ and a standard deviation $\sigma_Y$, then as $N$ becomes larger, the sampling distribution of sample means becomes approximately normal, with mean $\mu_{\bar{Y}}$ and standard deviation of the mean $\sigma_Y/\sqrt{N}$.

- The significance of the Central Limit Theorem is that it tells us that with sufficient sample size, the sampling distribution of the mean will be normal regardless of the shape of the population distribution. Therefore, even when the population distribution is skewed we can still assume that the sampling distribution of the mean is normal, given a large enough randomly selected sample size.

## KEY TERMS

Central Limit Theorem

disproportionate stratified sample

parameter

population

probability sampling

proportionate stratified sample

sample

sampling distribution

sampling distribution of the mean

sampling error

simple random sample

standard error of the mean

statistic

stratified random sample

systematic random sampling

## SPSS DEMONSTRATION

*Demonstration 1: Selecting a Random Sample*

This chapter discusses various types of samples and the definition of
the standard error of the mean. Usually, data entered into SPSS have
already been sampled from some larger population. However, SPSS does
have a sampling procedure that can take random samples of data in an
SPSS file. Systematic samples and stratified samples can also be drawn
with SPSS, but they require the use of the SPSS command language.

When might it be worthwhile to use the SPSS Sample procedure?
One common instance is when doing preliminary analysis of a very
large data set. For example, if you worked for the American Medical
Association and had data on all its members (tens of thousands), there
would be no need to use *all* the data during initial analysis. We could
select a random sample of members from the larger file and use this
subset of data (thus saving lots of time). Later, we could use the full
data set for doing the final analysis.

To use the Sample procedure, click on *Data* from the main menu,
then on *Select Cases*. The opening dialog box has four choices that will
select a subset of cases via various methods. By default, the *All cases*
radio button is checked.

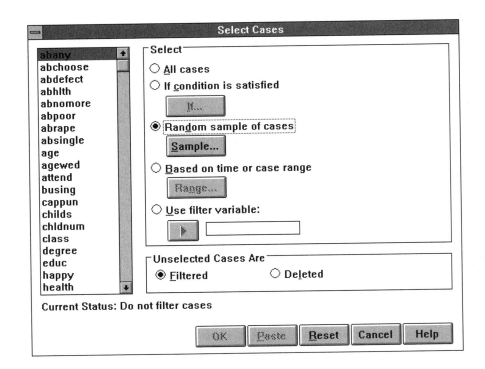

We click on the *Random sample of cases* radio button, then on the *Sample* push button to give SPSS our specification.

The next dialog box provides two options to create a random sample. The most convenient is normally the first, where we tell SPSS what percentage of cases to select from the larger file. Alternatively, we can tell SPSS to take an exact number of cases. The second option is available because SPSS will only take approximately the percentage specified in the first option.

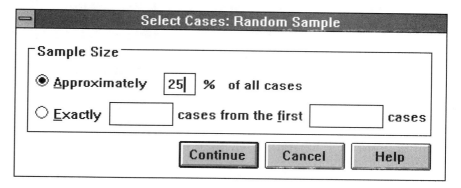

We type *25* in the box to ask for 25 percent of the original sample of 1,000 respondents from the GSS. Then click on *Continue* and *OK*, as usual, to process the request.

SPSS does not delete the cases from the active data file that aren't selected for the sample. Instead, they are filtered out (in the Data Editor window, you can identify them by the slash across their row number). This means that we can always return to the full data file by going back to the Select Cases dialog box and selecting the *All cases* radio button.

When SPSS processes our request, it tells us that the data have been filtered by putting the words "Filter On" in the status area on the bottom of the SPSS window (the status area has many helpful messages from SPSS).

To demonstrate the effect of sampling, we ask for univariate statistics for the variable CHILDS, measuring the number of children a respondent has. Click on *Statistics*, *Summarize*, then *Descriptives* to open this dialog box and place CHILDS in the variable list. Click on the *Options* button.

We'll add the standard error of the mean to the statistics that SPSS calculates by clicking the *S.E. mean* box. Then click *Continue* and *OK* to put SPSS to work.

The results show that we got lucky, as the number of valid cases is exactly 250, or 25 percent of the whole file. The mean of CHILDS is 1.85 and the standard error of the mean is .10.

```
                      SPSS for Windows Student Version - [!Output1]
  File  Edit  Data  Transform  Statistics  Graphs  Utilities  Window  Help

  Pause  Scroll   Round    Glossary   ▐▌    ▲   ▼    ±   ∓    ↑

◊ -> USE ALL.
  -> COMPUTE filter_$=(uniform(1)<=.25).
  -> VARIABLE LABEL filter_$ 'Approximately 25 % of cases (SAMPLE)'.
  -> FORMAT filter_$ (f1.0).
  -> FILTER BY filter_$.
◊ -> EXECUTE .
◊ -> DESCRIPTIVES
  ->    VARIABLES=childs
  ->    /FORMAT=LABELS NOINDEX
  ->    /STATISTICS=MEAN STDDEV MIN MAX SEMEAN
  ->    /SORT=MEAN (A) .




  Number of valid observations (listwise) =        250.00


                                                      Valid
  Variable      Mean S.E. Mean   Std Dev   Minimum   Maximum    N  Label

  CHILDS        1.85    .10       1.61        0         8      250  NUMBER OF C




  SPSS Processor is ready                                  Filter On
```

How closely does the mean for CHILDS from this random sample match that for the full file? The mean for all 1,000 respondents is 1.80, so it certainly appears that SPSS did take a random sample of this larger file. The standard error for the whole file is .05, or half of that for the 250 case random sample. This is no accident. Remember that the standard error of the mean has $\sqrt{N}$ in the denominator. Since the whole file has four times as many cases, it should have a standard error only half as large (the square root of 4). And that is what we found.

## EXERCISES

1. Explain which of the following is a statistic and which is a parameter.
   a. The mean age of Americans from the 1990 census
   b. The unemployment rate of the population of U.S. adults, estimated by the government from a large sample
   c. The percentage of Texans opposed to abortion from a poll of 1,000 residents
   d. The mean salaries of various categories of employees at a bank (tellers, loan officers, and so on)

2. Lately, the mayor of a large city has been talking about the need for a tax hike. The city's newspaper uses letters sent to the editor to judge public opinion about this possible hike. Do you think that these letters represent a random sample? Why or why not?

3. This question is concerned with selecting a sample and understanding how a sample relates to a population, in several common situations.

   a. A friend interviews every tenth shopper that passes by her as she stands outside a department store in a shopping mall. What type of sample is she selecting? How might you define the population from which she is selecting the sample?

   b. A political polling firm samples fifty potential voters from a list of registered voters in each county in a state to interview for an upcoming election. What type of sample is this? Do you have enough information to tell?

   c. Another political polling firm in the same state selects potential voters from the same list of registered voters with a very different method. First, they alphabetize the list of last names, then pick the first twenty names that begin with an A, the first twenty that begin with a B, and so on until Z (the sample size is thus $20 \times 26$, or 520). Is this a probability sample?

   d. A social scientist gathers a carefully chosen group of twenty people whom she selected to represent a broad cross-section of the population in New York City. She interviews them in-depth for a study she is doing on race relations in the city. Is this a probability sample? What type of sample has she chosen?

4. An upper-level sociology class at a large urban university has 120 students, including 34 seniors, 57 juniors, 22 sophomores, and 7 freshmen.

   a. Imagine that you choose one student at random from the classroom (perhaps by using a random number table). What is the probability that the student will be a junior?

   b. What is the probability that the student will be a freshman?

   c. If you are asked to select a proportionate stratified sample of size 30 from the classroom, stratified by class level (senior, junior, and so on), how many students from each group would be in the sample?

   d. If instead you are to select a disproportionate sample of size 20 from the classroom, with equal numbers of students from each class level in the sample, how many freshmen will be in the sample?

5. Can the standard error of a variable ever be larger than, or even equal in size to, the standard deviation for the same variable? Justify your answer by use of both a formula and a discussion of the relationship between these two concepts.

6. When taking a random sample from a very large population, how does the standard error of the mean change when:
   a. the sample size is increased from 100 to 1,600?
   b. the sample size is decreased from 300 to 150?
   c. the sample size is multiplied by 4?

7. Many television stations now do "instant" polls by providing an 800 number and asking an interesting (they hope) question of the day for viewers to call and answer.
   a. Do you think these polls are probability samples?
   b. What is the population from which the sample of calls is drawn? Be specific.

8. Use the data from exercise 6 in Chapter 10 concerning the percent of eligible adults who voted in the 1992 election, by state.
   a. Calculate the mean and standard deviation for the population.
   b. Now take ten samples of size 5 from the population. Use either simple random sampling or systematic sampling, with the help of the table of random numbers in Appendix A. Calculate the mean for each sample.
   c. After selecting the samples, calculate the mean and standard deviation for the ten sample means. How does the standard deviation of the sample means compare with that for the population of fifty states?
   d. Now select ten more samples of size 10 from the population of states, calculating the mean from each. Then, as before, calculate the mean and standard deviation for the ten sample means. How does the standard deviation here compare with that in (c)? Why?
   e. Now construct a histogram of the distribution of values in the population, and of the sampling distribution of means for the two sample sizes. Describe and explain any differences between the three distributions you observe.

9. You've been asked to determine the likely percentage of students who support a candidate for student government at your school, and you want to take a random sample to make the estimate. State whether or not each of the following scenarios describes a random sample. Explain your answers.

    a. You ask all students eating lunch in the cafeteria on a Tuesday.

    b. You ask every tenth student from the list of enrolled students.

    c. You ask every tenth student passing by the student union.

10. For the total population of a large southern city, mean family income is $34,000, with a standard deviation (for the population) of $5,000.

    a. Imagine that you take a sample of 200 city residents. What is the probability that your sample mean is between $33,000 and $34,000?

    b. For this same sample size, what is the probability that the sample mean exceeds $37,000?

11. A small population of $N = 10$ has values of 4, 7, 2, 11, 5, 3, 4, 6, 10, and 1.

    a. Calculate the mean and standard deviation for the population.

    b. Take ten simple random samples of size 3 and calculate the mean for each.

    c. Calculate the mean and standard deviation of all these sample means. How closely does the mean of all the sample means match the population mean? How is the standard deviation of the means related to the standard deviation for the population?

## GROUP PROBLEMS

1. This exercise involves sampling repeatedly from a population and comparing the results by sample size. Have one group member locate a reference source in the library that lists the population of all the countries of the world and copy this information for everyone. Then have one group member take ten samples of size 5 from the list, calculate the mean for each sample, and create a histogram to display the distribution of the means. Have another group member take ten samples of size 10 and do the same, another group member take ten samples of size 15, and a fourth take ten samples of size 20. Have another group member create a histogram of the population distribution for all the countries. After the histograms are created, compare them and discuss what they tell you about sample size, the relationship between a population distribution and the sampling distribution of the mean, and the Central Limit Theorem. Create a group report combining all this information and summarizing the discussion.

2. Have several group members find three or four newspaper or magazine articles that report on the results of a survey or poll. Record the information provided on the sample characteristics for each article. Was enough information supplied to determine whether the sample was a random sample, a stratified sample, or some other kind? Can you tell from what population each sample was drawn? What other information would you suggest be included for each article so that readers will have a complete understanding of the sampling used in the survey?

3. Your task is to estimate the proportion of students who have blond hair at your college. Sample 100 students to make this estimate. Have your group develop two different sampling schemes to make the estimate. Then go out and gather data using the two schemes. How closely do the estimates for the proportion of blond-haired students compare? Discuss the advantages and disadvantages of each sampling plan.

# 12    Estimation

**Introduction**

**Estimation Defined**
Reasons for Estimation
Point and Interval Estimation

**Confidence Intervals for Means**
Rationale for Confidence Intervals

**Box 12.1   Estimation as a Type of Inference**
Procedures for Estimating Means
  *Calculating the Standard Error of the Mean*
  *Deciding on the Level of Confidence and Finding the Corresponding
    Z Value*
  *Calculating the Confidence Interval*
  *Interpreting the Results*
Reducing Risk

**Estimating Sigma**
  *Calculating the Standard Error of the Mean*
  *Deciding on the Level of Confidence and Finding the Corresponding
    Z Value*
  *Calculating the Confidence Interval*
  *Interpreting the Results*

**Sample Size and Confidence Intervals**

**Box 12.2   What Affects Confidence Interval Width? A Summary**

**Statistics in Practice: Hispanic Migration and Earnings**

**Confidence Intervals for Proportions**
The Sampling Distribution of Proportions
Procedures for Estimating Proportions
  *Calculating the Standard Error of the Proportion*

## Introduction

In this chapter, we discuss the procedures involved in estimating population proportions and population means. These procedures are based on the principles of sampling and statistical inference discussed in Chapter 11. Knowledge about the sampling distribution enables us to estimate population means and proportions from sample outcomes and to assess the accuracy of these estimates.

*Example 1* An article published in *Time* magazine (May 20, 1996) reports the results of a survey conducted by a national polling organization for *Time*/CNN. Based on a sample of 826 registered voters, this poll estimated that 50 percent of all registered voters are Clinton supporters.

*Example 2* Each month, the Bureau of Labor Statistics interviews a sample of about 50,000 adult Americans to determine job-related activities. Based on these interviews, monthly estimates are made of vital statistics, such as the unemployment rate (the proportion who are unemployed), average earnings, the percentage of the workforce working part-time, and the percentage collecting unemployment benefits. These estimates are considered so vital that they cause fluctuations in the stock market and influence economic policies of the federal government.

*Example 3* Based on a telephone poll of 1,011 adult Americans conducted in 1996 by the Yankelovich polling organization, it was established that 78 percent of the population of adult Americans from which the sample was drawn favor a proposal to raise the minimum wage from $4.25 per hour to $5.15 per hour.

Each year the National Opinion Research Center (NORC) conducts the General Social Survey (GSS) on a representative sample of about 1,500 respondents. The GSS, from which many of the examples in this book are selected, is designed to provide social science researchers with a readily accessible database of socially relevant attitudes, behaviors, and attributes of a cross-section of the U.S. adult population. For example, in analyzing the responses to the 1991 GSS, researchers found the average income was $18,130. This average probably differs from the average of the population from which the GSS sample was drawn. However, we can establish that in most cases the sample mean (in this case $18,130) is fairly close to the actual true average in the population.

As you read through these examples you may have questioned the reliability of some of the numbers mentioned. Is it possible to establish the voting preferences of millions of Americans, to determine their opinion regarding the minimum wage, or to find their average income based on a sample of about 1,000 respondents? If elections were held the day the poll was conducted by the national polling organization, would 50 percent of all registered voters in the United States really vote for Bill Clinton? What is the actual percentage of adult Americans in the United States who favor raising the minimum wage from $4.25 to $5.15? How about the average income of $18,130? How close is it to the true average in the population from which the GSS sample was drawn?

## Estimation Defined

The average income of all adult Americans, the percentage of all registered voters who would vote for Bill Clinton, and the percentage of all adult Americans who favor raising the minimum wage are *population parameters.*

The average income calculated from the GSS, the percentage who stated that they would vote for Bill Clinton in the *Time*/CNN poll, and the percentage who favored raising the minimum wage in the Yankelovich survey are all *sample estimates of population parameters.* Thus, the responses to the *Time*/CNN political poll were used to estimate the percentage of registered voters in favor of Bill Clinton; the mean income of $18,130 calculated from the GSS sample can be used to estimate the mean income of all adults in the United States. Similarly, based on a national sample of adult Americans, the Yankelovich polling organization estimated the percentage of adults in the United States who favor raising the minimum wage.

These are all illustrations of *estimation.* **Estimation** is a process whereby we select a random sample from a population and use a sample statistic to estimate a population parameter. We can use sample proportions (or percentages) as estimates of population proportions, sample means as estimates of population means, or sample variances as estimates of population variances.

---

*Estimation*   A process whereby we select a random sample from a population and use a sample statistic to estimate a population parameter.

---

## Reasons for Estimation

Why estimate? The goal of most research is to find the population parameter. However, we hardly ever have enough time or money to collect information about the entire population. Therefore, we rarely know the value of the population parameter. Fortunately, we can learn a lot about a population by randomly selecting a sample from that population and obtaining an estimate of the population parameter from that sample. The major objective of sampling theory and statistical inference is to provide estimates of unknown parameters from sample statistics that can be easily calculated.

## Point and Interval Estimation

Estimates of population characteristics can be divided into two types: point estimates and interval estimates. **Point estimates** are sample statistics used to estimate the exact value of a population parameter.

When *Time* magazine projected that 50 percent of all registered voters are Clinton supporters, it was using a point estimate. Similarly, if we reported the average income of the population of adult Americans to be exactly $18,130, we would be using a point estimate.

The problem with point estimates is that sample estimates usually vary, and most result in some sort of sampling error. Therefore, when we use a sample statistic to estimate the exact value of a population parameter we never really know how accurate it is.

One method of establishing accuracy is to use an *interval estimate* rather than a point estimate (Figure 12.1). With interval estimation we establish a range of values within which the population parameter may fall. This range of values is called a **confidence interval**. Thus, instead of using a single value, $18,130, as an estimate of the mean earnings of adult Americans, we may say that the mean earnings is somewhere between $17,500 and $19,100.

When we use confidence intervals to estimate population parameters, such as the mean earnings, we can also evaluate the accuracy of this estimate by assessing the likelihood that any given interval will contain the mean. This likelihood, expressed as a percentage or a probability, is called a **confidence level**. Confidence intervals are defined in terms of confidence levels. Thus, by selecting a 95 percent confidence

Figure 12.1 **Point and Interval Estimates of Income**

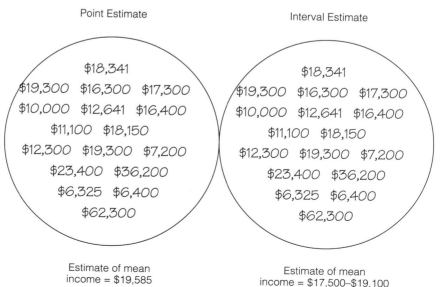

Point Estimate

Interval Estimate

Estimate of mean income = $19,585

Estimate of mean income = $17,500–$19,100

level, we are saying that there is a .95 probability—or 95 chances out of 100—that a specified interval will contain the population mean. Confidence intervals can be constructed for any level of confidence, but the most common ones are the 90 percent, 95 percent, and 99 percent levels.

---

*Point Estimate*   A sample statistic used to estimate the exact value of a population parameter.

*Confidence Interval (Interval Estimate)*   A range of values defined by the confidence level within which the population parameter is estimated to fall.

*Confidence Level*   The likelihood, expressed as a percentage or a probability, that a specified interval will contain the population parameter.

---

**Learning Check.**   *What is the difference between a point estimate and a confidence interval?*

## Confidence Intervals for Means

Confidence intervals can be constructed for many different parameters based on corresponding sample statistics. In this chapter, we describe the rationale and the procedure for the construction of confidence intervals for means and proportions. Let's begin with the rationale for establishing confidence intervals for means.

### Rationale for Confidence Intervals

To illustrate the procedure of establishing confidence intervals for means, let's reintroduce one of the research examples we discussed in Chapter 11—Example 1, assessing the needs of commuting students on our campus.

Recall that we have been given enough money to survey a random sample of 500 students. One of our tasks is to estimate the average commuting time, the population parameter, of all 15,000 commuters on our campus. To obtain this estimate we calculate the average commuting time for the sample. Suppose the sample average

### Box 12.1 *Estimation as a Type of Inference*

The goal of inferential statistics is to say something meaningful about the population, based entirely on information from a sample of that population. A confidence interval attempts to do just that: by knowing a sample mean, sample size, and sample standard deviation, we are able to say something about the population from which that sample was drawn.

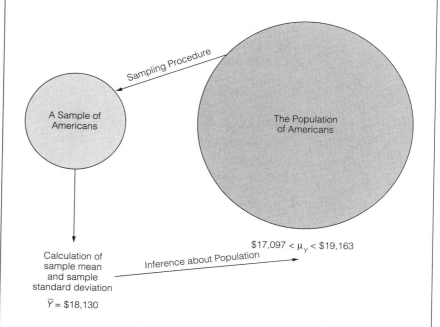

We know exactly what our sample mean is. Combining this information with the sample standard deviation and sample size gives us a range within which we can confidently say that the population mean falls.

is $\overline{Y}$ = 7.5 hours per week, and we want to use it as an estimate of the true mean commuting time for the entire population of commuting students.

Because it is based on a sample, this estimate is subject to sampling error. Therefore, we do not know how close it is to the true population mean. However, based on what the Central Limit Theorem tells us about the properties of the sampling distribution of the mean, we know that with a large enough sample size most sample means will tend to be quite close to the true population mean. Therefore, it is unlikely that our sample mean of $\overline{Y} = 7.5$ deviates much from the true population mean.

We know that the sampling distribution of the means is approximately normal with a mean $\mu_{\overline{Y}}$, equal to the population mean $\mu_Y$, and a standard error (standard deviation of the sampling distribution)

$$\sigma_{\overline{Y}} = \frac{\sigma_Y}{\sqrt{N}}$$

This information allows us to use the normal distribution to determine the probability that a sample mean will fall within a certain distance—measured in standard deviation (standard error) units or $Z$ scores—of $\mu_{\overline{Y}}$ or $\mu_Y$. For example, we can make the following assumptions:

■ 68 percent of all random sample means will fall between ±1 standard error from the true population mean

■ 95 percent of all random sample means will fall between ±1.96 standard errors from the true population mean

■ 99 percent of all random sample means will fall between ±2.58 standard errors from the true population mean

Based on these assumptions and knowing the value of the standard error, we can establish a range of values—a confidence interval—that is likely to contain the actual population mean. We can also evaluate the accuracy of this estimate by assessing the likelihood that this range of values will actually contain the population mean.

Let's suppose that the standard deviation for our population of commuters is $\sigma_Y = 1.5$. We calculate the standard error for the sampling distribution of the mean:

$$\sigma_{\overline{Y}} = \frac{\sigma_Y}{\sqrt{N}} = \frac{1.5}{\sqrt{500}} = 0.07$$

Using $\overline{Y} = 7.5$ as an estimate of $\mu_Y$—the average commuting time per week for all students—we can construct a confidence interval around it. For example, the 68 percent confidence interval for the mean commuting time is

$$68\% \text{ CI} = \overline{Y} \pm 1(\sigma_{\overline{Y}})$$

where

$\overline{Y}$ = the sample mean

$\sigma_{\overline{Y}}$ = the standard error of the sampling distribution of the mean

Applying this formula to our example, we get

$$68\% \text{ CI} = 7.5 \pm 1(0.07)$$
$$= 7.5 \pm 0.07$$
$$= 7.43 \text{ to } 7.57$$

We can then say there are 68 chances out of 100 (or we are 68% confident) that the procedure we are using will generate an interval (in this case from 7.43 to 7.57) that will contain the population mean. This interpretation is based on our assumption that if we took an *infinite number of samples* from the population, in the long run 68 percent of the sample means would be within ±1 standard error of the true population mean. Note that we can never be sure whether the population mean is actually contained within the confidence interval. Once the sample is selected and the confidence interval defined, the population mean either does or does not contain the population mean—but we will never be sure.

To illustrate the concept of confidence intervals, let's suppose that we draw ten different samples from the population of commuting students. For each sample mean we construct a 95 percent confidence interval. Figure 12.2 displays these confidence intervals. Each horizontal line represents a 95 percent confidence interval constructed around a sample mean (marked with a circle).

The vertical line represents the population mean. Note that the horizontal lines that intersect the vertical line are intervals that contain the true population mean. Only 1 out of the 10 confidence intervals does not intersect the vertical line; it does not contain the population mean. What would happen if we continued to draw samples of the same size from this population and constructed a 95 percent confidence

Figure 12.2 **95 Percent Confidence Intervals for Ten Samples**

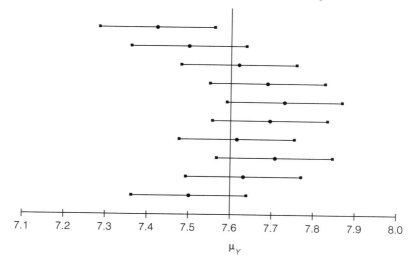

interval for each sample? For about 95 percent of all samples the specified interval would contain the true population mean and for about 5 percent of all samples it would not.

## Procedures for Estimating Means

The general formula for constructing confidence intervals for any level is

$$CI = \overline{Y} \pm Z(\sigma_{\overline{Y}})$$

Let's examine this formula in more detail. Notice that to obtain a confidence interval at a certain level, we take the sample mean and add to or subtract from it the product of a Z value and the standard error. The Z score we choose depends on the desired confidence level. We want the area between the selected ±Z to be equal to the confidence level. For example, to obtain a 95 percent confidence interval we would choose a Z of 1.96 because we know (from Appendix B) that 95 percent of the area under the curve is included between ±1.96 Z. Similarly, for a 99 percent confidence level we would choose a Z of 2.58. The relationship between the confidence level and Z is graphically illustrated in Figure 12.3 for the 95 percent and 99 percent confidence levels.

> **Learning Check.** *If you don't understand the relationship between the confidence level and Z, review the material in Chapter 10.*

Figure 12.3 **Relationship Between Confidence Level and Z for 95 and 99 Percent Confidence Intervals**

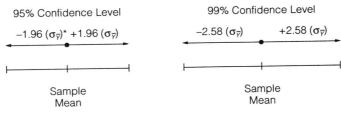

*Source:* Adapted from David Freedman et al., *Statistics*, 348. © 1991 by W. W. Norton & Co., Inc. Used by permission.

To determine the confidence interval for means follow these steps:

1. Calculate the standard error of the mean.
2. Decide on the level of confidence and find the corresponding $Z$ value.
3. Calculate the confidence interval.
4. Interpret the results.

Let's return to the problem of estimating the mean commuting time of the population of students on our campus. How would you find the 95 percent confidence interval?

*Calculating the Standard Error of the Mean*  The standard error for the sampling distribution of the mean commuting time is

$$\sigma_{\bar{Y}} = \frac{\sigma_Y}{\sqrt{N}} = \frac{1.5}{\sqrt{500}} = 0.07$$

*Deciding on the Level of Confidence and Finding the Corresponding Z Value*  We decided on a 95 percent confidence level. The $Z$ value corresponding to a 95 percent confidence level is 1.96.

*Calculating the Confidence Interval*  The confidence interval is calculated by adding and subtracting from the observed sample mean the product of the standard error and $Z$:

$$95\% \text{ CI} = 7.5 \pm 1.96(0.07)$$
$$= 7.5 \pm 0.14$$
$$= 7.36 \text{ to } 7.64$$

The 95 percent CI for the mean commuting time is illustrated in Figure 12.4.

Figure 12.4  **95 Percent Confidence Interval for the Mean Commuting Time ($N$ = 500)**

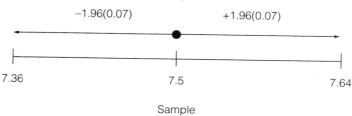

*Interpreting the Results* We can be 95 percent confident that the actual mean commuting time is not less than 7.36 hours and not greater than 7.64 hours. In other words, if we drew a large number of samples (*N* = 500) from the population of commuting students, then 95 times out of 100 the true population mean would be included within the computed interval. Note that with a 95 percent confidence level there is a 5 percent risk that we are wrong. That is, 5 times out of 100, the true population mean will not be included in the specified interval.

---

**Learning Check.** *What is the 90 percent confidence interval for the mean commuting time? (Hint: First, find the Z value associated with a 90 percent confidence level.)*

---

## Reducing Risk

One way to reduce the risk of being wrong is by increasing the level of confidence. For instance, we can increase our confidence level from 95 to 99 percent. The 99 percent confidence interval for our commuting example is

$$99\% \text{ CI} = 7.5 \pm 2.58(0.07)$$
$$= 7.5 \pm 0.18$$
$$= 7.32 \text{ to } 7.68$$

When using the 99 percent confidence interval we can be almost certain that the true population mean is included in the interval ranging from 7.32 to 7.68 hours per week. There is only a 1 percent risk that we are wrong and the specified interval does not contain the true population mean. Note, however, that by increasing the confidence level we have also increased the width of the confidence interval from 0.28 (7.36 − 7.64) to 0.36 hours (7.32 − 7.68), thereby making our estimate less precise. Thus, there is a trade-off between achieving greater confidence in making an estimate and the precision of that estimate. Although using a higher level of confidence, like the 99 percent level, increases our confidence that the true population mean is indeed included in our confidence interval, the estimate becomes less precise as the width of the interval increases. Although we are only 95 percent confident that the interval ranging between 7.36 and 7.64 hours includes the true population mean, it is a more precise estimate than the 99 percent interval ranging from 7.32 to 7.68 hours. The relationship between the confidence level and the precision of the confidence interval is illustrated in Figure 12.5.

Figure 12.5 **95 Percent vs. 99 Percent Confidence Intervals**

Among the population of black Americans, what is the mean number of children in a family? Using the 1994 GSS sample, we can construct the following confidence intervals:

**A 95% confidence interval**

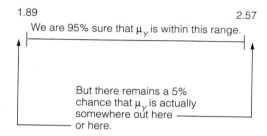

**A 99% confidence interval**

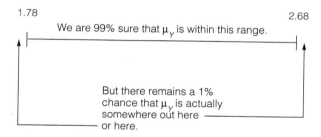

## Estimating Sigma

To calculate confidence intervals, we need to know the standard error of the sampling distribution, $\sigma_{\bar{Y}}$. The standard error is a function of the population standard deviation and the sample size

$$\sigma_{\bar{Y}} = \frac{\sigma_Y}{\sqrt{N}}$$

In our commuting example we have been using a hypothetical value of $\sigma_Y = 1.5$ for the population standard deviation. Typically, both the mean ($\mu_Y$) and the standard deviation ($\sigma_Y$) of the population are unknown to us. When $N \geq 50$, however, the sample standard deviation $S_Y$ is a good estimate of $\sigma_Y$. The standard error is then calculated as follows:

$$S_{\bar{Y}} = \frac{S_Y}{\sqrt{N}}$$

As an example, let's estimate the mean income for all adult Americans based on the 1991 GSS survey. The mean income for a sample of $N = 880$ is $\overline{Y}$ = \$18,130, and the standard deviation is $S_Y$ = \$15,639. Now let's determine the 95 percent confidence interval for these data.

*Calculating the Standard Error of the Mean*  The standard error for the sampling distribution of the mean is

$$S_{\overline{Y}} = \frac{S_Y}{\sqrt{N}} = \frac{15,639}{\sqrt{880}} = 527.19$$

*Deciding on the Level of Confidence and Finding the Corresponding Z Value*  We decided on a 95 percent confidence level. The Z value corresponding to a 95 percent confidence level is 1.96.

*Calculating the Confidence Interval*  The confidence interval is calculated by adding to and subtracting from the observed sample mean the product of the standard error and Z:

$$95\% \text{ CI} = 18,130 \pm 1.96(527.19)$$
$$= 18,130 \pm 1,033$$
$$= 17,097 \text{ to } 19,163$$

*Interpreting the Results*  We can be 95 percent confident that the actual mean income of the population of adult Americans from which the GSS sample was taken is not less than \$17,097 and not greater than \$19,163. In other words, if we drew a large number of samples ($N = 880$) from this population, then 95 times out of 100 the true population mean would be included within the computed interval.

## Sample Size and Confidence Intervals

Researchers can often increase the precision of their estimate by increasing the sample size. In Chapter 11 we learned that larger samples result in smaller standard errors and, therefore, in sampling distributions that are more clustered around the population mean (Figure 11.6). A more tightly clustered sampling distribution means that our confidence intervals will be narrower and thus more precise. To illustrate the relationship between the sample size and both the standard error and the confidence interval, let's calculate the 95 percent confidence interval for our GSS data with (1) a sample of $N = 440$, half the size of the original sample, and (2) a sample of $N = 1,760$, double the size of the original sample.

*Example 4* $N = 440$.

The standard error for the sampling distribution is

$$S_{\bar{Y}} = \frac{15,639}{\sqrt{440}} = 745.56$$

The 95 percent confidence interval is

$$
\begin{aligned}
95\% \text{ CI} &= 18,130 \pm 1.96(745.56) \\
&= 18,130 \pm 1,461 \\
&= 16,669 \text{ to } 19,591
\end{aligned}
$$

*Example 5* $N = 1,760$.

The standard error for the sampling distribution is

$$S_{\bar{Y}} = \frac{15,639}{\sqrt{1,760}} = 372.78$$

The 95 percent confidence interval:

$$
\begin{aligned}
95\% \text{ CI} &= 18,130 \pm 1.96(372.78) \\
&= 18,130 \pm 731 \\
&= 17,399 \text{ to } 18,861
\end{aligned}
$$

In Table 12.1 we present the 95 percent confidence intervals for the mean income for the three sample sizes: $N = 440$, $N = 880$, and $N = 1,760$. The 95 percent CIs for the mean income for all three sample sizes are also illustrated in Figure 12.6.

Notice that there is an inverse relationship between the sample size and the width of the confidence interval. The 95 percent confidence interval for the GSS sample of 440 cases is $2,922. But the interval widths decrease to $2,066 and $1,462, respectively, as the sample sizes increase to $N = 880$ and then to $N = 1,760$. Clearly, the increase in sample size is associated with increased precision of the confidence

Table 12.1  **95 Percent Confidence Interval and Width for Mean Income for Three Different Sample Sizes**

| Sample Size | Confidence Interval | Interval Width | $S_Y$ | $S_{\bar{Y}}$ |
|---|---|---|---|---|
| $N = 440$ | $16,669–$19,591 | $2,922 | $15,639 | 745.56 |
| $N = 880$ | $17,097–$19,163 | $2,066 | $15,639 | 527.19 |
| $N = 1,760$ | $17,399–$18,861 | $1,462 | $15,639 | 372.78 |

Figure 12.6 **The 95 Percent Confidence Intervals for Mean Income
($N$ = 440); ($N$ = 880); ($N$ = 1,760)**

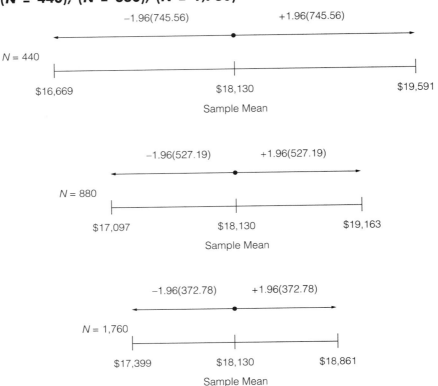

interval. However, notice that we had to quadruple the size of the sample (from 440 to 1,760) to reduce the confidence interval by half[1] (from \$2,922 to \$1,462). In general, whereas the precision of estimates increases steadily with sample size, the gains are rather modest after $N$ reaches about 400. An important factor to remember is the increased cost associated with a larger sample. In the final analysis researchers have to consider at what point the increase in precision is too small to justify the additional cost associated with a larger sample.

> **_Learning Check._** _Why do smaller sample sizes produce wider confidence intervals? (See Figure 12.7.)_ (Hint: _Compare the standard errors of the mean for the three sample sizes.)_

[1]The slight variation is due to rounding.

Figure 12.7 **The Relationship Between Sample Size and Confidence Interval Width**

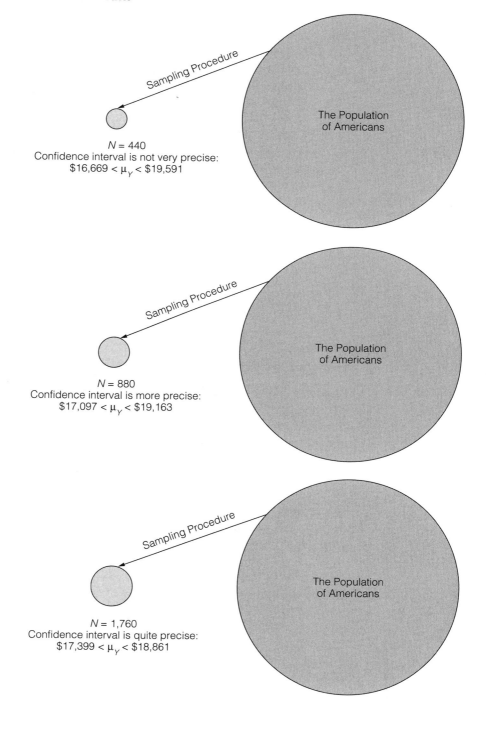

Sampling Procedure

The Population of Americans

$N = 440$
Confidence interval is not very precise:
$16,669 < \mu_Y < 19,591$

Sampling Procedure

The Population of Americans

$N = 880$
Confidence interval is more precise:
$17,097 < \mu_Y < 19,163$

Sampling Procedure

The Population of Americans

$N = 1,760$
Confidence interval is quite precise:
$17,399 < \mu_Y < 18,861$

## Box 12.2 What Affects Confidence Interval Width? A Summary

"Holding other factors constant . . . "

| | | |
|---|---|---|
| If the sample size goes up | ↑ | the confidence interval becomes more precise. → ← |
| If the sample size goes down | ↓ | the confidence interval becomes less precise. ← → |
| If the value of the sample standard deviation goes up | ↑ | the confidence interval becomes less precise. ← → |
| If the value of the sample standard deviation goes down | ↓ | the confidence interval becomes more precise. → ← |
| If the level of confidence goes up (from 95% to 99%) | ↑ | the confidence interval becomes less precise. ← → |
| If the level of confidence goes down (from 99% to 95%) | ↓ | the confidence interval becomes more precise. → ← |

## Statistics in Practice: Hispanic Migration and Earnings

Tienda and Wilson investigate the relationship between migration and the earnings of Hispanic men.[2] Their analyses focus on three major Hispanic groups—Mexicans, Puerto Ricans, and Cubans. They use a sample of the 1980 census, which included 5,726 Mexicans, 5,908 Puerto Ricans, and 3,895 Cubans. Tienda and Wilson argue that these three Hispanic groups vary markedly in socioeconomic characteristics as a result of differences in the timing and circumstances of their immigration to the United States. They claim that the period of entry and the circumstances prompting migration have affected the geographical distribution and the employment opportunities of each group. For example, Puerto Ricans are disproportionately located in the Northeast, where the labor market is characterized by the highest unemployment rates, whereas the majority of Cuban immigrants

[2]Adapted from Martha Tienda and Franklin D. Wilson, "Migration and the Earnings of Hispanic Men." *American Sociological Review,* Vol. 57, 1992, 661–678.

reside in the Southeast, where the unemployment rate is the lowest in the United States.

The contemporary profiles of Hispanic men also reveal persistent differences in educational levels among Mexicans and Puerto Ricans compared with Cubans. About 60 percent of Mexicans and Puerto Ricans had not completed high school compared with 42 percent of Cuban men. At the other extreme, 17 percent of Cuban men were college graduates compared with about 4 percent of Mexican men and Puerto Rican men.

These differences in migrant status and socioeconomic characteristics are likely to be manifested in disparities in earnings among the three groups. Tienda & Wilson anticipated that the earnings of Cubans would be higher than the earnings of Mexicans and Puerto Ricans. They compare the average earnings of the three groups. As anticipated, with an average earnings of $16,368 ($S_Y = \$3,069$) Cubans are at the top of the income hierarchy. Puerto Ricans are at the bottom of the income hierarchy, with earnings averaging $12,587 ($S_Y = \$8,647$). Mexican men are intermediate among the Hispanic groups, with average annual earnings of $13,342 ($S_Y = \$9,414$).

Although Tienda and Wilson do not calculate confidence intervals for their estimates, we will use the data they present to calculate a 95 percent confidence interval for the mean income for the three groups of Hispanic men.

*Example 6* The 95 Percent Confidence Interval for Cubans

Calculating the standard error:

$$S_{\bar{Y}} = \frac{3,069}{\sqrt{3,895}} = 49.17$$

Calculating the confidence interval:

$$\text{95\% CI} = 16,368 \pm 1.96(49.17)$$
$$= 16,368 \pm 96$$
$$= 16,272 \text{ to } 16,464$$

*Example 7* The 95 Percent Confidence Interval for Puerto Ricans

Calculating the standard error:

$$S_{\bar{Y}} = \frac{8,647}{\sqrt{5,908}} = 112.50$$

Calculating the confidence interval:

95% CI = 12,587 ± 1.96(112.50)

= 12,587 ± 220

= 12,367 to 12,807

*Example 8* The 95 Percent Confidence Interval for Mexicans

Calculating the standard error:

$$S_{\bar{Y}} = \frac{9,414}{\sqrt{5,726}} = 124.41$$

Calculating the confidence interval:

95% CI = 13,342 ± 1.96(124.41)

= 13,342 ± 244

= 13,098 to 13,586

The confidence intervals for Cuban, Puerto Rican, and Mexican immigrants are illustrated in Figure 12.8. Notice that the confidence intervals do not overlap, revealing great disparities in earnings among the three groups. As expected, the interval estimate for Cuban immigrants is considerably higher than the ones for Puerto Rican and Mexican immigrants.

## Confidence Intervals for Proportions

In the preceding sections, we looked at procedures for estimating means. Confidence intervals can also be computed for proportions or percentages. We saw earlier that researchers often use sample percentages to estimate population percentages. However, because they are based on a sample, estimated percentages, just like estimated means, are subject to sampling error. Therefore, we do not know how close they are to the actual population percentages.

For instance, let's take the *Time*/CNN report we discussed earlier. Based on a random sample of 826 registered voters the percentage favoring Bill Clinton was estimated to be 50 percent. Had we drawn another sample from the list of registered voters the percentage of voters favoring Bill Clinton would probably have been different. Thus, although it appears that half the registered voters would support Bill Clinton, it is also possible that such is not the case. To forecast the outcome of the election with any degree of accuracy, we need to assess the accuracy of the 50 percent result of this particular poll. In this

Figure 12.8  **The 95 Percent Confidence Intervals for the Mean Income of Puerto Ricans, Mexicans, and Cubans**

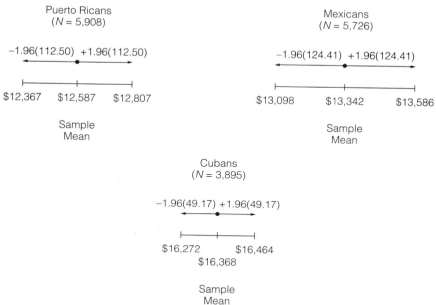

section, we learn to find confidence intervals for proportions. The procedures for estimating proportions and percentages are identical. Any of the formulas presented for proportions can be applied to percentages, and vice versa. We can obtain a confidence interval for a percentage by calculating the confidence interval for a proportion and then multiplying the result by 100.

## The Sampling Distribution of Proportions

The same conceptual foundations of sampling and statistical inference that are central to the estimation of population means are also central to the estimation of population proportions—namely, the selection of random samples and the special properties of the sampling distribution.

Earlier we saw that the sampling distribution of the means underlies the process of estimating population means from sample means. Similarly, the *sampling distribution of proportions* underlies the estimation of population proportions from sample proportions. Based on the Central Limit Theorem we know that with sufficient sample size the sampling distribution of proportions is approximately normal, with mean $\mu_p$ equal to the population proportion $\pi$ and with a standard error of proportions (the standard deviation of the sampling distribution of proportions) equal to

$$\sigma_p = \sqrt{\frac{(\pi)(1 - \pi)}{N}}$$

where

$\sigma_p$ = the standard error of proportions
$\pi$ = the population proportion
$N$ = the population size

However, since the population proportion, $\pi$, is unknown to us (that is what we are trying to estimate!), we can use the sample proportion, $p$, as an estimate of $\pi$. The estimated standard error then becomes

$$S_p = \sqrt{\frac{p(1 - p)}{N}}$$

where

$S_p$ = the estimated standard error of proportions
$p$ = the sample proportion
$N$ = the sample size

As an example, let's calculate the estimated standard error for the *Time*/CNN poll. With $p = .50$, $1 - p = (1 - .50) = .50$, and $N = 826$, the standard error is

$$S_p = \sqrt{\frac{(.50)(.50)}{826}} = .017$$

To meet the assumption of normality with the sampling distribution of proportions we will have to consider two factors: the sample size $N$ and the sample proportions $p$ and $1 - p$. When $p$ and $1 - p$ are about .50, a sample size of at least 50 is sufficient. But when $p > .50$ (or $1 - p > .50$), a larger sample is required to meet the assumption of normality. Usually, a sample that is 100 or more is adequate for any single estimate of a population proportion.

## Procedures for Estimating Proportions

Because the sampling distribution of proportions is approximately normal, we can use the normal distribution to establish confidence intervals for proportions in the same manner that we used the normal distribution to establish confidence intervals for means.

The general formula for constructing confidence intervals for proportions for any level of confidence is

$$CI = p \pm Z(S_p)$$

where

CI = the confidence interval
$p$ = the observed sample proportion
$Z$ = the $Z$ corresponding to the confidence level
$S_p$ = the standard error of proportions

Let's examine this formula in more detail. Notice that to obtain a confidence interval at a certain level we take the sample proportion and add to or subtract from it the product of a $Z$ value and the standard error. The $Z$ value we choose depends on the desired confidence level. We want the area between the mean and the selected $\pm Z$ to be equal to the confidence level. For example, to obtain a 95 percent confidence interval we would choose a $Z$ of 1.96 because we know (from Appendix B) that 95 percent of the area under the curve is included between $\pm 1.96$ $Z$. Similarly, for a 99 percent confidence level we would choose a $Z$ of 2.58. (The relationship between confidence level and $Z$ values was graphically illustrated earlier, in Figure 12.3.)

To determine the confidence interval for a proportion follow the same steps used to find confidence intervals for means:

1. Calculate the standard error of the proportion.
2. Decide on the desired level of confidence and find the corresponding $Z$ value.
3. Calculate the confidence interval.
4. Interpret the results.

To illustrate these steps we use the results of the *Time*/CNN presidential preference poll.

*Calculating the Standard Error of the Proportion* The standard error of the proportion .50 (50%) with a sample $N = 826$ is

$$S_p = \sqrt{\frac{(p)(1-p)}{N}} = \sqrt{\frac{(.50)(.50)}{826}} = .017$$

*Deciding on the Desired Level of Confidence and Finding the Corresponding Z Value* We choose the 95 percent confidence level. The $Z$ corresponding to a 95 percent confidence level is 1.96.

*Calculating the Confidence Interval* Calculate the confidence interval by adding to and subtracting from the observed sample proportion the product of the standard error and $Z$:

$$95\% \text{ CI} = .50 \pm 1.96(.017)$$
$$= .50 \pm .033$$
$$= .467 \text{ to } .533$$

*Interpreting the Results* We are 95 percent confident that the true population proportion is somewhere between .467 and .533. In other words, if we drew a large number of samples ($N = 826$) from the population of registered voters, then 95 times out of 100 the confidence interval we obtained would contain the true population proportion. We can also express this result in percentages and say that we are 95 percent confident that the true population percentage is included somewhere within the computed interval of 46.7 percent to 53.3 percent. The 95 percent CI for the percentage of Clinton supporters is illustrated in Figure 12.9.

---

**Learning Check.** *Calculate the confidence interval for the presidential preference poll using the percentages rather than the proportions. Your results should be identical with ours except that they are expressed in percentages.*

---

Note that with a 95 percent confidence level there is a 5 percent risk that we are wrong. That is, if we continued to draw samples of $N = 826$ from this population over and over again, then in 5 out of 100 samples the true population proportion would not be included in this specified interval.

Figure 12.9 **95 Percent Confidence Interval for the Percentage of Clinton Supporters**

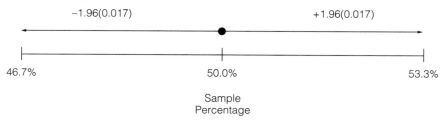

We can decrease our risk by increasing the confidence level from 95 to 99 percent.

$$99\% \ CI = .50 + 2.58(.017)$$
$$= .50 \pm .044$$
$$= .456 \ to \ .544$$

When using the 99 percent confidence interval we can be almost certain (99 times out of 100) that the true population proportion is included in the interval ranging from .456 (45.6%) to .544 (54.4%). However, as we saw earlier, there is a trade-off between achieving greater confidence in making an estimate and the precision of that estimate. Although using a 99 percent level increased our confidence level from 95 percent to 99 percent (thereby reducing our risk of being wrong from 5% to 1%), the estimate became less precise as the width of the interval increased.

## Increasing the Sample Size

The relationship between sample size and interval width when estimating means (illustrated in Table 12.1) also holds true for sample proportions. When the sample size increases, the standard error of the proportion decreases, and therefore the width of the confidence interval decreases as well. For instance, when we increase the sample of registered voters from $N = 826$ to $N = 1,500$, our standard error becomes

$$S_p = \sqrt{\frac{(.50)(.50)}{1,500}} = .013$$

and the 95 percent confidence interval is

$$95\% \ CI = .50 \pm 1.96(.013)$$
$$= .50 \pm .025$$
$$= .475 \ to \ .525$$

Notice that the width of the confidence interval decreased from .066 (.467 to .533) with $N = 826$ to .05 (.475 to .525) with $N = 1,500$. Thus, to increase the precision of our estimate only slightly we had to almost double our sample size! The increase in sample size is associated with increased cost, and therefore we need to consider whether the increased accuracy of the estimate justifies the associated increased cost of the project.

### Example 3 Revisited: Raising the Minimum Wage

We want to obtain a 95 percent confidence interval for the proportion of adult Americans who favor a proposal to raise the minimum wage from $4.25 to $5.15 per hour. We saw earlier that out of a random sample of 1,011 adult Americans, 78 percent favored raising the minimum wage.

*Calculating the Standard Error of the Proportion*  The standard error of the proportion .78 (78%) with a sample $N = 1,011$ is

$$S_p = \sqrt{\frac{(.78)(.22)}{1,011}} = .013$$

*Deciding on the Desired Level of Confidence and Finding the Corresponding Z Value*  We choose the 95 percent confidence level, with a corresponding $Z$ value of 1.96.

*Calculating the Confidence Interval*

$$\begin{aligned}
95\% \text{ CI} &= .78 \pm 1.96(.013) \\
&= .78 \pm .025 \\
&= .755 \text{ to } .805
\end{aligned}$$

*Interpreting the Results*  We are 95 percent confident that the true population proportion is somewhere between .755 and .805. In other words, if we drew a very large number of samples ($N = 1,011$) from the population of adult American voters, then 95 times out of 100 the true population proportion would be included within the obtained interval.

> **Learning Check.**  *Recalculate the confidence interval for the 78 percent who favor the increase in minimum wage, but decrease the sample size from $N = 1,011$ to $N = 500$. How did the change in the sample size affect the precision of your estimate? your risk level?*

## Statistics in Practice: Opinions About the Death Penalty

The results of public opinion polls are often reported in newspapers, in magazines, on television, and on the radio. Such reports almost routinely include a reference to the "sampling error" or the "margin of error" in connection with the poll results.[3] The margin of error and the sampling error are confidence intervals associated with the poll results. The format for presenting confidence intervals in the media usually differs from the format we employed in this chapter. Moreover, often these reports are incomplete and do not include a reference to the confidence level and/or the size of the sample.

We should have no problems interpreting estimates reported in the media provided they are complete and include a reference to the method of sampling, the sample size, the width of the confidence interval, and the confidence level.

For example, the Gallup organization estimated that the majority of adults living in the United States endorse the death penalty. According to a poll conducted in 1995, 77 percent say they favor the death penalty for a person convicted of murder.[4] Here is how the Gallup organization described the sampling error associated with their estimate:

> It should be borne in mind that all sample surveys are subject to sampling error, that is, the extent to which the results may differ from what would be obtained if the whole population surveyed had been interviewed. . . . The results of the whole sample are based on telephone interviews with a randomly selected national sample of 1,000 adults. For results based on a sample of this size, one can say with 95 percent confidence that the error attributable to sampling and other random effects could be plus [or] minus three percentage points.[5]

In this example the Gallup organization used the 95 percent confidence level, and the confidence interval was ±3 percent. We can interpret these results to mean that in 95 cases out of 100, the results obtained in a sample of this size are within ±3 percentage points of what would have been obtained had we interviewed the entire population from which this sample was drawn. In other words, we can say that in 95 cases out of 100 the true population percentage of adult Americans who favor the death penalty will be included within the obtained interval.

## Statistics in Practice: More on the Death Penalty

In this chapter our discussion was limited to single estimates of a parameter made for the total population. For instance, the *Time*/CNN

---

[3]See also Richard Maisel and Caroline Hodges Persell, *How Sampling Works*. Thousand Oaks, CA: Pine Forge Press, 1996, 134–135.

[4]*Gallup Poll Monthly*, June 1995, p. 23.

[5]Ibid.

poll reported the estimated percentage of Clinton supporters among registered voters in the United States. Similarly, the Yankelovich polling organization provided an estimate of the percentage of adult Americans who favor an increase in the minimum wage.

Most survey studies, however, are not limited to single estimates for the overall population. Often, separate estimates are reported for subgroups within the overall population of interest. For example, the Gallup survey compared level of support for the death penalty among whites (81%) and nonwhites (56%); men (80%) and women (74%); and Republicans (89%) and Democrats (67%). When estimates are reported for subgroups, the confidence intervals are likely to vary from subgroup to subgroup. Each confidence interval is based on the confidence level, the standard error of the proportion (which can be estimated from $p$), and the sample size. Therefore, even when a confidence interval is reported only for the overall sample, we can easily compute separate confidence intervals for each of the subgroups if the confidence level and the size of each of the subgroups are included in the report.

To illustrate this, let's calculate the 95 percent confidence intervals for the proportions of whites and nonwhites who support the death penalty for a person convicted of murder. These proportions were reported by the Gallup organization in its 1995 poll on opinions about the death penalty. Out of 846 whites included in its overall sample, .81 (or 81%) favor the death penalty. In contrast, .56 (or 56%) of the 154 nonwhites support the death penalty.

*Calculating the Standard Error of the Proportion* The standard error for the proportion of whites (.81) who support the death penalty ($N = 846$) is

$$S_p = \sqrt{\frac{(.81)(.19)}{846}} = .013$$

The standard error for the proportion of nonwhites (.56) who support the death penalty ($N = 154$) is

$$S_p = \sqrt{\frac{(.56)(.44)}{154}} = .04$$

*Deciding on the Desired Level of Confidence and Finding the Corresponding Z Value* We choose the 95 percent confidence level, with a corresponding $Z$ value of 1.96.

*Calculating the Confidence Interval* For whites

$$95\% \text{ CI} = .81 \pm 1.96(.013)$$
$$= .81 \pm .025$$
$$= .785 \text{ to } .835$$

Figure 12.10 **The 95 Percent Confidence Intervals for the Proportion of Whites and Nonwhites Supporting the Death Penalty**

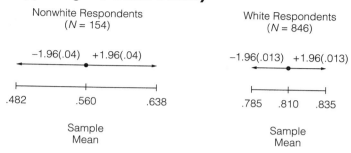

and for nonwhites

$$95\% \text{ CI} = .56 \pm 1.96(.04)$$
$$= .56 \pm .078$$
$$= .482 \text{ to } .638$$

The 95 percent confidence interval for the proportion of white and nonwhite respondents who support the death penalty is illustrated in Figure 12.10.

*Interpreting the Results* We are 95 percent confident that the true population proportion supporting the death penalty is somewhere between .785 and .835 (or between 78.5% and 83.5%) for whites, and somewhere between .482 and .638 (or between 48.2% and 63.8%) for nonwhites. Notice that the intervals vary considerably from .05 for whites to .156 for nonwhites. Because the sample for nonwhites ($N = 154$) is considerably smaller than the white sample ($N = 846$), the estimate for nonwhites is less precise than the estimate for white respondents.

## MAIN POINTS

■ The goal of most research is to find population parameters. The major objective of sampling theory and statistical inference is to provide estimates of unknown parameters from sample statistics.

■ Researchers make point estimates and interval estimates. Point estimates are sample statistics used to estimate the exact value of a population parameter. Interval estimates are ranges of values within which the population parameter may fall.

- Confidence intervals can be used to estimate population parameters like means or proportions. Their accuracy is defined with the confidence level. The most common confidence levels are 90 percent, 95 percent, and 99 percent.

- To establish a confidence interval for a mean or a proportion, add or subtract from the mean or the proportion the product of the standard error and the Z value corresponding to the confidence level.

### KEY TERMS

*confidence interval (interval estimate)*   *estimation*

*confidence level*   *point estimate*

### SPSS DEMONSTRATION

*Demonstration 1: Producing Confidence Intervals Around a Mean*

In this chapter, we learned how to create confidence intervals for interval-ratio data and for proportions. SPSS can calculate confidence intervals around a sample mean or proportion with the Explore procedure, which we encountered in an earlier chapter. Let's use it to investigate the mean age of marriage for women and men in 1994 with the 1994 GSS file.

Activate the Explore procedure by selecting the *Statistics* menu, *Summarize,* then *Explore.* The opening dialog box has spaces for both dependent and independent variables. Place AGEWED in the Dependent List: box, and SEX in the Factor List: box, as shown.

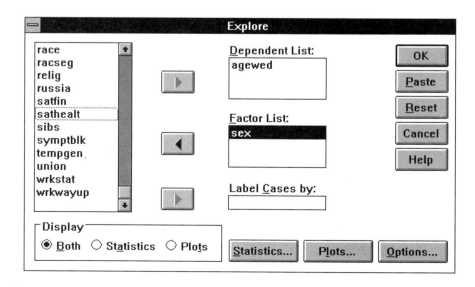

Click on the *Statistics* button. Notice that the Descriptives choice also includes the confidence interval for the mean, which by default is calculated at the 95 percent confidence level. Let's change that to the 99 percent level by erasing the "95" and substituting "99."

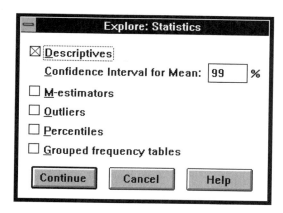

Click on *Continue* to return to the main dialog box. Recall that Explore produces several statistics and plots by default. For this example, we don't need to view the graphics, so click on the *Statistics* radio button in the *Display* section. Your screen should now look like this.

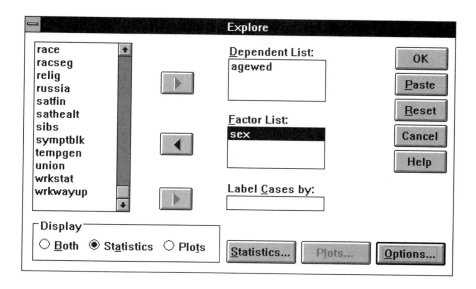

Click on *OK* to run the procedure.

The output from the Explore procedure is broken into two parts, one for males and one for females. The mean age of marriage for males is 23.9 years; for females it's 21.9. In American society, males tend to marry at a slightly later age than females, and males tend to marry slightly younger females (the latter observation is not proven by these mean differences but is compatible with them).

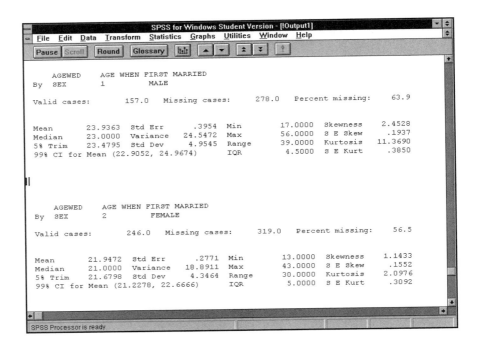

The 99 percent confidence interval for males runs from about 22.90 to 24.9 years. One way to interpret this result is to state that, in 100 samples of size 157 of males (note the number of males in this sample) from the U.S. adult population, we would expect the confidence interval we calculate to include the true population value for the mean age of marriage 99 times out of those 100. We can never be sure that in *this* particular sample the confidence interval includes the population mean. As explained in this chapter, any one sample's confidence interval either does or does not contain the (unknown) population mean, so no probability value can be associated with a particular confidence interval. Still, given all this, our best estimate for the mean age of male first marriage falls within a narrow range of only about 2.06 years.

For females, the 99 percent confidence interval is even narrower, varying from about 21.23 to 22.67 years, or only 1.44 years. This is because we have a larger sample of females, 246. Notice that the standard deviation of AGEWED is very similar for males and females.

In summary, despite the changes that have occurred since the 1960s in women's roles in society, people still are getting married at fairly young ages. On the other hand, if there is a trend toward slightly older marriages because of longer schooling and/or females entering the labor force, it may appear only when we examine people under, say, the age of 40. To take this demonstration one step further, use the Select Cases procedure to do that analysis.

### EXERCISES

1. In a study of crime, the FBI found that 13.2 percent of all Americans had been victims of crime during a one-year period. This result was based on a sample of 1,105 adults.

   a. Estimate the percentage of U.S. adults who were victims at the 90 percent confidence level. State in words the meaning of the result.

   b. Estimate the percent of victims at the 99 percent confidence level.

   c. Imagine that the FBI doubles the sample size in a new sample but finds the same value of 13.2 percent for the percentage of victims in the second sample. By how much would the 90 percent confidence interval shrink? By how much would the 99 percent confidence interval shrink?

   d. Considering your answers to (a), (b), and (c), can you suggest why national surveys, such as those by Gallup, Roper, or the *New York Times,* typically take samples of size 1,000 to 1,500?

2. Use the data in exercise 5 in Chapter 10 about income for this question.

   a. Construct the 95 percent confidence interval for the mean income of males.

   b. Construct the 99 percent confidence interval for the mean income of males.

   c. As our confidence in the result increases, how does the size of the confidence interval change? Explain why this is true.

3. The United States has often adopted an isolationist foreign policy designed to stay out of foreign entanglements (as George Washington advised his fellow citizens two hundred years ago). In 1995, the Times Mirror organization polled a random sample of Americans, asking, "Please tell me whether you agree or disagree that the United States should mind its own business internationally and let

other countries get along as best they can on their own." The poll found that .41 of the 1,007 respondents agreed with this statement.

   a. Estimate the proportion of all adult Americans who agree with the statement at the 95 percent confidence level.

   b. Estimate the proportion of all adult Americans who agree with the statement at the 99 percent confidence level.

   c. If you were going to write a report on this poll result, would you prefer to use the 99 percent or 95 percent confidence interval? Explain why.

4. Use the data in exercise 6 in Chapter 5 about occupational prestige for blacks and whites.

   a. Construct the 95 percent confidence interval for occupational prestige for blacks.

   b. Construct the 95 percent confidence interval for occupational prestige for whites. State in words the meaning of the result.

   c. Use these statistics to discuss differences in occupational prestige for blacks and whites. Does it appear that whites do have greater job prestige than blacks? Why?

5. Affirmative action has been a much-debated topic in this country since policies to implement quotas and preferences for minorities in hiring, university admissions, and other areas were begun in the 1960s. Many national surveys have asked questions designed to measure public support for affirmative action. In a 1994 NBC/*Wall Street Journal* poll, 81 percent of 751 respondents disagreed that "Blacks and other minorities should receive special preferences in hiring to make up for past inequalities."

   a. Calculate the 95 percent confidence interval for this percentage.

   b. Given your result in (a), is it likely that a majority of Americans favored special preferences in hiring?

6. A newspaper does a poll to determine the likely vote for the incumbent mayor, George Johnson, in the upcoming election. They find that 52 percent of the voters favor Johnson in a sample of 500 likely voters. The newspaper asks you, their statistical consultant, to tell them whether they should declare Johnson the likely winner of the election. What is your advice? Why?

7. The Chicago police department was asked by the mayor's office to estimate the cost of crime to citizens of Chicago. The police began their study with the crime of burglary, taking a random sample of 500 files (there is too much crime to calculate statistics for all the crimes committed).

   a. If the average dollar loss in a burglary, for this sample of size 500, is $678, with a standard deviation of $560, construct the

95 percent confidence interval for the true mean dollar loss in burglaries.

b. An assistant to the mayor, who claims to understand statistics, complains about your confidence interval calculation. She asserts that the dollar losses from burglaries are not normally distributed, which in turn makes the confidence interval calculation meaningless. Assume that she is correct about the distribution of money loss. Does that imply that the calculation of a confidence interval is not appropriate? Why or why not?

8. From the 1994 GSS we find that the mean number of hours worked last week in the U.S. population was 41.44, with a standard deviation of 13.95. A total of 636 adults answered this question.

a. What is the 95 percent confidence interval for the mean number of hours worked last week in the U.S. population?

b. Does the size of this confidence interval seem compatible with the fact that a sizable proportion of adults work only part-time? Why or why not?

9. A social service agency plans to do a survey of its clientele and would like to determine the mean income. The director of the agency prefers that you measure the mean income very accurately, to within ±$500. From a sample taken two years ago, you estimate that the standard deviation of income for this population is about $5,000. Your job is to figure out the necessary sample size to reduce sampling error to ±$500.

a. Do you need to have an estimate of the current mean income to answer this question? Why or why not?

b. What sample size should be drawn to meet the director's requirement at the 95 percent level of confidence? (*Hint:* Use the formula for a confidence interval and solve for $N$, the sample size.)

c. What sample size should be drawn to meet the director's requirement at the 99 percent level of confidence?

10. Data from the 1994 General Social Survey show that the mean number of children per respondent was 1.8, with a standard deviation of 1.62. A total of 997 people answered this question. Estimate the population mean number of children per adult using a 90 percent confidence interval.

11. A finance company took a random sample of their records to determine the proportion of auto loans they financed that were not repaid. In their sample of 500 they found that .12 of the loans defaulted (and the car had to be repossessed). Estimate at the 99 percent confidence level the proportion of all auto loans financed by the company that eventually default.

12. A psychologist is using the Inventory of Childhood Memories and Imaginings (ICMI) as a test designed to measure fantasy proneness, defined as the ability to engage in deep and profound fantasy and imagination on a regular basis. The ICMI scale runs from 0 to 52. She administers the test to 400 adults, trying to get a baseline mean for the normal population so that it can be used as a comparison in future studies of unusual or disturbed populations. She finds a mean ICMI score of 23.5, with a standard deviation of 9.5 in the sample.
   a. Estimate the population mean ICMI score at the 95 percent confidence level.
   b. Estimate the population mean ICMI score at the 99 percent confidence level.

13. The cost of health care continues to be a serious concern of Americans. This is especially true if you are without health insurance for any reason. To gauge the magnitude of this problem, the Gallup organization did a poll in May 1993 that asked whether a person had been without insurance at some point in the past. Out of the sample of 1,011, 41 percent answered yes to this question. What is the 95 percent confidence interval for the percentage of adult Americans who have been without insurance?

14. The Social Security system in the United States may encounter serious financial difficulties as baby boomers begin to retire in the future. Several polls have asked Americans their opinion about the financial condition of Social Security. In one poll taken in 1992 by CBS News and the *New York Times*, 53 percent of a sample of 1,281 adults said that they did not think "the Social Security system will have the money available to provide the benefits you expect for your retirement."
   a. Calculate the 95 percent confidence interval to estimate the percentage of Americans who don't think Social Security will be able to provide for them.
   b. Calculate the 99 percent confidence interval.
   c. Are both these results compatible with the view that *less* than 50 percent of Americans believe that the Social Security system will not be able to pay their benefits after retirement?

### SPSS PROBLEM

1. The question of the economic well-being of the American population is obviously an important issue. After adjusting for inflation, the average income increased fairly steadily in the years after World War II as the United States experienced the longest period

of economic expansion in its history. Then beginning in the early 1970s, real income, adjusted for inflation, went up only slowly, even declining in some years during economic downturns.

The 1987 to 1991 General Social Survey contains the variable REALRINC, which measures the respondent's income adjusted for inflation. It also contains the variable YEAR, which measures what year the data were collected. The income data were calculated for 1987, 1988, and 1989.

a. Use SPSS to explore how mean income changed over these three years at the end of the Reagan presidency. The Explore procedure will calculate the mean and a confidence interval around the mean. Have SPSS calculate the 95 percent confidence interval for REALRINC for each year. What is the width of the interval for 1989? for 1988? Why is the interval in 1989 narrower? (*Hint:* We are asking for statistical reasons here, not economic ones.)

b. Considering the width of the intervals, does it seem that REALRINC increased from 1988 to 1989? (*Hint:* Do the confidence intervals overlap?)

c. Now have SPSS calculate the 90 percent confidence intervals for REALRINC for each year. Does this change your evaluation of whether or not real income increased from 1988 to 1989? (*Note:* When the Bureau of Labor Statistics (BLS) calculates real income, it also uses a sample, but a very large one. Given what you know about the relationship of sample size and sampling error of the mean, this implies that the BLS 95 percent confidence interval for the mean is quite narrow, so that small yearly changes in the mean can be detected.)

A second critical statistical point leads into the topic of the next chapter. When comparing the means of two distributions, you should not, strictly speaking, compare two confidence intervals to see whether they overlap or not, even though this procedure can be helpful. The reason is somewhat technical, but the good news is that there are straightforward statistical tests to determine whether the means from two independent samples are different. These tests are discussed in Chapter 14.

## GROUP PROBLEMS

1. Are national election polls accurate? What is the typical size of the sampling error, or confidence interval, in these polls? Use data from the 1996 presidential election to answer this question. Review

preelection polls published in national media, including the *New York Times*, the *Washington Post, Time, Newsweek, USA Today*, or other national publications. Assign one group member to each publication to share the load, and gather information on polls conducted from about October 1 until the election in early November. For each poll, record the percentage predicted to vote for the three major candidates (Clinton, Dole, and Perot), the size of the sample, the sampling error (so you can place a confidence interval around the estimates), and any other characteristics that seem important (for example, was it a survey done by telephone or by personal interview?). Also, assign one group member to gather data on the actual election results. Remember that you can calculate a confidence interval for any poll if you know the sample size and response proportions (or percentages).

Now pool your results and see whether each poll's estimates (the confidence interval around a point estimate) included the actual percentage voting for a candidate in the general election. For example, if a poll predicted that Perot would receive 18 percent of the vote, plus or minus 3 percent, and Perot's actual vote total was 19.8 percent, then that poll was accurate. Have a group discussion where you consider this information and determine which polls were more accurate and which were less accurate. Was there any difference in accuracy by candidate? by polling organization? Can you suggest reasons, based on your research, why some polls are more accurate? Then work on a group presentation or report that summarizes your findings.

2. This exercise is designed to test how accurately you can estimate some characteristic of the students at your college or university from a sample. Pick some characteristic of a student for which it is possible to get accurate information for the total student body, such as the proportion of out-of-state undergrads, average age of all students, gender distribution, race, and so forth. Then construct a sampling scheme to gather this information from about fifty students (don't use members of the class). Once you have the data, construct a 95 percent confidence interval around your mean or proportion and see whether or not the true population value is contained within the confidence interval. If it is, congratulations! If not, suggest reasons why.

# 13     Testing Hypotheses: The Basics

**Introduction**

**Elements of Statistical Hypothesis Testing**

The Research Hypothesis ($H_1$)

The Null Hypothesis ($H_0$)

Assumptions of Statistical Hypothesis Testing

The Test Statistic and the *P* Value

Determining What Is Sufficiently Improbable

The Critical Value of the Test Statistic

One- and Two-Tailed Tests

Making a Decision and Interpreting the Result

The Six Steps in Hypothesis Testing: A Summary

*1. Making Assumptions*

*2. Stating the Research and the Null Hypotheses*

*3. Selecting the Sampling Distribution and Specifying the Test Statistic*

*4. Choosing Alpha (α) and Establishing the Region of Rejection*

*5. Computing the Test Statistic*

*6. Making a Decision and Interpreting the Results*

Statistics in Practice: The Earnings of White Women

*Applying the Six-Step Model*

*Comparing One- and Two-Tailed Tests*

**Errors in Hypothesis Testing**

MAIN POINTS

KEY TERMS

SPSS DEMONSTRATION

EXERCISES

SPSS PROBLEMS

GROUP PROBLEMS

## Introduction

A quarter of a century after Congress enacted major legislation aimed at equalizing opportunity in the workplace, black Americans continue to experience considerable earnings disadvantages relative to other workers in the labor market. Numerous studies have described the racial disparities in education, occupation, and income. For example, whites are almost twice as likely to be employed in managerial and professional fields, whereas blacks are much more concentrated in semiskilled labor and service occupations. Moreover, unemployment rates are considerably higher for African Americans. For instance, the differences in unemployment rates between black and white teenagers are striking: in 1992 the unemployment rate for black male teenagers was 42 percent compared with 18 percent for white male teenagers. The differences in education and in labor market experiences are reflected in persistent gaps in income. Thus, we would expect the average income of black Americans to be lower than the average earnings nationally.

We drew a random sample of African Americans ($N = 66$) working full-time from the GSS and calculated their mean income for 1990. Based on census information[1] we also know the mean earnings nationally of Americans who were employed full-time in 1990. We can thus compare the mean earnings of blacks in 1990 with the mean national earnings of all Americans who were employed full-time in 1990. By comparing these means we are asking whether it is reasonable to consider the sample of black Americans a random sample that is representative of the population of full-time workers in the United States. We expect to find the sample of blacks to be unrepresentative of the population of full-time workers because we assume that blacks

---

[1] *Current Population Survey,* March 1990, P-60 Series.

experience a considerable earnings disadvantage relative to other workers in the labor market.

The mean earnings for our sample of blacks is $\overline{Y}$ = $18,037. These earnings are considerably lower than $23,766, the mean earnings of the population of full-time workers obtained from the census.

But, is the observed gap of $5,729 ($23,766 – $18,037) large enough to convince us that the sample of blacks is not representative of the population? There is no easy answer to this question. The sample mean of $18,037 is considerably lower than $23,766, the average earnings nationally, but it is an estimate based on a single sample. It is possible that we happened by chance to draw a sample with a mean lower than $23,766. Had we selected another sample, we would have probably gotten another estimate; or, had we surveyed all black Americans who were employed full-time in 1990, we might have found that the average earnings were not lower than $23,766.

Thus, the sample average of $18,037 could mean one of two things: (1) the average earnings of the black population are indeed lower than average earnings nationally, or (2) the average earnings of the black population are about the same as the national average, and this sample happens to show a particularly low mean.

How can we decide which of these explanations makes more sense? Because most estimates are based on single samples and different samples result in different estimates, sampling results cannot be interpreted directly. We need a decision-making tool that enables us to evaluate hypotheses about population parameters on the basis of sample statistics. In Chapter 12 we saw that population parameters can be estimated from sample statistics. In this and the following two chapters, we learn how to use sample statistics to make decisions about population parameters. This process is called **statistical hypothesis testing**.

## Elements of Statistical Hypothesis Testing

In Chapter 1, we saw that hypotheses are usually defined in terms of interrelations between variables and are often based on a substantive theory. We also defined *hypotheses* as tentative answers to research questions. They are tentative because they can be verified only after they have been tested empirically. The testing of hypotheses discussed in this and the following two chapters is an important step in this verification process. The first step in this process is to express the substantive hypothesis (the *research hypothesis*) in more formal terms that are amenable to a statistical test.

## The Research Hypothesis ($H_1$)

The substantive hypothesis is called the **research hypothesis** and is symbolized by $H_1$. Research hypotheses are always expressed in terms of population parameters because we are interested in making statements about population parameters based on sample statistics. (Recall that the term *parameter* refers to a characteristic of a population.) Therefore, the symbols we use to state our research hypothesis are always population symbols and not sample statistics. Thus, in stating our hypothesis about the mean earnings of blacks, we use the symbol for the population mean, $\mu_Y$, not the sample mean symbol, $\overline{Y}$.

*Hypotheses* can be defined as statements of relationships between or among variables. Thus, by hypothesizing that the average wages of blacks are lower than average wages nationally, we are stating a relationship between race and wages. Our research hypothesis ($H_1$) suggests that the mean earnings of the black population are less than the mean national earnings of $23,766. Symbolically, this hypothesis can be expressed as

$H_1$: $\mu_Y < \$23,766$

In general, the research hypothesis ($H_1$) specifies that the population parameter is one of the following:

1. Not equal to some specified value: $\mu_Y \neq$ some specified value
2. Greater than some specified value: $\mu_Y >$ some specified value
3. Less than some specified value: $\mu_Y <$ some specified value

---

*Research Hypothesis ($H_1$)* A statement reflecting the substantive hypothesis. It is always expressed in terms of population parameters, but its specific form varies from test to test.

---

## The Null Hypothesis ($H_0$)

Before we use our sample observation to decide that the mean earnings of blacks are lower than the mean earnings nationally, we need to assure ourselves that the observed difference of $5,729 ($23,766 − $18,037 = $5,729) is not due to sampling error. Is it possible that in the population there is no difference between the mean wages of blacks and the mean wages nationally, and that the observed difference is due to the fact that this particular sample happened to contain a lot of cases with low earnings (although, on average, blacks earn about the same as everyone else)? Since statistical inference is based on probability theory, it is not possible to prove or disprove the research hypothesis directly. At best, we can estimate the likelihood that it is true or false.

Statisticians have come up with a solution to this dilemma by setting up a hypothesis that runs counter to the research hypothesis. The **null hypothesis**, symbolized as $H_0$, contradicts the research hypothesis and usually states that there is no difference between the population mean and some specified value.

Thus, for our example, the null hypothesis is stated symbolically as

$$H_0: \mu_Y = \$23,766$$

According to the null hypothesis, any observed difference between the mean earnings of blacks and the mean earnings nationally is due to the fact that this particular sample happened to contain a lot of cases with low earnings even though blacks, on average, earn about the same as everyone else.

Rather than directly testing the substantive hypothesis $(H_1)$ that there is a difference between the mean earnings of blacks and the mean earnings nationally, we test the null hypothesis $(H_0)$ that there are no differences in these earnings. The rejection of the null hypothesis will strengthen our belief in the substantive hypothesis. In testing statistical hypotheses we hope to reject the null hypothesis to provide support for the research hypothesis. Furthermore, the empirical support of the research hypothesis also increases our confidence in the importance and utility of the broader theory from which the research hypothesis was derived. In the following discussion, we illustrate how we go about testing the null hypothesis.

---

*Null Hypothesis ($H_0$)*   A statement of "no difference," which contradicts the research hypothesis and is always expressed in terms of population parameters.

---

## Assumptions of Statistical Hypothesis Testing

Statistical hypothesis testing involves several assumptions that must be met for the results of the test to be valid. These assumptions include considerations of the level of measurement of the variable, the method of sampling, the shape of the population distribution, and the sample size. The specific assumptions may vary, depending on the test or the conditions of testing. However, without exceptions, *all* statistical tests assume random sampling. Tests of hypotheses about means also assume interval-ratio level of measurement and require that the population under consideration is normally distributed or that the sample size is larger than 50.

The test we are considering for the mean income of blacks meets these conditions:

1. The sample is a subgroup in the GSS sample, which is a national probability sample, randomly selected.

2. The variable "income" is measured on an interval-ratio level of measurement.

3. We cannot assume that the population is normally distributed (remember that income distributions are usually *skewed*). However, because our sample size is sufficiently large ($N > 50$), we know, based on the Central Limit Theorem, that the sampling distribution of the mean will be approximately normal.

## The Test Statistic and the *P* Value

Having formulated the null hypothesis that the mean earnings of blacks are equal to the mean earnings nationally

$H_0$: $\mu_Y = \$23,766$

we now test it. The testing of the null hypothesis is based on determining the likelihood of getting the observed sample mean ($\overline{Y} = \$18,037$) given that the null hypothesis is true. In other words, we are going to determine the probability of obtaining a sample mean of $18,037 from a population in which the mean is actually $23,766. If the probability is very low, we will reject the null hypothesis as false in support of the alternative hypothesis that the average earnings of blacks are indeed lower than $23,766.

How do we go about determining the probability of the observed sample mean of $18,037 if the population mean is actually $23,766? We can determine this probability because of what we know about the sampling distribution and its properties. We know that because the sampling distribution includes all possible sample results, it allows us to compare our sample result with all possible sample outcomes and estimate the likelihood of its occurrence. We also know, based on the Central Limit Theorem, that if our sample size is larger than 50, the sampling distribution of the mean is approximately normal, with a mean $\mu_Y$ and a standard deviation $\sigma_Y/\sqrt{N}$.

So let's put all this information together. We are going to assume that the null hypothesis is true and then see if our sample evidence casts doubt on that assumption. We have a population mean $\mu_Y$ = $23,766 and a standard deviation $\sigma_Y$ = $16,101.[2] Our sample size is $N$ = 66 and the sample mean is $\overline{Y}$ = $18,037. Based on the Central Limit Theorem, we can assume that the distribution of means of all possible samples of size $N$ = 66 drawn from this distribution would be approximately normal, with a mean $23,766 and a standard deviation

$$\frac{16,101}{\sqrt{66}} = 1,982$$

This sampling distribution is shown in Figure 13.1. Also shown in Figure 13.1 is the mean earnings we observed for our sample of black Americans.

What is the probability of drawing a sample with a mean $\overline{Y}$ = $18,037 or smaller from this population if the mean was actually $\mu_Y$ = $23,766? Because this distribution of sample means is normal we can use Appendix B to determine the probability of drawing a sample mean of $18,037 or smaller from this population. But first we need to translate our sample mean into a $Z$ score so we can determine its location relative to the population mean. In Chapter 10, we learned how to translate a raw score into a $Z$ score by using formula 10.1:

$$Z = \frac{Y - \overline{Y}}{S_Y}$$

Figure 13.1  **Sampling Distribution of Sample Means Assuming $H_0$ Is True for a Sample $N$ = 66**

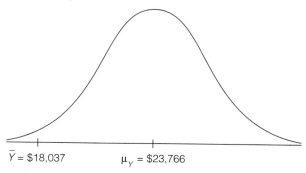

$\overline{Y}$ = $18,037          $\mu_Y$ = $23,766

[2]The standard deviation was calculated from the 1990 *Current Population Survey,* March 1990, P-60 Series.

Divide the difference between the score and the mean of the distribution by the standard deviation of the distribution. Because we are dealing with a sampling distribution in which our raw score is $\overline{Y}$, the mean is $\mu_Y$, and the standard deviation is $\sigma_Y/\sqrt{N}$, we need to modify the formula somewhat:

$$Z = \frac{\overline{Y} - \mu_Y}{\dfrac{\sigma_Y}{\sqrt{N}}} \qquad\qquad (13.1)$$

Thus, to translate a sample mean into a $Z$ score, we subtract from it the mean of the sampling distribution of the means (also the population mean) and divide the result by the standard deviation of the sampling distribution (its standard error). Converting the sample mean to a $Z$ score equivalent is called computing the *test statistic*. The $Z$ value we obtain is called the **obtained Z**. The obtained $Z$ gives us the number of standard deviations (standard errors) that our sample $\overline{Y}$ is from the hypothesized value $\mu_Y$, assuming the null hypothesis is true. For our example, the obtained $Z$ is

$$Z = \frac{\overline{Y} - \mu_Y}{\dfrac{\sigma_Y}{\sqrt{N}}} = \frac{18,037 - 23,766}{\dfrac{16,101}{\sqrt{66}}} = -2.89$$

---

**Z (obtained)**   The test statistic computed by converting a sample statistic to a $Z$ score. The formula for obtaining $Z$ varies from test to test.

---

To determine the probability of observing a $Z$ value of $-2.89$, given that the null hypothesis is true, look up the value in Appendix B to find the area to the left of (below) the negative $Z$ of 2.89. This area includes the proportion of all sample means of \$18,037 or lower. To find the area to the left of (below) a negative $Z$ score, refer to the entry in column C that corresponds to the specified $Z$ score (found in column A). The value is .0019 (see Figure 13.2). This means that .0019, or fewer than 19 out of 10,000 samples drawn from this population, are likely to have a mean that is 2.89 $Z$ scores below the hypothesized mean of \$23,766. Another way to say this: There are only 19 chances out of 10,000 (or .19%) that we would draw a random sample with a $Z \leq -2.89$ if the mean earnings of blacks were equal to mean earnings nationally. This value is the probability of getting a result as extreme

Figure 13.2   **The Probability (P) Associated with Z ≤ -2.89**

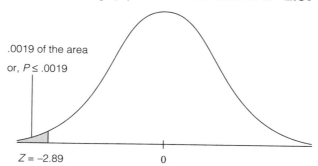

.0019 of the area

or, $P \leq .0019$

$Z = -2.89$       0

as the sample result if the null hypothesis is true; it is symbolized as *P*. Thus, for our example, $P \leq .0019$.

Our null hypothesis states that the earnings of blacks are identical with the mean earnings nationally, and, therefore, the observed sample mean of $18,037 was simply due to sampling error. We just established that the probability that this difference of $5,729 is due to sampling error is $P \leq .0019$ (or .19%). Is this probability sufficiently low to allow us to reject the null hypothesis (that is, that the sample mean of $18,037 came from a population with a mean of $23,766) in favor of the research hypothesis that the mean for blacks is less than $23,766? We still need to make a decision because there is still a .0019 probability that the observed difference is due to sampling error! (The risk of making such an error is discussed in more detail later in this chapter.) We need to make a decision about what would be considered sufficiently improbable to allow us to reject the null hypothesis *despite* the probability of making a mistake!

---

**P Value**   The probability associated with the obtained value of Z.

---

## Determining What Is Sufficiently Improbable

In the preceding section we determined the probability, expressed as *P*, of observing a $Z \leq -2.89$. The value of *P* tells us how likely it is to have observed a sample mean that is at least 2.89 standard deviations below the hypothesized mean of $23,766. If the likelihood is very low (*P* is very low) we reject the null hypothesis in favor of the research hypothesis.

Researchers usually define in advance what is a sufficiently improbable $Z$ value by specifying a cutoff point below which $P$ must fall to reject the null hypothesis. This cutoff point, called **alpha** and denoted by the Greek letter $\alpha$, is quite arbitrary but is customarily set at the .05, .01, or .001 level. For example, let's say that we decide to reject the null hypothesis that the sample mean of \$18,037 came from a population with a mean of \$23,766 if $P \leq .05$. The value .05 is referred to as $\alpha$ and it defines for us what result is sufficiently improbable to allow us to take the risk and reject the null hypothesis. Since our observed $P$ is less than .05 ($P =. 0019 < \alpha = .05$), we can reject the null hypothesis. We can then say that the null hypothesis was rejected at the .05 level of significance.

An alpha ($\alpha$) of .05 means that even if the observed sample result is due to sampling error, and so the null hypothesis is true, we have a 5 percent (or less) risk of rejecting it. Alphas of .01 and .001 are more stringent levels of significance. A .01 level means a 1 percent (or less) risk of making the error of rejecting a true null hypothesis; similarly, when we adopt a .001 level we are willing to take only a 0.1 percent (or less) risk of erroneously rejecting the null hypothesis.

---

*Alpha ($\alpha$)*   The level of probability at which the null hypothesis is rejected. It is customary to set alpha at the .05, .01, or .001 level.

---

The difference between $P$ and alpha is that whereas $P$ is the actual calculated probability associated with the obtained value of $Z$, alpha is the level of probability *determined in advance* at which the null hypothesis is rejected. The null hypothesis is rejected when $P \leq \alpha$.

> **Learning Check.**   *Can you think of some research examples where the researcher would be willing to take a 5 percent risk ($\alpha = .05$) of rejecting the null hypothesis if it were true? When might a 5 percent risk be too high?*

## The Critical Value of the Test Statistic

In our example, we calculated a $Z$ value for our sample mean of \$18,037, and then we found $P$, the probability associated with this $Z$ value. We then compared our obtained $P$ value with our chosen α (α = .05) and rejected the null hypothesis because $P < \alpha$ (.0019 < .05). In more formal applications of statistical hypothesis testing, rather than determining the $P$ value corresponding to our obtained $Z$ and comparing it with the selected α, we first determine the $Z$ value corresponding to our chosen α level. This $Z$ score is called the **critical value**. To find the **critical value of $Z$**, turn to Appendix B, column C, and then identify the $Z$ value associated with the desired α level. Thus, for a .05 level, we find .0500 (or the value closest to it) in column C and then identify the corresponding $Z$ value. The critical $Z$ associated with α = .05 is 1.65. Similarly, for .01 and .001 levels, the critical $Z$'s are 2.33 and 3.09, respectively.

The critical values of $Z$ associated with the .05, .01, and .001 levels are depicted in Figure 13.3. The shaded areas in Figure 13.3 are called the *regions of rejection*. The **region of rejection** is the area under the sampling distribution that includes all unlikely sample results. The critical $Z$, marking the beginning of the region of rejection, includes $Z$ values that are equal to or more extreme than the critical value and lead to the rejection of the null hypothesis.

---

*Region of Rejection*    The area under the sampling distribution that includes all unlikely sample results.

*Z (critical)*    The Z score associated with a particular α level and marking the beginning of the region of rejection.

---

## One- and Two-Tailed Tests

In Figure 13.3 the region of rejection is limited to only one tail—the left tail of the distribution. Figure 13.3 depicts what is known as a **one-tailed test**. The hypothesis we tested on the mean income of blacks is a one-tailed test. In a one-tailed test, the research hypothesis is directional; that is, it specifies that the mean of the tested population is either greater than (>) or less than (<) some specified value. Later in Chapter 14, we see that the research hypothesis in a one-tailed test states that a population mean is either less or greater than another population mean. When a one-tailed test specifies that the population mean is less than some specified value we call it a **left-tailed test** because the region of rejection is located in the left tail of the distribution. Our example was a left-tailed test because the research

Figure 13.3 **Regions of Rejection and Critical Zs for Alpha Levels of .05, .01, and .001 for One-Tailed Tests**

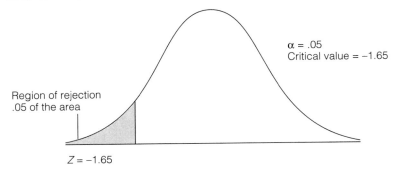

$\alpha = .05$
Critical value = −1.65

Region of rejection
.05 of the area

$Z = -1.65$

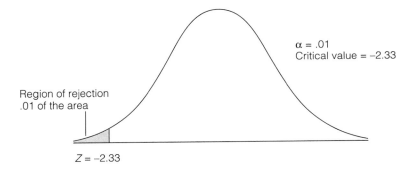

$\alpha = .01$
Critical value = −2.33

Region of rejection
.01 of the area

$Z = -2.33$

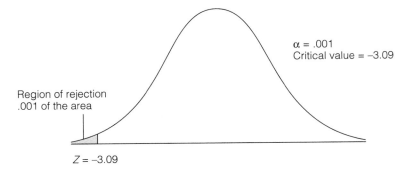

$\alpha = .001$
Critical value = −3.09

Region of rejection
.001 of the area

$Z = -3.09$

hypothesis stated that the mean earnings of the black population are less than $23,766, or

$$H_1: \mu_Y < \$23{,}766$$

---

***One-Tailed Test*** A type of hypothesis test in which the region of rejection is located on one side of the sampling distribution. A one-tailed test involves a directional research hypothesis.

---

In contrast, the research hypothesis can also specify that the mean of the population we are testing is larger than some specified value. We then call it a **right-tailed test** because the region of rejection is located at the right tail of the distribution. Had we hypothesized that the mean earnings of blacks are greater than the mean earnings nationally, our research hypothesis would have taken the form

$$H_1: \mu_Y > \$23{,}766$$

---

***Left-Tailed Test*** A one-tailed test in which the region of rejection is located in the left tail of the sampling distribution.

***Right-Tailed Test*** A one-tailed test in which the region of rejection is located in the right tail of the sampling distribution.

---

The location of the region of rejection for both types, a left- and a right-tailed test, is depicted in Figure 13.4. The critical Z for a .05 $\alpha$ level is also specified. Note that to reject the null hypothesis with a right-tailed test our obtained Z would need to be equal to or greater (more extreme) than a critical Z of +1.65, whereas to reject the null hypothesis with a left-tailed test we would be looking for an obtained Z equal to or less (more extreme) than a critical Z of −1.65.

In our example, we had theoretical reasons for believing that the mean earnings of blacks would be lower than mean earnings nationally. Therefore, the research hypothesis specified a direction, and we used a one-tailed test of the null hypothesis. However, there are numerous occasions when we may have some theoretical basis to assume that there might be differences between groups, but we cannot anticipate the direction of that difference. For example, we might have reason to believe that the average education of white men is *different* from 13.40 years, the average level of education nationally, but we may

Figure 13.4  **Regions of Rejection and Critical Zs for α = .05 for Right-and Left-Tailed Tests**

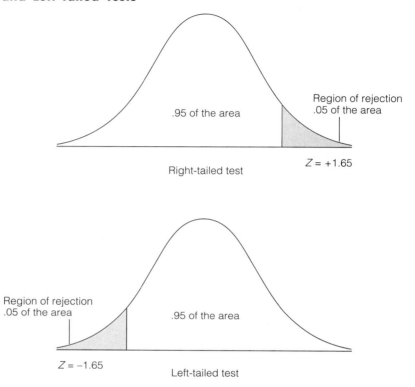

.95 of the area

Region of rejection
.05 of the area

*Z* = +1.65

Right-tailed test

Region of rejection
.05 of the area

.95 of the area

*Z* = −1.65

Left-tailed test

not have enough basis on which to predict that it is either *higher* or *lower* than the national average.

When we have no theoretical reason for specifying a direction to the research hypothesis, we conduct a two-tailed test. In such a test, the research hypothesis specifies that the population mean is *not equal* to some specified value. For example, we can express the research hypothesis about the mean education of white men as

$H_1$: $\mu_Y \neq 13.40$

The null hypothesis to be directly tested then takes the following form:

$H_0$: $\mu_Y = 13.40$

In a **two-tailed test** the region of rejection is located at both the high and the low ends of the sampling distribution—one half is located in the left tail and the other half in the right tail. For instance, a .05 alpha level means that $H_0$ will be rejected if our sample outcome falls either among the lowest or the highest 2.5 percent of the sampling distribution. To find the critical $Z$ for a two-tailed test, look up the area in column C of Appendix B that is equal to one-half the alpha level ($\alpha \div 2$); then find the $Z$ that corresponds to that area. For example, to find the critical $Z$ for $\alpha = .05$, look up .0250 (.05 ÷ 2 = .0250) in column C. The $Z$ value that corresponds to .0250 is ±1.96. The region of rejection and the critical $Z$ for a two-tailed test with $\alpha = .05$ are depicted in Figure 13.5.

---

***Two-Tailed Test*** A type of hypothesis test in which half the region of rejection is located at the left tail of the sampling distribution and half at the right tail of the sampling distribution. The test involves a nondirectional research hypothesis.

---

> ***Learning Check.*** *Would you use a one- or a two-tailed test to compare the mean statistics grades of social science majors with the mean statistics grades of all students? State the research and the null hypotheses. What alpha level would you use, and what is the critical value?*

Figure 13.5 **Region of Rejection and Critical $Z$ for a Two-Tailed Test at a .05 Alpha Level**

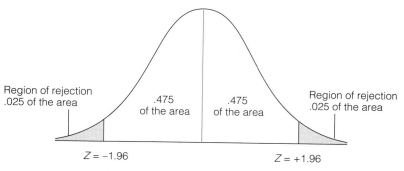

Region of rejection
.025 of the area

.475
of the area

.475
of the area

Region of rejection
.025 of the area

$Z = -1.96$          $Z = +1.96$

## Making a Decision and Interpreting the Result

Let's go back to our illustration of the average earnings of black Americans and determine the critical value for our test. We had previously selected an $\alpha$ level of .05 and, because our test is a left-tailed test, the region of rejection is located at the left tail of the distribution. The critical $Z$ for our test is therefore $-1.65$ (see Figure 13.3).

After identifying the critical $Z$, we compare it with our obtained $Z$. If the obtained value is equal to or more extreme (in the negative direction) than the critical value, it is considered *statistically significant* and leads to the rejection of the null hypothesis. Because our obtained $Z$ −2.89 is more extreme than the critical $Z$, −1.65, required for a one-tailed test with $\alpha = .05$, we reject the null hypothesis and conclude that the average earnings of blacks may indeed be lower than the national average of annual earnings. The critical $Z$ and the obtained $Z$ are depicted in Figure 13.6. Note that the obtained $Z$ (−2.89) falls within the critical region bounded by the critical $Z$, −1.65.

Figure 13.6 **Making a Decision—Comparing the Obtained Z with the Critical Z**

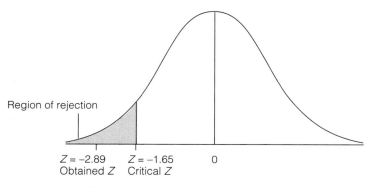

Region of rejection

$Z = -2.89$ $\quad$ $Z = -1.65$ $\quad$ 0
Obtained $Z$ $\quad$ Critical $Z$

We reject $H_0$ because $Z = -2.89 < $ critical $Z = -1.65$.

## The Six Steps in Hypothesis Testing: A Summary

In this chapter, we introduced all the elements used in the process of statistical hypothesis testing. We illustrated this process with an example involving a single sample of black Americans. We were interested in testing the statistical significance of the difference between the sample statistic—the mean earnings of full-time employed black Americans—and a population parameter—the mean earnings nationally. In the next chapter, we will apply the process of hypothesis testing to the problem of testing differences between two sample means and two sample proportions. Regardless of the particular application, however, every problem of statistical hypothesis testing can be organized into six basic steps. Before we conclude this section, let's summarize these steps:

1. Making assumptions
2. Stating the research and the null hypotheses
3. Selecting the sampling distribution and specifying the test statistic
4. Choosing alpha and establishing the region of rejection
5. Computing the test statistic
6. Making a decision and interpreting the results

*1. Making Assumptions*  Statistical hypothesis testing involves making several assumptions regarding the level of measurement of the variable, the method of sampling, the shape of the population distribution, and the sample size.

For our example we made the following assumptions:

a.  A random sample greater than 50 ($N = 66$) was selected
b.  The level of measurement of the variable "income" was interval-ratio.

*2. Stating the Research and the Null Hypotheses*  The substantive hypothesis is called the *research hypothesis* and is symbolized by $H_1$. Research hypotheses are always expressed in terms of population parameters because we are interested in making statements about population parameters based on sample statistics. Our research hypothesis was

$H_1: \mu_Y < \$23{,}766$

The *null hypothesis,* symbolized as $H_0$, contradicts the research hypothesis and is usually a statement of no difference between the population mean and some specified value. For our example, the null hypothesis was stated symbolically as

$H_0: \mu_Y = \$23{,}766$

*3. Selecting the Sampling Distribution and Specifying the Test Statistic*  The sampling distribution allows us to compare our sample result with all possible sample outcomes and estimate the likelihood of its occurrence. Based on the Central Limit Theorem, we selected the normal distribution as our sampling distribution. We used $Z$ as our test statistic and the following formula to translate the sample mean into a $Z$ score (the obtained $Z$):

$$Z = \frac{\overline{Y} - \mu_Y}{\dfrac{\sigma_Y}{\sqrt{N}}}$$

4. *Choosing Alpha (α) and Establishing the Region of Rejection* The level of probability at which the null hypothesis is rejected is the *α level*. It is customary to set the α level at .05, .01, or .001. An alpha of .05 means that even if the sample result is due to sampling error and the null hypothesis is thus true, we have a 5 percent (or less) risk of rejecting it.

The Z score corresponding to a particular alpha level is called the critical value (or critical Z). The critical value is a function of the alpha level and whether our test is one- or two-tailed. In our example, α = .05, our test was left-tailed, and the critical Z equaled −1.65.

5. *Computing the Test Statistic* Following formula 13.1 we computed the test statistic, Z. Our obtained Z was

$$Z = \frac{18,037 - 23,766}{\frac{16,101}{\sqrt{66}}} = -2.89$$

6. *Making a Decision and Interpreting the Results* We compared our obtained Z with the critical value. If the obtained value is equal to or more extreme than the critical value and falls into the region of rejection, it is considered *statistically significant* and leads to the rejection of the null hypothesis. Because −2.89, the obtained Z, is even more negative than −1.65, the critical Z required for an alpha of .05, we rejected the null hypothesis and concluded that the average earnings of black Americans are indeed lower than the average earnings nationally.

## Statistics in Practice: The Earnings of White Women

To illustrate these six steps, let's test a two-tailed hypothesis about a population mean $\mu_Y$. We drew a 1990 GSS sample ($N = 240$) of white women who work full-time. We found the mean earnings to be $\overline{Y} = \$16,653$. Based on the 1990 *Current Population Survey*,[3] we also know that the mean earnings nationally for adults working full-time is $\mu_Y = \$23,766$, and the standard deviation is $\sigma_Y = \$16,101$. We want to determine whether the sample of white women is representative of the population of all full-time workers. Although we suspect that white women experience relative disadvantage in earnings, we are not sure enough to predict that their earnings are indeed lower than the earnings nationally. Therefore, the statistical test is two-tailed.

---

[3] *Current Population Survey*, March 1990, P-60 Series.

*Applying the Six-Step Model*

1. Making assumptions.   A random sample greater than 50 ($N = 240$) is selected. The level of measurement of the variable "income" is interval-ratio.

> **Learning Check.**   *Note that because income distributions are skewed, we cannot assume that the population is normal. However, this is not a serious problem because our sample size is greater than 50.*

2. Stating the research and the null hypotheses.   The research hypothesis is

    $H_1$: $\mu_Y \neq \$23,766$

    and the null hypothesis states:

    $H_0$: $\mu_Y = \$23,766$

3. Selecting the sampling distribution and specifying the test statistic. The sampling distribution is a normal distribution. The test statistic is $Z$.

4. Choosing alpha ($\alpha$) and establishing the region of rejection.   We choose a .05 level of significance, and thus our critical $Z$ is $\pm1.96$. We will reject the null hypothesis if our obtained $Z$ is equal to or more extreme than $\pm1.96$.

> **Learning Check.**   *Why is the critical $Z$ for this test $\pm1.96$?*

5. Computing the test statistic.   To evaluate the probability of obtaining a sample mean of $16,653, assuming the average earnings of white women are equal to the national average of $23,766, we need to translate our obtained sample mean into a $Z$ statistic. To convert the sample mean of $16,653 to an obtained $Z$ statistic we use formula 13.1:

$$Z = \frac{16,653 - 23,766}{\frac{16,101}{\sqrt{240}}} = -6.84$$

6. Making a decision and interpreting the results.   Since our obtained $Z$, $-6.84$, is more extreme than $\pm1.96$, we can reject the null hypothesis at the .05 level of significance. We conclude that the mean earnings for white women are significantly different from the mean earnings nationally.

*Comparing One- and Two-Tailed Tests*  In comparing one- and two-tailed tests, note that because a two-tailed test divides the region of rejection in two, this area is smaller (and thus the critical Z is *more extreme, or greater in absolute value*) than with a one-tailed test. Thus, it is more difficult to reject a false null hypothesis with a two-tailed test. However, it should be emphasized that the choice of using a one- versus a two-tailed test should be guided only by substantive considerations and not by whether or not the test will make it easier to reject the null hypothesis.

## Errors in Hypothesis Testing

We began this chapter by exploring issues related to the mean earnings of black Americans. We wanted to learn about the mean earnings of the black population in the United States based on a random sample of black Americans. Based on the sample information and utilizing the process of statistical hypothesis testing, we were able to reject the null hypothesis, which stated that the mean earnings of black Americans are equal to the mean earnings nationally. We then concluded that the mean earnings of blacks in this country are lower than mean earnings nationally. We should emphasize that because our conclusion is based on sample evidence, we will never really know if the null hypothesis is true or false. In fact, as we illustrated earlier, there is a .19 percent probability that the null hypothesis is true and that we are rejecting it in error.

The null hypothesis can be either true or false, and in either case it can be rejected or not rejected. If the null hypothesis is true and we reject it nonetheless, we make an incorrect decision. This type of error is called a **Type I error**. Conversely, if the null hypothesis is false but we fail to reject it, the error is a **Type II error**. In Table 13.1 we show the relationship between the two types of errors and the decisions we make regarding the null hypothesis. The probability of a Type

Table 13.1  **Type I and Type II Errors**

|  | Null Hypothesis Is True | Null Hypothesis Is False |
|---|---|---|
| **Reject null hypothesis** | Type I error ($\alpha$) | Correct decision |
| **Do not reject null hypothesis** | Correct decision | Type II error |

I error—rejecting a true hypothesis—is equal to the alpha level chosen. For instance, when we set alpha at the .05 level, we know that if the null hypothesis is in fact true, the probability of rejecting it is .05 (or 5%). We can control the risk of rejecting a true hypothesis by manipulating alpha. For example, by setting alpha at the .01 level, we are reducing to 1 percent the risk of making a Type I error. Unfortunately, however, Type I errors and Type II errors are inversely related; thus, by reducing alpha and lowering the risk of making a Type I error we are increasing the risk of making a Type II error.

*Type I Error*   The probability (equal to alpha) associated with rejecting a true null hypothesis.

*Type II Error*   The probability associated with failing to reject a false null hypothesis.

Finally, let's reemphasize that we never know for sure whether we are making the correct decision regarding the null hypothesis. As long as we base our decisions on sample statistics and not population parameters, we have to accept a certain degree of uncertainty as part of the process of statistical inference.

**Learning Check.**   *The implications of research findings are not created equal. For example, researchers might hypothesize that eating spinach increases the strength of weight lifters. Little harm will be done if the null hypothesis that eating spinach has no effect on the strength of weight lifters is rejected in error. The researchers would most likely be willing to risk a high probability of a Type I error, and all weight lifters would eat spinach. But when the implications of research have important consequences, the balancing act between Type I and Type II errors becomes more important. Can you think of some examples where researchers would want to minimize Type I errors? When might they want to minimize Type II errors?*

## MAIN POINTS

■ Statistical hypothesis testing is a decision-making process that enables us to determine whether a particular sample result falls within a range that can occur by an acceptable level of chance. The process of statistical hypothesis testing consists of six steps: making assumptions; stating the research and the null hypotheses; selecting a sampling distribution and a test statistic; choosing alpha and establishing the region of rejection; computing the test statistic; and making a decision and interpreting the results.

## KEY TERMS

| | |
|---|---|
| *alpha ($\alpha$)* | *right-tailed test* |
| *left-tailed test* | *statistical hypothesis testing* |
| *null hypothesis ($H_0$)* | *two-tailed test* |
| *one-tailed test* | *Type I error* |
| *P value* | *Type II error* |
| *region of rejection (critical region)* | *Z critical* |
| *research hypothesis ($H_1$)* | *Z obtained* |

## SPSS DEMONSTRATION

*Demonstration 1: Producing a One-Sample T Test*

In this chapter, we discussed methods of testing differences in means between a sample and a population value. In the next chapter, we'll look at differences in means between two samples. SPSS includes two T Test procedures to do these tests. However, SPSS does not do any of these tests with the Z statistic; instead, the *t* statistic (discussed in Chapter 14) is used by SPSS to test for all mean differences.

SPSS takes this approach because it results in a more conservative test. That is, using a *t* statistic with larger samples makes it harder to reject the null hypothesis. This means that you can use the T Test procedure in any situation in which you want to compare sample means or proportions. If you wish, you can always take the calculated *t* statistic and use it in the standard normal table when sample sizes are above 50, but the results will be almost identical to those using the *t* statistic.

We'll use the 1994 GSS data for this demonstration. The standard workweek is thought to be 40 hours, so let's test to see whether or not American adults work that many hours each week. This is a different use of a one-sample test rather than simply using it to compare a sample mean with a population mean. Instead, we'll use it to test a theoretical or hypothesized relationship.

The One-Sample T Test procedure can be found under the *Statistics* menu, then under *Compare Means*. At least one variable must be placed in the Test Variable(s) box. Then a test value must be specified. In this example, place "40" in the box. Then click on *OK* to run the procedure.

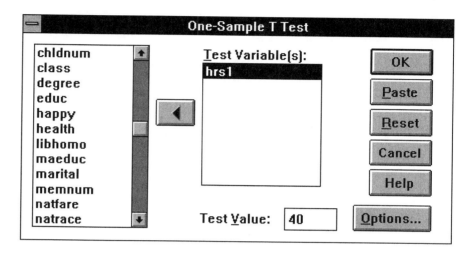

The output from the One-Sample T Test procedure is not too extensive. A total of 636 people answered the question about number of hours worked per week. The mean number of hours worked is 41.4371, with a standard deviation of 13.954. Below this, SPSS lists the test value, 40. At the bottom right of the output, SPSS prints the two-tailed significance, or probability, for the one-sample test. This value is .01, given the calculated $t$ statistic of 2.6, with 635 degrees of freedom. Thus, at the .05 significance level, we would reject the null hypothesis and conclude that adults do not work 40 hours a week, on average. In fact, they work slightly more than 40 hours.

One Sample t-tests

| Variable | Number of Cases | Mean | SD | SE of Mean |
|---|---|---|---|---|
| HRS1  NUMBER OF HOURS WORK | 636 | 41.4371 | 13.954 | .553 |

Test Value = 40

| Mean Difference | 95% CI Lower | Upper | | t-value | df | 2-Tail Sig |
|---|---|---|---|---|---|---|
| 1.44 | .351 | 2.524 | | 2.60 | 635 | .010 |

SPSS also supplies a 95 percent confidence interval for the mean difference between the test value and the sample mean. Here, the confidence interval runs from .351 to 2.524, providing estimates of how much more Americans work than 40 hours per week.

### EXERCISES

1. It is known that, nationally, doctors working for HMOs (health maintenance organizations) average 13.5 years of experience in their specialties, with a standard deviation of 7.6 years. The executive director of an HMO in a western state is interested in determining whether or not its doctors have less experience than the national average. A random sample of 150 doctors from the HMO shows a mean of only 10.9 years of experience.
   a. State the research and the null hypotheses to test whether or not doctors in this HMO have less experience than the national average.
   b. Using an alpha level of .10, make this test.

2. Consider the problem facing security personnel at a military facility in the Southwest. Their job is to detect infiltrators (spies trying to break in), and the facility has an alarm system to assist the security officers. However, sometimes the alarm doesn't work properly, and sometimes the officers don't notice a real alarm. In general, the security personnel must decide between these two alternatives at any given time:

   $H_0$: Everything is fine; no one is attempting an illegal entry.

   $H_1$: There are problems; someone is trying to break into the facility.

   Based on this information, fill in the blanks in these statements:

   A "missed alarm" is a Type _____ error, and its probability of occurrence is denoted by _____. A "false alarm" is a Type _____ error.

3. A sample of 180 SAT verbal test scores from a high school has a mean of 452. The past ten years of students' SAT verbal test scores from this same high school have a mean of 470, with a standard deviation of 100.

    a. Can we reject the null hypothesis that the current year's mean SAT verbal test score is significantly different from that for the past ten years of student tests at the .01 level?

    b. What is the probability that you have made a Type I error in answering this question?

4. One way to check on how representative a survey is of the population from which it was drawn is to compare various characteristics of the sample with the population characteristics. A typical variable used for this purpose is age. A survey done of the American adult population found a mean age of 44.88 for its sample of 1399 adults. Assume that we know from census data that the mean age of all American adults is 43.10 with a standard deviation of 19.20. Use this information to answer these questions.

    a. State the research and the null hypotheses for a two-tailed test.

    b. Calculate the Z statistic.

    c. Test this Z value at the .01 level of significance. What is the critical value of Z for that level of significance?

    d. What is your decision about the null hypothesis? What does this tell us about how representative the sample is of the American adult population?

5. A survey of 500 residents from one ward of a large city finds that they have a mean income of $22,523. Census figures tell us that, for the city as a whole, the mean income is $23,159 with a standard deviation of $9,500. Is the mean income of the ward's residents significantly different from that for the whole city at the .01 level?

6. Numerous studies indicate that Asian-American adults exceed other ethnic groups and often whites in their educational level. One way to test this is to compare the average educational level of a random sample of Asian Americans with the average educational level of all American adults. If earlier studies are correct, then the sample of Asian Americans would not be representative of the American adult population. Suppose that you were planning a study designed to test this hypothesis that Asian Americans have a higher level of education than the national average.

    a. State the research and the null hypotheses.

    b. Suppose you obtained a Z score of 1.70 when doing the test with actual data. Can you reject the null hypothesis at the .05 significance level? at the .01 level?

7. Faculty salary equity is a hot political issue debated on many campuses. Some argue that in today's climate of budget cuts and downsizing, the earnings of unionized faculty are considerably

higher than the earnings of faculty nationwide. Assume that we know from AAUP (the Association of American University Professors) data that the national mean salary of full-time faculty members is $45,000 with a standard deviation of $13,200. Suppose that for a random sample of 750 unionized faculty the average salary is $47,000. Are the salaries of unionized faculty significantly higher than the salaries of faculty nationwide?

   a. State the research and the null hypotheses.
   b. Calculate the Z statistic and test the null hypothesis at the .05 significance level. What did you find?

8. For each of the following situations determine whether a one- or a two-tailed test is appropriate. Also, state the research and the null hypotheses. Assuming that you use an alpha level of .01, indicate the critical value in each case.

   a. A researcher believes that the average income of elderly women is lower than the average income of women nationwide. Census figures tell us that the national mean income of women is $19,223.
   b. You are interested in finding out if the average income of elementary school teachers is different from the national average income for adults. According to the census the national average income is $23,766.
   c. You believe that students in small liberal arts colleges attend more parties per month than students nationwide. It is known that nationally, undergraduate students attend an average of 3.2 parties per month. The average number of parties per month will be calculated from a random sample of students from small liberal arts colleges.
   d. There are indications that people in public housing projects tend to watch television more often than other adults. Some think this is because watching television reduces the stress associated with living in a high-density environment. You plan to test this with data collected from a random sample of the residents of public housing projects in five major cities in the United States. You know that the national average for television watching is 10.4 hours per week.

9. In a sample of 350 black professional women selected in 1990 the mean annual income was $31,000. According to the 1990 census the mean annual income of all women was $19,223 with a standard deviation of $11,590. Is it reasonable to consider this sample of black professional women to be a representative sample of American women? Use an alpha level of .05 and do a two-tailed test to make your decision.

10. For each situation in exercise 8:
    a. Describe the Type I and Type II errors that could occur.
    b. What are the general implications of making a Type I error? of making a Type II error?
    c. When, generally speaking, would you want to minimize Type I error? Type II error?

11. The average final score of 1,200 students who took my class in social statistics between 1983 and 1994 is 70.7 with a standard deviation of 10.7. Since 1995 I have incorporated cooperative learning in my classes. I believe that students do better in cooperative learning situations and their performance is generally superior to the performance of students in more traditional settings. To test this hypothesis I have selected a random sample of 60 students who have participated in a cooperative learning situation since 1995. The average final score for these students is 78.6.
    a. Do a test to determine whether students in cooperative settings perform better, by calculating the Z statistic.
    b. Test the null hypothesis at the .05 level of significance.
    c. Interpret the results.

12. Fill in the blanks in these statements.
    a. The process of using sample statistics to make decisions about population parameters is called _____.
    b. The _____ is a statement reflecting the substantive hypothesis. It is always expressed in terms of population parameters.
    c. Tests of hypotheses about means require that the population under consideration is normally distributed or _____.
    d. The level of probability at which the null hypothesis is rejected is called _____.
    e. A _____ is a type of hypothesis test in which the region of rejection is located on one side of the sampling distribution.
    f. We reject the null hypothesis if the obtained Z is _____ than the critical Z.
    g. The probability associated with rejecting a _____ null hypothesis is called Type I error.

## SPSS PROBLEMS

1. Use the 1994 GSS file to investigate whether or not Americans have at least two children per person.
   a. Use the One-Sample T Test (Again, the t test will be discussed in Chapter 14.) procedure to do this test with the variable

CHILDS. Do the test at the .01 significance level. What did you find? Do Americans have two children, more, or less?

b. Try to explain the result substantively by offering reasons to explain what you found. These reasons can be related to characteristics of the General Social Survey sample or to processes affecting the American population as a whole. Keep in mind that the American population is continuing to increase, no matter what this test shows.

## GROUP PROBLEM

This exercise will allow you to compare your classmates with the rest of the student population. Have some of the group members investigate what information you can gather from the university or college administration about all the students at your school. This might include mean age, current GPA, mean SAT or ACT scores upon entrance, mean family income, or the amount of aid and scholarship money per student. Remember that you also need standard deviations in addition to the means. After you've gathered this information, have other group members collect the same data anonymously from all your classmates. Then your group can do one-sample $t$-tests to see whether or not the class mean for these variables is statistically equivalent to that for the student body as a whole. After you've got the results, write a report or do a class presentation. When you do, try to offer explanations for any differences you found.

# 14    Testing Hypotheses About Two Samples

## Reading the Research Literature: Reporting the Results of Statistical Hypothesis Testing

### Introduction

In Chapter 13, we illustrated the process of hypothesis testing with an example involving a single sample of black Americans. We were interested in testing the statistical significance of the difference between a sample value, the average earnings of black Americans, and a population value, the average earnings nationally. In practice, social scientists are much more interested in situations involving two parameters than those involving one. We may be interested in finding out, for example, whether the average earnings of black women in this country are lower than the average earnings of white men. Or, we may wish to know whether black women earn the same, less, or more than black men.

In earlier chapters we saw that comparisons between groups having different characteristics are quite common in the social sciences. We looked at numerous techniques that allow us to make such comparisons. For instance, in Chapter 3, we compared the percentages of elderly men and women on the basis of their living arrangements. We saw that 42 percent of elderly women versus 15.7 percent of elderly men who were surveyed by the census in 1990 live alone. Similarly, in Chapter 4, we compared the average number of traumatic events experienced by working-class black males and black females. We saw that the average is higher ($\overline{Y} = 1.76$) for the women than for the men ($\overline{Y} = 1.04$).

When social researchers make comparisons between groups, they are usually interested in identifying a relationship between variables. For example, the differences in the living arrangements of elderly men and women may mean that there is an association between gender and living arrangements among the elderly. Similarly, the differences in the average number of traumatic events experienced by working-class black males and black females may imply that gender is associated with the frequency of trauma among black Americans.

Earlier we encouraged you to begin thinking analytically about complex data and to draw some tentative conclusions about differences between groups and relationships between variables, but we also cautioned that you would need to consider the more complex techniques of sampling and statistical inference to make valid comparisons. Because most comparisons we make are based on information gathered from samples and not from studying the entire population, we need to consider the possibility that the observed differences—for instance between elderly men and women or between black women and black men—may not be real differences. Instead, the differences may be due to the fact that the estimates are based on single samples, and if we took other samples we would get different results.

The statistical procedures presented in this chapter allow us to test whether the differences we observe between two samples are large enough for us to conclude that the populations from which these samples are drawn are different as well. We present tests for the significance of the differences between two groups. Primarily, we consider differences between sample means and differences between sample proportions. Differences between means are considered in situations in which the variable about which the comparisons are made is measured on an interval-ratio level. Differences between proportions are discussed in situations in which the variable about which the comparisons are made is measured on a nominal or on an ordinal level.

## The Structure of Hypothesis Testing with Two Samples

Hypothesis testing with two samples follows the same structure as for single sample tests. The assumptions of the test are stated; the research and the null hypotheses are formulated; the sampling distribution and the test statistic are specified; the alpha level and the region of rejection are determined; and a decision is made whether or not to reject the null hypothesis following the calculation of the test statistic.

## The Assumption of Independent Samples

One important difference between one- and two-sample hypothesis testing involves sampling procedures. With a two-sample case we assume that the samples are independent of each other. This means that the choice of sample members from one population has no effect on the choice of sample members from the second population. This means that if we are comparing men and women, we are assuming that the selection of men is independent of the selection of women. Had we selected two samples, one of wives and the second of their husbands, our samples would not be considered independent of each other.

The requirement of independence is fairly easily satisfied by selecting one sample randomly and then dividing the sample into appropriate subgroups. For instance, we could randomly select a sample and then divide it into groups based on gender, race, ethnicity, or any other attribute we are interested in.

### Stating the Research and the Null Hypotheses

The second difference between one- and two-sample tests is in the form taken by the research and the null hypotheses. In one-sample tests both the null and the research hypotheses are statements about a single population parameter, $\mu_Y$. In contrast, with two-sample tests we compare two population parameters. For example, let's suppose that you have reason to believe that students on your campus who work fewer than 20 hours a week have a higher GPA than students who work 20 hours or more (not an unreasonable assumption!). You can select a random sample of students from the population of registered students in your school, divide the sample based on the number of hours worked each week, and record each student's GPA.

Symbolically, your research hypothesis is expressed as follows:

$$H_1: \mu_{Y_L} > \mu_{Y_M}$$

with $\mu_{Y_L}$ representing the mean GPA of students working less than 20 hours and $\mu_{Y_M}$ the mean GPA of students working 20 hours or more. Note that because $H_1$ specifies that the mean GPA for students working fewer than 20 hours is larger than the mean GPA for students working 20 hours or more, it is a directional hypothesis. Thus, our test is a one-tailed test. Alternatively, if there were not enough basis for deciding which population mean score is larger, the research hypothesis would state that the two population means are not equal:

$$H_1: \mu_{Y_L} \neq \mu_{Y_M}$$

In both cases the null hypothesis states that there are no differences between the two population means:

$$H_0: \mu_{Y_L} = \mu_{Y_M}$$

We are interested in rejecting the null hypothesis of no difference so that we have sufficient support for our research hypothesis that the GPAs of the two groups of students differ.

## The Sampling Distribution of the Difference Between Means

In Chapter 11, we learned about properties of the sampling distributions of sample means. The sampling distribution of sample means provides a basis for testing hypotheses about single sample means. Tests about differences between two sample means are based on another sampling distribution: the sampling distribution of the difference between two sample means. The **sampling distribution of the difference between two sample means** is a theoretical probability distribution that would be obtained by calculating all the possible mean differences $(\overline{Y}_1 - \overline{Y}_2)$ that would be obtained by drawing all possible independent random samples of size $N_1$ and $N_2$ from two populations.

The properties of the sampling distribution of the differences between two sample means are determined by a corollary to the Central Limit Theorem. This theorem assumes that our samples are independently drawn from normal populations, but that with sufficient sample size ($N_1 > 50$; $N_2 > 50$) the sampling distribution of the difference between means will be normal, even if the original populations are not normal. This sampling distribution has a mean $\mu_{Y_1} - \mu_{Y_2}$ and a standard deviation (standard error)

$$\sigma_{\overline{Y}_1 - \overline{Y}_2} = \sqrt{\frac{\sigma_{Y_1}^2}{N_1} + \frac{\sigma_{Y_2}^2}{N_2}} \tag{14.1}$$

which is based on the variances in each of the two populations ($\sigma_{Y_1}^2$ and $\sigma_{Y_2}^2$).

With this corollary to the Central Limit Theorem, we can utilize the normal distribution as our model of the sampling distribution of the difference between two sample means. Thus, we can use the probabilities associated with the normal distribution and the $Z$ statistic to test the null hypothesis that $\mu_{Y_1} = \mu_{Y_2}$, as long as the populations are normally distributed or the sample sizes are sufficiently large.

---

*Sampling Distribution of the Difference Between Means*  A theoretical probability distribution that would be obtained by calculating all the possible mean differences $(\overline{Y}_1 - \overline{Y}_2)$ that would be obtained by drawing all the possible independent random samples of size $N_1$ and $N_2$ from two populations.

---

To test the null hypothesis about differences between means, the sample means need to be translated into $Z$ statistics. The obtained $Z$ statistic is calculated using the following formula:

$$Z = \frac{(\overline{Y}_1 - \overline{Y}_2) - (\mu_{Y_1} - \mu_{Y_2})}{\sigma_{\overline{Y}_1 - \overline{Y}_2}}$$

(14.2)

where $\sigma_{\overline{Y}_1 - \overline{Y}_2}$ is the standard error of the sampling distribution of the difference between means. Note that the second term in the numerator contains the term $\mu_{Y_1} - \mu_{Y_2}$, which is assumed to be zero under the null hypothesis. Therefore, the actual formula we use to calculate $Z$ is

$$Z = \frac{(\overline{Y}_1 - \overline{Y}_2)}{\sigma_{\overline{Y}_1 - \overline{Y}_2}}$$

(14.3)

## Estimating the Standard Error

The problem with calculating the $Z$ ratio as displayed in formula 14.3 is that it assumes that the population variances are known and therefore we can easily calculate the standard error $\sigma_{\overline{Y}_1 - \overline{Y}_2}$ (the standard deviation of the sampling distribution) by using formula 14.1. However, in most practical situations when the only data available to us are sample data, we do not know the true value of the population variances $\sigma_{Y_1}^2$ and $\sigma_{Y_2}^2$, and thus we need to estimate the standard error from the sample variances ($S_{Y_1}^2$ and $S_{Y_2}^2$). The estimated standard error of the difference between means is symbolized by $S_{\overline{Y}_1 - \overline{Y}_2}$ (instead of $\sigma_{\overline{Y}_1 - \overline{Y}_2}$).

## The *t* Statistic

With an estimated standard error, the $Z$ statistic as described in formula 14.3 can no longer be used to test the null hypothesis of the difference between two sample means. Instead, another statistic, the *t* **statistic**, is employed.

The formula for computing the *t* statistic is

$$t = \frac{\overline{Y}_1 - \overline{Y}_2}{S_{\overline{Y}_1 - \overline{Y}_2}}$$

(14.4)

where $S_{\overline{Y}_1 - \overline{Y}_2}$ = estimated standard error.

## Calculating the Estimated Standard Error

The formula for calculating the estimated standard error will differ, depending on whether the two population variances are assumed to be equal.

## The Population Variances Are Assumed Equal

When we can assume that the two population variances are equal we combine information from the two sample variances to estimate the standard deviation of the sampling distribution:

$$S_{\bar{Y}_1-\bar{Y}_2} = \sqrt{\frac{(N_1-1)S_{Y_1}^2 + (N_2-1)S_{Y_2}^2}{(N_1+N_2)-2}} \sqrt{\frac{N_1+N_2}{N_1 N_2}} \qquad (14.5)$$

where $S_{\bar{Y}_1-\bar{Y}_2}$ is the estimated standard error of the difference between means, and $S_{Y_1}^2$ and $S_{Y_2}^2$ are the variances of the two samples. To calculate the $t$ statistic, substitute this computed value of $S_{\bar{Y}_1-\bar{Y}_2}$ into the denominator (formula 14.4).

## The Population Variances Are Assumed Unequal

If the variances of the two samples $S_{Y_1}^2$ and $S_{Y_2}^2$ are very different—when either sample variance is more than twice as large as the other—we can no longer assume that the two population variances are equal. Therefore, it no longer makes sense to pool the sample variances together to estimate the standard error $S_{\bar{Y}_1-\bar{Y}_2}$. The formula for the estimated standard error then becomes

$$S_{\bar{Y}_1-\bar{Y}_2} = \sqrt{\frac{S_{Y_1}^2}{N_1} + \frac{S_{Y_2}^2}{N_2}} \qquad (14.6)$$

This computed value of $S_{\bar{Y}_1-\bar{Y}_2}$ is then substituted into the denominator to calculate $t$ (formula 14.4).

## Comparing the *t* and the *Z* Statistics

Compare the $t$ statistic (formula 14.4) with the $Z$ statistic (formula 14.3) and note that they are quite similar; the only apparent difference between these two ratios is in the denominator. The denominator of $Z$ is $\sigma_{\bar{Y}_1-\bar{Y}_2}$—the standard error based on the population variances $\sigma_{Y_1}^2$ and $\sigma_{Y_2}^2$. In contrast, in the denominator of $t$ we replace $\sigma_{\bar{Y}_1-\bar{Y}_2}$ with $S_{\bar{Y}_1-\bar{Y}_2}$, the estimated standard error based on the sample variances.

However, there is another important difference between the $Z$ and the $t$ statistics: because it is estimated from sample data, the denominator of the $t$ statistic is *subject to sampling error.* Consequently, the sampling distribution of the test statistic is not normal and the standard normal distribution cannot be used to determine probabilities associated with it. The $t$ distribution is discussed next.

---

*t Statistic*   The test statistic computed when the population variance is unknown and the standard error is estimated.

---

## The *t* Distribution and the Degrees of Freedom (df)

The *t* distribution is actually a family of curves, each determined by the *degrees of freedom (df)*. The concept of degrees of freedom is used in calculating several statistics including the $t$ statistic. The **degrees of freedom** defines for each statistic the number of scores that are free to vary in calculating that statistic.

### Determining the Degrees of Freedom

To determine the degrees of freedom, we must know the sample size and whether there are any restrictions resulting from calculating that statistic. The number of restrictions is then subtracted from the sample size to determine the degrees of freedom. When calculating the $t$ statistic for two-sample tests, we lose 1 degree of freedom in estimating each population variance. Therefore, for a difference between means test, the df is equal to $N_1 + N_2 - 2$. For example, with $N_1 = 30$ and $N_2 = 40$, df is $(40 + 30) - 2 = 68$.[1]

### Adjusting for Unequal Variances

When the population variances are unequal, we use another, rather complicated formula to calculate the degrees of freedom associated with the $t$ statistic:

---

[1]The simplest way to think about it is in terms of subtracting one df for each prior estimate used to get the variance. In other words, to compute $S_{Y_1}$ we first had to compute $\overline{Y}_1$. Since the sum of the deviations about the mean must equal zero, only $N - 1$ of the deviation scores are free to vary with each variance estimate.

$$df = \frac{\left(\dfrac{S_{Y_1}^2}{N_1} + \dfrac{S_{Y_2}^2}{N_2}\right)^2}{\left(\dfrac{S_{Y_1}^2}{N_1}\right)^2 \left(\dfrac{1}{N_1 + 1}\right) + \left(\dfrac{S_{Y_2}^2}{N_2}\right)^2 \left(\dfrac{1}{N_2 + 1}\right)} - 2 \qquad (14.7)$$

However, this adjustment is necessary only for small samples (when the size of one or both samples is equal to or less than 50).

## The Shape of the *t* Distribution

The shape of the *t* distribution is determined by the degrees of freedom associated with a particular *t*. When df is small, the *t* distribution is much flatter than the normal curve, but as the degrees of freedom (remember that df is a function of the sample size!) increase, the shape of the *t* distribution gets closer to the normal distribution until the two are almost identical when df is greater than 120. Figure 14.1 shows the *t* distribution for several df's. Also shown is the standard normal curve as df approaches infinity (df = ∞). Notice that the *t* and Z distributions are quite different when df is small, but that with increasing size the *t* distribution approximates the normal curve.

## Critical Values of the *t* Distribution

Appendix C shows critical values of the *t* distribution for various df's. In Table 14.1, we have reproduced a small part of Appendix C for illustration purposes. Unlike in the Z table, the critical values of *t* are displayed in the body of the table. These values are a function of (1) the degrees of freedom, (2) the α level, and (3) whether the test is

Figure 14.1 **The Normal Distribution and *t* Distributions for 1, 5, 20, and ∞ Degrees of Freedom**

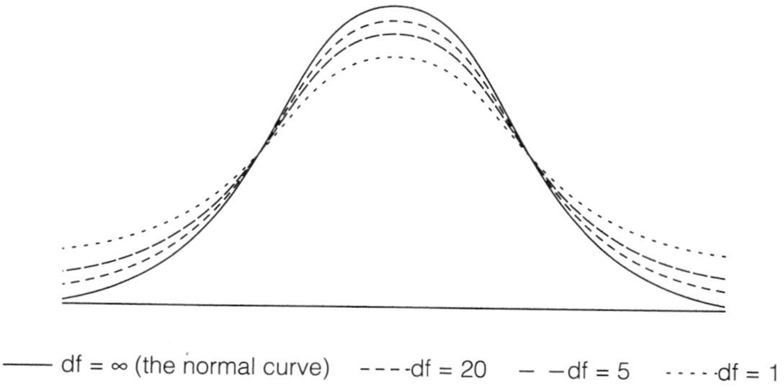

—— df = ∞ (the normal curve)    - - - -df = 20    – – df = 5    · · · · ·df = 1

Table 14.1  **Critical Values of the _t_ Distribution**

| | Level of Significance for One-Tailed Test | | | | | |
|---|---|---|---|---|---|---|
| | .10 | .05 | .025 | .01 | .005 | .0005 |
| | Level of Significance for Two-Tailed Test | | | | | |
| df | .20 | .10 | .05 | .02 | .01 | .001 |
| 1 | 3.078 | 6.314 | 12.706 | 31.821 | 63.657 | 636.619 |
| 2 | 1.886 | 2.920 | 4.303 | 6.965 | 9.925 | 31.598 |
| 3 | 1.638 | 2.353 | 3.182 | 4.541 | 5.841 | 12.941 |
| 4 | 1.533 | 2.132 | 2.776 | 3.747 | 4.604 | 8.610 |
| 5 | 1.476 | 2.015 | 2.571 | 3.365 | 4.032 | 6.859 |
| 10 | 1.372 | 1.812 | 2.228 | 2.764 | 3.169 | 4.587 |
| 15 | 1.341 | 1.753 | 2.131 | 2.602 | 2.947 | 4.073 |
| 20 | 1.325 | 1.725 | 2.086 | 2.528 | 2.845 | 3.850 |
| 25 | 1.316 | 1.708 | 2.060 | 2.485 | 2.787 | 3.725 |
| 30 | 1.310 | 1.697 | 2.042 | 2.457 | 2.750 | 3.646 |
| 40 | 1.303 | 1.684 | 2.021 | 2.423 | 2.704 | 3.551 |
| 60 | 1.296 | 1.671 | 2.000 | 2.390 | 2.660 | 3.460 |
| 120 | 1.289 | 1.658 | 1.980 | 2.358 | 2.617 | 3.373 |
| ∞ | 1.282 | 1.645 | 1.960 | 2.326 | 2.576 | 3.291 |

*Source:* Abridged from R. A. Fisher and F. Yates, *Statistical Tables for Biological, Agricultural and Medical Research.* London: Longman, 1974, Table 111. Used by permission of Addison Wesley Longman Ltd.

one- or two-tailed. The α levels are arrayed across the top of the table in two rows, the first for one-tailed and the second for two-tailed tests. The first column on the left side of the table shows the degrees of freedom. To find a critical $t$, choose the α level for either a one- or a two-tailed test and then enter the table in the appropriate row, depending on the df. For instance, let's find the critical $t$ for a two-tailed test with α = .05, $N_1$ = 15, and $N_2$ = 12 when the population variances are assumed equal. The df is (15 + 12) − 2 = 25, and, thus, the critical $t$ is 2.060.

**Degrees of Freedom (df)**   The number of scores that are free to vary in calculating a statistic.

**_t_ Distribution**   A family of curves, each determined by the degrees of freedom (df). It is used when the population variance is unknown and the standard error is estimated from the sample variances.

## Review

In the next section, we present a number of research examples illustrating the process of testing hypotheses about differences between means. These examples illustrate how to test for differences between sample means under different conditions. To help guide you in this discussion, we have summarized the assumptions and formulas associated with the different conditions discussed earlier. This summary is presented in Table 14.2.

## Hypotheses About Differences Between Means: Illustrations

In the following section, we illustrate tests about differences between means in which the population variances are unknown. Therefore, all the examples illustrate testing of hypotheses with the $t$ statistic. However, because the application of the $t$ statistic varies, depending on our assumptions about the population variances (see Table 14.2), we will consider the $t$ statistic under each of the following two conditions:

1. The population variances are assumed equal.
2. The population variances are assumed unequal.

### The Population Variances Are Assumed Equal: The Earnings of Asian American Men

Due to their socioeconomic achievement in American society, Asian Americans have been noted as a "model minority."[2] According to the 1980 census, the level of education and the average family income of Asian Americans is the highest among minority groups in the United States.[3] Among Asian Americans, the achievements of Chinese and Japanese have been particularly impressive. The 1980 census reports that the median years of schooling was 13.7 for Chinese Americans and 12.7 for Japanese Americans, as compared with 12.5 years of schooling for non-Hispanic whites. Similar trends have been observed in the relative earnings of these groups. For example, in 1990, the median income of

[2]Roger Daniels, *Asian Americans: Chinese and Japanese in the United States Since 1850.* Seattle, WA: University of Washington Press, 1988.

[3]Zhou Min and Yoshinori Kamo, "An Analysis of Earnings Patterns for Chinese, Japanese, and Non-Hispanic White Males in the United States." *The Sociological Quarterly,* Vol. 35, 1994, No. 4, 581–602.

**Table 14.2 Testing Hypotheses About Differences Between Two Means**

| Null Hypothesis | Level of Measurement | Sampling Method | Population Distribution | Population Variance | Test Statistic | Standard Error | df | Where to Locate the Critical Value |
|---|---|---|---|---|---|---|---|---|
| $\mu_{Y_1} = \mu_{Y_2}$ | Interval-ratio | Independent random | Assumed normal unless $N_1 > 50$ $N_2 > 50$ | Unknown and assumed equal | $t = \dfrac{\bar{Y}_1 - \bar{Y}_2}{S_{\bar{Y}_1 - \bar{Y}_2}}$ | Formula 14.5 | $(N_1 + N_2) - 2$ | $t$ distribution |
| $\mu_{Y_1} = \mu_{Y_2}$ | Interval-ratio | Independent random | Assumed normal unless $N_1 > 50$ $N_2 > 50$ | Unknown and assumed unequal | $t = \dfrac{\bar{Y}_1 - \bar{Y}_2}{S_{\bar{Y}_1 - \bar{Y}_2}}$ | Formula 14.6 | Large sample $\begin{pmatrix} N_1 > 50 \\ N_2 > 50 \end{pmatrix}$ $(N_1 + N_2) - 2$ Small sample $\begin{pmatrix} N_1 \leq 50 \\ N_2 \leq 50 \end{pmatrix}$ Formula 14.7 | $t$ distribution |

Chinese Americans was 99 percent that of white workers; the median income of Japanese Americans, 112 percent that of white workers.[4]

The success of Chinese and Japanese Americans and their image as a "model minority" challenges the predominant view that being nonwhite is an inherent liability to achievement in American society. It seems to reinforce the notion advanced by human capital theorists that the economic success of immigrant group members is solely determined by individual human capital (credentials and skills) and not by race or national origin. Thus, according to the human capital perspective, we would expect to find earning parity between Chinese and Japanese Americans and non-Hispanic whites who have similar credentials.

Other researchers argue that the "model minority" image diverts attention from problems such as employment discrimination and economic marginality confronting Asian Americans. They suggest that the earnings parity between Asian Americans and white workers may be due to the overachievement in educational attainment, longer working hours, and regional concentration of Asians in states such as California, where earnings are generally higher than in other states.[5] Thus, when factors such as education, work experience, and job training are controlled for, the earnings of Chinese and Japanese are lower than the earnings of white Americans. It is suggested that racial discrimination is the most likely explanation for these earning differentials.

To examine these competing explanations for the socioeconomic status of Chinese and Japanese Americans, Zhou and Kamo analyzed the earning patterns of Chinese and Japanese in the United States, relative to the earnings of non-Hispanic whites. They based their analysis on random samples from the 1980 census.[6] Their sample is limited to male workers between the ages of 25 and 64 who were in the labor force.[7]

Table 14.3 shows the mean earnings and standard deviations for U.S.-born Chinese, Japanese, and non-Hispanic whites who reside in California and who have a college degree.[8] The results in Table 14.3

[4]Zhou and Kamo, 1994; William P. O'Hare and Judy C. Felt, *Asian Americans: America's Fastest Growing Minority Group*. Washington, DC: Population Reference Bureau, Inc., 1991.

[5]Zhou and Kamo.

[6]U.S. Bureau of the Census. 1983. *Public-Use Microdata Samples*.

[7]To justify the exclusion of females from the analysis, Zhou and Kamo argue that the nature of female employment differs from that of male employment and that patterns of female labor participation vary among racial and ethnic groups.

[8]Zhou and Kamo analyzed the earnings of additional subsamples of Chinese, Japanese, and non-Hispanic whites. We are focusing on U.S.-born persons who reside in California and who have a college degree.

Table 14.3 **Means and Standard Deviations for Earnings of Chinese, Japanese, and Non-Hispanic Whites (in California)**

|  | Chinese | Japanese | Non-Hispanic Whites |
|---|---|---|---|
| Mean | $21,439 | $22,907 | $24,891 |
| Standard deviation | 10,289 | 11,120 | 14,225 |
| N | 471 | 758 | 2,123 |

*Source:* Adapted from M. Zhou and Y. Kamo, *The Sociological Quarterly,* Vol. 35, No. 4, November 1994, Table 2, p. 591. © 1994 by The Midwest Sociological Quarterly. Used by permission.

show that Chinese and Japanese Americans have not achieved earnings parity with whites, despite similar credentials (college degree) and employment in the same labor market (California). The mean earnings for whites ($\overline{Y}$ = $24,891) are higher than the earnings of either Japanese ($\overline{Y}$ = $22,907) or Chinese American ($\overline{Y}$ = $21,439) workers.

Does the gap of $3,452 ($24,891 − $21,439) or of $1,984 ($24,891 − $22,907) between the earnings of Chinese and Japanese Americans, respectively, and the earnings of whites provide support for Zhou and Kamo's argument that Chinese and Japanese Americans, as a group, have not achieved earnings parity with whites with identical credentials? We can use the data shown in Table 14.3 and the procedure of hypothesis testing about differences between means to answer this question. (This question is also illustrated in Figure 14.2.) We limit our discussion to a test of the differences in mean earnings between Chinese Americans and non-Hispanic whites.

We employ the *t* test to test whether the observed differences in earnings between these two groups are large enough for us to conclude that the populations from which these samples are drawn are different as well.

1. **Making assumptions.**
   a. Independent random samples are selected.
   b. Because $N_W$ > 50 and $N_C$ > 50, the assumption of normal population is not required.
   c. The level of measurement of the variable "income" is interval-ratio.
   d. The population variances are assumed equal.

2. **Stating the research and the null hypotheses.** If Chinese Americans as a group have not achieved earnings parity with whites with identical credentials as suggested by Zhou and Kamo, we would expect the earnings of non-Hispanic white men to be higher than

Figure 14.2 **Means Testing as a Type of Inference**

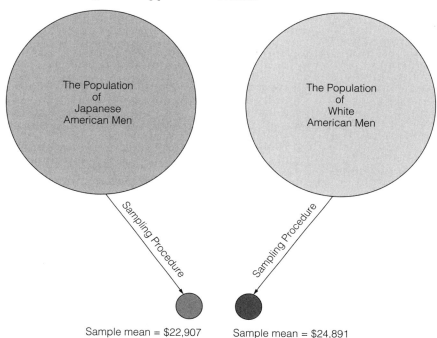

We select two random samples from two different populations and calculate means for the samples. We find that the means for the samples differ by $1,984.

But, is this observed difference *large enough* so that we can say with confidence that the population means differ?

Can we say, based on the data gathered, that white American men make more money than Japanese American men?

the earnings of Chinese American men. The research hypothesis we will test is that the mean earnings for the population of non-Hispanic white men are greater than the mean earnings of the population of Chinese American men.

Symbolically, the hypothesis is expressed as follows:

$$H_1: \mu_{Y_W} > \mu_{Y_C}$$

with $\mu_{Y_W}$ representing the mean earnings of white men and $\mu_{Y_C}$ the mean earnings of Chinese American men. Note that because $H_1$ specifies that the mean earnings for white men are greater than the mean earnings for Chinese men, it is a directional hypothesis. Thus, our test is a one-tailed test. Alternatively, if there were not enough basis for deciding which population mean score is larger, the research hypothesis would state that the two population means are not equal:

$$H_1: \mu_{Y_W} \neq \mu_{Y_C}$$

In both cases the null hypothesis states that there are no differences between the two population means:

$$H_0: \mu_{Y_W} = \mu_{Y_C}$$

We are interested in rejecting the null hypothesis of no difference so that we have sufficient support for our research hypothesis that white men's earnings are higher than Chinese men's.

3. **Selecting a sampling distribution and a test statistic.** We use the $t$ distribution and the $t$ statistic to test the significance of the difference between the two sample means.

4. **Choosing alpha and establishing the region of rejection.** To establish the region of rejection and choose a critical $t$ we first calculate the df associated with our test. Because the population variances are assumed equal, df is $N_W + N_C - 2 = 2{,}123 + 471 - 2 = 2{,}592$. Next, we turn to the $t$ distribution in Appendix C. Our test is one-tailed and $\alpha = .05$; thus we use the top line for a one-tailed test and select the column marked .05 in that line. We then read down the column marked "degrees of freedom" until we get to the last line marked $\infty$. Because the df is greater than 120 we must use this line for our df. The critical $t = +1.65$ is found in the body of the table at the intersection of our designated row and column.

5. **Computing the test statistic.** To test the null hypothesis about the differences between the mean earnings of Chinese Americans and non-Hispanic whites, we need to translate the ratio of the observed differences to its standard error into a $t$ statistic. The obtained $t$ statistic is calculated following formula 14.4:

$$t = \frac{\overline{Y}_W - \overline{Y}_C}{S_{\overline{Y}_W - \overline{Y}_C}}$$

where $S_{\overline{Y}_W - \overline{Y}_C}$ is the estimated standard error of the sampling distribution.

Because we assume that the population variances are equal, we can combine information from the two sample variances to estimate the standard error (formula 14.5):

$$S_{\overline{Y}_W - \overline{Y}_C} = \sqrt{\frac{(N_W - 1)S_{Y_W}^2 + (N_C - 1)S_{Y_C}^2}{(N_W + N_C) - 2}} \sqrt{\frac{N_W + N_C}{N_W N_C}}$$

For our example, the estimate for $S_{\bar{Y}_w - \bar{Y}_c}$ is

$$S_{\bar{Y}_w - \bar{Y}_c} = \sqrt{\frac{2,122(14,225)^2 + 470(10,289)^2}{(2,123 + 471) - 2}} \sqrt{\frac{2,123 + 471}{(2,123)(471)}} = 692.48$$

We substitute this value into the denominator for the $t$ statistic (formula 14.4):

$$t = \frac{24,891 - 21,439}{692.48} = 4.98$$

6. **Making a decision and interpreting the results.** We are now ready to compare the test statistic—the obtained $t$—with the critical value. Since the obtained $t$, 4.98, is greater than the critical value, ±1.645, we can reject the null hypothesis and conclude that the average earnings of non-Hispanic white males are probably higher than the average earnings of Chinese American men.

> **Learning Check.** *Using the data presented in Table 14.3, test the null hypothesis that the mean earnings of Japanese Americans are equal to the mean earnings of non-Hispanic whites. What is your conclusion?*

## The Population Variances Are Assumed Unequal: The Ratings of Ross Perot

For over twenty years, the Survey Research Center at the University of Michigan[9] has conducted election studies designed to measure the public reaction to numerous political issues, such as welfare reform and the federal budget deficit. These studies also ask respondents to evaluate elected officials as well as other political candidates. The election studies can be used to assess the political opinions of a cross-section of the American electorate as well as to examine how these opinions vary by gender, education, income, race, and ethnicity. In this section, we use the results of the 1994 survey to examine how Native Americans and Asian Americans rate Ross Perot.

[9]Steven J. Rosenstone, Warren E. Miller, Donald R. Kinder, and the National Election Studies. *American National Election Study, 1994: Post Election Survey.* Conducted by University of Michigan, Center for Political Studies. 2nd ICPSR ed. Ann Arbor, MI: University of Michigan, Center for Political Studies, and Inter-University Consortium for Political and Social Research, 1995.

The 1994 study, based on a random probability sample of 1,795 respondents representing the 1994 American electorate, included only 16 Native Americans and 26 Asian Americans. Under these circumstances (that is, when $N_1 \leq 50$; $N_2 \leq 50$) the sampling distribution of the difference between the means is no longer normal; therefore, we must assume that the population distributions are normal.

Table 14.4 shows the mean ratings of Ross Perot by Native Americans and Asian Americans. Also displayed are the standard deviations and the variances for each group. The mean ratings of Ross Perot were based on the following question asked of all respondents:

> I'd like to get your feelings toward some of our political leaders and other people who have been in the news. I'll read the name of a person and I'd like you to rate that person using something called the feeling thermometer. You can choose any number between 0 and 100. The higher the number, the warmer or more favorable you feel toward that person; the lower the number, the colder or less favorable. You would rate the person at the 50 degree mark if you feel neither warm nor cold toward them. . . . Using the thermometer, how would you rate . . . Ross Perot?

Table 14.4 shows that Ross Perot is favored more by Native Americans than by Asian Americans (a difference of 18.37 points). But do these differences reflect a true difference between the two groups, or are they a consequence of sampling error? The statistical significance of this observed difference can be tested by following the six steps of testing hypotheses.

Table 14.4 **Ratings of Ross Perot by Native Americans and Asian Americans in 1994**

| | Ross Perot | |
| --- | --- | --- |
| | Native Americans | Asian Americans |
| Mean | 47.22 | 28.85 |
| Standard deviation | 14.04 | 24.08 |
| Variance | 197 | 580 |
| $N$ | 16 | 26 |

*Source:* American National Election Survey, 1994.

In comparing the variances for the two groups, notice that the variance for Asian Americans is almost three times (580 ÷ 197 = 2.94) the size of the variance among Native Americans. Thus, we have to assume unequal variances.

1. **Making assumptions.**
   a. Independent random samples are used.
   b. Because $N_{NA} < 50$ and $N_{NA} < 50$ we have to assume that the populations are normally distributed.
   c. The level of measurement of the variable is interval-ratio.
   d. The population variances are assumed unequal.

---

**Learning Check.** *Why do we have to assume that the populations are normally distributed?*

---

2. **Stating the research and the null hypotheses.** The research hypothesis is that the mean ratings of Ross Perot for the population of Native Americans is different from that of the population of Asian Americans:

$$H_1: \mu_{Y_{NA}} \neq \mu_{Y_A}$$

The null hypothesis states that there are no differences between the two population means:

$$H_0: \mu_{Y_{NA}} = \mu_{Y_A}$$

3. **Selecting a sampling distribution and a test statistic.** The $t$ distribution and the $t$ statistic are used to test the significance of the difference between the two sample means.

4. **Choosing alpha and establishing the region of rejection.** To establish the region of rejection and choose a critical $t$ we first calculate the df associated with our test. Because the population variances are assumed unequal and the samples are small, df is

$$df = \frac{\left(\dfrac{S_{Y_{NA}}^2}{N_{NA}} + \dfrac{S_{Y_A}^2}{N_A}\right)^2}{\left(\dfrac{S_{Y_{NA}}^2}{N_{NA}}\right)^2 \left(\dfrac{1}{N_{NA}+1}\right) + \left(\dfrac{S_{Y_A}^2}{N_A}\right)^2 \left(\dfrac{1}{N_A+1}\right)} - 2$$

$$= \frac{\left(\dfrac{197}{16} + \dfrac{580}{26}\right)^2}{\left(\dfrac{197}{16}\right)^2 \left(\dfrac{1}{17}\right) + \left(\dfrac{580}{26}\right)^2 \left(\dfrac{1}{27}\right)} - 2$$

$$= 42$$

Always round df to the nearest whole number.

Next, we turn to the $t$ distribution in Appendix C. Our test is two-tailed and we choose $\alpha = .05$. Searching for 42 degrees of freedom we use the closest value—40. The critical $t = \pm 2.021$.

5. **Computing the test statistic.** Because the population variances are unequal, we use formula 14.6 to estimate the standard error $S_{\bar{Y}_{NA} - \bar{Y}_A}$:

$$S_{\bar{Y}_{NA} - \bar{Y}_A} = \sqrt{\frac{(14.04)^2}{16} + \frac{(24.08)^2}{26}} = 5.88$$

Substitute this value into the denominator for the obtained $t$ statistic:

$$t = \frac{47.22 - 28.85}{5.88} = 3.12$$

6. **Making a decision and interpreting the results.** The obtained $t$, 3.12, is greater (more extreme) than the critical $t$, $\pm 2.021$. Therefore, we reject the null hypothesis. We conclude that Native Americans and Asian Americans differ significantly in their ratings of Ross Perot.

## Testing the Significance of the Difference Between Two Sample Proportions (with Large Samples: $N_1 + N_2 > 100$)

In the preceding section, we learned how to test for the significance of the difference between two population means when the variable is measured on an interval-ratio level of measurement. Yet numerous variables in the social sciences are measured on a nominal or an ordinal level. These variables are often described in terms of proportions. For example, we might be interested in comparing the proportions of men and women who support federal funding for abortion or the proportions of Republicans and Democrats who believe in restricting social services for illegal immigrants. In this section, we present statistical inference techniques that are used when the objective is to test for significant differences between two sample proportions.

Hypothesis testing with two sample proportions follows the same structure as the statistical tests presented earlier. The assumptions of the test are stated; the research and the null hypotheses are formulated; the sampling distribution and the test statistic are specified; the alpha level and the region of rejection are determined; and a decision is made whether or not to reject the null hypothesis following the calculation of the test statistic. To illustrate hypothesis testing with proportions let's begin with an example.

### An Illustration: Public Opinion About the Environment

Most Americans consider protection of the environment one of the most important issues facing this country. According to a 1995 Gallup

Table 14.5 **Percentages of Democrats and Republicans Who Consider the Environment a Priority**

| Environment a Priority | Democrats (%) | Republicans (%) |
|---|---|---|
| Yes | 70 | 49 |
| No | 30 | 51 |
| Total | 100 | 100 |
| N | (342) | (341) |

poll,[10] 62 percent of Americans believe that protection of the environment should be given priority, even at the risk of curbing economic growth. However, environmental protection seems to be a partisan issue, with Democrats more willing to take aggressive measures and Republicans more cautious about the economic implications of such measures.[11] The responses of Democrats and Republicans to a 1995 Gallup poll are presented in Table 14.5.

More Democrats (70%) than Republicans (49%) consider environmental protection a priority, even at the risk of curbing economic growth. But does this difference of 21 percentage points (70% − 49%) represent a real difference in the opinions of Democrats and Republicans? These percentages are based on a single sample and it is possible that this particular sample happened to include a lot of Democrats who consider environmental protection a priority. Perhaps if we took another sample we would get a different result. To examine this question, we follow the structure of hypothesis testing that is applied throughout this chapter.

1. **Making assumptions.**
    a. Independent random samples of $N_D + N_R > 100$ are used.
    b. The level of measurement is nominal or ordinal.

2. **Stating the research and the null hypotheses.** The environment has been a major partisan issue in American politics for quite some time. We expect the population proportion of Democrats who consider the environment a priority to be higher than the population proportion of Republicans who do. Therefore, we formulate a directional hypothesis:

$$H_1: \pi_D > \pi_R$$

[10]*Gallup Poll Monthly,* April 1995, pp. 17–19.
[11]Ibid.

where $\pi_D$ and $\pi_R$ are the population proportions of Democrats and Republicans who consider environmental protection a priority.

Our null hypothesis states that there are no differences in the opinions of Democrats and Republicans:

$$H_0: \pi_D = \pi_R$$

3. **Selecting the sampling distribution and the test statistic.** The population distributions of dichotomies like yes/no (as shown in Table 14.5) are decidedly not normal. However, based on the Central Limit Theorem, we know that the sampling distribution of the difference between sample proportions is normally distributed when the sample size is large (when $N_1 + N_2 > 100$) with mean $\mu_{P_1-P_2}$ and the estimated standard error $S_{P_1-P_2}$. Therefore, we can follow the same procedure applied when testing the differences between means, using the normal distribution as the sampling distribution and calculating $Z$ as the test statistic.[12]

To calculate the test statistic $Z$, we follow formula 14.3 for testing the difference between means. Substituting $P_D$ and $P_R$ for $\overline{Y}_1$ and $\overline{Y}_2$ into the numerator and $S_{P_D-P_R}$ for $\sigma_{\overline{Y}_1-\overline{Y}_2}$ into the denominator, we get:

$$Z = \frac{P_D - P_R}{S_{P_D-P_R}} \tag{14.8}$$

where $P_D$ and $P_R$ are the sample proportions for Democrats and Republicans, and $S_{P_D-P_R}$ is the estimated standard error of the sampling distribution of the differences between sample proportions.

The estimated standard error is calculated using

$$S_{P_D-P_R} = \sqrt{\frac{P_D(1-P_D)}{N_D} + \frac{P_R(1-P_R)}{N_R}} \tag{14.9}$$

4. **Choosing the alpha level and establishing the region of rejection.** We set $\alpha$ at .05, and since $H_1$ is a directional hypothesis, our test is one-tailed. The critical $Z$ is +1.65.

5. **Calculating the test statistic.** Table 14.5 provides all the data we need to calculate $Z$ using formula 14.8. First, we calculate the standard error:

$$S_{P_D-P_R} = \sqrt{\frac{P_D(1-P_D)}{N_D} + \frac{P_R(1-P_R)}{N_R}}$$

[12]The sample proportions are unbiased estimates of the corresponding population proportions. Therefore, we can use the $Z$ statistic even though our standard error is estimated from the sample proportions.

$$= \sqrt{\frac{.70(.30)}{342} + \frac{.49(.51)}{341}} = .037$$

Substitute this value into the denominator for the Z statistic:

$$Z = \frac{P_D - P_R}{S_{P_D - P_R}} = \frac{.70 - .49}{.037} = 5.68$$

6. **Making a decision and interpreting the results.** Our obtained Z, 5.68, is more extreme than the critical Z, +1.65, and falls into the region of rejection. Therefore, we reject the null hypothesis at the .05 level of significance. We conclude that there are probably real differences between the population of Democrats and the population of Republicans regarding opinions about environmental protection.

## Statistics in Practice: Gender and Abortion Attitudes

Do men and women hold different attitudes about abortion? Some people feel that because women are more directly affected by abortion they will be more supportive of legal abortion. However, other studies[13] show that there is no significant difference between men's and women's views on abortion. We have randomly selected a subsample from the GSS survey and compared the proportion of men and women who reported that they "approve of abortion for any reason":

| Men | Women |
|-----|-------|
| $P_M = 0.42$ | $P_W = 0.44$ |
| $N_M = 421$ | $N_W = 392$ |

1. **Making assumptions.**
   a. Independent random samples of $N_W + N_M > 100$ are used.
   b. The level of measurement of the variable is nominal.

2. **Stating the research and the null hypotheses.**

   $H_1: \pi_W \neq \pi_M$

   $H_0: \pi_W = \pi_M$

3. **Selecting the sampling distribution and the test statistic.** The sampling distribution is the normal distribution, and the test statistic is Z.

4. **Choosing alpha and establishing the region of rejection.** Set $\alpha = .01$; our test is two-tailed. The critical Z is ±2.58.

5. **Calculating the test statistic.** Calculate the standard error using formula 14.9:

[13]See, for example, Elizabeth Addel Cook, Ted G. Jelen, and Clyde Wilcox, *Between Two Absolutes: Public Opinion and the Politics of Abortion*. Boulder, CO: Westview Press, 1992.

$$S_{P_W - P_M} = \sqrt{\frac{.44(.56)}{392} + \frac{.42(.58)}{421}} = .035$$

Substituting this value into the denominator for $Z$, we get:

$$Z = \frac{P_W - P_M}{S_{P_W - P_M}} = \frac{.44 - .42}{.035} = .57$$

6. **Making a decision and interpreting the results.** Our obtained $Z$, .57, is smaller in absolute value (less extreme) than the critical $Z$, ±2.58, and falls outside the region of rejection. Therefore, we cannot reject the null hypothesis. We conclude that the observed differences in the opinions of men and women regarding abortion probably *do not* reflect a difference that would have been seen had the entire population been measured.

## Reading the Research Literature: Reporting the Results of Statistical Hypothesis Testing

In this chapter, we discuss the process of hypothesis testing in terms of six basic steps: making assumptions; stating the research and the null hypotheses; specifying the sampling distribution and the test statistic; determining the alpha level and the region of rejection; calculating the test statistic; and making a decision on whether or not to reject the null hypothesis.

Let's conclude this chapter with two fairly typical examples of how the results of statistical hypothesis testing are presented in the social science research literature. Both examples demonstrate that when presented in the research literature, the results of statistical hypothesis testing usually do not follow either the format or the same degree of detail presented in this chapter. It is not uncommon for a single research article to include the results of ten to twenty statistical tests. Therefore, the results have to be presented succinctly and in summary form. As is illustrated in the two examples presented here, most research articles do not include a discussion of the null hypothesis, the sampling distribution, or the region of rejection. Instead, the results are usually presented in a summary table that may include the sample statistics (for instance, the sample means), the obtained test statistics ($t$ or $Z$), the alpha level, and an indication of whether or not the results are statistically significant.[14]

[14]Similar discussion is presented in Joseph F. Healey, *Statistics: A Tool for Social Research*, 3d ed. Belmont, CA: Wadsworth, 1993, p. 218.

The first example we present is drawn from a study that examines differences in the level of concern for environmental issues between people living in rich and poor countries. Table 14.6 summarizes the results of a study by Professors Brechin and Kempton. Their study challenges the conventional wisdom that only people in rich countries are concerned about the environment and that people in developing countries lack concern for environmental values. The researchers argue that pressures from increasing population growth and declining environmental resources, combined with little faith in meaningful assistance from their governments, have forced people from developing poor countries to take matters into their own hands to protect their families. Such decentralized, popularly supported action suggests considerable public support for environmental protection in developing countries. The research hypothesis tested in this study is that the level of environmental concern among citizens from developing countries is higher than the level of concern demonstrated by richer nations.

To test this hypothesis the researchers used survey data collected by the Gallup organization in 1992. Gallup interviewed some 22,000 citizens in 22 countries, with representative random samples from each country. Respondents were asked a series of questions about their concern with general and specific environmental issues. In each country the percentage of respondents who considered these problems as "very serious" was recorded. Countries were divided into poor ($N = 11$) and richer ($N = 11$) countries, and a mean percentage for each group of countries was then calculated. High means indicate a higher degree of environmental concern. To test the hypothesis, $t$ tests for differences between means were calculated. Table 14.6 displays the results of those calculations.

Let's examine this table carefully. Each row presents the results of a single statistical test of significance. Thus, in the first row, the researcher tests the statistical significance of the difference between the means of the concern with general environmental issues. In the second row, the comparison is between the means of the concern with air pollution; in the third, the comparison is between the means of the concern with contaminated soil; and in the fourth row, it is with loss of species.

Now examine the last column of the table. It presents the obtained $t$'s for each of these tests. The asterisks indicate which differences are statistically significant at the .05 level. Note that two of the four tests ("very serious for nation" and "air pollution and smog") are statistically significant; on both, the poorer nations demonstrate greater environmental concern, which is opposite from the common Western belief and supports the research hypothesis.

Table 14.6 **Tests of Environmental Concern Between Richer and Poorer Nations**

| Question | Poor Countries (N = 11) | | Rich Countries (N = 11) | | |
| | Mean ($\overline{Y}$) | SD (S) | Mean ($\overline{Y}$) | SD (S) | t |
| --- | --- | --- | --- | --- | --- |
| Very serious for nation | 55 | 9.8 | 42 | 15 | 2.50* |
| Air pollution and smog | 67 | 10.0 | 56 | 11 | 2.40* |
| Contaminated soil | 55 | 16.0 | 48 | 9 | 1.18 |
| Loss of species | 61 | 16.0 | 55 | 9 | 1.10 |

*Source:* Adapted from Steven R. Brechin and Willet Kempton, "Global Environmentalism: A Challenge to the Postmaterialism Thesis?" *Social Science Quarterly*, Vol. 75, No. 2, June 1994, 245–267. Used by permission.
* Statistically significant at the .05 level

The second example on abortion attitudes is taken from a study looking at racial differences in support for legalized abortion. Lynxwiler and Gay examined the hypothesis that blacks show lower support for legalized abortion than whites, using the 1972 to 1988 General Social Survey (GSS) data to examine racial differences in abortion attitudes. Their measure of abortion attitudes is a scale composed of answers to six questions that tap attitudes toward legalized abortion under differing circumstances. The scale's values range from 0 (for respondents' opposition to abortion under every circumstance) to 6 (for respondents' approval of abortion under every circumstance).

Table 14.7 presents year-by-year mean differences on the abortion scale for black and white respondents. The table illustrates a slightly different format for presenting the results of hypothesis testing. This table presents the sample values (the means for whites and blacks), the mean difference, and the sample size. However, unlike the previous example about environmental concerns, the value of the obtained test statistic is not shown here. Instead, the results of the differences between means tests for each year are indicated by asterisks. Typically, a single asterisk (*) indicates that the probability (P) associated with the obtained test statistic (t) is lower than .05 (* P < .05), and, therefore, the null hypothesis can be rejected at the .05 level. Double asterisks (**) indicate that P is lower than .01 (** P < .01), and the null hypothesis can be rejected at the .01 level. Note that except for the final year, all the mean differences in this example are significant at the .01 level, indicating that racial differences do exist. For all but one of the surveys (1988) occurring between 1972 and 1988, whites were more supportive of legal abortions than blacks.

Table 14.7 **Mean Comparisons: Differences Between White and Black Respondents on Abortion Attitudes by Survey Year**

| Year | Whites Mean ($\bar{Y}$) | (N) | Blacks Mean ($\bar{Y}$) | (N) | Difference |
|------|------|------|------|------|------|
| 1972 | 4.01 | (1,109) | 3.07 | (207) | .94** |
| 1973 | 4.27 | (1,178) | 3.33 | (161) | .94** |
| 1974 | 4.30 | (1,135) | 3.61 | (147) | .69** |
| 1975 | 4.19 | (1,148) | 3.66 | (135) | .53** |
| 1976 | 4.20 | (1,212) | 3.32 | (111) | .88** |
| 1977 | 4.23 | (1,183) | 3.47 | (156) | .76** |
| 1978 | 3.96 | (1,202) | 3.39 | (144) | .57** |
| 1980 | 4.19 | (1,162) | 3.51 | (117) | .68** |
| 1982 | 4.27 | (1,413) | 3.39 | (431) | .88** |
| 1984 | 4.02 | (1,114) | 3.25 | (150) | .77** |
| 1985 | 3.85 | (1,199) | 3.45 | (132) | .40** |
| 1987 | 3.95 | (1,342) | 3.43 | (455) | .52** |
| 1988 | 3.82 | (696) | 3.53 | (115) | .29 |

*Source:* Adapted from John Lynxwiler and David Gay, "Reconsidering Race Differences in Abortion Attitudes." *Social Science Quarterly,* Vol. 75, No. 1, March 1994, 73. Used by permission.
*P < .05.
**P < .01.

## MAIN POINTS

■ The most common type of statistical hypothesis testing involves a comparison between two sample means. If we knew the population variances when testing for differences between sample means, we would use the Z statistic and the normal distribution. However, in practice, we are unlikely to have this information.

■ When testing for differences between sample means when the population variances are unknown we use the *t* statistic and the *t* distribution to identify the critical *t* associated with the alpha level.

■ Tests involving differences between proportions follow the same procedure as tests for differences between means when population variances are known. The test statistic is Z and the sampling distribution is approximated by the normal distribution.

## KEY TERMS

*degrees of freedom*

*sampling distribution of the difference between means*

*t distribution*

*t statistic*

**SPSS DEMONSTRATION**

*Demonstration 1: Producing a Test of Mean Differences*

In this chapter, we discussed methods of testing differences in means or proportions between two samples (or groups). The two-sample T Test procedure can be found under the *Statistics* menu choice, then under *Compare Means*, where it is labeled *Independent-Samples T Test*.

The opening dialog box is fairly simple and requires that you specify various test variables (the dependent variable) and one independent or grouping variable.

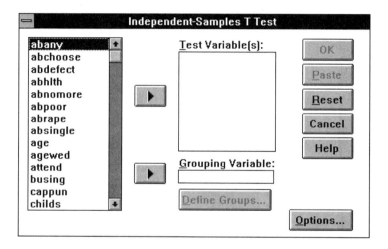

We'll test the null hypothesis that females and males work the same number of hours each week by using the variable HRS1. Place that variable in the Test Variable(s) box, then put SEX in the Grouping Variable box. When you do so, question marks appear next to SEX, indicating that you must supply two values to define the two groups (independent samples). Click on *Define Groups*. Then put "1" in the first box and "2" in the second box. Then click on *Continue* and *OK* to run the procedure.

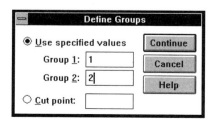

The output from T Test is fairly detailed and contains more information than was discussed in the chapter. The first part of the output displays the mean number of hours worked for males and females, the standard deviation (SD), the number of respondents in each group, and the standard error of the mean. We see that males worked about than 5 hours more per week than females.

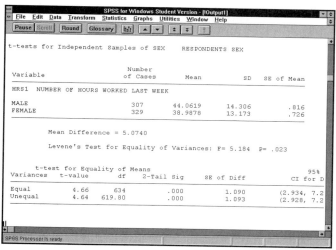

Recall from the chapter that an important decision of the *t* statistic calculation is whether the variances of the two groups are equal. If the variances are assumed equal, you can use a simple formula to calculate the number of degrees of freedom. However, SPSS can take account of those times when the variances are unequal and still calculate an appropriate *t* statistic and degrees of freedom. To do so, SPSS does a direct test of whether or not the variances for hours worked are identical for men and women (we did not discuss this test in the chapter). This is the Levene Test in the middle of the output screen. The test has a null hypothesis that the variances are equal. SPSS reports a probability of .023 for this test, so, for example, at the .01 level, we would conclude that the variances are equal. That is, we fail to reject the null hypothesis.

This then tells us which of the *t* tests to use in the bottom section of the output, the line for equal or unequal variances. Because the Levene Test suggests that the variances are equal, we use that line (this allows us to pool the variances). The actual *t* value is 4.66, with 634 degrees of freedom. The two-tailed exact significance (2-Tail Sig) is listed as .000, which means it is less than .0005. SPSS calculates the exact significance, so there is no need to look in a table. This probability is very small and well below the .05 or .01 levels, so we conclude that there is a mean difference in hours worked between males and females (we reject the null hypothesis).

What if we wanted to do a one-tailed test instead? SPSS does not directly list the probability for a one-tailed test, but it is easy to calculate. If we had specified a directional research hypothesis—such as that men work longer hours than women—we would simply take the probability reported by SPSS and divide it in half for a one-tailed test. Because the probability is so small in this case, our conclusion will be the same whether we do a one- or two-tailed test.

The last bit of output on each line is the 95 percent confidence interval for the mean difference in hours worked between the two groups. You should be able to understand this based on the discussion of confidence intervals in Chapter 12. It is helpful information when testing mean differences because the actual mean difference measured (here 5.074 hours) is a sample mean, which will vary from sample to sample. The 95 percent confidence interval gives us a range over which the sample mean differences are likely to vary.

### EXERCISES

1. A social psychologist has been studying the stress levels of people who live in cities compared with those who live in the suburbs. She had the people in her survey record the number of times during one week that they experienced a stressful situation, such as a driver cutting them off, a rude sales clerk, and so forth. Her null hypothesis is that suburban residents will have fewer stressful experiences or interactions than city dwellers. The data show that those who live in cities had an average of 14.2 stressful experiences; suburban residents had 12.5 stressful interactions, on the average. From many past studies she estimates that the standard deviation of the variable of interest is 2.3 interactions for both rural and city residents. She included 80 city dwellers and 80 suburbanites in the study.
   a. State the appropriate research and null hypotheses.
   b. Test the null hypothesis at the .01 level of significance. What do you conclude?

2. Do whites have jobs of higher prestige than nonwhites? Use data from the 1994 GSS to investigate this question. The variable PRESTG80 records job prestige for each respondent. The SPSS Means procedure was used to display means for job prestige, broken down into the racial classifications of white, black, and other. The standard deviation and number of respondents in each group are also listed. Assume that the standard deviations are unequal across the races.

a. Which two-sample test is appropriate to determine whether whites have higher job prestige than the other racial groups? Why?

b. Use this test to conduct a one-tailed test of the null hypothesis, comparing whites with blacks and whites with others. Use the .05 level of significance. What did you discover?

c. Would your conclusions have been different if you had used a two-tailed test?

| Summaries of By levels of | PRESTG80 RACE | | RS OCCUPATIONAL PRESTIGE SCORE (1980) RACE OF RESPONDENT | | | |
|---|---|---|---|---|---|---|
| Variable | Value | Label | | Mean | Std Dev | Cases |
| For Entire Population | | | | 43.9166 | 13.7219 | 959 |
| RACE | 1 | WHITE | | 44.6346 | 13.6347 | 810 |
| RACE | 2 | BLACK | | 39.7982 | 14.4468 | 114 |
| RACE | 3 | OTHER | | 40.7143 | 10.4194 | 35 |

3. In exercise 6 in Chapter 7 you studied the number of bills introduced to Congress on women's and family issues that passed during two time periods in the early 1990s. You used the statistic lambda to characterize the strength of the relationship in that previous exercise. Now you can further examine this same data with a two-sample test of proportions.

a. Test the null hypothesis that the proportion of bills passed was the same in 1990 and 1991 as in the 1992 and 1993 period. (For example, the proportion of bills passed in the earlier period is $19/231 = .082$.) Use the .01 level of significance.

b. How does this result add to or modify your conclusions based on the calculation of lambda in Chapter 7?

4. A social worker has been investigating the effect of residence on the lives of her clients. She randomly selected 35 people who live in public housing and 35 people who live in standard housing (a house, apartment, etc.), then studied several aspects of their lives. In particular, she was interested in whether people stay longer in a job if they are out on their own rather than living in public housing (for this study, she selected from only those people who had a job). She found that those who live in public housing have been working in their current job an average of 1.3 years with a standard deviation of 4.3 years. Those living in standard housing have been working in their current job an average of 2.4 years with

a standard deviation of 3.6 years. Assume that the standard deviations are equal.

    a. State the research and the null hypotheses.

    b. Test the null hypothesis at the .05 level.

5. A political scientist is measuring how Americans feel about Russia (Do they like the country?), now that the Cold War is over. One of his hypotheses is that people who are politically more liberal will feel more favorable toward Russia. He has conducted a small survey of adults, but the questionnaire unfortunately did not include a direct question on political position. However, it did include a question about support for the death penalty, which the political scientist believes is a good proxy, or substitute, for political position. (*Hint:* Conservatives are more likely to favor the death penalty.) The results follow. (*Note:* Liking for Russia is measured on a scale from 0 to 9, where a high score means *dislike.*)

| Attitude Toward Death Penalty | Liking For Russia | Std. Dev. | N |
|---|---|---|---|
| Favor | 4.06 | 2.49 | 123 |
| Oppose | 3.34 | 2.36 | 38 |

Using the data, answer these questions.

    a. What are the research and the null hypotheses for his study?

    b. What is the appropriate two-sample test? (Assume that the variances are equal.)

    c. Test the null hypothesis at the .05 significance level. Do your results support the political scientist's hypothesis?

6. You have previously examined the relationship between education and support for the busing of students to reduce segregation. Data from the 1994 GSS show that 36 percent (36 out of 100) of those with less than a high school education favor busing for this reason, whereas 31.48 percent (17 out of 54) of those with a graduate degree favor busing. You wonder whether there is any difference in support, in the population, between people with these two levels of education. Use a test of the difference between proportions when answering these questions.

    a. What is the research hypothesis? Should you conduct a one- or a two-tailed test? Why?

    b. Test the null hypothesis at the .05 level of significance. What do you conclude?

7. A friend suggests that people who are happier in life have more children than those who are unhappy. You think that she might be

correct but would prefer to investigate the question rather than speculate. You and she collect data from a random sample of people in the town in which you live, asking about happiness (happy or not happy) and the number of children. You find that those who are happy have an average of 1.81 children, with a variance of 2.21 (33 people in this group); those who are unhappy have an average of 2.12 children, with a variance of 2.99 (31 people in this group). Assume the variances are unequal.

a. What is the appropriate test statistic? Why?

b. Test the null hypothesis with a one-tailed test at the .01 significance level. What do you conclude about your friend's conjecture?

8. A study is done to see whether workers for a large manufacturing company support a new plan to allow flexible working hours. The company is so large that a random sample is taken to answer this question. The results of the study show that 45 percent of the employees who belong to a union at the company support the new plan (276 union employees were included in the sample). You've also been told by the researcher who did the study that 28 percent of the nonunion employees, chiefly management, support the plan (this figure also comes from a random sample).

a. Do you have enough information to test the null hypothesis that there is no difference in support between union and nonunion employees? If no, why not?

b. What if you learned that there are 19,546 employees at the company? Do you now have enough information? Why or why not?

c. What if you learned that the sample size for nonunion employees is 202? Can you now do the test? If so, test at the .05 level of significance, with a two-tailed test, whether or not union and nonunion employees differ in their support for the new plan.

9. The gender gap—differences in the political attitudes and behavior between men and women—was a central issue in the 1996 presidential election. The gender gap is evident in the tendency of women to hold more liberal views and to vote Democrat more often than men. A preelection poll found that, among 371 women, 53 percent supported Bill Clinton for president, whereas only 42 percent of 402 men did so. Do these differences reflect a real gender gap in the population of voters?

a. What are the research and the null hypotheses to test for a gender gap? Would you conduct a one- or a two-tailed test?

b. Test the null hypothesis at the .01 level of significance. What do you conclude?

10. Social class is an important sociological variable in many circumstances. Social class membership is related to many attitudes and behaviors, including marriage. For several reasons, including the fact that those of a higher social class have spent more time in school, it is quite possible that the age of first marriage is greater for those from the middle class than those from the working class. The 1994 GSS contains the variables AGEWED and CLASS, which allow a test of this hypothesis. The Means procedure in SPSS was used to produce this output.

```
Summaries  of      AGEWED        AGE  WHEN  FIRST  MARRIED
By  levels  of      CLASS         SUBJECTIVE  CLASS  IDENTIFICATION

Variable        Value   Label                   Mean    Std  Dev    Cases

For  Entire  Population                        22.7175    4.6682      400

CLASS               1    LOWER  CLASS          22.8400    5.1290       25
CLASS               2    WORKING  CLASS        21.9427    4.8055      157
CLASS               3    MIDDLE  CLASS         23.1805    4.2911      205
CLASS               4    UPPER  CLASS          24.5385    6.6032       13

   Total  Cases  =  1000
```

a. Use this information to see whether persons of self-perceived middle-class status were older when they married than were those in the working class. Test the hypothesis at the .01 significance level with a one-tailed test. Assume equal variances.

b. Test whether the upper class marries at a later age than those of middle-class status. Test at the .05 significance level. Assume unequal variances.

c. Imagine that there were 150 respondents from the upper class in the sample rather than the 13 actually in the study. Redo your calculations in (b). Does your conclusion change? What does this tell you about the effect of sample size on statistical tests?

11. In Chapter 12 we discussed a study by Tienda and Wilson on the relationship between migration and earnings of Hispanic men. Using a sample of the 1980 census, Tienda and Wilson found that the earnings of Cuban men are higher than the earnings of either Puerto Rican or Mexican men. In Chapter 12 we calculated the 95 percent confidence interval for the mean earnings of the three groups and found that the interval estimate for Cubans was considerably higher than the interval estimates for Puerto Ricans and Mexicans. A more direct way to investigate the question of whether

the earnings of Cuban men differ from the earnings of Puerto Rican and Mexican men is by testing directly for the differences between means. Use the data presented in Table 12.12 to conduct these tests.

   a. Which two-sample test is appropriate to determine whether Cuban men earn more than either Puerto Rican or Mexican men? Why?

   b. Use this test to conduct one-tailed tests of the null hypothesis that the earnings of Cuban men are equal to the other two groups. Use the .05 level of significance and interpret the results.

   c. Compare your results with the results we obtained in Chapter 12 using confidence intervals. Do your results confirm the conclusions we drew earlier?

12. In this chapter we used the results of the 1994 election study to show that Ross Perot was favored more by Native Americans than by Asian Americans. The same study shows that the mean rating of Bill Clinton was higher among Asian Americans than among Native Americans. The mean rating of Clinton among Native Americans ($N = 16$) was 45.57 with a variance of 597. Among Asian Americans ($N = 26$) it was 60.42 with a variance of 576. Conduct a test to find out whether there was a true population difference in the rating of President Clinton between these two groups.

   a. State the research and the null hypotheses for a two-tailed test.

   b. Test at the .01 significance level. What are your conclusions?

   c. Would your conclusions have been different had you tested the null hypothesis at the .10 level?

## SPSS PROBLEMS

1. Use the 1994 GSS file to investigate differences in educational attainment by class and race. The SPSS T Test procedure is the appropriate tool to test for any differences because SPSS doesn't directly calculate a Z statistic for the two-sample case. Race and class have more than two categories each, but they can be used in the T Test procedure by comparing two categories at a time (for example, blacks with whites, or the middle class with the lower class. Do all your tests at the .05 significance level as two-tailed tests. Write a report based on your findings. If you find any differences in educational level, do they seem to be large enough to make a critical difference in the real world? (*Note:* There is a more sophisticated method to make multiple-group comparisons, but it is beyond the scope of this textbook.)

2. Do males and females have the same average number of children (the variable CHILDS)? The answer to this question would seem to be obvious, but it is always best to test a hypothesis when data are available. Use the 1994 GSS to investigate the question, doing a two-tailed test at the .05 significance level. Write a report describing your finding and suggesting several causes for the result.

### GROUP PROBLEMS

1. Use the data you have collected from your classmates. Pick a few dependent variables that are measured on an interval scale and a couple of others that are dichotomies. Try to pick variables you've used before so you can compare these results with those from earlier exercises.
   a. Construct research and null hypotheses using the dependent variables and a few independent variables of the group's choosing. You don't have to pick independent variables with only two categories even though you've only learned two-sample tests in this chapter; as with SPSS exercise 1, you can always select only two categories to compare from a larger set.
   b. Choose appropriate test statistics and test your null hypotheses at the .05 significance level. Use either a one-tailed or a two-tailed test based upon your research hypotheses.
   c. Write a report or provide a verbal report to the class summarizing your group's findings. If you did use dependent variables you had used previously, compare your results from the earlier exercise.

2. By increasing sample size in a second study, it is often possible to make a difference in means between two groups statistically significant, even when it was not significant in a first study. Does this imply that we should always take very large samples so that statistical tests will show that all the differences between means or proportions are statistically significant? Discuss this question with other group members and be prepared to defend your conclusions to the class as a whole.

# 15     The Chi-Square Test

## Introduction

Figures collected by the U.S. Department of Justice suggest that violent crime is not an equal opportunity offender. Your chances of being a victim of a violent crime are strongly influenced by your age, race, gender, and neighborhood. For example, you are far more likely to be a victim of crime if you live in a city rather than in a suburb or in the country; if you are a young black male rather than a middle-aged white male; or if you are a black woman between the ages of 16 and 24 rather than a white woman of the same age.

The fear of being a crime victim—regardless of actual victimization—is greater for women at every age and of every race than for men.[1] Consider the cross-tabulation in Table 15.1 of the variables "fear of walking alone at night" and "gender." Based on a random sample taken from the 1987 to 1991 General Social Survey data set,[2] these data confirm the observation that fear of crime differs according to gender:

Table 15.1 **Percentage of Men and Women Afraid to Walk Alone in Neighborhood at Night**

| Afraid | Men | Women | Total |
|---|---|---|---|
| No | 75.00% | 38.06% | 56.57% |
| | (186) | (94) | (280) |
| Yes | 25.00% | 61.94% | 43.43% |
| | (62) | (153) | (215) |
| Total | 100.00% | 100.00% | 100.00% |
| (N) | (248) | (247) | (495) |

[1]Margaret L. Andersen, *Thinking about Women.* New York: Macmillan, 1997, 269.
[2]This table was discussed earlier, in Chapter 6. (See Table 6.3.)

61.94 percent of the women surveyed compared with only 25 percent of the men are afraid to walk alone in their neighborhoods at night.

The percentage differences in the perceptions of safety between males and females, as observed in Table 15.1, suggest that a relationship exists between gender and fear in the sample we analyzed. Our purpose in looking at this sample is to learn whether this relationship exists in the larger population from which we drew the sample. How do we know that the gender differences observed in Table 15.1 reflect a real difference in the perception of safety among the larger population? How can we be sure that these differences are not just a quirk of sampling and that had we taken another sample these differences would not be wiped out or perhaps even reversed?

Let's assume that men and women are equally likely to be afraid to walk alone at night, and that in the population from which this sample was drawn there are no real differences between them. What would be the expected percentages of men and women who would be afraid to walk alone at night? who would not be afraid to walk alone at night? If gender and fear were not associated, we would expect the same percentage of men as women to be fearful. (Similarly, we would expect to see the same percentage of men and women who are not fearful.) These percentages should be equal to the percentage of "fearful" respondents in the sample as a whole. The last column of Table 15.1, the row marginals, contains the percentage of "fearful" respondents in the sample as a whole. The row marginals show that 43.43 percent of all respondents were afraid to walk alone at night, whereas 56.57 percent were not afraid. Therefore, we would expect to see 43.43 percent of the men and 43.43 percent of the women in the sample afraid to walk alone at night; similarly, 56.57 percent of the men and 56.57 percent of the women would not be afraid to do so.

Table 15.2 shows these hypothetical expected percentages. Because the percentage distributions of the variable "fear" are identical for men and women, we can say that Table 15.2 demonstrates a perfect model of "no association" between the variable "fear" and the variable "gender."

If there is an association between gender and fear, then at least some of the observed percentages in Table 15.1 should differ from the hypothetical expected percentages shown in Table 15.2. On the other hand, if gender and fear are not associated, the observed percentages should approximate the expected percentages shown in Table 15.2. A cell-by-cell comparison of the actual data in Table 15.1 with the hypothetical data shown in Table 15.2 reveals that there is a great disparity between the observed percentages and the hypothetical percentages we generated. For example, whereas in Table 15.1, 75 percent of the

Table 15.2 **Percentage of Men and Women Afraid to Walk Alone in Neighborhood at Night (hypothetical data showing no association)**

| Afraid | Men | Women | Total |
|--------|-----|-------|-------|
| No | 56.57% | 56.57% | 56.57% (280) |
| Yes | 43.43% | 43.43% | 43.43% (215) |
| Total (N) | 100.00% (248) | 100.00% (247) | 100.00% (495) |

men reported that they were not afraid, the corresponding cell in Table 15.2 shows that only 56.57 percent of the men report no fear. The remaining three cells reveal similar discrepancies.

Are the disparities between the observed and expected percentages large enough to convince us that there is indeed a genuine pattern in the population? The *chi-square* statistic helps answer this question. It is obtained by comparing the actual observed frequencies in a bivariate table with the frequencies that are generated under an assumption that the two variables in the cross-tabulation are not associated with each other. If the observed and expected values are very close, the chi-square statistic will be small. If the disparities between the observed and expected values are large, the chi-square statistic will be large. In the next section, we will learn how to compute the chi-square statistic so we can determine whether the differences between men's and women's fear of walking alone in their neighborhood at night could have occurred simply by chance.

> *Learning Check.* *Calculating chi-square is fairly simple if you understand and follow each of the steps. In the next few learning checks we will provide you with the opportunity to practice calculating chi-square as we go through the steps. The value of chi-square for your practice data can be found in the learning check at the end of this chapter.*

## The Concept of Chi-Square as a Statistical Test

The **chi-square test** (pronounced kai-square and written as $\chi^2$) is an inferential statistics technique designed to test for significant relationships between two variables organized in a bivariate table. The test has a wide variety of research applications and is one of the most widely used tests in the social sciences. Chi-square requires no assumptions about the shape of the population distribution from which a sample is drawn. It can be applied to nominally or ordinally measured variables.

---

*Chi-Square Test* (pronounced kai-square and written as $\chi^2$) An inferential statistics technique designed to test for significant relationships between two variables organized in a bivariate table.

---

## The Concept of Statistical Independence

The question of whether gender is associated with fear can be restated in terms of the concepts of statistical independence and dependence. When two variables are not associated (as in Table 15.2), one can say that they are **statistically independent**. That is, respondents' scores on one variable are independent of their scores on the second variable. We can identify statistical independence in a bivariate table by comparing the distribution of the dependent variable in each category of the independent variable: When two variables are statistically independent, the percentage distributions of the dependent variable within each category of the independent variable are identical. The notion of statistical independence was concretely illustrated in Table 15.2. The distributions of the variable fear were identical within each category (men; women) of the independent variable gender: 43.43 percent of the men in the sample were afraid to walk alone at night and 56.57 percent were not afraid; the same percentages were observed among the women. Based on these hypothetical data one can say that in Table 15.2, level of fear is independent of one's gender.[3]

---

[3]Because statistical independence is a symmetrical property, the distribution of the independent variable within each category of the dependent variable will also be identical. That is, if gender and fear were statistically independent, we would also expect to see the distribution of gender identical in each category of the variable fear.

> **Learning Check.** *The data we will use to practice calculating chi-square should be familiar from Chapter 6 (Table 6.15). They are taken from the General Social Survey 1988 to 1991 and examine the relationship between "preferred family size" (the independent variable) and "support for abortion" (the dependent variable), as shown in the bivariate table:*
>
> **Preferred Family Size and Support for Abortion**
>
> | SUPPORT | PREFERRED FAMILY SIZE Large | Small | |
> |---|---|---|---|
> | Yes | 25% (38) | 50% (127) | 41% (165) |
> | No | 75% (112) | 50% (126) | 59% (238) |
> | Total (N) | 100% (150) | 100% (253) | 100% (403) |
>
> *Construct a bivariate table (in percentages) showing no association between "preferred family size" and "support for abortion."*

---

*Independence (Statistical)* The absence of association between two cross-tabulated variables. The percentage distributions of the dependent variable within each category of the independent variable are identical.

---

## The Structure of Hypothesis Testing with Chi-Square

The chi-square test follows the same six basic steps as the statistical tests first presented in Chapter 13: the assumptions of the test are stated; the research and the null hypotheses are formulated; the sampling distribution and the test statistic are specified; the $\alpha$ level and the region of rejection are determined; and a decision is made whether or not to reject the null hypothesis following the calculation of the test statistic. Before we apply the six-step model to a specific example, let's discuss some of the elements that are specific to the chi-square tests.

*The Assumptions* The chi-square test requires no assumptions about the shape of the population distribution from which the sample was drawn. However, like all inferential techniques it assumes random sampling. It can be applied to variables measured on a nominal and/or an ordinal level of measurement.

*Stating the Research and the Null Hypotheses* Like all other tests of statistical significance, the chi-square is a test of the null hypothesis. The null hypothesis $(H_0)$ states that no association exists between two cross-tabulated variables in the population, and therefore the variables are statistically independent.

The alternative (research) hypothesis $(H_1)$ proposes that the two variables are related in the population (therefore, the variables are not statistically independent).

> **Learning Check.** *Are the variables "preferred family size" and "support for abortion" statistically independent? Write out the null and alternative hypotheses for your practice data.*

*The Concept of Expected Frequencies* Assuming that the null hypothesis is true, the cell frequencies we would expect to find if the variables are statistically independent are computed. These frequencies are called **expected frequencies** (and are symbolized as $f_e$). The chi-square test is based on cell-by-cell comparisons between the expected frequencies $(f_e)$ and the frequencies actually observed (**observed frequencies** are symbolized as $f_o$).

---

**Expected Frequencies** $(f_e)$ The cell frequencies that would be expected in a bivariate table if the two variables in a bivariate table were statistically independent.

**Observed Frequencies** $(f_o)$ The cell frequencies actually observed in a bivariate table.

---

*Calculating the Expected Frequencies* The difference between $f_o$ and $f_e$ will determine the likelihood that the null hypothesis is true and that the variables are, in fact, statistically independent. When there is a large difference between $f_o$ and $f_e$ it is unlikely that the two variables are independent, and we will probably reject the null hypothesis. On the other hand, if there is little difference between $f_o$ and $f_e$, the variables are probably independent of each other as stated by the null hypothesis (and therefore we will not reject the null hypothesis).

The most important element in using chi-square to test for the statistical significance of cross-tabulated data is the determination of the expected frequencies. Because chi-square is computed on actual frequencies instead of on percentages, we need to derive the expected frequencies based on the null hypothesis. To illustrate this, let's go back to our example in Table 15.1. The expected frequencies are the numbers we would expect if men and women displayed the same level of fear as the entire sample. For instance, since 280 out of 495 of the respondents, or 56.57 percent, are not afraid, we expect 56.57 percent of the men, or $(56.57 \times 248)/100 = 140.29$, not to be afraid, and 56.57 percent of the women, or $(56.57 \times 247)/100 = 139.73$, not to be afraid. Similarly, if the null hypothesis were true, $(43.43 \times 247)/100 = 107.27$ women and $(43.43 \times 248)/100 = 107.71$ men would be afraid.

In practice, expected frequencies are more easily computed directly from the row and column frequencies than from percentages. Calculate the expected frequencies by following this formula:

$$f_e = \frac{(\text{Column marginal})(\text{Row marginal})}{N} \qquad \textbf{(15.1)}$$

To obtain the expected frequencies for any cell in any cross-tabulation in which the two variables are assumed independent, multiply the row and column totals for that cell and divide the product by the total number of cases in the table.

Let's use this formula to recalculate the expected frequencies for our data on gender and fear as displayed in Table 15.1. Consider the men who were not afraid to walk alone at night (the upper left cell). The expected frequency for this cell is the product of the row total (280) and the column total (248) divided by all the cases in the table (495):

$$f_e = \frac{280 \times 248}{495} = 140.28$$

For men who are afraid to walk alone at night (the lower left cell) the expected frequency is

$$f_e = \frac{215 \times 248}{495} = 107.72$$

Next, let's compute the expected frequencies for women who are not afraid to walk alone at night (the upper right cell):

$$f_e = \frac{280 \times 247}{495} = 139.72$$

Finally, the expected frequency for women who are afraid to walk at night (the lower right cell) is

$$f_e = \frac{215 \times 247}{495} = 107.28$$

These expected frequencies are displayed in Table 15.3.

Note that the table of expected frequencies contains the identical row and column marginals as the original table (Table 15.1). Although the expected frequencies usually differ from the observed frequencies (depending on the degree of relationship between the variables), the row and column marginals must always be identical with the marginals observed in the original table.

> **Learning Check.** *Calculate the expected frequencies for "preferred family size" and "support for abortion" and construct a bivariate table. Are your column and row marginals the same as in the original table?*

*Calculating the Obtained Chi-Square*   The next step in calculating chi-square is to compare the differences between the expected and observed frequencies across all cells in the table. In Table 15.4, the expected frequencies are shown in the shaded area in each cell below the corresponding observed frequencies. As you eyeball Table 15.4, note that the disparity between the observed and expected frequencies in each cell is quite large. Is it large enough to be significant? The way we decide is by calculating the **obtained chi-square** statistic:

$$\chi^2 = \sum \frac{(f_o - f_e)^2}{f_e} \qquad\qquad \textbf{(15.2)}$$

where

$f_o$ = observed frequencies
$f_e$ = expected frequencies

Table 15.3   **Expected Frequencies of Men and Women Afraid to Walk Alone in Neighborhood at Night**

| Afraid | Men $(f_e)$ | Women $(f_e)$ | Total $(f_e)$ |
|---|---|---|---|
| No | 140.28 | 139.72 | 280 |
| Yes | 107.72 | 107.28 | 215 |
| Total ($N$) | 248.00 | 247.00 | 495 |

Table 15.4 **Observed and Expected Frequencies of Men and Women Afraid to Walk Alone in Neighborhood at Night**

| | Men $(f_o)$ | Women $(f_o)$ | |
|---|---|---|---|
| **Afraid** | $(f_e)$ | $(f_e)$ | **Total** |
| No | 186.00 | 94.00 | |
| | 140.28 | 139.72 | 280.00 |
| Yes | 62.00 | 153.00 | |
| | 107.72 | 107.28 | 215.00 |
| Total ($N$) | 248.00 | 247.00 | 495.00 |

Table 15.5 **Calculating Chi-Square for "Fear"**

| Fear | $f_e$ | $f_o$ | $f_o - f_e$ | $(f_o - f_e)^2$ | $\dfrac{(f_o - f_e)^2}{f_e}$ |
|---|---|---|---|---|---|
| Men not afraid | 140.28 | 186.00 | 45.72 | 2090.32 | 14.90 |
| Men afraid | 107.72 | 62.00 | −45.72 | 2090.32 | 19.40 |
| Women not afraid | 139.72 | 94.00 | −45.72 | 2090.32 | 14.96 |
| Women afraid | 107.28 | 153.00 | 45.72 | 2090.32 | 19.48 |

$$\chi^2 = \sum \frac{(f_o - f_e)^2}{f_e} = 68.74$$

According to this formula, for each cell subtract the expected frequencies from the observed frequencies, square the difference, and divide by the expected frequency. After performing this operation for every cell, sum the results to obtain the chi-square statistic.

Let's follow these procedures using the observed and expected frequencies from Table 15.4. Our calculations are displayed in Table 15.5. The obtained $\chi^2$ statistic, 68.74, summarizes the differences between the observed frequencies and the frequencies we would expect to see if the null hypothesis were true and the variables—gender and fear of walking alone at night—were not associated.

> **Learning Check.** *Using the format of Table 15.5, construct a table to calculate chi-square for "preferred family size" and "support for abortion."*

*Chi-Square (Obtained)* The test statistic that summarizes the differences between the observed $(f_o)$ and the expected $(f_e)$ frequencies in a bivariate table.

Next, we need to interpret the magnitude of the number "68.74" and decide whether it is large enough to allow us to reject the null hypothesis.

*The Sampling Distribution of Chi-Square* In Chapters 11 through 14, we introduced the concept of the sampling distribution as a theoretical distribution used to evaluate hypotheses. We also saw that test statistics like $Z$ and $t$ have characteristic sampling distributions that tell us the probability of obtaining a statistic, assuming the null hypothesis is true. The sampling distribution of chi-square tells the probability of getting values of chi-square, assuming no relationship exists in the population.

Like other sampling distributions, the chi-square sampling distributions depend on the degrees of freedom. In fact, the $\chi^2$ sampling distribution is not one distribution, but—like the $t$ distribution—is a family of distributions. The shape of a particular chi-square distribution depends on the number of degrees of freedom. This is illustrated in Figure 15.1, which shows chi-square distributions for 1, 5, and 9 degrees of freedom. Here are some of the main properties of the chi-square distributions that can be observed in this figure:

■ The distributions are positively skewed.

■ Chi-square values will never be negative, and their minimum possible value will be zero. A $\chi^2$ of zero means that the variables are completely independent, and therefore the observed frequencies in every cell are equal to the corresponding expected frequencies.

■ As the number of degrees of freedom increases, the $\chi^2$ distribution becomes more symmetrical and, with df greater than 30, begins to resemble the normal curve.

Figure 15.1    **Chi-Square Distributions for 1, 5, and 9 Degrees of Freedom**

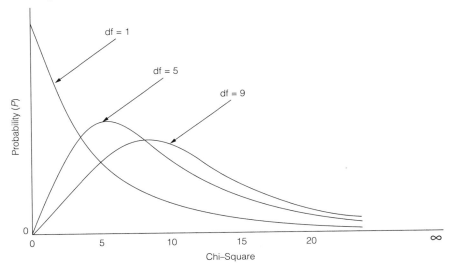

*Determining the Degrees of Freedom*  In Chapter 14, we defined degrees of freedom (df ) as the number of values that are free to vary. In cross-tabulation, we find the degrees of freedom using the following formula:

$$df = (r - 1)(c - 1) \tag{15.3}$$

where

$r$ = the number of rows
$c$ = the number of columns

Thus, Table 15.1 with 2 rows and 2 columns has $(2 - 1)(2 - 1)$ or 1 degree of freedom. If the table had 3 rows and 2 columns it would have $(3 - 1)(2 - 1)$ or 2 degrees of freedom.

The degrees of freedom in a bivariate table can be interpreted as the number of cells in the table for which the expected frequencies are free to vary, given that the marginal totals are already set. Let's illustrate this by referring to Table 15.3, which shows the expected frequencies for the cross-tabulation of fear and gender. Suppose we first calculate the expected frequencies for women who are not afraid to walk alone at night ($f_e$ = 139.72). Because the sum of the expected frequencies in the first row is set at 280, the expected frequency of men who are not afraid has to be 140.28 (280 – 139.72 = 140.28). Similarly, all other cells are predetermined by the marginal total and as a result are not free to vary. Therefore, this table has only 1 degree of freedom.

*Learning Check.* *Degrees of freedom is sometimes a difficult concept to grasp. Review this section and if you don't understand the concept of degrees of freedom, ask your instructor for further explanation. How many degrees of freedom are there in your practice example?*

*Critical Values of the Chi-Square Distribution* Appendix D shows critical values of the chi-square distribution for various df's. Note that the table is arranged with the degrees of freedom listed down the first column and the level of significance (the alpha level) arrayed across the top. The values in the body of the table are the critical values of $\chi^2$. A **critical chi-square** is a chi-square value obtained from the sampling distribution of all possible chi-square values. This critical value tells us how large the obtained chi-square must be if we are to reject the null hypothesis at the given df and level of significance. For instance, let's say we decide to test the null hypothesis at the .05 level of significance and that our df = 3. We would look at the third row and the column headed ".05." The corresponding critical $\chi^2$ value is 7.815. Our obtained chi-square needs to be at least this large to reject the null hypothesis at the .05 level. This number tells us that if the two variables were not associated in the population, a chi-square as high as 7.815 would occur only 5 times in 100 samples. Similarly, at the .01 level of significance, the critical $\chi^2$ is 11.341 (df = 3). This means that a chi-square as high as 11.341 would occur only once in 100 samples and that we need to obtain a $\chi^2$ at least as high to reject the null hypothesis at the .01 level.

Now let's get back to our example and find the probability of the chi-square we obtained, 68.74. We choose an alpha of .01. At that level of significance and with df = 1, the critical $\chi^2$ is 6.635. We need to have a chi-square equal to or larger than 6.635 to reject the null hypothesis. Because our obtained $\chi^2$, 68.74, exceeds this value, we can reject the null hypothesis that gender and fear are not associated in the population from which our sample was drawn. We can conclude, therefore, that the relationship we observed in our sample is statistically significant; that is, an association this large would occur by chance in only 1 percent of the samples drawn from a population having no association.

Note that our obtained $\chi^2$ is even larger than 10.827, which is the critical value needed to reject the null hypothesis at the .001 level. At that level we are even more confident of our conclusion that there is a relationship between gender and fear in the population because the probability of this result occurring due to sampling error is only .001.

*Chi-Square (Critical)*  A chi-square value obtained from the sampling distribution of all possible chi-square values. It is determined by the degrees of freedom (df) and the level of significance.

## Review

In the first part of this chapter we discussed the structure of hypothesis testing with chi-square. We illustrated the elements associated with this test, using an example about gender and fear. To summarize this discussion, we now apply the six-step process of hypothesis testing to this example.

1. **Making assumptions.**
   a.  A random sample of $N = 495$ was selected.
   b.  The level of measurement of the variable gender was nominal.
   c.  The level of measurement of the variable fear was nominal.

2. **Stating the research and the null hypotheses.**  The research hypothesis, $H_1$, was that there is a relationship between gender and fear (that is, gender and fear are statistically dependent). The null hypothesis, $H_0$, was that there is no relationship between gender and fear in the population (that is, gender and fear are statistically independent).

3. **Selecting the sampling distribution and the test statistic.**  The sampling distribution was chi-square. The test statistic was chi-square, with the df for Table 15.1:

$$df = (r - 1)(c - 1)$$
$$= (2 - 1)(2 - 1)$$
$$= (1)(1)$$
$$= 1$$

4. **Choosing alpha and establishing the region of rejection.**  We chose a .01 level of significance. At the .01 level of significance and with df = 1, the critical chi-square was 6.635. We needed to have a chi-square equal to or larger than 6.635 to reject the null hypothesis.

5. **Computing the test statistic.**  First, we determined the expected frequencies under the assumption of statistical independence. To obtain the expected frequencies for each cell, we multiplied its row and column marginal totals and divided the product by $N$.

Figure 15.2 **Chi-Square as a Type of Inference**
Study this diagram to visualize the relationships among a population, a sample, a crosstabulation, a chi-square test, and an inference. As noted in previous chapters, the goal of inferential statistics is to say something meaningful about the population, based entirely on information from a sample of that population.

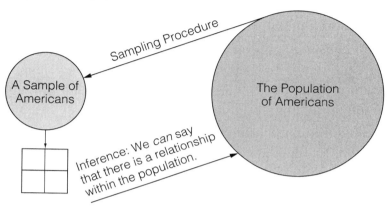

Creation of crosstabulation,
results of chi-square test:
Relationship in crosstabulation is significant

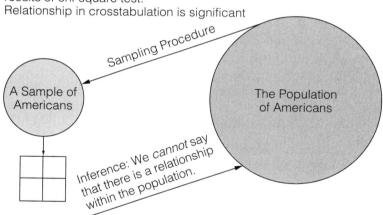

Creation of crosstabulation,
results of chi-square test:
Relationship in crosstabulation is not significant

The expected frequencies are displayed in Table 15.3. We asked, Are these expected frequencies different enough from the observed frequencies presented in Table 15.1 to justify the rejection of the null hypothesis?

To find out we calculated the chi-square statistic. The calculations are shown in Table 15.5. The obtained chi-square, 68.74, summarizes how much our sample result departs from independence.

6. **Making a decision and interpreting the results.** To determine if the observed frequencies are significantly different from the expected frequencies, we compared our obtained chi-square, 68.74, with the critical chi-square, 6.635. Because our obtained chi-square, 68.74, exceeded this value, we rejected the null hypothesis that there are no differences in the level of fear among men and women. Thus, we concluded that in the populations from which our sample was drawn, fear does vary by gender.

> ***Learning Check.*** *Find the critical value of chi-square for "preferred family size" and "support for abortion" at the .01 level of significance. Should you reject the null hypothesis?*

## The Limitations of the Chi-Square Test: Sample Size and Statistical Significance

Although we found the relationship between gender and fear to be statistically significant, this in itself does not give us much information about the *strength* of the relationship or its *substantive significance* in the population. Statistical significance only helps us to evaluate whether the argument (the null hypothesis) that the observed relationship occurred by chance is reasonable. It does not tell anything about the theoretical importance of the relationship or whether it is worth investigating further.

The distinction between statistical and substantive significance is an important one with the application of any of the statistical tests we discussed in Chapters 13–15. However, this distinction is of particular relevance in the case of the chi-square test because of the test's sensitivity to the sample size. The size of the calculated chi-square is directly proportional to the size of the sample, independent of the strength of the relationship between the variables. For instance, suppose that we cut the observed frequencies for every cell in Table 15.1

by exactly half—which is equivalent to reducing the sample size by one-half. This change will not affect the percentage distribution of fear among men and women; and therefore, the size of the percentage difference and the strength of the association between gender and fear will remain the same. However, reducing the observed frequencies by half will cut down our calculated chi-square by exactly half, from 68.74 to 34.37. (Can you verify this calculation?) In contrast had we doubled the frequencies in each cell, the size of the calculated chi-square would have doubled, thereby making it easier to reject the null hypothesis. Moreover, since the df for the table remains unchanged, the critical chi-square at the .01 level would still be 6.635.

This sensitivity of the chi-square test to the size of the sample means that a relatively strong association between the variables may not be significant when the sample size is small. Similarly, even when the association between variables is very weak, a larger sample may result in a statistically significant relationship. However, just because the calculated chi-square is large and we are able to reject the null hypothesis by a large margin does not imply that the relationship between the variables is strong and substantively important.

Another limitation of the chi-square test is that it is sensitive to small expected frequencies in one or more of the cells in the table. Generally, when the expected frequencies in one or more of the cells are below 5, the chi-square statistic may be unstable and lead to erroneous conclusions. There is no hard and fast rule regarding the size of the expected frequencies, but most researchers limit the use of chi-square to tables that either (1) have no $f_e$ values below 5 in value or (2) have no more than 20 percent of the $f_e$ values below 5 in value.

Testing the statistical significance of a bivariate relationship is only a small step, albeit an important one, in examining a relationship between two variables. A significant chi-square suggests that a relationship, weak or strong, probably exists in the population and is not due to sampling fluctuation. However, to establish the strength of the association, we need to employ measures of association such as gamma, lambda, or Pearson's $r$ (refer to Chapter 7). Used in conjunction, statistical tests of significance and measures of association help us determine the importance of a relationship and whether it is worth investigating further.

> **Learning Check.** If the total sample size of our practice data was reduced by 90 percent (we had only $\frac{1}{10}$ the total respondents), could we reject the null hypothesis at the .01 level of significance?

### Box 15.1 Comparing Chi-Square with Tests of Differences Between Proportions

In Chapter 14, we learned how to test for differences between proportions. Tests between proportions can always be expressed as 2 × 2 (a bivariate table with 2 rows and 2 columns) chi-square tests. We should obtain the same results from a chi-square test as from the test of the difference between proportions. For example, in Chapter 14 we tested the difference between the proportions of Democrats and Republicans who consider environmental protection a priority (Table 14.5). Our test resulted in a rejection of the null hypothesis that the proportions of Democrats and Republicans (in the population) who consider environmental protection a priority are equal. We rejected the null hypothesis at the .05 level of significance.

This problem can be reformulated as a chi-square test of independence between party affiliation and opinions about the environment. Here is the original table that was shown in Chapter 14 (we added the observed frequencies in the body of the table).

**Percentage of Democrats and Republicans Who Consider the Environment a Priority**

| Environment a Priority | Democrats | Republicans | Total |
|---|---|---|---|
| Yes | 70% | 49% | 59% |
| | (239) | (167) | (406) |
| No | 30% | 51% | 41% |
| | (103) | (174) | (277) |
| Total | 100% | 100% | 100% |
| (N) | (342) | (341) | (683) |

Our null hypothesis is:

$H_0$: There is no relationship between political party affiliation and opinions about environmental protection (that is, political party and opinions about the environment are statistically independent).

The research hypothesis is

$H_1$: There is a relationship between political party affiliation and opinions about the environment (that is, political party and opinions about the environment are statistically dependent).

The sampling distribution is chi-square; the test statistic is chi-square. The df for the table is

$$df = (r - 1)(c - 1)$$
$$= (2 - 1)(2 - 1)$$
$$= (1)(1)$$
$$= 1$$

We choose the same level of significance we chose to test the difference between the proportions, .05. The critical chi-square at the .05 level of significance and with df = 1 is 3.841. We need to have a chi-square equal to or greater than 3.841 to reject the null hypothesis.

To compute the obtained chi-square, we first determine the expected frequencies under the assumption of statistical independence. These expected frequencies follow.

**Expected Frequencies of Democrats and Republicans Who Consider Environmental Protection a Priority**

| Environment a Priority | Democrats $(f_e)$ | Republicans $(f_e)$ | Total $(f_e)$ |
|---|---|---|---|
| Yes | 203.30 | 202.70 | 406 |
| No | 138.70 | 138.30 | 277 |
| Total (N) | 342.00 | 341.00 | 683 |

Next, we calculate the obtained chi-square. These calculations follow.

**Calculating Chi-Square for Environmental protection**

| Protection | $f_e$ | $f_o$ | $f_o - f_e$ | $(f_o - f_e)^2$ | $\dfrac{(f_o - f_e)^2}{f_e}$ |
|---|---|---|---|---|---|
| Democrats/Yes | 203.30 | 239.00 | 35.70 | 1274.49 | 6.27 |
| Democrats/No | 138.70 | 103.00 | −35.70 | 1274.49 | 9.19 |
| Republicans/Yes | 202.70 | 167.00 | −35.70 | 1274.49 | 6.29 |
| Republicans/No | 138.30 | 174.00 | 35.70 | 1274.49 | 9.22 |

$$\chi^2 = \sum \frac{(f_o - f_e)^2}{f_e} = 30.97$$

To determine if the observed frequencies are significantly different from the expected frequencies, we compare our calculated chi-square, 30.97, to the critical chi-square, 3.841. Because our obtained chi-square exceeds this value, we can reject the null hypothesis that there are no differences in opinions about the environment between Republicans and Democrats. The null hypothesis is rejected at the .05 level of significance. This result is identical to the result of the difference between proportions test in Chapter 14.

## Statistics in Practice: Social Class and Health

In Chapter 6 (Table 6.11), we examined the relationship between health condition and social class in a random sample of GSS respondents. These data are shown again in Table 15.6. This bivariate table shows a clear pattern of a positive association between social class (the independent variable) and health condition (the dependent variable). For instance, whereas 39 percent of individuals of low social class suffered poor health, only 9 percent of those of high class reported the same condition. Similarly, only 25 percent of respondents of low class reported their health as good, whereas 63 percent of the respondents of high class fell into the same category.

The differences in the levels of health among the three social class groups seem sizable. However, it is not clear whether these differences are due to chance—that is, to sampling fluctuations—or whether they reflect a real pattern of association in the population. To answer these questions we perform a chi-square test following the six-step model of testing hypotheses.

1. **Making assumptions.**
    a. A random sample of $N = 495$ is selected.
    b. The level of measurement of the variable "class" is ordinal.
    c. The level of measurement of the variable "health" is ordinal.

2. **Stating the research and the null hypotheses.** $H_1$: There is a relationship between social class and health condition (that is, social class and health are statistically dependent).

Table 15.6  **Health Condition by Social Class: A Positive Relationship**

| HEALTH | CLASS Low | Middle | High | Total |
|---|---|---|---|---|
| Poor | 39% | 12% | 9% | 13% |
| | (15) | (31) | (18) | (64) |
| Fair | 36% | 45% | 28% | 37% |
| | (14) | (114) | (57) | (185) |
| Good | 25% | 43% | 63% | 50% |
| | (10) | (109) | (127) | (246) |
| Total | 100% | 100% | 100% | 100% |
| (N) | (39) | (254) | (202) | (495) |

$H_0$: There is no relationship between social class and health condition in the population (that is, social class and health are statistically independent).

3. **Selecting the sampling distribution and the test statistic.** Sampling distribution: chi-square; Test statistic: chi-square. The df for Table 15.6 is

$$df = (r - 1)(c - 1)$$
$$= (3 - 1)(3 - 1)$$
$$= (2)(2)$$
$$= 4$$

4. **Choosing alpha and establishing the region of rejection.** We choose a .05 level of significance. At the .05 level of significance and with df = 4, the critical chi-square is 9.488. We need a chi-square equal to or greater than 9.488 to reject the null hypothesis.

5. **Computing the test statistic.** First, we determine the expected frequencies under the assumption of statistical independence. To obtain the expected frequencies for each cell, we multiply its row and column marginal totals and divide the product by $N$. Here are the calculations for all cells in Table 15.6.

For low class/poor health

$$f_e = \frac{64 \times 39}{495} = 5.04$$

For low class/fair health

$$f_e = \frac{185 \times 39}{495} = 14.58$$

For low class/good health

$$f_e = \frac{246 \times 39}{495} = 19.38$$

For middle class/poor health

$$f_e = \frac{64 \times 254}{495} = 32.84$$

For middle class/fair health

$$f_e = \frac{185 \times 254}{495} = 94.93$$

For middle class/good health

$$f_e = \frac{246 \times 254}{495} = 126.23$$

For high class/poor health

$$f_e = \frac{64 \times 202}{495} = 26.12$$

For high class/fair health

$$f_e = \frac{185 \times 202}{495} = 75.49$$

and finally, for high class/good health

$$f_e = \frac{246 \times 202}{495} = 100.39$$

Are these expected frequencies different enough from the observed frequencies presented in Table 15.6 to justify the rejection of the null hypothesis? To find out we calculate chi-square. The calculations are shown in Table 15.7.

6. **Making a decision and interpreting the results.** To determine if the observed frequencies are significantly different from the expected frequencies, we compare our calculated chi-square, 44.62, with the critical chi-square, 9.488. Because our obtained chi-square exceeds this value, we can reject the null hypothesis that there are no differences in the level of health among the different social class groups. Thus, we conclude that in the population from which our sample was drawn, health condition does vary by social class.

Table 15.7  **Calculating Chi-Square for Health and Class**

| Class/Health | $f_e$ | $f_o$ | $f_o - f_e$ | $(f_o - f_e)^2$ | $\dfrac{(f_o - f_e)^2}{f_e}$ |
|---|---|---|---|---|---|
| Low/Poor | 5.04 | 15.00 | 9.96 | 99.20 | 19.68 |
| Low/Fair | 14.58 | 14.00 | −.58 | .34 | .02 |
| Low/Good | 19.38 | 10.00 | −9.38 | 87.98 | 4.54 |
| Middle/Poor | 32.84 | 31.00 | −1.84 | 3.39 | .10 |
| Middle/Fair | 94.93 | 114.00 | 19.07 | 363.66 | 3.83 |
| Middle/Good | 126.23 | 109.00 | −17.23 | 296.87 | 2.35 |
| High/Poor | 26.12 | 18.00 | −8.12 | 65.93 | 2.52 |
| High/Fair | 75.49 | 57.00 | −18.49 | 341.88 | 4.53 |
| High/Good | 100.39 | 127.00 | 26.61 | 708.09 | 7.05 |

$$\chi^2 = \sum \frac{(f_o - f_e)^2}{f_e} = 44.62$$

## Reading the Research Literature:
## AIDS Risks Among Women

In earlier chapters we examined a number of examples showing how the results of statistical analyses are presented in the professional literature. We learned that most statistical applications presented in the social science literature are a good deal more complex than those described in this book. The same can be said about the application and presentation of chi-square in the research literature. Rarely do research articles do not go through the detailed steps of reasoning and calculation that are presented in this chapter. In most applications the calculated chi-square is presented together with the results of a bivariate analysis. Occasionally, an appropriate measure of association summarizes the strength of the relationship between the variables.

Such an application is illustrated in Table 15.8, which is taken from an article written by Marie Withers Osmond et al., about AIDS risks among women. The article reports the results of a study that is part of a larger project designed to develop and evaluate interventions aimed at preventing perinatal AIDS. In this study, Osmond and her co-authors examine the ways that high-risk sexual behaviors are related to decisions about using condoms by low-income, culturally diverse women in South Florida. Research suggests that it is especially difficult for such women to initiate condom use with intimate sexual partners. The hypothesis of this study is that the relative power that women can assert in negotiating condom use directly influences the level of sexual risk.

The study focused on two subsamples of women who were randomly selected from various agencies, including county jails, public and community health services, and drug and alcohol treatment centers. The first subsample ($N = 268$), which became known as the "main partner" group, included women who stated that they had a main sexual partner with whom they were sexually active. The second subsample ($N = 109$), which was known as the "client" group, included women who stated that they had sex in exchange for money or drugs. To assess what power each group of women could assert in their relationships, the respondents were asked who actually makes the decision to use or not use a condom during sexual intercourse. Response categories for these questions were "myself," "both," "partner," and "never discuss." Each response category is viewed in terms of the relative power asserted by the women in their sexual relationships. Thus, "myself" is seen as being the least woman-subordinated response, and, at the other extreme, "never discuss" is seen as the most woman-subordinated response. The researchers measured sexual risk, the

Table 15.8    **Frequency of Condom Use by Who Decides to Use Condom**

| Condom Use | Who Decides to Use with Main Partner | | | | |
|---|---|---|---|---|---|
| | Never Discuss | Partner | Both | Myself | Total |
| 50% or more of the time | 0 (0%) | 2 (12%) | 40 (32%) | 27 (49%) | 69 (26%) |
| Less than 50% of the time | 73 (100%) | 15 (88%) | 83 (68%) | 28 (51%) | 199 (74%) |
| Total | 73 (100%) | 17 (6%) | 123 (46%) | 55 (21%) | 268 (100%) |

$\chi^2 = 45.68$, 3 df, $P < .0001$

| | Who Decides to Use with Client | | | | |
|---|---|---|---|---|---|
| 50% or more of the time | 0 (0%) | 5 (56%) | 15 (75%) | 56 (92%) | 76 (70%) |
| Less than 50% of the time | 19 (100%) | 4 (44%) | 5 (25%) | 5 (8%) | 33 (30%) |
| Total | 19 (17%) | 9 (8%) | 20 (18%) | 61 (56%) | 109 (100%) |

$\chi^2 = 58.96$, 3 df, $P < .0001$

*Source:* Adapted from Marie Withers Osmond et al., "The Multiple Jeopardy of Race, Class, and Gender for AIDS Risk among Women." *Gender & Society,* Vol. 7, No. 1, March 1993, 108. Reprinted by permission of Sage Publication, Inc.

dependent variable, by a behavioral indicator of frequency of condom use.

Table 15.8 shows the results for both subsamples cross-tabulated for the dependent variable indicator, condom use, by the independent variable, decision making with regard to condom use. The table displays the number of cases in each cell (the observed frequencies), the column percentages (in parentheses), and the row and column marginal frequencies and percentages. Below each set of figures the researchers report the obtained chi-square, the degrees of freedom, and the actual significance (the $P$ value) of the obtained chi-square.

Compare the column percentages to assess the relationship between decision making and condom use (with decision making being the independent variable) for both the main partner and the client sub-samples. Next, use the reported chi-square as the appropriate way to determine whether a statistically significant relationship exists between the variables depicted in the table.

The data in Table 15.8 support the researchers' hypothesis that the relative power that women can assert in negotiating condom use directly influences their level of sexual risk. One hundred percent of the women in both the main partner and client subsamples who indicate "never discuss" with regard to the decision to use condoms also report that condoms are used less than one-half the time. In contrast, when women make the decision whether to use a condom (the category "myself") only 8 percent of the women in the client subsample and 51 percent of the women in the main partner subsample use condoms in fewer than 50 percent of their sexual contacts.

A close examination of the percentages reveals some differences between the client and main partner subsamples. These differences are summarized by the authors:

> The major difference in the association between main partner and client subsamples has to do with whether the woman responds that both or "myself" make the decision. With the partner, 46 percent of the women say that both make the decision, and the result is less frequent condom use (68 percent use less than one-half of the time). With the client, the results are reversed: Only 18 percent report that both make the decision, but these women show more frequent condom use (75 percent use more than one-half of the time). There are also significant differences when the woman reports that she makes the decision. With the partner, making the decision herself is not directly associated with frequency of condom use. With the client, on the other hand, when the woman makes the decision to use, 92 percent use condoms more frequently (50 percent or more of the time). In sum, [Table 15.8] offers immediate evidence that power relations are different with clients than with the main partners: The women are more assertive and the men more compliant in the client relationship.[4]

Finally, the chi-square and the level of significance (indicated as *P* for probability) displayed in Table 15.8 indicate the existence of a very significant relationship between the frequency of condom use and who makes the decision within both partner and client populations. A level

---

[4]Marie Withers Osmond et al., "The Multiple Jeopardy of Race, Class, and Gender for AIDS Risk among Women." *Gender & Society,* Vol. 7, No. 1, March 1993, 109.

of significance less than .0001 means that a chi-square as high as 45.68 (in the main partner sample) or 58.96 (observed in the client sub-sample) would have occurred less than once in 10,000 if decision making and condom use were not associated in the population. Another way to say this is: the probability of this relationship occurring due to sampling fluctuations is less than 1 out of 10,000.

***Learning Check.*** *The value of chi-square for the practice data is 24.07. At the .01 level of significance the critical value for 1 degree of freedom is 6.635. Because the obtained chi-square is larger than the critical value, we reject the null hypothesis of no relationship between preferred family size and support for abortion. If we reduce our sample size by 90 percent, the obtained chi-square is 2.41, which is less than the critical value, 6.635. We could not reject the null hypothesis using this smaller sample.*

## MAIN POINTS

■ The chi-square test is an inferential statistics technique designed to test for a significant relationship between variables organized in a bivariate table. The test is conducted by testing the null hypothesis that no association exists between two cross-tabulated variables in the population and, therefore, the variables are statistically independent.

■ The obtained $\chi^2$ statistic summarizes the differences between the observed frequencies($f_o$) and the expected frequencies ($f_e$), the frequencies we would have expected to see if the null hypothesis were true and the variables were not associated.

■ The sampling distribution of chi-square tells the probability of getting values of chi-square, assuming no relationship exists in the population. The shape of a particular chi-square sampling distribution depends on the number of degrees of freedom.

■ To test for the significance of the obtained chi-square, compare it with the critical chi-square. The critical chi-square is found in the table of critical chi-square values. The values in the body of the table are the critical values of $\chi^2$. These values tell how large the obtained chi-square must be to reject the null hypothesis at the given df and level of significance.

## KEY TERMS

*chi-square (critical)*

*chi-square (obtained)*

*chi-square test (pronounced kai-square and written as χ²)*

*expected frequencies (f_e)*

*independence (statistical)*

*observed frequencies (f_o)*

## SPSS DEMONSTRATION

*Demonstration 1: Producing the Chi-Square Statistic for Cross-Tabulations*

The SPSS Crosstabs procedure was previously demonstrated in Chapters 6 and 7. The procedure is also used to calculate a chi-square value for a bivariate table. We will extend the analysis begun in Chapter 7 by calculating a chi-square value for the table of ABSINGLE and RELIG.

Click on *Statistics, Summarize,* and *Crosstabs,* then on the *Statistics* button. The following dialog box appears.

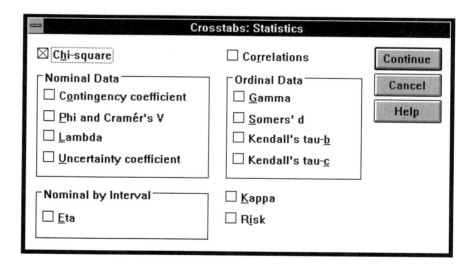

To request the chi-square statistic click on the Chi-Square box in the upper left corner. Notice that the chi-square choice is not grouped with the nominal or ordinal measures of association that we discussed in Chapter 7. SPSS separates it because the chi-square test is not a measure of association, but a test of independence of the row and column variables.

Click on *Continue.* Then place ABSINGLE in the Row(s) box and RELIG in the Column(s) box. Then click on *OK* to run the procedure.

```
                              SPSS for Windows Student Version - [!Output1]
  □  File   Edit  Data  Transform  Statistics  Graphs  Utilities  Window  Help
     Pause  Scroll  Round  Glossary  [▐▌▌  ▲  ▼  ▲  ▼  ?
```

ABSINGLE   NOT MARRIED   by   RELIG   RS RELIGIOUS PREFERENCE

|  | Count | RELIG | | | | | Page 1 of 1 |
|---|---|---|---|---|---|---|---|
|  |  | PROTESTA NT | CATHOLIC | JEWISH | NONE | OTHER | Row Total |
|  |  | 1 | 2 | 3 | 4 | 5 |  |
| ABSINGLE YES | 1 | 175 | 71 | 13 | 50 | 15 | 324 48.7 |
| NO | 2 | 221 | 93 |  | 18 | 9 | 341 51.3 |
| Column Total |  | 396 59.5 | 164 24.7 | 13 2.0 | 68 10.2 | 24 3.6 | 665 100.0 |

| Chi-Square | Value | DF | Significance |
|---|---|---|---|
| Pearson | 37.44336 | 4 | .00000 |
| Likelihood Ratio | 43.08953 | 4 | .00000 |
| Mantel-Haenszel test for linear association | 21.88570 | 1 | .00000 |

Minimum Expected Frequency -    6.334

```
SPSS Processor is ready
```

This is the same table we saw in Chapter 7, with the addition of the chi-square statistics. SPSS produces quite a bit of output, perhaps more than expected. We will concentrate on the first row of information, the Pearson chi-square.

The Pearson chi-square is the one we learned to calculate in this chapter. Its value is 37.44, with 4 degrees of freedom. SPSS calculates the significance of this value of chi-square with this many degrees of freedom to be less than .000005, which is rounded off to the value printed on the screen. The interpretation is that religious affiliation and support for legal abortions for single women are related. In particular, Jews and those with no religious affiliation are more likely to support abortions than are Protestants and Catholics.

The last portion of the output from SPSS allows us to check for the key assumption that all expected values in each cell of the table are 5 or greater. The minimum expected value is 6.334, above the threshold of 5, so the use of chi-square is justified for this table.

Refer to Chapter 7 and note that lambda, a measure of association for nominal variables, is .157 for this same table. This indicates a relatively weak relationship between religious affiliation and abortion attitude, yet the significance associated with the chi-square value for the table indicates there is little chance that the two variables are independent. These two statements are not contradictory. The magnitude of a relationship is not necessarily related to the statistical significance of that same relationship.

**EXERCISES**

1. In previous exercises we examined the relationship between race and the fear of walking alone at night. In Chapter 6 we created a bivariate table with these two variables to investigate their joint relationship. Now we can extend the analysis by calculating chi-square for the same table.

    a. Use the data from exercise 1 in Chapter 6 to calculate chi-square for the bivariate table of "race" and "fear of walking alone at night."

    b. What is the number of degrees of freedom for this table?

    c. Test at the .05 significance level the null hypothesis that race and fear of walking alone are independent. What do you conclude? Is your conclusion consistent with your description of the percentage differences in exercise 1 in Chapter 6?

    d. It's always important to test the assumption that the expected value in each cell is at least 5. Does any cell fail to meet this criterion?

2. Crime continues to be a major concern for many Americans, politicians, and, of course, police departments. To determine what policies Americans might support to reduce crime, CNN and the Gallup organization have conducted several polls asking for opinions about various policy and sentencing alternatives. Following are the results for one question from the 1989 and 1993 polls.

| DO YOU FAVOR MAKING BAIL MORE DIFFICULT FOR VIOLENT CRIMINALS? | YEAR | |
| --- | --- | --- |
| | 1989 | 1993 |
| No | 33% | 25% |
| Yes | 67% | 75% |

(Data taken from a *USA Today* article, October 28, 1993)

    a. It appears that Americans were more in favor of making bail more difficult for violent criminals in 1993 than in 1989. It would be interesting to calculate chi-square for this table to see whether there was a statistically significant change in attitude from 1989 to 1993. Can that be done from the information provided in the table? Why or why not?

b. What if you were told that the total combined number of people interviewed in both years was 2,156? Would you now have enough information to calculate chi-square?

3. In exercise 7 in Chapter 6 we investigated the relationship between sex and the respondent's self-rated health in the GSS from 1994. Now we can calculate chi-square for this table to determine whether our previous advice to the neighborhood clinic was correct.

a. Use the data from exercise 7 in Chapter 6. How many degrees of freedom does the table have?

b. Calculate chi-square for the table. What is the expected number of females who rate their health as poor?

c. Test at the .05 significance level the hypothesis that self-rated health and sex are independent. What is the critical chi-square value for the degrees of freedom in this table? What do you conclude? Is this consistent with your advice in Chapter 6?

4. The issue of whether and how minorities are able to advance in society is a complex matter, and people have diverse and conflicting ideas on these questions. Not surprisingly, blacks and whites often differ in their perception of how minorities overcome the problems of bias and prejudice. The 1994 GSS contains several questions on these topics, and following is the bivariate table relating race (limited to blacks and whites for this problem) and the variable WRKWAYUP, which asked whether blacks can overcome prejudice in society without favors. To make your task easier, the expected value ($f_e$) is also included as the second number in each cell.

RACE    RACE OF RESPONDENT by WRKWAYUP BLACKS OVERCOME PREJUDICE WITHOUT FAVORS

| Count Exp Val | AGREE S TRONGLY 1 | AGREE S OMEWHAT 2 | NEITHER AGREE N 3 | DISAGRE E SOMEWH 4 | DISAGRE E STRONG 5 | Row Total |
|---|---|---|---|---|---|---|
| RACE | | | | | | |
| 1 | 179 | 115 | 39 | 38 | 15 | 386 |
| WHITE | 161.3 | 117.1 | 39.0 | 39.9 | 28.6 | 86.7% |
| 2 | 7 | 20 | 6 | 8 | 18 | 59 |
| BLACK | 24.7 | 17.9 | 6.0 | 6.1 | 4.4 | 13.3% |
| Column Total | 186 41.8% | 135 30.3% | 45 10.1% | 46 10.3% | 33 7.4% | 445 100.0% |

a. What is the number of degrees of freedom for this table?

b. One cell has an expected value less than 5. Is this a serious violation of the expected value assumption?

c. Calculate chi-square for this table.

d. What is the critical chi-square value for the .01 level of significance? Test whether these two variables are independent at the .01 level of significance. What do you conclude?

e. To further specify the relationship, calculate an appropriate measure of association (refer to Chapter 7 if necessary).

5. A social scientist decided to study how job satisfaction varies with union membership. Her hypothesis was that union members would be more satisfied with their jobs because they have, on average, better benefits than nonunion members. She surveyed 400 workers, 200 union members and 200 nonunion members, and obtained the following result using SPSS.

```
UNIONMEM  by  JOBSAT

                          JOBSAT          Page  1  of  1
                 Count |
                 Row  Pct | Not  sati  Satisfie
                          | sfied      d                  Row
                          | 1.00   |   2.00   |   Total
      UNIONMEM    -------- +---------+ ------- +
                   1.00 |    75   |   125   |    200
      No               |    37.5  |   62.5  |    50.0
                        +---------+ ------- +
                   2.00 |    65   |   135   |    200
      Yes              |    32.5  |   67.5  |    50.0
                        +---------+ ------- +
                 Column     140       260       400
                 Total      35.0      65.0     100.0
```

| Chi-Square | Value | DF | Significance |
|---|---|---|---|
| Pearson | 1.09890 | 1 | .29451 |
| Continuity Correction | .89011 | 1 | .34545 |
| Likelihood Ratio | 1.09960 | 1 | .29435 |
| Linear-by-Linear Association | 1.09615 | 1 | .29511 |

a. Given this information, describe the relationship between union membership and job satisfaction. Was her research hypothesis supported by the data?

She decided to increase the sample size by a factor of four in her next survey to make it more likely that she would find the relationship between union membership and job satisfaction to be statistically significant. So she collected data from 1,600 employees in the next study, then used SPSS to create this crosstab table.

UNION by JOBSAT

```
                           JOBSAT          Page 1 of 1
                 Count |
                 Row Pct | Not sati  Satisfie
                         | sfied     d              Row
                         |  1.00   |   2.00   |    Total
    UNION        -------- + --------- + -------- +
                 1.00 |     300   |    500   |     800
    No                 |    37.5   |   62.5   |    50.0
                       + --------- + -------- +

                 2.00 |     260   |    540   |     800
    Yes                |    32.5   |   67.5   |    50.0
                       + --------- + -------- +

                 Column      560       1040         1600
                 Total      35.0       65.0        100.0
```

| Chi-Square | Value | DF | Significance |
|---|---|---|---|
| Pearson | 4.39560 | 1 | .03603 |
| Continuity Correction | 4.17857 | 1 | .04094 |
| Likelihood Ratio | 4.39842 | 1 | .03597 |
| Linear-by-Linear Association | 4.39286 | 1 | .03609 |

b. Does this table provide support for her research hypothesis (test at the .05 significance level)?
c. Looking at the percentages in the two tables, do you find any difference between the relationship of union membership and job satisfaction in the two surveys? If not, why is the chi-square larger (or, alternatively, significance lower) in the second table?
d. Would you consider the difference in job satisfaction to be substantively important? Why or why not?

6. In exercise 14 in Chapter 6 we studied whether there was a relationship between believing that pornography leads to a breakdown in morals and support for women working outside the home.
   a. Test whether the differences you found in the previous exercise are significant. Calculate chi-square for the table in exercise 14.
   b. Test the null hypothesis that the two variables are independent at the .01 significance level. What did you find? Is this consistent with what you decided in exercise 14?
   c. Which cell has the greatest difference between the expected value $(f_e)$ and the actual value $(f_o)$? What did you discover when you tried to answer this question?

7. Another policy that many have suggested to reduce crime is to make sentences for criminals more severe—longer with less chance of parole. Polls are done on this topic on a regular basis. The following table shows the results of a CNN/Gallup nationwide poll asking about this question.

| Do You Strongly Favor Making Sentences More Severe for All Crimes? | Race | |
| --- | --- | --- |
| | Whites | Blacks |
| No | 452 | 182 |
| Yes | 418 | 132 |

(Data from *USA Today*, January 6, 1994)

   a. What is the percentage difference between support for more severe sentences between blacks and whites?
   b. Calculate chi-square for this table and test the null hypothesis of independence at the .05 significance level.
   c. Use the information from (a) and (b) to characterize the relationship between race and support for sentence severity.

8. Use the data from exercise 6 in Chapter 7 to investigate the relationship between self-perceived social class and the belief that government should provide everyone a minimum income, controlling for race. In that earlier exercise, you used percentage differences and an appropriate measure of association for each table to study the relationships.
   a. Calculate chi-square for the two tables in exercise 6 in Chapter 7, one for whites and one for blacks.
   b. Test at the .05 significance level whether or not class and support for a minimum income are independent for whites or for blacks. What do you find?

c. Are your results compatible with what you concluded in exercise 6 in Chapter 7? Why or why not?

9. Continuing the investigation of attitudes toward criminals, we know that many people are in favor of the death penalty for murder (in the 1994 GSS file, over 80 percent said they were in favor). Nevertheless, there are differences in support across various demographic categories, and SPSS was used to create the following crosstab output to study how educational level is related to support for the death penalty.

```
CAPPUN FAVOR OR OPPOSE DEATH PENALTY FOR MURDER
by EDUC HIGHEST YEAR OF SCHOOL COMPLETED

                    EDUC                              Page 1 of 1
            Count |
          Exp Val | < high   High    Undergra Graduate
                  | school   school  d educ.  educ.        Row
                  |    1 |      2 |      3 |      4 |     Total
CAPPUN    ..... + ....... + ....... + ....... + ........ +
            1 |     129 |    252 |    287 |     78 |      746
FAVOR         |   134.6 |  237.2 |  286.9 |   87.3 |    80.1%
              + ....... + ....... + ....... + ........ +
            2 |      39 |     44 |     71 |     31 |      185
OPPOSE        |    33.4 |   58.8 |   71.1 |   21.7 |    19.9%
              + ....... + ....... + ....... + ........ +
       Column      168      296      358      109       931
        Total     18.0%    31.8%    38.5%    11.7%    100.0%
```

| Chi-Square | Value | DF | Significance |
|---|---|---|---|
| Pearson | 10.86566 | 3 | .01247 |
| Likelihood Ratio | 10.71985 | 3 | .01334 |
| Linear-by-Linear Association | 1.33835 | 1 | .24732 |

Minimum Expected Frequency - 21.6

a. Test at the .05 significance level the hypothesis that educational level and support for the death penalty are not related. What do you conclude?

b. The table displays the observed and expected counts, in that order, in each cell. You can use the difference between these two values to get a rough idea of which categories contribute the most to the chi-square value of 10.86566. Remember from the formula for chi-square, where the difference between the expected and observed values is divided by the expected value, that for two cells with the same difference between $f_e$ and $f_o$, the cell with the smaller expected value contributes more to chi-square. Where are the greatest differences between the observed and expected values? Which cells contribute most to the chi-square value?

c. Use the information from (b) to describe further how education is related to support for the death penalty.

10. Use the table from exercise 9.

a. Test whether the two variables are independent at the .01 significance level. What do you conclude?

b. Is there a dilemma because your conclusion differed from that in exercise 9 when you tested at the .05 significance level? Why or why not? What does this tell you about the choice of significance level?

11. In Chapter 6 we examined how attitude toward premarital sex was associated with age (grouped in categories). Now we will examine the association between the same attitude and educational level. Here is the table from the SPSS Crosstabs procedure displaying this relationship (the expected value is included to help you calculate chi-square) for the 1994 GSS file.

PREMARSX SEX BEFORE MARRIAGE by EDUC HIGHEST YEAR OF
SCHOOL COMPLETED

| | EDUC | | | | Page 1 of 1 |
|---|---|---|---|---|---|
| Count | < high | High | Undergra | Graduate | |
| Exp Val | school | school | d educ. | educ. | Row |
| Col Pct | 1 | 2 | 3 | 4 | Total |
| **PREMARSX** | | | | | |
| 1 | 42 | 49 | 50 | 10 | 151 |
| ALWAYS WRONG | 25.5 | 44.5 | 61.0 | 20.0 | 23.8% |
| | 39.3% | 26.2% | 19.5% | 11.9% | |
| 2 | 8 | 21 | 31 | 8 | 68 |
| ALMST ALWAYS WRG | 11.5 | 20.1 | 27.5 | 9.0 | 10.7% |
| | 7.5% | 11.2% | 12.1% | 9.5% | |
| 3 | 18 | 31 | 52 | 23 | 124 |
| SOMETIMES WRONG | 20.9 | 36.6 | 50.1 | 16.4 | 19.6% |
| | 16.8% | 16.6% | 20.3% | 27.4% | |
| 4 | 39 | 86 | 123 | 43 | 291 |
| NOT WRONG AT ALL | 49.1 | 85.8 | 117.5 | 38.6 | 45.9% |
| | 36.4% | 46.0% | 48.0% | 51.2% | |
| Column | 107 | 187 | 256 | 84 | 634 |
| Total | 16.9% | 29.5% | 40.4% | 13.2% | 100.0% |

a. Calculate chi-square for this table.

b. Test at the .01 significance level whether attitude toward pre-marital sex and educational level are independent.

c. Describe the relationship you found, using all available information.

d. Is the relationship between these two variables stronger or weaker than between age and attitude toward premarital sex? How can you answer this question?

12. Gun ownership is quite prevalent in the United States, but those who own a gun are not necessarily a cross-section of Americans. There are interesting differences in gun ownership between various groups. You suspect that there might be a difference by marital status and hypothesize that those individuals more likely to be living alone (those not married) are more likely to own guns (this is the alternative hypothesis $H_1$). You then use the 1994 GSS data to construct the following bivariate table and test your hypothesis.

```
OWNGUN  HAVE  GUN  IN  HOME  by  MARITAL  MARITAL  STATUS

                  MARITAL                                  Page  1  of  1
          Count |
                | MARRIED  WIDOWED  DIVORCED  SEPARATE  NEVER  MA
                |                                      D      RRIED        Row
                |    1  |    2  |    3  |    4  |    5  | Total
OWNGUN   ....... + ........ + ........ + ........ + ........ + ........ +
             1 |   176  |   23  |   28  |    3  |   41  |   271
YES            |        |       |       |       |       |    40.0
               + ........ + ........ + ........ + ........ + ........ +
             2 |   176  |   48  |   60  |   13  |  109  |   406
NO             |        |       |       |       |       |    60.0
               + ........ + ........ + ........ + ........ + ........ +
        Column     352      71      88      16     150      677
        Total     52.0    10.5    13.0     2.4    22.2    100.0
```

a. Calculate the value of chi-square for this table. What is the number of degrees of freedom for this table?

b. Test the null hypothesis at the .01 level of significance. Do you reject the null hypothesis?

c. If you rejected the null hypothesis, is your research hypothesis supported by the data in the table? What does your answer tell you about the implication of rejecting the null hypothesis in terms of support for a *specific* research hypothesis?

d. Can you suggest a substantive reason for the relationship you discovered between the variables?

13. During the long struggle to bring civil rights to minorities in the United States, churches and religious congregations have often been in the forefront of the movement. It seems reasonable, therefore, to suppose that those persons who are more religious (as demonstrated by their frequency of church attendance) are more likely to feel sympathy toward minorities (such sympathy, among other factors, may have motivated the more religious to offer assistance to the civil rights movement). The 1994 GSS data include a variable (SYMPTBLK) that measures sympathy toward blacks on a five-point scale. The following crosstab table displays the relationship between religious attendance and that variable.

SYMPTBLK  R  FEEL  SYMPATHY  TOWARDS  BLACKS
by  ATTEND  HOW  OFTEN  R  ATTENDS  RELIGIOUS  SERVICES

|  |  | ATTEND |  |  |  | Page 1 of 2 |
|---|---|---|---|---|---|---|
| Count | | NEVER | LT ONCE A YEAR | ONCE A YEAR | SEVRL TIMES A YR | ONCE A MONTH | Row |
|  |  | 0 | 1 | 2 | 3 | 4 | Total |
| SYMPTBLK | | | | | | | |
| VERY OFTEN | 1 | 7 | 6 | 11 | 11 | 9 | 85 / 18.0 |
| FAIRLY OFTEN | 2 | 30 | 23 | 22 | 21 | 12 | 176 / 37.2 |
| NOT TOO OFTEN | 3 | 35 | 12 | 27 | 29 | 13 | 175 / 37.0 |
| NEVER | 4 | 9 | 7 | 6 | 4 | 1 | 37 / 7.8 |
| Column (Continued) Total | | 81 / 17.1 | 48 / 10.1 | 66 / 14.0 | 65 / 13.7 | 35 / 7.4 | 473 / 100.0 |

SYMPTBLK  R  FEEL  SYMPATHY  TOWARDS  BLACKS
by ATTEND  HOW  OFTEN  R  ATTENDS  RELIGIOUS  SERVICES

| | ATTEND | | | | |
| --- | --- | --- | --- | --- | --- |
| Count | 2-3X A MONTH | NRLY EVERY WEEK | EVERY WEEK | MORE THN ONCE WK | Row Total |
| | 5 | 6 | 7 | 8 | |
| SYMPTBLK | | | | | |
| 1 VERY OFTEN | 5 | 7 | 14 | 15 | 85 / 18.0 |
| 2 FAIRLY OFTEN | 11 | 8 | 38 | 11 | 176 / 37.2 |
| 3 NOT TOO OFTEN | 13 | 8 | 31 | 7 | 175 / 37.0 |
| 4 NEVER | 1 | | 8 | 1 | 37 / 7.8 |
| Column Total | 30 / 6.3 | 23 / 4.9 | 91 / 19.2 | 34 / 7.2 | 473 / 100.0 |

a. Note that the table is so large that many cells have an expected value of less than 5. There are so many of these cells (about one-sixth of the table) that this assumption of the chi-square test is most definitely violated. Because you still hope to test the relationship, group the cells in logical subsets for each variable to create a table with only three categories for each variable. Display that table.

b. Check this table for the smallest expected frequency. What is its value?

c. Calculate chi-square for the new, collapsed table. How many degrees of freedom does this table have?

d. Test at the .05 significance level the null hypothesis that frequency of church attendance and sympathy for blacks are independent. What do you conclude?

## SPSS PROBLEMS

1. The 1994 GSS contains a question about whether the respondent favors job preferences in the hiring of blacks (JOBAFF). It is very likely that the responses to this question vary by race, but also by other variables as well.

   a. Use SPSS for Windows to investigate the relationship between SEX, RACE, and JOBAFF. Create crosstab tables and ask for appropriate percentages and expected values. Does either table have a large number of cells with expected values less than 5?

   b. If a table has a problem with low expected numbers, recode the variable causing the problem, or drop the category with only a few respondents, and then recreate the table.

   c. Have SPSS calculate chi-square for each table.

   d. Test the null hypothesis at the .05 significance level in each table. What do you conclude?

   e. Select another demographic variable and investigate its relationship with JOBAFF.

   f. Select a variable measuring an opinion or attitude and investigate its relationship with JOBAFF. Pick a variable you believe will be related to JOBAFF, and suggest the research hypothesis before creating the crosstab table.

2. In SPSS problem 3 in Chapter 6, we examined the relationship between attitudes about women working (FEWORK) and support for women having an abortion for any reason (ABANY).

   a. Study the same relationship using the 1987–1991 GSS, but this time request the chi-square statistic and use it to more completely characterize the relationship.

   b. Add SEX as a control variable and calculate chi-square in each subtable. What do you find about the effect of SEX?

   c. Now replace SEX with RACE as the control variable, and use chi-square to test for any relationship between the two attitudes in the subtables. Be careful that there aren't too few expected responses in any cell in the tables.

3. Throughout the textbook we have been illustrating the use of SPSS with items measuring support for abortion in various circumstances. Many variables are predictors of abortion attitudes (whether they are a *cause* of the attitudes is a question that can't be answered directly by statistics). In this exercise, we want you to explore the relationship of several variables and some of the abortion items. Good predictors to use are a general measure of political position (POLVIEWS), attitudes toward premarital sex (PREMARSX), and religious preference (RELIG) and religiosity (ATTEND).

a. Create bivariate tables with some or all of these predictors and some of the abortion items.

b. Calculate appropriate percentages and have SPSS calculate chi-square and the expected values to check that assumption. You may have to recode some tables or drop some categories to complete the analysis.

c. Summarize which variables are good predictors of which abortion attitudes. Did you find some general pattern?

d. Add the demographic variables RACE, CLASS, or SEX as control variables to a couple of these tables to see whether differences emerge between categories of respondents.

## GROUP PROBLEMS

1. Work with other group members to get newspaper or newsmagazine articles that present bivariate tables that are used to discuss the results from surveys. Be sure to pick tables with sufficient information to allow you to calculate a chi-square value.

a. Calculate chi-square for each table. Check for expected values less than 5 in each table.

b. Test the null hypothesis in each table at the .01 significance level.

c. Are the statistical tests consistent with the discussion in the article about the survey results? If not, describe any differences you found.

d. Do you and your group members think that a chi-square value (and its associated significance level) should be reported for most tables that are presented in newspaper or newsmagazine articles? Defend your position in a joint written report or before the class.

2. Continue to use the data collected from your classmates in the previous exercises.

a. Select three or four categorical variables, possibly the same ones you used in Chapter 6 or Chapter 7. Construct bivariate tables for each pair of variables.

b. Calculate chi-square for each table. Check for expected values less than 5; if you find a violation of that assumption, take action to correct it.

c. Test the null hypothesis of statistical independence at the .05 significance level in each table. What do you find?

d. Write a report or provide a verbal report to the class summarizing the group's findings. Are your conclusions consistent with what you determined about these variables in previous exercises?

# 16     Reviewing Inferential Statistics

### Introduction[1]

The goal of this chapter is to provide a concise summary of the information presented in Chapters 10 through 15. The organization of this chapter follows the order of presentation in these chapters. First, we discuss properties of the normal curve, provide formulas for calculating $Z$, and review uses for the standard normal table (Chapter 10). The next section reviews the aims of sampling and the concerns involved in sample selection (Chapter 11). Estimation is covered next, including the formulas and steps necessary to construct confidence intervals (Chapter 12). In the next section, we follow the process of statistical hypothesis testing, concentrating on two-sample situations using $t$ tests and chi-square. At the end of this section we provide a flowchart designed to help choose the proper statistical test for different types of sample data (Chapters 14 and 15).

The final sections of this chapter provide research examples that illustrate the use of some of the most common applications of statistical tests. The examples also represent the most typical formats for

---

[1]This chapter was co-authored with Pat Pawasarat.

presenting the results of statistical hypothesis testing in the social science research literature.

Chapter 16 is designed to help you sort out all you have learned in Chapters 10 through 15. Remember, it is a concise summary, and it is not all inclusive. If you are confused about any of the statistical techniques, please go back and review the relevant chapter.

## Normal Distributions

The normal distribution is central to the theory of inferential statistics. This theoretical distribution is bell-shaped and symmetrical, with the mean, the median, and the mode all coinciding at its peak and frequencies gradually decreasing at both ends of the curve. In a normal distribution a constant proportion of the area under the curve lies between the mean and any given distance from the mean when measured in standard deviation units.

Although empirical distributions never perfectly match the ideal normal distribution, many are near normal. When a distribution is near normal and the mean and the standard deviation are known, the normal distribution can be used to determine the frequency of any score in the distribution regardless of the variable being analyzed. But to use the normal distribution to determine the frequency of a score, the raw score must first be converted to a standard or $Z$ score. A $Z$ score is used to determine how many standard deviations a raw score is above or below the mean. The formula for transforming a raw score into a $Z$ score is

$$Z = \frac{Y - \overline{Y}}{S_Y}$$

where

$Y$ = the raw score
$\overline{Y}$ = the mean score of the distribution
$S_Y$ = the standard deviation of the distribution

A normal distribution expressed in $Z$ scores is called a standard normal distribution and has a mean of 0.0 and a standard deviation of 1.0. The areas or proportions under the standard normal curve are summarized in the standard normal table in Appendix B.

The standard normal curve allows researchers to describe many characteristics of any distribution that is near normal. For example, researchers can find:

1. the area between the mean and a specified positive or negative Z score.
2. the area between two Z scores on the same side of the mean.
3. the area between two Z scores on opposite sides of the mean.
4. the area above a positive Z score or below a negative Z score.
5. a raw score bounding an area above or below it.
6. the percentile rank of a score higher or lower than the mean.
7. the raw score associated with a percentile higher than 50.
8. the raw score associated with a percentile lower than 50.

Detailed explanations of the operations necessary to find any of these can be found in Chapter 10.

The standard normal curve can also be used to make inferences about population parameters, using sample statistics. Later, we will review how Z scores are used in the process of estimation and how the standard normal distribution can be used to test for differences between means or proportions (Z tests). But before we turn to those matters, let's review the aims of sampling and the importance of correctly choosing a sample as discussed in Chapter 11.

## Sampling: The Case of AIDS

All research has costs to researchers in terms of both time and money, and the subjects of research may also experience costs. Often the cost to subjects is minimal; they may be asked to·do no more than spend a few minutes responding to a questionnaire that does not contain sensitive issues. However, some research may have major costs to its subjects. For example, in the 1990s one of the main focuses of medical research is on the control of and a cure for AIDS. Statistical hypothesis testing allows medical researchers to evaluate the effects of new drug treatments on the progression of AIDS by administering them to a small number of people suffering from AIDS. If a significant number of the people receiving the treatment show improvement, the drug may be released for administration to all of the people who have AIDS. Not all of the drugs tested cause an improvement; some may have no effect and others may cause the condition to worsen. Some of the treatments may be painful. Because researchers are able to evaluate the usefulness of various treatments by testing a small number of people, the rest of the people suffering from AIDS can be spared these costs.

Statistical hypothesis testing allows researchers to minimize all costs by making it possible to estimate characteristics of a population— population parameters—using data collected from a relatively small subset of the population, a sample. Sample selection and sampling design are an integral part of any research project, and you will learn much more about sampling when you take a methods course. However, two characteristics of samples must be stressed here.

First, the techniques of inferential statistics are designed to be used only with probability samples. That is, researchers must be able to specify the likelihood that any given case in the population will be included in the sample. The most basic probability sampling design is the simple random sample; all other probability designs are variations on this design. In a simple random sample, every member of the population has an equal chance of being included in the sample. Systematic samples and stratified random samples are two variations of the simple random sample.

Second, the sample should—at least in the most important respects— be representative of the population of interest. Although a researcher can never know everything about the population he or she is studying, certain salient characteristics are either apparent or indicated by literature on the subject. Let's go back to our example of medical research on a cure for AIDS. We know that AIDS is a progressive condition. It begins when a person is diagnosed as HIV-positive and usually progresses through stages finally resulting in death. Some researchers are testing drugs that may prevent people who are diagnosed as HIV-positive from developing AIDS. When these researchers choose their samples, they should include only people who are HIV-positive, not people who have AIDS. Other researchers are testing treatments that may be effective at any stage of the disease. Their samples should include people in all stages of AIDS. AIDS knows no race, gender, or age boundaries, and all samples should reflect this. These are only a few of the obvious population characteristics researchers on AIDS must consider when selecting their samples. What you must remember is that when researchers interpret the results of statistical tests, they can only make inferences about the population their sample represents.

Every research report contains descriptions of the population of interest and the sample used in the study. Look carefully at the description of the sample when reading a research report. Is it a probability sample? Can the researchers use inferential statistics to test their hypotheses? Does the sample reasonably represent the population the researcher describes?

Although it may not be difficult to select, for example, a simple random sample (if a list exists of the population), it is often difficult to perfectly implement one. Subjects may be unwilling or unable to participate in the study, or their circumstances may change during the study. Researchers may provide information on the limitations of the sample in their research report, as we will see in a later example.

## Estimation

The goal of most research is to provide information about population parameters, but researchers rarely have the means to study an entire population. Instead, data are generally collected from a sample of the population, and sample statistics are used to make estimates of population parameters. The process of estimation can be used to infer population means, variances, and proportions from related sample statistics.

When you read a research report of an estimated population parameter, it will most likely be described as a point estimate. A point estimate is a sample statistic used to estimate the exact value of a population parameter. But, if we draw a number of samples from the same population we will find that the sample statistics vary. This is due to sampling error. Thus, when a point estimate is taken from a single sample, we cannot determine how accurate it is.

Interval estimates provide a range of values within which the population parameter may fall. This range of values is called a confidence interval. Because the sampling distributions of means and proportions are approximately normal, the normal distribution can be used to assess the likelihood expressed as a percentage or a probability that a confidence interval contains the true population mean or proportion. This likelihood is called a confidence level.

Confidence intervals may be constructed for any level, but the 90 percent, 95 percent, and 99 percent levels are the most typical. The normal distribution tells us that

1. 90 percent of all sample means or proportions will fall between ±1.65 standard errors.

2. 95 percent of all sample means or proportions will fall between ±1.96 standard errors.

3. 99 percent of all sample means or proportions will fall between ±2.58 standard errors.

The formula for constructing confidence intervals for means is

$$CI = \overline{Y} \pm Z(\sigma_{\overline{Y}})$$

where

$\overline{Y}$ = the sample mean

$Z$ = the $Z$ score corresponding to the confidence level

$\sigma_{\overline{Y}}$ = the standard error of the sampling distribution of the mean

If we know the population standard deviation, the standard error can be calculated using this formula

$$\sigma_{\overline{Y}} = \frac{\sigma_Y}{\sqrt{N}}$$

where

$\sigma_{\overline{Y}}$ = the standard error of the sampling distribution of the mean

$\sigma_Y$ = the standard deviation of the population

$N$ = the sample size

But, we rarely know the population standard deviation, so the standard error can be estimated using this formula

$$S_{\overline{Y}} = \frac{S_Y}{\sqrt{N}}$$

where

$S_{\overline{Y}}$ = the estimated standard error of the sampling distribution of the mean

$S_Y$ = the standard deviation of the sample

$N$ = the sample size

When the standard error is estimated, the formula for confidence intervals for the mean is

$$CI = \overline{Y} \pm Z(S_{\overline{Y}})$$

The formula for confidence intervals for proportions is similar to that for means

$$CI = p \pm Z(S_p)$$

where

$p$ = the sample proportion

$Z$ = the $Z$ score corresponding to the confidence level

$S_p$ = the estimated standard error of proportions

The estimated standard error of proportions is calculated using this formula

$$S_p = \sqrt{\frac{p(1-p)}{N}}$$

where

$p$ = the sample proportion
$N$ = the sample size

Interval estimation consists of the following four steps, which are the same for confidence intervals for the mean and for proportions.

1. Find the standard error.
2. Decide on the level of confidence and find the corresponding $Z$ value.
3. Calculate the confidence interval.
4. Interpret the results.

Interpreting the results consists of stating the level of confidence and the range of the confidence interval. If confidence intervals are constructed for two or more groups, they can be compared to show similarities or differences between the groups. If there is overlap in two confidence intervals, the groups are probably similar. If there is no overlap, the groups are probably different.

Remember, there is always some risk of error when using confidence intervals. At the 90 percent, 95 percent, and 99 percent confidence levels the respective risks are 10 percent, 5 percent, and 1 percent. Risk can be reduced by increasing the level of confidence. However, when the level of confidence is increased the width of the confidence interval is also increased and the estimate becomes less precise. The precision of an interval estimate can be increased by increasing the sample size, which results in a smaller standard error, but when $N \geq 400$ the increase in precision is small relative to increases in sample size.

## Statistics in Practice: The War on Drugs

If you pick up a newspaper, watch television, or listen to the radio, you will probably see the results of some kind of poll. Thousands of polls are taken in the United States every year, and the range of topics is almost unlimited. You might see that 75 percent of dentists recommend brand X or that 75 percent of all teenagers have tried drugs. Some polls may seem frivolous, whereas others may have important implications for public policy, but all of these polls use estimation.

The Gallup organization conducts some of the most reliable and widely respected polls regarding issues of public concern in the United States. In September 1995 a Gallup survey was taken to determine public attitudes toward combating the use of illegal drugs in the United States and public opinions about major influences on the drug attitudes of children and teenagers.[2]

The Gallup organization reports that 57 percent of Americans consider drug abuse to be an extremely serious problem. Forty percent of Americans favor education as the single most cost-efficient and effective strategy for halting the drug problem; 32 percent think efforts to reduce the flow of illegal drugs into the country would be most effective; 23 percent favor convicting and punishing drug offenders; and 4 percent believe drug treatment is the single best strategy. Seventy-one percent of Americans favor increased drug testing in the work-place, and 54 percent support mandatory drug testing in high schools. All of these percentages are point estimates.

Table 16.1 shows the percentage of Americans who think that peers, parents, professional athletes, organized religion, school programs, and television and radio messages have a major influence on the drug attitudes of children and teenagers. The table shows percentages for the total national sample and by subgroup for selected demographic characteristics. Notice that for most of the categories of influence the percentages are similar across the subgroups, and the subgroup percentages are similar to the national percentage for the category. One of the exceptions is the Peers category. The Gallup poll reports that 74 percent of Americans feel peers are a major influence on the drug attitudes of young people (the highest percentage for any of the categories).

Many of the subgroups show percentages fairly closely aligned with the national percentage. But look at the subgroups labeled "education." The percentages for respondents with bachelor's degrees (79%) and some college (76%) are similar to each other and to the national percentage. The percentages for college postgraduates (90%) and high school or less (66%) differ more widely. The comparison of the point estimates leads us to conclude that education has an effect on opinions about peer influence on drug attitudes. However, remember that point estimates taken from single samples are subject to sampling error so we cannot tell how accurate they are. Different samples taken from the populations of college postgraduates and people with a high school education or less might have resulted in point estimates closer to the national estimate, and then we may have reached a different conclusion.

[2]*Gallup Poll Monthly*, December 1995, pp. 16–19.

## Table 16.1 **Drug Attitudes of the Young: Major Influences**

|  | Peers | Parents | Pro Athletes | Organized Religion | School Programs | TV & Radio Messages | N |
|---|---|---|---|---|---|---|---|
| National | 74% | 58% | 51% | 31% | 30% | 26% | 1,020 |
| Sex |  |  |  |  |  |  |  |
| Male | 71 | 59 | 47 | 30 | 30 | 25 | 511 |
| Female | 76 | 57 | 55 | 32 | 30 | 27 | 509 |
| Age |  |  |  |  |  |  |  |
| 18–29 years | 72 | 55 | 54 | 26 | 23 | 26 | 172 |
| 30–49 years | 79 | 62 | 48 | 30 | 32 | 24 | 492 |
| 50–64 years | 74 | 57 | 54 | 39 | 31 | 27 | 187 |
| 65 & older | 60 | 52 | 42 | 34 | 31 | 29 | 160 |
| Region |  |  |  |  |  |  |  |
| East | 78 | 57 | 53 | 24 | 27 | 24 | 226 |
| Midwest | 73 | 56 | 46 | 28 | 31 | 26 | 215 |
| South | 73 | 61 | 56 | 42 | 33 | 31 | 363 |
| West | 72 | 57 | 48 | 27 | 29 | 21 | 216 |
| Community |  |  |  |  |  |  |  |
| Urban | 70 | 57 | 53 | 32 | 32 | 27 | 420 |
| Suburban | 77 | 60 | 50 | 29 | 29 | 24 | 393 |
| Rural | 72 | 57 | 51 | 34 | 28 | 28 | 199 |
| Race |  |  |  |  |  |  |  |
| White | 74 | 58 | 51 | 30 | 29 | 22 | 868 |
| Nonwhite | 73 | 56 | 54 | 42 | 37 | 47 | 143 |
| Education |  |  |  |  |  |  |  |
| College postgraduate | 90 | 58 | 44 | 24 | 17 | 12 | 155 |
| Bachelor's degree | 79 | 58 | 44 | 29 | 25 | 21 | 151 |
| Some college | 76 | 60 | 53 | 30 | 32 | 26 | 308 |
| High school or less | 66 | 56 | 54 | 35 | 33 | 31 | 400 |
| Income |  |  |  |  |  |  |  |
| $75,000 & over | 85 | 60 | 50 | 28 | 30 | 15 | 140 |
| $50,000–74,999 | 81 | 61 | 52 | 26 | 27 | 14 | 323 |
| $30,000–49,999 | 74 | 61 | 47 | 29 | 29 | 23 | 251 |
| $20,000–29,999 | 75 | 59 | 56 | 34 | 30 | 34 | 158 |
| Under $20,000 | 66 | 52 | 51 | 37 | 33 | 36 | 233 |
| Family drug problem |  |  |  |  |  |  |  |
| Yes | 78 | 55 | 55 | 28 | 29 | 23 | 191 |
| No | 73 | 59 | 50 | 32 | 30 | 27 | 826 |

*Source:* Adapted from *The Gallup Poll Monthly,* December 1995, pp. 16–19.

A comparison of confidence intervals can make our conclusions more convincing because we can state the probability that the interval contains the true population proportion. We can use the sample sizes provided in Table 16.1 to calculate interval estimates. In Box 16.1 we

## Box 16.1 Interval Estimation for Peers as a Major Influence on the Drug Attitudes of the Young

To calculate the confidence intervals for peer influence we must know the point estimates and the sample sizes for all Americans, college postgraduates, and Americans with a high school education or less. These figures are shown below:

| Group | Point Estimate | Sample Size (N) |
|---|---|---|
| National | 74% | 1,020 |
| College postgraduates | 90% | 155 |
| High school or less | 66% | 400 |

We follow the process of estimation to calculate confidence intervals for all three groups.

1. **Find the standard error.** For all groups we use the formula for finding the standard error of proportions:

$$S_p = \sqrt{\frac{p(1 - p)}{N}}$$

2. **Decide on the level of confidence and find the corresponding Z value.** We choose the 95 percent confidence level, which is associated with $Z = 1.96$.

3. **Calculate the confidence interval.** We use the formula for confidence intervals for proportions:

$$CI = p \pm Z(S_p)$$

4. **Interpret the results.**

Summaries of the calculations for standard errors and confidence intervals and interpretations follow.

| National | College postgraduates | High school or less |
|---|---|---|
| $S_p = \sqrt{\dfrac{(.74)(.26)}{1,020}}$ | $S_p = \sqrt{\dfrac{(.90)(.10)}{155}}$ | $S_p = \sqrt{\dfrac{(.66)(.34)}{400}}$ |
| $= .014$ | $= .024$ | $= .024$ |
| $CI = .74 \pm 1.96(.014)$ | $CI = .90 \pm 1.96(.024)$ | $CI = .66 \pm 1.96(.024)$ |
| $= .74 \pm .027$ | $= .90 \pm .047$ | $= .66 \pm .047$ |
| $= .713$ to $.767$ | $= .853$ to $.947$ | $= .613$ to $.707$ |

We can be 95 percent confident that the interval .713 to .767 includes the true population proportion.

We can be 95 percent confident that the interval .853 to .947 includes the true population proportion.

We can be 95 percent confident that the interval .613 to .707 includes the true population proportion.

> We can use the confidence intervals to compare the proportion for the three groups. None of the intervals overlap, which suggests that there are differences between the groups. The proportion of college postgraduates who think peer pressure is a major influence on the drug attitudes of young people is probably higher than the national proportion, and the proportion of the population with a high school education or less who think this is probably lower than the national proportion. It appears that education has an effect on opinions about this issue.

followed the process of interval estimation to compare the national percentage of Americans who think peers are a major influence on drug attitudes with the percentages for college postgraduates and those who have a high school education or less.

> **Learning Check.**   *Use Table 16.1 to calculate 99 percent confidence intervals for opinions about the influence of television and radio messages on drug attitudes of the young for the national sample and by race (three intervals). Compare the intervals. What is your conclusion?*

The primary purpose of estimation is to find a population parameter, using data taken from a random sample of the population. Confidence intervals allow researchers to evaluate the accuracy of their estimates of population parameters. Point and interval estimates can be used to compare populations, but neither allows researchers to evaluate conclusions based on those comparisons.

The process of statistical hypothesis testing allows researchers to use sample statistics to make decisions about population parameters. Statistical hypothesis testing can be used to test for differences between a single sample and a population or between two samples. In the following sections, we will review the process of statistical hypothesis testing, using $t$ tests, $Z$ tests, and chi-square in two-sample situations.

## The Process of Statistical Hypothesis Testing

In Chapter 13, we learned that the process of statistical hypothesis testing consists of the following six steps:

1. Making assumptions

2. Stating the research and the null hypotheses

3. Selecting a sampling distribution and a test statistic

4. Choosing alpha and establishing the region of rejection

5. Computing the test statistic

6. Making a decision and interpreting the results

Examine quantitative research reports, and you will find that all responsible researchers follow these six basic steps even though they may state them less explicitly. When asked to critically review a research report, your criticism should be based on whether the researchers have correctly followed the process of statistical hypothesis testing and if they have used the proper procedures at each step of the process. Others will use the same criteria to evaluate research reports you have written.

In this section, we follow the six steps of the process of statistical hypothesis testing to review Chapters 13 through 15. We provide a detailed guide for choosing the appropriate sampling distribution, test statistic, and formulas for the test statistics. In the following sections, we will present research examples to show how the process is used in practice.

## Step 1: Making Assumptions

Statistical hypothesis testing involves making several assumptions that must be met for the results of the test to be valid. These assumptions include the level of measurement of the variable, the method of sampling, the shape of the population distribution, and the sample size. The specific assumptions may vary, depending on the test or the conditions of testing. However, all statistical tests assume random sampling, and two-sample tests require independent random sampling. Tests of hypotheses about means also assume interval-ratio level of measurement and require that the population under consideration is normally distributed or that the sample size is larger than 50.

## Step 2: Stating the Research and the Null Hypotheses

In Chapter 1, we told you that hypotheses are tentative answers to research questions, which can be derived from theory, observations, or intuition. As tentative answers to research questions, hypotheses are generally stated in sentence form. For example, in Chapter 1 we asked a research question about gender and wage inequality. Based on dual labor market theory we stated the following hypothesis: Wages in occupations in which the majority of workers are female are lower than the wages in occupations in which the majority of workers are male. To verify this hypothesis using statistical hypothesis testing, it must be stated in a testable form called a research hypothesis. We use the symbol $H_1$ to denote the research hypothesis. Hypotheses are always stated in terms of population parameters. We are testing for a difference between means so the research hypothesis is

$H_1$: $\mu_{Y_F} = \mu_{Y_M}$

The null hypothesis ($H_0$) is a contradiction of the research hypothesis and is usually a statement of no difference between the population parameters. For our example of wage differences, the null hypothesis is

$H_0$: $\mu_{Y_F} = \mu_{Y_M}$

It is the null hypothesis that researchers test. If it can be shown that the null hypothesis is false, researchers can claim support for their research hypothesis.

Published research reports rarely make a formal statement of the research and the null hypotheses. Researchers generally present their hypotheses in sentence form as we did at the beginning of this section. This means that to evaluate a research report you must construct the research and the null hypotheses to determine whether the researchers actually tested the hypotheses they stated.

Although we discussed hypothesis testing with a single sample in Chapter 13, in this review we will concentrate on the more common two-sample situation discussed in Chapter 14. Box 16.2 shows possible hypotheses for comparing the sample means and for testing a relationship in a cross-tabulation.

## Step 3: Selecting a Sampling Distribution and a Test Statistic

The selection of a sampling distribution and a test statistic, like the selection of the form of the hypotheses, is based on a set of defining criteria. Whether you are choosing a sampling distribution to test your data or evaluating the use of a test statistic in a written research report, make sure that all of the criteria are met. Box 16.3 provides the criteria for the statistical tests for two-sample situations (Chapter 14) and for cross-tabulation (Chapter 15).

## Step 4: Choosing Alpha and Establishing the Region of Rejection

Statistical hypothesis testing always involves some risk of error because sample data are used to estimate or infer population parameters. Two types of error are possible—Type I and Type II. A Type I error occurs

---

### Box 16.2 Possible Hypotheses for Comparing Two Samples

When data are measured at the interval-ratio level, the research hypothesis can be stated as a difference between the means of the two samples in one of the following three forms:

1. $H_1$: $\mu_{Y_1} > \mu_{Y_2}$
2. $H_1$: $\mu_{Y_1} < \mu_{Y_2}$
3. $H_1$: $\mu_{Y_1} \neq \mu_{Y_2}$

Hypotheses 1 and 2 are directional hypotheses. A directional hypothesis is used when the researcher has information that leads him or her to believe that the mean for one group is either larger or smaller than the mean for the second group. Hypothesis 3 is a nondirectional hypothesis, which is used when the researcher is unsure of the direction and can only assume that the means are different.

The null hypothesis always states that there is no difference between means:

$H_0$: $\mu_{Y_1} = \mu_{Y_2}$

The form of the research and the null hypotheses for nominal or ordinal data is determined by the statistics used to describe the data. When the variables are described in terms of proportions, such as the proportions of elderly men and women who live alone, the research hypothesis can be stated as one of the following:

1. $\pi_1 > \pi_2$
2. $\pi_1 < \pi_2$
3. $\pi_1 \neq \pi_2$

The null hypothesis will always be:

$H_0$: $\pi_1 = \pi_2$

When a cross-tabulation has been used to descriptively analyze nominal or ordinal data, the research and the null hypotheses are stated in terms of the relationship between the two variables.

$H_1$: The two variables are related in the population (statistically dependent).

$H_0$: There is no relationship between the two variables in the population (statistically independent).

---

when a true null hypothesis is rejected; alpha ($\alpha$) is the probability of making a Type I error. In social science research alpha is typically set at either the .05, .01, or .001 level. At the .05 level researchers risk a 5 percent chance of making a Type I error. The risk of making a Type I error can be decreased by choosing a smaller alpha level—.01 or .001.

## Box 16.3  Criteria for Statistical Tests When Comparing Two Samples

When the data are measured at the interval-ratio level, sample means can be compared using either the normal distribution—$Z$ test—or the $t$ distribution—$t$ test.

### Criteria for using the normal distribution and a Z test with interval-ratio level data:

- population variances known
- independent random samples
- population distribution normal or $N_1 > 50$ and $N_2 > 50$

### Criteria for using the t distribution and a t test with interval-ratio level data:

- population variances unknown
- independent random samples
- population distribution assumed normal unless $N_1 > 50$ and $N_2 > 50$

When the data are measured at the nominal or ordinal level, either the normal distribution or the chi-square distribution can be used to compare proportions for two samples.

### Criteria for using the normal distribution and a Z test with proportions (nominal or ordinal data):

- population variances unknown but assumed equal
- independent random samples
- combined sample size greater than 100 ($N_1 + N_2 > 100$)

For this test, the population variances are always assumed equal because they are a function of the population proportion ($\pi$), and the null hypothesis is $\pi_1 = \pi_2$.

### Criteria for using the chi-square distribution and a $\chi^2$ test with nominal or ordinal data:

- independent random samples
- any size sample
- cross-tabulated data
- no cells with expected frequencies less than 5, or not more than 20 percent of the cells with expected frequencies less than 5

The chi-square test can be used with any size sample, but it is sensitive to sample size. Increasing the sample size results in increased values of $\chi^2$. This property can leave interpretations of the findings open to question when the sample size is very large. Thus, it is preferable to use the normal distribution if the criteria for a $Z$ test can be met.

However, as the risk of a Type I error decreases the risk of a Type II error increases. A Type II error occurs when the researcher fails to reject a false null hypothesis.

How does a researcher choose the appropriate alpha level? By weighing the consequences of making a Type I or a Type II error. Let's look again at research on AIDS. Suppose researchers are testing a new drug that may halt the progression of AIDS. The null hypothesis is that the drug has no effect on the progression of AIDS. Now suppose that preliminary research has shown this drug has serious negative side effects. The researchers would want to minimize the risk of making a Type I error (rejecting a true null hypothesis) so people would not experience the negative side effects unnecessarily if the drug does not affect the progression of AIDS. An alpha level of .001 or smaller would be appropriate.

Alternatively, if preliminary research has shown the drug has no serious negative side effects, the researchers would want to minimize the risk of a Type II error (failing to reject a false null hypothesis). If the null hypothesis is false and the drug might actually help people with AIDS, researchers would want to increase the chance of rejecting the null hypothesis. In this case the appropriate alpha level would be .05.

The critical value and region of rejection for the test statistic are determined by both the alpha level and whether the test is one- or two-tailed. Do not confuse alpha and $p$. Alpha is the level of probability—determined in advance by the investigator—at which the null hypothesis is rejected; $p$ is the actual calculated probability associated with the obtained value of the test statistic. The null hypothesis is rejected when $p \leq$ alpha, and $p \leq$ alpha when the calculated statistic is equal to or more extreme in value than the critical value of the test statistic. Let's review how critical values are located for the normal distribution, the $t$ distribution, and the chi-square distribution.

*Finding the Critical Value of Z* The standard normal table, found in Appendix B, is used to locate the critical value of Z. To determine the critical value of Z for directional hypotheses, first locate the alpha level—or the closest value to it—in column C. Then go across to the corresponding value in column A to locate the critical value of Z. For nondirectional hypotheses first divide the alpha level by 2, locate that value in column C, and then go across to the corresponding value in column A to locate the critical value of Z. The critical value denotes the lowest boundary of the critical region. Any obtained Z equal to or more extreme in value than the critical value will fall into the critical region. When the hypothesis is directional the critical value is positive for a right-tailed test and negative for a left-tailed test. When the hypothesis is nondirectional the obtained $Z$ must be equal to or more extreme in value than "±" the critical value to reject the null hypothesis. The critical values for directional hypotheses for $\alpha$ levels .05, .01, and .001 are 1.65, 2.33, and 3.09, respectively. The corresponding values for nondirectional hypotheses are ±1.96, ±2.58, and ±3.30.

*Finding the Critical Value of t* Before the $t$ distribution can be used to determine the critical value of $t$, the degrees of freedom for the distributions must be computed. For the difference between means test when the population variances are assumed equal, the degrees of freedom are computed by adding the number of cases in the distribution and subtracting two—$N_1 + N_2 - 2 = $ df. When the population variances are not assumed to be equal, the df will also be defined as $N_1 + N_2 - 2$ when both samples are large ($N_1 > 50$; $N_2 > 50$). However, when the samples are small ($N_1 \leq 50$; $N_2 \leq 50$), the df's are calculated using this formula:

$$df = \frac{\left(\dfrac{S^2_{Y_1}}{N_1} + \dfrac{S^2_{Y_2}}{N_2}\right)^2}{\left(\dfrac{S^2_{Y_1}}{N_1}\right)^2\left(\dfrac{1}{N_1+1}\right) + \left(\dfrac{S^2_{Y_2}}{N_2}\right)^2\left(\dfrac{1}{N_2+1}\right)} - 2$$

The $t$ distribution table is found in Appendix C. The degrees of freedom are shown in the left-most column of the table. To find the critical value of $t$ for a one-tailed test, locate the alpha level in the upper row of column headings and go down the column to the appropriate degrees of freedom. The critical value of $t$ will be positive for a right-tailed test or negative for a left-tailed test; any obtained $t$ equal to or more extreme in value than the critical value will fall into the critical region.

To locate the critical value of $t$ for a two-tailed test, locate the alpha level in the lower row of column headings and go down the column to the degrees of freedom. Any obtained $t$ equal to or more extreme in value than "±" the critical value will fall into the critical region.

*Finding the Critical Value of Chi-Square* The chi-square distribution is found in Appendix D. The left-most column shows the degrees of freedom for the distribution, and the alpha levels are shown in the column headings. The degrees of freedom are calculated by subtracting one from the number of columns and the number of rows and multiplying the results—$(r - 1)(c - 1) = $ df.

To find the critical value of chi-square, locate the alpha level in the column headings and go down the column to the appropriate degrees of freedom. The critical value of chi-square will always be positive; any obtained $\chi^2$ equal to or greater than the critical value will fall into the critical region.

## Step 5: Computing the Test Statistic

In Chapter 9, we told you that most researchers use computer software packages to calculate statistics for their data. Consequently, when you evaluate a research report there is very little reason to question the accuracy of the calculations. You, too, may use your computer to calculate statistics when writing a research report, but there may be times when you need to do manual calculations (such as your final exam!). The formulas you need to calculate $Z$, $t$, and $\chi^2$ statistics are shown in Box 16.4.

## Step 6: Making a Decision and Interpreting the Results

The last step in the formal process of statistical hypothesis testing is to determine whether or not the null hypothesis should be rejected. If the obtained statistic—$Z$, $t$, or $\chi^2$—is equal to or more extreme in value than the critical value, it is considered to be statistically significant and the null hypothesis is rejected.

If the null hypothesis is rejected the researcher can claim support for the research hypothesis. In other words, the hypothesized answer to the research question becomes less tentative, but the researcher cannot state that it is absolutely true because there is always some error involved when samples are used to infer population parameters.

The conditions and assumptions associated with the two-sample tests are summarized in the flowchart presented in Figure 16.1. Use this flowchart to help you decide which of the different tests ($Z$, $t$, or chi-square) is appropriate under what conditions and how to choose the correct formula for calculating the obtained value for the test.

## Statistics in Practice: Affirmative Action

In 1972 Congress passed the Equal Opportunity Employment Act in an effort to reduce and eventually eliminate the effects of past employment

## Box 16.4 Formulas for Z, t, and $\chi^2$

**Z: Comparing two samples with interval-ratio data (population variances known; population distribution normal or $N_1 > 50$ and $N_2 > 50$)**

$$Z = \frac{(\overline{Y}_1 - \overline{Y}_2)}{\sigma_{\overline{Y}_1 - \overline{Y}_2}} \qquad (14.3)$$

$$\sigma_{\overline{Y}_1 - \overline{Y}_2} = \sqrt{\frac{\sigma_{Y_1}^2}{N_1} + \frac{\sigma_{Y_2}^2}{N_2}} \qquad (14.1)$$

where

$\overline{Y}$ = the sample mean
$\sigma_{\overline{Y}_1 - \overline{Y}_2}$ = the standard error of the difference between two means
$\sigma_Y^2$ = the population variance
$N$ = the sample size

**Z: Comparing two samples with nominal or ordinal data (population variances unknown but assumed equal; $N_1 + N_2 > 100$)**

$$Z = \frac{P_1 - P_2}{S_{P_1 - P_2}} \qquad (14.8)$$

$$S_{P_1 - P_2} = \sqrt{\frac{P_1(1 - P_1)}{N_1} + \frac{P_2(1 - P_2)}{N_2}} \qquad (14.9)$$

where

$P$ = the proportion of the sample
$S_{P_1 - P_2}$ = the estimated standard error
$N$ = the sample size

**t: Comparing two samples with interval-ratio data (population variances unknown)**

$$t = \frac{\overline{Y}_1 - \overline{Y}_2}{S_{\overline{Y}_1 - \overline{Y}_2}} \qquad (14.4)$$

where

$\overline{Y}$ = the sample mean
$S_{\overline{Y}_1 - \overline{Y}_2}$ = the estimated standard error of the difference between two means

**Calculating the estimated standard error when the population variances are assumed equal (pooled variance)**

$$S_{\overline{Y}_1 - \overline{Y}_2} = \sqrt{\frac{(N_1 - 1)S_{Y_1}^2 + (N_2 - 1)S_{Y_2}^2}{(N_1 + N_2) - 2}} \sqrt{\frac{N_1 + N_2}{N_1 N_2}} \qquad (14.5)$$

where

$S_Y^2$ = the sample variance
$N$ = the sample size

## Calculating the estimated standard error when the population variances are assumed unequal

$$S_{\bar{Y}_1 - \bar{Y}_2} = \sqrt{\frac{S_{Y_1}^2}{N_1} + \frac{S_{Y_2}^2}{N_2}} \tag{14.6}$$

## Calculating df

$$df = (N_1 + N_2) - 2$$

## Adjusting for unequal variances (with small samples)

$$df = \frac{\left(\dfrac{S_{Y_1}^2}{N_1} + \dfrac{S_{Y_2}^2}{N_2}\right)^2}{\left(\dfrac{S_{Y_1}^2}{N_1}\right)^2 \left(\dfrac{1}{N_1 + 1}\right) + \left(\dfrac{S_{Y_2}^2}{N_2}\right)^2 \left(\dfrac{1}{N_2 + 1}\right)} - 2 \tag{14.7}$$

where

$S_Y^2$ = the sample variance
$N$ = the sample size

## $\chi^2$: Comparing two samples with nominal or ordinal data (cross-tabulated data; any sample size; no cells or less than 20 percent of cells with expected frequencies < 5)

$$\chi^2 = \sum \frac{(f_o - f_e)^2}{f_e} \tag{15.2}$$

where

$f_o$ = the observed frequency in a cell
$f_e$ = the expected frequency in a cell

$$f_e = \frac{(\text{Column marginal})(\text{Row marginal})}{N} \tag{15.1}$$

$$df = (r - 1)(c - 1)$$

where

$r$ = the number of rows
$c$ = the number of columns

Figure 16.1 **Flowchart of the Process of Statistical Hypothesis Testing: Two-Sample Situations**

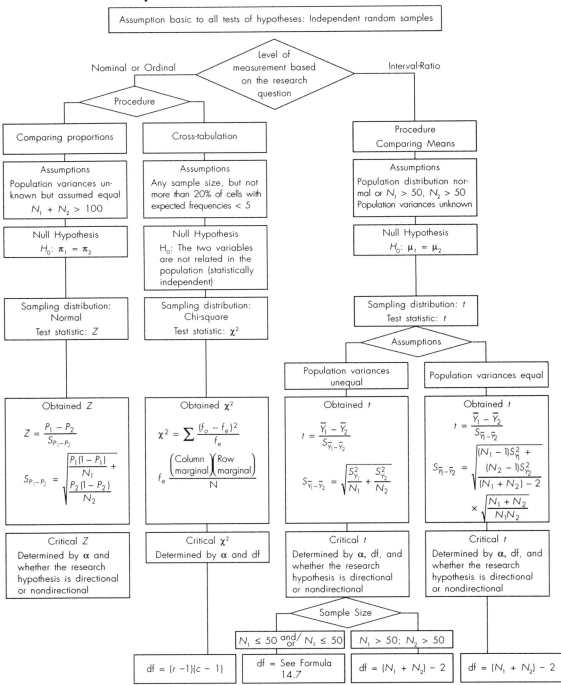

discrimination against women and minorities. Under this act colleges and universities must meet enrollment quotas in undergraduate, graduate, and postgraduate programs. Employers are required to implement affirmative action programs designed to increase the percentage of female and minority employees overall, but especially in upper-level positions.

Affirmative action programs have been in effect for over twenty years. Have they been effective? Have they resulted in discrimination against white males? Should they be continued? These are some of the questions addressed in a survey conducted by Gallup in 1995.[3]

One of the questions asked in the 1995 Gallup survey was: "In general, do you think blacks have as good a chance as white people in your community to get any kind of job for which they are qualified, or don't you think they have as good a chance?"[4] Table 16.2 shows the percentage distribution for responses to this question for all respondents and by race. For comparison purposes, the table also shows the results of similar surveys conducted in 1963 (before the Equal Opportunity Employment Act was passed) and 1993.

Table 16.2 shows that the percentage of all respondents who think the employment chances of qualified blacks are equal to whites increased between 1963 (43%) and 1993 (65%), then remained fairly stable between 1993 (65%) and 1995 (64%). The trend is similar for the percentages of whites: 46 percent in 1963; 70 percent in 1993; and 68 percent in 1995. The percentages for blacks, however, have steadily increased over time although the percentage for blacks is still very low: 24 percent in 1963; 30 percent in 1993; and 36 percent in 1995. Because we do not have information on the sample sizes in 1963 and 1993, we cannot calculate the standard errors for the groups in those years and, consequently, cannot use a statistical test to determine whether the percentage increases over time are significant. All we can say is that they appear to be moving, albeit slowly, in the desired direction.

Table 16.2 also shows that in all three years the percentage of whites was higher than the percentage of blacks who thought qualified blacks had job opportunity equal to whites (46% vs. 24% in 1963; 70% vs. 30% in 1993; and 68% vs. 36% in 1995). Are the opinions of whites and blacks significantly different? Again, we do not have the information to statistically test the data for 1963 and 1993, but because we have the sample sizes for the 1995 survey, we can test the data for 1995 as shown in Box 16.5. The results of the $Z$ test show that the

---

[3]*Gallup Poll Monthly*, July 1995, pp. 34–40.
[4]Ibid., p. 34.

Table 16.2 **Opinions About Equal Job Opportunity for Qualified Black Candidates for All Respondents and by Race: 1963, 1993, and 1995**

|  | Total | Whites | Blacks |
|---|---|---|---|
| **1963** | | | |
| Yes | 43% | 46% | 24% |
| No | 48 | 44 | 74 |
| No opinion | 9 | 10 | 2 |
| Total | 100% | 100% | 100% |
| (N) | * | * | * |
| **1993** | | | |
| Yes | 65% | 70% | 30% |
| No | 31 | 27 | 66 |
| No opinion | 4 | 3 | 4 |
| Total | 100% | 100% | 100% |
| (N) | * | * | * |
| **1995** | | | |
| Yes | 64% | 68% | 36% |
| No | 32 | 27 | 62 |
| No opinion | 4 | 5 | 2 |
| Total | 100% | 100% | 100% |
| (N) | (N = 1,161) | (N = 837) | (N = 324) |

*Source:* Adapted from *The Gallup Poll Monthly*, July 1995, p. 34.
*Sample size (N) not provided

---

### Box 16.5 *Affirmative Action: The Process of Statistical Hypothesis Testing, Using a Z test for Proportions*

To follow the process of statistical hypothesis testing we will calculate $Z$ for the percentages shown for the "yes" response for 1995 in Table 16.2.

#### Step 1. Making assumptions

1. Independent random samples with $N_1 + N_2 > 100$
2. Level of measurement: nominal

#### Step 2. Stating the research and the null hypotheses

We want to determine whether the percentage of whites is different from the percentage of blacks who think blacks have equal job opportunity. We can express our hypotheses in terms of differences between proportions. We have no basis for assuming that the percentage in one group is higher than the percentage in the other, so our research hypothesis is nondirectional.

$H_1: \pi_W \neq \pi_B$
$H_0: \pi_W = \pi_B$

### Step 3. Selecting a sampling distribution and a test statistic

We are analyzing data measured at the nominal level with $N_W + N_B > 100$.

Sampling distribution: The standard normal distribution
Test statistic: $Z$

### Step 4. Choosing alpha and establishing the region of rejection

$\alpha = .05$
Critical $Z = \pm 1.96$

### Step 5. Computing the test statistic

We use the formula for $Z$ for proportions:

$$Z = \frac{P_W - P_B}{S_{P_W - P_B}}$$

First, calculate the estimated standard error:

$$S_{P_W - P_B} = \sqrt{\frac{P_W(1 - P_W)}{N_W} + \frac{P_B(1 - P_B)}{N_B}}$$

$$= \sqrt{\frac{.68(.32)}{837} + \frac{.36(.64)}{324}} = .031$$

Then plug the values into the formula for $Z$:

$$Z = \frac{.68 - .36}{.031} = \frac{.32}{.031} = 10.32$$

### Step 6. Making a decision and interpreting the results

The obtained $Z$, 10.32, is more extreme in value than the critical $Z$, 1.96. We can conclude only that whites and blacks differ in the percentage who think blacks have job opportunity equal to whites.

percentages are significantly different for blacks and whites. Whites and blacks differ in the percentage who think that blacks have job opportunity equal to whites.

## Statistics in Practice: Attitudes Toward Illegal Immigrants

In Chapter 14, we introduced you to the American National Election Survey, which has been conducted by the Survey Research Center at the University of Michigan for over twenty years.[5] These surveys are designed to measure public attitudes toward elected officials, political candidates, and political issues. The election surveys provide data on selected demographic characteristics of the respondents including gender, race, and ethnicity; so researchers can compare attitudes between subgroups of respondents.

Illegal immigration and public obligations to illegal immigrants have been in the forefront of political and public debate in the 1990s. In this section, we use data from the 1994 National Election Study to compare the attitudes of Native Americans and Asian Americans toward illegal immigrants. We have chosen to compare these two groups because one group—Native Americans—is indigenous to this country and the other group—Asian Americans—is the product of immigration. Does a history of immigration make Asian Americans more sympathetic than Native Americans toward illegal immigrants?

In the American National Election Survey respondents were asked to use the feeling thermometer described in Chapter 14 to rate their feelings toward illegal immigrants. The feeling thermometer provides an interval-ratio scale from 0 to 100, with a rating of 0 indicating an extremely unfavorable attitude, 50 indicating neutrality, and 100 indicating an extremely favorable attitude. The mean ratings, standard deviations, and sample sizes for Native Americans and Asian Americans are shown in Table 16.3.

Table 16.3 **Feelings Toward Illegal Immigrants by Native Americans and Asian Americans in 1994**

|  | Native Americans | Asian Americans |
|---|---|---|
| Mean | 27.93 | 40.88 |
| Standard deviation | 27.65 | 24.97 |
| Variance | 765 | 624 |
| N | 16 | 25 |

*Source:* American National Election Survey, 1994.

[5]Steven J. Rosenstone, Warren E. Miller, Donald R. Kinder, and the National Election Studies. *American National Election Study, 1994: Post Election Survey,* 2d ICPSR ed. Conducted by University of Michigan, Center for Political Studies. Ann Arbor, MI: University of Michigan, Center for Political Studies, and Inter-University Consortium for Political and Social Research, 1995.

Table 16.3 shows that both Native Americans and Asian Americans have unfavorable feelings about illegal immigrants, but there is a difference of 12.95 in the mean ratings. Asian Americans appear to be more sympathetic than Native Americans toward illegal immigrants. But is there a true difference between the two groups or is the difference a result of sampling error? In Box 16.6 we follow the six steps of statistical hypothesis testing to test the significance of the difference. The results of the *t* test shown in Box 16.6 lead us to conclude that the observed difference is probably due to sampling error. Native Americans and Asian Americans do not differ significantly in their feelings toward illegal immigrants.

---

### Box 16.6 Attitudes Toward Illegal Immigrants: The Process of Statistical Hypothesis Testing, Using a t Test

To follow the process of statistical hypothesis testing we will calculate *t* for attitudes toward illegal immigrants from Table 16.3.

#### Step 1. Making assumptions
1. Independent random samples
2. Populations normally distributed
3. Level of measurement of the variable: interval-ratio
4. Population variances assumed equal

#### Step 2. Stating the research and the null hypotheses
Our hypothesis is directional because we have reason to believe that Asian Americans are more sympathetic than are Native Americans toward illegal immigrants:

$$H_1: \mu_{Y_A} > \mu_{Y_{NA}}$$
$$H_0: \mu_{Y_A} = \mu_{Y_{NA}}$$

#### Step 3. Selecting a sampling distribution and a test statistic
We will analyze data measured at the interval-ratio level with estimated variances that are assumed equal.

Sampling distribution: *t*
Test statistic: *t*

#### Step 4. Choosing alpha and establishing the region of rejection
We use a one-tailed test. Because the population variances are assumed equal, df is

$$df = N_{NA} + N_A - 2 = 16 + 25 - 2 = 39$$
$$\alpha = .05$$
Critical $t = \pm 1.684$

(continued)

### Step 5. Computing the test statistic

The formulas we need to calculate $t$ are

$$t = \frac{\overline{Y}_A - \overline{Y}_{NA}}{S_{\overline{Y}_{NA} - \overline{Y}_A}}$$

$$S_{\overline{Y}_{NA} - \overline{Y}_A} = \sqrt{\frac{(N_{NA} - 1)S_{NA}^2 + (N_A - 1)S_A^2}{(N_{NA} + N_A) - 2}} \sqrt{\frac{N_{NA} + N_A}{N_{NA}N_A}}$$

First, calculate the standard deviation of the sampling distribution:

$$S_{\overline{Y}_{NA} - \overline{Y}_A} = \sqrt{\frac{(15)(27.65)^2 + (24)(24.97)^2}{(16 + 25) - 2}} \sqrt{\frac{16 + 25}{(16)(25)}}$$

$$= \sqrt{\frac{11,467.84 + 14,964.02}{39}} \sqrt{\frac{41}{400}}$$

$$= 26.03(.32) = 8.33$$

Then plug this figure into the formula for $t$:

$$t = \frac{40.88 - 27.93}{8.33} = \frac{12.95}{8.33} = 1.55$$

### Step 6. Making a decision and interpreting the results

The obtained $t$, 1.55, is less extreme than the critical $t$, ±1.684. We cannot reject the null hypothesis, and we must conclude that there is no significant difference in attitudes toward illegal immigrants between Native Americans and Asian Americans. The observed difference is probably due to sampling error.

## Statistics in Practice: Education and Employment

Why did you decide to attend college? Whether you made the decision on your own or discussed it with your parents, spouse, or friends, the prospect of increased employment opportunities and higher income after graduation probably weighed heavily in your decision. Even though most college students expect that their major will prepare them to compete successfully in the job market and the workplace, undergraduate programs do not always meet this expectation.

In the introduction to a study of the efficacy of social science undergraduate programs, Velasco, Stockdale, and Scrams[6] note that sociology

[6]Steven C. Velasco, Susan E. Stockdale, and David J. Scrams, "Sociology and Other Social Sciences: California State University Alumni Ratings of the BA Degree for Development of Employment Skills." *Teaching Sociology*, Vol. 20, January 1992, 60–70.

programs have traditionally been designed to prepare students for gradu-ate school, where they can earn professional status. However, the vast majority of students who earn a BA in sociology do not attend gradu-ate school and must either earn their professional status through work experience or find employment in some other sector. The result is that many people holding a BA in sociology are underemployed.

According to Velasco et al., certain foundational skills are critical to successful careers in the social sciences. The foundational skills include logical reasoning, understanding scientific principles, mathe-matical and statistical skills, computer skills, and knowing the subject matter of the major. In their study the researchers sought to determine how well sociology programs develop these skills in students. Specifi-cally, they focused on the following research questions:

1. How do sociology alumni with BA degrees, as compared with other social science alumni, rate their major with respect to the helpfulness of their major in developing the "foundational skills"?

2. Has the percentage of sociology alumni who rate their major highly increased over time with respect to the development of these skills?

3. Do male and female alumni from the five social science disciplines differ in regard to ratings of the major in developing the founda-tional skills? Do male and female alumni differ with respect to occupational prestige or personal income?[7]

Clearly, surveying the entire population of alumni in five dis-ciplines to obtain answers to these questions would be a nearly insur-mountable task. To make their project manageable, the researchers surveyed a sample of each population and used inferential statistics to analyze the data. Their sampling technique and characteristics of the samples are discussed in the next section.

## Sampling Technique and Sample Characteristics

Velasco et al. used the alumni records from eight diverse campuses in the California State University system to identify graduates of BA programs in anthropology, economics, political science, psychology, and sociology. The population consisted of forty groups of alumni (5 disciplines × 8 campuses = 40 groups). The researchers drew a random sample from each group.[8] Potential subjects were sent a questionnaire

[7]Ibid., p. 62.

[8]All members of groups with fewer than 150 members were included as potential subjects. Up to three questionnaire and follow-up mailings were made to each alumnus to maximize responses from these groups.

and, if necessary, a follow-up postcard. If after follow-up fewer than fifty responses were received from a particular group, random replacement samples were drawn and new potential subjects were similarly contacted.

The final response rate from the combined groups was about 28 percent. Such a low response rate calls into question the representativeness of the sample and, consequently, the use of inferential statistics techniques. The researchers caution that because the sample may not be representative, the results of the statistical tests they performed should be viewed as exploratory.

A total of 2,157 questionnaires were returned. Some of the responses were from people holding advanced degrees, and some of the respondents were not employed full-time. Because the researchers were interested in examining how undergraduate programs prepare students for employment, they limited their final sample to full-time employed respondents with only a BA degree, thereby reducing the total sample size to 1,194. Table 16.4 shows selected demographic characteristics for the total final sample and for each discipline.

Table 16.4 **Selected Demographic Characteristics of the Sample Population with Bachelor's Degrees Who Are Employed Full-Time**

|  | All | Anthropology | Economics | Political Science | Psychology | Sociology |
|---|---|---|---|---|---|---|
| N | 1,194 | 181 | 288 | 222 | 220 | 283 |
| % sample in major | — | 15.2 | 24.1 | 18.6 | 18.4 | 23.7 |
| % female | 48.7 | 64.1 | 26.4 | 31.5 | 66.4 | 61.1 |
| % white | 84.8 | 87.3 | 87.2 | 83.3 | 86.4 | 80.6 |
| Mean age | 35.5 | 37.6 | 34.7 | 33.4 | 34.1 | 37.9 |
| SD age | 9.11 | 10.1 | 9.27 | 8.22 | 8.45 | 8.75 |
| Mean graduation age | 27.2 | 29.9 | 26.0 | 25.5 | 26.6 | 28.3 |
| SD graduation age | 7.75 | 9.90 | 6.79 | 6.38 | 6.98 | 8.01 |

*Source:* Steven C. Velasco, Susan E. Stockdale, and David J. Scrams, "Sociology and Other Social Sciences: California State University Alumni Ratings of the BA Degree for Development of Employment Skills." *Teaching Sociology*, Vol. 20, January 1992, 60–70.

## Comparing Ratings of the Major Between Sociology and Other Social Science Alumni

The first research question in this study required a comparison between sociology alumni ratings of their major on the development of foundational skills and the ratings given by alumni from other social science disciplines. To gather data on foundational skills, the researchers asked alumni to rate how well their major added to the development of each of the five skills, using the following scale: 1 = poor; 2 = fair; 3 = good; 4 = excellent. The mean rating for each of the foundational skills, by major, is shown in Table 16.5. The table shows that the skill rated most highly in all disciplines was subject matter of the major. Looking at the mean ratings, we can determine that economics alumni generally rated their major the highest, whereas sociology and political science alumni rated their majors the lowest overall.[9] The lowest rating in all disciplines was given to the development of computer skills.

Table 16.5 **Graduates' Mean Rating of Their Majors Regarding the Development of Foundational Skills**

|  | Anthropology | Economics | Political Science | Psychology | Sociology |
|---|---|---|---|---|---|
| Logical reasoning | 2.99 | 3.30 | 3.16 | 3.13 | 2.94 |
| Scientific principles | 3.01 | 2.98 | 2.41 | 3.07 | 2.70 |
| Mathematical and statistical skills | 2.23 | 3.22 | 2.16 | 2.90 | 2.54 |
| Computer skills | 1.63 | 2.23 | 1.67 | 1.93 | 1.89 |
| Subject matter of the major | 3.36 | 3.36 | 3.20 | 3.26 | 3.14 |

Scale: 1 = Poor; 2 = Fair; 3 = Good; 4 = Excellent

*Source:* Adapted from Steven C. Velasco, Susan E. Stockdale, and David J. Scrams, "Sociology and Other Social Sciences: California State University Alumni Ratings of the BA Degree for Development of Employment Skills." *Teaching Sociology,* Vol. 20, January 1992, 60–70.

[9]In this book we have limited our discussions to tests of differences between two sample means. Velasco et al. used a statistical test called the analysis of variance (ANOVA) to test for differences between several means (5 disciplines) and found that there were significant differences in the ratings given each foundational skill across majors.

### Ratings of Foundational Skills in Sociology: Changes over Time

In recent years many sociology departments have taken steps to more closely align undergraduate requirements with the qualifications necessary for a career in sociology. If these changes have been successful, then more recent graduates should rate program development of foundational skills higher than less recent graduates. This is the second research question addressed in this study. To examine the question of whether the percentage of sociology alumni who rate their major highly with respect to the development of foundational skills has increased over time, Velasco et al. categorized the sample of sociology alumni by number of years since graduation. The three resulting categories were 11+ years, 5–10 years, and 0–4 years. The two categories of ratings were "poor or fair" and "good or excellent." Table 16.6 shows percentage bivariate tables for each of the five foundation skills.

Cross-tabulation of the bivariate tables in Table 16.6 reveals the following relationship for all of the foundational skills: The percentage of alumni who rated the major as "good or excellent" in the development of the skill decreased as the number of years since graduation increased. For example, the bivariate table for scientific principles shows that 76.6 percent of the alumni who graduated 0 to 4 years ago rated the major as "good or excellent" compared with 64.1 percent of those who graduated 5 to 10 years ago and 46.4 percent of alumni who graduated 11+ years ago.

The researchers used the chi-square distribution to test for the significance of the relationship for each of the skills. (See Box 16.7 for an illustration of the calculation of chi-square for mathematical and statistical skills.) The chi-square statistic, degrees of freedom, and level of significance are reported at the bottom of each bivariate table in Table 16.6.

Look at the levels of significance. Remember that statistical software programs provide the most stringent level at which a statistic is significant, and researchers typically report the level indicated by the output. However, the alpha levels reported in Table 16.6 are somewhat deceptive. There is no problem with the levels reported for scientific principles ($p < .001$) or mathematical and statistical skills ($p < .01$) if we assume that the researchers set alpha at .05 or .01 because $p$ is less than either of these levels for both skills. We can agree with their conclusion that there is a significant relationship between recency of graduation and alumni ratings of the major, and we can further conclude that sociology programs may be improving in the development of the two skills.

Table 16.6  **Sociology Alumni Ratings of the Major in Developing Foundational Skills by Number of Years since Graduation**

|  | Number of Years since Graduation | | |
|---|---|---|---|
|  | **11+** | **5–10** | **0–4** |
| **Logical reasoning** | $(n = 112)$ | $(n = 93)$ | $(n = 65)$ |
| Poor or fair | 31.3 | 23.7 | 17.4 |
| Good or excellent | 68.5 | 76.3 | 81.5 |
|  | chi-square = 3.802; 2 df; $p$ = ns* | | |
| **Scientific principles** | $(n = 110)$ | $(n = 92)$ | $(n = 64)$ |
| Poor or fair | 53.6 | 35.9 | 23.4 |
| Good or excellent | 46.4 | 64.1 | 76.6 |
|  | chi-square = 16.46; 2 df; $p < .001$ | | |
| **Mathematical and statistical skills** | $(n = 109)$ | $(n = 92)$ | $(n = 64)$ |
| Poor or fair | 59.6 | 46.7 | 34.8 |
| Good or excellent | 40.4 | 53.3 | 65.2 |
|  | chi-square = 10.41; 2 df; $p < .01$ | | |
| **Computer skills** | $(n = 52)$ | $(n = 58)$ | $(n = 64)$ |
| Poor or fair | 84.4 | 72.4 | 65.4 |
| Good or excellent | 15.6 | 27.6 | 34.6 |
|  | chi-square = 4.57; 2 df; $p < .10$ | | |
| **Subject matter of the major** | $(n = 116)$ | $(n = 96)$ | $(n = 66)$ |
| Poor or fair | 21.6 | 15.6 | 9.1 |
| Good or excellent | 78.4 | 84.4 | 90.9 |
|  | chi-square = 4.82; 2 df; $p < .10$ | | |

*Source:* Adapted from Steven C. Velasco, Susan E. Stockdale, and David J. Scrams, "Sociology and Other Social Sciences: California State University Alumni Ratings of the BA Degree for Development of Employment Skills." *Teaching Sociology,* Vol. 20, January 1992, 60–70.
*ns = not significant

The problem arises when we compare the values presented for logical reasoning ($p$ = ns), computer skills ($p < .10$), and subject matter of the major ($p < .10$). None of the chi-square statistics for these skills are significant at even the .05 level, yet the researchers report the alpha levels differently. They clearly show that the chi-square statistic for logical reasoning skills is not significant ($p$ = ns), but they report $p < .10$ for both of the other skills, thereby giving the impression that these chi-square statistics are significant. The reason for this bit of misdirection can be inferred from the text accompanying the table. The researchers state that "the increases in ratings for computer skills and

---

### Box 16.7  Education and Employment: The Process of Statistical Hypothesis Testing, Using Chi-Square

To follow the process of statistical hypothesis testing, we will calculate chi-square for mathematical and statistical skills from Table 16.6.

#### Step 1. Making assumptions

A random sample of $N = 265$
Level of measurement of the variable "ratings": ordinal
Level of measurement of the variable "years since graduation": ordinal

#### Step 2. Stating the research and the null hypotheses

$H_1$:  There is a relationship between number of years since graduation and alumni ratings of the sociology major in developing mathematical and statistical skills. (statistical dependence)

$H_0$:  There is no relationship between number of years since graduation and alumni ratings of the sociology major in developing mathematical and statistical skills. (statistical independence)

#### Step 3. Selecting a sampling distribution and a test statistic
We will analyze cross-tabulated data measured at the ordinal level.

Sampling distribution: chi-square
Test statistic: $\chi^2$

#### Step 4. Choosing alpha and establishing the region of rejection

$\alpha = .05$
$df = 2 \ [(2 - 1)(3 - 1)] = 2$
Critical $\chi^2 = 5.991$

#### Step 5. Computing the test statistic
First, calculate the observed cell frequencies from the percentage table shown in Table 16.6. The frequency table follows.

| RATINGS | NUMBER OF YEARS SINCE GRADUATION | | | |
|---|---|---|---|---|
| | 11+ | 5–10 | 0–4 | |
| Poor or fair | 65 | 43 | 22 | 130 |
| Good or excellent | 44 | 49 | 42 | 135 |
| | 109 | 92 | 64 | 265 |

Next, calculate the expected frequencies for each cell:

$$f_e = \frac{\text{(Column marginal)(Row marginal)}}{N}$$

Poor or fair/11+ $\qquad f_e = \dfrac{(109)(130)}{265} = 53.47$

Good or excellent/11+ $\qquad f_e = \dfrac{(109)(135)}{265} = 55.53$

Poor or fair/5–10 $\qquad f_e = \dfrac{(92)(130)}{265} = 45.13$

Good or excellent/5–10 $\qquad f_e = \dfrac{(92)(135)}{265} = 46.87$

Poor or fair/0–4 $\qquad f_e = \dfrac{(64)(130)}{265} = 31.40$

Good or excellent/0–4 $\qquad f_e = \dfrac{(64)(135)}{265} = 32.60$

Calculate $\chi^2$.

**Calculating Chi-Square for Alumni Ratings**

| Rating | $f_e$ | $f_o$ | $f_o - f_e$ | $(f_o - f_e)^2$ | $\dfrac{(f_o - f_e)^2}{f_e}$ |
|---|---|---|---|---|---|
| Poor or fair/11+ | 53.47 | 65 | 11.53 | 132.94 | 2.49 |
| Good or excellent/11+ | 55.53 | 44 | −11.53 | 132.94 | 2.39 |
| Poor or fair/5–10 | 45.13 | 43 | −2.13 | 4.54 | .10 |
| Good or excellent/5–10 | 46.87 | 49 | 2.13 | 4.54 | .10 |
| Poor or fair/0–4 | 31.40 | 22 | −9.40 | 88.36 | 2.81 |
| Good or excellent/0–4 | 32.60 | 42 | 9.40 | 88.36 | 2.71 |

$$\chi^2 = \sum \frac{(f_o - f_e)^2}{f_e} = 10.60$$

## Step 6. Making a decision and interpreting the results

The obtained $\chi^2$, 10.60, exceeds the critical $\chi^2$, 5.991. We can reject the null hypothesis and conclude that there may be a relationship between the number of years since graduation and the rating given to the major. Sociology programs may have improved in the development of mathematical and statistical skills.

Notice that our calculation resulted in a $\chi^2$ value of 10.60, which differs from that in Table 16.6 ($\chi^2 = 10.41$). The difference of .19 is probably due to rounding as the researchers undoubtedly used a statistical program to do their calculations.

for understanding the subject matter of the major approached statistical significance."[10] In other words, the researchers would like us to believe that these results were almost significant. Although statements like this are not rare in research reports, they are improper. There is no such thing as an almost significant result. The logic of hypothesis testing dictates that either the null hypothesis is rejected or it is not, and there is no gray area in between. The researchers should have reported "$p$ = ns" for all three of the skills.

Does the lack of a significant result indicate that sociology programs are doing poorly in developing the skill in question? Does a significant finding indicate they are doing well? We need to analyze the results to answer these questions. For example, the chi-square statistic for subject matter of the major was not significant, indicating that the percentage of alumni who rate their major highly in this area has not increased. But let's look at the percentages shown in Table 16.6. Notice that a high percentage of the alumni graduating 11+ years ago (78.4%) felt their major did a good or excellent job of developing the skill. We would conclude that sociology programs have always performed pretty well in developing this skill and would not expect to see significant improvement.

> **Learning Check.**   *Analyze the results for the remaining four skills. Where is improvement necessary? Where is it less critical?*

## Gender Differences in Ratings of Foundational Skills, Occupational Prestige, and Income

The final research question explored by Velasco et al. concerned gender differences in alumni ratings of foundational skills, occupational prestige, and income. A foundational skills index was constructed by summing the responses for the five categories of skills for each alumnus. The index ranged from 5 to 20, and the mean index score was calculated for each of the disciplines by gender. Occupational prestige was coded using a recognized scale and job titles provided by respondents. Information on income was gathered by asking respondents to report their approximate annual income.

Table 16.7 shows the mean, standard deviation, and $t$ for each of the variables by discipline and gender. The researchers used $t$ tests for

---

[10]Velasco et al., p. 65.

Table 16.7 **Indicated Means and *t* Tests by Gender for Alumni from Each Major**

|  | Males | | Females | | |
|---|---|---|---|---|---|
|  | **Mean** | **SD** | **Mean** | **SD** | ***t*** |
| **Foundational skills index** | | | | | |
| Anthropology | 14.28 | 2.80 | 13.58 | 2.83 | 1.56 |
| Economics | 15.09 | 2.74 | 15.49 | 2.83 | −1.08 |
| Political science | 12.98 | 3.08 | 12.67 | 3.36 | .64 |
| Psychology | 15.23 | 2.84 | 14.42 | 2.22 | 2.06* |
| Sociology | 13.67 | 2.74 | 13.52 | 3.19 | .40 |
| **Occupational prestige** | | | | | |
| Anthropology | 49.83 | 14.01 | 48.75 | 11.04 | .53 |
| Economics | 49.94 | 10.53 | 51.42 | 8.90 | −1.08 |
| Political science | 48.19 | 10.18 | 49.54 | 9.05 | −.93 |
| Psychology | 49.37 | 10.43 | 49.56 | 9.22 | −.13 |
| Sociology | 47.27 | 10.32 | 48.81 | 9.45 | −1.25 |
| **Income (in thousands of dollars)** | | | | | |
| Anthropology | 32.78 | 22.10 | 23.30 | 13.78 | 3.15** |
| Economics | 40.09 | 22.73 | 31.43 | 15.44 | 3.53*** |
| Political science | 38.52 | 43.01 | 25.96 | 8.60 | 3.42*** |
| Psychology | 34.03 | 26.61 | 24.71 | 13.90 | 2.70** |
| Sociology | 39.36 | 44.40 | 25.66 | 10.47 | 3.13** |

*Source:* Adapted from Steven C. Velasco, Susan E. Stockdale, and David J. Scrams, "Sociology and Other Social Sciences: California State University Alumni Ratings of the BA Degree for Development of Employment Skills." *Teaching Sociology,* Vol. 20, January 1992, 60–70.
*$p < .05$
**$p < .01$
***$p < .001$

the difference between means because the variances were all estimated and the variables were measured at the interval-ratio level. Significant *t*'s are indicated by asterisks, with the number of asterisks indicating the highest level at which the statistic is significant. One asterisk indicates the .05 level, two asterisks indicate the .01 level, and three asterisks indicate the .001 level.

The mean ratings of foundational skills show that among males, psychology received the highest average rating (15.23), followed in order by economics (15.09), anthropology (14.28), sociology (13.67), and political science (12.98). Among females, economics received the highest average foundational skill rating (15.49) and political science received the lowest rating (12.67). Only one major, psychology, shows a significant difference between the mean ratings given by male and female alumni.

## Box 16.8 Occupational Prestige of Male and Female Sociology Alumni: Another Example Using a t Test

The means, standard deviations, and sample sizes necessary to calculate $t$ for occupational prestige as shown in Table 16.7 are shown below:

|         | Mean  | SD    | N   |
|---------|-------|-------|-----|
| Males   | 47.27 | 10.32 | 105 |
| Females | 48.81 | 9.45  | 162 |

### Step 1. Making assumptions

1. Independent random samples
2. Level of measurement of the variable "occupational prestige": interval-ratio
3. Population variances unknown but assumed equal
4. Because $N_M > 50$ and $N_F > 50$, the assumption of normal population is not required.

### Step 2. Stating the research and the null hypotheses

Our hypothesis will be nondirectional because we have no basis for assuming the occupational prestige of one group is higher than the occupational prestige of the other group:

$$H_1: \mu_{Y_M} \neq \mu_{Y_F}$$
$$H_0: \mu_{Y_M} = \mu_{Y_F}$$

### Step 3. Selecting a sampling distribution and a test statistic

We will analyze data measured at the interval-ratio level with estimated variances assumed equal.

Sampling distribution: $t$ distribution
Test statistic: $t$

### Step 4. Choosing alpha and establishing the region of rejection

$$\alpha = .05$$
$$df = (N_M + N_F) - 2 = (105 + 162) - 2 = 265$$
$$\text{Critical } t = \pm 1.96$$

### Step 5. Computing the test statistic

The formulas we need to calculate $t$ are

$$t = \frac{\overline{Y}_M - \overline{Y}_F}{S_{\overline{Y}_M - \overline{Y}_F}}$$

$$S_{\bar{Y}_M - \bar{Y}_F} = \sqrt{\frac{(N_M - 1)S_M^2 + (N_F - 1)S_F^2}{(N_M + N_F) - 2}} \sqrt{\frac{N_M + N_F}{N_M N_F}}$$

First, calculate the standard deviation of the sampling distribution:

$$S_{\bar{Y}_M - \bar{Y}_F} = \sqrt{\frac{(104)(10.32)^2 + (161)(9.45)^2}{(105 + 162) - 2}} \sqrt{\frac{105 + 162}{(105)(162)}}$$

$$= \sqrt{\frac{11,076.25 + 14,377.70}{265}} \sqrt{\frac{267}{17,010}}$$

$$= 9.801(.125) = 1.23$$

Then plug this figure into the formula for $t$:

$$t = \frac{47.27 - 48.81}{1.23} = \frac{-1.54}{1.23} = -1.25$$

**Step 6. Making a decision and interpreting the results**
The obtained $t$, $-1.25$ (which is the same as the $t$ shown in Table 16.7), is less extreme than the critical $t$, $\pm 1.96$. We cannot reject the null hypothesis, and we must conclude that there is no difference in occupational prestige between male and female sociology alumni.

---

The mean occupational prestige scores are similar across disciplines within genders. They are also similar across genders within disciplines. The results of the $t$ tests show no significant differences between the mean occupational prestige scores for male and female alumni from any major. In Box 16.8 we use the process of statistical hypothesis testing to calculate $t$ for occupational prestige among sociology alumni.

Economics majors have the highest mean annual income for both males ($40,090) and females ($31,430); anthropology majors have the lowest mean incomes (males, $32,780; females, $23,300). The results of the $t$ tests (for directional tests) show that the mean income of male alumni is significantly higher than the mean income of female alumni for each majors. This finding is not surprising given that we know that women typically earn less than men. It is interesting, however, since no significant differences were found between the mean ratings of occupational prestige of male and female alumni. This may indicate that females are paid less than males for similar work.

## Conclusion

We hope that this book has increased your understanding of the social world and helped you to develop your "foundational skills" in statistics.

As an undergraduate, you may need to use your statistics skills to complete a research project for a methods class; you almost certainly will be exposed to research reports that use the techniques you have learned. If you choose to pursue a graduate degree, the principles and procedures you have learned here will serve as the basis for more advanced statistics classes you will probably be required to take. If you choose a career in the social sciences, you may be required to conduct research, analyze data, or interpret the research reports of others. Even if you are not required to use statistics in your educational or occupational endeavors, your knowledge of statistics will help you to be a more knowledgeable consumer of the wide array of information we use in daily life.

## EXERCISES

1. The 1987–1988 National Survey of Families and Households found, in a sample of 6,645 married couples, that the average length a marriage had lasted was 205 months (about 17 years), with a standard deviation of 181 months. Assume that the distribution of marriage length is approximately normally distributed.
   a. What proportion of marriages lasts between 10 and 20 years?
   b. A marriage that lasts 50 years is commonly viewed as exceptional. What is the percentile rank of a marriage that lasts 50 years? Do you believe this justifies the idea that such a marriage is exceptional?
   c. What is the probability that a marriage will last over 30 years?
   d. Is there statistical evidence (from the data in this exercise) to lead you to question the assumption that length of marriage is normally distributed?

2. The 1994 National Election Study included a question on whether federal funding for AIDS research should be increased or decreased or stay about the same. Responses to this question are most likely related to many demographic and other attitudinal measures. The following table, created in SPSS, shows the relationship between this item and the respondent's political preference in five categories.
   a. Describe the relationship in this table by calculating appropriate percentages.

b. Test at the .01 significance level political preference and attitude toward AIDS funding are unrelated.

c. Are all the assumptions of doing a chi-square test met?

```
V821   94PO: AIDS RESEARCH -FED SPENDING (H1E.)
by V652 94PO: R REPUB, DEM OR INDEP (E11.)
                   V652                               Page 1 of 1
           Count |
                 |
                 | REPUBLIC   INDEPEND   NO PREFE   OTHER PA   DEMOCRAT
                 | AN         ENT        RENCE      RTY                  |  Row
                 |     1    +    2    +    3    +    4    +    5    +  Total
V821    ---------+---------+-------+-------+-------+-------+
          1 |      199  |    284  |    59   |    2    |   338   |   882
INCREASED        |                                                    50.7
                 +---------+-------+-------+-------+-------+
          2 |      230  |    165  |    31   |    2    |   190   |   618
SAME             +---------+-------+-------+-------+-------+   35.5
          3 |      111  |     73  |    11   |         |    44   |   239
DECREASED        |         |       |        |         |        |   13.7
                 +---------+-------+-------+-------+-------+
           Column      540       522       101         4        572       1739
           Total       31.1      30.0       5.8        .2       32.9      100.0
```

3. To investigate further the determinants for funding of AIDS research, the previous table is broken into the following two subtables for whites and blacks. Use them to answer these questions.

a. Test at the .05 significance level the relationship between political preference and support for AIDS research funding in each table. Are the results consistent or different by race?

b. Is race an intervening control variable, or is it acting to specify the relationship between political preference and attitude toward AIDS funding?

c. If the assumptions of calculating chi-square are not met in these tables, how might you group the categories of political preference to do a satisfactory test? Do this and recalculate chi-square in both tables. What do you find now?

d. Can you suggest substantive reasons for the differences between whites and blacks?

## WHITES ONLY

| | V652 | | | | | Page 1 of 1 |
|---|---|---|---|---|---|---|

| Count | REPUBLIC AN | INDEPEND ENT | NO PREFE RENCE | OTHER PA RTY | DEMOCRAT | Row |
|---|---|---|---|---|---|---|
| | 1 | 2 | 3 | 4 | 5 | Total |
| V821 1 INCREASED | 182 | 228 | 52 | 1 | 245 | 708 48.0 |
| 2 SAME | 217 | 152 | 26 | 2 | 161 | 558 37.8 |
| 3 DECREASED | 106 | 62 | 9 | | 32 | 209 14.2 |
| Column Total | 505 34.2 | 442 30.0 | 87 5.9 | 3 .2 | 438 29.7 | 1475 100.0 |

## BLACKS ONLY

| | V652 | | | | | Page 1 of 1 |
|---|---|---|---|---|---|---|

| Count | REPUBLIC AN | INDEPEND ENT | NO PREFE RENCE | OTHER PA RTY | DEMOCRAT | Row |
|---|---|---|---|---|---|---|
| | 1 | 2 | 3 | 4 | 5 | Total |
| V821 1 INCREASED | 5 | 45 | 5 | 1 | 84 | 140 74.9 |
| 2 SAME | 2 | 6 | 1 | | 20 | 29 15.5 |
| 3 DECREASED | 1 | 8 | 2 | | 7 | 18 9.6 |
| Column Total | 8 4.3 | 59 31.6 | 8 4.3 | 1 .5 | 111 59.4 | 187 100.0 |

4. A large labor union is planning a survey of its members to ask their opinion on several important issues. The members work in large, medium, and small-sized firms. Assume that there are 50,000 members in large companies, 35,000 in medium-sized firms, and 5,000 in small firms.
   a. If the labor union takes a proportionate stratified sample of their members of size 1,000, how many union members will be chosen from medium-sized firms?
   b. If one member is selected at random from the population, what is the probability that she will be from a small firm?

c. The union decides to take a disproportionate stratified sample with equal numbers of members from each size of firm (to make sure a sufficient number of members from small firms are included). If a sample size of 900 is used, how many members from small firms will be in the sample?

5. The Census Bureau reported that in 1991 66.9 percent of all Hispanic households were two-parent households. You are studying a large city in the Southwest and have taken a random sample of the households in the city for your study. You find that only 59.5 percent of all Hispanic households had two parents in your sample of 400.
   a. What is the 95 percent confidence interval for your population estimate of 59.5 percent?
   b. Do a test to determine whether the city's percentage of Hispanic two-parent households is significantly lower than the U.S. population figure. Set up appropriate research and null hypotheses and test at the .01 level.

6. It is often said that there is a relationship between religious belief and education, such that belief declines as education increases. On the other hand, the recent revival of fundamentalism may have weakened this relationship. The 1994 National Election Study data can be used to investigate this question. One item asked whether religion was important to the respondent, with possible responses of either "Yes" or "No." We find that those who answered yes have 12.96 mean years of education, with a standard deviation of 2.61; those who answered no have 13.36 mean years of education, with a standard deviation of 2.44. Altogether, 775 answered yes and 252 no.
   a. Using a two-tailed test, test at the .05 level the null hypothesis that there is no difference in years of education between those who do and those who don't find religion personally important.
   b. Now do the same test at the .01 level. If the conclusion is different from that (a), is it possible to state that one of these two tests is somehow better or more correct than the other? Why or why not?

7. Often, the same data can be studied with more than one type of statistical test. The following table displays the relationship between gender and whether the respondent approves or disapproves of Congress, with data taken from the 1994 National Election Study.

| Approval of Congress | Gender | |
| --- | --- | --- |
| | Male | Female |
| Approve | 249 | 303 |
| Disapprove | 564 | 540 |
| Total | 813 | 843 |

It is possible to study this table with both the chi-square statistic and a two-sample test of proportions.

  a. Conduct a chi-square test at the .01 level of the null hypothesis that females are more likely to disapprove of Congress than males.

  b. Conduct a two-sample proportion test at the .01 level to determine whether males and females differ in their disapproval of Congress.

  c. Construct a 95 percent confidence interval for the percentage of all respondents, both male and female, who disapprove of Congress.

  d. Were your conclusions similar or different in the two tests in (a) and (b)?

8. People who are self-employed are often thought to work more hours per week than those who are not self-employed. Study this question with data from 1994. Those who are self-employed (137 respondents) worked 44.80 hours per week, with a standard deviation of 20.70. Those not self-employed (1,035 respondents) worked an average of 41.69 hours per week, with a standard deviation of 12.21. Assume that the standard deviations are not equal.

  a. Test at the .05 level with a one-tailed test the hypothesis that the self-employed work more hours than others.

  b. The standard workweek is often thought to be 40 hours. Do a one-sample test to see whether those who are not self-employed work more than 40 hours at the .10 alpha level.

9. The Panel Study of Income Dynamics is a large ongoing survey that was developed to help us understand the functioning of the labor market. Data from the 1985 survey found that black males had an average hourly wage of $7.69, with a standard deviation of $3.96 (this from a sample of 395).

  a. Construct the 99 percent confidence interval for the mean hourly wage of black males in 1985.

  b. Is an appropriate interpretation that 99 percent of all black males have incomes within the calculated interval? Explain why or why not. If this is not a correct interpretation, provide one instead.

10. Ratings of the job being done by individuals can often differ from the overall job done by the organization to whom they belong. In an NBC/*Wall Street Journal* poll in October 1991, 60 percent of the respondents said that "In general, they disapproved of the job Congress is doing," whereas 40 percent approved. In an ABC/*Washington Post* poll done that same month, 70 percent of the respondents "Approved of the way your own representative to the U.S. House in Congress is handling his or her job," whereas 30 percent disapproved. The first poll contacted 716 people, and the second contacted 1,398.
   a. Test at the .01 level the null hypothesis that there is no difference in the approval ratings of Congress and individual representatives.
   b. If you find a difference, suggest reasons why people can believe their own representative is doing a good job but not the Congress as a whole. Try to think of reasons why there might be a difference even if the individual representative is performing similarly to his or her colleagues.

11. The National Survey of Families and Households in 1987/88 included several questions on the dissolution of marriages. One question asked, "Were you involved with someone else just before your marriage ended?" For non-Hispanic whites, 16.5 percent, or 141, of 855 males surveyed answered yes, whereas 163 of 1,143 females, or 14.3 percent, answered yes (these females and males were *not* married to each other). Based on this information, answer these questions.
   a. Do males and females differ in their reported involvement with someone other than their spouse? Test at the .01 level.
   b. Construct a 95 percent confidence interval for the U.S. non-Hispanic white population for the percentage of people who were involved with someone just before their marriage ended.

12. The MMPI test is used extensively by psychologists to provide information on personality traits and potential problems of individuals undergoing counseling. The test measures nine primary dimensions of personality, with each dimension represented by a scale normed to have a mean score of 50 and a standard deviation of 10 in the adult population. One primary scale measures paranoid tendencies. Assume the scale scores are normally distributed.
   a. What percentage of the population should have a Paranoia scale score above 70? A score of 70 is viewed as "elevated" or abnormal by the MMPI test developers. Based on your statistical calculation, do you agree?

b. What percentile rank does a score of 45 correspond to?

c. What range of scores, centered around the mean of 50, should include 75 percent of the population?

13. The 1994 National Election Study included a few questions that asked whether the respondent felt things are going to be better or worse next year, or have improved or gotten worse over the past year, for both the United States as a whole and the respondent himself or herself. The following table displays the relationship between answers to whether the respondent is doing better or worse than a year ago by marital status.

a. Describe the relationship between marital status and belief that things have improved or not by calculating appropriate percentages.

b. Test whether these two characteristics are related at the .05 level.

c. Offer some substantive reasons for the relationship you observe in the table.

| Better or Worse Off Than a Year Ago | Marital Status | | | | |
|---|---|---|---|---|---|
| | Married | Never Married | Divorced | Separated | Widowed |
| Better Off | 414 | 151 | 42 | 21 | 21 |
| Same | 388 | 83 | 48 | 8 | 63 |
| Worse Off | 276 | 90 | 57 | 16 | 40 |

## SPSS PROBLEMS

1. Three questions in the 1987–1991 GSS file are concerned with tolerance toward ideas from members of deviant groups. LIBCOM, LIBHOMO, and LIBRAC ask, respectively, whether a book by a communist (remember, this was before the end of the Cold War), homosexual, or racist should be retained or removed from a community library. Investigate the relationship between these questions and education, coded into four broad categories (EDLEV4). Calculate an appropriate statistical test and describe the relationships you find. Also, describe any differences in the relationships between education and the three attitudes.

2. The same relationships can be studied with tests of mean differences by using the variable EDUC that measures education in years.

   a. Test the null hypothesis that there is no difference in years of education between those who want a book removed and those who do not for the three attitude items. Do the test at the .05 level of significance.

   b. Are your results consistent with what you found in SPSS problem 1?

3. The variable TRAUMA5 measures the number of self-reported traumas of all types a respondent has experienced in the past five years. Use it to answer these questions.

   a. Calculate a 90 percent confidence interval for TRAUMA5 and provide an interpretation.

   b. A social scientist tells you that her data from the 1970s showed that the U.S. population experienced .90 traumas over a five-year period in that decade. Test whether the mean number of traumas has increased among respondents in the 1987–1991 GSS file.

   c. Study whether general happiness (HAPPY) varies with the number of traumas someone has experienced (it seems reasonable to suppose that as the number of traumas increases, happiness might decrease). Use whatever techniques are appropriate to study this relationship. (*Hint:* Although the variable HAPPY has three categories, you can use SPSS to compare only two categories at a time.)

# Appendix A
# Table of Random Numbers

## A Table of 14,000 Random Units

| Line/Col. | (1) | (2) | (3) | (4) | (5) | (6) | (7) | (8) | (9) | (10) | (11) | (12) | (13) | (14) |
|---|---|---|---|---|---|---|---|---|---|---|---|---|---|---|
| 1 | 10480 | 15011 | 01536 | 02011 | 81647 | 91646 | 69179 | 14194 | 62590 | 36207 | 20969 | 99570 | 91291 | 90700 |
| 2 | 22368 | 46573 | 25595 | 85393 | 30995 | 89198 | 27982 | 53402 | 93965 | 34095 | 52666 | 19174 | 39615 | 99505 |
| 3 | 24130 | 48360 | 22527 | 97265 | 76393 | 64809 | 15179 | 24830 | 49340 | 32081 | 30680 | 19655 | 63348 | 58629 |
| 4 | 42167 | 93093 | 06243 | 61680 | 07856 | 16376 | 39440 | 53537 | 71341 | 57004 | 00849 | 74917 | 97758 | 16379 |
| 5 | 37570 | 39975 | 81837 | 16656 | 06121 | 91782 | 60468 | 81305 | 49684 | 60672 | 14110 | 06927 | 01263 | 54613 |
| 6 | 77921 | 06907 | 11008 | 42751 | 27756 | 53498 | 18602 | 70659 | 90655 | 15053 | 21916 | 81825 | 44394 | 42880 |
| 7 | 99562 | 72905 | 56420 | 69994 | 98872 | 31016 | 71194 | 18738 | 44013 | 48840 | 63213 | 21069 | 10634 | 12952 |
| 8 | 96301 | 91977 | 05463 | 07972 | 18876 | 20922 | 94595 | 56869 | 69014 | 60045 | 18425 | 84903 | 42508 | 32307 |
| 9 | 89579 | 14342 | 63661 | 10281 | 17453 | 18103 | 57740 | 84378 | 25331 | 12566 | 58678 | 44947 | 05585 | 56941 |
| 10 | 85475 | 36857 | 43342 | 53988 | 53060 | 59533 | 38867 | 62300 | 08158 | 17983 | 16439 | 11458 | 18593 | 64952 |
| 11 | 28918 | 69578 | 88231 | 33276 | 70997 | 79936 | 56865 | 05859 | 90106 | 31595 | 01547 | 85590 | 91610 | 78188 |
| 12 | 63553 | 40961 | 48235 | 03427 | 49626 | 69445 | 18663 | 72695 | 52180 | 20847 | 12234 | 90511 | 33703 | 90322 |
| 13 | 09429 | 93969 | 52636 | 92737 | 88974 | 33488 | 36320 | 17617 | 30015 | 08272 | 84115 | 27156 | 30613 | 74952 |
| 14 | 10365 | 61129 | 87529 | 85689 | 48237 | 52267 | 67689 | 93394 | 01511 | 26358 | 85104 | 20285 | 29975 | 89868 |
| 15 | 07119 | 97336 | 71048 | 08178 | 77233 | 13916 | 47564 | 81056 | 97735 | 85977 | 29372 | 74461 | 28551 | 90707 |
| 16 | 51085 | 12765 | 51821 | 51259 | 77452 | 16308 | 60756 | 92144 | 49442 | 53900 | 70960 | 63990 | 75601 | 40719 |
| 17 | 02368 | 21382 | 52404 | 60268 | 89368 | 19885 | 55322 | 44819 | 01188 | 65255 | 64835 | 44919 | 05944 | 55157 |
| 18 | 01011 | 54092 | 33362 | 94904 | 31273 | 04146 | 18594 | 29852 | 71585 | 85030 | 51132 | 01915 | 92747 | 64951 |
| 19 | 52162 | 53916 | 46369 | 58586 | 23216 | 14513 | 83149 | 98736 | 23495 | 64350 | 94738 | 17752 | 35156 | 35749 |
| 20 | 07056 | 97628 | 33787 | 09998 | 42698 | 06691 | 76988 | 13602 | 51851 | 46104 | 88916 | 19509 | 25625 | 58104 |
| 21 | 48663 | 91245 | 85828 | 14346 | 09172 | 30168 | 90229 | 04734 | 59193 | 22178 | 30421 | 61666 | 99904 | 32812 |
| 22 | 54164 | 58492 | 22421 | 74103 | 47070 | 25306 | 76468 | 26384 | 58151 | 06646 | 21524 | 15227 | 96909 | 44592 |
| 23 | 32639 | 32363 | 05597 | 24200 | 13363 | 38005 | 94342 | 28728 | 35806 | 06912 | 17012 | 64161 | 18296 | 22851 |
| 24 | 29334 | 27001 | 87637 | 87308 | 58731 | 00256 | 45834 | 15398 | 46557 | 41135 | 10367 | 07684 | 36188 | 18510 |
| 25 | 02488 | 33062 | 28834 | 07351 | 19731 | 92420 | 60952 | 61280 | 50001 | 67658 | 32586 | 86679 | 50720 | 94953 |
| 26 | 81525 | 72295 | 04839 | 96423 | 24878 | 82651 | 66566 | 14778 | 76797 | 14780 | 13300 | 87074 | 79666 | 95725 |
| 27 | 29676 | 20591 | 68086 | 26432 | 46901 | 20849 | 89768 | 81536 | 86645 | 12659 | 92259 | 57102 | 80428 | 25280 |
| 28 | 00742 | 57392 | 39064 | 66432 | 84673 | 40027 | 32832 | 61362 | 98947 | 96067 | 64760 | 64584 | 96096 | 98253 |
| 29 | 05366 | 04213 | 25669 | 26422 | 44407 | 44048 | 37937 | 63904 | 45766 | 66134 | 75470 | 66520 | 34693 | 90449 |
| 30 | 91921 | 26418 | 64117 | 94305 | 26766 | 25940 | 39972 | 22209 | 71500 | 64568 | 91402 | 42416 | 07844 | 69618 |
| 31 | 00582 | 04711 | 87917 | 77341 | 42206 | 35126 | 74087 | 99547 | 81817 | 42607 | 43808 | 76655 | 62028 | 76630 |
| 32 | 00725 | 69884 | 62797 | 56170 | 86324 | 88072 | 76222 | 36086 | 84637 | 93161 | 76038 | 65855 | 77919 | 88006 |
| 33 | 69011 | 65797 | 95876 | 55293 | 18988 | 27354 | 26575 | 08625 | 40801 | 59920 | 29841 | 80150 | 12777 | 48501 |
| 34 | 25976 | 57948 | 29888 | 88604 | 67917 | 48708 | 18912 | 82271 | 65424 | 69774 | 33611 | 54262 | 85963 | 03547 |
| 35 | 09763 | 83473 | 73577 | 12908 | 30883 | 18317 | 28290 | 35797 | 05998 | 41688 | 34952 | 37888 | 38917 | 88050 |

*Source:* William H. Beyer, ed., *Handbook for Probability and Statistics,* 2nd ed. Copyright © 1966 CRC Press, Boca Raton, Florida. Used by permission.

| Line/Col. | (1) | (2) | (3) | (4) | (5) | (6) | (7) | (8) | (9) | (10) | (11) | (12) | (13) | (14) |
|---|---|---|---|---|---|---|---|---|---|---|---|---|---|---|
| 36 | 91567 | 42595 | 27958 | 30134 | 04024 | 86385 | 29880 | 99730 | 55536 | 84855 | 29080 | 09250 | 79656 | 73211 |
| 37 | 17955 | 56349 | 90999 | 49127 | 20044 | 59931 | 06115 | 20542 | 18059 | 02008 | 73708 | 83317 | 36103 | 42791 |
| 38 | 46503 | 18584 | 18845 | 49618 | 02304 | 51038 | 20655 | 58727 | 28168 | 15475 | 56942 | 53389 | 20562 | 87338 |
| 39 | 92157 | 89634 | 94824 | 78171 | 84610 | 82834 | 09922 | 25417 | 44137 | 48413 | 25555 | 21246 | 35509 | 20468 |
| 40 | 14577 | 62765 | 35605 | 81263 | 39667 | 47358 | 56873 | 56307 | 61607 | 49518 | 89656 | 20103 | 77490 | 18062 |
| 41 | 98427 | 07523 | 33362 | 64270 | 01638 | 92477 | 66969 | 98420 | 04880 | 45585 | 46565 | 04102 | 46880 | 45709 |
| 42 | 34914 | 63976 | 88720 | 82765 | 34476 | 17032 | 87589 | 40836 | 32427 | 70002 | 70663 | 88863 | 77775 | 69348 |
| 43 | 70060 | 28277 | 39475 | 46473 | 23219 | 53416 | 94970 | 25832 | 69975 | 94884 | 19661 | 72828 | 00102 | 66794 |
| 44 | 53976 | 54914 | 06990 | 67245 | 68350 | 82948 | 11398 | 42878 | 80287 | 88267 | 47363 | 46634 | 06541 | 97809 |
| 45 | 76072 | 29515 | 40980 | 07391 | 58745 | 25774 | 22987 | 80059 | 39911 | 96189 | 41151 | 14222 | 60697 | 59583 |
| 46 | 90725 | 52210 | 83974 | 29992 | 65831 | 38857 | 50490 | 83765 | 55657 | 14361 | 31720 | 57375 | 56228 | 41546 |
| 47 | 64364 | 67412 | 33339 | 31926 | 14883 | 24413 | 59744 | 92351 | 97473 | 89286 | 35931 | 04110 | 23726 | 51900 |
| 48 | 08962 | 00358 | 31662 | 25388 | 61642 | 34072 | 81249 | 35648 | 56891 | 69352 | 48373 | 45578 | 78547 | 81788 |
| 49 | 95012 | 68379 | 93526 | 70765 | 10593 | 04542 | 76463 | 54328 | 02349 | 17247 | 28865 | 14777 | 62730 | 92277 |
| 50 | 15664 | 10493 | 20492 | 38391 | 91132 | 21999 | 59516 | 81652 | 27195 | 48223 | 46751 | 22923 | 32261 | 85653 |
| 51 | 16408 | 81899 | 04153 | 53381 | 79401 | 21438 | 83035 | 92350 | 36693 | 31238 | 59649 | 91754 | 72772 | 02338 |
| 52 | 18629 | 81953 | 05520 | 91962 | 04739 | 13092 | 97662 | 24822 | 94730 | 06496 | 35090 | 04822 | 86772 | 98289 |
| 53 | 73115 | 35101 | 47498 | 87637 | 99016 | 71060 | 88824 | 71013 | 18735 | 20286 | 23153 | 72924 | 35165 | 43040 |
| 54 | 57491 | 16703 | 23167 | 49323 | 45021 | 33132 | 12544 | 41035 | 80780 | 45393 | 44812 | 12515 | 98931 | 91202 |
| 55 | 30405 | 83946 | 23792 | 14422 | 15059 | 45799 | 22716 | 19792 | 09983 | 74353 | 68668 | 30429 | 70735 | 25499 |
| 56 | 16631 | 35006 | 85900 | 98275 | 32388 | 52390 | 16815 | 69298 | 82732 | 38480 | 73817 | 32523 | 41961 | 44437 |
| 57 | 96773 | 20206 | 42559 | 78985 | 05300 | 22164 | 24369 | 54224 | 35083 | 19687 | 11052 | 91491 | 60383 | 19746 |
| 58 | 38935 | 64202 | 14349 | 82674 | 66523 | 44133 | 00697 | 35552 | 35970 | 19124 | 63318 | 29686 | 03387 | 59846 |
| 59 | 31624 | 76384 | 17403 | 53363 | 44167 | 64486 | 64758 | 75366 | 76554 | 31601 | 12614 | 33072 | 60332 | 92325 |
| 60 | 78919 | 19474 | 23632 | 27889 | 47914 | 02584 | 37680 | 20801 | 72152 | 39339 | 34806 | 08930 | 85001 | 87820 |
| 61 | 03931 | 33309 | 57047 | 74211 | 63445 | 17361 | 62825 | 39908 | 05607 | 91284 | 68833 | 25570 | 38818 | 46920 |
| 62 | 74426 | 33278 | 43972 | 10119 | 89917 | 15665 | 52872 | 73823 | 73144 | 88662 | 88970 | 74492 | 51805 | 99378 |
| 63 | 09066 | 00903 | 20795 | 95452 | 92648 | 45454 | 09552 | 88815 | 16553 | 51125 | 79375 | 97596 | 16296 | 66092 |
| 64 | 42238 | 12426 | 87025 | 14267 | 20979 | 04508 | 64535 | 31355 | 86064 | 29472 | 47689 | 05974 | 52468 | 16834 |
| 65 | 16153 | 08002 | 26504 | 41744 | 81959 | 65642 | 74240 | 56302 | 00033 | 67107 | 77510 | 70625 | 28725 | 34191 |
| 66 | 21457 | 40742 | 29820 | 96783 | 29400 | 21840 | 15035 | 34537 | 33310 | 06116 | 95240 | 15957 | 16572 | 06004 |
| 67 | 21581 | 57802 | 02050 | 89728 | 17937 | 37621 | 47075 | 42080 | 97403 | 48626 | 68995 | 43805 | 33386 | 21597 |
| 68 | 55612 | 78095 | 83197 | 33732 | 05810 | 24813 | 86902 | 60397 | 16489 | 03264 | 88525 | 42786 | 05269 | 92532 |
| 69 | 44657 | 66999 | 99324 | 51281 | 84463 | 60563 | 79312 | 93454 | 68876 | 25471 | 93911 | 25650 | 12682 | 73572 |
| 70 | 91340 | 84979 | 46949 | 81973 | 37949 | 61023 | 43997 | 15263 | 80644 | 43942 | 89203 | 71795 | 99533 | 50501 |
| 71 | 91227 | 21199 | 31935 | 27022 | 84067 | 05462 | 35216 | 14486 | 29891 | 68607 | 41867 | 14951 | 91696 | 85065 |
| 72 | 50001 | 38140 | 66321 | 19924 | 72163 | 09538 | 12151 | 06878 | 91903 | 18749 | 34405 | 56087 | 82790 | 70925 |
| 73 | 65390 | 05224 | 72958 | 28609 | 81406 | 39147 | 25549 | 48542 | 42627 | 45233 | 57202 | 94617 | 23772 | 07896 |
| 74 | 27504 | 96131 | 83944 | 41575 | 10573 | 08619 | 64482 | 73923 | 36152 | 05184 | 94142 | 25299 | 84387 | 34925 |
| 75 | 37169 | 94851 | 39117 | 89632 | 00959 | 16487 | 65536 | 49071 | 39782 | 17095 | 02330 | 74301 | 00275 | 48280 |
| 76 | 11508 | 70225 | 51111 | 38351 | 19444 | 66499 | 71945 | 05422 | 13442 | 78675 | 84081 | 66938 | 93654 | 59894 |
| 77 | 37449 | 30362 | 06694 | 54690 | 04052 | 53115 | 62757 | 95348 | 78662 | 11163 | 81651 | 50245 | 34971 | 52924 |
| 78 | 46515 | 70331 | 85922 | 38329 | 57015 | 15765 | 97161 | 17869 | 45349 | 61796 | 66345 | 81073 | 49106 | 79860 |
| 79 | 30986 | 81223 | 42416 | 58353 | 21532 | 30502 | 32305 | 86482 | 05174 | 07901 | 54339 | 58861 | 74818 | 46942 |
| 80 | 63798 | 64995 | 46583 | 09765 | 44160 | 78128 | 83991 | 42865 | 92520 | 83531 | 80377 | 35909 | 81250 | 54238 |
| 81 | 82486 | 84846 | 99254 | 67632 | 43218 | 50076 | 21361 | 64816 | 51202 | 88124 | 41870 | 52689 | 51275 | 83556 |
| 82 | 21885 | 32906 | 92431 | 09060 | 64297 | 51674 | 64126 | 62570 | 26123 | 05155 | 59194 | 52799 | 28225 | 85762 |
| 83 | 60336 | 98782 | 07408 | 53458 | 13564 | 59089 | 26445 | 29789 | 85205 | 41001 | 12535 | 12133 | 14645 | 23541 |
| 84 | 43937 | 46891 | 24010 | 25560 | 86355 | 33941 | 25786 | 54990 | 71899 | 15475 | 95434 | 98227 | 21824 | 19585 |
| 85 | 97656 | 63175 | 89303 | 16275 | 07100 | 92063 | 21942 | 18611 | 47348 | 20203 | 18534 | 03862 | 78095 | 50136 |

| Line/Col. | (1) | (2) | (3) | (4) | (5) | (6) | (7) | (8) | (9) | (10) | (11) | (12) | (13) | (14) |
|---|---|---|---|---|---|---|---|---|---|---|---|---|---|---|
| 86 | 03299 | 01221 | 05418 | 38982 | 55758 | 92237 | 26759 | 86367 | 21216 | 98442 | 08303 | 56613 | 91511 | 75928 |
| 87 | 79626 | 06486 | 03574 | 17668 | 07785 | 76020 | 79924 | 25651 | 83325 | 88428 | 85076 | 72811 | 22717 | 50585 |
| 88 | 85636 | 68335 | 47539 | 03129 | 65651 | 11977 | 02510 | 26113 | 99447 | 68645 | 34327 | 15152 | 55230 | 93448 |
| 89 | 18039 | 14367 | 61337 | 06177 | 12143 | 46609 | 32989 | 74014 | 64708 | 00533 | 35398 | 58408 | 13261 | 47908 |
| 90 | 08362 | 15656 | 60627 | 36478 | 65648 | 16764 | 53412 | 09013 | 07832 | 41574 | 17639 | 82163 | 60859 | 75567 |
| 91 | 79556 | 29068 | 04142 | 16268 | 15387 | 12856 | 66227 | 38358 | 22478 | 73373 | 88732 | 09443 | 82558 | 05250 |
| 92 | 92608 | 82674 | 27072 | 32534 | 17075 | 27698 | 98204 | 63863 | 11951 | 34648 | 88022 | 56148 | 34925 | 57031 |
| 93 | 23982 | 25835 | 40055 | 67006 | 12293 | 02753 | 14827 | 22235 | 35071 | 99704 | 37543 | 11601 | 35503 | 85171 |
| 94 | 09915 | 96306 | 05908 | 97901 | 28395 | 14186 | 00821 | 80703 | 70426 | 75647 | 76310 | 88717 | 37890 | 40129 |
| 95 | 50937 | 33300 | 26695 | 62247 | 69927 | 76123 | 50842 | 43834 | 86654 | 70959 | 79725 | 93872 | 28117 | 19233 |
| 96 | 42488 | 78077 | 69882 | 61657 | 34136 | 79180 | 97526 | 43092 | 04098 | 73571 | 80799 | 76536 | 71255 | 64239 |
| 97 | 46764 | 86273 | 63003 | 93017 | 31204 | 36692 | 40202 | 35275 | 57306 | 55543 | 53203 | 18098 | 47625 | 88684 |
| 98 | 03237 | 45430 | 55417 | 63282 | 90816 | 17349 | 88298 | 90183 | 36600 | 78406 | 06216 | 95787 | 42579 | 90730 |
| 99 | 86591 | 81482 | 52667 | 61583 | 14972 | 90053 | 89534 | 76036 | 49199 | 43716 | 97548 | 04379 | 46370 | 28672 |
| 100 | 38534 | 01715 | 94964 | 87288 | 65680 | 43772 | 39560 | 12918 | 86537 | 62738 | 19636 | 51132 | 25739 | 56947 |

# Appendix B
# The Standard Normal Table

The values in column A are Z scores. Column B lists the proportion of area between the mean and a given Z. Column C lists the porportion of area beyond a given Z. Only positive Z scores are listed. Because the normal curve is symmetrical, the areas for negative Z scores will be exactly the same as the areas for positive Z scores.

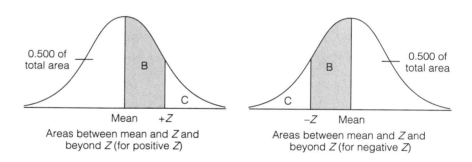

0.500 of total area

Areas between mean and Z and beyond Z (for positive Z)

0.500 of total area

Areas between mean and Z and beyond Z (for negative Z)

| A | B | C | A | B | C | A | B | C |
|---|---|---|---|---|---|---|---|---|
| | Area Between | Area Beyond | | Area Between | Area Beyond | | Area Between | Area Beyond |
| Z | Mean and Z | Z | Z | Mean and Z | Z | Z | Mean and Z | Z |
| 0.00 | 0.0000 | 0.5000 | 0.11 | 0.0438 | 0.4562 | 0.21 | 0.0832 | 0.4168 |
| 0.01 | 0.0040 | 0.4960 | 0.12 | 0.0478 | 0.4522 | 0.22 | 0.0871 | 0.4129 |
| 0.02 | 0.0080 | 0.4920 | 0.13 | 0.0517 | 0.4483 | 0.23 | 0.0910 | 0.4090 |
| 0.03 | 0.0120 | 0.4880 | 0.14 | 0.0557 | 0.4443 | 0.24 | 0.0948 | 0.4052 |
| 0.04 | 0.0160 | 0.4840 | 0.15 | 0.0596 | 0.4404 | 0.25 | 0.0987 | 0.4013 |
| 0.05 | 0.0199 | 0.4801 | 0.16 | 0.0636 | 0.4364 | 0.26 | 0.1026 | 0.3974 |
| 0.06 | 0.0239 | 0.4761 | 0.17 | 0.0675 | 0.4325 | 0.27 | 0.1064 | 0.3936 |
| 0.07 | 0.0279 | 0.4721 | 0.18 | 0.0714 | 0.4286 | 0.28 | 0.1103 | 0.3897 |
| 0.08 | 0.0319 | 0.4681 | 0.19 | 0.0753 | 0.4247 | 0.29 | 0.1141 | 0.3859 |
| 0.09 | 0.0359 | 0.4641 | 0.20 | 0.0793 | 0.4207 | 0.30 | 0.1179 | 0.3821 |
| 0.10 | 0.0398 | 0.4602 | | | | | | |

| A Z | B Area Between Mean and Z | C Area Beyond Z | A Z | B Area Between Mean and Z | C Area Beyond Z | A Z | B Area Between Mean and Z | C Area Beyond Z |
|---|---|---|---|---|---|---|---|---|
| 0.31 | 0.1217 | 0.3783 | 0.61 | 0.2291 | 0.2709 | 0.91 | 0.3186 | 0.1814 |
| 0.32 | 0.1255 | 0.3745 | 0.62 | 0.2324 | 0.2676 | 0.92 | 0.3212 | 0.1788 |
| 0.33 | 0.1293 | 0.3707 | 0.63 | 0.2357 | 0.2643 | 0.93 | 0.3238 | 0.1762 |
| 0.34 | 0.1331 | 0.3669 | 0.64 | 0.2389 | 0.2611 | 0.94 | 0.3264 | 0.1736 |
| 0.35 | 0.1368 | 0.3632 | 0.65 | 0.2422 | 0.2578 | 0.95 | 0.3289 | 0.1711 |
| 0.36 | 0.1406 | 0.3594 | 0.66 | 0.2454 | 0.2546 | 0.96 | 0.3315 | 0.1685 |
| 0.37 | 0.1443 | 0.3557 | 0.67 | 0.2486 | 0.2514 | 0.97 | 0.3340 | 0.1660 |
| 0.38 | 0.1480 | 0.3520 | 0.68 | 0.2517 | 0.2483 | 0.98 | 0.3365 | 0.1635 |
| 0.39 | 0.1517 | 0.3483 | 0.69 | 0.2549 | 0.2451 | 0.99 | 0.3389 | 0.1611 |
| 0.40 | 0.1554 | 0.3446 | 0.70 | 0.2580 | 0.2420 | 1.00 | 0.3413 | 0.1587 |
| 0.41 | 0.1591 | 0.3409 | 0.71 | 0.2611 | 0.2389 | 1.01 | 0.3438 | 0.1562 |
| 0.42 | 0.1628 | 0.3372 | 0.72 | 0.2642 | 0.2358 | 1.02 | 0.3461 | 0.1539 |
| 0.43 | 0.1664 | 0.3336 | 0.73 | 0.2673 | 0.2327 | 1.03 | 0.3485 | 0.1515 |
| 0.44 | 0.1700 | 0.3300 | 0.74 | 0.2703 | 0.2297 | 1.04 | 0.3508 | 0.1492 |
| 0.45 | 0.1736 | 0.3264 | 0.75 | 0.2734 | 0.2266 | 1.05 | 0.3531 | 0.1469 |
| 0.46 | 0.1772 | 0.3228 | 0.76 | 0.2764 | 0.2236 | 1.06 | 0.3554 | 0.1446 |
| 0.47 | 0.1808 | 0.3192 | 0.77 | 0.2794 | 0.2206 | 1.07 | 0.3577 | 0.1423 |
| 0.48 | 0.1844 | 0.3156 | 0.78 | 0.2823 | 0.2177 | 1.08 | 0.3599 | 0.1401 |
| 0.49 | 0.1879 | 0.3121 | 0.79 | 0.2852 | 0.2148 | 1.09 | 0.3621 | 0.1379 |
| 0.50 | 0.1915 | 0.3085 | 0.80 | 0.2881 | 0.2119 | 1.10 | 0.3643 | 0.1357 |
| 0.51 | 0.1950 | 0.3050 | 0.81 | 0.2910 | 0.2090 | 1.11 | 0.3665 | 0.1335 |
| 0.52 | 0.1985 | 0.3015 | 0.82 | 0.2939 | 0.2061 | 1.12 | 0.3686 | 0.1314 |
| 0.53 | 0.2019 | 0.2981 | 0.83 | 0.2967 | 0.2033 | 1.13 | 0.3708 | 0.1292 |
| 0.54 | 0.2054 | 0.2946 | 0.84 | 0.2995 | 0.2005 | 1.14 | 0.3729 | 0.1271 |
| 0.55 | 0.2088 | 0.2912 | 0.85 | 0.3023 | 0.1977 | 1.15 | 0.3749 | 0.1251 |
| 0.56 | 0.2123 | 0.2877 | 0.86 | 0.3051 | 0.1949 | 1.16 | 0.3770 | 0.1230 |
| 0.57 | 0.2157 | 0.2843 | 0.87 | 0.3078 | 0.1922 | 1.17 | 0.3790 | 0.1210 |
| 0.58 | 0.2190 | 0.2810 | 0.88 | 0.3106 | 0.1894 | 1.18 | 0.3810 | 0.1190 |
| 0.59 | 0.2224 | 0.2776 | 0.89 | 0.3133 | 0.1867 | 1.19 | 0.3830 | 0.1170 |
| 0.60 | 0.2257 | 0.2743 | 0.90 | 0.3159 | 0.1841 | 1.20 | 0.3849 | 0.1151 |

| A | B | C | A | B | C | A | B | C |
|---|---|---|---|---|---|---|---|---|
| z | Area Between Mean and z | Area Beyond z | z | Area Between Mean and z | Area Beyond z | z | Area Between Mean and z | Area Beyond z |
| 1.21 | 0.3869 | 0.1131 | 1.51 | 0.4345 | 0.0655 | 1.81 | 0.4649 | 0.0351 |
| 1.22 | 0.3888 | 0.1112 | 1.52 | 0.4357 | 0.0643 | 1.82 | 0.4656 | 0.0344 |
| 1.23 | 0.3907 | 0.1093 | 1.53 | 0.4370 | 0.0630 | 1.83 | 0.4664 | 0.0336 |
| 1.24 | 0.3925 | 0.1075 | 1.54 | 0.4382 | 0.0618 | 1.84 | 0.4671 | 0.0329 |
| 1.25 | 0.3944 | 0.1056 | 1.55 | 0.4394 | 0.0606 | 1.85 | 0.4678 | 0.0322 |
| 1.26 | 0.3962 | 0.1038 | 1.56 | 0.4406 | 0.0594 | 1.86 | 0.4686 | 0.0314 |
| 1.27 | 0.3980 | 0.1020 | 1.57 | 0.4418 | 0.0582 | 1.87 | 0.4693 | 0.0307 |
| 1.28 | 0.3997 | 0.1003 | 1.58 | 0.4429 | 0.0571 | 1.88 | 0.4699 | 0.0301 |
| 1.29 | 0.4015 | 0.0985 | 1.59 | 0.4441 | 0.0559 | 1.89 | 0.4706 | 0.0294 |
| 1.30 | 0.4032 | 0.0968 | 1.60 | 0.4452 | 0.0548 | 1.90 | 0.4713 | 0.0287 |
| 1.31 | 0.4049 | 0.0951 | 1.61 | 0.4463 | 0.0537 | 1.91 | 0.4719 | 0.0281 |
| 1.32 | 0.4066 | 0.0934 | 1.62 | 0.4474 | 0.0526 | 1.92 | 0.4726 | 0.0274 |
| 1.33 | 0.4082 | 0.0918 | 1.63 | 0.4484 | 0.0516 | 1.93 | 0.4732 | 0.0268 |
| 1.34 | 0.4099 | 0.0901 | 1.64 | 0.4495 | 0.0505 | 1.94 | 0.4738 | 0.0262 |
| 1.35 | 0.4115 | 0.0885 | 1.65 | 0.4505 | 0.0495 | 1.95 | 0.4744 | 0.0256 |
| 1.36 | 0.4131 | 0.0869 | 1.66 | 0.4515 | 0.0485 | 1.96 | 0.4750 | 0.0250 |
| 1.37 | 0.4147 | 0.0853 | 1.67 | 0.4525 | 0.0475 | 1.97 | 0.4756 | 0.0244 |
| 1.38 | 0.4162 | 0.0838 | 1.68 | 0.4535 | 0.0465 | 1.98 | 0.4761 | 0.0239 |
| 1.39 | 0.4177 | 0.0823 | 1.69 | 0.4545 | 0.0455 | 1.99 | 0.4767 | 0.0233 |
| 1.40 | 0.4192 | 0.0808 | 1.70 | 0.4554 | 0.0446 | 2.00 | 0.4772 | 0.0228 |
| 1.41 | 0.4207 | 0.0793 | 1.71 | 0.4564 | 0.0436 | 2.01 | 0.4778 | 0.0222 |
| 1.42 | 0.4222 | 0.0778 | 1.72 | 0.4573 | 0.0427 | 2.02 | 0.4783 | 0.0217 |
| 1.43 | 0.4236 | 0.0764 | 1.73 | 0.4582 | 0.0418 | 2.03 | 0.4788 | 0.0212 |
| 1.44 | 0.4251 | 0.0749 | 1.74 | 0.4591 | 0.0409 | 2.04 | 0.4793 | 0.0207 |
| 1.45 | 0.4265 | 0.0735 | 1.75 | 0.4599 | 0.0401 | 2.05 | 0.4798 | 0.0202 |
| 1.46 | 0.4279 | 0.0721 | 1.76 | 0.4608 | 0.0392 | 2.06 | 0.4803 | 0.0197 |
| 1.47 | 0.4292 | 0.0708 | 1.77 | 0.4616 | 0.0384 | 2.07 | 0.4808 | 0.0192 |
| 1.48 | 0.4306 | 0.0694 | 1.78 | 0.4625 | 0.0375 | 2.08 | 0.4812 | 0.0188 |
| 1.49 | 0.4319 | 0.0681 | 1.79 | 0.4633 | 0.0367 | 2.09 | 0.4817 | 0.0183 |
| 1.50 | 0.4332 | 0.0668 | 1.80 | 0.4641 | 0.0359 | 2.10 | 0.4821 | 0.0179 |

| A<br>Z | B<br>Area<br>Between<br>Mean and Z | C<br>Area<br>Beyond<br>Z | A<br>Z | B<br>Area<br>Between<br>Mean and Z | C<br>Area<br>Beyond<br>Z | A<br>Z | B<br>Area<br>Between<br>Mean and Z | C<br>Area<br>Beyond<br>Z |
|---|---|---|---|---|---|---|---|---|
| 2.11 | 0.4826 | 0.0174 | 2.41 | 0.4920 | 0.0080 | 2.71 | 0.4966 | 0.0034 |
| 2.12 | 0.4830 | 0.0170 | 2.42 | 0.4922 | 0.0078 | 2.72 | 0.4967 | 0.0033 |
| 2.13 | 0.4834 | 0.0166 | 2.43 | 0.4925 | 0.0075 | 2.73 | 0.4968 | 0.0032 |
| 2.14 | 0.4838 | 0.0162 | 2.44 | 0.4927 | 0.0073 | 2.74 | 0.4969 | 0.0031 |
| 2.15 | 0.4842 | 0.0158 | 2.45 | 0.4929 | 0.0071 | 2.75 | 0.4970 | 0.0030 |
| 2.16 | 0.4846 | 0.0154 | 2.46 | 0.4931 | 0.0069 | 2.76 | 0.4971 | 0.0029 |
| 2.17 | 0.4850 | 0.0150 | 2.47 | 0.4932 | 0.0068 | 2.77 | 0.4972 | 0.0028 |
| 2.18 | 0.4854 | 0.0146 | 2.48 | 0.4934 | 0.0066 | 2.78 | 0.4973 | 0.0027 |
| 2.19 | 0.4857 | 0.0143 | 2.49 | 0.4936 | 0.0064 | 2.79 | 0.4974 | 0.0026 |
| 2.20 | 0.4861 | 0.0139 | 2.50 | 0.4938 | 0.0062 | 2.80 | 0.4974 | 0.0026 |
| 2.21 | 0.4864 | 0.0136 | 2.51 | 0.4940 | 0.0060 | 2.81 | 0.4975 | 0.0025 |
| 2.22 | 0.4868 | 0.0132 | 2.52 | 0.4941 | 0.0059 | 2.82 | 0.4976 | 0.0024 |
| 2.23 | 0.4871 | 0.0129 | 2.53 | 0.4943 | 0.0057 | 2.83 | 0.4977 | 0.0023 |
| 2.24 | 0.4875 | 0.0125 | 2.54 | 0.4945 | 0.0055 | 2.84 | 0.4977 | 0.0023 |
| 2.25 | 0.4878 | 0.0122 | 2.55 | 0.4946 | 0.0054 | 2.85 | 0.4978 | 0.0022 |
| 2.26 | 0.4881 | 0.0119 | 2.56 | 0.4948 | 0.0052 | 2.86 | 0.4979 | 0.0021 |
| 2.27 | 0.4884 | 0.0116 | 2.57 | 0.4949 | 0.0051 | 2.87 | 0.4979 | 0.0021 |
| 2.28 | 0.4887 | 0.0113 | 2.58 | 0.4951 | 0.0049 | 2.88 | 0.4980 | 0.0020 |
| 2.29 | 0.4890 | 0.0110 | 2.59 | 0.4952 | 0.0048 | 2.89 | 0.4981 | 0.0019 |
| 2.30 | 0.4893 | 0.0107 | 2.60 | 0.4953 | 0.0047 | 2.90 | 0.4981 | 0.0019 |
| 2.31 | 0.4896 | 0.0104 | 2.61 | 0.4955 | 0.0045 | 2.91 | 0.4982 | 0.0018 |
| 2.32 | 0.4898 | 0.0102 | 2.62 | 0.4956 | 0.0044 | 2.92 | 0.4982 | 0.0018 |
| 2.33 | 0.4901 | 0.0099 | 2.63 | 0.4957 | 0.0043 | 2.93 | 0.4983 | 0.0017 |
| 2.34 | 0.4904 | 0.0096 | 2.64 | 0.4959 | 0.0041 | 2.94 | 0.4984 | 0.0016 |
| 2.35 | 0.4906 | 0.0094 | 2.65 | 0.4960 | 0.0040 | 2.95 | 0.4984 | 0.0016 |
| 2.36 | 0.4909 | 0.0091 | 2.66 | 0.4961 | 0.0039 | 2.96 | 0.4985 | 0.0015 |
| 2.37 | 0.4911 | 0.0089 | 2.67 | 0.4962 | 0.0038 | 2.97 | 0.4985 | 0.0015 |
| 2.38 | 0.4913 | 0.0087 | 2.68 | 0.4963 | 0.0037 | 2.98 | 0.4986 | 0.0014 |
| 2.39 | 0.4916 | 0.0084 | 2.69 | 0.4964 | 0.0036 | 2.99 | 0.4986 | 0.0014 |
| 2.40 | 0.4918 | 0.0082 | 2.70 | 0.4965 | 0.0035 | 3.00 | 0.4986 | 0.0014 |

| A | B | C | A | B | C | A | B | C |
|---|---|---|---|---|---|---|---|---|
| Z | Area Between Mean and Z | Area Beyond Z | Z | Area Between Mean and Z | Area Beyond Z | Z | Area Between Mean and Z | Area Beyond Z |
| 3.01 | 0.4987 | 0.0013 | 3.21 | 0.4993 | 0.0007 | 3.41 | 0.4997 | 0.0003 |
| 3.02 | 0.4987 | 0.0013 | 3.22 | 0.4994 | 0.0006 | 3.42 | 0.4997 | 0.0003 |
| 3.03 | 0.4988 | 0.0012 | 3.23 | 0.4994 | 0.0006 | 3.43 | 0.4997 | 0.0003 |
| 3.04 | 0.4988 | 0.0012 | 3.24 | 0.4994 | 0.0006 | 3.44 | 0.4997 | 0.0003 |
| 3.05 | 0.4989 | 0.0011 | 3.25 | 0.4994 | 0.0006 | 3.45 | 0.4997 | 0.0003 |
| 3.06 | 0.4989 | 0.0011 | 3.26 | 0.4994 | 0.0006 | 3.46 | 0.4997 | 0.0003 |
| 3.07 | 0.4989 | 0.0011 | 3.27 | 0.4995 | 0.0005 | 3.47 | 0.4997 | 0.0003 |
| 3.08 | 0.4990 | 0.0010 | 3.28 | 0.4995 | 0.0005 | 3.48 | 0.4997 | 0.0003 |
| 3.09 | 0.4990 | 0.0010 | 3.29 | 0.4995 | 0.0005 | 3.49 | 0.4998 | 0.0002 |
| 3.10 | 0.4990 | 0.0010 | 3.30 | 0.4995 | 0.0005 | 3.50 | 0.4998 | 0.0002 |
|  |  |  |  |  |  |  |  |  |
| 3.11 | 0.4991 | 0.0009 | 3.31 | 0.4995 | 0.0005 | 3.60 | 0.4998 | 0.0002 |
| 3.12 | 0.4991 | 0.0009 | 3.32 | 0.4995 | 0.0005 |  |  |  |
| 3.13 | 0.4991 | 0.0009 | 3.33 | 0.4996 | 0.0004 | 3.70 | 0.4999 | 0.0001 |
| 3.14 | 0.4992 | 0.0008 | 3.34 | 0.4996 | 0.0004 |  |  |  |
| 3.15 | 0.4992 | 0.0008 | 3.35 | 0.4996 | 0.0004 | 3.80 | 0.4999 | 0.0001 |
| 3.16 | 0.4992 | 0.0008 | 3.36 | 0.4996 | 0.0004 |  |  |  |
| 3.17 | 0.4992 | 0.0008 | 3.37 | 0.4996 | 0.0004 |  |  |  |
| 3.18 | 0.4993 | 0.0007 | 3.38 | 0.4996 | 0.0004 | 3.90 | 0.4999 | <0.0001 |
| 3.19 | 0.4993 | 0.0007 | 3.39 | 0.4997 | 0.0003 |  |  |  |
| 3.20 | 0.4993 | 0.0007 | 3.40 | 0.4997 | 0.0003 | 4.00 | 0.4999 | <0.0001 |

# Appendix C
# Distribution of *t*

| df | Level of Significance for One-Tailed Test | | | | | |
|---|---|---|---|---|---|---|
| | .10 | .05 | .025 | .01 | .005 | .0005 |
| | Level of Significance for Two-Tailed Test | | | | | |
| | .20 | .10 | .05 | .02 | .01 | .001 |
| 1 | 3.078 | 6.314 | 12.706 | 31.821 | 63.657 | 636.619 |
| 2 | 1.886 | 2.920 | 4.303 | 6.965 | 9.925 | 31.598 |
| 3 | 1.638 | 2.353 | 3.182 | 4.541 | 5.841 | 12.941 |
| 4 | 1.533 | 2.132 | 2.776 | 3.747 | 4.604 | 8.610 |
| 5 | 1.476 | 2.015 | 2.571 | 3.365 | 4.032 | 6.859 |
| 6 | 1.440 | 1.943 | 2.447 | 3.143 | 3.707 | 5.959 |
| 7 | 1.415 | 1.895 | 2.365 | 2.998 | 3.499 | 5.405 |
| 8 | 1.397 | 1.860 | 2.306 | 2.896 | 3.355 | 5.041 |
| 9 | 1.383 | 1.833 | 2.262 | 2.821 | 3.250 | 4.781 |
| 10 | 1.372 | 1.812 | 2.228 | 2.764 | 3.169 | 4.587 |
| 11 | 1.363 | 1.796 | 2.201 | 2.718 | 3.106 | 4.437 |
| 12 | 1.356 | 1.782 | 2.179 | 2.681 | 3.055 | 4.318 |
| 13 | 1.350 | 1.771 | 2.160 | 2.650 | 3.012 | 4.221 |
| 14 | 1.345 | 1.761 | 2.145 | 2.624 | 2.977 | 4.140 |
| 15 | 1.341 | 1.753 | 2.131 | 2.602 | 2.947 | 4.073 |
| 16 | 1.337 | 1.746 | 2.120 | 2.583 | 2.921 | 4.015 |
| 17 | 1.333 | 1.740 | 2.110 | 2.567 | 2.898 | 3.965 |
| 18 | 1.330 | 1.734 | 2.101 | 2.552 | 2.878 | 3.922 |
| 19 | 1.328 | 1.729 | 2.093 | 2.539 | 2.861 | 3.883 |
| 20 | 1.325 | 1.725 | 2.086 | 2.528 | 2.845 | 3.850 |

| df | Level of Significance for One-Tailed Test | | | | | |
|---|---|---|---|---|---|---|
| | .10 | .05 | .025 | .01 | .005 | .0005 |
| | Level of Significance for Two-Tailed Test | | | | | |
| | .20 | .10 | .05 | .02 | .01 | .001 |
| 21 | 1.323 | 1.721 | 2.080 | 2.518 | 2.831 | 3.819 |
| 22 | 1.321 | 1.717 | 2.074 | 2.508 | 2.819 | 3.792 |
| 23 | 1.319 | 1.714 | 2.069 | 2.500 | 2.807 | 3.767 |
| 24 | 1.318 | 1.711 | 2.064 | 2.492 | 2.797 | 3.745 |
| 25 | 1.316 | 1.708 | 2.060 | 2.485 | 2.787 | 3.725 |
| 26 | 1.315 | 1.706 | 2.056 | 2.479 | 2.779 | 3.707 |
| 27 | 1.314 | 1.703 | 2.052 | 2.473 | 2.771 | 3.690 |
| 28 | 1.313 | 1.701 | 2.048 | 2.467 | 2.763 | 3.674 |
| 29 | 1.311 | 1.699 | 2.045 | 2.462 | 2.756 | 3.659 |
| 30 | 1.310 | 1.697 | 2.042 | 2.457 | 2.750 | 3.646 |
| 40 | 1.303 | 1.684 | 2.021 | 2.423 | 2.704 | 3.551 |
| 60 | 1.296 | 1.671 | 2.000 | 2.390 | 2.660 | 3.460 |
| 120 | 1.289 | 1.658 | 1.980 | 2.358 | 2.617 | 3.373 |
| ∞ | 1.282 | 1.645 | 1.960 | 2.326 | 2.576 | 3.291 |

*Source:* Abridged from R. A. Fisher and F. Yates, *Statistical Tables for Biological, Agricultural and Medical Research,* 6th ed. (London: Longman, 1974), Table III. Used by permission of Addison Wesley Longman Ltd.

# Appendix D
# Distribution of Chi-Square

| df | .99 | .98 | .95 | .90 | .80 | .70 | .50 | .30 | .20 | .10 | .05 | .02 | .01 | .001 |
|---|---|---|---|---|---|---|---|---|---|---|---|---|---|---|
| 1 | $.0^3157$ | $.0^3628$ | .00393 | .0158 | .0642 | .148 | .455 | 1.074 | 1.642 | 2.706 | 3.841 | 5.412 | 6.635 | 10.827 |
| 2 | .0201 | .0404 | .103 | .211 | .446 | .713 | 1.386 | 2.408 | 3.219 | 4.605 | 5.991 | 7.824 | 9.210 | 13.815 |
| 3 | .115 | .185 | .352 | .584 | 1.005 | 1.424 | 2.366 | 3.665 | 4.642 | 6.251 | 7.815 | 9.837 | 11.341 | 16.268 |
| 4 | .297 | .429 | .711 | 1.064 | 1.649 | 2.195 | 3.357 | 4.878 | 5.989 | 7.779 | 9.488 | 11.668 | 13.277 | 18.465 |
| 5 | .554 | .752 | 1.145 | 1.610 | 2.343 | 3.000 | 4.351 | 6.064 | 7.289 | 9.236 | 11.070 | 13.388 | 15.086 | 20.517 |
| 6 | .872 | 1.134 | 1.635 | 2.204 | 3.070 | 3.828 | 5.348 | 7.231 | 8.558 | 10.645 | 12.592 | 15.033 | 16.812 | 22.457 |
| 7 | 1.239 | 1.564 | 2.167 | 2.833 | 3.822 | 4.671 | 6.346 | 8.383 | 9.803 | 12.017 | 14.067 | 16.622 | 18.475 | 24.322 |
| 8 | 1.646 | 2.032 | 2.733 | 3.490 | 4.594 | 5.527 | 7.344 | 9.524 | 11.030 | 13.362 | 15.507 | 18.168 | 20.090 | 26.125 |
| 9 | 2.088 | 2.532 | 3.325 | 4.168 | 5.380 | 6.393 | 8.343 | 10.656 | 12.242 | 14.684 | 16.919 | 19.679 | 21.666 | 27.877 |
| 10 | 2.558 | 3.059 | 3.940 | 4.865 | 6.179 | 7.267 | 9.342 | 11.781 | 13.442 | 15.987 | 18.307 | 21.161 | 23.209 | 29.588 |
| 11 | 3.053 | 3.609 | 4.575 | 5.578 | 6.989 | 8.148 | 10.341 | 12.899 | 14.631 | 17.275 | 19.675 | 22.618 | 24.725 | 31.264 |
| 12 | 3.571 | 4.178 | 5.226 | 6.304 | 7.807 | 9.034 | 11.340 | 14.011 | 15.812 | 18.549 | 21.026 | 24.054 | 26.217 | 32.909 |
| 13 | 4.107 | 4.765 | 5.892 | 7.042 | 8.634 | 9.926 | 12.340 | 15.119 | 16.985 | 19.812 | 22.362 | 25.472 | 27.688 | 34.528 |
| 14 | 4.660 | 5.368 | 6.571 | 7.790 | 9.467 | 10.821 | 13.339 | 16.222 | 18.151 | 21.064 | 23.685 | 26.873 | 29.141 | 36.123 |
| 15 | 5.229 | 5.985 | 7.261 | 8.547 | 10.307 | 11.721 | 14.339 | 17.322 | 19.311 | 22.307 | 24.996 | 28.259 | 30.578 | 37.697 |
| 16 | 5.812 | 6.614 | 7.962 | 9.312 | 11.152 | 12.624 | 15.338 | 18.418 | 20.465 | 23.542 | 26.296 | 29.633 | 32.000 | 39.252 |
| 17 | 6.408 | 7.255 | 8.672 | 10.085 | 12.002 | 13.531 | 16.338 | 19.511 | 21.615 | 24.769 | 27.587 | 30.995 | 33.409 | 40.790 |
| 18 | 7.015 | 7.906 | 9.390 | 10.865 | 12.857 | 14.440 | 17.338 | 20.601 | 22.760 | 25.989 | 28.869 | 32.346 | 34.805 | 42.312 |
| 19 | 7.633 | 8.567 | 10.117 | 11.651 | 13.716 | 15.352 | 18.338 | 21.689 | 23.900 | 27.204 | 30.144 | 33.687 | 36.191 | 43.820 |
| 20 | 8.260 | 9.237 | 10.851 | 12.443 | 14.578 | 16.266 | 19.337 | 22.775 | 25.038 | 28.412 | 31.410 | 35.020 | 37.566 | 45.315 |
| 21 | 8.897 | 9.915 | 11.591 | 13.240 | 15.445 | 17.182 | 20.337 | 23.858 | 26.171 | 29.615 | 32.671 | 36.343 | 38.932 | 46.797 |
| 22 | 9.542 | 10.600 | 12.338 | 14.041 | 16.314 | 18.101 | 21.337 | 24.939 | 27.301 | 30.813 | 33.924 | 37.659 | 40.289 | 48.268 |
| 23 | 10.196 | 11.293 | 13.091 | 14.848 | 17.187 | 19.021 | 22.337 | 26.018 | 28.429 | 32.007 | 35.172 | 38.968 | 41.638 | 49.728 |
| 24 | 10.856 | 11.992 | 13.848 | 15.659 | 18.062 | 19.943 | 23.337 | 27.096 | 29.553 | 33.196 | 36.415 | 40.270 | 42.980 | 51.179 |
| 25 | 11.524 | 12.697 | 14.611 | 16.473 | 18.940 | 20.867 | 24.337 | 28.172 | 30.675 | 34.382 | 37.652 | 41.566 | 44.314 | 52.620 |
| 26 | 12.198 | 13.409 | 15.379 | 17.292 | 19.820 | 21.792 | 25.336 | 29.246 | 31.795 | 35.563 | 38.885 | 42.856 | 45.642 | 54.052 |
| 27 | 12.879 | 14.125 | 16.151 | 18.114 | 20.703 | 22.719 | 26.336 | 30.319 | 32.912 | 36.741 | 40.113 | 44.140 | 46.963 | 55.476 |
| 28 | 13.565 | 14.847 | 16.928 | 18.939 | 21.588 | 23.647 | 27.336 | 31.391 | 34.027 | 37.916 | 41.337 | 45.419 | 48.278 | 56.893 |
| 29 | 14.256 | 15.574 | 17.708 | 19.768 | 22.475 | 24.577 | 28.336 | 32.461 | 35.139 | 39.087 | 42.557 | 46.693 | 49.588 | 58.302 |
| 30 | 14.953 | 16.306 | 18.493 | 20.599 | 23.364 | 25.508 | 29.336 | 33.530 | 36.250 | 40.256 | 43.773 | 47.962 | 50.892 | 59.703 |

Source: Table IV of Fisher & Yates: *Statistical Tables for Biological, Agricultural and Medical Research*. Published by Longman Group Ltd., London (1974), 6th edition (previously published by Oliver & Boyd Ltd., Edinburgh). Used by permission of Addison Wesley Longman Ltd.

# Appendix E
# How to Use SPSS™*

*by Joan Saxton Weber*

A *statistical package* is a set of computer programs that work together so that you can calculate many different statistics and perform other related tasks. There are many statistical packages available for mainframe (multi-user) and personal computers. Once you have learned how to use one or two of them, you should find it easy to use others (at least, if you have the right manual or guidebook). Here we will review the basic procedures for using the Statistical Package for the Social Sciences (SPSS), one of the most popular and best-documented comprehensive social science statistics packages. This appendix can be used with any SPSS Windows-based version, as all such versions operate in the same manner.

## Getting Acquainted with the Windows Environment

### Starting SPSS

If you are unfamiliar with the Windows environment (you have never touched a mouse), you may want someone to help you with your first Windows experience. Once you are comfortable with the environment, though, all the steps are similar to one another. Communicating with SPSS is simply a matter of using drop-down menus, toolbars, and dialog boxes.

To start SPSS for Windows, double-click on the SPSS icon. If you do not see the SPSS icon, click the *Start* button, then click on *Programs,* and then click on SPSS.

The program will begin to load, and soon you will see a new screen. The title in the blue strip along the top of the screen says "Untitled - SPSS Data Editor."

---

*This appendix has specifically been written to assist users of SPSS™ for Windows®, Versions 7.5, 8.0, or higher. Users of SPSS Base System for Windows, Releases 6.0, 6.3, or 6.3.1, may also profitably use this appendix because of the wealth of SPSS output and screens included in this book, from those specific versions. Another version of this appendix, exclusively written for SPSS 6.0, 6.3, or 6.3.1, is available by contacting the publisher at sales@pfp.sagepub.com.

Data Window (Empty)

Title bar

*Minimize* button

*Close* button

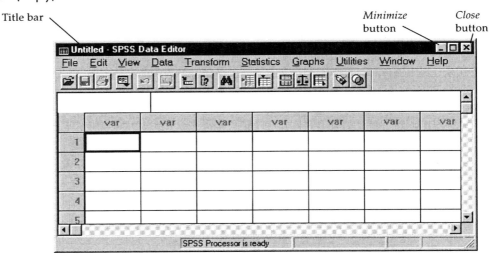

If you are using SPSS Version 8, a box will be superimposed on this screen. The box is titled "SPSS for Windows: What would you like to do?" For now, click on the *X* button (the *Close* button) in the upper right corner of the "What would you like to do?" box to get it out of the way.

"What would you like to do?" Dialog Box

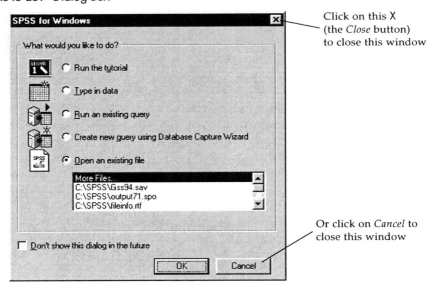

Click on this X (the *Close* button) to close this window

Or click on *Cancel* to close this window

Now you are looking at the SPSS Data Editor Window. By convention, it is called the "data window." As you can see, not a whole lot is going on. You will need to get some data before using this Untitled data window.

Drop-down menus appear at the top of the SPSS Data Editor screen.

**Menu Bar**

If you want to do something with a data file, you click on *File*, and that gives you a set of options, including opening a new file, saving a file, and closing a file. If you want to make a graph, click on *Graphs*.

A second way to tell SPSS what to do is through the use of toolbars. Even though you could use the drop-down menus to perform certain tasks, sometimes it is easier to click on a button in the toolbar. Here is the basic toolbar for SPSS:

**Tool Bar**

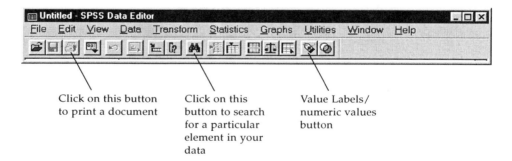

Click on this button to print a document

Click on this button to search for a particular element in your data

Value Labels/ numeric values button

The final way to communicate with SPSS is through the use of dialog boxes. You can get to a dialog box through the drop-down menus or through a button on a toolbar. For example, you can print documents in two ways. The first is to use the *File* menu.

Click on *File* in the menu bar, then click on *Print*, and the print dialog box opens up. The print dialog box lets you print all of your output or only certain selections, and it gives you choices of the type of printer and output you want. Decide what you want, and then click *OK*. (See why it is called a "dialog" box?)

File → Print

Print all of your output or highlight the selection you want to print

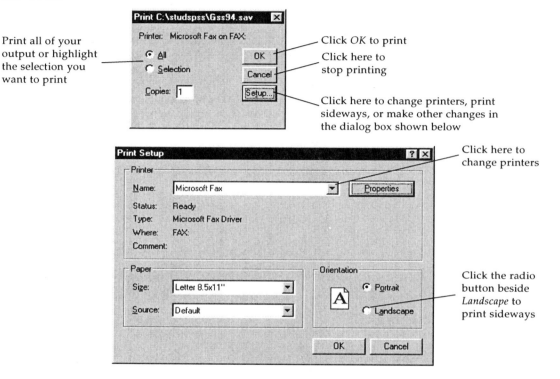

Click *OK* to print

Click here to stop printing

Click here to change printers, print sideways, or make other changes in the dialog box shown below

Click here to change printers

Click the radio button beside *Landscape* to print sideways

If you are certain that you want to print the entire output, and if you know the printer you will be using, you can just click on the print icon in the toolbar.

One caution about printing in a Windows environment: The computer will print whichever window is "active." Usually the active window is the one in front of other windows. We will discuss printing in more detail later; right now, just concentrate on getting used to the SPSS environment and the data visible on your screen.

The Windows environment is highly intuitive. All you need to do is look for the correct button and click on it.

### Setting Options in SPSS: Video Display Options

Before you go on, you should make changes and/or confirm settings in the options that SPSS uses to display information on your computer monitor while you work with data files. Click on *Edit*; then click on *Options*. From now on, such a list of directions will appear as follows:

Edit → Options

Edit → Options → General (Screen Display)

Click next to
*Alphabetical*

Click next to
/*Display names*

*General* tab
showing

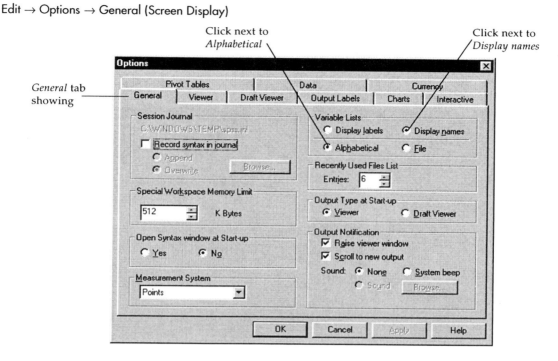

You will see the Options window open, with a series of "tabs" along the top of the window. The General options should be visible (if they aren't, click on the *General* tab). On the upper right side of the screen you will see the *Variable Lists* options. (Remember, the term *variable* usually refers to a question in a survey.) Under *Variable Lists*, the "radio button" next to *Display names* should be marked (with a small dot). If the radio button next to *Display labels* is marked instead, click on the button next to *Display names*. This tells SPSS to display the short names of the variables.

In the old days (that is, before Windows 95), variable names could be no more than eight characters long. Now the variables can have descriptions up to 25 characters long. The longer versions are less convenient to work with. The shorter variable names (called mnemonics) are used throughout this book. The short variable names can be thought of as nicknames. Nicknames such as EDUC for education are easy to spot. Others are not so easy to understand, but they are descriptive and are easy to remember once you become accustomed to them. For example, ABNOMORE is pronounced "Ab-No-More" and stands for a variable that asks about ABortion if a woman wants NO MORE children.

The other option to examine in the *Variable Lists* options is *Alphabetical*. The radio button next to *Alphabetical* should be marked with a dot. If the radio button next to *File* has a dot in it, click on the radio button next to *Alphabetical*. SPSS gives you the choice of seeing variables in alphabetical order or in the order in which they appear in the file. Listing variable names alphabetically is more convenient in most SPSS procedures.

By selecting these options, what you see on your computer screen will more closely resemble the examples in this book.

*Setting Options in SPSS: Viewing Output and Printing Options*

The next changes you should make in Options is for *Output Labels*—that is, how information will look on your monitor before it is printed and in the printed copy. Switch to these options by clicking on the *Output Labels* tab.

Edit → Options → Output Labels (Viewer Window and Print Format)

First, look at the settings under *Outline Labeling*. The box under "Variables in item labels shown as:" should say "Names." If not, click on the down arrow in the rectangle marked "Variables in item labels shown as:." You will see three choices; click on the *Names* option so it is highlighted in the rectangle.

Second, look at the settings in *Outline Labeling* for "Variable values in item labels shown as:." The box should say "Values and Labels." If not, click on the down arrow to highlight this choice.

Third, look at the settings for *Pivot Table Labeling*. "Variables in labels shown as:" should say "Names and Labels." If not, choose this option now. This way, your output will contain both the short variable "nicknames" (the mnemonic terms) and the longer descriptions of the variables.

Fourth, also under *Pivot Table Labeling*, the box "Variable values in labels shown as:" should show "Values and Labels." If not, choose this option now. This tells SPSS that you want to see both the numeric codes (values) for your variables and the labels assigned to those numbers in all the output you receive.

After you have made these Options changes, click *OK* and you will return to the SPSS data window. By selecting these options, your printed output will more closely resemble the examples in this book. If you have more experience, you may decide to keep or change these options.

### Getting Data

If you have collected your own data, at this point you would enter the data. More likely than not, though, you will be working with a set of data that already exists, such as a General Social Survey dataset or a dataset from one of the other national surveys. Instead of creating a brand new dataset, you will load a preexisting data file. Creating a dataset is easy enough, but we won't go into it here. For this appendix, we will be using the 1994 GSS dataset on the disk that accompanies this book.

To load a dataset, click on the *File* drop-down menu. From the *File* menu, click on *Open*. Another menu pops up. This takes you to the Open File dialog box where you will tell SPSS which file you want to open. If you are not using your own computer and the data are already stored on the computer, you will just need to highlight the name of the dataset and then click *Open*.

File → Open

STEP ONE: Tell the computer where to look for the file you want: the floppy drive (Drive A), the hard drive (Drive C), etc.

STEP TWO: Click on the name of the file you want to open.

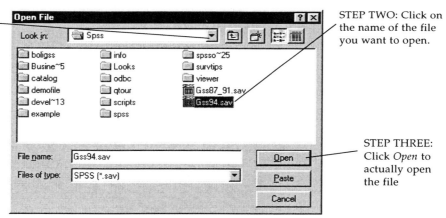

STEP THREE: Click *Open* to actually open the file

SPSS, having received its orders, retrieves your file and puts it into the data window. You will see something that looks like this:

Data Window (with GSS Data)

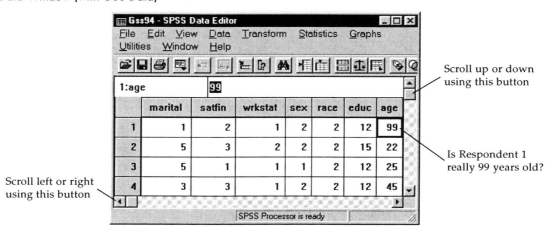

Scroll up or down using this button

Is Respondent 1 really 99 years old?

Scroll left or right using this button

The data window is divided up into rows and columns. Each row represents a person (a respondent to the survey, a "case"). This particular dataset has 1,000 rows, or 1,000 respondents. Each column represents a variable. The variable in the seventh column, AGE, is simply the age of the respondents. Many datasets have hundreds of variables and thus hundreds of columns. It is possible to print all 1,000 rows in this dataset, although the result is quite unwieldy. There are easier ways to examine the data. You can move around within the dataset in a number of ways: With the mouse, you can click on the scroll buttons at the right and bottom of the window; with the keyboard, you can use the arrow keys and the Page Up and Page Down keys. Try it.

### Looking at the Data

Something in the dataset may look funny to you: Is respondent 1 really 99 years old? Good question, and we will discuss that in a moment. First, though, from the data window, we see that respondent 4 is 45 years old and has 12 years of education. The respondent's race is a "2." The respondent's sex is a "2." The respondent's work status is a "1." All the responses to the GSS have been coded. That is, each possible response has been assigned a number (referred to as a *value*). For some variables, such as AGE and EDUC, the numbers simply correspond to the number of years. For other variables (such as RACE, SEX, and SATFIN), each number corresponds to a particular response or category. For example, for the variable RACE, white respondents were coded with the number 1, black respondents were coded with the number 2, and respondents of other races were coded with the number 3. Within SPSS, the response categories are given descriptive *value labels*.

Value labels and numeric value codes exemplify one of the most striking visual differences between SPSS version 8.0 and earlier versions; however, the meaning and categories of value labels and codes are the same in all versions of SPSS. There are several ways of locating the numeric codes, value labels, and missing data values for variables.

The most common way is by referring to a *codebook*. A codebook is similar to a dictionary. It contains pertinent information about each variable in the dataset. So we could open up the GSS codebook to the variable ABANY (or look at the codebook on the GSS website) and find out how it was coded by the GSS researchers.

What if there is no codebook? Never fear. Within SPSS it is quite easy to find the value labels. One way to look up value labels in SPSS is through the use of the Variables dialog box. To get to this dialog box, click *Utilities*.

Utilities → Variables

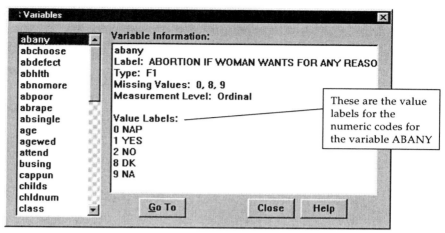

Another way to examine the value labels in SPSS is to click on the toolbar button that looks like a price tag. (It is the second-to-last button.) When you click on this, the numbers in the dataset will change to their respective labels. Or if the labels are what you are seeing, clicking on this button will turn them back to numbers.

Data Window Showing Value Labels

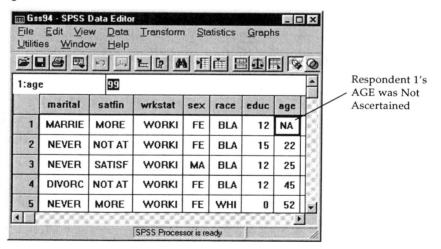

So why does AGE have a numeric code of 99 and a value label of NA for respondent 1? The answer involves *missing values*. Missing values are codes determined by the researcher to refer to missing data. If you use the Utilities → Variables command to look at the value labels for AGE, you will see that there are three codes labeled as missing: 0, 98, and 99. The code "99" describes people who did not want to answer. Fortunately, out of 1,000 people, only 3 refused to give their ages. The value labels for AGE shows that respondent 1's code of "99" (the value label NA) stands for Not Ascertained/No Answer.

From the value labels, we can learn a lot about respondent 4: She is a black high-school graduate who is 45 years old and divorced. She works full-time but is not at all satisfied with her current financial situation. You may want to "tell the story" of some other respondents just to make sure that you understand what all these numbers mean.

Let's compare the attitudes of respondents 1, 2, and 3 on abortion. Respondents 1 and 2 each oppose abortion (code "2") when a woman does not want any more children (ABNOMORE) or because she is poor (ABPOOR). However, their responses differ on the variable ABRAPE (abortion if a woman becomes pregnant as a result of being raped). Respondent 2 answered "1," which means that she agrees with abortion under these circumstances. Respondent 1's answer is recorded as "8." Respondent 3 was given a code of "0" for all three questions.

## Numeric Codes, Values, and Missing Data

Respondent 3 was not asked these questions; this is coded as "missing data."

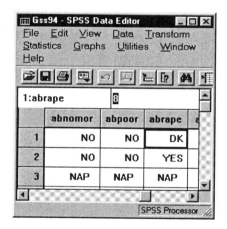

Respondent 1 said, "Don't know"; this response is coded as "missing data."

The numeric codes "0" and "8" again involve *missing values.* Let's face it, in a survey of 1,000 people, not everyone is willing to answer everything! To deal with such a situation, the GSS interviewer can pencil in responses such as "don't know" or "no answer," and for that one respondent, data on that variable will be considered "missing."

If you call up the value labels for ABPOOR and ABRAPE you will see that there are three missing values: 0, 8, and 9. Collectively, all of the "missing" codes are called *missing data.* "0" was the code given to people (such as Respondent 3) who weren't even asked the question. Respondents to the GSS are asked only certain sets, or modules, of questions. They are given a code of Not Applicable (NAP) for the questions that were not asked of them. "8" was the code given to people who said "don't know" (DK) when they were asked the question; "9" was the code given to people who did not want to answer the question (NA).

In calculations of statistics, SPSS takes those cases that had missing data "out of the equation" and calculates the statistics based on the data for the respondents who answered the questions. For example, in calculating the mean age of the respondents, SPSS calculates the mean based on the ages of 997 respondents. Some variables have more missing data than others, particularly variables for questions that are of a sensitive nature or variables for questions that were not asked of the entire sample.

To see and print responses for a subset of variables, you could use the Summarize Cases procedure (formerly known as the List Cases procedure) illustrated at the end of Chapter 2 by clicking Statistics → Summarize → Case Summaries. This feature of SPSS was essential in earlier versions of SPSS where the variable values and labels were encoded in *hexadecimal* (which was unreadable to most users). If you want to have a print copy of this information, the Case Summaries command is still useful. But for our purposes, it may be more instructive to view the data on your monitor in the manner illustrated above.

### Univariate Statistics

#### Frequencies

We could play around in the data window for hours without getting a good picture of who these 1,000 people are. It is much easier to analyze data by having SPSS make frequency distributions or graphs for your variables of interest, and such tools are only a dialog box away. Click on *Statistics* in the menu.

Statistics → Summarize → Frequencies

Put your variables of interest in this box (in this case, we've put in the variable ABANY)

Click here when you've finished telling SPSS what you want

Click here to get statistics on your variables

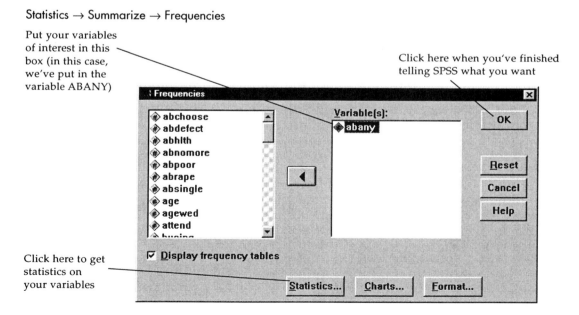

Here is what happens when you click *OK*. Scrolling down the output window below the Case Processing Summary, we can see the Frequency Distribution.

Output:
Frequency
Distribution

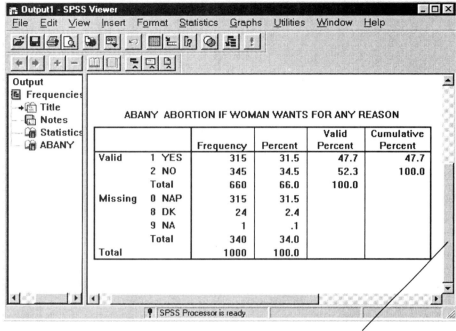

Scroll down the output
using this bar

SPSS has opened a new window called "Output 1 - SPSS Viewer," the output window. In this window, we can look at all the results of what we have asked SPSS to do. The viewer has two panes.[1] At the top of the left pane you can see the word "Ouput." To avoid confusion, this pane is referred to as the Outline pane. (Some of the default settings you changed earlier affect the appearance of this pane.) This is simply a list of everything we have asked SPSS to do since we began our session. Why is this pane useful? Well, imagine you have been working on SPSS for a couple of hours, and you have asked it to do many things. You have dozens of tables, graphs, and statistical models to pore over. If you want to go to a specific graph, you can find it in the Outline, click on it, and SPSS takes you there.

The right pane is the actual output for the commands you gave SPSS. In the pane shown here is a frequency distribution of the variable ABANY. If the entire table is not visible, which is often the case, you can move around in the output window with the arrow keys and the scroll buttons at the right and bottom of the output window. When you become more accustomed to SPSS you may want to use the Zoom/Print Preview feature.

At this point, we could print our output—that is, the right pane of the output window. Remember, the computer will print whichever window is "active." Therefore, if you want to print your output, make sure the output window is the active window. (If the data window is the active window instead, you will end up with a paper copy of the entire dataset—a stack of paper that could be several inches high!)

[1] Note: If you are using SPSS 6.1 for Windows, you will see only a single pane.

The SPSS version 8 output looks a bit different from output of earlier versions of SPSS, but the information about the distribution and statistical measures for the variable is the same.

## Data Transformation

### Recoding Variables

Not all variables are coded exactly as you would like them to be coded. Most of the time, to do what you want to do, you will need to recode variables. Let's say we want to recode EDUC (highest year of education completed) so that:

Everyone with less than a high school diploma is put into a single group.

Everyone with a high school diploma, but no more, is put into a second group.

Everyone with some college, but not a college diploma, is put into a third group.

Everyone with a college degree, but no more, is put into a fourth group.

Everyone with postcollege education is put into a fifth group.

Make sure you understand what we are doing here: We are taking the original 21 categories (years of education from 0 to 20) and collapsing them into five categories. We are going to accomplish this task by creating a new variable called ED5CAT. Click *Transform.* This takes us to the first of two dialog boxes involved in recoding variables.

Transform → Recode → Into Different Variables

STEP ONE: Select the variable you want to recode and put it in the Numeric Variable → Output box

STEP TWO: Type the name of the new variable, give it a label, and click on *Change*

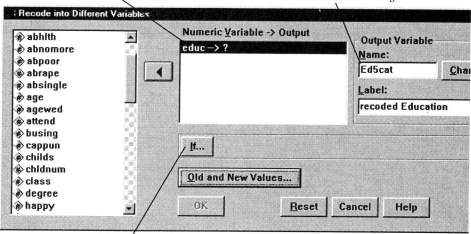

STEP THREE: Click this box to go to the second dialog box

In this first dialog box we are telling SPSS which old variable we are recoding *from* and which new variable we are recoding *to*. After doing this, we go to the second dialog box:

### Recode Old → New Values

STEP TWO: Tell SPSS the new value (E.g., 1)

STEP ONE: Tell SPSS which old values are to be recoded (E.g., 0 thru 11)

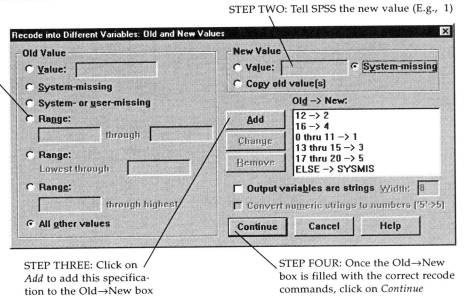

STEP THREE: Click on *Add* to add this specification to the Old→New box

STEP FOUR: Once the Old→New box is filled with the correct recode commands, click on *Continue*

In the Old → New box, our goal is to fill in the appropriate recode specifications. For example, we want everyone with less than a high school diploma to be put into one group. On the left side of the dialog box, we tell SPSS to take a particular value or set of values, such as the values ranging from 0 through 11 (those people with less than high school). On the right side of the dialog box, we tell SPSS to collapse these values into a single value: 1. Look through the list of recodes to make sure you understand what is going on here. When you have the list as you like it, click *Continue* to exit the second dialog box, then click *OK* to exit the first dialog box.

SPSS now creates a new variable named ED5CAT, giving all the respondents new values for their levels of education:

| GSS Respondent #: | Old Value on Variable EDUC | New Value on Variable ED5CAT |
|---|---|---|
| 1 | 12 | 2 |
| 2 | 15 | 3 |
| 3 | 12 | 2 |
| 4 | 12 | 2 |
| 5 | 0 | 1 |

Now, let's look at a frequency distribution for our new education variable:

Frequency
Distribution
for ED5CAT

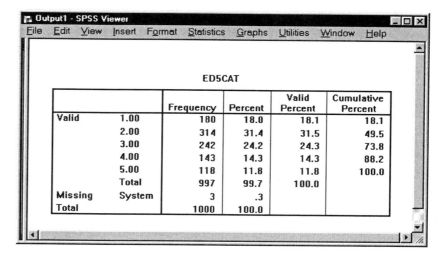

### ED5CAT

| | | Frequency | Percent | Valid Percent | Cumulative Percent |
|---|---|---|---|---|---|
| Valid | 1.00 | 180 | 18.0 | 18.1 | 18.1 |
| | 2.00 | 314 | 31.4 | 31.5 | 49.5 |
| | 3.00 | 242 | 24.2 | 24.3 | 73.8 |
| | 4.00 | 143 | 14.3 | 14.3 | 88.2 |
| | 5.00 | 118 | 11.8 | 11.8 | 100.0 |
| | Total | 997 | 99.7 | 100.0 | |
| Missing | System | 3 | .3 | | |
| Total | | 1000 | 100.0 | | |

As you can see, there are no value labels. Someone who was handed this output would have no way of knowing what "1" or "2" means. To make this output easier to read, we should attach value labels to our numeric codes. This requires using another dialog box.

In the data window, go to the rightmost column (this is where SPSS puts all the new variables you create). Double-click on the name of the variable ED5CAT. A dialog box pops up. In that dialog box, click on *Labels*. Up pops the dialog box you need. (If you have trouble remembering when to double-click versus when to single-click, you may find the menus easier to use. Click on your new variable in the data window, then click Data → Define Variable.)

Data → Define Variable

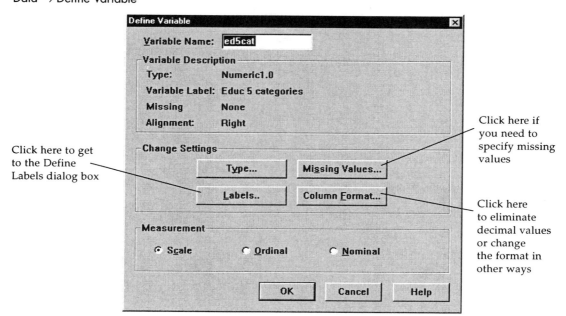

Notice that in the above dialog box (the one that takes you to the Define Labels dialog box), you can also tell SPSS what the missing values are for a variable and format the column in which the variable appears. Telling SPSS what values are the missing values is a *very* important step! You don't want SPSS to figure in its calculations, for example, that someone is 99 years old for a code of "99." Skipping this step can easily muddle any analysis.

Data → Define Variable → Labels

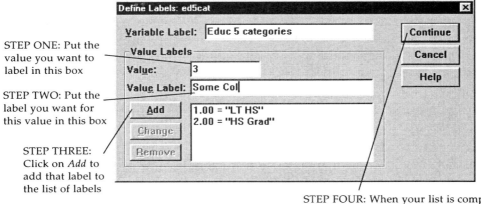

STEP ONE: Put the value you want to label in this box

STEP TWO: Put the label you want for this value in this box

STEP THREE: Click on *Add* to add that label to the list of labels

STEP FOUR: When your list is complete, click on *Continue* and then click *OK*

After you have created new variables, you will most likely want to save your work. Otherwise, the next time you use SPSS, you will have to start all over. Call up the Save Data As... dialog box by clicking:

File → Save As...

Then, specify the drive on which you want to save your file, specify the directory, give your file a name, and click *OK*. Note that if you are using the disk that comes with this book, you cannot save a new version of the GSS dataset onto that disk; the disk is already quite full. Give a new name to the data file that you save. Overwriting an existing data file can cause a lot of confusion.

### Computing a New Variable

Here is another way to modify data. On the disk we have data from GSS94 regarding the educational levels (in years) of the respondents' parents. The variable names are, appropriately enough, MAEDUC and PAEDUC. What if we want to know the mean level of education of the two? For example, if Joe's father had a high school education and his mother had a college education, the mean for the two would be 14 years of education: $(12 + 16)/2 = 14$. Let's create a new variable, PAREDUC, that provides this. Click *Transform*.

Transform → Compute

STEP ONE: Give
your new variable
a name

STEP TWO: Using
the correct variables
and mathematic
expressions, create
an equation

STEP THREE:
Click *OK*

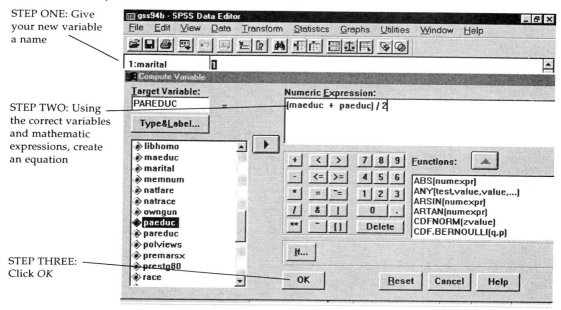

SPSS whirs away and computes PAREDUC. Here are some examples of values
of the new variable.

| MAEDUC: | PAEDUC | New Variable: PAREDUC |
|---------|--------|------------------------|
| 98 | 97 | • |
| 20 | 97 | • |
| 0 | 8 | 4 |
| 6 | 6 | 6 |
| 20 | 97 | • |

Some of the respondents will not have a value for the new variable PAREDUC
because, for one or both of the parents, the years of education was unknown,
and thus missing. (The symbol • is often used by SPSS for missing data.)

## Bivariate and Multivariate Statistics

### Crosstabulation

Now that we've gone through the basics of how to manipulate data in SPSS,
let's move on to some real statistics. You already know how to get descriptive
statistics on single variables, but how about looking at the relationships
between variables? Let's say we want to examine the relationship between

education (ED5CAT, the categorized measure of education we created earlier in this appendix with the *Recode* command) and attitudes about abortion (using the ABSINGLE variable). We will create a crosstab with these variables, using ED5CAT as our independent variable and ABSINGLE as our dependent variable. Choose *Statistics* from the menu.

Statistics → Summarize → Crosstabs

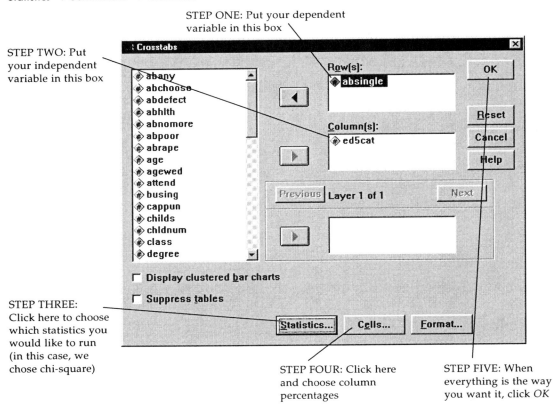

STEP ONE: Put your dependent variable in this box

STEP TWO: Put your independent variable in this box

STEP THREE: Click here to choose which statistics you would like to run (in this case, we chose chi-square)

STEP FOUR: Click here and choose column percentages

STEP FIVE: When everything is the way you want it, click *OK*

In the dialog box, click on *Statistics* to select *chi-square* and *measures of association,* and click *Continue.* Also click on *Cells* to get column percents for the variables, and click *Continue.* Then click *OK* to get the results:

## Output: Crosstabs

NOT MARRIED * recoded Education Crosstabulation

| | | | recoded Education | | | | | |
| | | | 1.00 LT High School | 2.00 High School | 3.00 Some College | 4.00 College Grad | 5.00 Post College | Total |
|---|---|---|---|---|---|---|---|---|
| NOT MARRIED | 1 YES | Count | 42 | 96 | 91 | 48 | 47 | 324 |
| | | % within recoded Education | 37.5% | 44.0% | 54.5% | 54.5% | 59.5% | 48.8% |
| | 2 NO | Count | 70 | 122 | 76 | 40 | 32 | 340 |
| | | % within recoded Education | 62.5% | 56.0% | 45.5% | 45.5% | 40.5% | 51.2% |
| Total | | Count | 112 | 218 | 167 | 88 | 79 | 664 |
| | | % within recoded Education | 100.0% | 100.0% | 100.0% | 100.0% | 100.0% | 100.0% |

Chi-Square Tests

| | Value | df | Asymp. Sig. (2-sided) |
|---|---|---|---|
| Pearson Chi-Square | 14.847 | 4 | .005 |

To print output that is wide, you may want to print it in landscape (sideways) format. Click on File → Page Setup; choose *Landscape*, adjust margins if necessary, and click *OK* to return to the main print dialog box. Click *OK* to actually print your output.

So we see that there definitely is a relationship between education and attitudes about abortion. As educational level rises, people are more likely to support abortion. The chi-square test tells us that the relationship is highly significant.

### Regression

Now let's use the combined education of parents, PAREDUC (the variable we created earlier in this appendix using the *Compute* command). Does parents' level of education affect the educational level of their children? Think about this for a moment in terms of your own life: If your parents had less (or more) education, how would this have affected your educational aspirations? With the data from the GSS respondents, use the variable PAREDUC to explain variation in the variable EDUC (respondent's education). To get to the Regression box, click *Statistics*.

Statistics → Regression → Linear

STEP ONE: Put your
dependent variable here

STEP TWO: Put your
independent variable(s) here

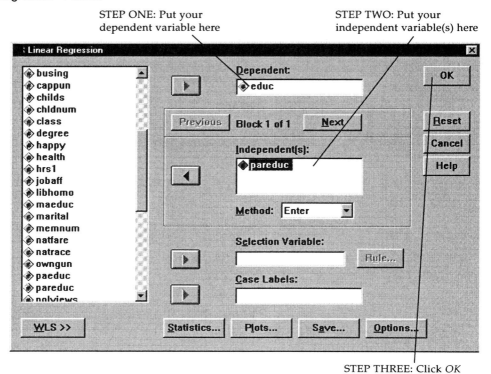

STEP THREE: Click *OK*

If you've ever calculated a regression equation by hand, you know that SPSS is one powerful program, since it can calculate an equation for 1,000 cases in a second or so.

Here are some of the most important statistics SPSS calculates for us.

Regression Output: R-Square and Test of Significance

The R², or proportion of variance, explained

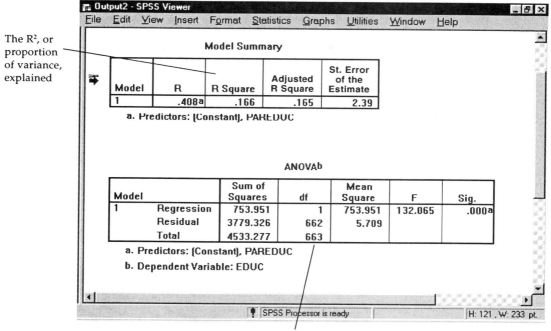

The number of cases involved
is 662 + 1 + 1 = 664

Regression Output: Unstandardized and Standardized Regression Coefficients

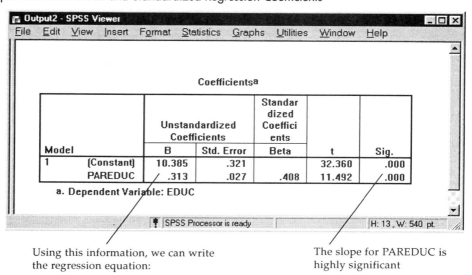

Using this information, we can write
the regression equation:

EDUC = 10.38 + .31(PAREDUC)

The slope for PAREDUC is
highly significant

More information than you can shake a stick at! First, we see that parents' education explains about 17 percent of the variation in respondents' education—quite a chunk, but certainly not everything. More than parents' education is at work; other variables may contribute as well, but we won't go into that here. Looking at the regression equation, we see that for each additional year of parents' education, respondents' education rises by .31. So if each of your parents has a college degree, your predicted educational attainment is 10.38 + .31(16), or 15.34 years of education.

### Comparing Means

One last statistical procedure often used is the *t*-test, which is used to compare the means of two groups on some variable of interest. Perhaps we are interested in whether whites make more money than nonwhites, or whether Protestants are more educated than Catholics. For purposes of example here, let's say we want to investigate the question: Do women marry younger than men? The GSS includes a variable called AGEWED, the age of the respondent at the time of first marriage. Choose *Statistics* from the menu to get to the appropriate dialog box:

Statistics → Compare Means → Independent Samples T-Test

STEP ONE: Put the variable you want to compare values of in this box

STEP TWO: Put the variable whose groups you want to compare in this box

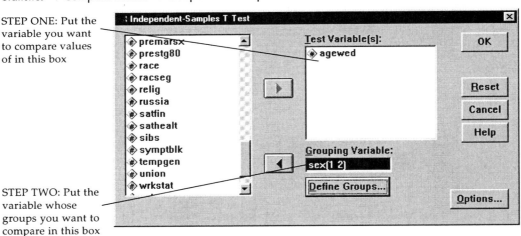

The only confusing part of this procedure is what occurs in the little *Grouping Variable* box. When you first put a variable in this box, the variable will appear with this after it:

(? ?)

This is how SPSS tells you that you have one more step to complete: choosing which groups you want to compare. With some variables, this will seem silly because there are only two possible groups. But with others, this step makes perfect sense: You can choose the variable RELIG, but you still need to tell SPSS whether you want to compare Protestants and Catholics, Catholics and

Jews, Protestants and Jews, and so on. To tell SPSS which groups you want, click on *Define Groups* and fill in the boxes. In this example, we have used the only two possible categories: "1" for men and "2" for women.

Output: T-Test Statistics

**Group Statistics**

| | SEX | N | Mean | Std. Deviation | Std. Error Mean |
|---|---|---|---|---|---|
| AGEWED | 1 MALE | 157 | 23.94 | 4.95 | .40 |
| | 2 FEMALE | 246 | 21.95 | 4.35 | .28 |

**Independent Samples Test**

| | | Levene's Test for Equality of Variances | | t-test for Equality of Means | | | | | | | |
|---|---|---|---|---|---|---|---|---|---|---|---|
| | | | | | | | | | | 95% Confidence Interval of the Difference | |
| | | F | Sig. | t | df | Sig. (2-tailed) | Mean Difference | Std. Error Difference | Lower | Upper |
| AGEWED | Equal variances assumed | .020 | .887 | 4.240 | 401 | .000 | 1.99 | .47 | 1.07 | 2.91 |
| | Equal variances not assumed | | | 4.120 | 300.687 | .000 | 1.99 | .48 | 1.04 | 2.94 |

We can see that the mean age of marriage for men is about 24, whereas the mean age for women is about 22—a difference of about two years. The significance level is .000, telling us that this difference within our sample can be generalized to the population at large: Women married at a younger age than men did.

Another question may come to mind: Did we get this result because the sample, like the population, contains many people who married before relatively recent social changes? Would the age of first marriage still be younger for women among people less than 30 to 35 years old? Would the age gap be as great? To answer these questions, you will need to perform multivariate analysis of the relationship among AGE, AGEWED, and SEX.

## Conclusion

If you have followed this appendix all the way, you should have a good grasp of the basics of using a statistical package. It's just like any other skill: The more you practice, the better you'll be. If you have difficulty with a procedure, just remember that there are many sources of assistance out there: this appendix (which, admittedly, won't answer all your questions), the Help drop-down menu in SPSS, the SPSS manual, your local computer lab consultant, and (let's not forget) your instructor. The computer is not a monster or your nemesis; it is merely a tool to help you do your work. You won't learn SPSS overnight, but after you have done some of the exercises in this book by hand, you may learn to appreciate just having SPSS do the computations for you. So try to have fun investigating questions about the diverse society in which we live.

# Appendix F
# The General Social Survey

In 1972 the National Opinion Research Center (NORC), funded by a grant from the National Science Foundation, began the General Social Survey (GSS). The GSS was designed to provide social science researchers with a readily accessible database of socially relevant attitudes, behaviors, and attributes of a cross-section of the U.S. population. With the continuing support of the National Science Foundation, the GSS has been conducted nearly every year since 1972. GSS data are not copyrighted; they are available to anyone for a minimal processing fee and may be shared between researchers without permission.

The GSS surveys a sample of approximately 1,500 people from across the United States every year. The data, obtained through a sampling design known as a multistage probability sample, are representative of Americans 18 years and older. This means that the GSS dataset allows us to estimate the characteristics, opinions, and behaviors of all noninstitutionalized, English-speaking, American adults in a given year.

Two data files are provided with this text, as described in the SPSS demonstration in Chapter 1. The codebook for the variables in both files is included on the disk that is enclosed with the textbook. The file is called GSSCODE.TXT and is stored in ASCII, or text only, format.

# Appendix G
# A Basic Math Review

*by James Harris*

You have probably already heard that there is a lot of math in statistics and for this reason you are somewhat anxious about taking a statistics course. Although it is true that courses in statistics can involve a great deal of mathematics, you should be relieved to hear that this course will stress interpretation rather than the ability to solve complex mathematical problems. With that said, however, you will still need to know how to perform some basic mathematical operations as well as understand the meanings of certain symbols used in statistics. Following is a review of the symbols and math you will need to know to successfully complete this course.

## Symbols and Expressions Used in Statistics

Statistics provides us with a set of tools for describing and analyzing *variables.* A variable is an attribute that can vary in some way. For example, a person's age is a variable because it can range from just born to over one hundred years old. "Race" and "gender" are also variables, though with fewer categories than the variable "age." In statistics, variables you are interested in measuring are often given a symbol. For example, if we wanted to know something about the age of students in our statistics class, we would use the symbol $Y$ to represent the variable "age." Now let's say for simplicity we asked only the students sitting in the first row their ages—19, 21, 23, and 32. These four ages would be scores of the $Y$ variable.

Another symbol that you will frequently encounter in statistics is $\Sigma$, or uppercase sigma. Sigma is a Greek letter that stands for summation in statistics. In other words, when you see the symbol $\Sigma$, it means you should sum all of the scores. An example will make this clear. Using our sample of students' ages represented by $Y$, the use of sigma as in the expression $\Sigma Y$ (read as: the sum of $Y$) tells us to sum all the scores of the variable Y. Using our example, we would find the sum of the set of scores from the variable "age" by adding each score together:

$$19 + 21 + 23 + 32 = 95$$

So, for the variable "age," $\Sigma Y = 95$.

Sigma is also often used in expressions with an exponent, as in the expression $\Sigma Y^2$ (read as: the sum of squared scores). This means that we should first square all the scores of the $Y$ variable and then sum the squared products. So using the same set of scores, we would solve the expression by squaring each score first and then adding them together:

$$19^2 + 21^2 + 23^2 + 32^2 = 361 + 441 + 529 + 1,024 = 2,355$$

So for the variable "age," $\Sigma Y^2 = 2,355$.

A similar, but slightly different, expression, which illustrates the function of parentheses, is $(\Sigma Y)^2$ (read as: the sum of scores, squared). In this expression, the parentheses tell us to first sum all the scores and then square this summed total. Parentheses are often used in expressions in statistics, and they always tell us to perform the expression within the parentheses first and then the part of the problem that is outside of the parentheses. To solve this expression, we need to sum all the scores first. However, we already found that $\Sigma Y = 95$, so to solve the expression $(\Sigma Y)^2$, we simply square this summed total,

$$95^2 = 9,025$$

So, for the variable "age," $(\Sigma Y)^2 = 9,025$.

You should also be familiar with the different symbols that denote multiplication and division. Most students are familiar with the times sign ($\times$); however, there are several other ways to express multiplication. For example,

$$3(4) \qquad (5)6 \qquad (4)(2) \qquad 7 \cdot 8 \qquad 9 * 6$$

all symbolize the operation of multiplication. In this text, the first three are most often used to denote multiplication. There are also several ways division can be expressed. You are probably familiar with the conventional division sign ($\div$), but division can also be expressed in these other ways:

$$4/6 \qquad \frac{6}{3}$$

This text uses the latter two forms to express division.

In statistics you are likely to encounter greater than and less than signs ($>$, $<$), greater than or equal to and less than or equal to signs ($\geq$, $\leq$), and not equal to signs ($\neq$). It is important you understand what each sign means, though admittedly it is easy to confuse them. Use the following expressions for review. Notice that numerals and symbols are often used together:

$4 > 2$ means 4 is greater than 2
$H_1 > 10$ means $H_1$ is greater than 10

$7 < 9$ means 7 is less than 9
$a < b$ means $a$ is less than $b$

$Y \geq 10$ means that the value for $Y$ is a value greater than or equal to 10
$a \leq b$ means that the value for $a$ is less than or equal to the value for $b$

$8 \neq 10$ means 8 does not equal 10
$H_1 \neq H_2$ means $H_1$ does not equal $H_2$

## Proportions and Percentages

Proportions and percentages are commonly used in statistics and provide a quick way to express information about the relative frequency of some value. You should know how to find proportions and percentages.

Proportions are identified by $P$; to find a proportion apply this formula:

$$P = \frac{f}{N}$$

where $f$ stands for the frequency of cases in a category and $N$ the total number of cases in all categories. So, in our sample of four students, if we wanted to know the proportion of males in the front row, there would be a total of two categories, female and male. Because there are 3 females and 1 male in our sample, our $N$ is 4; and the number of cases in our category "male" is 1. To get the proportion, divide 1 by 4:

$$P = \frac{f}{N} \qquad P = \frac{1}{4} = .25$$

So, the proportion of males in the front row is .25. To convert this to a percentage, simply multiply the proportion by 100 or use the formula for percentaging:

$$\% = \frac{f}{N} \times 100 \qquad \% = \frac{1}{4} \times 100 = 25\%$$

## Working with Negatives

Addition, subtraction, multiplication, division, and squared numbers are not difficult for most people; however, there are some important rules to know when working with negatives that you may need to review.

1. When adding a number that is negative, it is the same as subtracting:
   $$5 + (-2) = 5 - 2 = 3$$
2. When subtracting a negative number, the sign changes:
   $$8 - (-4) = 8 + 4 = 12$$
3. When multiplying or dividing a negative number, the product or quotient is always negative:
   $$6 \times -4 = -24, \qquad -10 \div 5 = -2$$
4. When multiplying or dividing two negative numbers, the product or quotient is always positive:
   $$-3 \times -7 = 21, \qquad -12 \div -4 = 3$$
5. Squaring a number that is negative always gives a positive product because it is the same as multiplying two negative numbers:
   $$-5^2 = 25 \text{ is the same as } -5 \times -5 = 25$$

## Order of Operations and Complex Expressions

In statistics you are likely to encounter some fairly lengthy equations that require several steps to solve. To know what part of the equation to work out first, follow two basic rules. The first is called the rules of precedence. They state that you should solve all squares and square roots first, then multiplication and division, and finally, all addition and subtraction from left to right. The second rule is to solve expressions in parentheses first. If there are brackets in the equation, solve the expression within parentheses first and then the expression within the brackets. This means that parentheses and brackets can override the rules of precedence. In statistics, it is common for parentheses to control the order of calculations. These rules may seem somewhat abstract here, but a brief review of their application should make them more clear.

To solve this problem,

$$4 + 6 \cdot 8 = 4 + 48 = 52$$

do the multiplication first and then the addition. Not following the rules of precedence will lead to a substantially different answer:

$$4 + 6 \cdot 8 = 10 \cdot 8 = 80$$

which is incorrect.

To solve this problem,

$$6 - 4(6)/3^2$$

First, find the square of 3,

$$6 - 4(6)/9$$

then do the multiplication and division from left to right,

$$6 - \frac{24}{9} = 6 - 2.67$$

and finally, work out the subtraction,

$$6 - 2.66 = 3.33$$

To work out the following equation, do the expressions within parentheses first:

$$(4 + 3) - 6(2)/(3 - 1)^2$$

First, solve the addition and subtraction in the parentheses,

$$(7) - 6(2)/(2)^2$$

Now that you have solved the expressions within parentheses, work out the rest of the equation based on the rules of precedence, first squaring the 2,

$$(7) - 6(2)/4$$

Then do the multiplication and division next:

$$(7) - \frac{12}{4} = (7) - 3$$

Finally, work out the subtraction to solve the equation:

$$7 - 3 = 4$$

The following equation may seem intimidating at first, but by solving it in steps and following the rules, even these complex equations should become manageable:

$$\sqrt{(8(4 - 2)^2)/(12/4)^2}$$

For this equation, work out the expressions within parentheses first; note that there are parentheses within parentheses. In this case, work out the inner parentheses first,

$$\sqrt{(8(2)^2)/3^2}$$

Now do the outer parentheses, making sure to follow the rules of precedence within the parentheses—square first and then multiply:

$$\sqrt{\frac{32}{3^2}}$$

Now, work out the square of 3 first and then divide:

$$\sqrt{\frac{32}{9}} = \sqrt{3.55}$$

Last, take the square root:

1.88

# Appendix H
# How to Use the GSS Data Files and Lotus ScreenCam

*by Mark Rodeghier*

The floppy disk that comes with this book has the data files for the exercises and SPSS demonstrations. It also has a set of the SPSS demonstrations that can be viewed with the help of the Lotus ScreenCam program.

### Data Files

Two SPSS data files are included on the disk in the DATA directory. One is named GSS87_91.SAV, and the other is named GSS94.SAV. Details of the files are explained in Appendix F: The General Social Survey and in the SPSS demonstration in Chapter 1.

Using SPSS, you can read these files directly from the floppy disk, but this will be slower than first copying them to the hard drive of your computer. You can copy them as you would any file, either with DOS commands or by using the File Manager program in Windows (see the next section on how to copy files in Windows).

### How to Install and Run the Lotus ScreenCam Examples

Several of the SPSS demonstrations have been recorded with the Lotus ScreenCam program. This allows you to see the exact mouse actions and keystrokes necessary to do analyses and create graphics with SPSS. Lotus ScreenCam allows you to record activity on a computer screen and then play it back at a later time. Only the playback file has been included on the floppy disk that comes with this book. To view the demonstrations, you will need to learn how to:

- Install the program and demonstration files on a hard disk.
- Load the program.
- Play the SPSS demonstration examples.
- Exit the program.

You can't run Lotus ScreenCam from the floppy disk because the files have been compressed, or zipped, so that more examples can be stored on one floppy disk. This means you must run ScreenCam from a hard drive. Also, ScreenCam is a Windows program and can't be run from DOS.

## Installing ScreenCam on a Hard Disk

To install ScreenCam, do the following:

1. Open the File Manager program from the Main program group in Windows. The File Manager icon looks like this:

File Manager

2. Check to make sure you have at least two megabytes of free disk space by looking in the lower left corner of the File Manager window, where you will see a number followed by "MB free."

3. Put the floppy disk in the appropriate drive, then click on that drive icon (usually either A: or B:) in File Manager. The icon should look like this:

4. There are two directories on the floppy disk. The one labeled SCRNCAM contains the ScreenCam program and demonstration files. You should see something like this

in the left-hand pane of the floppy drive window.

5. Make sure that windows for both drives are visible on the screen (you may first have to click on *Window...New Window* to create two windows, then click on *Window...Tile Horizontally* to see both windows). Now click on the SCRNCAM folder, hold the left button down, and drag the folder with the mouse to the root drive for C:

(or whichever drive is the hard disk), and release the button when the folder is over the root drive icon.

6. The computer will now create a new directory on the hard drive called SCRNCAM and copy three files from the floppy disk. The file SCREEN.ZIP contains the program and examples. The file PKUNZIP.EXE uncompresses the files. The file UNZIP.BAT runs the PKUNZIP program and applies it to the files in SCREEN.ZIP.

7. Double-click on the new SCRNCAM folder in the C: drive. You will see the three files that have been copied from the floppy disk. Now double-click on the file UNZIP.BAT. After a brief flurry of activity, you will be returned to the File Manager window. If you don't see any new files in the SCRNCAM directory, hit the F5 key to refresh the screen. You should

now see several files with the extension "SCM." These are the SPSS demonstration files. The other new file is SCPLAYER.EXE, the Lotus ScreenCam program you will use to view the demonstrations.

8. Congratulations! You've successfully installed the program and files.

## Loading and Running Lotus ScreenCam

To load ScreenCam:

1. Open the File Manager program as before, then click on the SCRNCAM folder in drive C:.

2. Double-click on the file SCPLAYER.EXE. When you do, this dialog box will appear on the screen. It will be superimposed over all windows while you are using the program.

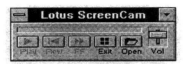

3. Using Lotus ScreenCam is like using a VCR. There is a *Play* button to run a demonstration, a *Rew* button to rewind, an *FF* button to fast forward, an *Open* button to open a demonstration file, and an *Exit* button to close the program. The *Vol* control is not used with these examples.

4. To open a demonstration, click on the *Open* button. When you do, a list of files with the extension "SCM" appears. The files have been named so you can probably tell what they demonstrate from their name (for example, XTABS.SCM produces a cross-tabulation), but there is also a description of each file when you click on the name. To open a file, double-click on it, or click once and then click on the *OK* button.

5. After the file is loaded, not much will have seemed to happen. However, the file name will be displayed in the control panel, and the Play button will now be highlighted. Click the *Play* button to begin the demonstration.

6. While the demonstration is playing, the Play button changes to a *Pause* button. This allows you to stop the movie at any moment to think about what you've been viewing. The demonstrations are also captioned to explain various actions as they occur.

7. When the demonstration is over, you can open another, rewind the current one, or exit the program.

8. Help is available by clicking on the control bar

in the upper left corner of the ScreenCam panel. When you do, you will see a list of options. Click on *Playback QuickHelp* to get help for each available action in ScreenCam.

# Answers to
# Odd-Numbered Exercises

## Chapter 1

1. Once a hypothesis is tested or evaluated, it is necessary to take the result and see what it tells us about how effective a theory is at predicting and understanding the social world. If the results show that the theory is not correct, then the theory should be modified.

3. a. Interval-ratio
   b. Nominal
   c. Interval-ratio
   d. Ordinal
   e. Nominal
   f. Ordinal
   g. Interval-ratio

5. The number of people in a household is a discrete variable because it can only take on certain values. The percentage who attended public high schools and the U.S. unemployment rate are both continuous measures.

9. Imagine that we asked people about their favorite songs and, also, about how well they could hear. We would probably find that people who liked certain types of music—show tunes and singers like Frank Sinatra—also had poorer hearing. Of course, type of music someone likes doesn't affect his or her hearing (unless you play rock music loud enough for a long enough time!); instead, age is the variable that causes the other two variables to be related. People of different ages like different types of music, and hearing deteriorates with age, on the average, so Sinatra fans might have poorer hearing.

## Chapter 2

1. a. Race is a nominal variable. Class is an ordinal variable because the categories can be ordered from lower to higher status.
   b. Frequency table for Race:

   | Race     | Frequency |
   |----------|-----------|
   | White    | 17        |
   | Nonwhite | 13        |

Frequency table for Class:

| Class | Frequency |
|---|---|
| Lower | 3 |
| Working | 15 |
| Middle | 11 |
| Upper | 1 |

   c. The proportion nonwhite is 13/30 = .43. The percentage white is (17/30) × 100 = 56.7%.

   d. The proportion middle class is 11/30 = .37.

3.  a. Relative frequency table for traumas experienced:

| Number of Traumas | Percentage |
|---|---|
| 0 | 50.0 |
| 1 | 36.7 |
| 2 | 13.3 |
| Total $N$ = 30 | |

Trauma is an interval-ratio level variable because it has a real zero point and a meaningful numeric scale.

   b. People in this survey are more likely to have experienced no traumas last year (50% of the group).

   c. The proportion who experienced one or more traumas is calculated by first adding 36.7 percent and 13.3 percent = 50 percent. Then divide that number by 100 to obtain .50, or half the group.

5.  a. Education is an interval-ratio variable.

   b. Frequency table for years of education:

| Years of Education | Frequency | Percentage | Cumulative Percentage |
|---|---|---|---|
| 1 | 4 | .2 | .2 |
| 2 | 4 | .2 | .4 |
| 3 | 13 | .6 | 1.0 |
| 4 | 18 | .8 | 1.8 |
| 5 | 14 | .6 | 2.4 |
| 6 | 33 | 1.5 | 3.9 |
| 7 | 30 | 1.4 | 5.3 |
| 8 | 100 | 4.6 | 9.8 |
| 9 | 79 | 3.6 | 13.4 |
| 10 | 123 | 5.6 | 19.0 |
| 11 | 156 | 7.1 | 26.1 |
| 12 | 684 | 31.1 | 57.3 |
| 13 | 194 | 8.8 | 66.1 |
| 14 | 252 | 11.5 | 77.6 |

| Years of Education | Frequency | Percentage | Cumulative Percentage |
|---|---|---|---|
| 15 | 113 | 5.1 | 82.7 |
| 16 | 214 | 9.7 | 92.5 |
| 17 | 53 | 2.4 | 94.9 |
| 18 | 62 | 2.8 | 97.7 |
| 19 | 18 | .8 | 98.5 |
| 20+ | 32 | 1.5 | 100.0 |
| Total | 2,196 | 100.0 | 100.0 |

   c. A total of 9.8 percent of the sample has eight years of education or less, which represents 206 respondents.

   d. Frequency table of grouped education:

| | Frequency | Percentage | Cumulative Percentage |
|---|---|---|---|
| Less than high school | 574 | 26.1 | 26.1 |
| High school graduate | 684 | 31.1 | 57.3 |
| Some college | 559 | 25.5 | 82.7 |
| College graduate | 379 | 17.3 | 100.0 |
| Total | 2,196 | 100.0 | 100.0 |

   e. A total of 17.3 percent of the sample has graduated from college.

   f. A total of 26.1 percent of the sample has not graduated from high school.

7. a. Relative frequency table for languages spoken at home (other than English):

| Language | Relative Percentage |
|---|---|
| Chinese | .9 |
| French | 1.5 |
| German | 1.8 |
| Hungarian | 5.4 |
| Indic | .9 |
| Italian | 2.6 |
| Other | .4 |
| Polish | 22.8 |
| Portuguese | 37.6 |
| Russian | 5.3 |
| Slavic | 7.7 |
| Spanish | 13.0 |
| Total | 100.0 |

A cumulative frequency table is less useful because this is a nominal variable.

   b. A total of 22.8 percent of the residents who speak a foreign language at home speak Polish. Another way to answer this question is to note that 831 out of 12,788 residents of South River speak Polish at home, which is only 6.5 percent.

c. A total of 13.0 percent speak Spanish at home.

d. The four most commonly spoken languages are Portuguese, Polish, Spanish, and Slavic.

e. The two least frequently spoken languages at home are Chinese and Indic.

9. a. Females are underrepresented on television. They compose 51 percent of the population but only 37 percent of characters on television.

b. Young adults and those defined as middle-aged are overrepresented.

c. It appears that Hispanics are the most underrepresented. They compose 9 percent of the American population but only 2 percent of television characters, for a difference of 7 percent (another way to put it is that Hispanics are underrepresented by a ratio of 4.5 to 1—9%/2%).

d. No. Professional/executive workers are greatly overrepresented; labor, service, and clerical workers are greatly underrepresented; and law enforcement officers are included on programs at a rate about ten times greater than they are found in the U.S. population.

e. Blacks are represented at about the relative frequency on television (13% to 12%).

f. Handicapped people are underrepresented, as are those who are overweight and those who wear glasses.

11. a. The relative frequencies for men and women:

| Reasons for Incarceration | Men | Women |
|---|---|---|
| Violent crime | 47.0% | 32.0% |
| Property crime | 25.0% | 29.0% |
| Drug crime | 21.0% | 33.0% |
| Other crime | 7.0% | 6.0% |
| Total (N) | 100.0% | 100.0% |
|  | 665,719 | 38,462 |

b. Men are incarcerated most often for violent crimes.

c. Women are incarcerated most often for drug crimes.

d. Men and women are most similar in property crime offenses (25% to 29%, respectively). Also, the category of "other crime" is about the same size for men and women.

13. a. The birth rate decreased from 1920 to 1945 by 0.8 of a child per woman. Then between 1945 and 1958 it increased by 1.3 births per woman, to a rate higher than in 1920. From 1958 to 1991 the rate declined to 2.1 births per woman (the lowest value was actually in 1976).

b. Birth rates seem to have been quite variable during the past seventy years, ranging from a high of 3.8 to a low of 1.7. In 1920 rates were well above the replacement level of about 2.2 births per female; they then declined in 1945, went up sharply during the baby boom, and have essentially declined since then, though not steadily. The low point for the birth rate was 1976, when the number of births was below replacement levels for the population.

15. a. A total of 85.7 percent of females think their family income is average or below; 77.2 percent of males believe the same about their family income.
   b. More blacks (88.9%) believe their family income is average or below than females.
   c. A total of 74.5 percent of all whites think their family income is average or above.
   d. A total of 25.4 percent of males think their family income is below average, whereas 22.8 percent think it is above average.

## Chapter 3

1. a. A total of .945 of all inmates are men.
   b. A total of 55 percent had a full-time job before being imprisoned.
   c. A total of 65 percent of the inmates did not graduate from high school.
   d. A total of 65 percent of inmates are nonwhite.

3. a. A total of 14 percent of all inmates were using both alcohol and drugs.
   b. A total of 49 percent were using either alcohol or drugs, or both.
   c. A total of 33 percent of women were incarcerated for drug crimes. Only 21 percent of men were incarcerated for the same crime.
   d. About 12,692 women were incarcerated for drug crimes.

5. a.

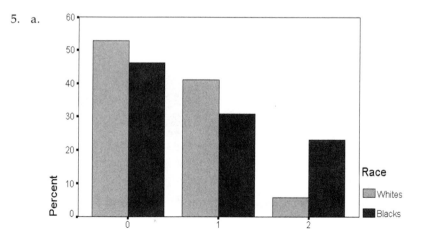

   b. Blacks are more likely to have experienced two traumas. About 23 percent of blacks experienced two traumas as compared with about 6 percent of whites.
   c. Frequencies don't control or adjust for the total number of people in each group. There are more whites (17) than blacks (13) in the survey, so percentages must be used to make the bars comparable.

7.  a. Either bar charts or pie charts can be used to display these data, and either graph type will accurately represent these data. However, comparing values across graphs is usually easier when bar charts are used; this is especially true when the proportions change greatly. Although that is not true in this case, because the number from each race receiving all four types of aid is relatively constant, we still recommend creating four bar graphs because the article will be comparing the relative frequencies by race.

    b.

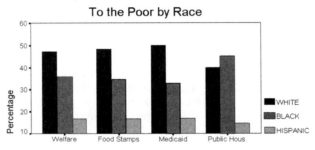

**Percentage of Recipients of Government Aid To the Poor by Race**

9.  a. Smoking by Grade Level

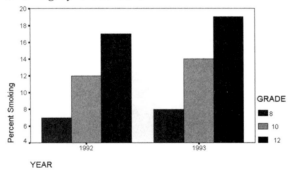

    b. Smoking by Year

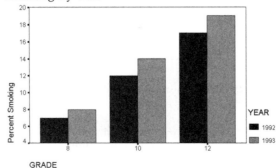

c.  The first bar graph shows that older students smoked more than younger students in each year, by placing the bars for the different grades next to each other. The second bar graph shows that students smoked more in 1993 than in 1992 at each grade level, by placing the bars for both years next to each other for each grade level. Either bar graph could be used to show that older teens smoked more and that smoking went up from 1992 to 1993, but it's easier to see the answer to each question with the data displayed in different formats.

11. a.

### Histogram for Whites

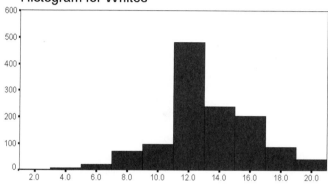

Years of Education

### Histogram for Blacks

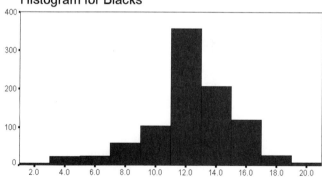

Years of Education

b.  The histograms show that whites have slightly more education than blacks. For example, about 22.1 percent of whites have at least a college degree, whereas only 10.7 percent of blacks have attained that level of education. However, the shapes of the histograms are very similar, which indicates that whites and blacks have roughly the same type of distribution of educational attainment. For example, both races show the largest category to be people who have completed about a high school education.

13. a.

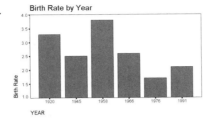

b.

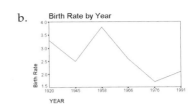

A time series bar chart is inherently more accurate because it only displays the data for the years we have information. A frequency polygon connects all the dots, which implies that birth rates changed steadily in between two dates (such as from 1920 to 1945). Of course, this is usually not true, so frequency polygons can give a somewhat distorted picture, especially when unequal time intervals are being used. On the other hand, statistical software, like SPSS, often presents bar charts with equal distances between each bar, as shown in (a). This can be misleading because the number of years between each data point is not equal; there are 25 years between 1920 and 1945, but only 13 between 1945 and 1958. So neither graph is perfect.

15. a.

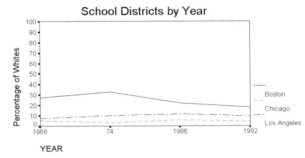

Chicago has had by far the most segregated school districts. At no time did blacks attend school in Chicago in districts where the percentage of white students was greater than 6 percent. On the other hand, in Boston whites have constituted as many as one-third of the students in predominantly black districts (in 1974). Los Angeles is more segregated than Boston and closer in percentages to Chicago. Over time, segregation has either increased, as in Boston, or stayed about the same, as in Chicago or Los Angeles.

b.

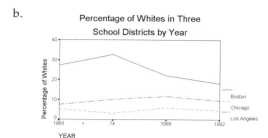

Percentage of Whites in Three School Districts by Year

One way to modify the percentage change in whites is to decrease the range of the Y-axis in the time series chart. The normal range for percentages is from 0 to 100, but you could reduce it so that the range ran from only 0 to 40 percent.

## Chapter 4

1. The mode for race is "white." The mode for class is "working class." The mode for traumas experienced is "0."

3. a. Education is measured on an interval-ratio scale. The mode is "12" years of education, or high school graduation. The median is also "12" years of education.
   b. The 25th percentile is 11 years; the 50th percentile is 12 years; the 75th percentile is 14 years. You don't need to calculate the 50th percentile because it is equivalent to the median.

5. a. For 18 to 29 year olds, the mode is once per day, and the median is several times a week. For 50 to 59 year olds, the mode is several times a day, and the median is once a day. For the 70- to 89-year-old group, the mode and median are both several times a day.
   b. Age is related to frequency of prayer because older people are more likely to pray. Thus, 50 to 59 year olds pray more than those in the 18 to 29 group, and those 50 to 59 year olds pray even more than 70 and above. The most common behavior in the two oldest groups is to pray several times a day. Moreover, over half of the oldest group prays at that frequency. On the other hand, the youngest respondents were most likely to pray once a day. At least as regards prayer behavior, there certainly seems to be a generation gap, as the differences between age groups are fairly large.

7. The mean number of persons per household is 2.72.

9. Distribution of Household Size, 1989 GSS

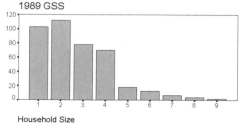

Household Size

a. Household size appears to be positively skewed. A bar chart for this variable shows a tail trailing toward larger values of household size.

b. The median for household size is 2, and the mode is also 2. Both of these values are below the mean, offering further proof that household size is positively skewed, as the mean is pulled toward the tail for skewed distributions. The distribution is not symmetrical because there is a smallest minimum value of household size (1), but no theoretical maximum, so the distribution is cut off at the low end and trails out at large household sizes.

11. Yes, both of these politicians can be correct, at least in a technical sense. One politician can be referring to the mean; the other could be using the median. The average or mean income of Americans can be greater than the median if income's distribution is positively skewed.

## Chapter 5

1. a. The maximum possible number of differences is 4,929,545.

b. The observed number of differences is 364,955.

c. The IQV is the ratio of the two answers in (a) and (b), or 0.074. This value is fairly close to 0, which means that, as measured by the IQV, Americans are not that diverse in their political position.

3. a. The range of poverty rates in the South is from 14.5 to 23.7 percent, or 9.2 percent. The range in the West is from 8.9 to 22.4 percent, or 13.5 percent. The West has a greater range.

b. For the South, the 25th percentile is 15.45 percent and the 75th percentile is 18.8 percent, so the IQR is 3.35 percent. For the West, the 25th percentile is 12.15 percent and the 75th percentile is 15.55 percent, so the IQR is 3.40 percent. The IQR for the West is just slightly larger.

c. The data support the idea that there is greater variability of poverty rates in western states. The range in poverty rates in western states is greater than in southern states by a factor of 13.5/9.2, or about 1.5. There is little difference in the IQRs for each region, though. The difference in variability seems to be because the West has more states with lower rates of poverty, such as Washington or Nevada.

5. a. The range of percent increase in the elderly population for the Mountain states is 68.2 percent. The range of percent increase for the West North Central states is 5.5 percent. The Mountain states have a much larger range.

b. The IQR for the Mountain states is 13.7 percent. The IQR for the West North Central states is 3.6 percent. Again, the value for the Mountain states is greater.

c. There is great variability in the increase in the elderly population in the Mountain states, chiefly caused by the large increases in Nevada, Arizona, and New Mexico, as measured by either the range or the IQR.

7. a. The standard deviation for states in the South is 2.79, and that for states in the West is 3.75.

b. As measured by the standard deviation, there is more variability in the West. This is consistent with the differences in the range between the two regions, although not with the IQR, which was essentially identical in both regions. Different measures of variability can give somewhat different results.

9. a. For traditional families, the variance is 78.56 and the standard deviation 8.86. For nontraditional families, the variance is 41.61 and the standard deviation 6.45.
   b. There is more variability in the number of hours that men do housework in traditional families each week.
   c. No, we didn't need the mean of $Y$ to calculate the variance or standard deviation.

11. a. The mean for violent crime rate is 464.8. The mean for federal and state prisoners is 2.3.
   b. The standard deviation for crime rate is 289.3. The standard deviation for prisoners is 0.9.
   c. The IQR for violent crime rate is 340.5, and the IQR for prisoner rate is 1.25.
   d. Because the mean is so much larger for the violent crime rate than the incarceration rate, it isn't appropriate to directly compare the standard deviation or IQR for one variable with the other. We do observe that the standard deviation for both variables is smaller than the mean, as is the IQR. However, it appears there is slightly more variability for the violent crime rate because the IQR and standard deviation are closer in size to the mean value. For violent crime rate, states like North Dakota, New York, Maine, New Hampshire, Vermont, and Illinois contribute more to its variability because they have values far from the mean. For incarceration rate, North Dakota, Minnesota, New York, Ohio, and Connecticut contribute more to its variability.

13. a. The standard deviation is 18.38.
   b. The IQR is 18 from Figure 5.4, so the standard deviation is slightly larger.
   c. Yes, the standard deviation would lead to about the same conclusion concerning the variability of the increase in elderly population as do the box plot and IQR. However, the box plot shows the actual range of values, which the standard deviation cannot (even though all values are used to calculate the statistic).

## Chapter 6

1. a. The independent variable is race; the dependent variable is fear of walking alone at night.

| FEAR | RACE | |
|------|-------|-------|
|      | Black | White |
| No   | 4     | 7     |
| Yes  | 6     | 4     |

b. A majority of whites (63.6%) are not afraid to walk alone in their neighborhoods at night, but a majority of blacks (60%) are afraid to walk alone. These differences undoubtedly have nothing to do with race as such, but rather with the fact that blacks are more likely to live in dangerous neighborhoods, where it is sometimes dangerous to be out at night alone.

**RACE**

| FEAR | Black | White |
|------|-------|-------|
| No | 40.0% | 63.6% |
| Yes | 60.0% | 36.4% |

3. Among the four majors, 89 percent of all students who get an engineering degree get a job related to their major. Only 57 percent of students who major in the humanities, though, find a job related to their major. Students who major in business are also likely to find a job related to their degree. Thus, based on just these statistics, you might counsel a new student to get a degree in engineering or business and avoid the humanities (assuming she finds the former subjects interesting).

5. a. Given how your classmate phrased the question, the dependent variable is belief about homosexuality, and the independent variable is whether or not someone has a gay or lesbian as a close friend or family member.

b. A total of $254/1,154 = .22$ have a close friend or family member who is gay or lesbian.

c. No, they are more likely to believe that homosexuality is not a choice. Only 36 percent of those who are close to a gay or lesbian think homosexuality is a choice, but 54.8 percent of those without close contact with gays or lesbians believe that homosexuality is a choice.

7. a. A total of 46.3 percent of the community think their health is good, 31.5 percent think their health is excellent, and 22.1 percent think their health is fair or poor.

b. There is very little difference in the perceived health of men and women. Men are slightly more likely to think they are in excellent health (32.4% to 30.8%), but they are also very slightly more likely to think they are in fair or poor health (22.5% to 21.9%).

c. It would seem that the clinic should focus equally on men and women, given that their perceived differences in health are so slight.

9. a. Yes, there is definitely a relationship between age and attitude toward premarital sex. About 17.6 percent of the youngest group believe premarital sex is always wrong, but 53.3 percent of the oldest respondents believe this. Then, 49.5 percent of the youngest think that premarital sex is not wrong at all, but only 19.2 percent of the oldest group believe this.

b. The direction of this relationship is such that older people are more likely to think premarital sex is wrong. It would be fair to say that

the relationship is reasonably strong. The difference in attitude between the oldest and youngest respondents is 35.7 percent for those who believe premarital sex is always wrong, and the difference is 30.3 percent for those who believe it is not wrong at all.

11. a. Residential segregation patterns have changed for both blacks and Hispanics between 1980 and 1990. Blacks increasingly live in more integrated neighborhoods; the percentage living in neighborhoods that are predominantly black has dropped from 35 to 13 percent. Hispanics have increasingly come to live in neighborhoods that are more segregated, as the percentages for them have increased from 17 to 27 percent.

b. There is a relationship between ethnicity and changes in segregation, such that segregation increased for Hispanics and decreased for blacks. In fact, it would appear that Hispanics in 1990 live in more segregated neighborhoods than blacks, which was not true in 1980.

13. a. In three of the four cities, Los Angeles, Dallas, and Chicago, there has been little change in school segregation from 1968 to 1992, though in the two former cities, segregation did decrease slightly. In New York, segregation has increased over time; 23.2 percent of black students had predominantly white classmates in 1968, but that was true for only 8.4 percent of blacks in 1992.

b. The trend is much stronger in New York. The percentage change was 14.8 percent in New York and only 3.7 percent in Dallas.

c. In Los Angeles, segregation decreased from 1968 to 1986 (92.5% to 88.3%), then increased in 1992 (to 90.4 percent). In Dallas, segregation decreased from 1968 to 1974 (94.4% to 86.6%), but then increased in 1986 and 1992. In Chicago, segregation increased from 1968 to 1972 (94.6% to 98.8%), then decreased in 1986, then increased in 1992. In New York, segregation increased steadily from 1968 to 1992, so it was the only city to show a steady trend.

15. a. For whites, 72 percent of those who disapprove of women working outside the home think that pornography leads to a breakdown in morals, whereas only 60.6 percent of those who approve of women working think the same about the effect of pornography. For blacks, 71.4 percent of those who disapprove of women working outside the home think that pornography leads to a breakdown in morals, whereas only 56.3 percent who approve of women working think the same about pornography.

b. These differences between blacks and whites are small, so we conclude that race does not have a conditional effect on the relationship between attitudes toward women and the effect of pornography.

## Chapter 7

1. a. We will make 496 errors, because we predict that everyone falls in the modal category that considers homosexuality to be a choice. The category of "Don't know" should be ignored.

b. We will make 81 errors of prediction for those respondents who had a close friend or family member who is gay or lesbian. We will make 352 errors for those who don't have such a relationship.

c. The proportional reduction in error is then (496 − 433)/496 = 12.7 percent, so we can increase our ability to predict attitude toward homosexuality by 12.7 percent (and equivalently, decrease the errors of prediction) by knowing whether or not someone has a close friend or family member who is lesbian or gay.

3. a. The number of same order pairs, $Ns$, is 165,958. The number of inverse order pairs, $Nd$, is 84,958.

b. Gamma for the table is .324 and is positive. This implies that older people are more likely to believe that premarital sex is wrong. This value of gamma is moderate in size.

5. a. Time is the independent variable. Without knowing time, we would make 83 errors by predicting that all bills didn't pass. Knowing time period, we would make 19 + 64 = 83 errors. Thus, lambda is (83 − 83)/83 = 0. This value seems to indicate that knowing the time period doesn't help to predict whether or not bills passed; put another way, it might be seen as evidence that there was no change in the proportion of bills passed on women's and family issues in the 1992/93 period versus 1990/91.

b. Lambda has a value of exactly zero because the modal category for both time periods is the same—didn't pass—which is also the mode for the bill passage variable as a whole. The value of lambda does seem surprising, as 12.8 percent of the bills passed in 1992/93 versus 7.6 percent in 1990/91.

7. a. Gamma is equal to .28.

b. That gamma is positive means that more bills passed in the later time period than in the earlier. That gamma is not close to 1 means that the relationship is fairly weak, which we have also seen by looking at the percent difference in bill passage.

9. a. Somers' $d$, with attitude toward the death penalty the dependent variable, is .025.

b. This is a very weak relationship because the value of Somers' $d$ is so close to zero. People with a graduate education are more likely to oppose the death penalty. However, those most in favor of the death penalty are not people with the least education, but instead people with a high school education.

11. a. Gamma is −.28.

b. Somers' $d$ is −.13.

c. The values of these two statistics are negative because disapproval of women working outside the home is associated with a greater belief that pornography leads to a breakdown in morals. In exercise 14, Chapter 6, we found a 12.8 percent difference between belief about the effect of pornography, depending on whether one approved or disapproved of women working outside the home. Now we see that these differences translate into a modest statistical association between these two attitudes: both gamma and Somers' $d$ are closer to 0 than to −1.

## Chapter 8

1. a. On the scatterplot the regression line has been plotted to make it easier to see the relationship between the two variables.

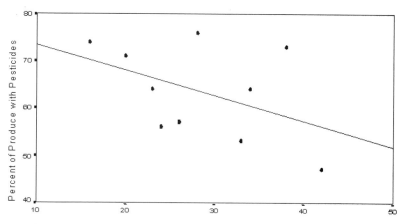

Number of Types of Pesticides

b. The scatterplot shows that there is a general linear relationship between the two variables, even though there is a fair amount of scatter about the straight line describing the relationship. As the number of pesticides detected increases, the percentage of a particular food type with pesticides decreases.

c. The Pearson correlation coefficient between the two variables is −.45. This seems rather odd, because it means that as the percent of a produce with pesticides increases, the different number of pesticides in that food decreases. It is hard to explain, but one possibility is that when a type of food is more often contaminated with pesticides, it is because of a few specific pesticides, rather than a large number.

3. a. The correlation between the number of AIDS cases in each year is the same, .996.

b. The correlation coefficient is the same as in exercise 2, even though 20 was added to each value for 1992. Adding a constant to a variable, or both variables, in a scatterplot, simply shifts the position of the best-fitting line, but it doesn't change the slope of the line or the correlation coefficient.

5. a. The correlation coefficient between percent of unwed births is .95.

b. The correlation coefficient is very close to 1, which means that high values of unwed births for whites are closely associated with high values of unwed births for nonwhites, and vice versa.

7. a. Yes, it is true that as wealth, as measured by GNP per capita, increases, infant mortality decreases. This is a negative relationship.

b. At very low values of GNP per capita, say under $1,000, infant mortality can range widely from near 0 to over 200 deaths per 1,000 births, though the majority of countries have values near 100 and above. As GNP per capita increases, there is less variation, and fewer high values of infant mortality are observed. Above $10,000, only one country has an infant mortality rate of about 100 and most are well below that value.

c. A straight line doesn't seem to be the best fit. Notice how it falls below the bulk of points at low values of GNP. Instead, a curved line that curves up at low values of GNP would seem to be a better fit. Not all relationships in the world are linear.

9. a.

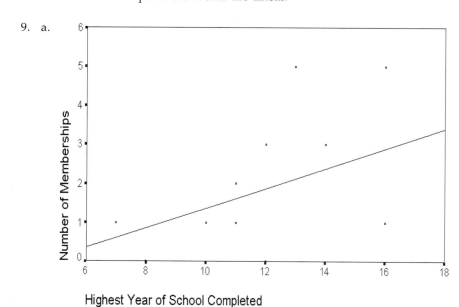

Highest Year of School Completed

b. The slope of the regression equation is .25. The intercept is –1.16. A straight line fits the data reasonably well, but it fits people with less education better. This is because the scatter about the line is less for people with less than 12 years of education than for those who have completed more education. In general, people with more education have more formal memberships.

c. The error of prediction for the second case is about 2.15 memberships. That is, we predicted that he or she would have 2.85 memberships, but this person actually belongs to 5 organizations. The error of prediction for a person with 10 years of education and 1 membership is –.34 membership. Here, we predicted a value of 1.34, but the person has less than that amount.

d. For someone with 14 years of education, we predict about 2.3 memberships. For someone with 4 years of education, we predict less than 0 memberships. This can't be right. This prediction illustrates the problem of making predictions beyond the range of the independent variable (also, the relationship between these two variables is most likely nonlinear at low values of education).

11. a.  A straight line fits the data rather well, as shown in the scatterplot.

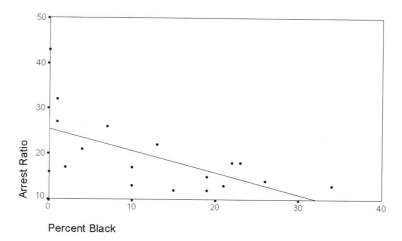

Percent Black

b.  The slope of the regression equation is –.48. The intercept is 25.48. The city that falls farthest from the line is Livonia, Michigan, with no blacks and an arrest ratio of 43.
c.  A value of 51 percent for the black population yields a predicted arrest ratio of 1.

## Chapter 9

1.  a.  Nominal
    b.  Interval-ratio
    c.  Ordinal
    d.  Nominal
    e.  If an exact time, interval-ratio; if an approximate time, ordinal
    f.  Ordinal

3.

Willingness to Accept a Cut in Living Standards to Help the Environment

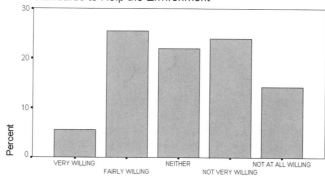

5. a. Yes, there appears to be a relationship. Whites are more willing to accept a cut in living standards to help the environment, as compared with other races. Combining the categories of "very willing" and "fairly willing" includes 34.7 percent of whites, 29.3 percent of blacks, and 33.3 percent of others. Fewer whites are "not at all willing" to accept a cut in living standards. Nevertheless, more blacks, 8.3 percent, than whites or other races say they are "very willing" to accept a cut.

   b. Lambda = .008. This value is very close to zero, and although the relationship between GRNSOL and race is weak, it doesn't quite seem this nonexistent.

7. The median amount of sales tax paid is $338.84.

9. The 25th percentile is $171.15 and the 75th percentile is $538.96, so the IQR is $367.81.

11. The bar chart uses a scale for the $Y$-axis that runs from only 2.60 to 2.75, thus exaggerating the difference in self-rated health between males and females. It would have been better to use a scale running from 1 to 7 on the $Y$-axis. Obviously, an unsuspecting reader might think that females rate their health much lower than do males.

13. a. The mean for feelings toward Clinton is 60.42. The mean feelings toward Dole is 51.67.

   b. The variance for feelings toward Clinton is 875.91, and the standard deviation is 29.60.

   c. The 25th percentile for Dole is 35. The 75th percentile is 70, so the IQR for feelings toward Dole is 35.

15. a. Working-class people are more likely to approve of Clinton: 22.3 percent of this group give the highest approval rating to Clinton, compared with 15.9 percent of the middle class. Over one-third of the middle class (35.4%) "strongly disapprove" of Clinton, but only 22.5 percent of the working class do.

   b. Somers' $d$ for the table is −.164, with class as the predictor. The sign is negative because "working class" is coded lower than "middle class." This value of Somers' $d$ indicates that there is a weak negative relationship between class and approval of President Clinton. It also indicates that by using the order of pairs of cases on class, we can improve the prediction of the order or relative ranking of pairs of cases on approval of President Clinton by 16.4 percent over a prediction without using class.

## Chapter 10

1. a. Yes, the applicant would be accepted because a score of 115 is at the 90.5th percentile.

   b. The cutoff score is about 113 for the 88th percentile.

   c. The $Z$ score for 113 is 1.17.

3. a. China's $Z$ score equivalent is 10.16.

   b. For any normal distribution, about 15.9 percent of all cases should fall less than 1 standard deviation below the mean. For the distribution of population values, 1 standard deviation below the mean is less than zero (27.3 − 105.7), so clearly no countries have population values lower than 1 standard deviation below the mean.

  c. The distribution of population must not be normal, because a true normal distribution would have cases well below the mean. Therefore, the median would be a better measure of central tendency.

5. a. About .17 of the males have incomes between $30,000 and $40,000. About .08 of the females have incomes in this range.
  b. For a male drawn at random, the probability of having an income above $50,000 is .058. For females, the probability is only about .002.
  c. The upper limit is $22,543.18; the lower limit is $6,119.24.
  d. If income is positively skewed, then the proportion of cases at high incomes will be greater than for a normal distribution. This means, for example, that the probabilities of an income above $50,000 should be larger.

7. a. About 13 percent of whites should have scores above 60.
  b. About 8 percent of blacks should have scores above 60.
  c. About .83 of all whites should have prestige scores between 30 and 70.
  d. About 18 blacks should have prestige scores between 50 and 60.

9. a. About .282 of all burglaries had dollar losses above $1,000.
  b. About 5.5 percent of burglaries had dollar losses between $200 and $300.
  c. The probability is about .69 that a dollar loss was above $400.

11. a. $Z = 2.0$
  b. About .308 of the sample reads less than 10 magazines, or about 154 people.
  c. 6.8
  d. 68.3 percent, because this corresponds to the proportion of a normal curve within 1 standard deviation of the mean

13. For any $Z$ distribution, the value of the mean is 0. The standard deviation of a $Z$ distribution is 1. $Z$ distributions are based on the mean of a variable and are centered around that value, so they have a mean of 0 by definition. A $Z$ score of 1 or −1 is equivalent to a score in the original distribution that is 1 standard deviation above or below the mean, respectively. This direct mapping from the original distribution to a $Z$ score means that the standard deviation of a $Z$ distribution must be equal to 1.

## Chapter 11

1. a. Although there are problems with the collection of data from all Americans, the census is assumed to be complete, so the mean age would be a parameter.
  b. A statistic because it is estimated from a sample
  c. A statistic because it is estimated from a sample
  d. A parameter because the bank has information on all employees

3. a. She is selecting a systematic random sample. The population might be defined as all persons shopping at that mall that day of the week. A more precise definition might limit it to all persons passing by the department store at the mall that day.

    c. This is neither a simple random sample nor a systematic random sample. It might be thought of as a sample stratified on last name, but even then, choosing the first twenty names is not a random selection process.

5. No.

7. a. They are undoubtedly not probability samples.

9. b. This is a systematic random sample because names are drawn systematically from the list of all enrolled students.

11. a. Mean = 5.3; standard deviation = 3.27
    b. Here are ten means from random samples of size 3: 6.33, 5.67, 3.33, 5.00, 7.33, 2.33, 6.00, 6.33, 7.00, 3.00.
    c. The mean of these ten sample means is 5.23. The standard deviation is 1.76. The mean of the sample means is very close to the mean for the population. The standard deviation of the sample means is much less than the standard deviation for the population. The standard deviation of the means from the samples is an estimate of the standard error of the mean we would find from one random sample of size 3.

# Chapter 12

1. a. The best estimate at the 90 percent confidence level runs from 11.52 to 14.88 percent. This means that there are 90 chances out of 100 that the confidence interval we calculate in this manner will contain the percentage of victims in the U.S. population. The calculated interval for this particular sample either does or does not contain the population mean.
    b. The confidence interval at the 99 percent level is 13.2 percent ± 2.63 percent.
    c. Both confidence intervals will shrink by a factor of $1/\sqrt{2}$.

3. a. .41 ± .03
    b. .41 ± .04

5. a. 81 percent ± 2.8 percent
    b. No, a majority of Americans do not favor special preferences in hiring.

7. a. $678 ± $49.08
    b. The calculation of a confidence interval is still appropriate.

9. a. No estimate of the mean is needed. The error in a sample is related to the standard deviation, not directly to the mean.
    b. Sample size should be about 384.
    c. Sample size should be about 666.

11. .12 ± .037

13. 41 percent ± 3.0 percent

# Chapter 13

1. a. $H_0$: $\mu_Y$ = 13.5 years; $H_1$: $\mu_Y$ < 13.5 years
    b. For a one-tailed test at an alpha level of .10, the critical value of Z is −1.28 (negative because the sample mean is less than the population

mean). The $Z$ value obtained is $-4.19$. This exceeds the critical value, so we reject the null hypothesis and conclude that the doctors at the HMO do have less experience than the population of doctors at all HMOs.

3.  a.  The appropriate test is a one-sample test of a mean, with $H_0$: $\mu_Y = 470$ and $H_1$: $\mu_Y \neq 470$. At the .01 significance level for a two-tailed test, the critical value of $Z$ is $-2.58$. The obtained value of $Z$ is $-2.41$, so we fail to reject the null hypothesis.
    b.  Even though we failed to reject $H_0$, the probability of a Type I error when doing the test is still the alpha level of .01.

5.  At the .01 level of significance, for a two-tailed test, the critical value of $Z$ is $\pm 2.58$. The obtained value of $Z$ is $-1.50$, so we fail to reject the null hypothesis. This means that the mean income of the ward's residents is not significantly different from that for the whole city.

7.  a.  $H_0$: $\mu_U = \$45,000$; $H_1$: $\mu_U > \$45,000$
    b.  At the .05 significance level, the critical value of $Z$ is 1.65 for a one-tailed test. The obtained value of $Z$ is 4.15, so we reject the null hypothesis. Unionized faculty do earn more than all faculty nationwide.

9.  At an alpha level of .05 with a two-tailed test, the critical value of $Z$ is $\pm 1.96$. The obtained value of $Z$ is very large, 19.01. We reject the null hypothesis of no difference and conclude that this sample of black professional women is not representative of all women.

11.  a.  The obtained value of $Z$ is 5.72.
    b.  We should do a one-tailed test because we predict cooperative learning leads to higher scores. At the .05 level of significance, the critical value of $Z$ is 1.65. The obtained value of $Z$ exceeds this, so we reject the null hypothesis of no difference.
    c.  We conclude that cooperative learning does lead to higher final scores.

## Chapter 14

1.  a.  $H_0$: $\mu_{Y_C} = \mu_{Y_S}$. The research hypothesis is $\mu_{Y_C} > \mu_{Y_S}$.
    b.  At the .01 level of significance, the critical value of $t$ is 2.33. We use the two-sample test with the variance in the two populations known, yielding a $t$ value of 4.67. This leads to a rejection of the null hypothesis, and we conclude that the researcher is correct that city residents do experience more stressful events than suburban residents.

3.  a.  This is a two-tailed test. At the .01 level, the critical value of $Z$ is $\pm 2.58$. Using the two-sample test for proportions, we find a $Z$ of $-2.32$. This is less, in absolute value, than the critical value, so we fail to reject the null hypothesis and conclude that the proportion of bills passed was equal in both two-year intervals.
    b.  This result is compatible with a lambda of zero, as calculated before, which also indicates no relationship. However, the value of gamma calculated was .28, which indicates a weak relationship. Different statistical tests can yield somewhat different results on the same data.

5.  a.  The null hypothesis is $\mu_{Y_L} = \mu_{Y_C}$. The research hypothesis is $\mu_{Y_L} < \mu_{Y_C}$ because more favorable attitudes are associated with lower scores.

    b.  The appropriate two-sample test is a $t$ test where the variances are unknown but assumed to be equal. It will have $123 + 38 - 2 = 159$ degrees of freedom.

    c.  At the .05 significance level the critical value of $t$ for a one-tailed test is –1.65 (negative because of the direction of $H_1$). The obtained value of $t$ is –1.58, so we fail to reject $H_0$. This result fails to support the political scientist's hypothesis.

7.  a.  The variances cannot be assumed to be equal, so we must use a $t$ test that meets these restrictions (Equation 14.6).

    b.  The degrees of freedom for the test are approximately 8.6 (or 9), calculated from Equation 14.7. The critical value of $t$ for a one-tailed test at the alpha level of .01 is 2.39. The obtained $t$ value is .767, so we fail to reject the null hypothesis of no difference in the number of children for happy and unhappy people. The friend was wrong.

9.  a.  The appropriate test is the $Z$ test for differences in two proportions with large samples.

    b.  The critical value of $Z$ at the .05 significance level for a two-tailed test is 1.96. The obtained value of $Z$ is 1.13, so we fail to reject the null hypothesis. Males and females have an equal level of support for abortion for single women.

11. a.  To compare Cuban with Puerto Rican men, we use the $t$ test for unequal variances. But to compare Cuban with Mexican men, we can use the $t$ test for equal variances.

    b.  For a one-tailed test with 9,801 degrees of freedom, the critical value of $t$ is 1.65. For the Cuban–Puerto Rican comparison, the obtained $t$ is 28.59, so we reject the null hypothesis. For the Cuban–Mexican comparison, the obtained $t$ is 48.31, so we again reject the null hypothesis.

    c.  These results confirm the previous results from Chapter 12. These large obtained values of $t$ make it very, very unlikely that the earnings of Cuban men are equal to those of Mexican or Puerto Rican men in the U.S. population.

13. a.  $H_0$: $\pi_F = \pi_M$. $H_1$: $\pi_F > \pi_M$. We should conduct a one-tailed test because females are predicted to have a higher level of support.

    b.  The obtained value of $Z$ is 3.08. The critical value for a one-tailed test at the .01 level of significance is 2.33, so we reject the null hypothesis. This means that there was a gender gap based on the poll results.

## Chapter 15

1.  a.  $\chi^2 = .883$

    b.  Degrees of freedom = 1

    c.  The critical value of $\chi^2$ is 3.84 at the .05 significance level. Thus, we fail to reject the null hypothesis of independence between race and fear. This conclusion is not consistent with the description of the table in Chapter 6. Using percentages, it appeared that whites are less fearful than blacks of walking alone at night.

    d. The cell for blacks who are afraid of walking alone has an expected valuᶜ of 4.76.

3. a. 3 degrees of freedom
   b. $\chi^2 = 2.32$. The expected number of females who rate their health as poor is 14.
   c. The critical value of $\chi^2$ is 7.81. We conclude that sex and self-rated health are independent.

5. a. A total of 67.5 percent of union members are satisfied with their job compared with 62.5 percent of workers who don't belong to a union, so it appears that union membership and job satisfaction may be related. However, the probability of the chi-square test is .294, above the .05 level, so her alternative hypothesis is not supported.
   b. The new study does support her alternative hypothesis, because the chi-square significance level is .036, below the .05 level.
   c. There is no difference in percentages between the two tables, as the percentages of union and nonunion members who are satisfied are identical. The chi-square value is larger in the second table because sample size was increased.

7. a. There is a 6 percent difference, with whites having more support: 48 percent of whites support more severe sentences compared with 42 percent of blacks.
   b. $\chi^2 = 3.37$ with 1 degree of freedom. This value is not significant at the .05 level, so we fail to reject the null hypothesis.
   c. Although there is a 6 percentage point difference in support by race, it appears that race and support for sentence severity are independent.

9. a. The chi-square value of 10.866 has a significance (or probability) of .012, so at the .05 level we conclude that education is related to support for the death penalty.
   b. The greatest differences are for those in high school and persons with graduate education. The cells that contribute most to chi-square are those with larger differences between the expected and observed values and with relatively smaller expected values. The two cells that contribute the most are high school graduates and those with a graduate education who oppose the death penalty for murder.
   c. The relationship between education and support for the death penalty is driven by people with a graduate education, who tend to oppose the death penalty more than expected, and high school graduates, who favor the death penalty more than expected.

11. a. $\chi^2 = 26.61$
    b. The degrees of freedom for the table is 9. The critical value of $\chi^2$ is 21.67. At the .01 significance level, we conclude that educational level and attitude toward premarital sex are related.
    c. There is a roughly linear relationship between the two variables because as education increases, the belief that premarital sex is "not wrong at all" increases: 51.2 percent of those with a graduate education but only 36.4 percent of those with less than a high school education believe this. The reverse is true for those who believe that premarital sex is always wrong, where 39.3 percent of the least educated but only

11.9 percent of those with graduate education have this opinion. The cells that contribute most to chi-square are associated with the lowest and highest values of education. The cell that contributes the most is for those with less than a high school education who believe pre-marital sex is always wrong.

13. a.

```
                          ATTEND
              Count |
                    | ONCE A Y   MONTHLY   WEEKLY O
                    | EAR OR L   BUT LESS  R MORE O      Row
                    |    1     |    2    |    3    |   Total
SYMPTBLK     ------- + --------- + ------- + -------- +
                  1 |    24    |    25   |    36   |     85
     VERY   OFTEN   |          |         |         |   18.0
                    + --------- + ------- + -------- +
                  2 |    75    |    44   |    57   |    176
     FAIRLY OFTEN   |          |         |         |   37.2
                    + --------- + ------- + -------- +
                  3 |    96    |    61   |    55   |    212
   NOT  TOO  OFTEN  |          |         |         |   44.8
                    + --------- + ------- + -------- +
              Column    195       130       148       473
              Total     41.2      27.5      31.3     100.0
```

b. The smallest expected frequency is 23.36.
c. Degrees of freedom is 4; $\chi^2 = 10.38$
d. The critical value of $\chi^2$ at the .05 significance level is 9.49, so we reject the null hypothesis. Those who are more sympathetic toward blacks attend religious services more frequently.

# Chapter 16

1. a. About .258 of all marriages last between 10 and 20 years.
   b. A marriage that lasts 50 years is at the 98.5th percentile. This is certainly a rare value, so it justifies the exceptional nature of such marriages.
   c. The probability is about .196.
   d. Yes, length of marriage is probably not normally distributed because there are few cases below 1 standard deviation from the mean.

3. a. For whites, $\chi^2 = 64.25$ with 8 degrees of freedom. We reject the null hypothesis. For blacks, $\chi^2 = 6.97$ with 8 degrees of freedom. This is less than the critical value, so we fail to reject the null hypothesis. The results are thus different by race.
   b. Race is a control variable that specifies the relationship between support for AIDS research funding and political preference. In other words, there is a conditional relationship between the latter two variables because of race.
   c. The main problem comes about because of the small number of people who say they prefer a third, or other, party. Combine the "Other Party" category with the "Independent" and "No Preference" groups. These

categories are not exactly comparable but this groups political preference into Republican, Democrat, and Other. In the table for whites, the relationship remains significant (chi-square 60.87). In the table for blacks, the relationship remains nonsignificant (chi-square 5.44).

5. a. The 95 percent confidence interval is 59.5 percent ± 4.8 percent.
   b. The upper end of the confidence interval is at 64.3 percent, which is below the census figure of 66.9 percent as a whole. This indicates that it is likely that the percentage of Hispanic two-parent households is lower in the city.

7. a. $\chi^2 = 5.26$. The critical value of $\chi^2$ is 6.63 at the .01 level, so we fail to reject $H_0$.
   b. The proportion of males disapproving is .694; for females it is .640. The obtained $Z$ is 2.34. The critical value of $Z$ is 2.58, so we fail to reject the null hypothesis.
   c. The 95 percent confidence interval is 66.7 percent ± 2.3 percent
   d. The conclusions are similar.

9. a. The 99 percent confidence interval is $7.69 ± .51.
   b. No, this is not an appropriate interpretation.

11. a. A two-sample difference of proportions test is appropriate. The obtained $Z$ is 1.343, which is below the critical value of 2.58, so we conclude that males and females are equally likely to have been involved with someone else before their marriage ended.
    b. The 95 percent confidence interval is 15.2 percent ± 1.6 percent.

13. a. People who are divorced, separated, or widowed say they are worse off than they were a year ago. People who are married are the least likely to say this (25.6%). However, singles (46.6%) and those separated (46.7%) are the most likely to say they are better off. Only a majority of those widowed say they are about the same (50.8%).
    b. The chi-square for this table is 56.90 with 8 degrees of freedom. The critical value of chi-square is 15.51, so we reject the null hypothesis and conclude that the two variables are related.

# Index/Glossary

## A

*a*, 359, 360, 369

Abortion
    gender, and, 605, 606
    job security, and, 248, 249
    morality, and, 272–274
    prediction error, 299, 300
    race, and, 608, 609
    religious affiliation, and, 265–272
    trauma, and, 301
    worldview, and, 329–333

Absolute frequencies, 246, 248

Accuracy of predictions, 373, 374

Affirmative action, 679–685

Age at first marriage, 146, 147

AIDS, 664, 665

AIDS risks among women, 641–644

Algebraic sum of errors, 361

**Alpha** ($\alpha$) the level of probability at which the null hypothesis is rejected. It is customary to set alpha at the .05, .01, or .001 level, 564

Anxiety about statistics, 28, 182

Association. *See* Measures of association

**Asymmetrical measure of association** a measure whose value may vary depending on which variable is considered the independent variable and which the dependent variable, 309

Average, 149. *See also* Mean

## B

*b*, 359, 360, 369

$b_{yx}$, 367–369

**Bar graph** a graph showing the differences in frequencies or percentages among categories of a nominal or an ordinal variable. The categories are displayed as rectangles of equal width with their height proportional to the frequency or percentage of the category, 93–96, 113, 114

Bell-shaped curve, 443. *See also* Normal distribution

**Best-fitting line** *See* Least-squares line, 361, 362

**Bivariate analysis** a statistical method designed to detect and describe the relationship between two variables, 236

Bivariate regression analysis, 350

Bivariate relationship, 255–260

**Bivariate table** a table that displays the distribution of one variable across the categories of another variable, 240–255
    computing percentages, 244–246
    constructing, 242–244
    defined, 242
    features, 243, 244
    percentaging, 247
    research literature, 250–255
    theoretical question, and, 249

Book, overview, 23–25

Box plot, 202–205

## C

Causally prior variable, 262

Cause-and-effect relationships, 11, 12

**Cell** the intersection of a row and a column in a bivariate table, 244

Center of gravity, 156

**Central limit theorem** an important principle in statistical inference that relates the normal distribution and the sampling distribution of the means with a sufficient sample size, 501–506

Central tendency. *See* Measures of central tendency

Chain migration, 191

**Chi-square (critical)** a chi-square value obtained from the sampling distribution of all possible chi-square values. It is determined by the degrees of freedom (df) and the level of significance, 631, 632

**Chi-square (obtained)** the test statistic that summarizes the differences between the observed $(f_o)$ and the expected $(f_e)$ frequencies in a bivariate table, 627–629

Chi-square distribution, 629–631, App. D

**Chi-square test** (pronounced kai-square and written as $\chi^2$) an inferential statistics technique designed to test for significant relationships between two variables organized in a bivariate table, 619–659
  critical chi-square, 631, 632
  defined, 623
  degrees of freedom, 630
  example, 694, 695
  influence, as type of, 633
  limitations, 634, 635
  obtained chi-square, 627–629
  research literature, 641–644
  sample size, and, 634, 635
  sampling distributions, 629
  six steps, summarized, 624
  small expected frequencies, and, 635

Class interval, 54, 56, 68

**Coefficient of determination ($r^2$)** a PRE measure reflecting the proportional reduction of error resulting from utilizing the linear regression model. It reflects the proportion of the total variation in the dependent variable, $Y$, explained by the independent variable, $X$, 374, 376–378

Collecting data, 14

Column percentages, 248–250

**Column variable** a variable whose categories are the columns of a bivariate table, 243

Comparable worth discrimination, 381–386

Comparisons, 43–45, 47

Computer commands/operations. *See* SPSS for Windows

**Conditional relationship** a relationship between the independent and dependent variables that differs for different categories of the control variable, 272

**Confidence intervals** a range of values defined by the confidence level within which the population parameter is estimated to fall, 666
  defined, 521, 522
  general formula, 526
  means, and, 522–529
  proportions, and, 536–541
  reducing risk, 528
  sample size, and, 530–534
  width, and, 534

**Confidence levels** the likelihood, expressed as a percentage or a probability, that a specified interval will contain the population mean, 521, 522, 666

Continuous variable, 20

Control variable, 260, 262

Counting pairs, 316–321

Covariance, 363–365, 367

Critical chi-square, 631, 632

Critical region, 576. *See also* Region of rejection

Critical value, 565

**Critical Z (value)** the $Z$ score corresponding to a particular alpha level, 565

**Cross-tabulation** a technique for analyzing the relationship between two variables that have been organized in a bivariate table, 238

**Cumulative frequency distribution** a distribution showing the frequency at or below (or at or above) each category (class interval or score) of the variable, 55–59

**Cumulative percentage distribution** a distribution showing the percentage at or below (or at or above) each category of the variable, 58–60

**D**

**Data** information represented by numbers, which can be the subject of statistical analysis, 3

Data collection, 14

Death penalty, 542–545

Defense spending, 145, 146

**Degrees of freedom (df)** the number of scores that are free to vary in calculating a statistic, 590–592, 630

Demonstrations. *See* SPSS for Windows

**Dependent variable** the variable to be explained (the "effect") by the researcher, 11–13, 239

Descriptive data analysis, 407–440
  flowchart (systematic approach), 409, 410

an interval-ratio variable. Points representing the frequencies of each category are placed above the mid-point of the category and are joined by a straight line, 103–105, 114, 115

### G

**Gamma** a symmetrical measure of association suitable for use with ordinal variables or with dichot-omous nominal variables. It can vary from 0.0 to ±1.0 and provides us with an indication of the strength and direction of the association between the variables. When there are more $Ns$ pairs gamma will be positive; when there are more $Nd$ pairs gamma will be negative, 316
    defined, 323
    how to calculate, 322
    practical example, 324, 325
    PRE measure, as, 323, 324
    range of values, 322, 323
    research literature, 329–333
    Somers' $d$, compared, 327
Gender. *See also* Women
    abortion, and, 605, 606
    local political party activism, and, 411–425
    segregation in workplace, 6, 7
General Social Survey (GSS), 22, 519, App. F, H
Graph, 90
Graphic presentation, 89–131
    bar graph, 93–96, 113, 114
    box plot, 202–205
    distortions, 110–112
    frequency polygon, 103–105, 114, 115
    histogram, 99–103
    pie chart, 91–93
    statistical map, 96–99
    stem and leaf plot, 105–107
    time series charts, 108–110, 116
Graying of America, 101–103
Grouped data
    median, 144
    percentile, 149
GSS87_91.SAV, 30
GSS94.SAV, 30

### H

$H_0$, 558, 559
$H_1$, 558
Health care, 138–140
Hispanic migration and earnings, 534–536

**Histogram** a graph showing the differences in frequencies or percentages among categories of an interval-ratio variable. The categories are displayed as contiguous bars, with width proportional to the width of the category and height proportional to the frequency or percentage of that category, 99–103
Home ownership and race, 242–246, 306–308
**Hypothesis** a tentative answer to a research problem, 7, 8
Hypothesis testing. *See* Statistical hypothesis testing

### I

Illegal immigration, 685–688
Immigration, 191, 685–688
**Independence (statistical)** the absence of association between two cross-tabulated variables. The percentage distributions of the dependent variable within each category of the independent variable are identical, 623, 624
**Independent variable** the variable expected to account for (the "cause" of) the dependent variable, 11–13, 239
**Index of qualitative variation (IQV)** a measure of variability for a nominal variable. It is based on the ratio of the total number of differences in the distribution to a maximum number of possible differences within the same distribution
    calculate maximum possible differences, 186–188
    calculate total number of differences, 185, 186
    calculation of, from percentage/ proportion distribution, 189
    compute ratio, 188, 189
    defined, 184
    demystifying, 190
    general characteristics, 183
    how to calculate, 189
    percentage, expressed as, 189
    practical examples, 191–195, 197
**Inferential statistics** the logic and procedures concerned with making predictions or inferences about the population from observations and analyses of a sample, 22
Infinite population, 492n